Reforming Juvenile Justice

A DEVELOPMENTAL APPROACH

Committee on Assessing Juvenile Justice Reform

Richard J. Bonnie, Robert L. Johnson,
Betty M. Chemers, and Julie A. Schuck, *Editors*

Committee on Law and Justice

Division of Behavioral and Social Sciences and Education

NATIONAL RESEARCH COUNCIL
OF THE NATIONAL ACADEMIES

THE NATIONAL ACADEMIES PRESS
Washington, D.C.
www.nap.edu

THE NATIONAL ACADEMIES PRESS   500 Fifth Street, NW   Washington, DC 20001

NOTICE: The project that is the subject of this report was approved by the Governing Board of the National Research Council, whose members are drawn from the councils of the National Academy of Sciences, the National Academy of Engineering, and the Institute of Medicine. The members of the committee responsible for the report were chosen for their special competences and with regard for appropriate balance.

This study was supported by Contract/Grant No. 2009-JF-FX-0102 between the National Academy of Sciences and Office of Juvenile Justice and Delinquency Prevention. Any opinions, findings, conclusions, or recommendations expressed in this publication are those of the author(s) and do not necessarily reflect the views of the organizations or agencies that provided support for the project.

Library of Congress Control Number: 2013939486

Additional copies of this report are available from the National Academies Press, 500 Fifth Street, NW, Keck 360, Washington, DC 20001; (800) 624-6242 or (202) 334-3313; http://www.nap.edu.

Suggested citation: National Research Council. (2013). *Reforming Juvenile Justice: A Developmental Approach*. Committee on Assessing Juvenile Justice Reform, Richard J. Bonnie, Robert L. Johnson, Betty M. Chemers, and Julie A. Schuck, Eds. Committee on Law and Justice, Division of Behavioral and Social Sciences and Education. Washington, DC: The National Academies Press.

THE NATIONAL ACADEMIES
Advisers to the Nation on Science, Engineering, and Medicine

The **National Academy of Sciences** is a private, nonprofit, self-perpetuating society of distinguished scholars engaged in scientific and engineering research, dedicated to the furtherance of science and technology and to their use for the general welfare. Upon the authority of the charter granted to it by the Congress in 1863, the Academy has a mandate that requires it to advise the federal government on scientific and technical matters. Dr. Ralph J. Cicerone is president of the National Academy of Sciences.

The **National Academy of Engineering** was established in 1964, under the charter of the National Academy of Sciences, as a parallel organization of outstanding engineers. It is autonomous in its administration and in the selection of its members, sharing with the National Academy of Sciences the responsibility for advising the federal government. The National Academy of Engineering also sponsors engineering programs aimed at meeting national needs, encourages education and research, and recognizes the superior achievements of engineers. Dr. Charles M. Vest is president of the National Academy of Engineering.

The **Institute of Medicine** was established in 1970 by the National Academy of Sciences to secure the services of eminent members of appropriate professions in the examination of policy matters pertaining to the health of the public. The Institute acts under the responsibility given to the National Academy of Sciences by its congressional charter to be an adviser to the federal government and, upon its own initiative, to identify issues of medical care, research, and education. Dr. Harvey V. Fineberg is president of the Institute of Medicine.

The **National Research Council** was organized by the National Academy of Sciences in 1916 to associate the broad community of science and technology with the Academy's purposes of furthering knowledge and advising the federal government. Functioning in accordance with general policies determined by the Academy, the Council has become the principal operating agency of both the National Academy of Sciences and the National Academy of Engineering in providing services to the government, the public, and the scientific and engineering communities. The Council is administered jointly by both Academies and the Institute of Medicine. Dr. Ralph J. Cicerone and Dr. Charles M. Vest are chair and vice chair, respectively, of the National Research Council.

www.national-academies.org

Preface

Recent findings from research on adolescent development, and particularly increasing knowledge about the adolescent brain, have led to deep and growing concerns about the treatment of juveniles in the nation's justice system. There is a fundamental disconnect between what is now known about the characteristic features of adolescents and the apparent assumptions of that system. One reflection of that disconnect is a recent series of decisions from the U.S. Supreme Court forbidding the most severe penalties for adolescent offenders, especially the death penalty. There has also been a wide range of reforms in the administration of juvenile justice over the past 15 years, some of which reflect the emerging knowledge about adolescents and some of which do not.

The committee's charge was to take stock of the juvenile justice reforms undertaken over the past 15 years in light of current knowledge about adolescent development. The study was requested by the Office of Juvenile Justice and Delinquency Prevention (OJJDP), an agency of the U.S. Department of Justice. In an austere fiscal environment with so many pressing priorities, OJJDP naturally wants to ensure that it supports the research and programs that best harness the available scientific evidence.

During the two years of our study, we have been struck by the energy and dedication of all the stakeholders and participants in the juvenile justice system who took the time to appear before the committee and to help us to carry out our charge. A diverse array of the nation's institutions and leaders, both private and public, are playing key roles in the movement for juvenile justice reform, including elected officials in the states and localities, judges, foundations, advocacy organizations, and research organizations.

The central premise of this report is that the goals, design, and operation of the juvenile justice system should be informed by the growing body of knowledge about adolescent development. If designed and implemented in a developmentally informed way, procedures for holding adolescents accountable for their offending, and the services provided to them, can promote positive legal socialization, reinforce a prosocial identity, and reduce reoffending. However, if the goals, design, and operation of the juvenile justice system are not informed by this growing body of knowledge, the outcome is likely to be negative interactions between youth and justice system officials, increased disrespect for the law and legal authority, and the reinforcement of a deviant identity and social disaffection.

Scientists commonly complain that policy makers are not paying attention to the scientific evidence. Our experience in studying juvenile justice has been quite the reverse. We have detected an impressive consensus among stakeholder groups and public officials regarding the goals of the juvenile justice system, a genuine hunger for evidence about what works, and a willingness to embrace evidence-based policies and programs. This report aims to consolidate the progress that has been made in both science and policy making and to establish a strong platform for a 21st century juvenile justice system.

Advancing knowledge has helped to foster a climate of optimism. However, this energizing spirit of change has not taken root in all parts of the country, and it could dissipate if institutional structures are not put in place to sustain it and to assure a continuing partnership among practitioners, researchers, and policy makers. The locus of reform lies at the state, local, and tribal levels, and most of this report focuses on the opportunities and challenges facing the courts, law enforcement agencies, schools, social service agencies, and mental health agencies in communities throughout the nation. However, OJJDP support and leadership are critically important if the reform process is to succeed, and the report urges Congress to embrace the cause of juvenile justice reform by clarifying and reaffirming the mission of OJJDP.

Many people may argue that the lives of nation's youth most deeply ensnared by the juvenile justice system will not be substantially improved simply by reforming the juvenile justice system. We do not claim that juvenile justice reform can carry the burden of overcoming the many causes of juvenile crime. Also needed are stronger families, better schools, truly equal opportunity, and safe and healthy communities for the nation's youth. However, this report shows that a harsh system of punishing troubled youth can make things worse, while a scientifically based juvenile justice system can make an enduring difference in the lives of many youth who most need the structure and services it can provide.

> Robert L. Johnson, *Chair*
> Richard J. Bonnie, *Vice Chair*
> Committee on Assessing Juvenile Justice Reform

Acknowledgments

This report would not have been possible without the efforts of many people, each of whom has contributed time and expertise. The committee had the assistance and close cooperation of the staff of the Office of Juvenile Justice and Delinquency Prevention (OJJDP), the report's sponsor. The committee benefited greatly from briefings received from senior staff such as Andrea Coleman, disproportionate minority coordinator; Melodee Hanes, deputy administrator for policy; Elissa Rumsey, compliance monitor coordinator; Jeff Slowikowski, acting deputy administrator; and Greg Thompson, associate administrator, State Relations and Assistance Division. The committee also appreciates the assistance and insight of other OJJDP staff that briefed National Research Council (NRC) staff, including Janet Chiancone, associate administrator, Budget and Planning Division; Brecht Donahue, research coordinator; and Kathi Grasso, senior juvenile justice policy and legal advisor. Robin Delany-Shabazz, director, Concentration of Federal Efforts Program, and Anita Butler, program analyst, also provided information. Kellie Dressler-Tetrick, acting associate administrator, Demonstration Programs, and Marilyn Roberts, deputy administrator for programs, helped coordinate the committee's activities and assure that all funding requirements were met.

The committee drew on the expertise of many people during the course of its information gathering. The committee extends its thanks to Kristin N. Henning, J.D., LL.M., of Georgetown University Law School for her thoughtful analysis of procedural justice and adolescent's perceptions of law and legal authority that has been incorporated into Chapter 7; Alex R. Piquero, Ph.D., of the University of Texas at Dallas, for a review of research on racial disparities for Chapter 8; Simon Singer, Ph.D., of Northeastern University, for assisting committee member Jeff Butts with a paper on current juvenile justice practices; Beth Huebner, Ph.D., of the University of Missouri at St. Louis, for her paper on the Missouri Model that appears in Appendix B of this report; Jessica Kostelnik, Ph.D., a postdoctoral fellow at the Institute of Law, Psychiatry and Public Policy at the University of Virginia, for a background paper on socializing agents and unique characteristics of adolescents relevant to their sense of accountability; Kyle Frankiewich, M.P.A., and Daniel J. Evans, School of Public Affairs, University of Washington, for developing material used in Appendix A on costs and benefits of juvenile justice interventions. The committee also relied on a paper prepared for the NRC/Institute of Medicine Board on Children, Youth, and Families by a member of the committee, Kenneth A. Dodge, Ph.D., of Duke University, and Nancy Gonzales, Ph.D., of the University of Arizona, for a portion of the material on parental and peer influences on adolescent behavior in Chapter 4.

The committee would also like to acknowledge the following people for giving presentations at committee meetings: Neelum Arya, Campaign for Youth Justice; James Bell, W. Haywood Burns Institute; Shay Bilchik, Center for Juvenile Justice Reform, Georgetown University Public Policy Institute; Marcia I. Cohen, Development Services Group, Inc.; Susan Davis, Division of Criminal Justice, Colorado Department of Public Safety; Lindsey Draper, Office of Justice Assistance, State of Wisconsin; William Feyerherm, Hatfield School of Government, Portland State University; Laurie Garduque, John D. and Catherine T. MacArthur Foundation; Amy Holmes Hehn, District Attorney's Office, Multnomah County, Oregon; Nancy Gannon Hornberger, Coalition for Juvenile Justice; James C. Howell, National Gang Center, Institute for Intergovernmental Research; Lisa Hutchinson, Department of Criminal Justice, University of Arkansas at Little Rock; Candice Jones, John D. and Catherine T. MacArthur Foundation; Valerie LaMotte, Criminal Justice Policy and Planning Division, Connecticut Office of Policy and Management; Akiva Liberman, Urban Institute; Mark W. Lipsey, Peabody Research Institute, Vanderbilt University; Daniel J. Losen, Civil Rights Project, University of California, Los Angeles; Bart Lubow, Annie E. Casey Foundation; Katyoon Majid, Public Welfare Foundation; Ashley Nellis, The Sentencing Project; Laura Nissen, Robert Wood Johnson Foundation; Judy Preston, Special Litigation Unit, Office of Civil Rights, U.S. Department of Justice; Patricia Puritz, National Juvenile Defender Center; Brad Richardson, University of Iowa School of Social Work, National Resource Center for Family Centered Practice; Pili Robinson, Missouri Youth Services Institute; John Ryals, Department of Juvenile Services, Jefferson Parish, Louisiana; Vincent N. Schiraldi, New York City Department of Probation; Dana Shoenberg, Center for Children's

Law and Policy; Mark Soler, Center for Children's Law and Policy; Thomas Stickrath, Ohio Bureau of Criminal Identification and Investigation; Joe Vignati, Governor's Office for Children and Families, State of Georgia; John Wilson, Institute for Intergovernmental Research; and Jennifer Woolard, Department of Psychology, Georgetown University. Special thanks goes to Dwayne Betts who graciously appeared before the committee and shared his experiences as an adolescent offender confined in adult institutions and the obstacles he overcame on his way to achieving academic and professional success.

Thanks and acknowledgments are due to the members of the committee, all of whom gave generously of their time. Several members took primary responsibility for drafting sections of the report. We wish to thank Terence Thornberry for Chapter 1; Elisabeth Scott for Chapters 2 and 5; Jeff Butts for Chapter 3; B.J. Casey, Kenneth Dodge, Sandra Graham, and Edward Mulvey for Chapter 4; Edward Mulvey and Robert Plotnick for Chapter 6; and Richard Bonnie for Chapter 7. Finally, we would like to thank the NRC staff for valuable assistance with this project: project coordinator Barbara Boyd, for facilitating the panel's meetings; senior research associate Julie A. Schuck, for providing critical budgetary and programmatic information on OJJDP and pulling together other research materials for the committee; study director Betty M. Chemers, for filling in numerous gaps and turning the report into a coherent whole; Kirsten Sampson Snyder for help guiding the report through reviews, Christine McShane and Eugenia Grohman for skillful editing, and Yvonne Wise for managing the production process.

This report has been reviewed in draft form by individuals chosen for their diverse perspectives and technical expertise, in accordance with procedures approved by the NRC's Report Review Committee. The purpose of this independent review is to provide candid and critical comments that assist the institution in making its report as sound as possible, and to ensure that the report meets institutional standards for objectivity, evidence, and responsiveness to the study charge. The review comments and draft manuscript remain confidential to protect the integrity of the deliberative process.

We thank the following individuals for their participation in the review of this report: Shay Bilchik, Center for Juvenile Justice Reform, Georgetown University Public Policy Institute; Barry C. Feld, Centennial Professor of Law, University of Minnesota Law School; Anne Holton, AECF Child Welfare Strategy Group Consultant, Richmond, Virginia; Antoinette Kavanaugh, Forensic Clinical Psychologist, Chicago, Illinois; Mark W. Lipsey, Peabody Research Institute, Vanderbilt University; Diane Nunn, Center for Families, Children and the Courts, Judicial Council of California, Administrative Office of the Courts; Alex R. Piquero, Program in Criminology, University of Texas at Dallas; Steven Raphael, Richard and Rhoda Goldman School of Public Policy, University of California, Berkeley; Carol Wilson Spigner (emerita), University of Pennsylvania, and Child Welfare Services and Policy Consultant, Harrisburg, Pennsylvania; and Laurence Steinberg, Department of Psychology, Temple University.

Although the reviewers listed above provided many constructive comments and suggestions, they were not asked to endorse the conclusions and recommendations nor did they see the final draft of the report before its release. The review of this report was overseen by Alfred Blumstein, The H. John Heinz III College of Public Policy and Information Systems, Carnegie Mellon University, and Ellen Wright Clayton, Center for Biomedical Ethics and Society, Vanderbilt University. Appointed by the NRC, they were responsible for making certain that an independent examination of this report was carried out in accordance with institutional procedures and that all of the review comments were carefully considered. Responsibility for the final content of this report rests entirely with the authoring committee and the institution.

Contents

Acronyms

AAG	Assistant Attorney General
Act4JJ	Act 4 Juvenile Justice Campaign
Archive	National Juvenile Court Data Archive
ART	aggression replacement therapy
BCA	benefit-cost analysis
BJS	Bureau of Justice Statistics
CEA	cost-effectiveness analysis
Centers	Community Learning Centers
CIUS	*Crime in the United States*
CJRP	Census of Juveniles in Residential Placement
CPC	Correctional Program Checklist
CRIPA	Civil Rights of Institutionalized Persons Act of 1980
CV	contingent valuation
DMC	disproportionate minority contact
DOJ	U.S. Department of Justice
DSO	deinstitutionalization of status offenders
DTI	diffusion tensor imaging
DYS	Department of Youth Services
EUDL	Enforcing Underage Drinking Laws Program

FACJJ	Federal Advisory Committee for Juvenile Justice
FASD	fetal alcohol spectrum disorder
FBI	Federal Bureau of Investigation
FFLIC	Family and Friends of Louisiana's Incarcerated Children
FFT	functional family therapy
fMRI	functional magnetic resonance imaging
GAO	U.S. Government Accountability Office
GGI	guided group interaction
IAP	Intensive Aftercare Program
IDEA	Individuals with Disabilities Education Act
IOM	Institute of Medicine
JABG	Juvenile Accountability Block Grant
JAIBG	Juvenile Accountability Incentive Block Grant
JDAI	Juvenile Detention Alternatives Initiative
JJDPA	Juvenile Justice Delinquency Prevention Act of 1974
JJPL	Juvenile Justice Project of Louisiana
JRFC	Juvenile Residential Facility Census
JUMP	Juvenile Mentoring Program
MCAA	Missing Children's Assistance Act
MIP	minor in possession
MRI	magnetic resonance imaging
MST	multisystemic therapy
MTFC	multidimensional treatment foster care
MVPP	Multisite Violence Prevention Project
NCJJ	National Center for Juvenile Justice
NCLB	No Child Left Behind Act
NCVS	National Crime Victimization Survey
NIJ	National Institute of Justice
NLSY97	National Longitudinal Survey of Youth 1997
NRC	National Research Council
NREPP	National Registry of Evidence-based Programs and Practices
NTTAC	National Training and Technical Assistance Center
ODYS	Ohio Department of Youth Services
OJJDP	Office of Juvenile Justice and Delinquency Prevention
OJP	Office of Justice Programs
OMB	U.S. Office of Management and Budget

PbS	Performance-based Standards Program
PEP	Parent Empowerment Program
PLRA	Prison Litigation Reform Act of 1995
PPC	Positive Peer Culture Program

RNR	risk-need-responsivity
RRI	Relative Rate Index

SACWIS	Statewide Automated Child Welfare Information System
SAGs	State Advisory Groups
SAMHSA	Substance Abuse and Mental Health Services Administration
SFY	Strategies for Youth
SYRP	Survey of Youth in Residential Placement

TTA	training and technical assistance
TYP	Tribal Youth Program

UCR	Uniform Crime Report

VCO	valid court order
VOCA	Victims of Child Abuse Act

WSIPP	Washington State Institute for Public Policy

Summary

Recent research on adolescent development has underscored important behavioral differences between adults and adolescents with direct bearing on the design and operation of the justice system, raising doubts about the core assumptions driving the criminalization of juvenile justice policy in the last decades of the 20th century. It was in this context that the Office of Juvenile Justice and Delinquency Prevention (OJJDP) asked the National Research Council to convene a committee to conduct a study of juvenile justice reform. The committee's charge was to review recent advances in behavioral and neuroscience research and draw out the implications of this knowledge for juvenile justice reform, to assess the new generation of reform activities occurring in the United States, and to assess the performance of OJJDP in carrying out its statutory mission as well as its potential role in supporting scientifically based reform efforts.

ADOLESCENT DEVELOPMENT

Adolescence is a distinct, yet transient, period of development between childhood and adulthood characterized by increased experimentation and risk taking, a tendency to discount long-term consequences, and heightened sensitivity to peers and other social influences. A key function of adolescence is developing an integrated sense of self, including individuation, separation from parents, and personal identity. Experimentation and novelty-seeking behavior, such as alcohol and drug use, unsafe sex, and reckless driving, are thought to serve a number of adaptive functions despite their risks. Research indicates that for most youth, the period of

1

risky experimentation does not extend beyond adolescence, ceasing as identity becomes settled with maturity. Much adolescent involvement in illegal activity is an extension of the kind of risk taking that is part of the developmental process of identity formation, and most adolescents mature out of these tendencies.

Adolescents differ from adults and children in three important ways that lead to differences in behavior. First, adolescents have less capacity for self-regulation in emotionally charged contexts, relative to adults. Second, adolescents have a heightened sensitivity to proximal external influences, such as peer pressure and immediate incentives, relative to children and adults. Third, adolescents show less ability than adults to make judgments and decisions that require future orientation. The combination of these three cognitive patterns accounts for the tendency of adolescents to prefer and engage in risky behaviors that have a high probability of immediate reward but can have harmful consequences.

Evidence of significant changes in brain structure and function during adolescence strongly suggests that these cognitive tendencies characteristic of adolescents are associated with biological immaturity of the brain and with an imbalance among developing brain systems. This imbalance model implies dual systems: one involved in cognitive and behavioral control and one involved in socioemotional processes. Accordingly, adolescents lack mature capacity for self-regulation because the brain system that influences pleasure-seeking and emotional reactivity develops more rapidly than the brain system that supports self-control.

Adolescent risk taking and delinquent behavior result from the interaction between the normal developmental attributes of adolescents described above and the environmental influences to which they are exposed before and during this stage of development. Put simply, the brain plays an enormous role in determining behavior, but individual development is affected strongly by the interplay between the brain and an adolescent's environment. In particular, the likelihood and seriousness of offending, as well as the effects of interventions, are strongly affected by the adolescent's interactions with parents, peers, schools, communities, and other elements of his or her social environment.

THE JUVENILE JUSTICE SYSTEM

The vast majority of youth who are arrested or referred to juvenile court have not committed serious offenses, and half of them appear in the system only once. Regardless of how serious delinquency is defined, the evidence indicates that youth who commit serious offenses constitute a very small proportion of the overall delinquent population and that their behavior is driven by the same risk factors and developmental processes that influence the behavior of other juvenile offenders.

During the past two decades, many youth have come to the attention of the juvenile justice system from schools, child welfare agencies, and the mental health system. Zero-tolerance policies are increasing the number of suspensions and expulsions from schools, leading to increased risk of drop-out and juvenile justice involvement. Crossover youth, who move between the child welfare and juvenile justice systems, and youth with mental health disorders are more likely to be treated harshly in the juvenile justice system. Furthermore, black and ethnic minority youth make up a disproportionate number of adolescents disciplined by the schools, managed by the child welfare system, and diagnosed with the kinds of mental disorders (e.g., emotional disturbances) that are less likely to make them eligible for smaller, more specialized treatment programs.

The scientific literature shows that three conditions are critically important to healthy psychological development in adolescence: (1) the presence of a parent or parent figure who is involved with the adolescent and concerned about his or her successful development, (2) inclusion in a peer group that values and models prosocial behavior and academic success, and (3) activities that contribute to autonomous decision making and critical thinking. Schools, extracurricular activities, and work settings can provide opportunities for adolescents to learn to think for themselves, develop self-reliance and self-efficacy, and improve reasoning skills.

Yet the juvenile justice system's heavy reliance on containment, confinement, and control removes youth from their families, peer groups, and neighborhoods—the social context of their future lives—and deprives them of the opportunity to learn to deal with life's challenges. For many youth, the lack of a positive social context during this important developmental period is further compounded by collateral consequences of justice system involvement, such as the public release of juvenile records that follow them throughout their lives and limit future educational and employment opportunities.

Economically disadvantaged and minority youth are particularly affected by a juvenile justice system in which they are disproportionately represented. There is evidence that "race matters" above and beyond the characteristics of an offense. With few exceptions, data consistently show that youth of color have been overrepresented at every stage of the juvenile justice system. The evidence for race effects is greatest at the earlier stages of the process, particularly at the stages of arrest, referral to court, and placement in secure detention. And in nearly all juvenile justice systems, youth of color also remain in the system longer than white youth.

During the past 15 years, substantial progress has been made by various states and local jurisdictions in embracing and implementing a more developmentally appropriate way of handling youth who come to the attention of the juvenile justice system. However, when viewed nationally, the pace of reform has been sluggish. Many changes that have occurred have not been evaluated in a sufficiently rigorous and systematic manner to enable other reform-minded jurisdictions to undertake similar initiatives. The lack of critical data on youth characteristics, including race/ethnicity, processing at various stages of the system, and outcomes, significantly impedes tracking and evaluation of reform activities. At the local level, a lack of transparency regarding the decisions of police, prosecutors, and judges makes it difficult to understand and improve system functioning. Advances in information technology allow organizations to share data, but the complex laws governing privacy and confidentiality, as well as entrenched organizational practices, create barriers to collaboration and efficiency.

TRANSFORMING JUVENILE JUSTICE

The overarching goal of the juvenile justice system is to support pro-social development of youth who become involved in the system and thereby ensure the safety of communities. The specific aims of juvenile courts and affiliated agencies are to hold youth accountable for wrongdoing, prevent further offending, and treat them fairly. It is often thought that these specific aims are in tension with one another. However, when these aims and the actions taken to achieve them are viewed from a developmental point of view, the evidence shows that they are compatible with one another. This evidence is summarized below, and guiding principles for implementing a developmentally informed approach to juvenile justice reform are set forth in Box S-1.

Accountability

Holding adolescents accountable for their offending vindicates the just expectation of society that responsible offenders will be answerable for wrongdoing, particularly for conduct that causes harm to identifiable victims, and that corrective action will be taken. It does not follow, however, that the mechanisms of accountability for juveniles should mimic criminal punishments. Condemnation, control, and lengthy confinement ("serving time"), the identifying attributes of criminal punishment, are not necessary features of accountability for juveniles. The research demonstrates that, if designed and implemented in a developmentally informed way, procedures specifically designed for holding adolescents accountable for their offending can promote positive legal socialization, reinforce a prosocial identity, and facilitate compliance with the law. However, unduly harsh interventions and negative interactions between youth and justice system officials can undermine respect for the law and legal authority and reinforce a deviant identity and social disaffection. A developmentally informed juvenile justice system can promote accountability by providing a setting and an opportunity for juveniles to accept responsibility for their actions, make amends to individual victims and the community for any harm caused, and to participate in community service or other kinds of programs. Restorative justice programs involving victims and adjudication programs that involve restitution and peers are examples of developmentally appropriate instruments of accountability.

Preventing Reoffending

Assessing the risk of rearrest and the intervention needs of each youth is the necessary first step in achieving the overall goal of a more rational and developmentally appropriate array of preventive interventions in the juvenile justice system. Researchers have confirmed the validity of methods to do this. The central challenge is to incorporate these risk/needs assessments effectively into standard court and probation practice. Research is needed on whether and how information generated in screens or assessments is translated in the receipt of appropriate services and whether these services tend to reduce criminal behavior and increase successful adjustment in the community. Also, continued research is needed to eliminate racial/ethnic and gender bias in the design and administration of these tools.

The introduction of risk/needs assessment is a significant shift in how juvenile justice agencies conceptualize the potential impact of court involvement. This approach implies a dynamic view of juvenile justice involvement, reflects a shift from predicting risk to managing risk, and puts less stock in determining categories of offenders than on the malleable factors that might contribute to criminal involvement.

Using risk/needs assessments at critical points can reduce idiosyncratic decision making and maximize the impact of resources by targeting them to the risk level of each offender. Whatever the specific mechanism, the appropriate focusing of more intense (and costly) interventions on higher risk adolescents produces a greater reduction in subsequent offending and limits the negative effects of unwarranted intensive intervention on less serious offenders.

No single risk marker is very strongly associated with serious delinquency. Risk for delinquency is generated across multiple developmental stages from infancy to adolescence. Serious delinquents do commit more offenses and in many cases more violent offenses, but that is because they experience a greater accumulation of risk markers, in comparison with others. Consequently, interventions targeted at just one "key" factor during a limited period of development are likely to have little sustained impact on reoffending. This does not mean that secondary prevention efforts to reduce future offending are for naught. Multiple effective strategies for working with troubled and troubling youth have been shown to have positive effects.

Whether conducted in institutions or in communities, programs are more likely to have a positive impact when they focus on high-risk offenders, connect sound risk/needs assessment with the treatment approach taken, use a clearly specific program rooted in a theory of how adolescents change and tailored to the particular offender, demonstrate program integrity, involve the adolescent's family, and take into account community context. Expanding the role of families in juvenile justice appears to be a critical challenge, and additional research regarding the processes of family involvement in juvenile justice and methods for successfully involving parents in these processes are urgently needed.

If implemented well, evidence-based programs in both institutions and residential and nonresidential community placement reduce reoffending and produce remarkably large economic returns relative to their costs. But effective evidence-based practice cannot be achieved if service providers alter program characteristics in a misguided effort to make them more appropriate to the clients, culture, or resources of their communities. To offset this tendency, service providers should increase efforts to ensure model fidelity throughout the life of the intervention. A refinement of this approach is to help programs move toward consistent use of practices that have been shown to improve performance across a range of programs.

In general, multifaceted community-based interventions show greater reductions in rearrests than institutional programs. Once they are in institutional care, adequate time (arguably up to about six months) is needed to provide sufficiently intense services for adolescents to benefit from this experience. There is no convincing evidence, however, that confinement of juvenile offenders beyond the minimum amount needed for this purpose, either in adult prisons or juvenile correctional institutions, appreciably reduces the likelihood of subsequent offending.

Fairness

Treating youth fairly and ensuring that they perceive that they have been treated fairly and with dignity contribute to positive outcomes in the normal processes of social learning, moral development, and legal socialization during adolescence. Based on perceptions of procedural fairness as well as constitutional requirements, juvenile courts should ensure that youth are represented by properly trained counsel, that adjudications do not occur unless youth are able to understand the proceedings and assist counsel, and that youth have an opportunity to participate. However, lawyers in juvenile courts are often under-resourced and overburdened by high caseloads. To improve the quality of representation and enhance the youth's perception of justice, states should clarify the duties and obligations of juvenile defense counsel at every stage of the case and should specify caseload limits in accordance with recommended standards. Courts and juvenile justice agencies should also collaborate to formulate and implement performance measures for fairness (based on legal criteria and on perceptions of participants) during all phases of the juvenile justice process.

Reducing racial/ethnic disparities in the administration of juvenile justice is critical to achieving a fair juvenile justice system. The literature reflects continuing uncertainty about the relative contribution of differential offending, differential enforcement and processing, and structural inequalities to these disparities. However, the current body of research suggests that poverty, social disadvantage, neighborhood disorganization, constricted opportunities, and other structural inequalities—which are strongly correlated with race/ethnicity—contribute to both differential offending and differential selection, especially at the front end of juvenile justice decision making. Because bias (whether conscious or unconscious) also plays some role, albeit of unknown magnitude, juvenile justice officials should embrace activities designed to increase awareness of unconscious biases and to counteract them, as well as to detect and respond to overt instances of discrimination. Although the juvenile justice system itself cannot alter the underlying structural causes of racial/ethnic disparities in juvenile justice, many conventional practices in enforcement and administration magnify these underlying disparities, and these contributors *are* within the reach of justice system policy makers.

Several intervention efforts and policy initiatives have been undertaken to reduce disparities, but there is little scientific evidence bearing on their effectiveness so far. Activities that have shown some promise for reducing disparities include using periodic public reports as a tool for heightening awareness and promoting accountability of state and local governments, modifying policies and practices that tend to disadvantage minority youth, concentrating efforts to reduce or structure discretionary decision making at the arrest and detention stages, eliminating punitive and discretionary school discipline practices likely to result in a referral to the juvenile justice system, and initiating a comprehensive research and data program on the causes and consequences of racial/ethnic disparities.

OFFICE OF JUVENILE JUSTICE AND
DELINQUENCY PREVENTION

OJJDP is the federal agency that has responsibility for providing state, local, and tribal jurisdictions with the scientific knowledge and programmatic and technical support they need to improve their juvenile justice systems.

OJJDP's 1974 authorizing legislation reflects several basic understandings that have set the nation on the path toward developmentally appropriate juvenile justice policies and practices. The guiding premises are that youth who offend should be treated differently from adults who offend, that juvenile offending is preventable, and that youthful offenders should receive individualized treatment and services. The legislation's core requirements reflect key normative principles underlying developmentally appropriate policies and practices: the prohibition against detaining offenders whose offense (e.g., truancy, running away) would not be a crime if committed by an adult reflects the principle that youth who are not a risk to society or themselves should not be detained or removed from existing support systems; the requirements of "sight and sound separation" from adults and removal from adult jails reflect the idea that youth are vulnerable and should not be subject to punitive and potentially harmful conditions of incarceration; and the obligation to address racial disparities reflects the principle that youth should be treated fairly and equitably as a matter of justice.

Congress envisioned a strong partnership between the federal government, state juvenile justice agencies, and tribal governments as well as a strong leadership role for OJJDP. However, OJJDP's capacity to carry out this role has dramatically declined over the past decade because of inadequate funding and a severe restriction of its discretion in determining how its resources should be used. Its core requirements have been weakened by exceptions and a lack of clarifying federal regulations. Although reduced funding has continued, OJJDP's authorizing legislation expired in 2007 and 2008, and there has been no presidentially appointed administrator since 2009.

OJJDP's weakened state comes at a time when the juvenile justice field is moving toward a more developmentally appropriate system, but the field needs technical assistance, training, and other kinds of consultative services to help achieve that goal. OJJDP has the necessary congressional mandate and the support of the juvenile justice field. However, the agency will not be able to provide robust guidance and assistance to the juvenile justice field unless Congress removes the budgetary and political roadblocks that prevent it from doing so.

RECOMMENDATIONS

Knowledge about the developmental stage of adolescence has important implications for juvenile justice policy, providing the framework for a system that is fair to young offenders and effective in reducing youth crime. There are admittedly many gaps in this understanding. But the research is sufficiently robust to provide a solid foundation for juvenile justice policy and for general guidance about the design and operation of interventions and programs as knowledge continues to develop.

The recommendations that follow set forth the core components of a sustained process for reforming the nation's juvenile justice systems in a developmentally informed manner, for incorporating new evidence into policy and practice on a continuing basis, and for solidifying and sustaining these changes.

Political Commitment to Reform by
State, Local, and Tribal Governments

Given the current fiscal realities regarding the role of OJJDP and the role of the federal government in general, the immediate momentum for change will need to come from state, local, and tribal governments. Numerous state and local jurisdictions appear to be making progress toward more developmentally appropriate juvenile justice policies and practices. But many jurisdictions lack political support for reforms or the readiness to take the first necessary steps. Even among reform-minded jurisdictions, many have not yet undertaken system-wide improvements; they appear to be progressing on some fronts and backsliding on others. Moreover, some specific reforms, such as reducing racial/ethnic disparities and improving access to counsel, are being addressed at a very slow pace and by relatively few jurisdictions.

Every state should undertake a comprehensive, sustained and transparent process for achieving juvenile justice reform guided by the developmentally informed principles enunciated in this report (see Box S-1).

A key element in building and sustaining organizational and constituent support for reform has been the willingness of policy makers at all levels to be engaged in the process and to be transparent regarding the effectiveness and costs of their current programs and policies. Two strategies have been helpful: (1) the use of bipartisan, multistakeholder task forces or commissions to promote consensus and long-term follow-through and (2) collaboration with foundations, OJJDP, and other youth-serving organizations to leverage resources.

Many reform activities have not been adequately documented or evaluated, particularly those aimed at reducing racial/ethnic disparities. System-

---

BOX S-1
Guiding Principles for Juvenile Justice Reform

The overarching goal of the juvenile justice system is to support prosocial development of youth who become involved in the system and thereby ensure the safety of communities. Juvenile courts and affiliated agencies specifically aim to hold youth accountable for wrongdoing, prevent further offending, and treat youth fairly. Actions taken to achieve these aims should be designed and carried out in a developmentally informed manner.

Accountability

- Use the justice system to communicate the message that society expects youth to take responsibility for their actions and the foreseeable consequences of their actions.
- Encourage youth to accept responsibility for admitted or proven wrongdoing, consistent with protecting their legal rights.
- Facilitate constructive involvement of family members in the proceedings to assist youth to accept responsibility and carry out the obligations set by the court.
- Use restitution and community service as instruments of accountability to victims and the community.
- Use confinement sparingly and only when needed to respond to and prevent serious reoffending.
- Avoid collateral consequences of adjudication, such as public release of juvenile records, that reduce opportunities for a successful transition to a prosocial adult life.

Preventing Reoffending

- Use structured risk/needs assessment instruments to identify low-risk youth who can be handled less formally in community-based

---

wide reform efforts as well as individual programs should have clearly stated goals and objectives that can be measured scientifically, either on an individual site basis or across many sites. A plan for collecting and analyzing the necessary data should also be developed and the assessment made public.

Recommendation 1: State and tribal governments should establish a bipartisan, multistakeholder task force or commission, under the aus-

settings, to match youth with specialized treatment, and to target more intensive and expensive interventions on high-risk youth.

- Use clearly specified interventions rooted in knowledge about adolescent development and tailored to the particular adolescent's needs and social environment.
- Engage the adolescent's family as much as possible and draw on neighborhood resources to foster positive activities, prosocial development, and law-abiding behavior.
- Eliminate interventions that rigorous evaluation research has shown to be ineffective or harmful.
- Keep accurate data on the type and intensity of interventions provided and the results achieved.

Fairness

- Ensure that youth are represented throughout the process by properly trained counsel unless the right is voluntarily and intelligently waived by the youth.
- Ensure that youth are adjudicated only if they are competent to understand the proceedings and assist counsel.
- Facilitate participation by youth in all proceedings.
- Intensify efforts to reduce racial/ethnic disparities, as well as other patterns of unequal treatment, in the administration of juvenile justice.
- Ensure that youth perceive that they have been treated fairly and with dignity.
- Establish and implement evidence-based measures for fairness based on both legal criteria and perceptions of youth, families, and other participants.

pices of the governor, the legislature, or the highest state court, charged with designing and overseeing a long-term process of juvenile justice reform. This body should

a. Undertake a formal, authoritative, and transparent review of its juvenile justice system aiming to align laws, policies, and practices at every stage of the process with evolving knowledge regarding adolescent development and the effects of specific juvenile justice interventions and programs.

b. Develop a strategy for modifying current laws, policies, and practices, for implementing and evaluating necessary changes on an ongoing basis, and for reviewing any proposed juvenile justice legislation.

c. Intensify efforts to identify and then modify policies and practices that tend to disadvantage racial/ethnic minorities at various stages of the juvenile justice process and publish periodic reports on the nature and extent of disparities and the effects of specific interventions undertaken to reduce them.

Strong Supporting Role for OJJDP

The policies and principles reflected in OJJDP's legislation are now buttressed by a strong body of scientific knowledge regarding adolescent development as well as an impressive array of research on juvenile offending. Strengthening the legislation will send a strong message regarding the need for state, local, and tribal jurisdictions to assume greater responsibility for complying with the requirements and achieving a developmentally appropriate juvenile justice system. It will also enable OJJDP to redirect its resources in a way that best supports the efforts of state, local, and tribal jurisdictions.

Recommendation 2: The role of OJJDP in preventing delinquency and supporting juvenile justice improvement should be strengthened.

a. OJJDP's capacity to carry out its core mission should be restored through reauthorization, appropriations, and funding flexibility. Assisting state, local, and tribal jurisdictions to align their juvenile justice systems with evolving knowledge about adolescent development and implementing evidence-based and developmentally informed policies, programs, and practices should be among the agency's top priorities. Any additional responsibilities and authority conferred on the agency should be amply funded so as not to erode the funds needed to carry out the core mission.

b. OJJDP's legislative mandate to provide core protections should be strengthened through reauthorizing legislation that defines status offenses to include offenses such as possession of alcohol or tobacco that apply only to youth under 21; precludes without exception the detention of youth who commit offenses that would not be punishable by confinement if committed by an adult; modifies the definition of an adult inmate to give states flexibility to keep youth in juvenile facilities until they reach the age of extended juvenile court jurisdiction; and expands the protections to all youth under age 18 in pretrial detention, whether charged in juvenile or in adult courts.

c. OJJDP should prioritize its research, training, and technical assistance resources to promote the adoption of developmentally appropriate policies and practices by jurisdictions throughout the country, particularly helping those that have not yet achieved a state of readiness to undertake reform.

d. OJJDP should support state and local efforts to reduce racial/ethnic disparities by using its technical and financial resources to expand the number of local jurisdictions currently participating in activities aimed at reducing disproportionate minority contact (DMC); support efforts to design and implement programs and policies aiming to reduce disparities; support scientifically valid methods for understanding the causes of racial/ethnic disparities and for evaluating the impact of DMC interventions; and enhance the transparency of its oversight activities by identifying impediments being encountered and assisting localities to overcome them.

Federal Support for Research

Traditionally, OJJDP has been the primary funder of research on juvenile crime and juvenile justice, but its capacity is limited. It is essential that OJJDP and other funding agencies continue to support research that has far-reaching implications beyond that of juvenile justice. But it is critical that the research agenda, outlined in Chapter 11 of our report, adhere to the highest standards of scientific rigor. The evidence-based movement in treatment and prevention did not gain traction until the programs were evaluated with experimental designs and benefit-cost analyses were undertaken.

Recommendation 3: Federal research agencies, including the National Science Foundation, the Centers for Disease Control and Prevention, and the National Institutes of Health, as well as OJJDP, should support research that continues to advance the science of adolescent development and expands our understanding of the ways in which developmental processes influence juvenile delinquency and juvenile justice responses.

Data Improvement

State, local, and tribal jurisdictions are dependent on a variety of data sources from the federal government and from various agencies within their own jurisdictions, including law enforcement and juvenile justice agencies and courts, as well as education, social services, and health and mental health agencies. They often lack the clout to influence the providers of relevant juvenile justice and other systems' data. This challenge must be pursued at the federal level, and OJJDP is the logical agency to lead the effort and provide the training and technical assistance on automated data systems and support for data analysis activities to assess reform initiatives.

Recommendation 4: Under OJJDP's leadership, the Bureau of Justice Statistics and other governmental and private statistical organizations should develop a data improvement program on juvenile crime and juvenile justice system processing that provides greater insight into state, local, and tribal variations. OJJDP should also be involved in any effort undertaken by other U.S. Department of Justice agencies with the Federal Bureau of Investigation to improve the federal collection of juvenile arrest and incident data. At the state, local, and tribal levels, data should be collected on the gender, age, race/ethnicity of offenders as well as the offense charged or committed; arrest, detention, and disposition practices; and recidivism. OJJDP should provide training and technical assistance on data collection, automated data systems, and methods of protecting the confidentiality of juvenile records.

1

Introduction

In 2001, the National Research Council (NRC) report, *Juvenile Crime, Juvenile Justice,* focused on the causes and responses to juvenile crime (National Research Council and Institute of Medicine, 2001). The study came on the heels of rising violent juvenile crime and a wave of state statutes imposing tougher sanctions on juvenile offenders, including the transfer of juveniles to criminal courts at younger ages. The NRC panel observed that the spike in serious juvenile crime during the late 1980s and early 1990s was mainly attributable to gun homicides associated with the crack epidemic and that serious juvenile crime was already declining when most of the punitive statutes were being enacted.

Much has occurred since the publication of *Juvenile Crime, Juvenile Justice.* First, there has been an explosion of knowledge regarding adolescent development, especially in increased understanding of the neurobiological underpinnings of the behavioral differences associated with this distinct period of human development. In addition, much has been learned about the pathways to delinquency and patterns of offending, the efficacy and cost-effectiveness of prevention and treatment programs, and the long-term effects of confining youth in secure or harsh conditions and transferring them to the adult system. Significantly, the rate of offending among both juveniles and adults has continued to decline.

The wisdom of the "get-tough" policies of the 1990s has been widely questioned based on growing doubts about their effectiveness in reducing offending and increasing concern about their high costs in the face of declining state budgets. As a result, many state and local jurisdictions have undertaken significant steps to reverse these measures and, more generally, to overhaul their juvenile justice systems. This impressive reform movement has been propelled by a coalition of child advocacy organizations, private foundations, and political leaders. Juvenile justice reform is once again "in the air," just as it was during the 1990s—this time, however, the emerging consensus is that the juvenile justice system should be strengthened rather than contracted and that it should be grounded in the advancing science of adolescent development rather than treating offending youth as emerging adult criminals.

It was in this context that the Office of Juvenile Justice and Delinquency Prevention (OJJDP) asked the NRC to take stock of the new wave of reforms undertaken since the 2001 study. OJJDP, established in 1974, is the agency through which the federal government can help state and local governments prevent and control juvenile delinquency and improve juvenile justice systems. A key aim was to protect juveniles from harm, both physical and psychological, that could occur as a result of inappropriate placements and from exposure to adult inmates. Through funding incentives, OJJDP encourages states to incorporate core protections[1] into their juvenile justice practices. For more information on OJJDP's role and its assistance to state and local governments, see Chapter 10.

THE CHARGE

The Committee on Assessing Juvenile Justice Reform was charged with conducting a study to assess the implications of recent advances in behavioral and neuroscience research for the field of juvenile justice, to assess the new generation of reform activities occurring in the United States, and to assess the performance of OJJDP in carrying out its statutory mission as well as its potential role in supporting scientifically based reform to improve the fair and equal treatment of delinquent youth.

The specific primary tasks of this study were to:

- review the science of childhood and adolescent development and identify relevant findings for juvenile justice;
- describe the history of juvenile justice reform, its stages, major legislative and judicial changes, and the driving forces behind the current rethinking of policies and programs;
- provide a current context for understanding the implications of developmental behavioral and neuroscience research for juvenile justice policies and programs;

---

[1]OJJDP's authorizing legislation ties four core requirements to state formula funding: deinstitutionalization of status offenders, removal from adult jail and lockup, sight and sound separation, and reduction of disproportionate minority contact.

- identify current juvenile justice reform efforts occurring at the state and local level and review available evidence regarding the effectiveness of these initiatives;
- review the activities of OJJDP in carrying out the legislative mandates in the Juvenile Justice and Delinquency Prevention Act (JJDPA) of 1974 as subsequently amended;
- assess OJJDP's capacity to promote and support scientifically based reforms aimed at reducing crime and providing for the fair and safe treatment of juveniles; and
- make recommendations to advance theory and research and to improve state and federal juvenile justice policies and practices.

The current report builds on and complements the earlier NRC report but differs substantially from it. Rather than focusing on the causes and characteristics of juvenile crime, we focus solely on the policies and practices of the juvenile justice system and on the aspects of adolescent development that bear on its design and operation. We aim, in short, to contribute to the transformation of juvenile justice that is already under way by consolidating its scientific foundation and pointing the way toward effective implementation. This report is being written at a time when policy makers seem particularly receptive to evidence-based policies, programs, and practices that are known to be effective in preventing juvenile crime. After a period of serious conflict about the mission of the juvenile justice system (sometimes questioning its very existence), a new consensus is emerging regarding the need for a separate justice system for adolescents. However, this consensus is neither fully developed nor deeply rooted. This report has two goals: (1) to show that the emerging consensus rests on strong scientific and normative foundations and (2) to set forth a framework for a developmentally informed juvenile justice system, for incorporating new evidence into policy and practice on a continuing basis, and for solidifying and sustaining these changes over the long term.

STUDY METHODS

The committee held six meetings during the course of the study. The first three were information-gathering meetings at which we heard presentations from a variety of stakeholders, including representatives from OJJDP, foundations, academia, state and local juvenile justice agencies, and research and legal institutions, as well as a young adult who had served time in the adult criminal justice system as an adolescent. The last three meetings were closed to the public in order for the committee to deliberate on the report and finalize our conclusions and recommendations.

The committee reviewed multiple sources of information as background for the study: research literature on adolescent development, juvenile crime, and the treatment of juvenile offenders, as well as materials on the legislative history of the JJDPA; the grant programs of OJJDP and other federal agencies, including available financial data; current reform efforts at national, state, and local levels; and practitioner experiences with implementing the core requirements of JJDPA and responding to shifts in youth crime prevention and control policies. We also commissioned a paper on the Missouri juvenile justice system.

TERMINOLOGY

A word is in order regarding some of the terminology used in this report. There is no common agreement in the juvenile justice field about a number of terms used in this report. The committee struggled with this and in an effort to provide uniformity it has tried to use the definitions that follow. But it is important to point out that we have had some difficulty always applying these definitions when reviewing the literature, because they are ours and not necessarily those of the field.

As with the earlier 2001 NRC report on juvenile crime, the committee uses the term "juvenile" to refer to anyone under the age of 18, unless otherwise specified.[2] Other terms used synonymously with juvenile include "young person" and "youth." For the analyses of crime trends in this chapter, "juvenile" refers to those between ages 10 and 17, because those under age 10 are seldom arrested.

"Adolescence" is the pivotal concept used in this report. Scientifically speaking, adolescence has no finite chronological onset or end-point, and there is no legal definition of adolescence per se because the law regards different ages as being legally relevant in different contexts. The science of adolescence refers to a phase in development between childhood and adulthood beginning at puberty, typically about 12 or 13 and ending in the late teens or early 20s. Generally speaking, however, the committee focuses on youth under age 18, typically the age of majority and the ceiling of delinquency adjudication in most states. In the few instances in which we mean to encompass youth older than age 18, a specific statement is made.

The terms "delinquency" refers to acts by a juvenile that would be considered a crime if committed by an adult, as well as to actions that are illegal only because of the age of the offender. "Juvenile crime" or "criminal delinquency" refers to more serious acts that would be crimes if commit-

---

[2]Technically, "juvenile" is a legal definition referring to the jurisdictional age of each state's juvenile court or family court system and includes those youth who fall under the purview of the state's delinquency code and not the criminal code.

ted by adults. "Status delinquency" offenses include truancy, running away from home, incorrigibility (i.e., habitually disobeying reasonable and lawful commands of a parent, guardian, or custodian; also referred to in various statutes as unruly, uncontrollable, or ungovernable behavior), and liquor law violations.[3] In some states, status delinquents are referred to the child welfare or social service systems, and in others status delinquents are dealt with in the juvenile justice system.

"Adjudicated delinquent" or "delinquent" is used synonymously to describe the individual who has been found by the juvenile court to have committed a juvenile crime. The committee uses the term "justice-involved youth" to refer to youth who have contact with any form of legal authority, including police diversion, and "juvenile offenders" or "youthful offenders" for those who are referred to court or juvenile intake after police intake. For reasons mentioned below, this report does not distinguish between serious juvenile offenders and the general population of youthful offenders, except where noted.

Finally, one of the most controversial issues in the administration of juvenile justice relates to the use of confinement, either after the juvenile has been taken into custody and charged with delinquency or as a formal disposition after an adjudication of delinquency. This report uses the term "confinement," depending on the context, to refer to detention before adjudication or to placement in a custodial setting as a disposition after a finding of delinquency. In the dispositional context, it encompasses what are typically called institutional placements or out-of-home residential placements. It is not meant to encompass day treatment or nonresidential, community-based therapeutic programs.

THE COMPLEX MISSION OF JUVENILE JUSTICE

America's system of juvenile justice was founded on the premise that, because of their immaturity, young people accused of crimes should be treated differently from adults. Ideally, the juvenile justice system is more responsive than the criminal justice system would be to the developmental characteristics of children and youth. The sanctions prescribed and services provided by the juvenile system should be designed not only to hold youth accountable but also to address the causes of their misbehavior, reduce reoffending, and facilitate positive and healthy adolescent development. The long-term goal of any intervention is to restore the youth to full and responsible membership in his or her family as well as the larger community.

---

[3]Legally, delinquent acts are akin to criminal acts, and status offenses are noncriminal acts akin to civil violations based on age. It is important to note also that states vary considerably in the language they use to denote status offenses.

A developmental approach to juvenile justice recognizes that illegal acts committed by adolescents occur in the context of a distinct period of human development, a time of life when individuals are more likely to exercise poor judgment, take risks, and pursue thrills and excitement. This naturally results in a higher incidence of illegal behavior. Most young people involved with the juvenile justice system will desist from criminal behavior simply as a result of maturation, although the timing and trajectories of desistance vary considerably (Laub and Sampson, 2001).

The U.S. system of juvenile justice authorizes legal intervention in all forms of adolescent offending, from nearly trivial to life-threatening offenses. As traditionally understood, the purpose of intervention in each case is to prevent the escalation of illegal behavior while not damaging the life chances of young people with punitive and permanently stigmatizing criminal sanctions. However, the boundaries between juvenile court dispositions and criminal sanctions have become blurred during the past two decades, allowing delinquency adjudications to establish the legal predicate for sex offender registration and to count as prior convictions for criminal sentencing purposes.

The legal traditions of juvenile justice rest on an awkward blend of civil and criminal law. That is why the juvenile justice system is sometimes described using terms from the realm of social welfare, and at other times drawing on the vocabulary of criminal law. The judicial discretion and more flexible procedures characteristic of the juvenile legal system (for example, the absence of a jury trial) are intended to achieve a number of important goals simultaneously.

The goal of delivering services to reduce the risk of reoffending is deeply grounded in the origins of juvenile justice. For more than a century since the founding of the first juvenile court in 1899, the juvenile justice system has justified its existence by being more treatment oriented and more rehabilitative than its criminal counterpart—indeed rehabilitation has been abandoned as a goal of criminal justice in most modern criminal codes. By contrast, treatment is the juvenile justice system's very reason for being. An industry of treatment providers has emerged to support this treatment mission by delivering therapeutic interventions to address family conflict, cognitive deficits, drug abuse, and mental health issues, including a growing number of programs that are now supported by high-quality evaluation evidence.

The successful juvenile court must deliver needed services while ensuring accountability and protecting the community. The young person before the court is at once a potential beneficiary of the intervention and a target of accusation and judgment. If these tensions were not already complicated enough, it is essential to remember that the young person is also a holder of rights. Whatever the society's motivation for intervening (rehabilitation or accountability), the young person is legally entitled to be treated fairly, and the Constitution requires juvenile justice to adhere to the basic requirements of due process, including representation by counsel in a trial at which the prosecution is required to prove the elements of the delinquent offense beyond a reasonable doubt. But fairness is also important from a social science perspective and, while the research is limited, there is some indication that perceptions of fairness on the part of youth and families also are important in achieving the juvenile court's objectives.

In the committee's view, looking at juvenile justice through the prism of adolescent development helps to reconcile these tensions. Holding youth accountable for wrongdoing and treating them fairly can facilitate successful socialization and thereby reduce the risk of reoffending. That is not to say that the task is an easy one. Many obstacles must be overcome to initiate and sustain juvenile justice reform. However, the committee is optimistic about the prospects for success.

JUVENILE DELINQUENCY

Two important topics must be addressed before undertaking the basic narrative of the committee's report. First, the committee's focus on juvenile justice should not be understood as deemphasizing the importance of investing in programs and services that can prevent delinquency in the first place. Second, we also want to take note of the heterogeneity of adolescent offending. Policy makers might imagine that the best way to reconcile the tensions in the mission of juvenile justice is to sort offenders into categories, using seriousness of offending as proxies for maturity, culpability, social danger, or amenability to rehabilitation. However, it is important to recognize from the outset that this strategy is generally not scientifically supportable. There may be other reasons to draw legal distinctions based on offense categories, but they are generally unsupported by criminological data.

Preventing Delinquency

This report focuses on the role of the juvenile justice system in promoting accountability and preventing reoffending once a youth is already in contact with the system. However, we are certainly mindful that serious adolescent behavior problems do not spring up suddenly in adolescence. From a developmental perspective, youth at highest risk accumulated these risks from childhood and often from infancy and before birth. Moreover, we are also mindful that poverty, social disorganization, and other serious structural issues in many communities propel vulnerable adolescents toward delinquency, and that local officials in these communities all too often tend to see the juvenile justice system as the standard intervention rather than as a last resort. For this reason, it is important to emphasize at the outset of this report that findings in developmental science provide a strong rationale for investing in early prevention programs, that empirical evidence regarding the efficacy of specific prevention programs is growing, and that OJJDP is charged with providing federal leadership in delinquency prevention.

Developmental science findings indicate that children who are at risk for persistent delinquency can be identified early in life with relative accuracy (Moffitt et al., 2011), providing targets for prevention programs. Findings also identify theoretically coherent risk and protective factors, beginning at or before birth, that provide substantive foci for interventions. The findings provide the rationale for early prevention programs that have been evaluated through randomized controlled trials and found to reduce risk for delinquency. The most effective programs are ones that target multiple domains of parenting, children's social-cognitive skills, and school success. Programs directed toward demographically high-risk families in the first several years of life focus on supporting parenting and/or delivery of high-quality preschool day care, including the Abecedarian Project (Campbell and Ramey, 1995), the Child-Parent Center Education Program (Reynolds et al., 2011), the Nurse Family Partnership (Olds et al., 1998), and the Perry Preschool Program (Heckman et al., 2010). A meta-analysis by Piquero et al. (2009) revealed that these programs, on average, are not only effective but also may be wise economic investments because of the savings that accrue over a youth's life course.

Programs in middle childhood target parenting and social-cognitive skills among early-starting children with conduct problems, including Anger Coping (Lochman and Wells, 2004), the Fast Track Program (Conduct Problems Prevention Research Group, 2010), GREAT Schools and Families (Multisite Violence Prevention Project, 2009), and the Montreal Longitudinal Experiment (Boisjoli et al., 2007). An effective approach with African American boys is to help them alter hostile attributional biases (Hudley and Graham, 1993). Middle school curricula in social-cognitive development, such as Life Skills Training (Botvin et al., 2006), prevent adolescent substance use and antisocial behaviors. In order for these programs to have a population-level effect, major systems in children's lives—school, family, health, housing, community—must support and coordinate their services. For a recent review of the prevention literature, the reader is also referred to *Preventing Mental, Emotional, and Behavioral Disorders Among Young People: Progress and Possibilities* (National Research Council and Institute of Medicine, 2009).

Heterogeneity of Juvenile Offending

Although this report focuses on the design and operation of the juvenile justice system, it is important to have a sense of some general characteristics of the offending behavior to which the system is expected to respond. Research on juvenile offending[4] reflects substantial heterogeneity in the population of youth who can be considered delinquent. At one extreme, some youth commit only a few trivial offenses; at the other extreme, some youth commit many offenses, some of which are quite serious and violent.

The epidemiological literature shows that, regardless of how serious delinquents are defined,[5] they constitute a very small proportion of the overall delinquent population. They do commit many offenses, but most of their offenses are relatively minor and there are extraordinarily few chronic violent offenders. The vast majority of youth who are arrested or referred to juvenile court are not serious delinquents, and half of them appear in the system only once.

Concern over serious delinquents emerged from the pioneering longitudinal studies of Wolfgang and colleagues (Wolfgang et al., 1972, 1987; Wolfgang, 1983) in their study of the 1945 birth cohort of males in Philadelphia. Using official arrest data to measure delinquency, they identified a group they called chronic offenders, youth who had been arrested five or more times. Although constituting only 6 percent of the total cohort and 18 percent of the delinquents (those who had been arrested at least once), chronic offenders were responsible for 52 percent of all the offenses committed. They also committed serious and violent offenses at a higher than average rate. Their disproportionate contribution to the overall delinquency rate garnered great attention, in terms of both research and policy. Although the identification of this group of chronic offenders was important to juvenile justice policy, it is also worth recalling another finding from the Philadelphia study: almost half of the delinquents (46 percent) were one-time offenders and almost two-thirds (65 percent) of the offenders were arrested no more than twice. Similar results were also found in the 1958 Philadelphia birth cohort (Kempf-Leonard et al., 2001).

---

[4]It is also important to bear in mind that there are important methodological differences across criminological studies with respect to who is studied and how. All of this variation can influence the observed results and needs to be kept in mind in interpreting research findings. For further discussion of this, see Box 1-1 at the end of this chapter.

[5]There is no clear, generally agreed-upon definition of what it means to be a serious delinquent. Some studies of serious delinquents focus just on the seriousness of the offenses that are committed, some on the frequency of their offending, and others on involvement in violent behavior (Loeber and Farrington, 1998). In addition, some studies focus on the co-occurrence of these dimensions as they tend to be interrelated (Loeber, Farrington, and Waschbusch, 1998; see also Kempf-Leonard et al., 2001). For example, youth who are high-frequency offenders are also more likely to commit violent and serious offenses at a higher rate than others.

Since this early work, a number of studies have examined serious chronic offenders (Loeber and Farrington, 1998). Perhaps the most thorough investigation was conducted by Snyder (1998) who found that a majority of the youth referred to juvenile court in Maricopa County, Arizona, did not meet criteria to be placed into the categories of chronic offender (referred four or more times), violent offender, or serious but nonviolent offender. Indeed, 63.9 percent of all referred youth were not considered as any of these, and 29.5 percent were considered serious but nonviolent offenders. Moreover, the majority of referred youth were one-time offenders. This finding is echoed by Kempf-Leonard et al. (2001) and van der Geest et al. (2009), both of whom found that the majority of their sample did not commit violent offenses.

Snyder (1998) also found that the chronic offenders were responsible for a disproportionate proportion (44.6 percent) of all offenses referred to the court. Perhaps the public's greatest fear is focused on chronically violent delinquents, that is, youth who frequently commit violent offenses. Yet this group is exceedingly rare. Of the 151,209 referred youth, Snyder found that only 168 were referred for four or more violent offenses. This represents only 0.1 percent of all referred youth and 1.4 percent of those youth ever referred for a violent offense. This finding continues to be reflected in recent estimates where Esbensen et al. (2010) presented concordant national-level data: "a rough approximation can be made that only .74 percent of all juveniles [aged 10 to 17 in the United States] were arrested for simple assault in 1995" (2010, p. 42). Similarly only .29 percent were arrested for aggravated assault and .20 percent for robbery. Examining the most serious offense type, homicide and nonnegligent manslaughter, the actual prevalence and proportion of offenses committed by those under age 15 is negligible (.08 percent).

Piquero (2008b) conducted an extensive review of the trajectory literature (e.g., Nagin and Land, 1993; Sampson and Laub, 1993a; Brame, Mulvey, and Piquero, 2001; Ezell and Cohen, 2005) based on over 80 longitudinal studies. He reports considerable consistency across these studies which were conducted with very different samples and in several countries. Although the number of trajectory groups varies somewhat across studies, these studies overwhelmingly find evidence that there is a large group of youth who are either nonoffenders or who offend at a very low rate at one extreme and a numerically small group of chronic offenders at the other extreme. This pattern is similar to that found in the earlier studies by Wolfgang, Figlio, and Sellin (1972) and Snyder (1998).

Recent summaries of analyses of longitudinal data sets indicate that approximately one-third of adolescents with an arrest record go on to an adult arrest; two-thirds do not. The consistency of offending varies by era, gender, race/ethnicity, and age of onset of offending, with adolescents who begin offending at a younger age more likely to be adult offenders (Kazemian, Farrington, and LeBlanc, 2009; Piquero, Hawkins, and Kazemian, 2012). Estimates of the continuity of offending also vary depending on whether self-report or arrest is used as the indicator of criminal activity (Loeber et al., 2008). Depending on where the sample of juvenile offenders is drawn from in the juvenile justice system, in almost all studies, however, only a minority of juvenile offenders do become adult criminals. Even in a sample of serious (felony level) juvenile offenders, the majority of adolescents report very low levels of offending three years after court involvement (Mulvey et al., 2010).

In addition, juvenile and adult offenders reduce criminal behavior over time enough to be indistinguishable in their risk of offending from individuals who have never committed a crime (Kurlychek, Brahm, and Bushway, 2007; Blumstein and Nakamura, 2009). The time until an individual reduces his risk of offending to that of others his age varies by offense and age of the first arrest. It is worth noting, though, that a juvenile arrested at age 16 for robbery has the same likelihood of arrest as his peers when they are 24.5 years old (Blumstein and Nakamura, 2009).

Numerous theories exist about why youth persist or desist from crime, and it is generally recognized that the factors that promote desistance may be distinct from the factors that support the maintenance of a criminal lifestyle. Theories about desistance revolve around the relative influence of stable, individual differences (in traits like self-control or intelligence), the effects of developmental factors associated with late adolescence (like increased consideration of others, sense of agency, or brain maturation), and the impact of dynamic life changes (like romantic relationships or stable employment). While there is considerable empirical support for a number of these ideas, the evidence overall appears to support an interactionist view of an individual's psychological and social assets, their current developmental challenges, and the occurrence of normative and unexpected life events (see Thornberry et al., 2012). The extant capacity of adolescents and young adults to address the emerging challenges and roles of early adulthood, interacting with the skills and social resources that they might acquire during this period, make the difference in reducing antisocial activity. There is considerable work ahead, however, to fill in the picture of how these multiple factors mesh together to promote desistance (Laub and Boonstoppel, 2012).

The juvenile justice system needs to respond forcefully to serious, chronic, and violent offenders, but it should always be recognized that the proportion of youth who fall in this category, even among youth referred to the juvenile justice system, is quite small. We recognize that serious chronic delinquents may need to be dealt with differently from other offenders, including more reliance on secure confinement in order to protect public safety. But as the report discusses, the behavior of these youth is still driven by the same risk factors and developmental processes that influence the behavior of other delinquents. For that reason, the committee has not included a separate chapter singling out this small subgroup of serious delinquents. Instead, we consider the entire population of juvenile offenders, noting when appropriate specific differences that arise for serious, violent, or chronic offenders.

REPORT ORGANIZATION

Chapter 2 describes the history of the juvenile court and its shifting goals, with a particular emphasis on the harsh policies of the 1990s and the emergence of a contemporary model of juvenile justice in the 21st century. It explains the role of scientific research in this most recent reform period and its influence on attitudes, policies, and programs. Chapter 3 provides an overview of the current practice of juvenile justice in the United States and the characteristics of juvenile justice administration that make reform difficult and uneven. Chapter 4 reviews the body of behavioral, psychological, and neuroscience research demonstrating that adolescence is a distinct period of human development differing in fundamental ways from both childhood and adulthood. Chapter 5 draws out the implications of a developmental perspective for design and operation of a fair and effective system of juvenile justice. Chapter 6 focuses specifically on the body of research bearing on the most effective policies and programs for preventing reoffending by youth who have come to the attention of the juvenile court. Chapter 7 explores the implications of the developmental perspective for designing a fair and effective process for holding youth accountable for their wrongdoing. Chapter 8 provides an overview of the problem of racial/ethnic disparity in the juvenile justice system, reviews the contending explanations for minority overrepresentation, and identifies strategies for moving beyond the current impasse. Chapter 9 describes the major juvenile justice reform initiatives undertaken over the past two decades and identifies the key lessons that can be drawn from these experiences to guide jurisdictions embarking on the path of developmentally informed reform. Chapter 10 is an overview of OJJDP's legislatively mandated role in helping state and localities strengthen their juvenile justice systems and make them more fair and equitable. It describes OJJDP's current weakened status and the steps that will be needed to restore its leadership capacity to promote the developmentally appropriate treatment of juveniles by the justice system. Chapter 11 concludes the report with the committee's recommendations for achieving a fairer and effective system of juvenile justice based on a developmental approach.

The report contains four appendixes. Appendix A supplements the report's discussion of the benefits and costs of juvenile offender programs by describing the methodological challenges in undertaking such analyses and the strong evidence regarding the financial benefits of evidence-based programs. Appendix B provides detailed information on the history and characteristics of the widely replicated Missouri model of juvenile justice and an assessment of its effectiveness. Appendix C examines OJJDP's role in mentoring, a program heavily supported by Congress, and reviews research bearing on its effectiveness as a prevention program. Appendix D presents biographical sketches of committee members and staff.

BOX 1-1
Methodological Differences of Criminological Studies

Many studies are based on representative, community samples of adolescents, some of whom are delinquent and some of whom are not. The purpose of these studies is to compare delinquents with nondelinquents, for example, to identify risk and protective factors. Studies of this type include Wolfgang et al. (1972), Elliott et al. (1989), Farrington (1989), and the projects of OJJDP's Research Program on the Causes and Correlates of Delinquency (Huizinga, Loeber, and Thornberry, 1995). Many other studies focus solely on youth who have already had contact with the juvenile justice system. Although these studies examine different types of young offenders, recidivism and desistance, and related topics, the sample numbers are based on youth officially identified as delinquent. Studies of this nature include Snyder (1998), Ezell and Cohen (2005), and Mulvey et al. (2010).

In addition to variability by type of sample, there is also a fundamental difference in the manner in which delinquent behavior is measured in criminological studies. Many studies use official or archival data to assess whether a participant is a delinquent and, if so, the number and types of offenses committed. The most typical measures are arrest or adjudication records. Many other studies use self-reported data in which the study participants are surveyed and asked to report on their own involvement in delinquent behavior. In addition, some studies use both types of information—official measures and self-report measures—for the same participants. There is some relationship between the type of sample and the type of measure likely to be found in a given study. That is, studies of general community samples are likely to use self-reported measures, and studies of youth in the juvenile justice system are likely to use official measures. But that correlation is far from perfect. For example, the study by Wolfgang and colleagues (1972), based on a community cohort, uses only official data, whereas the study by Mulvey and colleagues (2010), based on an adjudicated sample, relies extensively on self-report measures.

Each strategy for sampling and for measurement has strengths and weaknesses. With respect to sampling, community samples are more representative of the total adolescent population and allow for important comparisons between youth who have committed delinquent acts and those who have not.* They often contain few very serious offenders, however, and are hampered in their investigation of juvenile justice system processes. In contrast, studies based on only adjudicated youth are likely to contain a higher representation of serious offenders and more direct information about how the juvenile justice system operates and how it influences delinquent careers. But, by definition, these studies do not include a comparison group of nondelinquents, and findings based on these samples cannot be generalized to the total adolescent population. Similarly, with respect to measurement, official measures may provide greater certainty that those identified as delinquent are, in fact, delinquents, but the heavy screening that occurs between the commission of an offense and the likelihood of arrest and adjudication means that the vast majority of youth who actually commit delinquent behaviors are not categorized as delinquent. In other words, they grossly undercount the number of delinquents and the number of delinquencies. In contrast, the self-report method provides a fuller accounting and is much more apt to identify all the youth who commit delinquent acts as delinquents, but they often underestimate the rate of serious and violent offending (Thornberry and Krohn, 2000).

These methodological issues can influence the results observed in studies and provide somewhat different images of the delinquent population and the developmental processes that lead to offending. Even something as basic as estimates of the prevalence of delinquency—the percentage of the population that engages in this behavior—differ. Based on self-reported delinquency studies, virtually everyone commits at least some delinquent acts during adolescence, and most report committing several (Short and Nye, 1958; Elliott, Huizinga, and Ageton, 1985; Huizinga et al., 1993). From this perspective, delinquent behavior could be considered "age-normative"—a part of the normal developmental process of moving through the teenage years. In contrast, in studies based on official measures, such as arrest or adjudication, delinquent behavior, especially repeated delinquent behavior, is committed only by a distinct minority of the adolescent population.

There are also differences in the basic correlates of delinquency, for example, by race/ethnicity, social class, and gender. In general, subgroup differences are greater when official data are used and considerably reduced when self-reported data are used.

Neither of these approaches to research—community versus juvenile justice samples or official versus self-report measures—is better than the other. As noted above, each has advantages and disadvantages. They are also designed to address somewhat different questions. For example, representative, community samples are more appropriate for identifying risk factors and causes of offending. Juvenile justice samples are more appropriate for studying the impact of new policies and practices in the juvenile justice system on various outcomes. Throughout this report, we rely on both types of studies and both types of measures as appropriate to the question at hand.

---

* It is important to point out that youth who are classified as nondelinquent may, in fact, have committed a delinquent act but have managed to evade detection.

2

Historical Context

Juvenile justice policy in the United States has evolved since the first juvenile court was established in Chicago in 1899. In this chapter, we characterize this evolution as four stages or periods of reform (Beuttler and Bell, 2010; Scott and Steinberg, 2010). Although there has been much overlap and continuity, and others might describe the history of the juvenile court differently during each of these periods, policy makers adopted an approach to juvenile crime that was different in important ways from the perspective and policies of other periods.

The first stage, which persisted into the 1960s, embodied the rehabilitative vision of the Progressive Era founders of the juvenile court (Lindsey and O'Higgins, 1970). These reformers viewed young offenders as innocent children and saw youthful criminal activity as symptomatic of an impoverished social context. Under the rehabilitative model, the purpose of correctional interventions was to provide the treatment young offenders needed to avoid a life of crime.

The second period of juvenile justice reform in the 1960s and 1970s was driven by the belief that the juvenile court was failing in its rehabilitative mission and that young offenders were actually being harmed by its paternalistic approach (Allen, 1964; Handler, 1965). Beginning in the 1960s with the landmark Supreme Court opinion of *In re Gault* (1967),[1] courts and legislatures introduced procedural due process into juvenile delinquency proceedings. Lawmakers in this period recognized that a jus-

---

[1] *In re Gault,* 387 U.S. 1 (1967).

tice system that aims to protect youth and promote their welfare must also adhere to the principles of justice and deal fairly with young offenders.

By the late 1980s, a harsher attitude toward juvenile crime had emerged, leading to a third period of policy reform, which lasted through the 1990s. Some even referred to youthful offenders as "super-predators" who posed a serious threat to public safety (Dilulio, 1995). During this period, the foundational premise of juvenile justice policy—that delinquent youth were different from adult criminals in ways that influenced their criminal conduct and should guide appropriate dispositions—seemed to carry little weight (Regnery, 1985). Lawmakers across the country radically reformed juvenile crime policy to facilitate the adult prosecution and punishment of young offenders and increase the length of confinement for those who remained in the juvenile system (Zimring, 1998). By 2000, the vision and commitments that led to the establishment of a separate juvenile justice system seemed to have disappeared, and some critics suggested that the system was obsolete and should be abolished altogether (Feld, 1998b).

In the past decade, policy makers and the public have had second thoughts about this harsh approach, and the country has moved toward a fourth period of juvenile justice reform. Many factors have contributed to widespread dissatisfaction with the policies of the past generation and to an interest in a less punitive response to youth crime. First, juvenile crime rates have been relatively low. Second, incarceration-based policies have strained state budgets, a burden that became more onerous during the economic recession of 2008-2009 and the period of anemic growth that has followed. More importantly perhaps, mounting evidence indicates that imposing harsh sentences on young offenders is unlikely to reduce reoffending or contribute to public safety in the way that supporters of get-tough policies assumed; indeed, sending youth to prison may increase the likelihood of recidivism (Task Force on Transforming Juvenile Justice, 2009). At the same time, a growing body of research on adolescent development, particularly brain development, has captured the attention of courts (including the U.S. Supreme Court) and policy makers. This research reinforces the conventional wisdom that adolescents *are* different from adults in ways that affect their criminal conduct, and it has probably contributed to the reemergence of less punitive attitudes toward juvenile offenders. Moreover, treatment programs in nonsecure settings that are based on developmental knowledge and implemented with fidelity have been shown to be effective in reducing crime at a lower cost than incarceration (Henggeler, Melton, and Smith, 1992; Aos et al., 2001; Aos, 2002; Barnoski and Aos, 2004; Greenwood and Turner, 2011).

In response, some states have repealed laws mandating transfer to adult court, and others have raised the general age of criminal court jurisdiction. In three important opinions, the Supreme Court held that imposing the most severe punishments on juveniles violates the ban on cruel and unusual punishment under the Eighth Amendment of the Constitution, sending a powerful signal that adult punishment of juveniles is problematic on moral grounds. The Court in these opinions emphasized that juveniles, because of their developmental immaturity, are less culpable than adults and therefore deserve less punishment.[2,3,4]

At the same time, states and localities have embraced evidence-based programs, sometimes shifting resources from expensive institutional facilities to communities (Bray, 2009). In general, pragmatic policy makers care about holding youth accountable for the harms they cause, but they also want to adopt effective programs that reduce crime at the lowest cost. These conditions create an opportunity to implement reforms grounded in scientific knowledge that serve the public interest as well as the interests of the youth involved in criminal activity.

FOUR STAGES OF JUVENILE JUSTICE REFORM

Stage One: The Rehabilitative Model

The establishment of the juvenile court was at the heart of the Progressive Era social reforms of the late 19th and early 20th centuries. In Chicago, progressive reformers such as Jane Addams sought to promote the welfare of poor immigrant children and, in 1899, established the first juvenile court in pursuit of this goal (Howell, 1997; Beuttler and Bell, 2010). Before this time, most youth charged with crimes were tried and punished as adults; only very young children were not held criminally responsible (Walkover, 1984). Whether based on mixed or benign motivations, an important Progressive Era goal was to define a role for the state as the protector of children—and to shift the boundary of childhood to include adolescents in that protection (Mack, 1909; Van Waters, 1925). Aside from the juvenile court, other important progressive reforms included compulsory school attendance and child labor laws (Davis et al., 2008). In promoting the juvenile court, the reformers envisioned a system that aimed to promote the welfare of youth involved in crime as well as those who had suffered abuse and neglect by their parents. Indeed, abused and delinquent children were described in similar terms; delinquent youth were thus often depicted as innocent children who had gone astray because their (usually immigrant) parents had failed them (Lindsey and Borough, 1931).

---

[2]*Roper v. Simmons*, 541 U.S. 1040 (2005).
[3]*Graham v. Florida*, U.S. Supreme Court, 560 U.S. (2010) (Slip Op., at 23).
[4]*Miller v. Alabama*, U.S. Supreme Court, 567 U.S. (2012).

The rehabilitative model was the foundation of the juvenile court and shaped its operation until the late 1960s. Criminal responsibility had no place in the jurisprudence of juvenile justice; the purpose of delinquency dispositions was to rehabilitate young offenders and not to punish them for their crimes (Mack, 1909; Lindsey and O'Higgins, 1970). Thus, although the purpose of delinquency proceedings was to respond to alleged criminal conduct, the original architects of the juvenile court insisted that it did not conduct criminal trials. Indeed, the traditional juvenile court was hardly a court at all. Because its announced purpose was diagnosis and prescription rather than adjudication and punishment, the proceedings were not adversarial (Lindsey and O'Higgins, 1970). Youth in delinquency proceedings were not afforded (and were presumed not to need) the procedural rights that are deemed essential to protect criminal defendants facing prosecution by the state. These include the right to an attorney, the right to confront witnesses, and the privilege against self-incrimination. Without attorneys testing the state's evidence and enforcing the rights of the accused, delinquency adjudications were informal proceedings (Stapleton and Teitelbaum, 1972). This informality was reflected in the qualifications of juvenile court judges, many of whom lacked legal training.

Under the rehabilitative model, judges prescribed individualized treatment based on the needs of the offender, presuming that treatment would correct youthful criminal tendencies. Consistent with the court's rehabilitative purpose, dispositions were indeterminate and open-ended; in theory, rehabilitation should end when the child was "cured" (Davis et al., 2008). Furthermore, the duration of dispositions bore no necessary relation to the seriousness of the offense. The principle of proportionality, like criminal responsibility, had no place in delinquency proceedings, and judges exercised broad discretion, ordering dispositions they deemed appropriate (Paulsen, 1957; Allen, 1964; Glueck, 1964).

At one level, the Progressive Era reformers were very successful in accomplishing their mission; between 1899 and 1925, every state established a separate juvenile court for dealing with youth charged with crimes—a remarkable institutional transformation (Dawson, 1990; Davis et al., 2008). However, the traditional juvenile court and the rehabilitative model on which it was based began to crumble in the 1960s. From the left and the right, critics claimed that the court's rehabilitative mission had never been achieved (Allen, 1964; Handler, 1965; Regnery, 1985; Dawson, 1990). Child advocates argued that the juvenile court harmed the youth whose interests it claimed to serve, and conservative critics emphasized its failure to protect the public from young criminals. These two challenges eventually led to successive waves of reform of juvenile justice policy in the last third of the 20th century.

Stage Two: The Due Process Reforms

In the 1960s, youth advocates argued that adolescents charged with crimes were getting a bad deal from a juvenile justice system that ostensibly was designed to serve their needs (Allen, 1964). The system failed to provide young offenders with the promised treatment, but the myth of rehabilitation continued to be offered as justification for denying juveniles the procedural rights of adult criminal defendants (Paulsen, 1957; Glueck, 1964; Handler, 1965). Juveniles charged with crimes had no right to an attorney, and the informal hearings in which their guilt was determined lacked the rigorous evidentiary protections of a criminal trial; on the basis of often casual fact-finding, many youth were adjudicated delinquent and sentenced to dispositions in prisonlike facilities (Allen, 1964; Handler, 1965).

Ultimately, the Supreme Court agreed with critics that youth in the juvenile system had the worst of both worlds.[5] In *In re Gault*, the Court extended many of the procedural rights enjoyed by criminal defendants to juveniles facing delinquency charges in juvenile court. The case of Gerry Gault represented a stark example of the deficiencies of the rehabilitative model of juvenile justice. Fifteen-year-old Gerry was accused of making lewd phone calls to his neighbor. He was brought before a juvenile court judge without notice of the charge or an attorney to defend him. The neighbor never appeared as a witness; instead, the arresting officer reported her complaint to the judge. At the end of the proceeding, the judge committed Gerry to the Arizona State Industrial School for up to six years—for a misdemeanor for which an adult would receive, at most, a $50 fine and jail term of up to 12 months. In Gerry's case and many others, the outcome of an informal nonadversarial delinquency proceeding was a potentially severe deprivation of liberty.

The Supreme Court rejected the state's justification for the court's informality. Writing for the Court, Justice Abe Fortas called the proceedings a "kangaroo court" (*In re Gault* at 28).[6] He observed that delinquent juveniles got little rehabilitation and that the high rates of recidivism among juvenile offenders showed that whatever treatment they received was ineffective. The Court in *Gault* held that youth in delinquency proceedings faced a serious loss of liberty and therefore were entitled to protection under the due process clause of the Fourteenth Amendment of the Constitution. Like adult criminal defendants, juveniles have a right to counsel, a right to notice of charges, a right to confront witnesses against them, and a privilege against self-incrimination. The introduction of due process

---

[5]*In re Gault*, 387 U.S. 1 (1967).
[6]Ibid.

(and particularly of attorneys) brought greater formality and regularity to delinquency proceedings.

It says much that these reforms were initiated by child advocates who argued that the rehabilitative model, which insistently focused on the objective of promoting children's welfare, actually harmed youth who came before the court (Paulsen, 1957; Allen, 1964). What the liberal critics realized was that this idealistic purpose obscured a tension at the heart of the rehabilitative model. The state's interest in responding to youth crime was more complex than the architects of the juvenile court acknowledged. When a young offender has intentionally caused social harm, the state's announced interest in promoting his welfare is in tension with powerful if unexpressed conflicting interests in public protection and accountability (Scott and Steinberg, 2010). In criminal proceedings, it is well understood that the state's interest is adverse to that of the defendant; it is for that reason that the Constitution requires procedural protections (Allen, 1964; Scott and Steinberg, 2010). The child advocates who challenged the informality of delinquency proceedings realized that the juvenile system's professed mission conflicted with these more conventional purposes of criminal justice.

Had the "treatment" offered by the juvenile system been effective, the tension might have been manageable. But policy makers and elected officials were increasingly frustrated by evaluations of rehabilitative programs that failed to generate strong and consistent effects (Martinson, 1974). As Justice Fortas pointed out, 66 percent of youth referred to juvenile court were recidivists (*In re Gault* at 28).[7] But when dispositions failed to rehabilitate young offenders, courts not surprisingly lost confidence in rehabilitation and imposed more restrictive and punitive correctional interventions. The rehabilitative model's inherent weakness eventually became clear to those who aimed to promote the interests of children; youth adjudicated without procedural protections were at the mercy of judges who were free to punish them while claiming to act in their best interests. The procedural changes mandated by the Supreme Court in *Gault* and later opinions[8,9] had a powerful impact on juvenile justice policy, transforming delinquency proceedings into adversarial hearings. Most importantly, juveniles after *Gault* have a right to be represented by attorneys, who can challenge prosecutors' evidence and raise defenses. During the adjudicative stage of the proceeding, as in a criminal trial, the prosecutor is required to prove that the youth committed the crime beyond a reasonable doubt. In contrast to the informal practice of the traditional court, the juvenile court judge is no

---

[7]*In re Gault*, 387 U.S. 1 (1967).
[8]*In re Winship*, 397 U.S. 358 (1970).
[9]*Breed v. Jones*, 421 U.S. 519 (1975).

longer free to question the juvenile about his conduct unless the juvenile waives his rights. Although adherence to the rules of evidence is somewhat less rigorous in juvenile proceedings, in many regards they became similar to criminal trials in the post-*Gault* era. The extension of procedural rights to juveniles in delinquency hearings proceeded with little attention to the question of whether juveniles were competent to exercise their rights. This may be due to an implicit assumption that the level of competence required for a juvenile to function as a defendant in a delinquency proceeding is less demanding than that required of an adult facing prosecution (Scott and Grisso, 2005). But adjudicative competence became a key issue in the 1990s as more youth were tried in criminal court.

These due process reforms made sense, of course, only if rehabilitation were not the sole aim of the hearings. But the due process reforms did not constitute an explicit rejection of the juvenile system or even of rehabilitation as one of its goals.[10] During the dispositional stage of the delinquency proceeding, courts are expected to exercise discretion and to respond to the individual needs of offenders. Although the due process reformers challenged the rosy characterization of young offenders as innocent children, they supported the proposition that juveniles were different from adults and should receive different treatment in the justice system (Zimring, 1978; Shepherd, 1996). In the 1970s and 1980s, most juveniles continued to be dealt with in a separate system in which dispositions continued to have a rehabilitative focus.

Nonetheless, the due process revolution created a conceptual vacuum, by destabilizing the rehabilitative model that had provided a coherent rationale for a juvenile justice system and borrowing adversarial procedures and sanctions from the adult criminal justice system. In the 1970s and 1980s, a few law reform groups responded by offering a new model of juvenile justice—one that emphasized accountability and public protection but retained a commitment to lenience and a concern for the needs of young offenders (Zimring, 1978, 1998; Shepherd, 1996). The Juvenile Justice Standards, an ambitious law reform project, sponsored by the Institute for Judicial Administration and the American Bar Association, emphasized the importance of expansive procedural protections for youth in delinquency proceedings and challenged the tradition of discretionary dispositions. The standards envisioned proportionate but lenient sanctions, which for most youth could be undertaken in their communities (Singer, 1980). But before this new approach could become established, youth advocates lost control of the law reform process. A third wave of reform took hold that explicitly rejected the goal of rehabilitation, along with the assumption that young offenders were different from adults in ways that were important to justice

---

[10]*McKeiver v. Pennsylvania*, 403 U.S. 528 (1971).

policy. Ironically, the procedural reforms that youth advocates had promoted appeared to support the legitimacy of an adversarial regime that
ignored developmental differences between juveniles and adults.

Stage Three: Getting Tough on Juvenile Offenders

The sweeping legal reforms in the 1980s and 1990s resulted in juvenile
justice policies quite different from both the traditional rehabilitative model
and the due process model of the 1960s and 1970s. This third period of
reform was triggered by an increase in violent juvenile crime, particularly
homicide, in the late 1980s that generated hostility and fear of young
offenders. Advocates for the punitive reforms offered a dramatically revised
account of delinquent youth; no longer were they depicted as wayward
children whose welfare was a key concern to the justice system. Indeed, an
important theme of these reforms was that young offenders were not different from their adult counterparts in ways that were relevant to criminal
responsibility or to the justice system's response to their crimes. Youthful
immaturity might warrant a more lenient response toward youth engaged in
petty criminal conduct, but those who committed serious (and particularly
violent) crimes should be punished as adults (Doherty, 1998). The mantra
of punitive reform, "adult time for adult crime," captured the sentiment of
the period (Wagman, 2000).

Public concern about violent juvenile crime was an important (and
legitimate) catalyst for reform during this period, but the legal changes
were often undertaken under conditions that had the hallmarks of a "moral
panic" (Cohen, 2002; Goode and Ben-Yehuda, 2009; Howell, 2009). Young
offenders were characterized as super-predators who posed a grave threat to
society—a threat that advocates predicted would worsen unless drastic measures were taken (Dilulio, 1995; Fox, 1996). In several states, legal changes
followed high-profile juvenile crimes—school shootings (as in Arkansas
following the Jonesville shootings) or gang killings of innocent bystanders.
The media focused on these incidents, politicians expressed grave concern,
and the public responded with alarm—contributing to an increasingly
urgent sense that "something must be done" (Scott and Steinberg, 2010).
Legislatures in turn rushed to pass laws that would respond to the concerns
expressed by their constituents to protect the public and punish young
offenders. Legitimate concerns about public safety became exaggerated in
response to salient incidents or political campaigns, so that in some states
harsh laws were enacted even though youth crime had been declining for
several years.

In pushing for major legal reform, critics targeted the juvenile court for
its ineffectiveness in controlling crime (Zimring, 1998). As mentioned earlier, beginning in the 1970s, critics pointed to mounting evidence that cor-

rectional programs were ineffective at reducing crime (Martinson, 1974). But disillusionment with the juvenile system was particularly acute. Many observers (including much of the public, according to many polls) thought the juvenile court's lenient treatment of young offenders and failure to hold them accountable for their criminal offenses encouraged youthful criminal activity (Flanagan and Maguire, 1991). Juvenile court judges were assumed to be too soft on young offenders, punishing them with slaps on the wrist and sending them back to the streets to offend again (Sprott, 1998; Zimring, 1998). It seems clear that a lack of confidence in the juvenile court played a key role in exacerbating the fear of juvenile crime and fueling the reforms of this period.

Around the country, reformers used several legislative strategies to facilitate the prosecution and punishment of juveniles as adults. First, laws governing the juvenile court were amended to facilitate judicial transfer of youth to criminal court and to expand the category of youth eligible for trial as adults (Torbet et al., 1996). Under traditional laws in most states, the transfer hearing functioned as a safety valve to exclude from juvenile court jurisdiction the occasional older youth charged with a serious violent felony who was deemed not amenable to treatment as a juvenile, thereby acknowledging that not every youth could be rehabilitated in the justice system (Wagman, 2000). During the period of punitive reforms, the category of transfer-eligible youth was expanded substantially to include young adolescents and even children (Wagman, 2000). For example, by 2000, 10-year-old youth charged with murder could be prosecuted and punished as adults in most states, and, in a large minority of states, there is no minimum age of transfer at all (Office of Juvenile Justice and Delinquency Prevention, 1995b; Griffin et al., 2011). Moreover, whereas traditional statutes focused on the maturity of the youth and his or her lack of amenability to treatment in the justice system, the new generation of statutes ignores or discounts these factors, emphasizing instead the seriousness of the charged crime (Feld, 1988). Finally, some statutes limit judicial discretion by creating presumptions favoring transfer for certain offenses.

Although many more youth became eligible for transfer in the wake of these reforms, another legal reform that expanded during this period has had a far greater impact on the adjudication of youth in adult court. Under "legislative waiver" or automatic transfer statutes, juveniles of a designated age are categorically excluded from juvenile court jurisdiction and tried as adults when charged with particular serious offenses (Torbet et al., 1996). For example, under California law, a 14-year-old charged with murder or rape is automatically prosecuted as an adult (California Welfare and Institutions Code, 2000). Between 1992 and 1995, 24 states either created or expanded (by adding more crimes) legislative waiver statutes (Torbet et al., 1996). These statutes implicitly shift the discretionary power to determine whether a youth will be tried as a juvenile or as an adult from the juvenile court judge to the prosecutor (who can decide whether to charge the waivable offense instead of a less serious crime in juvenile court). Under "direct file" statutes, another reform adopted in some states, prosecutors have explicit discretionary authority to charge juveniles as adults or as juveniles (Office of Juvenile Justice and Delinquency Prevention, 1997b). Moreover, in several states, the minimum age of *general* adult criminal court jurisdiction is set at 16 or 17 (Griffin et al., 2011), an age at which adolescents are legal minors for most other purposes. In New York, for example, all 16-year-olds are dealt with in the adult system.[11] Together, these reforms have resulted in a substantial increase in the number of youth tried as adults to 250,000 per year by most estimates (National Center for Juvenile Justice, 2011).

Many states also have expanded the range of offenses that can make youth eligible for criminal court adjudication. Traditionally, only youth charged with the most serious violent crimes (murder, rape, kidnapping, aggravated assault) could be tried as adults. Today, many statutes include long lists of transferrable offenses or crimes subject to automatic waiver; some states allow transfer for any felony (Torbet et al., 1996; Feld, 1998). Thus, although supporters of the punitive reforms emphasized the threat to public safety posed by violent youth, legislative reforms undertaken in a climate of moral panic have resulted in laws facilitating criminal prosecution of youth for nonviolent felonies as well. Indeed, more than half of the youth in prison in the 1990s were convicted of property and drug offenses (Puzzanchera et al., 2004).

Public and political hostility toward young offenders also had an important impact on the operation of the juvenile justice system (Sprott, 1998). Despite (or perhaps because of) the criticism of the juvenile court's excessive leniency, dispositions became much harsher during this period, with greater use of secure placement and longer periods of time. Moreover, some states introduced so-called blended sentencing, under which youth adjudicated in juvenile court who received lengthy sentences would be committed to a juvenile facility but upon turning 18 could complete their sentence in an adult prison (Duggan, 1999).

The punitive reforms of juvenile justice policy in the 1980s and 1990s responded to a legitimate concern; violent youth crime rates were high and, in the eyes of many policy makers and the public, the response of the juvenile justice system appeared to be inadequate. But extensive legal and policy changes were often undertaken with little deliberation in a climate of fear, and they were broader in scope than the concerns that triggered the reforms. Moreover, these legal challenges represented a radical departure

---

[11]*New York Family Court Act* § 301.2(1).

from the law's conventional approach toward minors generally. In virtually every other domain, a core assumption guides policy—that children and adolescents differ from adults in critically important ways and that society has an obligation to nurture their healthy development to adulthood. It is also assumed that promoting child welfare furthers the interest of society (Scott, 2000). They rejected the relevance to justice policy of the developmental differences between adolescents and adults—not questioning the efficacy or fairness of punishing juveniles as adults (Wagman, 2000). Moreover, they apparently assumed that the interests of society were wholly adverse to those of young offenders, who were portrayed as predators and enemies of society (Dilulio, 1995). Reformers saw harsh policies as the only means to protect the public from the threat of youth crime, paying little attention to the longer term consequences of these policies (Zimring, 1998; Scott and Steinberg, 2010).

The punitive reforms that effectively dismantled the rehabilitative model of juvenile justice did not proceed unchallenged. Youth advocates persisted in promoting traditional policies, but in the 1990s researchers and major private foundations also began to challenge the wisdom of criminalizing juvenile justice. For example, the Annie E. Casey Foundation undertook a national program of alternatives to detention, and in the mid-1990s the John D. and Catherine T. MacArthur Foundation launched a 10-year research network to study differences between juveniles and adults relevant to justice policy (Mendel, 2009; John D. and Catherine T. MacArthur Foundation, 2011). An important study sponsored by MacArthur indicated that younger juveniles might be incompetent to participate in criminal proceedings because of their developmental immaturity (Grisso et al., 2003). Meanwhile, a growing body of research indicated that evidence-based treatment programs implemented with fidelity to their design might be far more effective in changing youth behavior than incarceration (Henggeler, Melton, and Smith, 1992; Aos et al., 2001; Barnoski and Aos, 2004). Although these developments did not have an immediate impact, they paved the way for rethinking juvenile justice reform during the first decade of the 21st century.

Stage Four: A Window of Opportunity for Rethinking Juvenile Justice

By the mid-1990s, juvenile crime rates began to decline, and by 2004 youth crime rates were at a two-decade low (Snyder and Sickmund, 2006). Although supporters might argue that the harsh legal response caused the decline, juvenile crime rates had begun to decline long before the era of punitive reforms ran its course. A new attitude toward adolescent offenders and juvenile crime emerged, along with a reevaluation of incarceration-based correctional policies. The underlying premise of the juvenile court—that juvenile offenders are different from adult criminals and that the justice system should treat them differently—seems to be reemerging. Today, policy makers have the benefit of recent scientific knowledge about adolescence and about the features of effective interventions, knowledge that can provide a sounder basis for policies than was available to early 20th-century reformers.

Several pragmatic considerations have influenced lawmakers to revise their approach to youth crime. One is that the high costs of incarceration-based policies adopted in the 1990s have become increasingly clear, with escalating juvenile justice expenditures straining state budgets across the country (Aos, 2002; Aos et al., 2006). These costs became more onerous with the economic recession in 2008, forcing difficult trade-offs between corrections and other government programs. Moreover, states increasingly had good reason to question the social value of the costly reforms and to ask whether resources could not be better expended elsewhere. Recidivism rates were high for youth coming out of prison and juvenile institutions, suggesting that policies based heavily on incarceration were not serving their avowed purpose of protecting the public and reducing crime (Harp and Walker, 2007; Task Force on Transforming Juvenile Justice, 2009; Lippman, 2010). At the same time, a growing body of evidence, including comprehensive benefit-cost analyses, indicated that some community-based programs were effective at reducing recidivism—and at a much lower cost than incarceration (Aos et al., 2001). In combination, these factors have contributed to a new wave of policy initiatives and to a rethinking of juvenile justice policy.

The 1990s reforms were also challenged on racial justice grounds in the early years of the new century, when it became clear that minority youth received disproportionately harsh treatment in many states. In Illinois, for example, a statute mandating transfer for 15-year-olds charged with selling drugs overwhelmingly resulted in adult prosecutions of African American youth (Illinois Juvenile Justice Commission, 2005). The statute was repealed in 2005. In a Georgia case that received national publicity, a 17-year-old African American youth, Genarlow Wilson, received a 10-year prison sentence for aggravated child sexual molestation on the basis of consensual oral sex with a 15-year-old white girl. The sentence generated angry protests of racial bias and was reversed on the ground that it was excessive by the Georgia Supreme Court.[12] Thereafter, the legislature amended the law to make the crime a misdemeanor (Joyner, 2007).

The recent characterization of juvenile offenders in legal and policy contexts and by the media provides striking evidence of a change in attitude. Seldom is the term "super-predator" used today. Instead juvenile offenders are described as youth whose criminal activity is the product of

___
[12] *Wilson v. State*, 282 Ga. 520 (2007).

developmental immaturity (Wallis, 2004; Huff, 2007; Schrader, 2007). To some extent, this change in the public image of young offenders might simply represent the reemergence of deep-seated benevolent attitudes toward minors that were obscured during the "get tough" period of the 1990s. But today, scientific knowledge about adolescence informs a more sophisticated account of juveniles and their criminal activity than was available to reformers in earlier periods. This account not only does not support the traditional depiction of juveniles as children who bear no responsibility for their crimes, but it also clarifies that young offenders are quite different from their adult counterparts in ways that influence their criminal activity and response to correctional interventions. Lawmakers, from local and state government to the U.S. Supreme Court, increasingly accept that young offenders are adolescents and that their developmental immaturity is important to justice policy (Wallis, 2004).

A substantial body of research over the past generation (see Chapter 4) supports this new understanding of young offenders. Many behavioral studies show that psychosocial factors associated with adolescence may influence adolescent decision making in ways that contribute to criminal activity (Scott and Steinberg, 2010). These include susceptibility to peer influence, poor impulse control, sensation-seeking, and a tendency to focus on immediate rather than future consequences of choices. The impact of this research in the policy arena has been amplified by recent studies of adolescent brain development that have begun to shed light on the biological underpinnings of some of these psychosocial influences on decision making (see Chapter 4). Politicians and the public appear to give substantial weight to developmental neuroscience research, even at an early stage, and it is often invoked by policy makers in support of differential policies toward juvenile offenders (Begley, 2000; Wallis, 2004; Schrader, 2007).

The Supreme Court has relied on developmental research in three recent opinions prohibiting the use of the harshest criminal penalties with juvenile offenders. In a 2005 opinion, *Roper v. Simmons*,[13] the Court held that the use of the death penalty for a crime committed by a juvenile was a violation of the Constitution's prohibition of cruel and unusual punishment under the Eighth Amendment. The Court drew heavily on psychological research in reaching the conclusion that juveniles, because of their developmental immaturity, were not sufficiently blameworthy to be subject to a punishment reserved for the worst offenders. Five years later, in *Graham v. Florida*,[14] the Court extended its analysis to the sentence of life without parole for a nonhomicide offense. Like *Roper*, *Graham* emphasized that the immaturity of youth makes their crimes less reprehensible than those of

---

[13]*Roper v. Simmons*, 541 U.S. 1040 (2005).
[14]*Graham v. Florida*, U.S. Supreme Court, 560 U.S. (2010) (Slip Op., at 23).

adults and suggested that juvenile offenders cannot be assumed to be irre-deemable. *Graham* pointed to developments in psychology and brain sci-ence that "continue to show fundamental differences between juvenile and adult minds" (at 2026). Most recently, in *Miller v. Alabama*,[15] the Court again drew on developmental psychology and neuroscience in holding unconstitutional a mandatory sentence of life without parole for homicide.

Although the holdings of *Roper, Graham,* and *Miller* affect a relatively small category of young offenders, these opinions carry great symbolic importance. Following a long period in which the differences between juvenile and adult offenders were either ignored or denied as irrelevant to criminal punishment, the opinions are forceful statements by America's highest court that young offenders are different from and less culpable than adults. The Court bases this opinion not on conventional wisdom, but on developmental psychology and neuroscience research.

Some states have retreated from laws facilitating the adjudication of juveniles in adult court. For example, Washington State repealed an auto-matic transfer law enacted in 1994 and narrowed the category of offenses eligible for transfer,[16] and Illinois, as mentioned, abolished a statute man-dating adult prosecution of 15-year-olds charged with selling drugs near schools (Illinois Juvenile Justice Commission, 2005). Connecticut raised the general age of criminal court jurisdiction from 16 to 18, following a cam-paign that emphasized the developmental immaturity of young offenders and the need to separate them from adults (Connecticut Juvenile Jurisdic-tion Planning and Implementation Committee, 2007). Some states have abolished sentences of life imprisonment without parole altogether for juve-niles. In Colorado, Governor Bill Owens explained his support for abolition by pointing to research suggesting a link between immature adolescent brain development and youthful criminal activity (Moffeit and Simpson, 2006). Some states have also enacted statutes that facilitate the assessment of competence to stand trial of juveniles,[17] addressing concerns that some youth, because of their immaturity, may be unable to function adequately as defendants in criminal trials or, in some cases, even in juvenile adjudi-cations (Bonnie and Grisso, 2003; Scott and Grisso, 2005). The upshot is that adult adjudication and punishment of young offenders has lost some of its appeal in recent years and differences between youth and adults have become more salient in the policy arena.

Several jurisdictions also have systematically reduced the number of youth confined to institutions, shifting resources to community-based pro-grams that have been shown to reduce recidivism (Bray, 2009; National

---

[15]*Miller v. Alabama*, U.S. Supreme Court, 567 U.S. (2012).
[16]HB 1187, 59th Leg. Reg. sess. (Washington, 2005).
[17]Virginia Code Ann. Section 16.1-356.

Center for Juvenile Justice, 2011). A 2009 governor's task force report in New York evaluated the state's troubled juvenile institutions, in which youth (most convicted of misdemeanors) were confined at a cost to citizens of $210,000 a year. The report sharply criticized the system's punitive approach, which "damaged the future prospects of these young people, wasted millions of taxpayers' dollars and violated the fundamental principles of positive youth development" (Task Force on Transforming Juvenile Justice, 2009, p. 8). After the report was issued, New York City officials announced that the number of city delinquents sent to state institutions would be drastically reduced (Bosman, 2010). (See Chapter 9 for a detailed discussion of federal, state, and local jurisdictional reforms.)

Around the country, enthusiasm for evidence-based community programs and practices has become a dominant theme in juvenile justice reform. These programs seek to contribute to the healthy development of delinquent adolescents by enhancing key elements of their social environment and providing them with the tools to deal with environmental influences that have contributed to their criminal activity. The combination of the crime-reducing potential of these programs together with their lower cost, in comparison to institutional placement, has made them central to juvenile justice reform in many states.

A DEVELOPMENTAL APPROACH

Scientific research has played a significant role in influencing attitudes and in shaping policies and programs in juvenile justice reform over the past decade. First, research on adolescent development, particularly brain development, has been invoked to underscore that juvenile offenders are different from and less culpable than their adult counterparts—and that these differences should result in more lenient punishment of juveniles. This scientific knowledge challenges the core assumption driving the criminalization of juvenile justice policy in the last decades of the 20th century. Second, scientific research on adolescent psychosocial development has underscored the importance of social context to healthy development; this knowledge has informed the approach of evidence-based interventions and programs that have proven to be effective in reducing crime. Third, outcome research on these programs and on institutional placement of juveniles has been important in generating enthusiasm for evidence-based programs and has resulted in resource reallocation from institutions to communities.

The current period of reform shares some general objectives with earlier periods, but its perspective on how key goals can best be implemented is importantly influenced by scientific knowledge not available to early reformers—and not deemed relevant to the punitive reformers of the 1990s. Thus, public safety and the reduction of crime continue to be critically important policy objectives, but policy makers increasingly believe that incarceration may not be an effective means of accomplishing these goals with many youth (Task Force on Transforming Juvenile Justice, 2009). Instead, they are receptive to the crime-reducing potential of programs that address the developmental needs of adolescents (see Chapter 5). The presumption that the interests of society inherently conflict with those of young offenders is gradually yielding to a view that delinquent youth and society have convergent interests that can be realized through interventions that support the development of young offenders into law-abiding adults. Moreover, while contemporary policy makers continue to emphasize the importance of holding youth accountable for their crimes, scientific knowledge about adolescence now informs the meaning of this principle; accountability is less likely to be interpreted to mean "adult time for adult crime." It is also understood that holding youth accountable for their crimes functions to inculcate norms of personal responsibility, and thus it may have an important role in preventing future offending (see Chapter 6).

The current period of juvenile justice reform bears some similarity to the traditional rehabilitative model. Contemporary policy makers express more benign sentiments toward juvenile offenders than would have been heard a generation ago, and confidence in evidence-based programs is sometimes equated with a revival of rehabilitation as a key goal of juvenile justice. But the goal of rehabilitation is more closely linked to crime prevention than in the days of the traditional juvenile court. Moreover, developmental knowledge has undermined the Progressive Era myth that teenage offenders are children who lack criminal responsibility. Today it is accepted that adolescence is an intermediate developmental stage between childhood and adulthood and that justice policy should deal with most young offenders as adolescents.

An important objective of the current period—a growing commitment to substantive fairness in the adjudication of juveniles—is also grounded in modern developmental knowledge but has its origins in the due process reforms of the 1960s and 1970s. Neuroscience and behavioral research supports the intuition first offered by reformers in the 1970s that the criminal acts of juveniles are less culpable than those of adults, and that young offenders deserve less punishment than their adult counterparts (Zimring, 1978). Proportionality is a core principle of a fair system of criminal punishment (Bonnie, Coughlin, and Jeffries, 2010), but it was given short shrift in the 1990s (Steinberg and Scott, 2003). This has changed; the recent Supreme Court opinions emphasize the reduced culpability of juveniles, and this lesson has had far-reaching impact. Several states have raised the jurisdictional age or restricted their transfer laws in recent years, recognizing that the adult prosecution and punishment of juveniles should be reserved for a narrow category of older youth charged with particularly serious offenses or who have been chronic offenders.

Concerns about procedural fairness have also become increasingly salient, as courts and legislatures have realized that youth may need special protections when they face law enforcement and adult prosecution (Scott and Grisso, 2005). Several states have created procedures for evaluating the competence to stand trial of juveniles, in response to research indicating that younger teens may be unable to participate effectively in their defense in criminal proceedings (Grisso et al., 2003). Moreover, very recently the Supreme Court held that the age of a young suspect must be a factor in evaluating whether police questioning is "custodial."[18] In general, policy makers have recognized that juveniles in the justice system differ from adults in important ways, and this has challenged them to reconcile policies with principles of fairness.

Recognition of the important differences between adolescents and adults and the other social and legal developments described in this chapter have distinct implications for policy making in the two key domains of juvenile crime policy—the design and operation of the juvenile justice system and the treatment of juveniles in the criminal justice system. The committee's charge focuses exclusively on reforming the juvenile justice system, and the report accordingly does not address the policies and practices of criminal courts toward young offenders (the setting for the Supreme Court's influential decisions over the past decade). Nor does the report undertake a comprehensive review of the still-controversial issues relating to the boundaries between the juvenile and the criminal justice systems; the circumstances under which adolescents should be subject to criminal court jurisdiction are mentioned only when necessary to draw out the implications of findings and conclusions reached about the juvenile justice system.[19]

---

[18]*JDB v. North Carolina*, 131 S. Ct. 2394 (2011).

[19]See Loeber and Farrington (2012) for a review of offending careers during the age period between midadolescence and early adulthood (roughly ages 15-29) and the implications of this research for juvenile and criminal justice systems.

3

Current Practice in the Juvenile Justice System

Juvenile justice is a highly varied process that is shaped by law and driven by local practice. Youth coming into the justice system—usually after an arrest by law enforcement—are screened and assessed by various organizations and individuals. The charges against them are reviewed for legal sufficiency, and a formalized court process may be used to establish their culpable commission of a criminal act. If the case merits some type of intervention, other actors in the justice system attempt to match the youth with an appropriate and cost-effective program or sanction. The availability and suitability of an intervention often influences the outcome of earlier decisions.

As expressed in most state statutes and understood by participants, the goals of the process are to hold youth accountable, to satisfy the demands of due process, and to prevent crime, ideally by providing rehabilitative interventions in the most serious and high-risk cases while keeping costs to a minimum and avoiding the use of expensive interventions for low-risk youth and youth charged with less serious offenses. A wide variety of professionals, semiprofessionals, citizens, and volunteers participate in the juvenile justice process. Although all participants share a general commitment to the declared goals, they rely on their own professional perspectives and values in making decisions and recommending particular actions for individual cases. Law enforcement officers want to identify young offenders quickly and to ensure that every youth receives an effective and appropriate sanction for each offense. Prosecutors want the legal system to run efficiently and to protect the rights and feelings of crime victims while deterring future crime. Defense attorneys want their clients to be treated fairly and for all youth meriting rehabilitation to receive services that will help them to stay out of trouble. The public wants the entire process to be cost-effective and their neighborhoods and homes to be safe.

Balancing the varying perspectives and expectations of the people involved in the juvenile justice process can be difficult, contentious, and somewhat unpredictable. Young people charged with committing similar acts of delinquency may be handled quite differently, depending on the state or county in which they live, the characteristics of their families and neighborhoods, their sex, their race or ethnicity, their demeanor, their involvement with drugs and alcohol, any mental health issues involved, and the actual harm their behavior has inflicted on individuals or the community. Some youth are treated harshly and receive severe punishments, including long periods of confinement, and others are handled informally and even diverted from the process without any legal record of the encounter. The seriousness of the offense and the past record of the offender help to determine but do not ordinarily control the outcome. Many factors govern the path that an individual delinquency case takes through the justice process. The juvenile justice process is organizationally complex, value-driven, and often politicized. It does not necessarily involve careful and accurate assessments of needs or treatment. Thus, it is not possible to infer the dangerousness and harmfulness of a youth's behavior solely on the basis of how that individual is handled in the juvenile justice system. There are too many other factors involved, some of which stem from the youth's behavior, but others originate in bureaucracy, fiscal and political issues, and cultural definitions of social problems.

This chapter aims to provide an overview of the practice of juvenile justice in the United States—that is, the patterns and variations that emerge in 50 states and the District of Columbia as well as those that characterize what is often a highly localized process. After describing the characteristics of youth (and charges) that can bring them within the jurisdiction of the juvenile court, the chapter provides an overview of juvenile justice administration and summarizes the aggregated decisions made at each stage of the process by police, intake officers, prosecutors, and judges. Having presented a portrait of juvenile justice, we return to the theme of complexity with which the chapter began.

DEFINING JUVENILE DELINQUENCY

The juvenile justice system is the combined effect of decisions and actions taken by the police, the courts, and a wide variety of human services agencies as they respond to incidents of juvenile delinquency. What is a "juvenile"? The answer varies from place to place and from case to case. What is "delinquency"? Some illegal behaviors by underage minors are considered to be acts of delinquency; some are not. How does one define the system that responds to cases of delinquency? Do youth have to be arrested to have contact with the system? Must they be formally charged, adjudicated, or placed in a program to be in the system? Discussions about juvenile justice policy and practice are confusing if these elements are not clear. In short, it must be remembered that juvenile delinquency (i.e., conduct for which a juvenile is subject to a delinquency adjudication) is a legally defined concept that varies substantially from state to state. (See the "Terminology" section in Chapter 1 for the committee's definitions.)

Most people would say that a juvenile delinquent is a badly behaved teenager under age 18 who gets into trouble frequently—or, more precisely, one who gets into trouble with police frequently. The image that comes to mind is an adolescent who skips school, drinks alcohol, uses illegal drugs, steals, is often belligerent, and may be prone to violence. This popular notion of delinquency, however, is not an adequate definition for a discussion of juvenile justice practice and policy. It is far too broad. Not all misbehaving teenagers under age 18 are subject to the jurisdiction of the juvenile court. Even when they are legally defined as a minor (or juvenile), not all of their law violations are defined as acts of "juvenile delinquency." A law violation by a young person is considered an act of juvenile delinquency only if the behavior meets all three of the following criteria: (1) the act involved would be a criminal offense if it were committed by an adult; (2) the young person charged with committing the act is below the age at which the criminal court traditionally assumes jurisdiction; and (3) the juvenile is charged with an offense that must be adjudicated in the juvenile court (or some other court with jurisdiction over noncriminal but illegal acts of juveniles) or the prosecution and the juvenile court judge exercise their discretion to lodge and retain jurisdiction in the juvenile court.

In all states, the legal status of a young person charged with an illegal act is largely determined by the person's age, but the exact definitions are governed by state law. Most states consider people to be adults for the purposes of criminal prosecution as of their 18th birthday, but some jurisdictions use the 17th birthday as the cutoff (e.g., Georgia, Louisiana, Massachusetts, Michigan, Missouri, and Texas) and a few prefer the 16th birthday (e.g., New York and North Carolina). States periodically revisit these age boundaries (Office of Juvenile Justice and Delinquency Prevention, 2011c). Since the mid-1990s, the legislatures of Connecticut, Illinois, New Hampshire, and Wisconsin, all redefined the original jurisdiction of their juvenile courts, either raising the boundary for entire age groups (Connecticut, New Hampshire, and Wisconsin) or raising it for certain classes of offenses (Illinois). Whatever age is specified by state law as the upper limit of original juvenile jurisdiction, young people who commit offenses after that age are automatically under the jurisdiction of the criminal (adult) court. Whatever happens to them as a result of being arrested is outside the scope of the juvenile justice system. States may also set a lower boundary for the age of original juvenile court jurisdiction (Snyder and Sickmund, 2006). Children below the specified age do not fall under the jurisdiction of the juvenile court when they commit delinquent acts. Such matters are referred instead to a child welfare or social services agency. In Pennsylvania, for example, children below age 10 are not brought into juvenile court for delinquent charges. Youth under age 10 are juveniles in the legal sense but their law violations are not defined as delinquency. North Carolina sets a lower age limit of 6 years, and Maryland, Massachusetts, and New York, set it at age 7. A total of 34 states and the District of Columbia have no statutory age limit for when children may face delinquency charges in juvenile court, but it is often assumed, based on common law principles, that the minimum age for juvenile court jurisdiction in these states is age 7.

Youth may also be subject to juvenile court jurisdiction for behaviors that would not be considered illegal for adults. Generally these are called "status offenses"—not acts of delinquency—because they apply only to persons whose legal status is that of a juvenile. The most common status offenses are running away from home, refusing to attend school (truancy), violating curfew ordinances, and refusing to obey parents, teachers, or other lawful authorities (incorrigibility). Other common status offenses are underage drinking of alcoholic beverages or smoking tobacco and engaging in underage, consensual sexual activities. Not all jurisdictions use the term "status offense." Some states refer to these youth simply as "nonoffenders." Other states use names that imply that a young person has not been charged with criminal violations but may be still subject to court intervention—such as "children in need of supervision" or "persons in need of supervision."

The last, and essential, criterion for defining a young person's illegal behavior as an act of delinquency is that the case remains under the delinquency jurisdiction of a court empowered to handle delinquent matters. Every state has some form of "transfer" law that removes particular youth or particular cases from the delinquency jurisdiction of the juvenile court, placing them under the criminal jurisdiction of another court (see Box 3-1). State laws define the scope of these transfer provisions differently, using various combinations of age, offense, and prior record (Griffin et al., 2011). In most states, youth may be transferred by order of a juvenile court judge who "waives" the juvenile court's jurisdiction and allows the case to be tried in criminal court. In some states, however, it is not necessary to obtain the consent of a judge. Youth may be transferred by prosecutors on an individual basis or by a preemptive act of the legislature, known as "statutory exclusion" or "automatic transfer." For example, a 15-year-old who steals something of value will typically be charged with an act of delinquency

---

BOX 3-1
Mechanisms Used to Transfer Youth Out of the
Juvenile Justice System

Judicial Waiver. The most commonly available method of sending juveniles to criminal court (i.e., used by the most states). Juvenile court judges can decide to waive their jurisdiction over a particular case and transfer it instead to the adult court. This is also referred to as a discretionary waiver.

Legislative Exclusion. The most frequently used method of transfer (i.e., affects the most youth). State legislators pass a law requiring all youth charged with certain offenses to be prosecuted in criminal court even if they are below the age of criminal court jurisdiction. Sometimes it is called "automatic transfer."

Prosecutor Discretion. The second most frequently used method of sending youth to adult court. State law gives prosecutors the authority to decide whether to send certain youthful offenders to juvenile court or to criminal court. Also known as "concurrent jurisdiction" because certain cases (those involving serious offenses committed by youth at least age 14, age 15, etc.) start out under the jurisdiction of both courts, adult and juvenile.

---

akin to theft or burglary and the matter will be handled in juvenile court. A 15-year-old who steals using a threat of force, however, may be charged with robbery and in some states that offense will fall automatically under the jurisdiction of the criminal court, depending on the youth's age at the time of the offense. In such a state, a youth charged with robbery after the cutoff age immediately loses the protection of his or her juvenile status.

THE JUVENILE JUSTICE PROCESS

Each state, county, and sometimes each city creates its own processes for responding to delinquent youth. Law violations by young people may be handled by probate courts, juvenile divisions of a circuit court, or even comprehensive family courts. In every community, some form of court is charged with responding to cases in which a person under the age of adulthood (a juvenile) is suspected of breaking the law. Because these courts have jurisdiction over juveniles and they follow the same general principles of juvenile law, it is conventional to refer to them simply as juvenile courts.

But they are far from standardized. Many juvenile courts handle other types of cases. They often handle dependency cases (or matters involving abused and neglected children) and youth charged with noncriminal acts (i.e., status offenses). Other juvenile courts (especially family courts) handle domestic violence and child custody matters (Butts, 2002).

As the juvenile court concept spread across the United States in the early 20th century, lawmakers invented a variety of structures for the new courts in order to incorporate juvenile court ideals into existing procedures and policies (Watkins, 1998). Frequently, the court responsible for handling young people accused of law violations is a division of the trial court with general jurisdiction (Butts, 2002). However, some states and localities have created a separate juvenile court that is also a court of general jurisdiction. Other states operate juvenile courts within a single, statewide structure of limited jurisdiction courts.

Certain processing steps, of course, are common to most juvenile justice systems, regardless of terminology, the configuration of the court, or the allocation of service delivery responsibilities. These include intake screening, filing a formal petition, adjudication, and disposition (National Research Council, 2001a). Several kinds of hearings occur during these stages. They include the detention hearing, the waiver or fitness hearing, the adjudicatory hearing, the dispositional hearing, and the postdisposition review. Hearings to review the youth's violation of the court-approved plan (Binder et al., 1997; National Council of Juvenile and Family Court Judges, 2005) are also held.

Juvenile Court Administration

Intake Screening and Petition

Before any court processes come into play, a juvenile must be referred to the court. Referral can be made by the police, parents, schools, social service agencies, probation officer, or victims. Generally police are the primary referring agents, but, in approximately 20 percent of the arrests, referral will come from a source other than the police (Snyder and Sickmund, 2006).

Police affidavits explaining the alleged facts and circumstances are filed with the juvenile court, and at this stage the juvenile court process is said to begin. The affidavit is then forwarded to the prosecutor or handled by juvenile court intake, most commonly the probation department. The legal sufficiency of the case is determined during this first stage as well as whether the case is better resolved informally through diversion to a program or a specified set of conditions without formal adjudication (National Research Council, 2001a). A decision is also made whether to continue detention for those youth brought into custody. Unlike adults, juveniles do not have a constitutional right to bail but instead may be released to parents or a guardian.

Virtually all cases that are handled by the juvenile courts have contact with a probation officer. Probation departments are generally responsible for screening cases, making detention decisions on some of them, preparing investigative reports on most of them, providing supervision to more than a third of all cases processed by the juvenile court, and delivering aftercare services to many youth released from out-of-home placement. Youth may be assigned to the probation department at the front end as a pretrial alternative to formal adjudication or as an alternative to detention. Usually, the pretrial alternative is offered only to first-time low-risk offenders. As described below, not all probation departments execute all of the intake functions (Torbet et al., 1996).

The detention decision is reviewed by a judge in a *detention hearing*. This hearing is also referred to as an arraignment, initial hearing, pretrial hearing, probable cause hearing, or plea hearing. Numerous issues may be handled: appointment of counsel, the youth's admission or denial of allegations, a determination of the youth's detention status or condition of release pending trial, and a determination of the need for additional services. The judge determines whether the youth is competent to stand trial (which may lead to a separate hearing), reviews the youth's due process rights, and addresses the youth's right to a jury trial if one is available under state law. Unlike adults, youth in juvenile court do not have a constitutional right to a jury trial,[1] although 20 states do provide them as either an absolute right or a right under limited special circumstances (Szymanski, 2008). Options available to the court at this first stage include dismissal, unofficial handling by the court that may include informal or voluntary probation without filing a petition, or initiating the formal process by filing a petition (Binder et al., 1997). Some youth will voluntarily agree to probation (known as voluntary probation) with the understanding that if they successfully complete their probationary period (usually 3-6 months), their case will be terminated without any formal processing.

A petition may be filed if the factual allegations provide a legally sufficient basis for prosecution and no adequate alternative responses to the youth's behavior are available outside the juvenile justice system. Whereas prosecutors focus on the legal sufficiency, the role of an intake officer is usually broader—to determine whether the youth is a risk to himself or herself, to determine whether he or she should be detained, and to make recommendations whether the case should be handled formally (filing a petition) or informally. In many jurisdictions, the petition will be filed by the court intake officer (or probation officer) (Snyder and Sickmund, 2006), and the

---

[1] *McKeiver v. Pennsylvania*, 403 U.S. 528 (1971).

prosecutor's role will be limited to reviewing cases petitioned by the intake officer. In other jurisdictions, the prosecutor will review all police referrals and take complete responsibility for court intake screening. Regardless of the roles of court intake or the prosecutor, front-end juvenile processing decisions, because of the discretion they involve, have an enormous impact on court operations and how youth are handled. However, no national inventory exists of these arrangements or intake practices (Mears, 2012).

Prior to making a determination to proceed to adjudication, the court may also schedule a *waiver* or *fitness hearing* prior to proceeding to or in lieu of an adjudicatory hearing if the prosecutor has filed a motion asking the court to waive juvenile court jurisdiction and transfer the youth to the criminal court. Whether transfer is mandatory or discretionary under the terms of state law, the court must determine whether there is probable cause to believe the youth has committed the alleged offense. If the court finds probable cause, a second decision involves whether the court will retain jurisdiction or transfer the case. Unless transfer is mandatory, the court's decision will depend on the statutory criteria, which vary widely from state to state. Typically, the state bears the burden of proving that the criteria are met, but a youth can contest the waiver motion by challenging or producing evidence. If the waiver is presumptive under the statute upon proof of probable cause and previous delinquency, the burden of proof may shift to the youth to prove that he or she is amenable to treatment in the juvenile justice system (National Council of Juvenile and Family Court Judges, 2005).

Adjudication and Disposition

The *adjudicatory hearing* is similar to a trial in criminal court. All youth have a constitutional right to counsel at the adjudicatory stage (*In re Gault*, 1967). *Gault* also established the rights to a speedy trial, timely notice, cross-examination of witnesses, and to remain silent at adjudicatory hearings when there is a possibility of incarceration (Binder et al., 1997) (see Chapters 2 and 7). According to the model court guidelines of the National Council of Juvenile and Family Court Judges (2005), the youth's counsel has responsibility for investigating all circumstances behind the allegations, seeking discovery for all court documents, appointing an investigator, and informing the youth and his family about the nature of the proceedings and the consequences. The guidelines also propose that statements of a juvenile made during court intake or during the detention hearing should not be admissible at trial. The state is required to prove every element of the allegation beyond a reasonable doubt. Finally, the guidelines also note the importance of juvenile delinquency courts' rendering timely decisions and the avoidance of continuances (National Council of Juvenile and Family Court Judges, 2005).

The *adjudicatory hearing* may result in the youth being found to have committed the delinquent act (and equivalent to a finding of guilt and a conviction in a criminal trial), in which case a disposition hearing will be scheduled. The youth is now considered an "adjudicated delinquent." The youth may be found not guilty and the case dismissed, or the case may be continued in contemplation of dismissal. The latter may occur if the judge orders the youth to undertake some kind of action prior to the final decision being made (National Research Council, 2001a). Similar to criminal courts, plea agreements between the prosecutor and the youth's counsel may also occur during the adjudicatory phase.

The *dispositional hearing* is similar to the sentencing hearing in the criminal court. Some states allow a dispositional hearing immediately after the adjudicatory hearing if the youth admits to the offense, but usually time is required to complete a social history or receive evidence. In several states, there are time limits to the period between the adjudication and disposition phases (Binder et al., 1997). Unlike the adjudicatory hearing, virtually any information that bears on the youth's life, family, schooling, etc., is admissible.

A judge can decide on probation, placement in a foster home, institutionalization, or some other alternative for the youth, such as referral to a treatment program, imposition of a fine, community service, victim-offender mediation, or restitution. Probation is the most common disposition for youth who receive a juvenile court sanction (Snyder and Sickmund, 1999).

Finally, during the period the youth is under the court's jurisdiction, the judge may require a *postdisposition hearing* or *review* to determine if the youth, parent, and/or legal guardian is following the court's orders and services are being provided. However, for many youth, counsel are not often involved in the postdisposition stage and as a result are not available to advise on many important postdisposition matters (see Chapter 7). Youth who commit technical violations of the court-approved plan (not new alleged delinquent acts) will be handled in the same manner as a new delinquency petition alleging a misdemeanor or felony (National Council of Juvenile and Family Court Judges, 2005).

The Impact of Due Process Requirements

A full and accurate description of juvenile court administration is incomplete without addressing the impact of the due process requirements mandated by various decisions of the Supreme Court in the 1960s and 1970s. These decisions[2] are discussed in Chapter 2. Among the pro-

---

[2]*Kent v. United States*, 383 U.S. 541 (1966); *In re Gault*, 387 U.S. 1 (1967); *In re Winship*, 397 U.S. 358 (1970); *Breed v. Jones*, 421 U.S. 519 (1975).

cedural safeguards these decisions established are the right against self-incrimination, the right to counsel, the right to timely notice of allegations, the right to confront and cross-examine witnesses, a prohibition against double jeopardy, and a requirement of proof beyond a reasonable doubt in adjudicatory hearings. Other due process requirements, such as right to bail and the right to trial by jury found in criminal courts, were not mandated for the juvenile court.

Although the states incorporated due process requirements into their state codes, it is difficult to generalize about the extent of their implementation given the diverse practices of juvenile courts. Little research exists on the contemporary juvenile court more generally or on the philosophies and practices of those who administer and work in it (Bishop, 2006; Tanenhaus, 2012). Scholars who have studied juvenile courts typically describe the gap between the intent of due process requirements (the ideal) and actual practice (Feld, 1991, 2012; Binder, 1997; Mears, 2012). Mears, in particular, concludes that genuine due process probably constitutes the exception rather than the norm (2012, p. 600). Feld takes a somewhat different tack, arguing that the current due process rights are inadequate to begin with and additional procedural safeguards are needed to protect youth from their immaturity and vulnerability (2012).

This gap is reflected in findings relating to access to counsel (e.g., barriers to appointed counsel, frequency of waiver of counsel) and the effectiveness of counsel (e.g., high caseloads, public defender staff turnover, inexperience). Almost three decades after *Gault*, a national survey of the defense bar (Puritz et al., 1995) showed that more than a third of public defender offices reported some youth waiving their right to counsel at the detention hearing. They also reported enormous caseloads of more than 500 cases a year and large turnovers of staff, with 55 percent of public defenders staying less than 24 months. More recently, state-by-state assessments conducted during 2001 and 2007 reflect large numbers of youth waiving counsel, failing to have counsel appointed, or not availing themselves of counsel early in the process. Other state findings reflect inadequate legal representation, with states reporting limited contact with juvenile clients, failure to perform necessary background investigations, and a lack of training (Mlyniec, 2008). These findings have implications for whether fairness is being achieved but also whether the process is being perceived as fair by youth and their families. See Chapter 7 for more detail on the status of defense representation.

Despite the change from the traditional rehabilitation model to a more adversarial one with its due process requirements, the juvenile court retains broad powers over those who come under its jurisdiction (Tanenhaus, 2012). Court intake officers, in particular, continue to exercise enormous discretion and make decisions that can "affect case flows, the frequency and manner in which detention is used, the amount of informal and formal sanctioning that occurs, the use of various services and treatments, and differences in how different groups (e.g., males versus females, minorities, the mentally ill) are processed" (Mears, 2012, p. 593). Having defense counsel can serve as a check against decisions that are unfounded or not in the best interest of the youth (National Council of Juvenile and Family Court Judges, 2005), and all 50 states provide some statutory right to counsel for youth accused of delinquency in the juvenile justice system. Nonetheless, access to counsel and the quality of legal representation for youth appear to be uneven and haphazard (Puritz et al., 1995; Mlyniec, 2008) in many jurisdictions. Finally, most juvenile courts allow young offenders to waive those rights; others have been noted for their aggressiveness in encouraging waivers (Binder et al., 1997).

Juvenile Crimes Not Handled by the Justice System

Analyzing the operations of juvenile justice systems is not the same as analyzing juvenile crime itself. The workloads of law enforcement agencies and courts are partly the result of the scale and intensity of illegal activity by youth, and partly a function of how likely it is that citizens report crimes and how likely it is that police and courts decide to intervene. The likelihood that any particular youth will be arrested and referred to court depends on the amount of personnel and resources available to the police and the court system, as well as the effect of each agency's policies and practices about the appropriate response to juvenile offending. The combined effect of these factors can be profound. The odds of a particular crime being reported vary, and the odds of that report resulting in an arrest and that arrest resulting in a referral to the justice system also vary. In the end, the youth processed by the juvenile justice system are merely a sample of all young people involved in illegal behavior.

The "sampling" effect of the juvenile justice system is clear when official data are compared with self-reported data. Self-reported delinquency data (obtained from youth directly) suggest that half of all 15-year-old youth may have done something in the previous year that could have resulted in their arrest. According to the annual Monitoring the Future surveys administered by the Institute for Social Research at the University of Michigan, 27 percent of all tenth graders (or 15-year-olds) report having used an illegal drug in the previous 12 months (Johnston et al., 2012). According to the U.S. Census Bureau, in 2008, the resident population of 15-year-olds in the United States was approximately 4.2 million. If 27 percent of these youth used illegal drugs, this would suggest that the pool of violators among 15-year-olds could be as high as 1.1 million each year. According to Federal Bureau of Investigation (FBI) data, however, police nationwide made approximately 150,000 drug arrests involving 15-year-olds in 2008 (Snyder and Mulako-Wangota, 2011). Juvenile courts nationwide report that they handled just 36,600 delinquency cases in 2008 involving 15-year-old juveniles charged with drug offenses (Puzzancheraet, Adams, and Sickmund, 2011). Thus, the juvenile justice system handles roughly 3 percent of all the "actual" 15-year-old drug offenders each year.

A similar heuristic exercise can be undertaken for other offenses. For example, the National Survey on Drug Use and Health[3] (Substance Abuse and Mental Health Services Administration, 2012) estimates that 4 percent of all 15-year-olds carried a handgun at least once in the past year. Thus, the pool of 15-year-old violators for weapon charges (not even counting other types of weapons) in 2008 was perhaps 168,000 of the nation's 4.2 million 15-year-olds. Yet law enforcement agencies across the United States reported just 27,200 weapon arrests involving youth who were age 15 (Snyder and Mulako-Wangota, 2011), suggesting that police may have had contact with just 16 percent of the 15-year-olds who could have been arrested for weapon possession at least once if their offense had been detected.

The committee recognizes that the Fourth Amendment and general respect for individual privacy substantially limits the detection of drug and weapons offenses and that arrests will and should necessarily be limited. However, these data are useful reminders that the scale of the juvenile justice system, the number and characteristics of arrestees, and the odds of any particular youth being involved in the justice system may vary depending on political decisions and structural disparities that influence the level of resources and personnel that will be deployed to detect, apprehend, and prosecute young offenders in various communities. For a further explanation of how these factors can contribute to racial/ethnic disparities, see Chapter 8.

Juvenile Crimes Reported to Police

Several methods are used to measure the amount of juvenile crime and delinquency in the United States. Of course, there is no perfect way to estimate the total volume of juvenile crime or to predict future changes in juvenile offending. Official data from law enforcement and courts, however, allow one to appreciate the scale of juvenile crime trends and to place current crime levels in the proper context.

The most reliable source of official data about juvenile crime is the

---

[3]The authors offer a caveat. The National Survey on Drug Use and Health is based on a randomly selected sample of 70,000 individuals. Although the methodology aims at ensuring as representative a sample as possible, the results are an approximation and cannot be assumed to be true for the entire U.S. population.

Uniform Crime Reports (UCR) series maintained by the FBI in the U.S. Department of Justice (see http://www.fbi.gov/stats-services/crimestats). The UCR data represent reported crimes and the arrests made by police in thousands of cities and towns across the country. When Americans hear media stories about changes in the official "crime rate," they are probably encountering the latest figures from the UCR. A regular compilation of UCR data is published each year by the FBI as *Crime in the United States* (CIUS). The annual CIUS report and the various preliminary and supplemental reports associated with it constitute the nation's primary source of data about crime trends.

It is not possible to analyze the crimes committed by juveniles because, until an arrest is made in response to a crime, the age of the offender is unknown. Thus, all law enforcement data about "juvenile crime" is actually a measure of arrests rather than crime. Nor is an arrest dispositive of guilt. Because youth tend to commit crime in groups more often than adults do (Snyder and Sickmund, 2006), they may be committing fewer crimes than aggregated arrest numbers suggest. It also means that the available measures of juvenile crime are affected by law enforcement resources. The first step in using this information for analyzing juvenile crime is to create national estimates of juvenile arrests. The UCR reports do not include data from all jurisdictions in the country, only those jurisdictions able to report data on time and in the format required by the FBI. In recent years, the jurisdictions included in the UCR reporting sample accounted for 70 to 78 percent of the U.S. population. The FBI creates one national arrest estimate for each major offense by taking the total number of arrests reported in each offense category and weighting the number to represent the national population (see Federal Bureau of Investigation, 2011, Table 29). For example, in 2010 the FBI estimated that law enforcement agencies across the country made a total of 13.1 million arrests, including more than 552,000 arrests for violent crimes and 1.6 million arrests for property crimes. These arrests, however, involved offenders of all ages. To track arrests of juveniles (i.e., offenders under age 18) requires an additional step.

Beginning in the 1990s, the U.S. government began publishing national estimates of arrests for specific age groups. Using a method developed by Howard N. Snyder (now with the Bureau of Justice Statistics at the U.S. Department of Justice), data from UCR-participating jurisdictions was analyzed to determine the proportion of arrests reported for each offense that involved individuals of various ages. Those proportions were then applied to the national estimate for each offense as published by the FBI (2011, Table 29). Next, per capita rates of arrest were determined by dividing each of these national arrest estimates over the appropriate population data from the U.S. Census Bureau. National arrest estimates created with this method were routinely published in reports from the Office of Juvenile

Justice and Delinquency Prevention (Butts, 2010). More recently, similar estimates were made available from the Bureau of Justice Statistics (BJS) (see http://bjs.ojp.usdoj.gov/).

Using these methods of estimation, the total number of juvenile (under age 18) arrests made by law enforcement in 2010 was more than 1.6 million (see Table 3-1). Of these arrests, 75,800 involved one of the offenses included in the FBI's Violent Crime Index, including murder and non-negligent manslaughter (1,000), forcible rape (2,800), robbery (27,000), and aggravated assault (44,900).[4] Another 369,200 juvenile arrests involved one of the four offenses included in the Property Crime Index, including arson (4,600), burglary (65,700), larceny/theft (283,100), and motor vehicle theft (15,800). The remainder of arrests (1,204,400) were for nonindex crimes, such as simple assaults, property crimes (buying, receiving, possessing stolen property; vandalism), white-collar crimes (forgery, counterfeiting), nuisance crimes (vagrancy, curfew and loitering violations), nonviolent sex offenses (prostitution and commercialized vice), and offenses involving alcohol, drugs, gambling, and domestic issues.

The majority of juvenile arrests involved youth ages 16 or older. In 2010, these older teens were involved in 54 percent of all juvenile arrests. They accounted for 55 percent of arrests under age 18 for the FBI's four Violent Crime Index offenses and 52 percent of juvenile arrests for the four Property Crime Index offenses (arson, burglary, larceny/theft, and motor vehicle theft). Youth over age 16 accounted for 76 percent of juvenile arrests for murder, 62 percent of juvenile arrests for robbery, and more than 50 percent of all juvenile arrests for aggravated assault, burglary, drug law violations, and larceny/theft.

The volume and rate of juvenile arrests fluctuated from 1980 through 2010. Beginning in 1983, the total number of juvenile arrests grew more than 40 percent, from 1.9 to nearly 2.9 million arrests in 1996 (see Figure 3-1). Arrests then fell dramatically, reaching a 30-year low of 1.6 million in 2010. The direction and scale of change varied significantly by offense. Property offenses in general fell generally consistently through 2010. Juvenile arrests for burglary, for example, plummeted from just under 230,000 in 1980 to slightly fewer than 66,000 in 2010. The offenses included in the FBI's Violent Crime Index, however, swelled from the mid-1980s through the mid-1990s and then fell back to approximately the level of the early 1980s, or about 80,000 arrests per year. Juvenile arrests for weapon offenses followed a pattern similar to that of the Violent Crime Index offenses.

When viewed as per capita rates (arrests per 100,000 people ages 10-17 in the U.S. population), the wave of juvenile violence experienced during

---

[4]The figure for forcible rape arrests made in 2010 does not reflect the new definition of sexual offenses announced by the FBI in 2011.

TABLE 3-1 Arrests Involving Youth Under Age 18

	National Estimate of Juvenile Arrests in 2010	Percentage Involving Youth Age 16 or Older
Total	1,649,300	54
Violent Crime Index Offenses	*75,800*	*55*
Murder	1,000	76
Forcible rape	2,800	49
Robbery	27,000	62
Aggravated assault	44,900	51
Property Crime Index Offenses	*369,200*	*52*
Burglary	65,700	54
Larceny/theft	283,100	52
Motor vehicle theft	15,800	58
Arson	4,600	25
Other Offenses		
Other assaults	209,400	43
Forgery and counterfeiting	1,700	74
Fraud	5,900	68
Embezzlement	400	89
Stolen property: buying, receiving, possessing	14,800	58
Vandalism	77,400	42
Weapons carrying, possessing, etc.	31,500	49
Prostitution and commercialized vice	1,000	75
Sex offense (except forcible rape and prostitution)	13,100	35
Drug abuse violations	171,000	65
Gambling	1,400	73
Offenses against the family and children	3,900	49
Driving under the influence	12,100	95
Liquor laws	97,100	75
Drunkenness	12,700	71
Disorderly conduct	154,500	43
Vagrancy	2,200	48
All other offenses (except traffic)	299,400	57
Suspicion (not always in total)	100	62
Curfew and loitering law violations	94,800	53

NOTE: These estimates may vary slightly from those published by the Bureau of Justice Statistics (BJS) later in 2012, as the BJS estimates typically include additional data not counted in the Federal Bureau of Investigation's annual report. Detail may not add to totals due to rounding.
SOURCE: Estimates calculated using data from Federal Bureau of Investigation (2011).

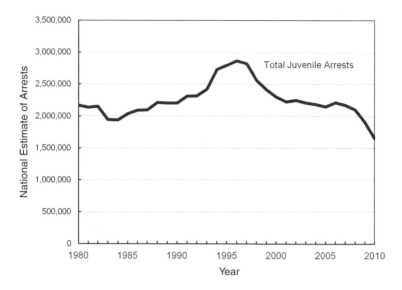

FIGURE 3-1 Total juvenile arrests in the United States, 1980 to 2010.
SOURCES: Snyder and Mulako-Wangota (2011). Estimates for 2010 calculated directly using data from Federal Bureau of Investigation (2011).

the late 1980s and early 1990s is clearly apparent (see Figure 3-2). The total arrest rate for offenses in the FBI's Violent Crime Index grew from 299 to 503 juvenile arrests per 100,000 between 1980 and 1994, before falling to 270 per 100,000 in 2004. After fluctuating for several years, the violent crime arrest rate dropped below 230 per 100,000 in 2010. With few exceptions, juvenile arrest rates for the most serious property offenses (i.e., those included in the FBI Property Crime Index) have been falling since the 1990s (see Figure 3-3). The juvenile arrest rate for burglary has been in a steep decline, from 751 arrests per 100,000 in 1980 to fewer than 200 arrests per 100,000 in 2010. After rising during the 1980s, the juvenile arrest rate for larceny/theft declined steadily between 1994 and 2005 and then grew slightly before dropping again to just above 800 arrests per 100,000 in 2010. Juvenile arrests for motor vehicle theft reached a peak of nearly 350 per 100,000 in the late 1980s and plummeted to below 50 per 100,000 in 2010.

Other offense types show a very different pattern. For example, juvenile arrests for drug abuse violations, disorderly conduct, and "other assaults" (usually misdemeanor) increased during the period of growing violent crime—from the mid-1980s through the mid-1990s (see Figure 3-4). But unlike arrests for violent offenses, the number of juvenile arrests for these offenses never quite returned to pre-1990 levels. They remained at the

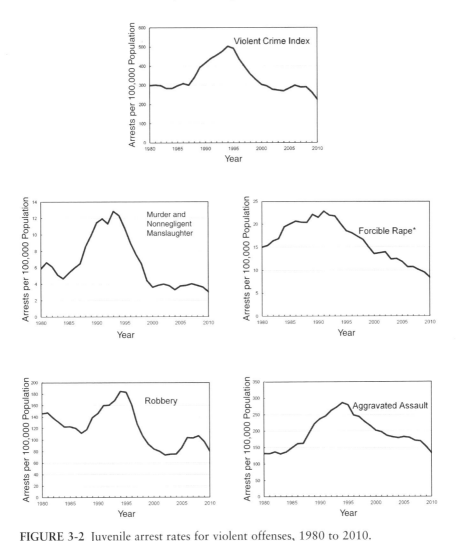

FIGURE 3-2 Juvenile arrest rates for violent offenses, 1980 to 2010.
*As defined by the FBI prior to 2011.
SOURCES: Snyder and Mulako-Wangota (2011). Estimates for 2010 calculated directly using data from Federal Bureau of Investigation (2011).

elevated levels they reached during the height of youth violence in the early 1990s. As a result, the composition of delinquency cases processed by police after the youth violence peak of the 1990s and the workload of the juvenile court system at that time were not identical to the caseload mix that existed prior to the mid-1990s. When the number of juvenile arrests for these other

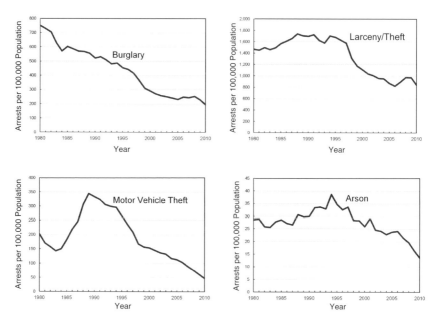

FIGURE 3-3 Juvenile arrest rates for property offenses, 1980 to 2010.
SOURCES: Snyder and Mulako-Wangota (2011). Estimates for 2010 calculated directly using data from Federal Bureau of Investigation (2011).

offenses is compared directly with the number of arrests for violent crime, it is clear that the juvenile justice system in 2010 handled a different mix of offenses than in the 1990s (see Figure 3-5). Specifically, the caseload included more youth arrested for misdemeanor assaults, drug offenses, and disorderly conduct and fewer youth charged with violent offenses and serious property offenses.

Juvenile Crimes Referred to Courts

The several thousand juvenile courts across the United States are not required to report case-processing data for national statistics, but, through the efforts of the National Juvenile Court Data Archive at the National Center for Juvenile Justice, the nation has a source of information that comes very close to being nationally representative. Funded since 1975 by the Office of Juvenile Justice and Delinquency Prevention, the National Juvenile Court Data Archive (Archive) collects, stores, and analyzes data about youthful offenders referred to court for delinquency and status offenses. Juvenile and family courts provide the Archive with demographic

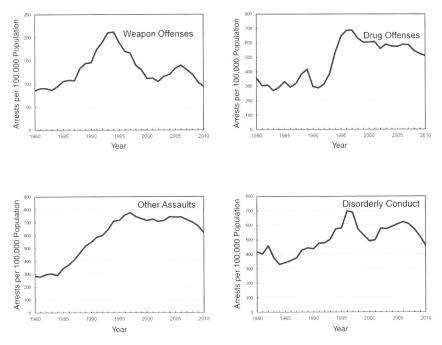

FIGURE 3-4 Juvenile arrest rates for offenses not included in the FBI Violent Crime Index, 1980 to 2010.
SOURCE: Snyder and Mulako-Wangota (2011). Estimates for 2010 calculated directly using data from Federal Bureau of Investigation (2011).

information about the juveniles, the reasons for their referral to court, and the court's handling of each case, including whether the case involved detention, whether it resulted in formal charges and adjudication, and the final disposition of the matter. In recent years, the Archive received data about more than 1 million new juvenile court cases every year from jurisdictions covering more than 80 percent of the U.S. juvenile population (Puzzanchera, Adams, and Sickmund, 2011). This information was analyzed by the Archive staff and weighted to represent the nation as a whole.

In 2008 (the most recent data available at the time of publication), the national estimates generated from the National Juvenile Court Data Archive suggested that juvenile courts throughout the United States handled an estimated 1.65 million delinquency cases (see Figure 3-6). The national caseload in 2008 was more than 40 percent larger than the number of cases handled by juvenile courts in 1985 (1.16 million). A property offense was the most serious charge involved in 37 percent of delinquency cases in

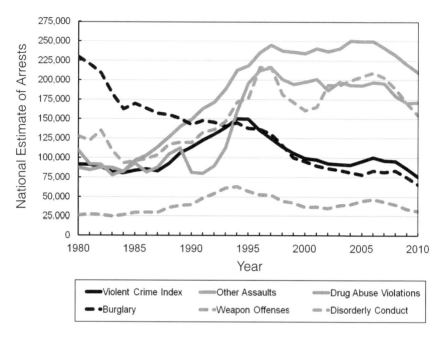

FIGURE 3-5 Juvenile arrests by offense, 1980 to 2010.
SOURCES: Snyder and Mulako-Wangota (2011). Estimates for 2010 calculated directly using data from Federal Bureau of Investigation (2011).

2008. The most serious charge was a person offense in 24 percent of the cases, a drug offense in 11 percent, and a public order offense in 28 percent (i.e., obstruction of justice, disorderly conduct, weapon offenses). Larceny/theft, simple assault, obstruction of justice, and disorderly conduct were the most common delinquency offenses seen by juvenile courts in 2008 (see Table 3-2). Together, these offenses accounted for more than half (54 percent) of all delinquency cases processed by juvenile courts nationwide.

Formal Processing by the Juvenile Court

Most (56 percent) of the delinquency cases handled by U.S. courts with juvenile jurisdiction in 2008 were processed formally (i.e., a petition was filed charging the youth with delinquency). This was higher than the proportion of petitioned cases in 1985 (46 percent). Of all the cases that were formally petitioned and scheduled for an adjudication or waiver hearing in juvenile court in 2008, 61 percent were adjudicated delinquent and approximately 1 percent were transferred to adult court through a judicial waiver of juvenile court jurisdiction. The handling of formal delinquency

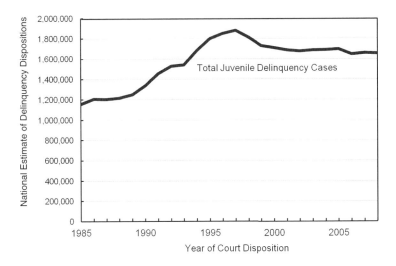

FIGURE 3-6 Total delinquency cases handled by U.S. Juvenile Courts, 1985 to 2008.
SOURCES: Sickmund, Sladky, and Kang (2011). *Easy Access to Juvenile Court Statistics: 1985-2008.* Online. Available: http://www.ojjdp.gov/ojstatbb/ezajcs/. Data source: National Center for Juvenile Justice. (2011). National Juvenile Court Data Archive: Juvenile court case records 1985-2008 [machine-readable data files]. Pittsburgh, PA: NCJJ [producer].

cases in juvenile courts did not vary significantly by offense. Adjudication in juvenile court was most common for cases involving drug offenses and public order offenses (63 percent), but this was only slightly higher than the odds of adjudication for cases involving property offenses (61 percent) and person offenses (60 percent).

Detention

One of the first decisions made in processing juvenile delinquency cases is whether or not the juvenile should be detained in a secure facility pending the completion of court processing. Depending on state and local law, youth may be detained prior to adjudication to protect the community, to ensure their appearance at subsequent court hearings, or to secure the juvenile's own safety. In some jurisdictions, detention can also be ordered following adjudication as a short-term sanction. Other youth are held in detention following court disposition while awaiting placement in a long-term youth correctional facility.

TABLE 3-2 Number of Delinquency Cases by Offense

	National Estimate of Delinquency Cases	Percentage Involving Youth Age 16 or Older
All Offenses	1,653,300	47
All Person Offenses	403,300	40
Violent Crime Index Offenses	86,500	46
Murder	*1,400*	66
Forcible rape	*4,400*	40
Robbery	*32,800*	50
Aggravated assault	*48,000*	43
Simple assault	270,200	38
Other violent sex offenses	14,500	29
Other person offenses	32,000	43
All Property Offenses	**616,700**	**46**
Property Crime Index Offenses	421,300	47
Burglary	*109,000*	46
Larceny/theft	*281,300*	47
Motor vehicle theft	*23,200*	51
Arson	*7,900*	24
Vandalism	105,500	38
Trespassing	54,100	46
Stolen property offenses	17,700	52
Other property offenses	18,000	56
Drug Law Violations	**179,500**	**62**
All Public Order Offenses	**453,900**	**50**
Obstruction of justice	211,600	58
Disorderly conduct	127,200	47
Weapons offense	39,300	43
Liquor law violations	24,400	71
Nonviolent sex offenses	11,900	35
Other public order offenses	39,500	51

NOTE: Detail may not add to totals due to rounding.
SOURCE: Puzzanchera, Adams, and Sickmund (2011, p. 9).

In 2008, juveniles were held in detention at some point during court processing in 21 percent of all delinquency cases (see Table 3-3). Cases involving property offenses were least likely to be detained. Those involving person offenses were most likely to involve detention. In 2008, 17 percent of property offense cases involved detention, compared with 27 percent of person offense cases, 23 percent of public order offense cases, and 18 percent of drug law violation cases. The use of detention changed only slightly between 1985 and 2008 and generally fluctuated between 18 and 22 percent. A similar pattern was seen in each of the four major offense categories,

TABLE 3-3 Use of Detention by Offense

Cases Involving Detention	1985	1990	1995	2000	2005	2008
All offenses	245,822	288,970	320,135	363,478	375,859	347,774
Person offenses	46,593	64,315	89,210	98,296	115,476	109,958
Property offenses	126,348	139,067	126,738	118,022	107,877	102,611
Drug law violations	17,192	25,522	35,605	41,653	38,583	32,741
Public order offenses	55,689	60,065	68,583	105,507	113,924	102,464

Detention Cases as Percentage of Cases Referred	1985	1990	1995	2000	2005	2008
All delinquency cases	21	22	18	21	22	21
Person offenses	25	25	22	25	27	27
Property offenses	18	18	14	17	18	17
Drug law violations	22	36	22	22	21	18
Public order offenses	29	26	21	25	24	23

NOTE: Detail may not add to totals due to rounding.
SOURCES: Sickmund, Sladky, and Kang (2011). *Easy Access to Juvenile Court Statistics: 1985-2008*. Online. Available: http://www.ojjdp.gov/ojstatbb/ezajcs/. Data source: National Center for Juvenile Justice. (2011). National Juvenile Court Data Archive: Juvenile court case records 1985-2008 [machine-readable data files]. Pittsburgh, PA: NCJJ [producer].

although the chances of detention once (in 1990) reached as high as 36 percent in drug offenses cases. However, as noted earlier, the caseload in 2008 was 40 percent higher than that of 1985. As such, the actual number of youth held in detention has increased.

Although the use of detention is least likely in property offense cases, such cases once accounted for the largest share of detained cases due to the large volume of property offenders overall. In 1985, for example, property offense cases represented more than half of all detained cases (126,300 of 245,800). By 2005, however, person offenses (115,500) outnumbered property offenses (107,900) among cases involving detention.

Diversion

One of the distinguishing characteristics of the juvenile court process is that, at numerous stages, a youth may be offered alternatives from formal processing. Diversion can occur at intake processing, normally for first offenders or for those whose charge is a minor one. It can also occur at the detention stage, whereby the youth is released and free pending adjudication. However, as Mears points out, no consensus exists as to how diversion should be defined (2012), with the consequence that generalizations about them or their effect on youth outcomes are difficult to make (National Research Council and Institute of Medicine, 2001, p. 169). (Also see Chapter 6 for a discussion of the community-based programs.)

Juvenile Court Dispositions

In 2008, juveniles were adjudicated in more than three of four cases brought before a judge. Given the large proportion (44 percent) of cases handled informally, however, adjudicated cases account for just 341 of every 1,000 delinquency referrals (see Figure 3-7). Once adjudicated, most cases (57 percent) resulted in a final disposition of probation, accounting for 195 of every 1,000 delinquency referrals, whereas 50 of every 1,000 referrals ended with other dispositions (referral to an outside agency, community service, restitution, etc.).

Out-of-Home Placements

Juvenile courts rely on a variety of dispositions for youth adjudicated as delinquent offenders. Short of transfer to the criminal court system, the most restrictive form of disposition for youth in juvenile court is placement out of the home in some form of residential setting, including foster homes and group homes, residential treatment centers, and juvenile correctional facilities. Between 1985 and 2008, the number of cases in which an adjudicated delinquent was ordered by the court to be placed in a residential facility increased 51 percent, from 104,500 to 157,700 cases (see Figure 3-8). Out-of-home placements peaked in the late 1990s, reaching 180,000 cases before starting to decline over the last decade. This was largely due to the growing number of delinquency referrals handled by juvenile courts rather than an increasing use of placement. The total probability of placement did not change substantially. In 2008, 28 percent of adjudicated delinquency cases resulted in out-of-home placement (Sickmund, Sladky, and Kang, 2011), a figure slightly lower than the rate in 1985, when 31 percent of adjudicated cases resulted in out-of-home placement. In 2008, adjudicated

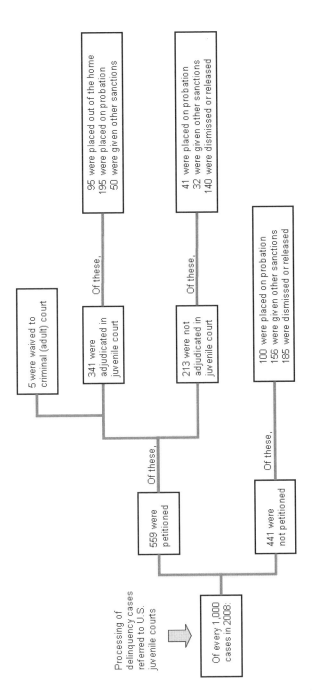

FIGURE 3-7 Number of cases resulting in out-of-home placement, 2008.
NOTE: Detail may not add to totals due to rounding.
SOURCE: Puzzanchera, Adams, and Sickmund (2011, p. 59).

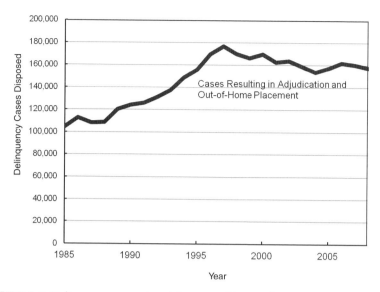

FIGURE 3-8 Delinquency cases involving out-of-home placement, 1985 to 2008. SOURCES: Sickmund, Sladky, and Kang (2011). *Easy Access to Juvenile Court Statistics: 1985-2008*. Online. Available: http://www.ojjdp.gov/ojstatbb/ezajcs/. Data source: National Center for Juvenile Justice (2011). National Juvenile Court Data Archive: Juvenile court case records 1985-2008 [machine-readable data files]. Pittsburgh, PA: NCJJ [producer].

and placed cases accounted for 9.5 percent of all delinquency referrals. In 1985, the rate of placement was 9 percent.

The probability of placement did change for specific offenses during this period. The largest relative change in the odds of placement was observed among the small category of "other public order"[5] offenses. The placement rate for cases involving these charges more than doubled, growing from 2.5 percent in 1985 to 5.1 percent by 2008 (see Table 3-4). The increase resulted in 1,200 more placements in 2008 compared with 1985. The next largest change in placement was observed for vandalism cases. The placement rate for cases involving charges of vandalism nearly doubled, climbing from 3.5 percent in 1985 to 6.4 percent by 2008. Almost 4,000 more vandalism cases received out-of-home placement as the final court disposition in 2008 than was true in 1985. Other large relative increases were seen in the placement rate for cases involving stolen property offenses (rising from

---

[5]This category includes other offenses against government administration or regulation, such as bribery, escape from confinement, false fire alarms, fish and game violations, gambling, health violations, hitchhiking, immigration violations, etc. (Sickmund, Sladky, and Kang, 2011).

TABLE 3-4 Use of Out-of-Home Placement by Offense, 1985 and 2008

	Cases Referred		Cases Placed		Percentage Placed		Change
	1985	2008	1985	2008	1985	2008	1985-2008
All Offenses	1,155,100	1,653,300	104,500	157,700	9.0	9.5	+53,200
Violent Crime Index	64,400	86,500	11,100	18,600	17.2	21.5	+7,500
Simple assault	100,300	270,200	6,200	19,900	6.2	7.4	+13,700
Other violent sex offenses	8,300	14,500	1,100	2,400	13.3	16.6	+1,300
Other person offenses	10,700	32,000	700	2,600	6.5	8.1	+1,900
Property Crime Index	516,300	421,300	48,600	38,300	9.4	9.1	−10,300
Vandalism	84,900	105,500	3,000	6,800	3.5	6.4	+3,800
Trespassing	52,500	54,100	1,900	2,500	3.6	4.6	+600
Stolen property offenses	27,300	17,700	2,800	2,900	10.3	16.4	+100
Other property offenses	18,200	18,000	1,700	1,900	9.3	10.6	+200
Drug law violations	76,700	179,500	5,700	15,200	7.4	8.5	+9,500
Obstruction of justice	66,200	211,600	15,700	33,500	23.7	15.8	+17,800
Disorderly conduct	44,500	127,200	1,200	4,600	2.7	3.6	+3,400
Weapon offense	19,800	39,300	1,600	4,700	8.1	12.0	+3,100
Liquor law violations	20,100	24,400	600	600	3.0	2.5	—
Nonviolent sex offenses	12,600	11,900	1,700	1,200	13.5	10.1	−500
Other public order offenses	32,200	39,500	800	2,000	2.5	5.1	+1,200

NOTE: Detail may not add to totals due to rounding.
SOURCES: Sickmund, Sladky, and Kang (2011). *Easy Access to Juvenile Court Statistics: 1985-2008.* Online. Available: http://www.ojjdp.gov/ojstatbb/ezajcs/. Data source: National Center for Juvenile Justice (2011). National Juvenile Court Data Archive: Juvenile court case records 1985-2008 [machine-readable data files]. Pittsburgh, PA: NCJJ [producer].

10.3 to 16.4 percent), weapon offenses (growing from 8.1 to 12 percent), and disorderly conduct (2.7 to 3.6 percent).

Some of the offenses with the largest increases in the odds of placement, however, involved relatively few cases (e.g., stolen property offenses). As a result, the change in placement rates for these offenses contributed little to the overall growth in placements. The higher placement rate for stolen property cases, as an example, generated an increase of just 200 placement cases between 1985 and 2008. Offense categories with more volume some-times resulted in many new cases placed out of the home, even when the relative increase in their rate of placement was smaller. When one considers the number of new placement cases generated rather than changes in the relative rate of placement, the top five offense categories responsible for expanding the number of juveniles involved in out-of-home placement cases were obstruction of justice, simple assault, drug law violations, the Violent Crime Index offenses, and vandalism. Together, the growth in placements for these offenses accounted for an increase of 52,300 cases between 1985 and 2008, nearly equal to the increase in placement overall (see Table 3-5).

Length of Confinement

The amount of time youthful offenders spend confined to an out-of-home placement depends on many factors, such as time in detention prior to adjudication, the severity of their offense(s), their commitment status, and the jurisdiction's particular policies and practices. There are no national data to examine trends in the lengths of stay in out-of-home placements. Current surveys measure how long youthful offenders have been in a facility at the time of the survey. The Census of Juveniles in Residential Placement (CJRP), described further in Chapter 10, collects individual records on each

TABLE 3-5 The Top Five Offense Categories in the Expansion of Juvenile Out-of-Home Placements

Offense Category	Increase in Placements
Obstruction of justice	17,800 cases
Simple assault	13,700 cases
Drug law violations	9,500 cases
Violent Crime Index	7,500 cases
Vandalism	3,800 cases
Total	52,300 cases

SOURCES: Sickmund, Sladky, and Kang (2011). *Easy Access to Juvenile Court Statistics: 1985-2008*. Online. Available: http://www.ojjdp.gov/ojstatbb/ezajcs/. Data source: National Center for Juvenile Justice (2011). National Juvenile Court Data Archive: Juvenile court case records 1985-2008 [machine-readable data files]. Pittsburgh, PA: NCJJ [producer].

juvenile held in public and private residential juvenile facilities across the United States on a given day. According to the most recent survey, from more than 70,000 records, about 47 percent of youth confined to residential placement had been there for 60 days or less and 28 percent had been there between 61 and 180 days. Only 8 percent had been in the facility for more than a year (Sickmund, Sladky, and Kang, 2011). This percentage breakdown in days because admission has been fairly constant across the biennial survey since 1997. However, the number of juveniles in out-of-home placement at the time of the survey has steadily declined from 105,055 in 1997 to 70,792 in 2010.

Relationship Between Detention, Disposition, and Race

In 2008, the likelihood of formal handling was higher for cases involving black youth (61 percent) than for cases involving white youth (53 percent) (see Table 3-6). The largest discrepancy was for drug cases, in which black youth were significantly more likely to be handled formally than were white youth (70 versus 54 percent). Detention was used slightly more in cases involving black youth (25 percent) than white youth (19 percent) or youth of other races (22 percent). The use of detention was relatively unchanged from 1985 to 2008 for white youth but has declined for black youth (see Table 3-7).

In 2008, cases involving black youth were less likely to result in adjudication once petitioned. Even in cases involving drug charges, cases of black youth were less frequently adjudicated than those of white youth (59 compared with 64 percent). The bias in favor of white youth returned, however, at the dispositional stage. In all offense categories, cases involving black youth were more likely to end in out-of-home placement (32 versus 26 percent), and once again the difference was most striking in drug law violation cases (35 versus 19 percent).

A COMPLEX SYSTEM

The juvenile justice system is a complex, interorganizational setting (Cicourel, 1967; Hasenfeld and Cheung, 1985; Jacobs, 1990; Stapleton, 1993). Part of the reason for this complexity is that there is no single system of juvenile justice, but a multitude of systems to consider (Singer, 1996). The juvenile justice system is not a place or an organization. It is not a courthouse, a detention center, or a reformatory. The juvenile justice system includes all of these entities—and much more. The system encompasses all of the organizations, institutions, and individuals responsible for handling acts of juvenile delinquency, from the moment a juvenile offense is observed or reported to the final delivery of services, sanctions, and follow-up super-

TABLE 3-6 Handling of Delinquency Cases by Offense and by Race, 2008

	White	Black	American Indian*	Asian**
Delinquency Cases in 2008				
Total Cases	1,043,600	563,500	23,500	22,700
Person offenses	226,400	167,100	5,200	4,500
Property offenses	405,900	191,200	9,400	10,200
Drug law violations	131,200	43,500	2,700	2,000
Public order offenses	280,100	161,600	6,200	6,000
Petitioned Cases as Percentage of Total Cases				
All delinquency cases	53	61	61	58
Person offenses	55	64	61	64
Property offenses	51	57	59	51
Drug law violations	54	70	58	57
Public order offenses	55	59	68	66
Adjudicated Cases as Percentage of Petitioned Cases				
All delinquency cases	63	57	70	61
Person offenses	61	55	69	63
Property offenses	63	56	69	57
Drug law violations	64	59	70	60
Public order offenses	65	59	72	65
Cases Placed Out-of-Home as Percentage of Adjudicated Cases				
All delinquency cases	26	32	31	25
Person offenses	29	34	35	31
Property offenses	25	30	32	24
Drug law violations	19	35	24	27
Public order offenses	29	30	31	23

NOTE: Detail may not add to totals due to rounding.
*Includes Alaskan Native.
**Includes Native Hawaiian and Other Pacific Islanders.
SOURCES: Sickmund, Sladky, and Kang (2011). *Easy Access to Juvenile Court Statistics: 1985-2008*. Online. Available: http://www.ojjdp.gov/ojstatbb/ezajcs/. Data source: National Center for Juvenile Justice (2011). National Juvenile Court Data Archive: Juvenile court case records 1985-2008 [machine-readable data files]. Pittsburgh, PA: NCJJ [producer].

vision for each youth held responsible for an offense. The juvenile justice system is the people and organizations that move young offenders through the legal process, including judges, prosecutors, defense attorneys, court administrators, court intake workers, counselors, and probation officers. It is the institutions and organizations that sometimes hold and house juveniles, such as juvenile detention centers, juvenile correctional facilities and training schools, residential treatment centers, foster homes, group homes, and drug treatment and mental health facilities. Depending on each individual case, the system that responds to the illegal behaviors of juveniles

TABLE 3-7 Likelihood of Detention in Cases by Offense, Gender, Race, and Age (in percentage)

	1985	2000	2008
Person offenses	25	25	27
Property offenses	18	17	17
Drug offenses	22	22	18
Public order offenses	29	25	23
Male youth	22	23	23
Female youth	18	17	16
White youth	19	19	19
Black youth	27	28	25
Youth of other races	26	21	22
Youth age 15 and younger	20	20	20
Youth age 16 and older	23	23	22
Total delinquency cases	21	21	21

SOURCES: Sickmund, Sladky, and Kang (2011). *Easy Access to Juvenile Court Statistics: 1985-2008*. Online. Available: http://www.ojjdp.gov/ojstatbb/ezajcs/. Data source: National Center for Juvenile Justice (2011). National Juvenile Court Data Archive: Juvenile court case records 1985-2008 [machine-readable data files]. Pittsburgh, PA: NCJJ [producer].

may also include a variety of diversion programs that are nonresidential and voluntary and provide informal services and supports, such as social services, housing assistance, education, health care, and occupational or vocational training.

Nonetheless, the juvenile justice system is not synonymous with social welfare in general. The juvenile justice system may draw on the resources and expertise of many partners from the broader social welfare sector, but it does so when youth have been brought to the attention of justice authorities due to acts of delinquency, whether or not those acts resulted in arrest or formal prosecution, and whether the justice system learns of the delinquency from law enforcement or from education and child welfare authorities. As outlined in Chapter 1, the goal of juvenile justice intervention, in responding to acts of delinquency, is to hold youth accountable for their illegal behavior and to deliver treatments and services that will address the causes of this misbehavior and will facilitate positive and healthy adolescent development to prevent the youth from becoming involved in the justice system again.

The administration of juvenile justice in the United States reflects continuing ambivalence about the goals of the system and the differences in perspective of the various participants and decision makers. These tensions are evident not only in the disagreements that can arise in individual cases but also at a structural level. Over time, variations in juvenile justice have generated subsystems. The term "subsystem" suggests a hierarchy of decision making, and such a hierarchy often exists by design (Weick, 2001). In this hierarchical juvenile justice system, the judge may render the ultimate decision about the status of an individual juvenile, but many decisions affecting the final outcome are made before the judge has even reviewed the case (Hagan, 1975). The preferences and actions of police, intake, and probation officials as well as social workers and prosecutors determine the delinquent status of individual offenders prior to judicial review (Feeley and Lazerson, 1983). The perceptions and values of each official are likely to be affected by public opinion, although the views of the American public have not always been clear (Cullen, Golden, and Cullen, 1983). Surveys find consistent evidence that the public supports the preventive and rehabilitative mission of the juvenile system (Nagin et al., 2006; Mears et al., 2007; Piquero et al., 2010). Yet the same public elected those officials who largely criminalized juvenile justice in recent decades, especially for youth charged with relatively serious offenses (Feld, 1984; Bishop et al., 1996). The criminalization of juvenile justice may not have eliminated the public's support for treatment and rehabilitation, but it created more complexity in how justice officials balance rehabilitation with sanctions, or how they determine whether youth are delinquents who need treatment or criminals who deserve punishment (Singer, 1996).

Today's highly complex version of juvenile justice is certainly not the one envisioned by reformers at the beginning of the 20th century (Mack, 1909; Levine and Levine, 1992). The Progressive Era reformers who created the juvenile court believed that it should be the only court with jurisdiction over youth below the age of criminal responsibility (Tanenhaus, 2004). In the contemporary juvenile justice system, the legal status of individual juveniles is determined in more than one organizational setting and by a range of individual actors who may decide to initiate or transfer the case to criminal court. Even within the juvenile court, various subsystems and even separate, specialized courts or dockets have emerged as alternative arenas for deciding the most appropriate services and sanctions for youth (Butts, Roman, and Lynn-Whaley, 2012). Drug courts, gun courts, teen courts, and mental health courts were organized within the juvenile justice system because they were seen as better able to focus on each youth's circumstances and to provide more treatment options. Juveniles who fail in these diversionary courts often find themselves back in juvenile court. As a consequence, the juvenile court in the 21st century is less of a true diversionary court and more of a unit within the larger justice system from which some juveniles are now diverted for differential processing.

The growing complexity of juvenile justice makes the system more difficult to comprehend. Traditionally, much of the system was hidden from public view. The lack of transparency was often required by state confidentiality laws designed to protect adolescents from the stigma of a delinquent label. In practice, of course, the veil of confidentiality also protected juvenile justice officials from the effects and implications of their decision making. Recently states have relaxed these confidentiality laws (Sanborn, 1998) for a number of reasons, including a desire to increase the collateral consequences of a juvenile adjudication (Feld, 2012); to hold youth accountable for public scrutiny, contrary to the founders' intent; and to ensure public safety by putting the public on notice about the risk of harm (e.g., schools, public housing authorities, victims) (National Research Council and Institute of Medicine, 2001). Yet the system's complexity continues to make it difficult to understand and improve system functioning.

The availability of justice data is even more contentious today due to advances in information technology. The broader availability of automation allows organizations to share client data instantly and in greater detail, but the laws governing privacy and confidentiality remain a complex patchwork that creates barriers to collaboration and efficiency. Juvenile court records follow young adults into criminal court in many states. By allowing criminal court judges to consider a defendant's prior juvenile court record at the time of sentencing, states have altered the terms of the historical agreement that created the juvenile justice system in the first place. Under the traditional juvenile court model, less formal procedures were coupled with nonstigmatizing and nonpermanent dispositions. By the 1990s, policies that permitted juvenile court records to enhance the severity of criminal court sentences essentially revoked this arrangement (Sanborn, 1998). Adult defendants could be punished more severely, including receiving longer prison sentences, as a direct result of previous juvenile adjudications. All 50 states and the District of Columbia have statutes, court rules, or case law allowing this practice.

Each subsystem in juvenile justice embraces different reasons for adjudicating and sanctioning individual adolescents. Psychologists and mental health providers may advise the court that a youth's delinquent behavior is a function of mental or emotional troubles or a history of trauma and abuse. Prosecutors may have little use for this kind of assessment and instead present a narrative based on rational choice and the need for punishment. Jacobs observed that juvenile justice systems routinely overcharge some youth to justify needed treatment (Jacobs, 1990). A less serious offense may be handled severely because an offender's drug use is thought to require intervention, just as medical systems may alter their characterization of a patient's illness to conform to the requirements of insurance coverage. Representatives of other subsystems may view the resources of the justice system as a respite from their own overtaxed agencies. Teachers may view a referral to the juvenile justice system as an effective alternative for a disruptive student. Child welfare officials may welcome the intervention of the juvenile justice system when resources for older youth in foster care and group homes become strained.

Schools and the Justice System

For the most part, school disciplinary practices have traditionally had only a tangential relation to juvenile justice. However, over the past two decades, as a by-product of school zero-tolerance policies, discussed further in Chapter 4, schools appear to have lowered their threshold for misbehaving students (Wald and Losen, 2003; Kim, Losen, and Hewitt, 2010). Also, many school districts have opted to have a law enforcement presence on school campuses, either through school resource officers for whom districts contract with local policing agencies or through in-house school district police departments overseen by superintendents. Several states have seen a rise in school-based arrests as a result. For example, in Pennsylvania, the number of school-based arrests nearly tripled from 4,563 in 1999-2000 to 12,918 in 2006-2007; in North Carolina, there were 16,499 delinquency referrals to juvenile court directly from schools in 2008-2009 (Advancement Project, 2010). However, for many states and on a national level, the data are such that untangling arrests made on school grounds from overall police arrests is difficult. In a recent study of school discipline in Texas (Fabelo et al., 2011), researchers found it difficult to take stock of tickets issued and arrests made on school campuses because school district police are not required to report such data to the Texas Education Agency (Texas Appleseed, 2011). As such, school-based arrests are counted as any other juvenile arrest. Even if one cannot identify the number of school-based arrests from nonschool-based ones, the same Texas study identified large numbers of students with repeated disciplinary actions, ending up in the juvenile justice system (Fabelo et al., 2011).

The Texas study is highlighted here because it is a recent, large-scale, longitudinal look at school discipline, and its findings mirror other analyses (Puzzanchera, Adams, and Sickmund, 2011; Saunders, 2011). This study examined student records over the course of at least six years for every student in the Texas school system who was in seventh grade in 2000, 2001, or 2002, a total of 928,940 records (Fabelo et al., 2011). The researchers sought "to investigate whether students' involvement in the school disciplinary system could predict subsequent juvenile justice contact" (Fabelo et al., 2011, p. 64). They found that more than one in seven students had contact during their middle or high school years. They found that the likelihood of contact with the juvenile justice system increased with repeated discretionary disciplinary actions[6] by schools. The Texas study (Fabelo et al., 2011) also added to the research on the disproportionate impact on black and Hispanic students (see Chapters 4 and 8). It confirmed the extent of disparities for black, Hispanic, and white youth on such issues as juvenile justice involvement, specific disciplinary actions, use of discretion, and minority students with disabilities.

Children's Services and the Justice System

Many children involved in the child welfare system later come to the attention of the juvenile justice system as adolescents. These youth are known as "crossover youth," a term most commonly applied to those who have experienced maltreatment and engaged in delinquency.[7] Crossover youth are of particular interest in understanding the juvenile justice process because youth from the same families and the same neighborhoods are often at higher risk of involvement in both systems, and because the link between child maltreatment and subsequent delinquency is well documented. Children who experience abuse and neglect are not predestined to become youthful offenders, but the odds are greater. One longitudinal study found that maltreated youth were more likely than their nonabused counterparts to be arrested as juveniles (27 versus 17 percent), to be younger at the time of their first arrest (average age 16.5 versus 17.3), and to be arrested for a violent crime at some point in the future (18 versus 14 percent) (Widom and Maxfield, 2001). Furthermore, abused or neglected children are likely to have more complex and varied service needs, and the fact that they are often simultaneously involved in both the child welfare and the juvenile justice systems complicates the capacity of either system to deal with them effectively (Wiig, Widom, and Tuell, 2003). Crossover youth are also of particular concern because, like youth with mental health disorders and substance abuse problems, they are more likely to be treated harshly within the juvenile justice system and their numbers tend to accumulate proportionately as delinquency cases move deeper into the system (Wasserman et al., 2010).

There are several ways that youth become involved with both the child welfare and the juvenile justice systems. The most common way is for a youth to commit a delinquent offense while under the care and custody of child protective services, most often through the dependency jurisdiction of the juvenile or family court. A second way is for youth to be adjudicated

---

[6]Discretionary disciplinary actions are those suspensions, expulsions, and out-of-school placements made at the discretion of the administrator usually for violations of student codes of conduct as opposed to mandatory violations listed in statute that require student removal from classroom.

[7]This section relies heavily on the research summary by Herz and Ryan (2008a) and Herz et al. (2012).

for delinquency at some point after a period of involvement in the child welfare system. Another pathway is followed by youth who are victims of maltreatment, but without any contact with child welfare, enter the juvenile delinquency system and then are referred by probation authorities to child protective services. Finally, there are youth who exit the juvenile justice system and enter the child welfare system because of an absence of a guardian or parent.

Researchers have sometimes followed these crossover youth as they navigated the juvenile justice system. In one study, youth with child welfare involvement were much more likely to penetrate further into the juvenile justice system. The researchers followed youth in Arizona's juvenile justice system and found that only 1 percent of all informal diversion cases were dual jurisdiction youth (i.e., involved in both the child welfare and the delinquency systems), compared with 7 percent of probation supervision cases and 42 percent of cases placed in private group homes or residential treatment facilities (Halemba et al., 2004). Other studies show that crossover youth are perceived as higher risk by juvenile justice decision makers and receive harsher dispositions than their noncrossover counterparts (Herz and Ryan, 2008a; Herz, Ryan, and Bilchik, 2010), that detention is used more often for youth with prior foster care episodes, and that crossover youth are less like to receive probation dispositions (Ryan et al., 2007) and more likely to receive out-of-home placements (Conger and Ross, 2001; Ross and Conger, 2009). See Chapter 8 for a discussion of racial/ethnic disparities among crossover youth.

Mental Health Disorders and the Justice System

Youth held in juvenile detention centers and other residential facilities exhibit high rates of mental health problems (Teplin et al., 2002; Cauffman and Grisso, 2005; Shufelt and Cocozza, 2006; Illinois Models for Change Behavioral Assessment Team, 2010). Approximately 65 to 70 percent have at least one diagnosable mental health disorder, and more than 60 percent of the youth met criteria for three or more diagnoses.[8] It also appears that the prevalence of mental disorders among juvenile offenders is approximately 40 to 60 percent higher than the prevalence of mental disorders among community samples of adolescents (approximately 17-22 percent) (Cauffman and Grisso, 2005).

---

[8] Youth with a diagnosable mental health disorder are those that meet the formal criteria in the *Diagnostic and Statistical Manual of Mental Disorders: Fourth Edition* (DSM-IV 1994), such as psychotic, learning, conduct, and substance abuse disorders. Youth with schizophrenia, major depression, and bipolar disorder are classified as having serious mental disorders (Cocozza and Skowyra, 2000).

The failure of states to provide adequate mental health services for youth may have contributed to these high numbers. During the 1990s, many states closed their residential facilities for youth and cut back on community-based treatment services. The result was that parents began to seek help for their children from the juvenile justice system (Grisso, 2006, 2008; Skowyra and Cocozza, 2006). In some cases, youth were brought to detention centers in lieu of a psychiatric emergency room, or parents had their children arrested in order to obtain the medical services they needed (Grisso, 2006). A congressional report found that, in 33 states, detained youth with mental health needs were being held in detention with no charges but were awaiting mental health services (Waxman and Collins, 2004).

A recent survey of all youth in residential commitment programs confirmed the high prevalence of mental health problems (Sedlak and McPherson, 2010).[9] Among committed youth in all types of juvenile facilities, more than 60 percent of youth included in the survey had anger management issues. Half exhibited elevated symptoms for anxiety and half for depression as well. More than two-thirds reported serious substance abuse problems, and 59 percent said that they had been getting drunk or high several times per week (or daily) in the months leading up to their arrest (Sedlak and McPherson, 2010a). For many youth, their mental health needs will remain unmet (Skowyra and Cocozza, 2006; Mendel, 2009). The survey also found that more than half of the survey youth were held in facilities that do not conduct mental health assessments for all residents and that two of five youth in these facilities had not received any mental health counseling (Sedlak and McPherson, 2010b).

DIFFERENCES IN POLICY AND PROCEDURE

Despite federal efforts to create a more unified response to delinquency, juvenile justice still depends on state law and the practices established in local jurisdictions. The intensity and diversity of interventions are determined by where the youth happens to reside: "justice by geography" (Feld, 1991). In densely populated urbanized areas, there may be more specialized divisions in which to consider the needs of youthful offenders. In affluent communities, there may be diversionary programs that are not available to youth in impoverished communities. For youth living in impoverished areas, the juvenile justice process may be more similar to the criminal system, with fewer alternatives. In affluent areas, the existence of alternatives

---

[9]The authors point out that the Survey on Youth in Placement, a survey of 7,073 youth in 2003, reflects the general scope of self-reported mental and emotional problems but is not diagnostic of specific disorders.

and diversionary programs may lead police to divert rather than to arrest youth.

The varying level of a youth's personal resources could affect system behavior as well. Youth who are disrespectful or contemptuous of authority are more likely to find themselves arrested and handled harshly (Black and Reiss, 1970). Youth who have the skills to be articulate and polite are more likely to be warned than arrested, offered services rather than sanctions, and treated rather than incarcerated (Cohen, 1985). In other words, decisions about the status of juveniles as delinquents are determined not just by the characteristics of the offense, but also by the personal characteristics of the juveniles and the social and emotional resources of their families. This kind of decision making is not only performed by law enforcement as the first line of decision makers, but also by intake, probation, and judicial officials (Emerson, 1991, 1974). Familial resources are equally relevant and serve as an indicator of the likelihood that an adolescent is in need of more intrusive interventions. Sons and daughters of single parents may be more at risk of harsher penalties because their families have less ability and opportunity to supervise their behavior (Bishop and Frazier, 1992).

Complexity is an unavoidable quality of modern life, and it is not surprising that complexity affects juvenile justice decision making. There is a variety of subsystems that make up the larger juvenile justice system, and each of these subsystems has its own set of goals and values. The organizational interests of probation officers are different from those of the police or prosecutors. A social worker sees delinquent behavior through a lens that is very different from that of a judge. Each of the central actors in the juvenile justice system may express different values and preferences depending on their location. These systems and subsystems may be more complex in urban areas than in rural areas or sparsely populated small towns. Juvenile justice is resource dependent, and the resources available for youth matter (Mulvey and Reppucci, 1988). In affluent areas, the existence of more treatment options may lead to greater numbers of youth being eligible for diversionary or treatment-oriented programs.

Organizational theorists sometimes employ the phrase "loose coupling" to describe decision making in large and complex systems, including juvenile justice (Singer, 1996). A prosecutor's office is loosely connected to the probation department, but prosecutors have an interest in advocating a particular disposition that might conflict with the preferences of probation officials. Each group may be aware of the other's position in an individual case, but each will act to further its own goals and purposes whether or not the other agrees. In contrast, the response of police may be more in sync with that of the prosecutor, and in this regard these subsystems may be more tightly coupled. Their interests are more naturally aligned. Justice systems are likely to bring greater agreement to the decision-making process in individual cases by considering the seriousness of the offense, but extra-legal factors are involved almost immediately (Matza, 1964). This is when it becomes relevant whether subsystems are loosely or tightly connected. If there is plenty of residential space, for example, more offenders will be viewed as appropriate for out-of-home placement. If residential space is limited, probation may be the only feasible option. In other words, one part of the system is loosely connected to the other, influencing each stage of decision making. The juvenile justice system is more tightly coupled around serious violent offenses, but such charges account for only 1 in 20 arrested juveniles (Federal Bureau of Investigation, 2011). The system can operate in a tightly coupled manner when responding to cases of murder, rape, and robbery, but in the vast majority of cases the system functions in a more loosely coupled way.

SUMMARY

Policies and practices that guide the handling of justice involved youth vary substantially among local and state jurisdictions. These differences are rooted in large part in ambivalence about juvenile justice system goals as well as different perspectives of its participants and decision makers. The ages at which youth are handled by the juvenile court—both in law and in practice—have been subject to significant modifications in recent years, often symbolizing this ambivalence.

Juvenile crime data are difficult to interpret because they measure arrests and not actual crime. What we do know is that juvenile crime has declined since its peak in the 1990s and that the juvenile court is handling a different mix of offenses than in the 1990s—more youth being processed with misdemeanor assaults, drug offenses, and disorderly conduct, and fewer youth with violent offenses and serious property crimes. Similar to the adult system, the juvenile justice system operates like a funnel with only a fraction of cases referred to juvenile court ending up being formally processed and adjudicated. For example, in 2008, a little more than half of all cases were formally petitioned. Of those petitioned, again slightly less than two-thirds were adjudicated. Cases falling into the nonadjudicated category include cases either waived to adult court or those in which the youth received some form of informal probation or other voluntary disposition.

For those youth whose cases were adjudicated, slightly more than half received probation while slightly more than a quarter resulted in place-ment outside the home in a residential facility. Large increases in out-of-home placement were experienced by youth adjudicated for obstruction of justice, simple assault, drug law violations, violent crime index offenses, and vandalism. In terms of actual numbers of cases, however, property offense cases consumed the largest share of adjudicated delinquent cases that resulted in out-of-home placement.

Certain steps are common to most juvenile justice systems, regardless of terminology, court organization, or the allocation of service delivery responsibilities. Court processes are also shaped by due process requirements although it is difficult to generalize about their implementation and impact. Race appears to play a part in arrests and juvenile court processes. For example, in 2008, black youth were more likely to be formally handled than white youth, more likely to be detained, and less likely to result in adjudication once petitioned. The bias in favor of white youth returned at the dispositional stage with that of black youth is more likely to end in out-of-home placement.

Finally, the chapter noted that during the past two decades, many youth have come to the attention of the juvenile justice system from schools, child welfare agencies, and the mental health system. This phenomenon is explored in greater depth in Chapters 4 and 8.

4

Adolescent Development

Adolescence is a distinct, yet transient, period of development between childhood and adulthood characterized by increased experimentation and risk taking, heightened sensitivity to peers and other social influences, and the formation of personal identity. Although this developmental period has been recognized for centuries by philosophers and educators (Scott and Steinberg, 2010), the law has embraced this understanding only gradually and imperfectly, especially in relation to offending by juveniles. This report brings a developmental perspective to the century-old confusion about the purposes and proper design of a separate legal court for adolescents and builds on advances in the science of adolescent development. This advancing knowledge provides an empirical basis for a renewal of the juvenile justice system. The framework for reform set forth in this report aims to enable juveniles to make a successful, prosocial transition to adulthood, while holding them accountable for their wrongdoing, treating them fairly, and protecting society from further offending.

The purpose of this chapter is to summarize relevant aspects of the rapidly developing knowledge of adolescent development most pertinent to the purposes, design, and operation of the juvenile justice system and thereby lay the scientific foundation for the proposals for reform set forth in the rest of the report. The first section reviews key cognitive and behavioral features of the normal process of adolescent development, including poor self-control, sensitivity to peer influence, and a tendency to be especially responsive to immediate rewards while failing to take account of long-term consequences. The section then reviews brain imaging findings strongly suggesting that adolescents lack these abilities because of biological immaturity of the brain.

The second section highlights aspects of the adolescent's social environment (the social context in which ongoing neurobehavioral development occurs) that have been shown to affect the probability that any given youth will offend, will desist during adolescence or young adulthood or will continue offending. It also focuses on the impact of interventions designed to reduce such offending.

THE SCIENCE OF NORMAL ADOLESCENT DEVELOPMENT

By definition, adolescence is a transitional period of normal development, distinct from both childhood—when regulation of behavior is the responsibility of the parents—and adulthood—when regulation of behavior is viewed as the responsibility of the individual (Casey et al., 2010). This definition applies to all adolescents, regardless of ethnicity, culture, or nationality, and it is not special to humans but observed across species as a period for acquiring the basic skills needed to transition from dependence to relative independence from parental care (Spear, 2010).

A key function of adolescence is developing an integrated sense of self, including individuation, separation from parents, and personal identity (Collins and Steinberg, 2006). Age-typical ways in which adolescents form their identities and develop adult skills include experimentation and novelty-seeking behavior that tests limits (Spear, 2010). These behaviors are thought to serve a number of adaptive functions including socialization and procreation. In testing limits and experimenting, however, the adolescent may engage in alcohol and drug use, unsafe sex, and reckless driving (Irwin and Millstein, 1986; Crockett and Pope, 1993; Spear, 2010), despite the risks that this can pose to the individual and others (National Research Council and Institute of Medicine, 2011). Often these actions occur in the presence of peers and are exacerbated by their influence (Gardner and Steinberg, 2005).

Research indicates that, for most youth, the period of risky experimentation does not extend beyond adolescence, ceasing as identity becomes settled with maturity. Only a small percentage of youth who engage in risky experimentation persist in their problem behavior into adulthood (Moffitt, 1993; Snyder, 1998). Thus, it is not possible to predict enduring antisocial traits on the basis of risky behavior during adolescence. Much adolescent involvement in illegal activity is an extension of the kind of risk taking that is part of the developmental process of identity formation, and most adolescents mature out of these tendencies.

Evolutionary theorists (Ellis et al., 2012) have identified adaptive functions of adolescent risky behavior, based on the recognition that the task of adolescence is to move from a childhood state of dependence on parents to an emerging adult state characterized by acquiring independence and self-identity, enabling procurement of additional resources, increasing the probability of reproductive success, improving life circumstances, and exploring adult liberties (Csikszentmihalyi and Larson, 1987; Daly and Wilson, 1987; Belsky, Steinberg, and Draper, 1991; Meschke and Silbereisen, 1997). Thus, adolescence by definition is a transient period of development that involves disruption of an old, secure state in favor of an uncertain but exciting new state. Antisocial behaviors, such as disobedience and lawbreaking, serve the function of disrupting ties to "old" parents and authority figures. Drug use, driving after drinking, and unprotected sex are exemplars of exciting new states that the adolescent may explore, as he or she seeks the new state of adulthood. The adolescent is primed to embrace exciting risk-taking behaviors and may even need to fail at some of these behaviors in order to succeed eventually at the tasks required of adults. The balance that parents and a justice system must find is how to encourage the transition to adulthood while keeping adolescents, and society as a whole, safe.

Cognitive and Behavioral Adolescent Development

Current empirical evidence from the behavioral sciences suggests that adolescents differ from adults and children in three important ways that lead to differences in behavior. First, adolescents lack mature capacity for self-regulation in emotionally charged contexts, relative to adults and children (Somerville, Fani, and McClure-Tone, 2011a). Second, adolescents have a heightened sensitivity to proximal external influences, such as peer pressure and immediate incentives, relative to adults (Gardner and Steinberg, 2005; Figner et al., 2009). Third, adolescents show less ability to make judgments and decisions that require future orientation (Steinberg, 2009). The combination of these three cognitive patterns accounts for the tendency of adolescents to prefer and to engage in risky behaviors that have a high probability of immediate reward but in parallel can lead to harm to self or to others. The preference for risky behaviors rises by a third of a standard deviation between ages 10 and 16, and then it declines by a half standard deviation by age 26. Figure 4-1 depicts this pattern based on research by Steinberg (2009). One can conclude from the body of behavioral and brain studies that adolescents clearly differ from adults in crucial ways that suggest the need for a different response from the justice system. One can also conclude that age 18 does not suddenly mark complete transition to adulthood. The most recent empirical evidence for each of these three behavioral patterns is provided below, although they are interrelated.

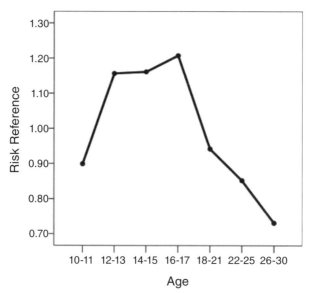

FIGURE 4-1 Age differences in preference for risky behaviors (e.g., unprotected sex, shoplifting, smoking).
SOURCE: Steinberg (2009).

Self-Control

Lack of self-control, that is, the inability to control one's behavior and emotions in order to optimize future gains, is the central hypothesized psychological process related to criminal behavior, according to some theories of crime (e.g., Gottfredson and Hirshi, 1990). Studies of self-control, measured in a variety of ways, show a gradual but steady increase through adolescence, with gains continuing into late adolescence and young adulthood. Self-control, mainly in boys, has been linked to positive adjustment in several domains (although with varying magnitude of effects), including less aggressive and delinquent behavior (Krueger et al., 1996; de Ridder et al., 2012).

These observations are supported by a wealth of behavioral evidence from laboratory tasks requiring participants to override one response in order to achieve a correct one (Luna et al., 2001; Somerville, Fani, and McClure-Tone, 2011). Similarly, self-report measures of lack of self-control as a general trait of impulsiveness decline linearly between adolescence and adulthood (Galvan et al., 2007; Steinberg et al., 2008). In emotionally charged contexts, the capacity for self-control is challenged, especially in adolescents. For example, in a recent laboratory study that explicitly tested the successful ability to inhibit responses to emotional relative to nonemotional stimuli, Tottenham and colleagues (2011) showed that emotional control (e.g., suppressing a response to an emotional cue) was slower to develop than other forms of self-control. Moreover, adolescent males showed the greatest difficulty when having to suppress a response to an emotional cue. Self-control in the context of positive social cues (such as happy faces) shows a similar lag in development (Somerville, Fani, and McClure-Tone, 2011a). These data together suggest that adolescent decision making and judgment are compromised when made in emotionally charged situations, especially for young men. The findings are consistent with observations that criminal acts by adolescents often occur in emotionally charged situations, especially by young men.

Sensitivity to Social Influences

Adolescents are particularly sensitive to exogenous stimuli that relate to psychological development in, and in interaction with, the social environment. Two important social influences on adolescent behavior that are relevant to this report are incentives that have come to take on basic reward properties (such as a smiling face and money) and peer influence.

Incentives. Incentives can modulate behavior by enhancing or diminishing the behavior. Rewarding an individual for appropriate behavior can make him or her work harder and perform better than when not rewarded. In contrast, behaviors can be diminished when they require not responding to rewarding cues in the environment. Recent studies of adolescent development show a change in sensitivity to reward-based cues, suggesting that they have a unique influence on cognition during the adolescent years.

Empirical evidence for how adolescent behavior is differentially biased in external motivational contexts comes from several experiments. Using a gambling task in which reward feedback was provided during a decision or held until after the decision, Figner and colleagues (2009) showed that adolescents made disproportionately more risky gambles compared with adults, but only in the immediately rewarded condition. Steinberg and colleagues, using a similar gambling task (Cauffman et al., 2010) and a delay discounting task (Steinberg et al., 2009b), have shown that this sensitivity to rewards and incentives actually peaks during adolescence, with a steady increase from late childhood to adolescence and subsequent decline from late adolescence to adulthood. More recently, Somerville and colleagues (2011a) specifically tested how well adolescents could suppress a response to a rewarding social cue relative to a nonrewarding cue. Adolescents made more commission errors to the rewarding social cue than children or adults. These findings reveal an increasing sensitivity to rewards that peaks between 13 and 17 and then declines. Taken together, these studies suggest that during adolescence, motivational cues of potential reward are particularly salient and can lead to risk taking and otherwise suboptimal choices.

Incentives can not only impair performance, but can also enhance it. Recent work by Ernst and colleagues (Jazbec et al., 2006; Hardin et al., 2009) suggests that adolescents show improved cognitive performance if an immediate incentive is at stake. They used an impulse control task (antisaccade task) to measure cognitive performance and promised a financial reward for accurate performance on some trials but not others. The results showed that promise of a reward facilitated adolescent performance on the task more than it did for adults. These findings suggest that immediate incentives can alter both desirable and undesirable behavior in adolescents and may be used to positively alter behavior.

Peer Influence. Substantial empirical evidence shows that teens are more oriented toward peers and conforming to peer views than are either adults or younger children (Steinberg and Monahan, 2007). They are more likely than adults to engage in reckless driving (Simons-Morton et al., 2005), substance abuse (Chassin, Hussong, and Beltran, 2009), and criminal offenses (Zimring, 1998) in groups. The strongest experimental evidence of heightened peer influence in early adolescence has come from Costanzo and Shaw (1966), who manipulated "peer" feedback to cognitive judgment tasks and found an inverted U-shaped function of conformity to peers across adolescence, with 13-year-olds demonstrating greater conformity with peers' judgments than younger and older participants. Costanzo and Shaw (1966) found a complementary U-shaped function for conformity to adult judgments. The decline of adult influence and growth of peer influence during this period of life is consistent with an evolutionary perspective under which individuals depart from parental protection and strive instead for reproductive success and peer integration with puberty.

Peers can influence individual decision making even without direct interaction. To the extent that an adolescent seeks favor with the peer group, she or he may try to emulate peer behavior and attitudes. Prinstein and Wang (2005) found that adolescents tend to overestimate the frequency and seriousness of problem behavior of their peers. Given the high sensation value and salience of deviant talk in peer interactions (Dishion et al., 1996a), these overestimates may be self-perpetuating (Gonzales and Dodge, 2010).

Recent empirical studies (Gardner and Steinberg, 2005; Chein et al., 2011) show that adolescents' decisions and actions are influenced by the mere presence of peers. Specifically, Gardner and Steinberg (2005) examined risk taking in adolescents and adults during a simulated driving task. Half the subjects performed the task alone, and the other half performed the task in the presence of two friends. The adolescents, but not the adults, took a substantially greater number of risks when observed by peers. Together, these findings suggest that adolescence is a transient stage of development during which peer psychosocial influences have powerful effects that can contribute to risk taking.

Future Orientation and Reasoning

Adolescents are similar to adults in their reasoning and abstract thinking abilities (Hale, 1990; Overton, 1990; Kail, 1997; Keating, 2004; Kuhn, 2009). However, they lack a mature ability to consider the long-term consequences of actions given a heightened sensitivity to psychosocial influences and a lack of experience-based knowledge for making decisions (Steinberg and Monahan, 2007; Steinberg et al., 2008). A converging literature of studies that use a range of methodologies, from observation to interviews to questionnaires, has shown a lack of mature future orientation abilities in adolescence (Greene, 1986; Nurmi, 1991; Cauffman and Steinberg, 2000; Grisso et al., 2003). More recently, scientists have attempted to measure this ability with controlled laboratory tasks in addition to self-report measures. Steinberg and colleagues (2008) examined age differences in future orientation using both a self-report measure and a delay-discounting paradigm. Delay-discounting tasks assess the preference of an individual to choose between a smaller immediate reward versus a larger delayed reward. The results showed that adolescents were less oriented to the future than adults on both measures.

One possible explanation for less future orientation in adolescents relative to adults is that adolescents have been alive for a shorter amount of time and have had far fewer experiences than adults to inform judgments and decisions about the future (Gardner, 1993). The limited experiences of adolescents may also explain why they are more likely than adults to overestimate their own understanding of a situation, underestimate the probability of negative outcomes, and make judgments based on incorrect or incomplete information (Quadrel, Fischhoff, and Davis, 1993; Zimring, 1998). Together these findings suggest that adolescents are less capable than adults of envisioning the longer term consequences of their decisions and actions.

As youth often make decisions about experimentation with drugs and alcohol, risk taking, and criminal activity in situations involving peer pressure, emotions, and little time to consider a decision thoroughly (Zimring, 1998), it is important to understand how decision making differs across the period of development from childhood to adulthood. Indeed, the deficiencies in adolescent decision making that have been documented so clearly in laboratory experiments are probably magnified in actual social settings in which they cannot be studied directly. A full account of adolescent decision making must include the examination of social and emotional influences on these cognitive abilities (Scott et al., 1995; Steinberg and Cauffman, 1996; Piquero et al., 2011).

Adolescent Brain Development

The last decade has provided evidence of significant changes in brain structure and function during adolescence with a strong consensus among neuroscientists about the nature of these changes (Steinberg, 2009). Much of this work has resulted from advances in magnetic resonance imaging (MRI) techniques that provide the opportunity to safely track the development of brain structure, brain function, and brain connectivity in humans. Consistent with the previously described behavioral findings that adolescents have poor self control, are easily influenced by their peers, and do not think through the consequences of some of their actions, the brain imaging findings strongly suggest that adolescents lack these abilities because of biological immaturity of the brain.

Structural Brain Development

Several studies have used MRI to map the developmental time course of the structural changes in the normal brain. Even though the brain reaches approximately 90 percent of its adult size by age 6, the gray and white matter subcomponents of the brain continue to undergo dynamic changes throughout adolescence and well into young adulthood. Data from longitudinal MRI studies indicate that increases in white matter are linear and continue well into young adulthood, whereas gray matter volume shows an inverted U-shaped course, first increasing and then decreasing during adolescence (Sowell et al., 2003, 2004; Giedd, 2004; Gogtay et al., 2004). These changes do not occur uniformly across development, but rather there are regional differences in the brain's development (Thompson and Nelson, 2001; Amso and Casey, 2006; Casey et al., 2010). In general, regions that involve primary functions, such as motor and sensory systems, mature earliest compared with brain regions that integrate these primary functions for goal-directed behavior (Gogtay et al., 2004; Sowell et al., 2004). Similar to sensorimotor regions, subcortical regions involved in novelty and emotions (e.g., striatum, amygdala) mature before the control region of the brain and show greater changes in males than in females during adolescence (Caviness et al., 1996; Giedd et al., 1996a, 1996b; Reiss et al., 1996; Sowell et al., 1999). These developmental and gender findings are important in the context of this report, given the increase in criminal behavior during the period of adolescence, especially in males (Steffensmeier et al., 2005).

Functional Brain Development

The most influential method for studying human brain development is that of functional magnetic resonance imaging (fMRI). This method allows for seeing what areas of the brain are active when an individual is behaving by indexing changes in blood oxygen levels in the brain. In the last decade, there has been an explosion of fMRI studies examining adolescent brain development (Casey et al., 2008). This work challenges the traditional view that changes in behavior during adolescence are due simply to immature cognitive control capacities and the underlying neural substrates (e.g., prefrontal cortex). Instead, the latest studies suggest that much of what distinguishes adolescents from children and adults is an imbalance among developing brain systems (Casey, Getz, and Galvin, 2008; Steinberg et al., 2008). This imbalance model implies dual systems: one that is involved in cognitive and behavioral control and one that is involved in socioemotional processes. Accordingly, adolescents lack mature capacity for self-regulation because the brain system that influences pleasure-seeking and emotional reactivity develops more rapidly than the brain system that supports self-control.

Empirical evidence to support this view comes from three areas of work. First, prefrontal circuitry implicated in self-regulation and planning behavior continues to develop into young adulthood (Casey et al., 1997, 2002; Luna et al., 2001; Bunge et al., 2002; Klingberg, Forssberg, and Westerberg, 2002; Bitan et al., 2006). This development is slow and linear in nature. Specifically, adolescents tend to recruit prefrontal regions less efficiently than adults, and these areas become more fine-tuned with age and experience (Casey et al., 1995; Brown et al., 2005; Durston et al., 2006). For example, imaging studies using tasks in which children and adolescents are asked to suppress a compelling response or to look away from a target have shown less focal prefrontal recruitment than in adults (Casey et al., 1995; Luna et al., 2001; Durston et al., 2006). These studies provide insights into the role of prefrontal circuitry in behavior regulation across development, but they do not speak to the heightened sensitivity of adolescents to rewards and emotional cues.

Several research teams (May et al., 2004; Ernst et al., 2005; Galvan et al., 2006; Geier et al., 2010; Van Leijenhorst et al., 2010) have examined brain systems involved in reward to address this issue. Their studies (Bjork et al., 2004) have shown enhanced sensitivity to rewards in adolescents, relative to children and adults. For example, Van Leijenhorst and colleagues (2010) showed exaggerated ventral striatal responses in adolescents during the anticipation and receipt of a monetary reward. The magnitude of activity in this region is associated with real-world behavior. Specifically, greater ventral striatal activity to rewards is predictive of risk-taking tendencies (Galvan et al., 2007).

A second form of support for the imbalance model of adolescent development comes from studies that directly examine how brain systems interact when self-control is required in a motivational or emotional context. Incentives can both motivate (Hardin et al., 2009) and interfere with (Somerville, Fani, and McClure-Tone, 2011) cognitive functioning in adolescents. Geier and colleagues (2010) have shown enhancement of behavioral control by adolescents as compared with adults when a financial reward was promised for accurate performance relative to when it was not. Relative to adults, adolescents had exaggerated activation in the ventral striatum when preparing and executing a response that would be reinforced and an increase in prefrontal activity important for controlling the movements, suggesting a reward-related up-regulation in control regions. In contrast, Somerville and colleagues (2011) have shown that adolescents' performance is worse than both children and adults when having to suppress a response to an alluring social cue relative to a neutral one. This inverted-U pattern of performance is paralleled by a similar inflection in ventral striatal activity and heightened prefrontal activity.

Perhaps the most compelling imaging findings supportive of the imbalance model are those by Chein and colleagues (2011). They examined the neural basis of riskier driving decisions by adolescents relative to adults in the presence of peers during a simulated driving task. Adolescents, but not adults, showed heightened activity in reward-related circuitry, including the ventral striatum, in the presence of peers. This activity was inversely correlated with subjective ratings on resistance to peer influences. Individuals rating themselves low on this scale showed more reward-related brain activity in the presence of peers. Not only are peers influential but also positive exchanges with others may be powerful motivators (Baumeister and Leary, 1995; Steinberg et al., 2008). Asynchronous development of brain systems appears to correspond with a shift from thinking about self to thinking about others from early adolescence to young adulthood (van den Bos et al., 2011). Together these studies suggest that in the heat of the moment, as in the presence of peers or rewards, functionally mature reward centers of the brain may hijack less mature control systems in adolescents.

the brain is fighting itself?

Brain Connectivity

Although regional changes in brain structure and function are important in understanding how behavior changes during adolescence, development in the connections between brain regions with age and experience are equally important (Casey et al., 2005). There are two relatively new approaches to indexing human brain connectivity. The first is that of diffusion tensor imaging (DTI). DTI detects changes in white matter tracts related to myelination, the process through which nerve fibers become sheathed in myelin, thereby improving the efficiency of neural signaling. DTI-based connectivity studies of prefrontal white matter tracts suggest an association between connection strength and self-regulation (Liston et al., 2006; Casey et al., 2007; Asato et al., 2010). Combining DTI and fMRI, Casey and colleagues have linked connection strength between prefrontal cortex and subcortical brain regions with the capacity to effectively engage in self-control in both typically and atypically developing individuals (Casey et al., 2007). A similar increase in number and strength of prefrontal connections to cortical and subcortical regions from age 13 to young adulthood has been shown to be associated with improvements in self-control by Hwang and colleagues (2010).

The second method, resting state fMRI, assesses the strength of functional connections within a network by quantifying correlated spontaneous activity between brain regions at rest. Resting state fMRI studies show that brain maturity involves connections between distal brain regions increasing while connections between proximal or local brain regions simultaneously decrease (Fair et al., 2007; Dosenbach et al., 2010). Together, these findings support the claim that cognitive maturation occurs not in unitary structures but in the connectivity and interactions between developing structures (Fair et al., 2007; Thomason et al., 2010; Uddin, Menon, and Supekar, 2010). Thus, the relative immaturity of adolescent abilities will rely on specific immaturity of the circuitry.

Overall the findings suggest that in emotionally charged situations with limited time to react, as may be the case for most juvenile offenses, basic emotional circuits may drive adolescent actions. In more neutral contexts, more top-down cortical circuits may have a greater impact on decisions (Steinberg, 2009; Casey and Jones, 2010; Somerville, Fani, and McClure-Tone, 2011).

Pubertal Influences on Brain and Behavior

Puberty involves physical changes to the body initiated by gonad hormones to which the adolescent must adjust. These hormones also impact brain and behavior by binding to testosterone and estrogen receptors in the brain. These hormonal and brain changes coincide with increased sexual activity and interest (Sisk and Zehr, 2005) and with changes in arousal and the salience of motivational stimuli (Friemel, Spanagel, and Schneider, 2010). Brain changes specifically associated with puberty are consistent with broader brain and behavior patterns that occur during adolescence—that is, poor self-control, heightened sensitivity to peer influence, and heightened responsivity to immediate rewards.

Importantly, individual differences in the timing of puberty affect long-term outcomes. Early puberty has been associated with poor outcomes in both sexes. These outcomes include earlier use of alcohol and illegal substances, earlier sexual behavior, higher risk for mental health problems, and increased risk for delinquency (Kaltiala-Heino et al., 2003; Waylen and Wolke, 2004; Deardorff et al., 2005; Bratberg et al., 2007).

Early maturation creates particular risks for girls. Early puberty coupled with stressors such as conflict with parents and involvement with delinquent and often older male peers is a risk factor for delinquency unique to girls (Zahn et al., 2010). Using data from the National Study of Adolescent Health, Haynie (2003) found that earlier puberty among girls was associated with higher levels of delinquency and that conflict with parents, exposure to peer deviance, and involvement in romantic relationships strengthened the link between puberty and delinquency. Furthermore, early onset of puberty among girls continued to predict increased risk behavior into adulthood (Zahn et al., 2010). Unfortunately, the limited number of studies specific to girls' delinquency that include biological factors precludes any definitive conclusions at this time (Zahn et al., 2010).

THE SOCIAL CONTEXT OF ADOLESCENT DEVELOPMENT

From a developmental perspective, adolescent risk taking and delinquent behavior can be understood as resulting from the interaction between the normal developmental attributes of adolescents described above and the environmental influences to which they are exposed during this key stage of development. There are, of course, substantial individual differences among adolescents, not only in their pace of maturation but also in the type and frequency of risky behavior in which they engage. The likelihood of engaging in risky behavior is correlated with brain activity in anticipation of immediate rewards regardless of age, is highest for adolescents as a group, and varies among adolescents as well as among children and adults. To a large extent, the differences within age groups can be linked to variations in social influences.

With specific reference to delinquency, self-reports indicate that most adolescents engage in some form of delinquent behavior. However, many adolescents do not offend and, among those who do offend, most desist and only a small fraction become persistent offenders who commit crimes against persons or property crime as adults. (See Chapter 1 for a review of the research on heterogeneity of juvenile offending.) Based on decades of research, behavioral and social scientists have identified factors affecting the probability that a youth will offend initially and continue offending during adulthood (Loeber and Farrington, 1998). More broadly, the literature also addresses the factors that promote healthy development and forestall continued offending (Howell, 1995a; Hawkins et al., 1998; Loeber and Farrington, 2000). These factors include the biological characteristics of the individual, the ever-changing environment to which the developing individual is exposed from gestation onward, and the interaction between biology and environment. As noted in Chapter 1, this research suggests that interventions designed to support strong families and otherwise foster a safe and supportive social environment can contribute to healthy psychosocial development in adolescence. These investments can reduce the risk that normal adolescent tendencies will lead to drug or alcohol problems, serious delinquency, or other harmful behaviors.

The committee does not think it necessary to summarize the voluminous literature on early child development and the etiology and prevention of delinquency for purposes of this report. Instead, we focus on factors that bear most directly on adolescent involvement in criminal activity and on the optimal design and operation of the juvenile justice system. With this limited purpose in mind, we focus on the social context of adolescent development, including the influence of families, peers, schools, and organized community activities. This knowledge sheds light on why some youth get involved in crime and others do not (and why most desist but a few become career criminals), and it also has important implications for designing interventions for offenders that will reduce delinquency and facilitate successful transitions to adulthood.

Research on the particular influences that promote desistance from criminal activity in adolescents who continue to offend is less well developed. A range of relevant studies point to the importance of such factors as positive romantic relationships, successful work experiences, psychosocial development, and the achievement of adult roles (Laub and Sampson, 2001; Mulvey et al., 2004; Laub and Boonstoppel, 2012). However, considerable work still needs to be done in this area regarding the mapping of the desistance process and identification of relevant behavioral and psychological factors. (See Chapter 6 for a discussion of the implications of desistance for sanctions and intervention.)

The scientific literature shows that three conditions are critically important to healthy psychological development in adolescence (Steinberg, Chung, and Little, 2004). The first is the presence of a parent or parent figure who is involved with the adolescent and concerned about his or her successful development. This adult relates to the adolescent with a combination of warmth, firmness, and encouragement of individuation—what is known as authoritative parenting. The impact of parents and other adults during adolescence can be powerful and positive. A positive relationship with a prosocial adult during this period is known to act as a protective factor against exposure to external risks and the adverse impact of that exposure. Laird and colleagues (2003a, 2003b) found that a positive parent-adolescent relationship in high school, as reflected by parent and adolescent reports of how much they enjoy being with each other, predicted declines in adolescent antisocial behaviors over time, and that influence operated through increased parent-adolescent time together, increased parental knowledge and monitoring of the adolescent's whereabouts, and increased acceptance by the adolescent that parental monitoring is appropriate.

Second, healthy development is promoted by inclusion in a peer group that values and models prosocial behavior and academic success (Brown et al., 2008). An antisocial peer group, in contrast, can undermine healthy development; thus, weakening the influence of a delinquent peer group is a major challenge for juvenile justice interventions. Third, activities that contribute to autonomous decision making and critical thinking contribute to healthy development. Schools, extracurricular activities, and work settings can provide opportunities for adolescents to learn to think for themselves, develop self-reliance and self-efficacy, and improve reasoning skills. The absence of these opportunities in these settings will undermine developmental progress.

These three dimensions of the adolescent's social environment provide the conditions needed to make progress in accomplishing key developmental tasks and to allow the acquirement of skills essential to the transition to conventional adult roles. First, adolescents acquire basic educational and vocational skills that allow them to function in the workplace. Second, they acquire social skills that are the basis of intimate relationships and cooperation in groups. Finally, through normal developmental processes, adolescents begin to set personal goals and to make responsible choices without external supervision. The process of maturation is one of reciprocal interaction between the individual and a social context that provides opportunity structures facilitating normative development. If the adolescent's social context lacks these opportunity structures, of course, it can undermine healthy development.

Parental Influences[1]

There is a vast literature on parental and other family influences on child and adolescent development. For purposes of this report, the most important aspect of parental influence relates to parental behavior that can be modified or relied on, as appropriate, in connection with juvenile justice interventions. Parental behavior can affect the occurrence of delinquent behavior in three main ways: hostile and coercive family processes, parent-

---

[1]The material on parental and peer influences was drawn from a paper prepared for the National Research Council and Institute of Medicine's Board on Children, Youth, and Families, dated April 26, 2010, by a member of this committee, Kenneth Dodge, and Nancy Gonzales, ASU Foundation Professor at Arizona State University. The material itself was edited, reorganized, and integrated into the chapter's structure and subjected to scientific review. The paper can be found at http://www.BCYF.org/dodge_gonzales_pdf.

ing styles and practices, and family modeling and socialization about risky behaviors. These family factors are not exhaustive of the broad array of family influences that have been implicated in the prediction of adolescent risk taking. Additional family characteristics, such as family psychopathology, parents' socioeconomic status, maternal age at the birth of the child, ethnicity, and family size and structure (intact versus nonintact) play contributing roles as well.

One of the most replicated findings in developmental research is that early physical maltreatment predicts a range of difficulties for adolescents, including increased risk for delinquent and dysregulated behavior (Smith and Thornberry, 1995; Swanston et al., 2003; Bergen et al., 2004). Maltreatment is associated with earlier initiation of delinquent behaviors (Rivera and Widom, 1990), more violent offenses (Lansford et al., 2002), and higher recidivism (Chang, Chen, and Brownson, 2003). Numerous mechanisms account for the consistent link between early harsh parental behavior and adolescent delinquency. The developmental model of antisocial behavior of Patterson posits that behavioral undercontrol and high negative affectivity of a vulnerable child underlie oppositional behavior. This behavior, in turn, incites negative affective responses and restrictions from parents, producing increasingly aversive parent-child exchanges (Patterson, 1982; Patterson, Reid, and Dishion, 1992). Patterson (1982) coined the term "coercion cycle" to describe the escalation in negativity that occurs between parents and children.

Adolescent delinquency is strongly influenced by the type of caregiving that youth receive prior to and during adolescence. Adolescents who are raised in homes characterized by authoritative parenting (i.e., parenting that is warm but firm) are more mature and less likely to engage in delinquent behavior (Baumrind, 1985; Steinberg, 2001). Dimensions of effective parenting include parental nurturance; active interest and involvement in the life of the child; clear, reasonable expectations and standards for appropriate behavior, with explicit rules and consequences for transgressions; and effective monitoring or supervision of the youth's activities and peers.

Disengaged parenting raises the risk for adolescent problem behavior due to the absence of emotional bonding or attachment to parents and a lack of supervision and consistent behavioral control. Disengaged parents fail to provide a clear communication of parental values and also undermine motivation for adolescents to attend and comply, thus weakening their internalization of parental values and socialization (Baumrind, 1991; Grusec and Goodnow, 1994). Highly supportive and responsive caregiving, particularly when combined with clear and consistent discipline, also facilitates the gradual increase in youths' self-regulatory capacities and decision-making abilities (Martin, Martin, and Jacklin, 1981; Shaw, Keenan, and Vondra, 1994; Shaw et al., 1998). Consistent with this view, recent research has shown that maltreatment that occurs during adolescence also has a pronounced impact on increasing involvement in later delinquency and related problem behaviors (Eckenrode et al., 2001; Stewart, Livingston, and Dennison, 2008; Thornberry et al., 2010).

Evidence suggests that the parenting context begins to shape pathways to adolescent risk taking very early in development. Keenan and Shaw (2003) explain development of antisocial behavior as the result of both individual deficits in the capacity to regulate emotions and behaviors and a caregiving environment that exacerbates these deficits by not providing the appropriate level of developmental guidance in important socialization processes. Contingent and sensitive responding in infancy and early childhood provides a foundation for caregivers to facilitate development of self-regulatory skills (Martin, Maccoby, and Jacklin, 1981; Shaw, Keenan, and Vondra, 1994; Calkins and Johnson, 1998; Shaw et al., 1998), internalization of moral standards (Kochanska, 1995), and the development of empathy (Eisenberg et al., 1996), and it also sets the stage for parents to have greater impact in middle childhood and adolescence.

As youth enter adolescence, parents' knowledge and supervision of their child's whereabouts and settings become increasingly important in influencing outcomes. During elementary and middle school, parents can directly manage a child's behavior by actively steering a child toward desired peers and activities (Parke et al., 1996). In mid- to late adolescence, parents have much less direct influence on peer group affiliation. However, they still exert control by monitoring the whereabouts of an adolescent and ensuring that the adolescent does not spend time in unsupervised settings in which exposure to deviant peers and opportunities for delinquent behavior abound. One of the controversies in the field is whether troublesome adolescents make it difficult for their parents to monitor them—in which case parental monitoring has little causal impact on an adolescent who is destined to engage in delinquent behavior (Kerr and Stattin, 2000)—or parental supervision actually controls behavior. Longitudinal studies provide compelling evidence that parental supervision indeed matters a great deal (Fletcher et al., 2004; Dick et al., 2009).

The family context also provides socialization specific to deviant behaviors through modeling (e.g., parent or sibling involvement with drugs and alcohol), transmission of family attitudes that are favorable or prohibitive of risk taking (Johnson and Pandina, 1991; Ellis, Zucker, and Fitzgerald, 1997), and communication about such topics as adolescent sexuality, drinking, and drug use (Webster, Hunter, and Keats, 1994; Chassin, Fora, and King, 2004).

Peer Influences

By early adolescence, the youth's growing independence affords access to peers over which the parent has less control. The onset of puberty and other biologically based changes lead early adolescents to direct greater attention toward the peer group; 85 percent of American adolescents report being a member of a peer crowd (Brown, 2004). Not only do peers hold high value and exert strong influence over individual youth during adolescence, but they also spend a great deal of time with each other. Gradually, as adolescents move into adulthood, self-regulatory skills improve and peer conformity declines. General skill in making independent decisions and resisting peer influence increases steadily across the adolescent years (Steinberg and Monahan, 2007), so that the older adolescent becomes cognitively and socially more able to make independent decisions. However, both peers and families continue to exert influence as adolescents mature, and a key developmental task of emerging adulthood becomes balancing peer and family influences through self-regulation (Arnett, 2000).

Positive and Deviant Peer Influences

Although peers are typically cast as solely negative agents in adolescent development, the fact is that the peer group as a context and specific peers as relationship partners exert mostly positive influence on adolescent development (Brown et al., 2008). Peers provide normative regulation (Eder, Evans, and Parker, 1995) that defines, clarifies, maintains, and enforces norms for behavior in dyadic and group settings. For example, peers provide feedback about family rules, curfews, and privileges that help an adolescent understand when his or her behavior has gone beyond normative practice and when parents are acting normatively. Peers also provide a staging ground for the practice of social behaviors, leading to social cognitive competence and experimentation with roles, leading to identity development. Peer friendships offer an adolescent the opportunity to explore intimacy, and groups offer opportunities for leadership, competition, conformity, and rebellion. Peers provide feedback so the adolescent can experience the consequences of trial behaviors and develop a comfortable, stable identity.

Prolonged exposure to peers during adolescence without authoritative adult supervision can also have negative effects on development and behavior. The impact of the peer-centered social context on deviance has been studied in a variety of settings.

Unstructured Settings. When the peer context is unstructured and attracted to risk taking and deviance, the result can be a dramatic increase in offending. High levels of informal contact with peers without adult supervision during the middle school years have been found to predict growth in antisocial behavior across time, primarily among adolescents who were initially at least slightly antisocial (Osgood et al., 1996; Pettit et al., 1999). The interrelation between peer influence and parental influence suggests, however, that the progression toward deviance often starts even earlier. Dishion and colleagues (1995) found that ineffective parental monitoring and supervision predicted which adolescents would gravitate toward deviant peer groups. Likewise, Oxford and colleagues (2001) reported that parental rules and high levels of monitoring in grade 5 reduced their children's association with deviant peers in middle school and subsequent drug use. Thus, it appears that unsupervised contact with deviant peers is the catalyst for deviant behavior, but the process starts earlier with a lack of parental supervision.

Structured Interventions. Peer influences operate not only in naturally occurring peer groups but also in groups that are assembled by adults for purposes of intervention. Aggregation of deviant adolescents with other deviant adolescents is the single most common public policy response to deviant behavior in education, juvenile justice, and mental health (Dodge, Lansford, and Dishion, 2006). In juvenile justice, it occurs in detention centers, training schools, boot camps, and wilderness camps. Over the past decade, evidence has emerged that these well-intentioned interventions have adverse effects on participants under some, but not all, conditions. A similar phenomenon occurs in the child welfare field, where it has been shown that foster care youth living in group settings are more likely to "cross over" into juvenile justice than other child welfare youth (Herz, Ryan, and Bilchik, 2010). Adverse effects are most likely to occur when there is enhanced opportunity for deviant peer group exposure, leading to learning and copying of deviant behavior, a pattern that has been characterized as "deviancy training" (Dishion, McCord, and Poulin, 1999).

Deviancy training in intervention groups is relatively likely to occur when (1) participants are of early adolescent age; (2) participants have begun a trajectory toward deviance but are not extremely deviant; (3) participants are exposed to slightly older, slightly more deviant peers; and (4) the setting is unstructured and allows for free interaction without well-trained adult supervision (Dishion, Dodge, and Lansford, 2006; Gottfredson, 2010). This subject is explored further in Chapter 6.

Gangs. Participation in a gang is perhaps the most striking case of exposure to deviant peer influences. Longitudinal studies have revealed convincingly that entering a gang is associated with increases in deviant behavior and exiting a gang is associated with subsequent decreases in deviant behavior (Battin et al., 1998; Thornberry et al., 2003; Gatti et al., 2005). Klein

(2006) has described the gang process as one of peer influence that is fueled by promotion of rivalry with other gangs, group norms of loyalty and commitment to the deviant gang, and cohesiveness and group identity. These processes contribute to criminal activity during gang membership.

Neighborhoods

Numerous studies have examined peer effects in neighborhood settings. Chase-Lansdale and colleagues (1997) found that once family factors are controlled, neighborhood peer effects on behavioral and academic outcomes persist but are modest. Experimental evidence on the impact of peer group exposure in neighborhoods comes from the Moving to Opportunity study, in which economically disadvantaged families were randomly assigned to move to new neighborhoods through housing vouchers (Kling and Liebman, 2004; Sanbonmatsu et al., 2007). As hypothesized by peer influence models, shortly after being assigned to move to less deviant neighborhoods, boys displayed fewer violent and other problem behaviors relative to control boys who stayed in neighborhoods of origin (Katz, Kling, and Liebman, 2001). The long-term findings are perplexing, however. As expected, girls who had been assigned to live in neighborhoods in which they were exposed to fewer deviant peers experienced fewer arrests for violent, property, and other crimes and improvements in well-being on several measures (Kling and Liebman, 2004). However, boys who moved to less deviant neighborhoods experienced more arrests and worse behavior than control boys (Kling, Ludwig, and Katz, 2005). The most persuasive finding and parsimonious explanation of this pattern (but admittedly post hoc by the authors) is one that is consistent with the deviant peer influence hypothesis: girls in less deviant neighborhoods participated more in team sports and structured after-school organizations, whereas boys in less deviant neighborhoods returned to interact with peers from their old neighborhoods and spent time with new peers who used drugs (Orr et al., 2003; Ludwig and Duncan, 2008).

Organized Community Activities

After-school youth development programs bring together peers for ostensibly positive purposes, but they also may expose children to deviant peers (Lansford, 2006). Because a disproportionate number of children who enroll in these programs come from disadvantaged backgrounds and have histories of deviant behavior, these programs offer a test of the hypothesis of deviant peer influences. Evaluation of a randomized controlled trial involving 18 centers (called Community Learning Centers) for elementary school children revealed that program children reported safer after-school experiences than control children, but school records indicated that program children were suspended more frequently than controls and teachers reported more behavior problems for treatment children. Among middle school students in Community Learning Centers, experimental evidence is lacking, but analyses with statistical controls indicated that participants in these programs later had higher rates of substance use, drug dealing, and property destruction (James-Burdumy et al., 2005). Mahoney and colleagues (2001, 2004, 2005) have reached similar conclusions following analyses of publicly funded after-school programs that aggregate deviant youth: participation in unstructured after-school programs increases antisocial behavior, and the most likely cause is exposure to deviant peer influences.

It is misleading to characterize all peer group activities as harmful, however. Mahoney and Stattin (2000) reported that participation in highly structured activities with peers that are led by an adult and that meet regularly (such as sports, music, scouts, church) is associated with a lower level of antisocial outcomes, although selection effects account for these outcomes as well as participation. But a randomized controlled trial of participation in Boys and Girls Clubs (which meet regularly with trained adult leaders who follow structured curricula in addition to affording structured fun activities) found that participants showed higher levels of social competence than controls (St. Pierre et al., 2001).

School Influences

Adolescents spend more time in school than any other place except home: at least 7 hours a day, 5 days a week, for 180 days a year. Schools are therefore an important context in which the psychosocial capacities discussed earlier in this chapter are developing. School is also the major setting for the development and expression of academic competence and for attainment of the assets needed for a successful transition to young adulthood.

We focus on three specific topics that are important for understanding adolescent development and schooling in relation to juvenile justice: school transitions (to middle school and high school), the academic achievement gap, and school discipline.

School Transitions

Students undergo two, possibly three, school transitions during the adolescent years—from elementary school to middle school, from middle school to high school and, for many, from high school to some form of postsecondary education. At each transition, schools become larger, more bureaucratic, impersonal, competitive, and discipline-oriented, as well as more focused on public displays of ability. Research on these transitions sheds light on the degree to which there is a match between the developmental needs of adolescents and the opportunities afforded them in school settings (Simmons and Blyth, 1987; Eccles et al., 1993; Eccles and Roeser, 2009). Much of the research suggests that there is more mismatch than match, which partly explains why school transitions can be challenging for many students.

The school transition literature is also compatible with what is known about successful schools from the school effectiveness literature. That literature attempts to identify the features of schools that predict good student achievement over and above students' background characteristics, as well as the features of schools that are especially effective for low-income and/ or poorly performing students (Lee, 2000; Rutter and Maugham, 2002). At the secondary level, the most effective schools have teachers who communicate high academic expectations for students in a supportive and safe environment as well as strong leaders who focus on academic outcomes. Effective schools are also smaller, in part because they allow more opportunities for students to establish close relationships with teachers. Unfortunately, the characteristics of secondary schools often are at odds with the developmental challenges of adolescence, which include the need for close peer relationships, autonomy, support from adults other than one's parents, identity negotiation, and academic self-efficacy. Stage-environment mismatch during secondary school transitions can undermine students' self-confidence, feelings of belonging, and motivation to do well in school, factors which can, in turn, contribute to poor school performance (Cook et al., 2008).

Achievement Disparities

About 75 percent of American students graduate from high school in four years (National Research Council and National Academy of Education, 2011); most never become involved with the juvenile justice system. Thus, secondary schools are doing a reasonably good job of providing students with the skills, values, and motivation to successfully transition to adult roles.

What about the 25 percent who fail to achieve on-time high school graduation? Many of these students encountered school failure early in their academic careers, and these difficulties were magnified by the middle school and high school transitions and by attendance at low-performing schools. Many of these students are also ethnic minority members. One of the most consistent findings in the education literature is the achievement gap between different racial/ethnic groups in American schools. On just about every standardized measure of academic achievement and just about every indicator of educational attainment, African American and Latino students are doing more poorly than their white (and Asian descent) counterparts. For example, at eighth grade, they lag considerably behind whites in mathematics achievement and reading (Vanneman et al., 2009). On average only about 50 percent of African American and Latino youth are graduating from high school on time (National Research Council and National Academy of Education, 2011).

The achievement gap between different racial/ethnic groups is partly explained by differential opportunity and preparation for high school. Among the educational practices widely used by secondary schools to address the achievement gap are academic tracking and high-stakes testing. Although motivated by good intentions, neither of these practices has been successful in reducing the achievement gap, and neither seems to be well informed by the science of adolescent development. Very importantly, both practices also appear to disadvantage ethnic minority adolescents.

Academic Tracking. Academic tracking, also known as ability grouping, describes teaching practices in which students who are similar in ability are grouped together for instruction. By the time students transition to high school, academic tracking in some form is nearly universal (Lucas, 1999). Tracking patterns also mirror the achievement gap, with white and Asian students more likely to be in the high-ability tracks and Latino and African American youth more likely to be placed in the low-ability tracks. Some have argued that tracking frequently operates to perpetuate racial inequality and social stratification in American society (Gamoran, 1992; Oakes, 2005).

Tracking remains controversial as a way to organize instruction because it is clear that the main beneficiaries of tracking are the high-ability youth placed in high-track classes (Oakes, 2005; Eccles and Roeser, 2009). In contrast, being in a low (e.g., vocational) track is often related to decelerated academic growth. Students in low-track streams also experience the stigma of being designated as low ability: diminished self-esteem, lower aspirations, and more negative attitudes about school.

Tracking also has an impact on students' peer group affiliations. Tracking inhibits the formation of cross-ethnic friendships, an important social competency (Hallinan and Williams, 1989; Moody, 2001; Hamm, Brown, and Heck, 2005). In addition, by restricting peer exposure to same-ability classmates, tracking can also contribute to deviant behavior. As discussed previously, disengaged students in the low tracks are more likely to affiliate with similarly disengaged peers and engage in risky or deviant behavior.

High-stakes Testing. Since its passage in 2001, the No Child Left Behind (NCLB) Act mandates annual testing in reading and mathematics of all students, with federal funding and other rewards contingent on performing at a certain level. Some states have added other forms of high-stakes testing, such as high school exit exams, which impact individual students more directly.

Requiring schools to regularly assess student progress can help various stakeholders—including parents—put pressure on schools and school districts to do a better job of providing quality education. In practice, however, NCLB and other forms of high-stakes testing have been controversial (National Research Council, 2001b; Posner, 2004; Advancement Project, 2010). Whatever else may be said, however, it is clear that the act's testing requirements particularly impact low-performing students and students of color. Failure to pass the high school exit exam—a particular challenge for African American and Latino youth—greatly increases the odds of school dropout (Jacob, 2001), a major risk factor for involvement in the juvenile justice system.

School Discipline

Schools have an obligation to maintain a safe and orderly learning environment and to discipline students who undermine these goals. Since the 1990s, one of the main approaches to school discipline has been "zero tolerance." Zero tolerance is a label given to a collection of school discipline policies that began when Congress passed the Gun-Free Schools Act in 1994. That legislation required states to enact laws mandating expulsion of students found with firearms on school property. Most states and school districts responded to the federal mandate by adopting so-called zero-tolerance policies requiring expulsion or suspension of students not only for possessing firearms but also for possessing other weapons, possessing drugs, or committing any serious violations on or off school. Surveillance of students also increased with the implementation of school resource officer programs; the installation of hardware, such as metal detectors and cameras; and more intrusive searches. Thus far, however, the research on the impact of these practices on school safety has been mixed—ranging from reports that they enhanced school security to findings that they actually led to more school disorder (Theriot, 2009). The connection between school-based arrests and referral to the juvenile justice system is also less established (see Chapter 3).

What is clear is that rates of suspension and expulsion have increased dramatically. For example, the U.S. Department of Education reported that there were 250,000 more students suspended from school in 2006-2007 than there were four years earlier, and the number of expelled students increased by 15 percent (Advancement Project, 2010). In large urban school districts, such as Chicago, Houston, Los Angeles, and New York, increased suspension and expulsion rates greatly exceed the national averages.

Zero-tolerance policies fall disproportionately on racial/ethnic minority youth, particularly African American youth. Across the K-12 spectrum, the American Psychological Association Zero Tolerance Task Force (2008) found that African American students were about three times more likely to be suspended from school than whites, whereas Latinos and Native Americans were about 1.5 times more likely to be suspended than whites. Even after controlling for structural factors, such as poverty, or individual character-istics, such as academic achievement or the severity of school infractions, racial differences in suspensions and expulsions persist (Gregory, Skiba, and Noguera, 2010). More recently, the Department of Education released data based on approximately 85 percent of the nation's students that showed that African American students are more than 3.5 times more likely to be suspended or expelled than their white peers (U.S Department of Education, 2012), and more than 70 percent of students involved in school-related arrests or referred to law enforcement are Hispanic or African American. Texas data also confirmed the large numbers of students being suspended and expelled (15 percent of nearly 1 million students) and that only a small percentage (3 percent) of these actions were in response to conduct for which state law mandated suspensions and expulsion; the rest were made at the dis-cretion of school officials primarily in response to violations of local schools' conduct codes (Fabelo et al., 2012). The study also showed that suspension or expulsion greatly increased a student's risk of being held back a grade, dropping out, or landing in the juvenile justice system (Fabelo et al., 2012).

How effective are zero-tolerance policies in reducing school misbehav-ior and providing a safer learning environment for students? The Ameri-can Psychological Association Zero Tolerance Task Force (2008) reviewed the evidence and concluded that zero-tolerance policies were not effec-tive. Mandated punishment for particular offenses—a hallmark of zero tolerance—did not appear to increase the consistency of school discipline policies. There was no evidence that zero tolerance created a school climate more conducive to learning for students who remain, and zero tolerance did not have the intended deterrence effect on individual student behavior.

Zero tolerance as a philosophy of school discipline creates a discipline gap that closely mirrors the racial achievement gap. Suspensions and expul-sions increase the disconnection between youth and their schools, causing them to be less invested in school rules and coursework and less motivated to achieve academic success. The disproportionate suspension and expulsion of minority students raises issues of fundamental fairness and increases the likelihood that they will be targets of school-based arrests for even relatively minor offenses. For these reasons, school reformers have called for restor-ing discipline responsibilities to educators, decreasing reliance on school resource officers, and mandating alternatives to harsh discipline (New York Civil Liberties Union and Annenberg Institute for School Reform, 2009).

Experiences with Racial Discrimination

One of the major challenges faced by racial/ethnic minority groups in the United States is the experience of discrimination. By discrimination, we mean negative or harmful behavior toward a person because of his or her membership in a particular racial/ethnic group (Jones, 1997). Our focus is the perception of bias and harmful treatment because of one's race rather than actual (documented) discrimination in the legal sense. Despite the economic, political, and social gains of the past 50 years for people of color, experiences with racial discrimination continue to be quite prevalent in contemporary America. Survey data reveal that at least two-thirds of African Americans report that they have been discriminated against in a one-year period (Broman, Mavaddat, and Hsu, 2000; Pager and Shepherd, 2008) and that middle-class samples are just as likely to be targets of racial discrimination as their economically disadvantaged counterparts (Feagin, 1991; Cose, 1993).

Personal interactions experienced as racially discriminatory are part of everyday life for youth of color. Many studies now document that reported discrimination is common among ethnic minority youth in schools and in other public spaces (Kessler, Mickelson, and Williams, 1999; Rosenbloom and Way, 2004). Among the most prevalent kinds of unfair treatment reported by ethnic minority youth are receiving a lower grade than deserved from teachers, being the recipient of unusually harsh discipline from authority figures, such as school administrators and police officers, and being accused of behaving suspiciously in public places (Fisher, Wallace, and Fenton, 2000). In criminology research, a few studies have focused on adolescents' perception of unfair treatment by police officers in particular. Net of actual police contact, African American youth perceive a high degree of police-instigated discrimination, especially when they live in more racially integrated neighborhoods (Stewart et al., 2009) or attend more racially integrated high schools (Hagan, Shedd, and Payne, 2005). Thus, regular contact with a more privileged racial group (whites) can heighten black youth's awareness of and sensitivity to perceived police discrimination. More recently, the research has zeroed in on how a youth's experiences help to shape and form perceptions about the police. Lee and colleagues in two different studies showed that youth with a stronger sense of ethnic identity perceived more police discrimination but also reported more positive beliefs about police legitimacy (Lee, Steinberg, and Piquero, 2010; Lee et al., 2011).

Consequences of Perceived Discrimination

Discrimination can take its toll on the mental, physical, social, and academic well-being of youth. Its adverse effects have been examined in three different developmental domains: health, academic achievement, and antisocial behavior.

Mental and Physical Health. Adolescents who perceive or experience repeated discrimination report elevated levels of depression, more general psychological distress, and lower self-worth (Simons et al., 2002; Prelow et al., 2004; Huynh and Fuligni, 2010). In addition to these mental health challenges, new programs of research are documenting that these kinds of race-based discrimination experiences are also linked to long-term physical health problems, such as hypertension and heart disease—the very diseases that disproportionately affect African Americans (Mays, Cochran, and Barnes, 2007). If stressful enough, perceived or actual discrimination experiences are thought to set in motion a series of physiological responses (e.g., elevated blood pressure and heart rate) that eventually result in disease.

Academic Achievement. Perceived discrimination also affects academic outcomes. Several studies have now documented that as reports of unfair race-based treatment by teachers increase, adolescents' grades decline (DeGarmo and Martinez, 2006; Neblett et al., 2006; Berkel et al., 2010). Studies of mediating mechanisms suggest that multiple perceived discrimination experiences undermine the motivation to do well in school (Wong, Eccles, and Sameroff, 2003), and promote the perception of a school climate that is unresponsive to the needs of ethnic minority youth (Benner and Graham, 2011). Low motivation and perceived negative school climate are both known predictors of academic decline. The growing literature on racial disparities in the use of punishment in schools (Losen, 2011) suggests that perceived unfair treatment by teachers is likely to be increasing among ethnic minority youth and contributing to academic disengagement.

Antisocial Behavior. Third, and most germane to the focus of this report, there is a small but growing empirical literature documenting relations among perceived discrimination, externalizing symptoms, and antisocial behavior. For some adolescents of color, repeated experiences with perceived discrimination are correlated with attitudes and behaviors that suggest a weakened commitment to conventional rules and values. For example, in cross-sectional studies, personal experiences with unfair treatment due to race were significantly correlated with teacher reports of externalizing behavior for Latino youth (Vega et al., 1995), substance abuse for American Indian youth (Whitbeck et al., 2001) and delinquent behavior for Chinese American youth (Deng et al., 2010). Among black youth, with whom most of the discrimination research has been conducted, perceived unfair treatment has been linked to anger and a hostile view of relationships (Simons et al., 2003) as well as self-reported delinquency (DuBois et al., 2002b; Prelow et al., 2004; Simons et al., 2006). In one particularly rigorous analysis of longitudinal data covering five years, reported personal experiences with discrimination predicted increases in self-reported delinquency by black youth (Martin et al., 2011). However, the reverse set of relations (delinquency predicting increases in reported discrimination) was not found.

Why is perceived discrimination predictive of delinquent behavior? Although research on mediating mechanisms is limited, the general belief is that cumulative experiences with perceived discrimination by authority figures in the larger society can lead adolescents to question whether members of their racial/ethnic groups are treated fairly and respectfully by society's institutions and whether, in fact, outgroup members who represent those institutions can be trusted (Smith, 2010; Benner and Graham, 2011). To the degree that society's institutions are untrustworthy, aggressive actions may be perceived as both necessary and legitimate to defend oneself.

Although not linked to the developmental literature on perceived discrimination, criminology research indicates that adolescents of color often do not trust the legal system, endorsing the belief that they and members of their racial/ethnic group will not be treated fairly. For example, Woolard and colleagues (2008) studied anticipated legal system injustice in a sample of adolescents from multiple ethnic groups, half of whom had become involved in the juvenile justice system. These researchers reported that black youth were particularly likely to report that they expected to be treated more unfairly than others by the legal system if they were accused of a crime, helped less by their lawyer, more likely to be found guilty, and punished more harshly. The race differences were more striking among youth who had not been involved with the justice system, suggesting that there may be a shared consensus within the African American community that people from their racial group should expect to be treated less fairly in the justice system than members of other racial/ethnic groups, particularly whites. Anticipated legal injustice, we suggest, can be traced back to more widespread experience with perceived discrimination in the larger society.

Racial Identity and Racial Socialization as Buffers

Not all ethnic minority youth who perceive or experience discrimination suffer the negative consequences described above. A strong racial identity and parental socialization about race appear to buffer some of those negative developmental outcomes Regarding racial identity, a number of studies document that feeling connected to one's racial group (centrality) and awareness of societal views about one's racial group (public regard) reduces the adverse mental health consequences of perceived discrimination (Sellers and Shelton, 2003; Sellers et al., 2006). As briefly described earlier, a strong ethnic identity can also result in more positive beliefs about police legitimacy even when there is perceived discrimination (Lee, Steinberg, and Piquero, 2010; Lee et al., 2011). Indeed, the development of a strong racial identity has positive consequences in just about every developmental domain in which it has been studied. Concerning parental socialization, when parents teach their offspring to expect unfair treatment (preparation for bias) and at the same time instill pride in racial group membership, adolescents are able to thrive academically and emotionally despite perceived discrimination (Hughes et al., 2006). Studies of racial identity and racial socialization processes underscore the resilience of ethnic minority youth and the ways in which their unique experiences contribute to healthy development.

These buffers notwithstanding, the literature on perceived discrimination during adolescence shows that efforts must be made to increase awareness among teachers, juvenile justice personnel, police officers, merchants, and other authority figures of the adverse consequences of perceived discrimination. Consciousness-raising about the ways in which adult authority figures contribute to perceptions of unfair treatment is also needed. For example, it is known that racial stereotypes are often precursors of unfair treatment and that these stereotypes can be activated outside conscious awareness. (See Chapter 8 for a description of research by Graham and Lowery [2004] that involved police and juvenile probation officers.) Just because stereotypes are unconscious does not mean that they cannot be changed. This awareness should be part of any long-term strategies aimed at reducing differential treatment of ethnic minority youth that is biased or perceived to be biased, and the well-documented negative consequences of such treatment.

SUMMARY

Although knowledge of behavioral and brain development in adolescence is advancing, it is still an emerging area of investigation. There is clear behavioral evidence that adolescence is characterized by poor self-control, increased risk taking, emotional dysregulation, and susceptibility to peer and environmental influences. In recent years, an impressive body of neuroscience research has identified likely neural correlates of these behavioral phenomena, and the inference that brain immaturity underlies these characteristic features of adolescent behavior is reasonable and intuitive. Nonetheless, it is important to note that research on developmental neuroscience is still in a relatively early stage and has some important limitations. For example, few studies measure both neurobiological immaturity and psychological immaturity concurrently in the same individuals (Somerville, Fani, and McClure-Tone, 2011), across a variety of legally relevant psychological capacities, and across a broad age range (Steinberg, 2009). Many of the existing studies are speculative and correlative, providing an enticing invitation for further investigation. However, the committee concludes that the basic contribution of the fast-developing body of brain development research is that it has provided plausible and informative neurobiological grounding for well-documented behavioral differences between adolescents and adults, and that these differences are sufficiently well established to provide a sound basis for juvenile justice policy making and for consideration in developing juvenile justice interventions.

The research summarized here has identified the developmental forces and settings through which peers influence adolescent risk taking, suggesting that some risk taking is normative, biologically driven, and, to a certain degree, an inevitable outcome of increased salience and time spent with peers during adolescence. Evidence also shows that two peer conditions, in particular, can serve as a catalyst for risk taking and other forms of deviant behavior—unsupervised peer groups and peer groups constituted by a greater number of deviant peers—the latter often occurring as a result of well-intentioned policies and practices for managing youth. The literature highlights the influence of peers' behaviors and attitudes on an adolescent, most likely through processes of deviancy training, modeling, and reinforcement. A relative gap in the literature concerns the way in which qualities of adolescent peer relationships (e.g., reciprocation, mutual support) affect development.

Moreover, peer influences do not operate independently but remain interconnected with family and school influences in complex ways. Family and peer influences operate sequentially, competitively, or in a compensatory fashion at different stages of development, and parental factors can contribute to deviant peer involvement (Dick et al., 2009) However, even during adolescence, the family can provide a source of supervision, guidance, and protection. Hawkins and colleagues (1992) have proposed that strong bonds between an adolescent and his or her parents reduce the likelihood of problem behaviors and substance use because they tend to reduce the salience and value of peer influences, and vice versa. Efforts of parents to monitor, structure, and limit peer activities are also important to delay or reduce exposure to risky peer contexts, which may be especially important during early adolescence, when youth are most vulnerable to heightened reward processing coupled with a still immature self-regulatory system.

School transitions, attendance at low-performing schools and school discipline practices are critical contextual factors influencing poor school performance, a major risk factor for involvement in juvenile crime. Schools can promote adaptive student outcomes by adopting best practices of highly functioning schools identified by the school effectiveness literature and giving greater attention to the disparities in school achievement and discipline practices.

Many studies document that interactions perceived as racially dis-criminatory are common among ethnic minority youth in schools and in other public spaces and that perceived discrimination adversely affects the mental, physical, social, and academic well-being of youth. A strong racial identity and parental socialization about race can buffer the adverse effects that either actual or perceived discrimination can have on a young person. Teachers, juvenile justice personnel, and other authority figures should be part of long-term strategies aimed at reducing interactions with minority youth that are perceived as discriminatory or unfair.

Given the pivotal influences during adolescent development, and par-ticularly those that increase the risk of juvenile offending, it is clear that preventive interventions, including those undertaken by the juvenile justice system, must take into account interactions with peers and adults and attempt to shape them in positive rather than negative ways.

The concordant evidence from both behavioral science and neuro-science research shows that there are changes in both behavior and brain development during adolescence that are transient rather than persistent. Most criminal conduct in adolescence is driven by developmental influ-ences that will change with maturity. Moreover, most adolescent offenders desist during adolescence and many more desist during young adulthood. The sensitivity of adolescents to environmental influences, such as rewards, peers, adversity, and discrimination, has important implications for the design of preventive interventions, including those that occur in the juve-nile justice system. Family members, teachers, and other adults aiming to promote healthy and successful adolescent development, including juvenile justice agencies, should focus on rewards and immediate consequences while creating avenues for developing self-control and self-confidence.

5

A Framework for Reform

The developmental science of adolescence suggests that juveniles differ from adults in ways that are centrally important to both the juvenile justice system and criminal justice system. This body of scientific knowledge helps to explain adolescents' involvement in criminal activity and also enhances our ability to design interventions that will serve the interests of both society and young offenders. The often postulated goals of the justice system are to hold offenders accountable for wrongdoing and to reduce crime. The committee's view is that these purposes are best served when the legal response to juvenile offending is grounded in scientific knowledge about adolescent development.

Four broad lessons for juvenile justice policy can be derived from the psychological and neuroscience research discussed in Chapter 4. Attending to these lessons can contribute to a justice system that serves the important goals of fairness and crime reduction better than a regime that ignores differences between juveniles and adults. First, psychosocial factors, characteristic of adolescence as a developmental stage, are likely to contribute in important ways to the involvement of adolescents in criminal activity. Major influences on adolescent decision making include susceptibility to peer influence, impulsivity, reward seeking, and a tendency to focus on immediate consequences of decisions and to discount the future consequences (Scott and Steinberg, 2003). A growing body of research indicates that these explanatory factors are grounded in neurobehavioral tendencies associated with normal maturation (Steinberg, 2010b). The normal adolescent brain is not fully mature and functions in a way that predisposes the adolescent to risk-taking behavior. This is not to suggest that all adolescents are likely to engage in criminal activity. Moreover, as explained in Chapter 1, adolescent offending is heterogeneous, ranging from the great majority who offend infrequently or whose offending is limited primarily to alcohol or drug use, to a small group of adolescents whose delinquencies are repeated and serious. Individual differences, reflecting each youth's biological characteristics, experiences, and social environment, which includes family, peer, and neighborhood influences, affect the occurrence, intensity, and frequency of offending. Even taking variations in individual risk factors into account, however, psychosocial influences on decision making during adolescence distinguish juvenile choices from those of adults and indicate that, at a quite fundamental level, the determinants of criminal involvement among juveniles generally differ from the determinants of adult criminality. This etiological difference makes the criminal choices of adolescents less culpable than those of adults and bears directly on the justice system's response to adolescent offending.

Second, if the influences on much teenage criminal activity are developmental in nature, most youth are likely to mature out of their tendency to become involved in crime unless justice system interventions themselves impede or prevent a successful transition to a law-abiding adult life. Thus, research indicates that most adolescent criminal behavior is outgrown and that only a small percentage of teenage offenders are young "career criminals" who will persist in their offending into adulthood (Farrington, 1989; Moffitt, 1993). This pattern of criminal involvement among teenagers suggests that a society's goal of reducing crime will be furthered by ensuring that interventions holding young offenders accountable for their misdeeds do not have the unwanted effect of increasing the risk of reoffending and or otherwise impeding successful maturation.

The third lesson provides guidance for accomplishing this goal. The research indicates that adolescence is a period during which teenagers normally make important progress toward acquiring skills and capacities necessary to successfully assume conventional adult roles of spouse (or partner), employee, and citizen. This developmental process involves a dynamic interaction between the individual and the social environment; a healthy social environment provides "opportunity structures" that facilitate development. Three crucial environmental conditions are important: authoritative parents or adult parent figures, prosocial peer affiliates (and limited access to antisocial peers), and participation in activities that promote autonomy and critical thinking (Chung, Little, and Steinberg, 2005). Facilities or programs in which justice involved youth are placed become an important social context for their ongoing development, and these dispositions therefore have a strong potential for either facilitating or undermining healthy maturation. Juvenile justice interventions, both residential and community-based, that genuinely aim to reduce recidivism will seek to provide opportunity structures that can promote young offenders' development into productive adults.

Finally, knowledge about adolescent development has several important implications for the fairness of the justice system when it holds adolescents accountable for their offending. First, because adolescents lack mature capacities for judgment and self-regulation, the justice system should apply the principle of mitigation, avoiding interventions or sanctions that are excessive or disproportionate to their culpability. Second, justice system participants must also recognize that younger juveniles, due to their developmental immaturity, may be less capable than adults of participating in proceedings to adjudicate their offenses and determine sentences, and some may not meet minimum standards of competence. The ability to understand the trial process and to assist one's attorney is a part of fundamental fairness under the Constitution, and it is essential to the legitimacy of any criminal proceeding (Bonnie and Grisso, 2003; Scott and Grisso, 2005). Third, adolescents' tendencies to question adult authority are often accompanied by sensitivity to whether they and their peers have been treated fairly by adults. The justice system should therefore make special efforts to adhere to fair procedures and to avoid practices and outcomes that appear biased or discriminatory, particularly in cases involving minority youth.

ADOLESCENTS IN THE JUVENILE JUSTICE SYSTEM

Advancing knowledge of adolescent development solidifies and strengthens the normative foundations of the juvenile court. The architects of a separate system of justice for youthful offenders embraced rehabilitation rather than punishment as its central mission. Viewed from a contemporary perspective, the juvenile justice system has three complementary goals—promoting accountability, preventing reoffending, and treating youth fairly—each of which is served by a rehabilitative orientation. Promoting accountability refers to the process of inculcating and reinforcing norms of personal responsibility, thereby helping to foster adolescents' healthy moral development and socialization and satisfying society's expectations that corrective action will be taken in response to wrongdoing. Reducing the occurrence of reoffending is a distinct objective of juvenile justice, but it is also the most concrete measure of whether adolescents who have come to the attention of the juvenile justice system have embraced a law-abiding way of life. The duty to assure "due process of law" is, of course, a constitutional obligation, but treating adolescents fairly can also promote positive legal socialization. Scientific study can ascertain whether juvenile justice interventions are achieving these objectives.

Crime Prevention

Legal mechanisms of prevention operate at two levels: at a population level (general prevention) and at the individual level (specific prevention) (Bonnie, Coughlin, and Jeffries, 2010). At the population level, there are two basic legal tools of prevention: (1) declarative or expressive strategies, which aim to inculcate norms of conduct by expressing social disapproval and punishing violators and (2) deterrent strategies, which attempt to discourage the target population from engaging in the prohibited activity by threatening to impose sanctions if they do. Mechanisms of specific prevention operate at the individual level after an offender is apprehended, with the goal of preventing that particular person from committing future crimes. This can be accomplished by a variety of legal mechanisms, including intimidation by threat of future penalties (sometime called specific deterrence), incapacitation, or rehabilitation. The goal of specific crime prevention has always been important in juvenile crime policy, but the form of prevention has differed in different periods. During the period of the traditional juvenile court, the emphasis (in theory at least) was solely on rehabilitation. During the 1980s and 1990s, lawmakers assumed that incapacitation was the only effective means of preventing juvenile crime. Modern policy makers, guided by the scientific knowledge of adolescence, seek to prevent juvenile offenders from reoffending not only through specific rehabilitative programs, but also by fostering a healthy social environment. It is important to reemphasize that many programs and interventions are available to promote healthy development and prevent delinquency during childhood and adolescence before youth become involved with the juvenile justice system. We are focusing here only on the preventive role of the juvenile justice system itself.

General Prevention

The punitive reforms of the 1980s and 1990s aimed to send a strong message to juveniles generally that their crimes would be severely punished. But the science of adolescence would seem to indicate that general prevention, and particularly deterrent threats, may operate less effectively with adolescents than with adults. First, the available evidence indicates that the anticipated response of peers has a greater impact on juveniles' choices about criminal activity than does the threat of sanctions (Foglia, 1997). Moreover, adolescents' tendency to focus on immediate consequences may lead them not to attend to abstract or remote threats. Even increasing the severity of the threatened sanction may add little to its deterrent effect for adolescents, when the punishment is projected far into the future, especially if the probability of detection is perceived to be low. Conversely, an immediate sanction combined with a high probability of detention is more likely to deter offending.

Individual Prevention

The goal of protecting the public from violent young offenders was an important rationale for the harsh reforms of juvenile crime policy in the 1980s and 1990s. But these reforms relied heavily on incapacitation to achieve their crime prevention goal. At one level, incapacitation is effective at reducing crime—young offenders who are locked up are not out on the streets engaging in crime. But placement in institutions is very expensive and, as discussed below, confinement under punitive conditions may increase recidivism in young offenders after release rather than reducing it. Scientific knowledge about adolescence sheds light on the possible harmful developmental impact of harsh or extended confinement; although it may be effective in achieving public protection in the short term, it may be ineffective at reducing the risk of future offending (Fagan, 1999; Bishop and Frazier, 2000). To be clear, secure institutional confinement sometimes has a place in juvenile justice policy, but it should be used only for youth who pose a serious and immediate threat to public safety. As Chapters 6 and 7 demonstrate, the research also suggests that other justice system interventions (aside from confinement) can reduce juvenile crime while holding young people accountable for their conduct.

As noted above, most youth crime is what psychologist Terrie Moffitt (1993) has called "adolescence-limited" offending, and most young offenders will desist from offending as they age into adulthood. The statistics uniformly show that crime rates increase steadily from early adolescence to age 17 and then decline sharply thereafter; 17-year-olds commit more crimes than any other age group (Piquero, 2008b; Piquero et al., 2012). This developmental pattern in criminal activity parallels laboratory-based findings showing heightened risk taking (Steinberg et al., 2008; Figner et al., 2009) and enhanced activity in the emotional brain region (Galvan et al., 2006; Hare et al., 2008; Somerville, Hare, and Casey, 2011) in adolescents from approximately age 13 to age 17 that "may be due to the combination of relatively higher inclinations to seek excitement and relatively immature capacities for self-control that are typical during this period of development" (Steinberg et al., 2008, p. 1,764). The research is inconclusive regarding the specific or definitive boundaries (i.e., onset and offset) because they vary by specific behavior and brain system, making it difficult to narrow the age range as to when this occurs. If the criminal activity of many young offenders is driven by developmental influences, dispositions that hold them accountable for their crimes while providing opportunity structures essential for healthy development are more likely to reduce recidivism than either "slaps on the wrist" or harsh punishment.

This account of the connection between adolescent development and teenage criminal activity underscores that an important preventive goal of the justice system in responding to juvenile crime is to maximize the prospects that young offenders will make a successful transition to adulthood with their expected range of opportunities intact. Public protection is an important objective of the justice system; no regime that sacrifices this goal will be viable over time. Incapacitation may be a justifiable public response for cases involving repetitive violent offenders, but in focusing on short-term public safety, lawmakers should be careful not to increase the social costs of juvenile crime over the long term. For most young offenders, the ultimate goal of preventing future offending may be best served through interventions that do not compromise public safety in the short term and most importantly that prepare them for conventional adult roles as workers, intimate partners, and citizens.

At least in its rhetoric, the traditional juvenile court signaled that juvenile offenders bore no responsibility for their crimes. This rhetoric not only exacerbated public fears that the justice system was failing to protect the public from juvenile offenders, but also probably diluted accountability in young offenders. However, as discussed below, harsh sanctions in institutional settings may contribute to recidivism. The committee concludes that juvenile dispositions that incorporate developmental knowledge may assist delinquent youth to complete essential developmental tasks, including the task of learning to take responsibility for their own mistakes and to live law-abiding lives (Bazemore and Schiff, 2005).

Delinquency Dispositions

The goal of preventing juvenile crime and reducing its social costs can be furthered by incorporating developmental knowledge into dispositional policies and practices of the juvenile justice system. Perhaps the most important lesson of the developmental research for designing delinquency dispositions that are likely to reduce reoffending juvenile crime is that the social context plays a critical role in psychological development during the formative stage of adolescence (Bronfenbrenner and Morris, 1998; Chung, Little, and Steinberg, 2005). A youth's social setting—family, peer group, school, and community—can either inhibit or facilitate healthy development. For the youth in the justice system, the program or facility in which he or she is placed becomes the developmental setting and thus can have a substantial impact—positive or negative—on the youth's future developmental trajectory in ways that may affect recidivism. Juvenile justice programs can either further or undermine the law's crime prevention goals on the basis of the kind of developmental setting they provide.

Juvenile justice interventions should be structured to help adolescents acquire skills that are essential for fulfilling conventional adult roles. These include not only educational and vocational skills but also social skills that allow individuals to form intimate relationships and cooperate in groups, as well as the ability to act responsibly without supervision (Lipsey, 1995). The attributes of programs that are likely to exert positive influence on psychosocial development will vary depending on young offenders' needs and the level of security and culture of the program. The research suggests that supportive adult authority figures; prosocial peer affiliations; and educational, employment, and other activities that promote autonomous decision making and critical thinking are important in providing opportunity structures that facilitate normative development. Moreover, young offenders need to acquire the tools to deal with the challenges they face in their families, peer groups, and neighborhoods—the social context of their future lives. It is thus not surprising that many successful juvenile justice programs adopt an ecological approach in which parents, families, peers, schools, and communities play a prominent part (Henggeler, Melton, and Smith, 1992).

Chapter 4 makes clear that parents play a very important role in their children's psychological development and can either support healthy development and prosocial behavior or contribute to their children's inclinations to engage in delinquent behavior. The Progressive Era reformers who established the traditional juvenile court assumed that parents were the source of their children's delinquent proclivities and aimed to substitute the benevolent state as *parens patriae* (Tiffan, 1982). This view had a lasting influence on juvenile justice policy; until recently, juvenile justice programs paid little attention to parents. But the research described in Chapter 4 confirms that parents can play pivotal roles in preventing reoffending if the courts work with them.

Several justice system programs most effective at reducing recidivism involve an emphasis either on parental involvement or on providing a parent-like alternative when parents are unable or unwilling to assume a positive parental role. Multisystemic therapy, functional family therapy, and multidimensional treatment foster care all put parents and the parent-child relationship at the center of their treatment programs (Henggeler, Melton, and Smith, 1992; Barnoski, 2004; Greenwood, 2006). The importance of including parents as key participants in programs directed at young offenders supports a policy of keeping delinquent youth in their communities whenever possible. Even when they must be placed in residential facilities, including parents in their treatment program is important. On this basis, the Missouri model of small residential facilities located near offenders' homes is superior to large institutions located far from urban centers (Task Force on Transforming Juvenile Justice, 2009). The caregivers in these programs also engage in practices that are consistent with the actions required of parents to support healthy adolescent development.

Chapter 4 also makes clear that another important element of adolescents' social context is peer affiliations; peer relationships can have a positive or negative impact on psychological development and on the inclination of juveniles to get involved in criminal activity. Not surprisingly, many young offenders have antisocial peer affiliates who may reinforce their delinquent tendencies. An important challenge for the justice system in designing interventions is to limit the influence of antisocial peers while providing youth with the tools to resist negative peer pressure. One deficiency of large juvenile correctional facilities (and adult prisons) is that these settings are likely to involve unsupervised contact with antisocial peers and no contact with prosocial peers (Scott and Steinberg, 2010). A key lesson of the developmental research is that association with antisocial peers should be limited; interaction should be either avoided or highly structured, visible, and transparent. Community programs and small residential facilities are better situated than are large institutions to restrict interaction among delinquent youth and to provide the necessary structure and visibility, although they must also actively address this issue. Size and community location do not solve this problem. Community programs are in a better position to promote contact with prosocial peers.

The scientific evidence reviewed in Chapter 6 shows that well-designed community-based programs are more likely than institutional confinement to facilitate healthy development and reduce recidivism for most young offenders. Aside from the importance of involving parents and limiting and structuring contact with antisocial peers (and encouraging contact with prosocial peers), these programs can more readily be designed to provide a social context with opportunity structures for healthy development and the tools to deal with negative influences in the setting in which the youth will live in the future. For the small proportion of youth who require confinement in residential facilities, proximity to their community is likely to be less disruptive of developmental progress than commitment to distant facilities. As suggested above, large facilities that are located far from young offenders' homes may be particularly harmful (Bishop and Frazier, 2000). The practice of committing youth to large institutions that fail to provide for their developmental needs is both costly in financial terms and ineffective in furthering the goal of crime prevention. A 2009 governor's task force report in New York delivered a harsh rebuke of that state's juvenile justice system, pointing to the high recidivism rates among the large number of youth incarcerated in secure juvenile institutions far from their homes in New York City (Task Force on Transforming Juvenile Justice, 2009).

Collateral Consequences of Delinquency Adjudication

Developmental research indicating that most juvenile crime is adolescence-limited offers another lesson for designing policies that serve the long-term goal of reducing juvenile crime. Society has an interest in juvenile offenders maturing into productive adulthood; thus, policies and practices that impede that progress or impose burdens that follow youth into their adult lives harm society as well as young offenders.

Criminal conviction is often accompanied by collateral consequences required or permitted by law, such as disenfranchisement, limitation of employment opportunities, and, for certain offenses, registration in publicly accessible databases. Whatever the justification for these practices for adults, they are fundamentally at odds with a developmentally informed system of juvenile justice. Adolescent-limited juvenile offending does not reflect on a youth's character or disposition. Moreover, a criminal record may impede the development of prosocial peer and intimate relationships in adulthood (Laub and Sampson, 2001). Except in extraordinary circumstances involving a compelling need to protect public safety, official records of a juvenile's encounters with the justice system should be strictly confidential so as to fully preserve the youth's opportunities for successful integration into adult life. Similarly, citizens should not be disenfranchised on the basis of youthful conduct that has limited or no predictive relevance to community safety.

Fairness

Notwithstanding its continuing commitment to rehabilitation, the contemporary juvenile justice system still jeopardizes many adolescents who become enmeshed in it. As the Supreme Court declared in *In re Gault* (1967),[1] the protective ambition of the juvenile court does not weaken society's obligation to ensure fundamental fairness all the way through the process—including police decisions to question a youth, take custody, or file a charge; prosecutorial and court decisions to initiate proceedings; adjudication; and dispositional placements. Even when invoked for the ostensible benefit of the youth, exercise of the state's power deprives him or her of liberty and may result in harm. This power must accordingly be exercised sparingly and fairly.

Like other aims of juvenile justice, achieving fairness is developmentally grounded. First, interventions or sanctions that are intended to hold adolescents accountable for their wrongdoing should not be excessive or disproportionate to the seriousness of the wrongdoing or to the blame-

---

[1]*In re Gault,* 387 U.S. 1 (1967).

worthiness of the youth. Second, procedures that may be regarded as fair
to adults may not be fair to juveniles, because they are less able than adults
to protect their own interests. (See Chapter 7.) Third, adolescents are very
sensitive to perceived injustice (Tyler and Huo, 2002; Fagan and Tyler,
2005; Fagan and Piquero, 2007; Woolard, Harvell, and Graham, 2008),
and unfair treatment by the legal system may accentuate antisocial tendencies, whereas fair official responses to wrongdoing may enhance respect for
and obedience to law and reduce the likelihood of reoffending (Sherman,
1993). These points will be addressed in turn.

Proportionality

It has long been recognized that children below a certain age lack sufficient moral understanding of their conduct to deserve any official punishment by the state. Under the rules of common law, criminal punishment was
categorically precluded for children younger than age 7, and older children
could also be found to lack the requisite moral understanding on a case-by-
case basis under the so-called infancy defense (Walkover, 1984). Although
the juvenile justice system has largely displaced the infancy defense, many
states set a minimum age (e.g., 8 or 10) for the juvenile court's delinquency
jurisdiction, reflecting the judgment that children younger than the jurisdictional age, as a class, are not sufficiently blameworthy to be subject to
delinquency adjudication and that their misconduct should be dealt with in
the child welfare or education systems rather than the delinquency system.

Historically, delinquency jurisdiction has served as an alternative to
criminal court jurisdiction for adolescents; it aims to hold adolescents
accountable for their offending while undertaking interventions designed
to reduce reoffending. Seen in this way, the policies and practices guiding
dispositions in the juvenile justice system are predicated on a widely shared
moral judgment that punishment in the adult criminal justice system in itself
is presumptively disproportionate to the culpability of younger adolescent
offenders as a class. However, despite the legislative reticence to embrace
the language of retribution, use of lengthy or harsh periods of confinement
for adolescents in juvenile courts are problematic under the principle of proportionality as well as on utilitarian grounds. Concerns about excessive sentences for adolescents are, of course, magnified if the juvenile is prosecuted
in criminal court. (This issue is explored in the next section in this chapter.)

Procedural Fairness

The developmental immaturity of juveniles may affect their ability to
exercise their rights and to participate competently in proceedings adjudicating their criminal charges, whether these proceedings occur in juvenile

courts or criminal courts. The U.S. Constitution requires that defendants be afforded certain rights when they are suspected of and charged with crimes to ensure that the proceedings are fair. Because of adolescents' reduced capacity for reasoning and understanding and psychosocial immaturity, they may be less capable of exercising their rights than are adults (Grisso, 1981). The Supreme Court recognized this point indirectly in *JDB v. North Carolina* (2010) in rejecting the statement of a 13-year-old made without Miranda warnings. The Court held that the age of the youth questioned by a police officer in a school conference room must be considered in evaluating whether it was reasonable for him to believe he was not free to leave. Research shows that juveniles are far more likely than adults to waive their right to remain silent (Grisso, 1980) and to confess to crimes (and even to make false confessions) than are adults (Scott, Reppucci, and Woolard, 1995). Juveniles under age 15 have a poorer comprehension of their right to remain silent, as do 15- and 16-year-olds with below-average intelligence (Grisso, 1981). Juveniles are also more likely to waive their right to an attorney than are adults charged with crimes, despite the fact that they are less capable of protecting their interests in the justice system. (See Chapters 3 and 7.)

A criminal defendant must be competent to stand trial for a criminal proceeding to meet the requirements of constitutional due process. According to the Supreme Court, to satisfy this constitutional requirement, the defendant must be capable of assisting his or her attorney with his defense and must have a rational as well as a factual understanding of the proceedings against him or her.[2] The competence requirement has typically been applied to protect mentally ill and disabled adults; it has also been applied in juvenile delinquency proceedings involving youth with mental disabilities. However, as greater numbers of youth have become eligible for prosecution in adult criminal court under law reforms in recent decades, courts and legislatures have recognized the concept of *developmental incompetence* (Scott and Grisso, 2005). Research evidence indicates that about 33 percent of 11- to 13-year-olds and 20 percent of 14- and 15-year-olds may not be competent to stand trial under the standard applied to adults due to their developmental immaturity (Grisso et al., 2003). Many younger teens may simply lack the capacity for understanding and reasoning to comprehend the trial and its consequences or to be able to assist the attorney. Even older adolescents may be less capable of making decisions that criminal defendants must make—such as the decision to accept a plea offer. Justice Anthony Kennedy in *Graham v. Florida* (2010)[3] recognized that the developmental immaturity of adolescent defendants could undermine the ability of their

---

[2]*Dusky v. U.S.*, 362 U.S. 402 (1960).
[3]*Graham v. Florida*, U.S. Supreme Court, 560 U.S. _ (2010) (Slip Op., at 23).

attorneys to adequately represent them in criminal proceedings, unfairly resulting in erroneous convictions. The possibility that many younger teens are not competent to participate in criminal proceedings poses a serious challenge to the prosecution of juveniles as adults and raises an important concern that must be addressed even in juvenile delinquency proceedings.

Perceived Fairness

Recent research indicates that individuals' perceptions of fairness are important to legal socialization (Piquero, Moffitt, and Lawton, 2005; Tyler and Fagan, 2008). As explored in Chapter 7, the still-nascent literature on legal socialization during adolescence suggests that juveniles may be more likely to accept responsibility for less serious offenses early in the process if they perceive delinquency proceedings to be fair and transparent and any sanctions imposed to be proportionate to their offenses. And the converse is also true. For example, youth in prison are more likely to perceive sentences to be unfair and less likely to forswear future offending than those in the juvenile system (Sherman, 1993). More generally, the well-documented pattern of disproportionate minority contact throughout the process, together with disproportionately harsh sentences imposed on minority youth, are likely to contribute to perceptions by African American youth and those who are members of other ethnic and racial minorities that the justice system is fundamentally unfair. These perceptions, which begin to form even before initial contact with the justice system, impede efforts to encourage minority youth to accept responsibility for their criminal acts and to internalize prosocial values. As important aim of juvenile justice reform is to heighten the awareness of all participants of the ways in which their conduct can affect and influence the legal socialization of minority youth.

ADOLESCENTS IN THE CRIMINAL JUSTICE SYSTEM

As a rule of thumb, interventions shown to be effective in preventing juvenile reoffending at reasonable cost are also likely to satisfy society's expectations that corrective action will be taken in response to wrongdoing. However, for serious violent offending, additional policy considerations may be relevant. Perhaps the greatest political challenges that juvenile crime policy makers face are those relating to whether juveniles should ever be subject to lengthy confinement. a response that rarely can be justified as a means of preventing reoffending (because it is more likely to be criminogenic) but is nonetheless thought to be a necessary response to especially serious offenses, such as homicide or armed robbery. In such cases, a lengthy period of confinement may be sought by prosecutors to register societal disapproval and to incapacitate youth who are thought to present a severe risk of serious reoffending based on their offense histories and other risk factors. These decisions require delicate judgments in which many considerations will be weighed, including public safety and the need to satisfy victims of crime and communities. Developmental knowledge will not, and should not, be the only factor that determines the jurisdictional boundaries between the adult and juvenile courts. But as the Supreme Court and policy makers across the country have recognized in recent years, developmental knowledge should inform legal policies that govern adult punishment of juveniles in important ways. Specifically, the boundaries between juvenile justice and criminal justice, and the sentencing options available for juveniles who are being tried in criminal courts, should be compatible with two normative principles derived from the developmental precepts summarized above and from recent decisions of the Supreme Court: proportionality and individualization.

Diminished Culpability

The proportionality principle implies that a person whose conduct was not blameworthy should not be punished at all, and that even blameworthy offenders should not be punished by sanctions that are excessive, as measured by the harm caused by the offense and the degree of the offender's culpability (Duff, 1993). Thus, for example, a criminal defendant who was insane at the time of the offense may be excused from criminal responsibility altogether, whereas a defendant whose admittedly unlawful aggression was provoked by the victim's wrongdoing may receive a more lenient sentence than he would have received in the absence of provocation (Bonnie, Coughlin, and Jeffries, 2010).

An expanding body of developmental science supports the traditional supposition that adolescent offenders (as a class) are less culpable than adult offenders because their choices are influenced by psychosocial factors that are integral to adolescence as a developmental stage and are strongly shaped by still-developing brain systems (Scott and Steinberg, 2010). Taken together, susceptibility to peer influence, deficiencies in risk perception, sensation-seeking, the tendency to discount future consequences, and weak impulse control are likely to play an important role in shaping adolescent choices that lead to offending. It is not surprising, for example, that adolescents typically offend in groups, whereas adult criminals are much more likely to act alone (Reiss and Farrington, 1991; Farrington and Welsh, 2007; Piquero, 2008b). Moreover, adolescent criminal activity may represent the risky experimentation that is part of the developmental process of identity formation for many adolescents (Gardner and Herman, 1990). As Chapter 4 demonstrates, recent research on adolescent brain development provides evidence that the developmental factors that seem to contribute to adolescent offending have biological underpinnings. Of course, it is not possible to study the decision making of teenagers actually engaging in criminal activity. But the current body of research can be applied to these decisions, supporting the conclusion that much teenage criminal activity is probably a product of developmental forces rather than deeply rooted deficiencies in character (Albert and Steinberg, 2011). To the extent that this is so, juvenile offenders are appropriately seen as less culpable than their adult counterparts.

The psychosocial immaturity that characterizes adolescence does not lead every adolescent to get involved in crime. Individual factors and social context also play important roles in the etiology of adolescent offending. Some youth have individual characteristics and vulnerabilities that place them at higher risk for criminal offending, and others have what are often described as "protective" characteristics; some family, peer, and neighborhood settings contribute to teenage offending more than others. However, the research supports the conclusion that much adolescent involvement in crime is driven by developmental influences and is not indicative of incipient character pathology or the early stage of a criminal career. Indeed, normal teenagers growing up in neighborhoods in which many peers are involved in crime may be subject to substantial pressure to participate (Fagan, 1999).

That adolescents are generally understood to be less culpable than adult offenders does not mean that they should be regarded as children who lack moral or legal responsibility for their crimes. As Chapter 2 explained, this was the view of the social reformers who established the juvenile court a century ago. But modern science says that adolescence is different from both childhood and adulthood in ways that mitigate the criminal blameworthiness of adolescents. In short, developmental knowledge challenges the fairness of subjecting juvenile offenders to the same punishment as their adult counterparts.

Mitigated Punishment

The U.S. Supreme Court has provided powerful support for the mitigation principle as a foundation of juvenile crime policy in three recent landmark decisions. In each of these opinions, the Court pointed to developmental psychology and neuroscience evidence in holding that offenders who were younger than age 18 at the time of their offenses cannot be subject to the most severe criminal penalties because of their reduced culpability. In a 2005 opinion, *Roper v. Simmons*, the Court held that the Eighth Amendment ban on cruel and unusual punishment prohibited the use of the death penalty for a crime committed by a juvenile. Drawing on scientific knowledge, the Court pointed to the decision-making deficits of adolescents that contribute to impulsive risk taking, their vulnerability to external pressures from peers and families, and their unformed characters. Because of these distinctive aspects of adolescence, punishments reserved for the worst offenders are excessive as applied to juveniles. "Retribution is not proportional if the law's most severe penalty is imposed on one whose culpability or blameworthiness is diminished, to a substantial degree, by reason of youth and immaturity."[4] Five years later, in *Graham v. Florida* (2010), the Court prohibited the sentence of life without parole for a non-homicide offense on the same constitutional ground. Most recently, the Court in *Miller v. Alabama* (2012) rejected a mandatory sentence of life without parole even for juvenile offenders who committed homicide.

Although juveniles seldom received these sentences even before the Supreme Court proscribed them, the general principle of mitigation has a broader reach than the two specific rules enunciated in these decisions because it supports more lenient dispositions for adolescents as a general policy. This translates into dispositions that are shorter in duration than those imposed on adults for similar crimes. Moreover, when judged from the constricted time perspective of an adolescent, even sentences that are shorter than those imposed on adults may be experienced as longer.

Transfer to the Criminal Court

Developmental science strongly reinforces the long-standing legal tradition of holding juveniles accountable in a separate juvenile justice system. However, even after traditional juvenile court was established, some youth were prosecuted in criminal court and punished in the adult system. How the boundary is drawn between the two systems has always been controversial, and the laws governing transfer of jurisdiction from juvenile to adult courts (as well as the sentences available for punishment of youthful offenders in the adult system) have undergone pendular swings. As Chapter 2 describes, laws enacted in the 1990s in many states expanded substantially the category of youth subject to prosecution and punishment as adults. To be sure, many youth dealt with in the adult system were placed on probation and some proportion were even sent back to the juvenile system, but the number of youth who experienced preadjudication detention in adult jails and were ultimately sent to prison increased substantially as a result of these laws. However, legislatures have shown a willingness to reexamine transfer rules (Feld and Bishop, 2012). The policy determination of where to draw the lines—in relation to the age of transfer, the offenses that should trigger transfer, and restrictions on the severity of sentences of juveniles for particularly serious offenses—requires a number of complex value judgments that cannot be resolved based solely on developmental evidence.

---

[4] *Roper v. Simmons*, 541 U.S. 1040 (2005, p. 568).

But as the Supreme Court has made clear, developmental science does play an important role in determining the conditions under which juveniles are subject to prosecution and punishment in the adult criminal court. The committee believes that these policies can and should be informed by the two important principles announced by the Court—proportionality and individualization—as well as the policy goal of crime prevention.

Both proportionality and prevention support a policy of retaining youth in the juvenile justice system; adult prosecution and punishment should be "uncommon."[5] First, from the standpoint of proportionality, the ceiling for punishment of juveniles should be lower than it is for adults committing similar offenses, and juvenile court dispositions (which include residential placement in appropriate cases) constitute sufficient sanctions for almost all youth. Second, confinement in adult jails and prisons is likely to be counter-productive in many cases (Austin et al., 2000; Mulvey and Schubert, 2011) and should therefore be regarded as exceptional rather than routine—and should not be mandatory in any event.

Although supporters of the punitive reforms of the 1990s argued that getting tough on juvenile offenders was necessary to protect the public, developmental knowledge indicates that punishing juveniles as adults is not likely to reduce recidivism and is likely to increase the social cost of juvenile crime. Prisons have been characterized as developmentally toxic settings for adolescents (Task Force on Community Preventive Services, 2007; Redding, 2008); they contain none of the attributes of a social environment that are likely to facilitate youthful progress toward completion of the developmental tasks that are important to functioning as law-abiding adults (Forst, Fagen, and Vivona, 1989; Bishop and Frazier, 2000). The available adult authority figures are prison guards whose job is to maintain order and security and who are typically in distant hostile relationships with prisoners (Bishop and Frazier, 2000). Not surprisingly, young prisoners perceive prison staff as unconcerned about their welfare and uninterested in helping them acquire social skills or deal with problems. In the juvenile system, in contrast, youth generally view staff as concerned about their welfare (Bishop and Frazier, 2000).

Moreover, although some prisons segregate juveniles, in most adult facilities they associate with other prisoners, who may teach them to become more proficient criminals or victimize them but who are unlikely to provide the support and authoritative adult guidance needed for healthy development. Even segregation is problematic as young prisoners can sometimes be quite isolated—effectively in solitary confinement (American Academy of Child and Adolescent Psychiatry, 2012). Indeed, youth are sometimes purposely isolated to protect them from adult predators (McShane and

---

[5] *Miller v. Alabama* (2012, p. 19).

Williams, 1989). In comparison to juvenile facilities in many states, most prisons have few educational, vocational, or therapeutic programs and generally are unlikely to provide the opportunity structures needed for healthy psychological and social maturation during this critical developmental stage (Beck et al., 1993; Bishop and Frazier, 2000). In short, the experience of imprisonment is more aversive for adolescents than for adult prisoners, because adolescents are in a formative developmental stage in which their social context is likely to shape the trajectory of their future lives. While some may view this experience as one that is deserved due to the harm caused to any victim of crime, it does not accomplish the purpose that most victims desire for a juvenile offender, i.e., that the result of incarceration will be no future victims. Moreover, as suggested above, a criminal record may severely limit employment prospects and educational opportunities, as well as hampering the ability to develop relationships with noncriminal affiliates. The harmful effects of the prison experience and of a criminal record are likely to have a lasting negative effect on psychosocial development and to make the transition to noncriminal adult life extremely difficult if not impossible.

As noted earlier, however, older juveniles who have committed serious violent offenses may be deemed to pose too great a risk to public safety to be dealt with in the juvenile system, and they may be sufficiently mature that adult punishment is less unfair than with younger teens. For this very small group of offenders, longer periods of incarceration available in the adult system may be regarded as necessary to protect public safety. But even for youth charged with serious violent crimes (e.g., felonious assault, robbery, kidnapping, rape, carrying a firearm in the commission of a felony), an individualized decision by a judge in a transfer hearing should be the basis for the jurisdictional decision. The committee counsels against allowing the prosecutor to make the jurisdictional decision, as is allowed under direct-file statutes. The committee also opposes automatic transfer based solely on the offense with which the youth is charged because it fails to consider the maturity, needs, and circumstances of the individual offender or even his or her role in the offense or past criminal record—all of which should be considered in a transfer hearing.[6] Similarly, mandatory sentences of confinement for young offenders should be avoided. The committee draws support for these recommendations from the Supreme Court's rejection of the mandatory sentence in *Miller* and its insistence on an individualized hearing to determine the appropriateness of such a sentence. More generally, as a matter of policy, the Court's proportionality analysis supports shorter sentences for juveniles, compared with those received by adults

---

[6]A similar conclusion was reached by Loeber and Farrington (2012, p. 350) in their review of adolescent and young adult criminal careers and its implications for criminal justice policy.

for the same offenses. Furthermore, when youth are detained in adult jails and/or sentenced to adult prisons, their developmental needs as adolescents should not be ignored—as happens in some states that provide few services to teenage prisoners. Educational, vocational, and therapeutic programs directed at juveniles serve the goal of maximizing the potential of young offenders to become law-abiding adults.

The committee's recommendations regarding transfer to adult court are solidly based on the larger lessons of the Supreme Court's decisions in *Roper* (2005), *Graham* (2010), and *Miller* (2012). Juvenile offenders as a class are less culpable than their adult counterparts and the decision to prosecute a juvenile as an adult is one that should be made with careful deliberation on an individualized basis. Moreover, although politicians may believe that the public will insist that youth charged with serious crimes be tried as adults, substantial research evidence indicates that the public does not support transfer of young juveniles and generally favors rehabilitation of juvenile offenders (Nagin et al., 2006; Scott et al., 2006; Piquero et al., 2010).

CONCLUSION

In recent decades, developmental psychologists and neuroscientists have learned a great amount about the developmental stage of adolescence. This knowledge has important implications for juvenile justice policy, providing the framework for a system that is fair to young offenders and that also is likely to reduce youth crime by maximizing the potential of young offenders to become productive, law-abiding adults and minimizing the harmful impact of involvement in the juvenile justice system. This developmental model of juvenile justice rejects many of the punitive law reforms of the late 20th century as often excessively harsh and therefore unfair to young offenders and as likely to increase rather than decrease the threat they pose to public safety. Public safety is a legitimate and important goal of justice policy, but there is good reason to believe that this goal was not being effectively served by this harsh approach. Although some juvenile offenders pose such a grave threat to public safety that trial as adults and lengthy incarceration may be regarded as necessary, the policies introduced in the 1980s and 1990s have resulted in the confinement of many youth whose lives and developmental trajectories have probably been harmed, with little compensating public safety benefit. Indeed, the evidence suggests that incarceration likely increased the risk of recidivism for many youth.

It is important to emphasize that policies based on developmental research do not represent a return to the outmoded and naive rehabilitative model of the traditional juvenile court. The traditional model was built around an idealized vision of young offenders as innocent children whose parents had failed them and whose offending conduct could readily be redirected by the benevolent state. Today a more sophisticated understanding of adolescent development recognizes that young offenders are neither children nor adults, but adolescents whose criminal activity is often a predictable, and transient, feature of adolescence itself. This knowledge provides a foundation for a juvenile system that takes proper account of the formative nature of adolescence, by both ensuring genuine accountability for the harms young offenders cause while responding to their criminal conduct through interventions that are likely to decrease its incidence and enhance their prospects for productive adult lives.

Lawmakers around the country have shown an increasing interest in developmental knowledge and its potential to provide new understandings of juvenile crime and of effective dispositions. Over the past decade, legislatures and other policy makers have come to accept a proposition that was vehemently rejected only a few years earlier: that adolescent offenders are different from adults and these differences are important to juvenile justice. In part, the interest in developmental knowledge is a pragmatic response to evidence that the punitive policies of the 1990s were very costly and failed to reduce juvenile crime (which subsequently did drop for unexplained reasons), and some evidence-based programs promised to be more effective. But attitudes toward young offenders have changed in important ways from the days when young offenders were labeled "super-predators" (Dilulio, 1995), and the research has reinforced these changes; today there seems to be a genuine concern to deal fairly with young offenders in the justice system and to intervene in their lives in ways that preserve their future prospects.

The committee concludes that the incorporation of contemporary scientific knowledge about adolescence and juvenile crime is likely to result in juvenile justice policies and practices that are both fairer and more effective at reducing crime than policies of earlier periods. Today an important opportunity for major policy reform exists, created by a substantial body of developmental knowledge and policy makers receptive to its importance. Knowledge about adolescent offending and about optimal preventive and rehabilitative responses is far from complete. There are many gaps in understanding. But the research is sufficiently robust to offer general guidance to lawmakers and practitioners about an effective approach to juvenile justice policy.

This chapter has sketched a framework for policy reform based on advances in developmental science. The next two chapters focus on the three complementary goals of the juvenile justice system—preventing reoffending (see Chapter 6) and assuring accountability of juveniles and treating them fairly (see Chapter 7).

6

Preventing Reoffending

A core function of the juvenile justice system is to prevent reoffending by adolescents who have committed acts that would be considered crimes if committed by adults. Even if the court is an active partner in the broad prevention activities of the community, it will retain the primary responsibility for responding to adolescents who were not prevented from engaging in illegal behavior. Whether imposing sanctions or providing services, the court will continue to determine the type and intensity of interventions for the adolescents and families that come before it.

Whether the court can reduce reoffending depends on its ability to accomplish two interrelated tasks. Effectiveness lies in the system's ability to (a) intervene with the right adolescent offenders and (b) use the right type and amount of intervention. Achieving this ideal, or at least moving toward it, requires the court to examine its methods for assessing adolescents at different points of contact with the system, its thresholds and approaches for intervening in their lives, and how court resources and practices can promote the core task of preventing reoffending.

As explained in Chapter 5, consideration of the unique capacities and needs of adolescents is a necessary starting point for designing a theoretically coherent, just, and effective juvenile justice system. It is thus appropriate to consider how knowledge about adolescent development can be applied to the prevention of reoffending. In this chapter, we consider how efforts to keep juvenile offenders from continuing criminal activity might be extended and refined by consideration of advancing knowledge regarding adolescent development.

GENERAL RISK AND SERIOUS ADOLESCENT OFFENDING

Intervening with adolescent offenders to prevent continued offending would be a relatively straightforward task if one could identify those who would be chronic, serious, and/or violent offenders early in their offending careers and correct the factors that were most influential in producing this pattern of behavior. As noted in Chapter 1, however, this amounts to predicting and intervening to stop a relatively rare event; serious, violent, chronic adolescent offenders are a small proportion of the general adolescent offending population. This group is both proportionately and numerically quite small, and when the focus is restricted to the most serious delinquent offenders, for example, the chronically violent offender, it is exceedingly small (Snyder, 1998). In addition, the markers that differentiate this group cleanly at the start of their offending careers are rather limited in their predictive power.[1]

The power of a risk marker to predict future arrest or the impact of an intervention to reduce the likelihood of future arrest is often depicted in terms of an "effect size." An effect size is a metric that can be compared across multiple studies; it indicates how much impact a particular risk variable or intervention has on whether an individual is arrested. It is useful for comparing results across studies because, unlike indicators of statistical significance, it is less affected by the size of the samples examined. In the studies of interventions considered later in the chapter, the effect size indicates the average observed difference in arrest rate between a treated group and a comparison group. If a study indicates that a treated group has an arrest rate of 25 percent and the comparison group has an arrest rate of 35 percent, that intervention has an effect size of .10, a 10 percent lower rate of rearrest. Effect sizes across multiple studies are examined using a technique called *meta-analysis*, which uses regression approaches to identify aspects of programs that are related to larger or smaller effect sizes among the pool of studies examined.

---

[1]The term "risk marker" is used throughout this section. This is in keeping with the distinction made by Kraemer and colleagues (1997), in which a marker has a documented association with a later outcome, and a factor has substantiation that the observed association with the later outcome is causal (i.e., changing the risk factor has been shown to reduce the likelihood of the outcome). Overwhelmingly, the research on risk for future delinquency has demonstrated the presence of risk markers, with much less evidence that these risk indicators are risk factors related to later delinquency. The literature uses these terms loosely and interchangeably. The wording used here is believed to be reflective of the general state of the literature, and further specific distinctions would be distracting.

PREDICTING SERIOUS DELINQUENCY

Over the years, a number of studies have examined risk markers for or predictors of serious delinquency, chronic offending, and violent delinquency. Several excellent summaries of that literature exist (Hawkins et al., 1998; Lipsey and Derzon, 1998; Biglan et al., 2004; Farrington and Welsh, 2007). Lipsey and Derzon (1998, p. 88), using meta-analytic techniques, identified 793 effect sizes from 66 reports of 34 independent studies, and Hawkins and colleagues (1998) identified 39 studies and provided a substantive summary of the identified risk markers. Summarizing the rather voluminous findings from these reviews in a short space is a difficult task. For an overview, see Table 6-1.

This table shows the largest effect sizes for particular risk markers at different ages. As the table shows, the identified risk markers cut across a number of developmental domains, including prior offending and aggression, as well as peer, family, and school factors. Hawkins and colleagues (1998) also found significant risk markers in all of the developmental domains they examined: individual, family, school, peer, and community. To illustrate their findings, we summarize risk markers from the area of the family: "Within the family, living with a criminal parent or parents, harsh discipline, physical abuse and neglect, poor family management practices, low levels of parent involvement with the child, high levels of family conflict, parental attitudes favorable to violence, and separation from family have all been linked to later violence" (Hawkins et al., 1998, p. 146). We can draw several important conclusions from the results presented in these and other reviews.

First, there is no single risk marker that is very strongly associated with serious delinquency. As is true of other problem behaviors, there are multiple risk markers drawn from multiple domains, each of which, alone, is only modestly related to these outcomes. In other words, there is no single solution on which to focus efforts to prevent serious delinquency. This behavior pattern appears to come about from the accumulation of risk across many domains (Hawkins et al., 1998; Lipsey and Derzon, 1998; Biglan et al., 2004; Farrington and Welsh, 2007; Howell, 2009).

Second, risk for serious delinquency is generated across multiple developmental stages from infancy through childhood and into adolescence, with risk markers at each stage making contributions to the origins of serious delinquency. Although early risk markers have a role to play, they are clearly not determinative of these outcomes. However, early risk markers are predictive of the development of new risk markers for delinquency at subsequent ages. For example, risk indicators during early childhood, such as increased aggression and hyperactivity, are predictive of peer rejection and either peer isolation or attachment to delinquent peers; both of these

TABLE 6-1 Ranking of Ages 6-11 and Ages 12-14 Predictors of Violent or Serious Delinquency at Ages 15-25

Ages 6-11 Predictor (r)	Ages 12-14 Predictor (r)
Rank 1 Group	
General offenses (.38)	Social ties (.39)
Substance use (.30)	Antisocial peers (.37)
Rank 2 Group	
Gender (male) (.26)	General offenses (.26)
Family socioeconomic status (.24)	
Antisocial parents (.23)	
Rank 3 Group	
Aggression (.21)	Aggression (.19)
Ethnicity (.20)	School attitude/performance (.19)
	Psychological condition (.19)
	Parent-child relations (.19)
	Gender (male) (.19)
	Physical violence (.18)
Rank 4 Group	
Psychological condition (.15)	Antisocial parents (.16)
Parent-child relations (.15)	Person crimes (.14)
Social ties (.15)	Problem behavior (.12)
Problem behavior (.13)	IQ (.11)
School attitude/performance (.13)	
Medical/physical (.13)	
IQ (.12)	
Other family characteristics (.12)	
Rank 5 Group	
Broken home (.09)	Broken home (.10)
Abusive parents (.07)	Family socioeconomic status (.10)
Antisocial peers (.04)	Abusive parents (.09)
	Other family characteristics (.08)
	Substance use (.06)
	Ethnicity (.04)

SOURCE: Lipsey and Derzon (1998).

place a child at increased risk for delinquent behavior during puberty and adolescence (Biglan et al., 2004).

Third, there is no evidence that there are unique risk markers associated with serious delinquency, chronic delinquency, or violent delinquency. The risk markers listed in Table 6-1 and the illustrative family risk markers from the Hawkins and colleagues (1998) review quoted above have been linked to general delinquency, conduct disorder, substance use, and a host of other adolescent problem behaviors, as well as to serious delinquency

(Lorion et al., 1987; Farrington, 1989; Yoshikawa, 1994; Catalano and Hawkins, 1996; Biglan et al., 2004).

Other studies of risk markers for serious delinquency reached similar conclusions. Porter and colleagues (1999) used data from the three projects of the Office of Juvenile Justice and Delinquency Prevention's Program of Research on the Causes and Correlates of Delinquency in Denver, Pittsburgh, and Rochester. They compared three groups—nonoffenders, general but nonviolent delinquents, and violent delinquents—on 19 risk markers representing 7 domains—community, family structural characteristics, parent-child relations, school, peers, individual, and problem behaviors. They conclude that "there is not a different set of risk factors for serious violent offenders . . . [but] the serious violent offenders have greater deficits, or more extreme scores, on many of these risk factors as compared to general delinquents [and] are also more likely to experience risk in multiple domains" (Porter et al., 1999, p. 15). More recently, Esbensen and colleagues (2010) examined risk markers for serious delinquency in a sample of 5,935 eighth graders drawn from 11 different communities throughout the United States. They compared nonoffenders to nonviolent offenders and to serious violent offenders across 18 risk markers. In general, level of risk increased from nonoffenders to nonviolent offenders to violent offenders, but the differences appeared to be a matter of degree rather than kind. Similar results were also found when examining a high-risk sample of adolescents from Los Angeles (MacDonald, Haviland, and Morral, 2009). Once again, frequent and violent offenders differed from nonviolent and low-rate offenders, not in the presence of certain risk markers, but rather in that frequent and violent offenders had higher than average values across their baseline assessment of risk markers for delinquency, such as delinquent peers, family criminality, and substance use.

Comparing Delinquents and Nonoffenders

Few studies directly compare serious delinquents to both general delinquents and nonoffenders. Among those that do, however, the weight of the available evidence suggests that serious delinquents are influenced by the same risk markers and developmental processes as other youth. Some preliminary evidence of associations between neuropsychological or physiological indicators and serious adolescent offending exists (e.g., Cauffman, Steinberg, and Piquero, 2005), but there is no body of evidence of which we are aware to indicate that serious delinquents are qualitatively different from other delinquents who are involved in the juvenile justice system. They do commit more offenses and some more violent offenses, but that is because they appear to experience a greater accumulation of risk markers in comparison to others. But the individual risk markers that they experience, such as impulsivity and risk taking, family distress, school failure, and peer influence, are, by and large, similar to those experienced by all youth caught up in delinquent behavior and in the juvenile justice system. More serious offenders may well experience more powerful and prevalent environmental influences, such as neighborhood disorder or deviant peer involvement, and these in turn may exacerbate existing intraindividual vulnerabilities for involvement in antisocial behavior. The processes by which these contextual and individual risk characteristics interact to increase the risk of criminal involvement, however, appear more similar than different among serious, nonserious, and nonoffending adolescents.

It is important to note that the findings summarized above and in Table 6-1 are inherently limited, in light of new, possible risk markers that might be examined if this type of research were done today. When the referenced studies were conducted, there was little awareness of the wide range of biological, neuropsychological, or psychosocial variables that might be considered as highly relevant to adolescent development. Examination of these new constructs of interest might elucidate powerful interactions or moderated effects that simply were not imagined as relevant when the reviewed studies were conducted.

IMPLICATIONS FOR DEVELOPING STRATEGIES

The above findings are nonetheless relevant for developing strategies for assessing and intervening with adolescent offenders. First, there is currently no clearly applicable approach for identifying the adolescent offender who will go on to commit the most horrific and troubling crimes. Hindsight often makes it seem like these adolescents must be readily detectable, but foresight for doing so has not been found (Mulvey, Schubert, and Odgers, 2010). Adolescent offenders differ on a gradient of risk for future offending, with no distinct set of risk markers associated with the most serious and chronic offending, and approaches that use this general framework for risk have the most solid empirical basis. In addition, the risk markers associated with future offending, either serious and chronic or not, cover a broad array of personal and social features and differ with developmental period. This means that interventions limited to just one "key" factor during a limited period of development are likely to have an equally limited sustained impact on reoffending.

This does not mean that secondary prevention efforts to reduce involvement in antisocial activities and future offending are for naught. Multiple effective prevention strategies for working with troubled and troubling youth have been shown to have positive effects (Office of the Surgeon General, 2001). The implication of the above findings about the limited specificity of risk markers is that interventions of this sort will have only so much usefulness forestalling future offending, despite notable positive effects. Without the ability to identify the most serious juvenile offenders cleanly, prevention efforts will necessarily enroll and treat a proportion of adolescents who would otherwise have had a trouble-free adolescence in the absence of the intervention and will overlook another proportion who will become serious, chronic, or violent adolescents at a later developmental stage. The challenge of assessing adolescent offenders regarding the most reasonable level and type of intervention once they have come to the attention of the juvenile justice system remains unsolved.

ASSESSING RISK OF FUTURE CRIME AND NEED FOR SERVICE INTERVENTION

Many areas of health and social service practice have come to rely more on actuarial methods for screening and assessing individuals. These methods include checklists to identify particular problems for further assessment and structured protocols to determine the severity of a problem (e.g., screens for depression in primary care practices [Zuckerbrot et al., 2007], instruments for assessing intimate partner or sexual violence [Basile, Hertz, and Back, 2007; Rabin et al., 2009]). In some instances, structured instruments are used to assess the readiness of an individual to leave a restrictive environment or to identify potentially high-risk individuals if grave outcomes, such as imminent serious violence, might be avoided by admission into an institutional environment. Structured risk assessments have even made their way into court deliberations about the imposition of specialized laws, such as violent sexual predator statutes.

Use of Risk/Needs Assessment Instruments

Actuarial or structured professional judgment measures have also become more commonplace throughout the juvenile justice system. Detention screening instruments are now often used to determine an adolescent's risk of failing to appear in court or of committing another criminal act if released into the community. In addition, screening instruments for mental disorders have become a standard instrument used at detention intake to identify adolescents with incipient mental health problems (Desai et al., 2006). Finally, beginning in the 1980s, instruments for assessing the risk of reoffending by adjudicated adolescent offenders have also permeated practice in many locales, as a way for communities to establish a consensus about the appropriate threshold for sending an adolescent to institutional placement (Baird, Storrs, and Connelly, 1984; Wiebush et al., 1995). Many locales have developed slightly modified versions of early structured approaches, and a limited number of these have been validated and received widespread distribution (Howell, 2003a). Researchers continue to refine assessment instruments by exploring innovative algorithms for identifying subgroups of offenders with differing levels of risk for reoffending (Grann and Langstrom, 2007; Yang, Liu, and Coid, 2010; Walters, 2011), and focusing on predicting reoffending in special populations of juvenile offenders (e.g., juvenile sex offenders) (Prentky and Righthand, 2003). Several initiatives (e.g., MacArthur Foundation's Models for Change) have promoted the use of structured instruments as a method to increase juvenile justice efficiency and effectiveness by limiting institutional placement to adolescents who are most likely to reoffend and investing intervention resources in those adolescents for whom they will make the most difference.

Newer juvenile assessment instruments consider not only risk of reoffending, but also attempt to identify the needs of the adolescent that might be addressed with interventions. The intent of these instruments is to go beyond calculating a single score of how likely a juvenile might be to reoffend, and acknowledge that risk of reoffending is not a fixed attribute of the adolescent, but rather a partially contextually dependent estimate that might be lowered by particular interventions, monitoring in the community, or changes in life situation. Newer structured risk/needs instruments include an assessment of potential protective factors or treatment needs that might be considered when planning interventions (Andrews and Bonta, 1995; Wiebush et al., 1995; Dembo et al., 1996; Hoge, Andrews, and Leschied, 1996), as well as an assessment of the adolescent's likely responsivity to interventions for these identified needs (Kennedy, 2000).

In line with the review of the risk marker literature cited above, most risk/needs instruments include an array of factors to consider, covering such considerations as prior offending history, family history of criminality, school performance, current peer associations, and antisocial attitudes. Based on the level of overall risk, an adolescent could be considered for more or less intensive services (e.g., institutional placement or community supervision). If appropriate dynamic risk factors for offending could be identified and assessed adequately, interventions for a particular adolescent could then be based on the number and type of dynamic factors related to continued offending. For example, an adolescent with high antisocial attitudes and levels of offending could be considered a good candidate for cognitive interventions aimed at altering these attitudes or promoting positive social skills, or an adolescent with a drug and alcohol problem might be considered a candidate for positive community adjustment if these issues can be addressed effectively. These methods, if built into an ongoing system of readministration and monitoring of services, hold considerable promise for assessing whether an adolescent offender has received appropriate services and whether intermediate goals of the interventions have been met.

Integrating Assessments and Case Management

Methods for integrating the findings from structured risk/needs assessments with case management planning and implementation have been developed (e.g., Bonta, 2002), but the effectiveness of these strategies is untested. The development of risk/needs instruments is instead at an early stage of sorting out whether it has identified the dynamic predictors of risk most associated with offending and the needs that will really make a difference if they are the targets of intervention (Baird, 2009). The groundwork for a more systematic assessment of risk and needs in juvenile offenders has been laid, but there is considerable work to be done on further development of instruments and application of these instruments to improve practice.

Risk/needs assessment instruments perform well for assigning adolescent offenders to groups with different likelihoods of future offending, and the predictive accuracy of these approaches has increased as refinements have been developed (Andrews, Bonta, and Wormith, 2006; Howell, 2009). The proportion of youth screened who will be classified high, medium, or low risk will vary depending on the sample examined and the cutoffs deemed acceptable in each locale. The use of risk/needs assessment instruments in the earlier phases of juvenile justice involvement will gain most of their predictive power from identifying "true negatives"—adolescents who have a low probability of continued offending. Across studies of adolescents on probation, the correlations between risk assessment scores and involvement in subsequent criminal offending are between .25 and .30 (Schwalbe, 2004, 2008a), with slightly higher associations ($r = .41$ for general delinquency) reported for the use of the Youth Level of Service/Case Management Inventory in some studies (Andrews, Bonta, and Wormith, 2006). Even given the modesty of these associations, these instruments do provide adequate guidance for the important task of identifying adolescent offenders who warrant more intensive intervention or supervision and those who should be diverted from intervention programs (Wiebush, 2002; Latessa, 2004; DeComo and Wiebush, 2005; Grisso, Vincent, and Seagrave, 2005; Borum and Verhaagen, 2006; Gottfredson and Moriarty, 2006a).

Predicting and Managing Risk

The introduction of risk/need assessment is a significant shift in how juvenile justice conceptualizes the potential impact of court involvement. This approach implies a more dynamic view of juvenile justice involvement, looking at both static and dynamic factors that might be relevant to reoffending. It reflects a shift in thinking more generally among service providers about the need to move from predicting risk to managing risk in certain populations, like individuals with mental illness who are involved in violence (Mulvey and Lidz, 1998; Douglas and Skeem, 2005). It is also congruent with the risk-need-responsivity (RNR) approach taken in correctional rehabilitation (Andrews and Bonta, 2010; Skeem, Manchak, and Peterson, 2011). This orientation puts less stock in determining categories of offenders and places greater emphasis on the malleable factors that might contribute to continued criminal involvement.

Current Challenges

The orientation described above opens up the possibility for probation staff or the court to match adolescents more effectively with specialized treatment providers and for the court to monitor the provision of appropriate services. This latter task is rarely done effectively by the courts and represents perhaps the most fundamental payoff from advances in the assessment of adolescent offenders. Valid methods exist for assessing the risk of reoffending and intervention needs; the current challenge is to incorporate these effectively into standard court and probation practice.

Clarifying Outcomes. Integrating these instruments effectively into routine practice requires clarification of the mechanisms related to community service provision, reoffending, and subsequent systems involvement. In both research and practice, a variety of outcomes are often considered when determining the ideas of "risk" and "need" as well as the connection between these two concepts. Some instruments are developed to indicate the risk of being returned to a particular institutional setting during program involvement; others are developed to indicate the risk of rearrest or the general risk for multiple possible negative outcomes (e.g., dropping out of school) in some time period after program involvement. Moreover, the nexus of the particular need assessed (e.g., mental health disorder) and future offending is often more assumed than demonstrated (Grisso, 2008). Instruments thus often indicate risk markers that might or might not be appropriate foci for intervention or the need for services that might or might not actually reduce the likelihood of reoffending for that adolescent.

The Potential for Bias. It is worth noting that the most commonly used instruments are developed with rearrest or reconviction as the only relevant outcomes. These instruments thus provide estimates of the likelihood of detection, apprehension, and prosecution for illegal acts, not involvement in illegal activity. Given the well-documented patterns of selective law enforcement, gender differences in processing, and disproportionate minority contact (DMC), this means that risk/needs instruments might be conflating risk with the ongoing biases in the juvenile justice system and enforcing the status quo in juvenile justice processing. The potential for the application of risk/need assessments to propagate system inequities seems to exist, although there is no available research that documents whether this possibility actually occurs.

Limited research on racial/ethnic and gender differences in risk/need and screening instruments has indicated different proportions of risk classifications and different patterns of problem identification by race/ethnicity and gender, as well as differential rates of rearrest and service involvement (Schwalbe et al., 2006; Schwalbe, Fraser, and Day, 2007; Vincent et al., 2008; Onifade, Davidson, and Campbell, 2009; Vincent, Chapman, and Cook, 2011; Baglivio and Jackowski, 2012; Desai et al., 2012). The amount and type of bias in assessment and processing in the juvenile justice system connected with the use of these instruments, however, has not been adequately documented. This research is a high priority, because the application of these instruments has become (and will become even more) widespread. While the application of risk/need and screening instruments is a clear improvement over unfettered discretion, there is a long way to go in determining the unintended, and possibly harmful, effects connected with their use.

Need for Monitoring. Putting these instruments into practice thus requires a collaborative process in which practice professionals, researchers, and policy makers/administrators come to a consensus about the reasons for adoption of risk/needs instruments as well as the procedures and expectations regarding the use of these instruments (Howell, 2009). Effective use of structured screening and assessment procedures implies changes beyond simply the agreement to endorse the use of a previously developed measure. The process of integrating risk/need principles involves an ongoing examination of how courts process adolescents with different risk profiles and monitoring of how dispositions and interventions fit the risk profile of adolescents coming to different decision points in the juvenile justice system (Coordinating Council on Juvenile Justice and Delinquency Prevention, 1996; National Conference of State Legislatures, 1996; Howell, 2009). By monitoring the appropriateness of the court actions taken and the interventions provided, a local juvenile justice system can implement a system of graduated sanctions, assigning more intensive interventions to the most serious adolescent offenders with the most cumulative risk.

Potential of Risk/Need Assessment Systems

There are two benefits of developing systems of risk/need assessment at critical points in the juvenile justice system. First, the introduction of these methods reduces idiosyncratic decision making, increasing the uniformity of juvenile justice practice. Unstructured decision making introduces individual biases and contextual influences that generally lower the overall accuracy of judgments about future behavior (Dawes, Faust, and Meehl, 1989). Having juvenile justice personnel follow a protocol for decision making reduces the variability in these determinations and increases the overall rate of sound decisions in the process. The use of actuarial instruments, however, can be seen as formulaic and clinically vacuous when confronted with the complexities of a particular adolescent's life situation (Mulvey, 2005). It is therefore recommended that overrides to the determination reached by the instrument alone be permitted, but that the proportion of cases that can qualify for such an override be limited to a set proportion of cases and that the procedures for documenting these be clear (Office of Juvenile Justice and Delinquency Prevention, 1995a). If implemented carefully, systematic consideration of relevant risk/need variables should produce more consistency than would unstructured professional judgment, while allowing adequate flexibility.

In addition, making focused improvements in accuracy at specific points in juvenile justice processing can have ripple effects. Evidence from the Juvenile Detention Alternatives Initiative (JDAI) indicates that many locales have seen this type of payoff in detention decision making: they have lowered the overall rate of detention as well as the rate of detaining minority adolescents after implementing a structured decision-making protocol at this single point in juvenile justice processing (Mendel, 2009). Limiting system involvement among adolescent offenders is often considered an indicator of progress in and of itself.

There is a commonly held belief among juvenile justice professionals that further systems penetration is associated with increasingly negative outcomes (National Research Council and Institute of Medicine, 2001). Research on adult incarceration identifies an iatrogenic effect from prison confinement, resulting mainly from postrelease obstacles in housing, employment, and family relationships (Vieraitis, Kovandzic, and Marvell, 2007; Nagin, Cullen, and Jonson, 2009; Cullen, Jonson, and Nagin, 2011). The limited research on juvenile processing indicates a small, and somewhat inconsistent, negative effect from juvenile justice system processing compared with diversion at the point of initial referral (Huizinga et al., 2003; Gatti, Tremblay, and Vitaro, 2009; Petrosino, Turpin-Petrosino, and Gluckenburg, 2010). There is not a convincing body of research, however, demonstrating that increasing penetration across the points of juvenile justice system processing significantly increases offending beyond what might be attributable to individual risk characteristics. This type of research is extremely difficult to do, given the strong selection effects that have to be accounted for. It is, however, an important area for future investigation.

The second benefit of introducing risk/needs assessments is that they can maximize the impact of resource investment by targeting resources to the risk level of the juvenile offender. The impact of both institutional and community-based programs generally varies with the risk level of the adolescent. Higher risk adolescents show larger reductions in reoffending, while lower risk offenders show only modest positive effects or even negative effects—such as increased recidivism in some instances (Lowenkamp and Latessa, 2005c; Greenwood, 2008). These findings could well be the result of high-risk offenders having the most room for improvement in their levels of offending, whereas interventions for lower risk offenders are disrupting potentially positive developmental experiences or exposing them to antisocial peers (Smith, Gendreau, and Swartz, 2009). Whatever the specific mechanism, the appropriate focusing of more intense (and costly) interventions on higher risk adolescents produces a greater reduction in subsequent offending and limits the negative effects on less serious offenders from unwarranted intensive interventions (Aos et al., 2004; Howell, 2009).

The use of structured risk/need assessment at the initial stages of court processing can produce a substantial benefit. More than half of the adolescents seen at the initial phases of juvenile justice processing system do not have further involvement with it (54 percent of males and 73 percent of females) (Snyder and Sickmund, 1999). Structured instruments can be especially useful for identifying low-risk adolescents who are unlikely to reappear in the court system and releasing these adolescents outright or referring them to appropriate diversionary services. Relying on inferential clinical judgment about the need for further intervention with an adolescent inevitably leaves this judgment open to the market demands of diversionary service providers to generate referrals or the potential overreaching of court personnel on issues that might not be best addressed in the juvenile justice system.

Improved risk/needs assessment is not a panacea but a key component of a more informed and targeted juvenile justice system. The potential of these approaches lies in the juvenile justice system's ability to obtain reliable assessments, ensure that the information is used in decision making, and track the outcomes of interventions (Mulvey and Iselin, 2008). Making risk/needs assessment a functional component of juvenile court practice thus takes professional commitment, adequate data systems, accurate information about service provision, and a reorientation of judges and court personnel about the mission of the juvenile court.

RESEARCH NEEDS

Although the broad potential of risk/needs assessment lies in its role as a component of a data-informed juvenile court system, there is currently little empirical work to support the widespread use of risk/needs instruments beyond the face-valid argument for their use. There are numerous reports documenting the adoption of these instruments (Vincent, 2011), but a striking lack of evidence regarding the effects of such instruments on the types of services received by adolescent offenders or the impact of altered service provision patterns on institutional or community adjustment (Chung, Schubert, and Mulvey, 2007). Studies of the introduction of risk/needs instruments or other structured decision-making approaches in juvenile justice have been largely restricted to assessments of how well received and implemented these approaches have been among practitioners. It is possible, however, that these assessment forms become a part of the adolescent's court file in many locales, with little impact on the types of services provided.

Implementation and outcome research is needed on whether and how information generated in screens or assessments is translated into receipt of appropriate services and, if so, whether these services tend to reduce criminal behavior or increase community adjustment for juvenile offenders. Risk/needs assessment is the first necessary step to achieving the overall goal of a more rational juvenile justice system. As pointed out earlier, however, it is important to remember that much of the literature tests the accuracy of these instruments by asking whether they predict future arrest or continued system involvement. As a result, these instruments and approaches can be seen as effectively predicting future system response to an adolescent offender as well as the future offending behavior of that adolescent. Given that DMC seems to be an enduring feature of the juvenile justice system and that mental health service involvement for adolescents shows consistent race/ethnicity differences, it is imperative that future research in this area sort out the possible racial/ethnic biases connected with the use of any risk/needs assessment strategy. Mere tests of accuracy regarding these approaches could reinforce a system of inequity in service provision and sanctions; careful examination of patterns of service provision and community adjustment are needed to determine the benefits and limits of risk/needs assessment. Finding out how to make these instruments contribute to a larger vision of effective and fair service involvement is a key challenge for future applied research.

EVIDENCE-BASED SERVICES FOR JUVENILE OFFENDERS

Academics and practitioners have pursued a number of related activities over the last two decades that have enriched our understanding of what interventions work with juvenile offenders. Most notably, evidence about the effectiveness of intervention programs with adolescent offenders has expanded in scope and strength. Numerous controlled trials of interventions have been completed, producing several documented approaches with convincing evidence of reduced offending for treated adolescents. Meta-analyses of existing data about interventions with adolescent offenders have been conducted, highlighting both the relative impact of interventions and the characteristics of the interventions with notable and consistent effects. In addition, several groups have established criteria for demonstrating effectiveness of an intervention and provided easily accessible information to practitioners and policy makers about what programs meet these standards. State funding agencies and legislatures have become knowledgeable about the idea of evidence-based practices and have attempted to create a policy context to support such activities. These developments have pushed the field toward better informed and focused practice, although considerable challenges lie ahead for creating integrated and effective service systems for juvenile offenders.

Program Effectiveness Research

Clinical trials of interventions with adolescent offenders over the past 25 years have become increasingly sophisticated scientifically and, as a result, more convincing in their claims that interventions can actually produce sizeable reductions in criminal involvement of adolescents. Recent research on interventions with juvenile offenders has, in general, been more rigorous than previous work in documenting the adolescents treated, the interventions tested, and the effects of treatment involvement. The general ethos that "nothing works" has clearly been supplanted by the belief that many things do work.

Effective Programs

Several programs for adolescent offenders with demonstrated effectiveness have been identified (Office of the Surgeon General, 2001; Greenwood, 2008).[2] The most commonly recognized and often cited approaches include functional family therapy (FFT) (Alexander and Parsons, 1973; Barton et al., 1985; Alexander et al., 2000), multisystemic therapy (MST) (Henggeler et al., 1998; Schaeffer and Borduin, 2005), and multidimensional treatment foster care (MTFC) (Chamberlain, 2003; Eddy, Whaley, and Chamberlain, 2004). Each of these programs intervenes with the family and/or the community context of an adolescent offender, and each has repeatedly produced convincing evidence of reductions in offending behavior in samples of juvenile offenders. Each also provides clear information about the characteristics of the intervention. A number of other more specialized interventions targeting mediators of criminal involvement—most notably aggression

---

[2]In this section, the outcome of interest is rearrest, measured as either police reports or juvenile court petitions. Interventions are presented as effective or not in terms of how much they reduce rearrest. Programs often target and change other behaviors, but these effects are not considered in detail here.

replacement therapy (ART) (Goldstein et al., 1987) and cognitive-behavioral therapy approaches (Milkman and Wanberg, 2007)—have also produced convincing evidence of their positive effects (Sherman et al., 1998; Mendel, 2000). Unfortunately, efforts to identify effective programs for female adolescent offenders have been less successful (Larance, 2009). In a nationwide review of 61 girls' delinquency programs, only 17 had published evaluations, no programs could be rated as effective, and most programs were rated as having insufficient evidence (Zahn et al., 2008). Most recently, Kempf-Leonard (2012) noted that "The current body of knowledge is not sufficient to allow us to make informed decisions about accurate and effective responses to female delinquents" (p. 511).

Ineffective Programs

Many popular programs, like Scared Straight and boot camps, have consistently shown marginal, null, or negative effects. Individual counseling and peer group interventions relying on loosely structured group discussions (e.g., the guided group interaction model) have unimpressive records for preventing reoffending (Sherman et al., 1998). Repeated evaluations of the Scared Straight program, in which convicts confront groups of adolescent offenders with the horrors of prison life, show no effect or increased reoffending among the adolescents taking part (Finckenauer and Gavin, 1999; Petrosino, Turpin-Petrosino, and Buehler, 2003; Klenowski, Bell, and Dodson, 2010). Boot camp programs, widely adopted as a method for instilling discipline in adolescent offenders, have generally been shown to have no, or a negative, impact on reoffending (MacKenzie, Wilson, and Kider, 2001; Bottcher and Ezell, 2005), with some reviews showing that boot camps and other disciplinary programs increase recidivism by about 8 percent (Lipsey, 2009).

Measuring Effects

Meta-analyses of published reports of the effects of delinquency intervention programs (Lipsey and Wilson, 1993; Latimer, 2001) have provided quantitatively based estimates of the relative effects of a variety of interventions. In this approach, findings across studies are aggregated and summary statistics are generated regarding the effects found and the characteristics of certain interventions associated with larger or smaller effects. Using well-defined methods for determining the adequacy of a program evaluation as well as combining the reports, the analyst can derive a general estimate of the effect size of an intervention approach, that is, the reduction in the rate of rearrest associated with programs of a particular type. Meta-analyses of intervention programs with adolescent offenders (Andrews, Bonta, and

Hoge, 1990; Lipsey and Wilson, 1998; Cullen, 2005; Lipsey and Cullen, 2007; Lipsey, 2009) have not all agreed in their estimates of effects, given different sets of programs examined and the time periods covered. In general, however, these analyses have identified several features of interventions related to smaller and larger effects. Institutional programs show approximately a 10 percent reduction in rearrest, and generally show smaller effects than multifaceted community-based interventions, with about a 25 percent differential reduction in rearrest over a period of approximately a year or longer in one analysis. The important point of these meta-analyses, however, is the demonstration that there are a number of different types of interventions that have relatively large effects, and that these effects can be found even when these interventions are applied in community settings with relatively high-risk adolescents. Many of these specific program effects are presented later in this chapter, when consideration is given to the potential costs and benefits of different intervention approaches.

The average effect size attributed to a particular type of program or intervention in a meta-analysis is obviously dependent on the reports considered to be representative of that category of programs or interventions. There is often considerable variability of effect sizes within program types, with even more recognized "model" program types varying in their effect sizes (Lipsey et al., 2010). Not surprisingly, there are often reports of programs or interventions that illustrate the conditions under which a certain approach might be more or less effective.

Institutional Programs. Analyses indicate that institutional treatment programs generally have an unimpressive record for reducing reoffending and that large, overcrowded facilities with limited treatment programs (in which custody trumps treatment concerns) often have high recidivism rates (Ezell, 2007; Trulson et al., 2007). At the same time, there are empirically sound and convincing reports indicating that theoretically grounded, adequately staffed, and well-documented programs for seriously violent youth that involve institutional care can produce impressive and fiscally advantageous effects (Barnoski, 2004; Caldwell, Vitaceo, and Van Rybrock, 2006; Caldwell et al., 2006). General reviews also note that institutional programs that adopt a cognitive-behavioral approach show higher reductions in reoffending (Lipsey and Cullen, 2007; Lipsey, 2009). There is also an emerging literature demonstrating that the social climate of an institutional setting (e.g., its orderliness or harshness) affects the subsequent community outcomes of adolescent offenders in that setting (Schubert et al., 2012).

Counseling. Differential effects have also been observed in assessments of the impact of counseling as an approach in both institutional and community-based settings. A meta-analysis of these types of programs

(Lipsey, 2006) found a positive mean effect size of .12 for individual counseling and a smaller effect (.08) for counseling administered in groups of offending peers. Many juvenile justice models, such as guided group interaction (GGI) (Empey and Rabow, 1961) and positive peer culture (PPC) (Vorrath and Brendtro, 1985) bring groups of adolescent offenders together with the idea that peer influences are powerful but can be converted to a positive influence in institutional settings led by adult staff members (Gonzales and Dodge, 2010).

Contagion Effect. Some researchers have raised the possibility that group treatments create a "contagion effect," in which adolescent offenders learn about and are reinforced for criminal involvement. The evidence for such an effect is at best equivocal, with results indicating that the level and structure of adult supervision is key to producing a positive effect from group interventions. There is some evidence of contagion effects promoting antisocial behavior in group interventions with younger adolescents (Dishion and Andrews, 1995; Dishion et al., 1996). In addition, a field experiment conducted by Feldman and colleagues (1983) that randomly assigned delinquent and nondelinquent adolescents to all-deviant groups, all-nondeviant groups, or mixed groups (predominantly nondelinquent) found that assignment to all-deviant groups was associated with worse outcomes (Gonzales and Dodge, 2010). Also, incarcerated adolescents placed in cells with peers arrested for drug-related crimes appear to be more likely to be arrested subsequently for drug-related crimes themselves than if placed in other cells (Bayer, Pintoff, and Posen, 2003), but this effect was found only for younger adolescents, those who were placed with slightly older peers, or those with prior experience with dealing drugs. A meta-analysis of this literature indicates that the strength of this effect is marginal and apparent mainly in younger adolescents (Weiss et al., 2005). Evidence for such an effect in juvenile justice interventions with more serious offenders is not available; the power of this influence, either positively or negatively, in juvenile justice interventions is still unclear and previously held views that institutional youth suffer a contagion effect have been called into question. Moreover, it appears that any potential adverse effect can be mitigated by a highly trained leader or a lack of opportunity for unsupervised peer interaction, and many interventions with demonstrated positive effects (cognitive-behavioral approaches) are usually done in group settings.

Characteristics of Effective Interventions

The above examples illustrate that certain conditions of an intervention, whether it is institutional or community-based, can alter its impact, over and above its categorization as a particular type of program. Meta-analyses or other lines of research can provide valuable information about some of the general characteristics of interventions that might be influential in producing an enhanced or blunted effect. By coding the features of programs and assessing how well these features account for observed reductions in rearrest, analysts are able to identify certain practices that might increase effectiveness across different program types.

Program Developer's Role

More positive effects for a program are seen when the implementation and follow-up are done by the program developers, rather than by other agencies adapting a model program (Karoly et al., 1998; Dodge, 2001; Lipsey and Landenberger, 2006). In addition, the use of a clear treatment strategy (especially the use of cognitive-behavioral approaches), a focus on the most serious adolescent offenders, a matching of the needs of the offenders and the program orientation, and a demonstration that the program implementation has followed the program model are all associated with larger reductions in rearrests (Lipsey et al., 2010). Application of these practice principles is a key to improving both institutional and community-based interventions.

Program Duration

Any intervention must be provided with enough intensity to have an effect. This simple observation is recognized even by adolescent offenders who comment that longer stays in juvenile facilities (compared to shorter stays in adult facilities) offer adequate time to benefit from programming (Bishop and Frazier, 2000). Certain types of treatments have standards regarding the amount of time or number of sessions that must be provided to expect a desirable outcome. It is recommended, for example, that substance use treatment should have at least a 90-day duration to produce stable behavioral change (National Institute on Drug Abuse, 2006). Analyses of institutional treatment for juvenile offenders indicate that shorter and longer stays may each produce deleterious outcomes (Lipsey and Wilson, 1998; MacKenzie, 2001; Piquero, Gomez-Smith, and Langton, 2004). A recent meta-analysis (Lipsey et al., 2010) indicates that both institutional and community-based program treatment effects are most powerful when an adolescent has spent at least, but about, the approximate average amount of time observed for that type of program—that is, shorter stays do not produce positive effects and longer stays do not increase the effect appreciably. An investigation with stringent controls for selection but small samples at each time point substantiates this position, finding no reductions in rearrest or self-reported offenses from longer institutional stays (greater than six months, the average institutional stay in the sample), and a possible detrimental effect from shorter (less than three months) stays for serious adolescent offenders (Loughran et al., 2009).

Based on work in adult corrections (Lowenkamp, Latessa, and Holsinger, 2006), it seems reasonable to posit that more time in a program ensures that an individual has sufficient exposure to a program's effect, but also that the largest effect from program involvement will occur when sufficient resources are provided only to the most high-risk individuals. The exact mechanisms or standards for program involvement that might produce these effects in interventions for juvenile offenders, however, are far from clear. In some, too little program involvement and too much program involvement undercut effectiveness. On one hand, there is no credible evidence that very brief, shock programs, either institutional or community-based, produce reductions in reoffending. On the other hand, there is evidence that extended program involvement beyond the average program length does not increase effectiveness.

Family Involvement

It is worth highlighting two general consistencies in the broad set of findings about program effectiveness presented above. First is the potential importance of family involvement in community-based treatment. Several of the interventions with positive program effects include the youth's family and give focused consideration to the particular features of the adolescent's social environment. This regularity is not too surprising, given the centrality of family dynamics (particularly parental monitoring) in the continuation of antisocial behavior in adolescents (Patterson and Stouthamer-Loeber, 1984; Chung and Steinberg, 2006) and the importance of family involvement in other areas of intervention with adolescents, such as substance use treatment (National Institute on Drug Abuse, 2006; Chassin et al., 2009). Such a finding is also in line with theoretical approaches positing that continued involvement in crime is the product of ongoing interactions between vulnerable individuals and their social world across the life span (Sampson and Laub, 2005), and that the interplay between parents and peers is particularly powerful in maintaining adolescent antisocial behavior (Laird et al., 2003a, 2003b; Dodge and Rutter, 2011).

There is a commonsense argument for engaging parents and family members in programming. Most adolescent offenders maintain contact with their families throughout and in spite of court involvement, and parents are usually the constant thread through the patch of service providers working with these adolescents. That is not to say that parents and family members are always positive influences on adolescents; some unknown percentage of parents and family members contribute to the chaos and corruption in an adolescent's development. Even in circumstances in which parenting behavior may have contributed negatively to the development of antisocial child behaviors, though it seems axiomatic that positive change will have to include parent involvement (Romanelli et al., 2009). Given all that is known regarding the significance of parenting and of the parent-child relationship, expecting that a youth might experience significant and lasting change with only superficial family involvement seems illogical. The juvenile justice system, however, appears to have a long way to go toward integrating parents and families into interventions and court processes.

Despite the centrality of parental involvement in many successful programs, focus groups reveal that parents continue to be, or perceive being, blamed for the youth's problems, to be regarded as obstacles, and to be insufficiently involved in crucial decision-making and planning processes during disposition, placement, and preparation for aftercare (Osher and Shufelt, 2006; Luckenbill and Yeager, 2009). Parental involvement is often overlooked as a program priority, prompting many to demand greater effort to attain full and positive family-provider collaboration in services and service planning in the juvenile justice system (MacKinnon-Lewis, Kaufman, and Frabutt, 2002). Some efforts are under way to involve families more in the juvenile justice process, but most models for parental involvement are still in the early stages of development, needing further refinement and validation. For example, the Parent Empowerment Program (PEP) (Olin et al., 2010), a manualized training and consultation program designed to prepare family peer advocates to help empower families during involvement with child welfare services, has been adapted to juvenile justice, and initial pilot efforts of PEP in juvenile justice populations are under way. In addition, the Systems of Care approach in mental health (MacKinnon-Lewis, Kaufman, and Frabutt, 2002; Hoagwood, 2005), which takes an avowedly "family first" approach, has been adapted to juvenile justice in a few locales (e.g., Missouri), but no empirical validation of these programs is yet available. Expanding the role of families in juvenile justice appears to be a critical, unmet challenge, but the potential contributions of families in many interventions and in the juvenile justice process remain ill defined. Additional research regarding the processes of family involvement in juvenile justice and methods for successfully involving parents in these processes is urgently needed.

Other Factors Influencing Effectiveness. It is worth emphasizing the connection between the specificity and focus of an intervention and impact. Programs with clear guidelines and methods developed over successive trials appear to have positive effects when administered by the program developers. The success of these efforts is less clear when moved into general practice with existing service providers, where there is less control over practice. Attenuation in effect is even built into assessments of program impact when implementation is not done by the demonstration team (Aos, Miller, and Drake, 2006; Welsh, Sullivan, and Olds, 2010). Moreover, structured forms of intervention, like cognitive-behavioral approaches, appear to exert a more consistent positive effect, mirroring research on effective approaches in adult corrections programs. Careful, quality program implementation has been identified as one of only a few factors (in addition to the presence of therapeutic intervention philosophy and serving high-risk offenders) linked to better outcomes for adolescent offenders after other aspects of programming were controlled (Lipsey, 2009). These findings highlight the importance of documenting the procedures of an intervention in sufficient detail to allow replication and to enhance the chances of consistent implementation. In addition, it raises the challenge of finding ways to monitor program implementation and to identify factors that contribute to, or undermine, the eventual effectiveness of an intervention.

Accreditation Efforts

More refined assessments of program impact and the development of clear program models have prompted the establishment of several accreditation bodies that judge the adequacy of the results supporting claims of effectiveness. Four highly visible and widely used examples illustrate these efforts.

1. The Blueprints for Violence Prevention Project (Mihalic et al., 2001), an initiative of the Center for the Study and Prevention of Violence at the University of Colorado, started as an effort to identify effective programs and implement them in Colorado. It rated delinquency prevention and treatment programs for their demonstrated effectiveness (e.g., a model program, a promising program) according to a set of criteria regarding the strength of the research design evaluating the program's impact and replicability.[3] With support from the Office of Juvenile Justice and Delinquency Prevention (OJJDP), the project evolved to a larger scale to both identify model programs and provide technical assistance to implement them nationwide (Mihalic et al., 2004). To date, the Blueprints initiative has identified 11 model and 29 promising prevention and intervention programs effective in reducing adolescent violent crime, aggression, delinquency, and substance abuse.

---

[3]The Annie E. Casey Foundation recently began supporting the Blueprints program. With this funding, outcomes have been expanded to include not only behavior but also education, emotional well-being, health, and positive relationships. The program is now being called Blueprints for Healthy Youth Development. (E-mail exchange with Sharon Mihalic, director of Blueprints initiative, Center for the Study and Prevention of Violence, University of Colorado, May 21, 2012.)

2. The Substance Abuse and Mental Health Services Administration (SAMHSA) also operates a National Registry of Evidence-based Programs and Practices (NREPP) (http://nrepp.samhsa.gov) with a searchable database of interventions to prevent or treat a variety of mental health and/or substance use problems, including adolescent violence and antisocial behavior.

3. In addition, in the widely disseminated *Youth Violence: A Report of the Surgeon General* (Office of the Surgeon General, 2001), a set of standards is presented for determining best practices for violence prevention in several settings (e.g., schools, community agencies), and specific programs are identified in groups based on a scale of demonstrated effectiveness (e.g., model, promising).

4. Finally, OJJDP and its parent agency, the Office of Justice Programs (OJP), provide information about model programs for juvenile justice interventions in two locations (OJJDP Model Programs Guide at http://www.ojjdp.gov/mpg and OJP CrimeSolutions at http://www.crimesolutions.gov).

These centralized repositories of information about programs with solid evidence to support their use have been valuable resources for policy makers and funders sorting through the voluminous and scattered program evaluations in juvenile justice. These accreditation systems have also provided a goal for many program developers and service providers. Becoming a Blueprints program, for example, is a certification of achievement and opportunity to develop beyond current operations; a certified status such as this makes an agency stand out in its field of competitors and gives it a marketing tool for expansion to other locales. Government funding agencies have also been able to use these systems to mount focused research agendas by limiting service research activities to programs that have met the standards of these reviews (evidence-based practices). These systems indicate a major reorientation of the juvenile justice field toward recognition of the importance of empirical demonstrations of effectiveness.

However, standards and judgments across these different systems vary significantly, with each of the accrediting entities using slightly different categories and criteria for designating a program as having sufficient validity to warrant use or replication. The domain of programs with some certification as "evidence based" has thus become wider over time, and the meaning of this designation has become blurred and its value has become denigrated as the number of accrediting entities has grown (and continues to grow). Continued expansion of certification entities with different, and increasingly scientifically lax, standards could devalue the designation of a program as evidence-based and slow progress toward overall service improvement.

Having a sound scientific basis for designating program quality is a timely concern because legislators and public officials have been paying increased attention to information about what appears to work to reduce juvenile offending. In several states (e.g., North Carolina, Pennsylvania), there are efforts to direct funding for juvenile programs only to initiatives that have an empirically demonstrated record of success. Some state legislatures have passed provisions that lay out a plan over several years to restrict funding to only certain programs demonstrated to be effective (Howell, 2009). Pressed by fiscal realities and pushes for government accountability, state officials are now trying to create environments that build knowledge about what works with juvenile offenders into their prescriptive mandates and revise regulatory practices to increase monitoring of relevant program features.

Putting Evidence-Based Services into Practice

Based on the above review, it is apparent a significant number of existing programs have reduced criminal offending. The evidence from evaluation studies indicates that these programs are as effective, and usually even more effective, with the highest risk youth rather than the more prevalent low-risk adolescents in the juvenile justice system. This suggests that future research and policy should continue to investigate how far inclusion criteria for program involvement can be expanded to incorporate even more serious delinquents. After all, programs that are effective for these youth will be particularly beneficial given their disproportionate involvement in offending.

Although it would be ideal for all delinquent youth to receive a service with documented effectiveness, the reality of service provision is more complicated than simply finding something that works. While creating and documenting effective programs for juvenile offenders is a large step toward ensuring public safety and improving outcomes for these adolescents, it is still only one step toward these larger goals (Bickman and Hoagwood, 2010). Estimates are that, even with the current level of knowledge about what constitutes effective intervention with adolescent offenders, only about 5 percent of youth eligible for evidence-based programs participate in one (Hennigan et al., 2007; Greenwood, 2008). As seen in medicine and other areas of clinical care (Kazdin, 2008), having evidence-based practices is a necessary but not sufficient condition for changing how services are delivered every day, either within an organization or across a locale. Getting effective programming into practice requires both the identification of what works and the development of a framework for ensuring that programming as applied produces the effects expected.

One strategy for increasing the use of evidence-based practices is to market demonstrated programs broadly to practitioners and then ensure that they are implemented with fidelity to the original model. This is usually accomplished by providing a renewable "license" to use the program materials that is contingent on provision of data indicating that certain standards of service provision have been met. This strategy is somewhat akin to franchising retail establishments, with product quality specifications that must be met to use the recognizable name and fees that are paid for services or products, like staff training or supervision rating forms, to promote consistency.

Program Drift

The distribution of brand-name programs has proven successful for introducing local service providers to evidence-based practices and giving them a method to implement these programs without having to reinvent the program anew. Local practitioners, however, often see certain aspects of the program as ill suited to their clients or community in particular, and additions or alterations to the standard program are made so that local stakeholders can "own" the program more enthusiastically. Changes to the program operations or requirements are also often made to accommodate the skills of the workforce in a particular locale. As a result, program operations drift toward less stringent or clearly defined practice, and local program monitors are usually unable to either document these shifts or enforce changes in a contracted agency's practice. Research is still limited on the components of many programs that are essential to its previously documented effect (Real and Poole, 2005; Schoenwald, 2008), and changes in operations or slippage in fidelity in seemingly inconsequential program aspects may undermine program effectiveness. Moreover, as mentioned above, some states make funding contingent on the use of specified program approaches, and providers often retrofit existing programs to meet these new standards, with only some of the specified program components found in the program going by the name needed to meet the funding requirements. Recognizing and accounting for the tendency of service providers to alter program characteristics to make them more appropriate to the clients, culture, or resources of their locale poses a serious challenge to the effort to move juvenile justice services toward more effective, evidence-based practice.

One way to address the issue of program drift is to increase efforts to ensure model fidelity throughout the life of the intervention. More effort, energy, and data collection can be put toward documenting that the program as implemented meets the operational standards of the model as developed. The resources needed to do this well are considerable, however, and the funding for such activities is usually difficult to find in already tight budgets. Program implementation efforts have historically kept the costs of monitoring relatively low compared with service delivery costs. Moreover, this approach assumes that evidence-based programs, as developed, are very robust to alterations in the population of adolescents and families enrolled or the community context in which they are implemented. In other words, if one could just get practitioners to follow the program protocol, the intervention would work almost anywhere and everywhere. This assumption is generally faulty, as several seemingly well-designed and implemented applications of sound evidence-based programs with juvenile offenders have failed to produce impressive outcomes (Barnoski, 2002; Landenberger and Lipsey, 2005; Lipsey, 2006; Welsh, Sullivan, and Olds, 2010; Washington State Institute for Public Policy, 2011).

Programs Versus Practices. Pinning hopes for a better juvenile justice system solely on expanding the currently limited sets of evidence-based, brand name programs seems ill advised. The task is more complicated than that. Certainly more controlled trials of intervention models and critical reviews of existing evidence bases are required. The number of programs with rigorous research designs and positive results is still strikingly small, and cumulative knowledge of how model programs actually work is thin. In the end, however, it is difficult to envision a broad range of empirically validated practices carried out by sufficiently trained and supervised individuals applying these approaches at the right point in development with the right types of problems. Although information about evidence-based practices is critical in showing the way toward more effective intervention, the efforts at knowledge generation cannot stop there. Valuable lessons must be also drawn from inquiries into evidence-based practices, and these must focus on the identification of general principles of effective care.

Monitoring. The application of evidence-based practices, no less than the application of sound but not empirically tested interventions, must occur in an environment that documents and monitors its operations and impacts. Even if a program is implementing a brand name approach, it is necessary to collect data on youth/family characteristics, program practices, and outcomes for enrolled adolescents. Programs for delinquents, whether evidence-based or not, should be subjected to rigorous evaluation to determine whether or not they are helpful, not just assumed to be so. It is important to bear in mind that intervention programs for delinquents can be iatrogenic as well as effective (Gottfredson, 1997, 2010; Dishion, McCord, and Poulin, 1999), and only rigorous scientific designs can separate the wheat from the chaff. Continuous evaluation can provide information about how well any program is specifically addressing the needs and behaviors of adolescent offenders involved with it (Thornberry, 2010).

A refinement of this approach is to monitor program implementation closely and to document adherence to *practices* that typify successful evidence-based programs. In this formulation, it is not simply a question of whether a program did what it said it would do and if it worked in reducing reoffending. Instead, data about program operations is used to apply a quality improvement model to help programs move toward consistent use of practices that have been shown to improve performance across a range of programs. As stated above, careful reviews of meta-analysis results as well as reviews of the organizational features of successful interventions have identified general principles that increase the likelihood of putting a program into place that works with serious adolescent offenders (Lipsey et al., 2010). In general, programs are more likely to have a positive impact when (a) they focus on high-risk offenders (Lowenkamp and Latessa, 2005c), (b) connect sound risk/need assessment with the treatment approach taken (Schwalbe, 2008), (c) use a clearly specified intervention program rooted in a theory of how adolescents change and tailored to the particular offender (Andrews et al., 1990; Barnoski, 2004), (d) demonstrate program integrity (Gendreau, 1996), and (e) take into account the community context (Altschuler and Armstrong, 1994). Operationalizing and measuring how well organizations or locales follow the principles of effective practice is an important challenge, one that is critical to actually changing what happens to adolescents in the system.

Assessments of how well these principles guide practice can be done across the full spectrum of juvenile justice services. A variety of methods have been devised for determining how well institutional or community-based programs adhere to a theoretical model, focus on high-risk offenders, or demonstrate program integrity. It is equally important, however, to develop and apply sound principles of effective programming for probation practice, particularly surrounding the reentry process. The emphasis on probation practices during reentry seems particularly important in light of the potential benefits of increasing family involvement during this critical transition. Probation officers are in a pivotal position for increasing family involvement to promote positive community adjustment; identifying and promoting effective practices to achieve this potential is a pressing challenge for practitioners and researchers. Although a large proportion of juvenile offenders have repeated contact with probation officers, the development and testing of sound practice in this area is relatively undeveloped (Schwalbe and Maschi, 2009).

There is some reason to be optimistic about taking on the challenge of monitoring the principles of effective practice. Researchers in other areas of clinical practice (Donabedian, 1988; Berwick, 1989; Chowanec, 1994; Counte and Meurer, 2001; Heinemann, Fisher, and Gershon, 2006) have shown that principles of effective programming can be rated regularly, and settings can work toward improving their adherence to best practices as time goes on. Efforts along this line have begun in juvenile justice (Lipsey et al., 2010).

This does not mean that recognized, evidence-based programs will not be valuable as templates for best practice. Such an approach instead recognizes that building a system of effective services for adolescent offenders implies more than simply amassing a collection of evidence-based programs. For purposes of innovation, juvenile justice service systems will include programs that are variants of more established practices, and the challenge is to ensure that these services, as well as those touted as evidence-based, provide quality care. By measuring program adherence to the principles marking effective programs, a locale can increase the chances that all programs promote positive change in enrolled adolescents.

Looking Forward. The central point of this section on evidence-based services is that improving services in the juvenile justice system requires an ongoing process of program development and monitoring of the delivery of services. Although it is clearly necessary to develop more innovative and proven methods for intervening with adolescent offenders, it is also critical to make sure that these services can be put into practice as designed. Ongoing organizational assessment and quality improvement are essential tasks for improving the design, delivery, and ultimate effectiveness of services for juvenile offenders.

A first, necessary step in this effort would be the development of methods for collecting information about the organizational features and regularities of service provision in both institutions and community-based services for juvenile offenders. Efforts at measuring organizational and community-based program climates have been undertaken (Altschuler and Armstrong, 1996; Armstrong and McKenzie, 2000; Mulvey, Schubert, and Odgers, 2010), some quality improvement strategies have been developed (e.g., Performance Based Standards for Youth Correction and Detention Facilities at http://pbstandards.org/initiatives/performance-based-standards-pbs) (Torbet et al., 1996), and some research has been done on the effects of organizational dimensions and program content on outcomes (Glisson, 2007; Schubert et al., 2012). The scope of this work, however, is very limited, given the centrality of these issues for improving services for these adolescents.

The overall vision for improving services in the juvenile justice system does not rest solely with the development of more evidence-based interventions or with the establishment of quality improvement processes. Both are necessary, and neither alone is sufficient. Refining intervention models without getting them into practice does little; not knowing what interventions accomplish or how to improve them when they are put into place probably does even less. As John F. Kennedy and others have noted, "A rising tide lifts all boats." Evidence-based programs provide valuable lessons in how to design a boat that floats well, and an ongoing process of quality improvement provides a process for raising the level of performance for those that stay above water.

COSTS AND BENEFITS OF JUVENILE JUSTICE INTERVENTIONS

Because there is compelling evidence that a variety of intervention programs for juvenile offenders significantly reduces one-year rearrest (by anywhere from about 6 to 40 percentage points), it remains to ask if it is really worth it from a broader social policy perspective to promote these types of programs. Even if a juvenile offender intervention program is effective, it is still necessary to ask a number of questions about the wisdom of widespread adoption. Is the program more valuable than other opportunities that could be pursued with the resources devoted to it? That is, does the value of its effects exceed the cost of producing them? Information relevant to these questions can be obtained using the technique of benefit-cost analysis.

The fundamental idea of benefit-cost analysis is straightforward. These approaches comprehensively identify and measure the benefits and costs of a program, including those that arise in the longer term, after youth leave it, as well as those occurring while they participate. If the benefits exceed the costs, the program improves economic efficiency in the sense that the value of the output (i.e., the program's impacts) exceeds the cost of producing it. As a result, society is economically better off because certain measurable, positive outcomes have been achieved as the result of having the program in place, and the value of these outcomes is greater than the costs of putting the program into place. If costs exceed benefits, society would be economically better off not operating the program at all and devoting the scarce resources that would be used to run it to other programs with the same goal that do pass a benefit-cost test or to other worthwhile purposes.

Benefit-cost analysis may be viewed as a way to calculate society's return from investing in an intervention. In a sense, it is the public-sector analog to private-sector decisions about where to invest resources. Benefit-cost analysis, however, considers benefits and costs for all members of society, not just those for one enterprise.

Our analysis covers benefit-cost analyses of programs explicitly designed to reduce juvenile crime.[4] There are a number of analyses of program effects on a range of outcomes for children and youth, including schooling, earnings, teen pregnancy, and sometimes crime as well (Aos et al., 2004; Small et al., 2005; National Research Council and Institute of

---

[4]Appendix A provides a more extensive discussion of how benefit-cost analysis is applied to juvenile justice programs.

Medicine, 2009), but these are not considered here. Although there are more than 500 impact evaluations of juvenile offender programs (Drake, Aos, and Miller, 2009; Lipsey, 2009), benefit-cost analyses of these programs are sparse.

The benefit-cost analyses produced by the Washington State Institute for Public Policy (WSIPP) are widely regarded as the most thorough and comprehensive in the juvenile justice literature. WSIPP's studies are notable for several reasons. First, they examine a wide variety of juvenile justice interventions that have been carefully evaluated. These include model programs endorsed by the Blueprints for Violence Prevention Project (http://www.colorado.edu/cspv/blueprints), such as multisystemic therapy, multidimensional treatment foster care, and functional family therapy. They also include other interventions that WSIPP judges to be effective, such as drug courts, as well as interventions shown to be ineffective, such as Scared Straight and juvenile intensive probation supervision. The studies use meta-analytic methods to combine findings from different evaluations of the same intervention to derive the effects on crime outcomes used in the benefit-cost analyses. Second, they use established methods to project the reductions in crime that an intervention is likely to produce over a 13-year follow-up period. They then use the projections to estimate the resulting cost savings for the criminal justice system and victims. The projected reductions in crime and the criminal justice system cost savings are meticulously derived from Washington state data. Victim costs are taken from Miller and colleagues (1996). Finally, WSIPP analysts are transparent in describing their assumptions and methods.[5]

Table 6-2 presents the findings for the juvenile justice programs analyzed in Drake and colleagues (2009) and Washington State Institute for Public Policy (2011). The message is clear: Whether one chooses to intervene with juvenile offenders when they are institutionalized, in group or foster homes, or on probation, states and localities can adopt programs that produce remarkably large economic returns. The same is true for programs that seek to divert juveniles before they are convicted of further crimes. Indeed, some programs deliver $10 or more of benefits for each $1 of cost. Although impressive, these findings are actually conservative; existing benefit-cost analyses measure the interventions' costs well but usually omit some important and possibly large categories of benefits.

For juvenile offenders in group or foster homes, the benefits of multidimensional treatment foster care exceed its costs by $33,300. For juveniles on probation, the benefits of aggression replacement therapy and functional family therapy both exceed their costs by about $34,500 per

---

[5]For further discussion of methods of estimating the benefits of preventing crime, including reductions in victim costs, see Appendix A.

participant. Multisystemic therapy also easily passes a benefit-cost test: a recent benefit-cost analysis of a program in Missouri shows large economic returns (Klietz, Borduin, and Schaeffer, 2010). For institutionalized juveniles, the benefits of aggression replacement therapy, functional family therapy, and family integrated transitions (Trupin et al., 2004) exceed their costs by roughly $65,500, $57,300, and $16,000 per participant, respectively. For the small group of juvenile sex offenders, sex offender treatment yields large benefits that exceed the high treatment cost by nearly $25,000 per participant.[6]

Six program models meant to limit the penetration of adolescent offenders into the juvenile justice system have benefits that substantially exceed costs. The benefits per participant of adolescent diversion (for lower risk offenders) are about $51,000 greater than the costs. The corresponding figures for teen courts, drug courts, restorative justice, coordination of services, and victim offender mediation are $16,800, $9,700, $9,200, $4,900, and $3,400, respectively.

Other programs clearly do not make sense economically. Boot camp programs do not reduce crime, but they cost less if one considers institutional care as the alternative and assumes that all individuals enrolled in these programs would be in an institutional setting if not enrolled. It is important to recognize that some programs are economically inferior to conventional practice (i.e., the benefits are lower than the costs). This is the case for alternative parole programs. Wilderness challenge, intensive probation supervision, and Scared Straight are all economically inferior to conventional practice. In these cases, the benefits are less than the costs; running these programs costs money for no gain in the long run.

Parole is the only custody status for which no alternative programs pass a benefit-cost test. There may be parole practices that are economically better than standard practice, but they have not yet been developed or successfully tested. Juvenile justice officials may consider supporting the development and testing of new parole models that might prove successful and pass a benefit-cost test. Alternatively, they can use their scarce resources to implement the already proven programs that intervene during a different custody status.

These bottom-line estimates of total benefits and costs have a degree of uncertainty because estimates of some of the underlying parameters needed

---

[6]Of the 14 programs that pass a benefit-cost test when all benefits are counted, 10 still pass even if one compares program costs only with the benefits to the criminal justice system (i.e., ignoring the large benefits to victims). The four that do not are family integrated transitions, sex offender treatment, multisystemic therapy, and drug courts. The sources for Table 6-2 provide separate benefit estimates for victims and the criminal justice system.

TABLE 6-2 Benefits and Costs per Participant of Juvenile Offender Programs (net present value, 2010 dollars)

Custody Status of Juvenile Participants[a]	Program	Benefits to Victims and Criminal Justice System	Program Costs (compared with cost of alternative)	Benefits Minus Costs	Benefit-Cost Ratio	Probability That Benefits Exceed Costs
Institution	Aggression replacement therapy[c]	$66,954	$1,473	$65,481	45.5	.93
	Functional family therapy[c]	60,639	3,198	57,341	19.0	.99
	Family integrated transitions[c]	27,020	10,968	16,052	2.5	.86
	Sex offender treatment[b]	60,477	35,592	24,885	1.7	n/a
	Boot camp[b]	0	-8,661	8,661	n/a	n/a
	Wilderness challenge[b]	0	3,350	-3,350	n/a	n/a
Group or Foster Home	Multidimensional treatment foster care[c]	40,787	7,739	33,047	5.3	n/a
Parole	Regular surveillance-oriented parole (versus no parole supervision)[b]	0	1,301	-1,301	n/a	n/a
	Intensive parole supervision[b]	0	7,015	-7,015	n/a	n/a
Probation	Aggression replacement therapy[c]	36,043	1,476	34,566	24.4	.93
	Functional family therapy[c]	37,739	3,190	34,549	11.9	.99
	Multisystemic therapy[c]	29,302	7,206	22,096	4.1	.91
	Intensive probation supervision[b]	0	1,735	-1,735	n/a	n/a

Diversion	Adolescent diversion project (for low-risk offenders)[b]	53,072	2,077	50,995	25.6	n/a
	Teen courts[b]	17,782	985	16,797	18.0	n/a
	Drug courts[c]	12,737	3,024	9,713	4.2	.80
	Restorative justice[b]	10,106	954	9,152	10.6	n/a
	Coordination of services[c]	5,270	386	4,884	13.6	.78
	Victim offender mediation[c]	3,922	566	3,357	6.9	.90
	Scared Straight[c]	−6,031	63	−6,095	n/a	n/a

Benefits (Costs not available)

Institution	Behavior modification[b]	42,706
	Cognitive-behavioral therapy[b]	7,744
	Counseling, psychotherapy[b]	50,304
	Education programs[b]	109,834
	Life skills education programs[b]	13,908
Diversion	Diversion with services (versus regular juvenile court)[b]	3,982
	Other family-based therapy programs[b]	40,281

NOTE: n/a = estimate not available. Monetary figures are converted into 2010 dollars.
[a]Adapted from Greenwood (2008).
[b]Adapted from Drake et al. (2009).
[c]Adapted from Washington State Institute for Public Policy (2011).

to conduct a benefit-cost analysis are themselves uncertain.[7] The Washington State Institute for Public Policy's (2011) recent analyses, however, take this uncertainty into account in calculating their costs and benefits. They use Monte Carlo methods, repeating the computations under thousands of variations to test the sensitivity of the overall findings to the inherent uncertainty of the underlying parameters. Columns 3 and 4 of Table 6-2 show the best point estimates of benefits and costs, using these methods.

The Monte Carlo results in the last column of Table 6-2 imply that one can be highly confident that aggression replacement therapy, family integrated transitions, functional family therapy, multisystemic therapy, and victim offender mediation are successful programs from a benefit-cost perspective. The probabilities that these approaches pass a benefit-cost test are all at least .86. Most exceed .90. The probabilities are somewhat lower for drug courts and coordination of services (.80 and .78), but one can still be quite confident that both are successful.

Because WSIPP uses Washington data to estimate changes in crime and the costs of the criminal justice system, the findings on program application from this locale are technically not generalizable to other states or to the nation as a whole. Washington's crime and the costs of its criminal justice system, however, in all likelihood do not differ substantially from those of other states, and the application of these findings to other locales is probably appropriate. Indeed, even if the savings in criminal justice costs and the benefits to victims (not shown separately in the table) were both 25 percent smaller, all programs that pass a benefit-cost test in WSIPP's analysis would still pass by a wide margin in this adjusted analysis. WSIPP's findings provide reliable guidance for other states and localities.

Seven other types of programs examined in Drake and colleagues (2009) also generate benefits to victims and the criminal justice system, as shown in the lower panel of Table 6-2. Four of the seven have benefits exceeding $40,000 per participant, so they are likely to pass a benefit-cost test. We cannot draw this conclusion with certainty, however, because WSIPP had not computed cost estimates at the time of publication. WSIPP is currently developing a tool that other jurisdictions can use to derive benefit-cost estimates of criminal justice programs (Aos and Drake, 2010). The tool will allow analysts to use crime and cost data for their jurisdictions and vary the assumptions needed to compute cost savings.

---

[7]Suppose an evaluation reports that a program reduced crime by 12 percent, with a standard error of 1.4. This means that although the most likely impact is 12 percent, there is a 95 percent chance that the true impact lies between 9.3 and 14.7 percent. Similarly, estimates of program costs, estimates of victim costs, and the methods used by Drake and colleagues (2009) to combine findings from several studies are not perfectly precise.

Although the program cost estimates in Table 6-2 are essentially complete, all benefit estimates are understated for several reasons. These shortcomings apply to all other benefit-cost analyses of juvenile justice programs as well. First, although they assess the benefits of less crime to victims and to the justice system (police, prosecutors, courts, parole officers, etc.), they ignore possible benefits to nonvictims (e.g., less fear of being victimized) and to offenders and their families (e.g., increased productivity from substance use treatment). The latter could be especially large if programs help offenders to attain more schooling or reduce the likelihood that younger siblings engage in delinquent acts.[8] Second, they count the savings of less crime for the justice system but not for other public or nonprofit agencies that may see savings (e.g., less money spent on mental health hospitalizations). Third, methods for measuring some types of victim costs have not yet been developed.[9] Finally, because adolescent behavior, including delinquency, is heavily influenced by peers, programs that reduce a participant's delinquency may reduce their peers' antisocial activities as well. Because program evaluations have not measured this second-round impact on crime, benefit-cost analyses cannot include its benefits.[10]

Recognizing these reasons why benefits are understated further strengthens our earlier conclusion: states and localities can invest in a variety of programs for juvenile offenders that, if implemented well, have demonstrated effectiveness for reducing reoffending and pay large dividends.

SPECIFIC DETERRENCE

So far, we have focused mainly on the role of providing appropriate rehabilitative services to move an adolescent onto a more positive developmental track, away from continued offending. Adolescents may also refrain from future offending, however, by simply learning their lesson from their encounter with the juvenile justice system. Being held accountable for an offense may teach an adolescent that his or her own conduct is beyond the bounds of what the community will tolerate and well short of what is

---

[8]For example, if a program raises the probability of completing high school by .10. And in 2009, male high school graduates earned $11,600 and female high school graduates earned $8,900 more per year than those without a degree (U.S. Census Bureau, 2010a, 2010b), then the average increase in earnings would be $1,160 for males and $890 for females. Over a 40-year working life, the present value of $1,160 and $890 is $20,900 and $16,000 making the conservative assumption that it does not grow over time and using a discount rate of 5 percent.

[9]Some other studies are further limited because they estimate cost savings to the criminal justice system but not victim benefits (Robertson et al., 2001; Cowell et al., 2010).

[10]Butts and Roman (2009) observe that some potentially valuable program models, such as community-based interventions, lack the rigorous evaluations required to assess benefits and costs. This is less a limitation of the technique of benefit-cost analysis per se than of the funding priorities of agencies and researchers.

expected. Experience with the juvenile justice system could also lead the adolescent to rethink the risks and rewards of future criminal involvement (i.e., they are deterred from future crime). (The potential normative function of the juvenile justice system is addressed in Chapter 7.)

There is a very large literature in criminology on deterrence (Zimring and Hawkins, 1973; Andenaes, 1974), generally rooted in the position that criminal activity is reduced when criminal sanctions are seen as certain, severe, and swift. This happens because the risk and costs of sanctions will exceed the perceived returns from crime (Becker, 1968). Deterrence theorists usually distinguish between two types of deterrence: for society as a whole (general deterrence) and for individuals (specific deterrence). General deterrence is based on the idea of vicarious learning; widely known laws—accompanied by strong enforcement, prosecution, and punishment—send a clear message that crime will not be tolerated. Potential offenders, seeing or hearing about the experiences of others, decide that it is not wise to engage in that criminal activity or others. Specific deterrence is based on experiential learning; one's own prior offending and sanction experiences provide a framework for judging the likely costs and benefits of criminal activity involvement and determine whether one will offend again. We are concerned here with the idea of specific deterrent effects in adolescents who have already offended (consideration of general deterrent effects in adolescents is discussed in Chapter 5).

In general, punishment that is more certain should reduce crime, and the stronger a penalty connected with a crime, the less likely it should be that a person will do it. The majority of deterrence research indicates that the certainty of the punishment, rather than its severity, is the primary mechanism through which deterrence works (Nagin, 1998; Paternoster, 2010; Durlauf and Nagin, 2011). In other words, offenders typically respond to a punishment that is more likely than one that is more severe.

There is good reason to believe that adolescents might respond differently than adults to factors related to deterrence. As mentioned throughout this report, distinctive features of adolescent decision making (e.g., heightened risk taking and reduced sensitivity to threat of punishment, especially its long-term consequences) would be expected to affect an adolescent's weighing the consequences of criminal involvement. Moreover, the objective characteristics of certainty and severity are not the prime determinant of deterrence; subjective perceptions are more influential (Matsueda, Kreager, and Huizinga, 2006). How an adolescent might distinctly frame the issue of the certainty and severity of punishment then becomes an even more important concern.

The research on the applicability of deterrence models to adolescent decision making about criminal involvement, however, is rather limited. Most of the studies of the mechanisms of deterrence, with both adults and adolescents, have used samples of nonoffenders or primarily nonserious offenders (Nagin and Pogarsky, 2001, 2003). As a result, there are very few findings regarding specific deterrence among adolescent offenders in particular. The best known of these (Shannon, 1980, 1985; Schneider, 1990) indicate that adolescents do not respond in accordance with the posited mechanisms of deterrence; that is, perceptions of higher costs of crime are not associated with decreased offending in serious juvenile offenders, and processes other than cost-benefit calculations (e.g., labeling oneself as an offender) may be operating in less serious offenders.

A series of relevant studies done on serious adolescent offenders from the Pathways to Desistance project has recently expanded this literature, finding that the elements of deterrence do operate in a sample of serious adolescent offenders over time, but that these effects are heterogeneous (Anwar and Loughran, 2011; Loughran et al., 2011a, 2011b, 2012). Some initial findings from these investigations indicate that, even in serious adolescent offenders, certainty of arrest appears to play a more important role in deterring future criminal activity than severity of punishment, offenders with more extensive histories of antisocial activity are less likely to change their risk perceptions after being arrested, and there may be a threshold level of risk that must be perceived (about a 30 percent chance of being arrested) to exert an effect on involvement in later offending. Most notably, this line of research so far indicates that deterrence operates to curtail future offending in serious adolescent offenders, although the mechanisms of its operations may still be different in some dimensions from those observed in adult samples.

There is a body of research on the effects of transfer to adult court, which could be considered a specific deterrent policy meant to dissuade serious offenders from continued involvement in crime. Numerous studies have compared the arrest histories of samples of juvenile offenders processed in the juvenile system with those processed in the adult court system. Analyses of these studies have repeatedly asserted that transfer laws are ineffective (i.e., they do not prevent future crime among those transferred) (Redding, 2008) and may in fact be harmful (i.e., counterproductive for the purpose of reducing crime and enhancing public safety) (McGowan et al., 2007). There is some indication that transfer to adult court may have a differential effect on adolescent offenders, with violent offenders reducing, and property offenders increasing, their subsequent offending levels (Loughran et al., 2010). Most of the analyses of these results, however, align with the assessment of Bishop and Frazier (2000, p. 261) that transferred adolescents are "more likely to reoffend, and to reoffend more quickly and more often, than those retained in the juvenile system." Other work has examined the effects of placement in a juvenile facility compared with community-based treatment, finding that the latter in general produces higher levels of successful adjustment after adjudication (Garrett, 1985; Andrews, Bonta, and Hoge, 1990; Sherman et al., 1997; Lipsey, 1999; Lipsey, Wilson, and Cothern, 2000). A recent, well-controlled analysis of the effects of institutional placement versus probation, however, indicated no reduction, or increase, in rearrest or self-reported offending among serious adolescent offenders associated with placement in a juvenile institution versus assignment to probation (Loughran et al., 2009). Across the studies of deterrence and the effects of transfer, there is no evidence that more severe punishments reduce the likelihood of future offending.

TAKING A DEVELOPMENTALLY ORIENTED APPROACH

Clearly, juvenile justice policy and practice have to respond to so-called serious delinquents and hold them accountable for their behavior, especially because of the frequency and seriousness of the offenses committed by this small proportion of adolescent offenders. At the same time, concerns about serious offending delinquents should not dominate the approaches taken across the juvenile justice system. Over the past 20 years, the juvenile system has become increasingly punitive: for example, reducing the jurisdiction of the juvenile court, increasing transfer to adult court, and increasing sentence lengths (Logan, 1998; Feld, 1999; Howell, 2009). Much of this reorientation of the court to a "war on juveniles" (Howell, 2003a) appears to have been driven by concern over serious, chronic delinquency; a result of the moral panic about juvenile crime in the 1990s and the super-predator myth (Dilulio, 1995; Bennett, Dilulio, and Walters, 1996). In the midst of this uproar, the simple fact that serious delinquents represent a small minority of the total population of delinquents has become lost. The extreme end of the distribution of juvenile offenders, that is, youth who are chronically violent, is extraordinarily small. Thus, although it is essential to make every effort to successfully prevent and deter serious delinquent behavior, these efforts will not be behaviorally appropriate for the vast majority of less serious delinquents who make up the bulk of the delinquent population. Recall that approximately half of the delinquents are referred to the juvenile justice system only once. It is just as important to respond appropriately to the behavior and needs of this very large group as it is to respond to the very small group of serious, chronic offenders.

Consideration of knowledge regarding adolescent development can help refine the approaches taken to assess and intervene with juvenile offenders. Current approaches to processing and intervening with adolescents often build on models adapted from the adult criminal justice system or conceptions about behavioral disorders from mental health treatment. An alternative is to recognize that adolescent offenders, whether serious or not, all share common processes of risk and development. There may be a greater accumulation of risk in serious offenders, but the underlying processes by which risk and protective factors affect outcomes appear to be the same for all juvenile offenders. Based on the studies cited earlier regarding differential program effects and reports of prevention work increasing stimulation of environmentally deprived young children (Masten and Coatsworth, 1998; Masten, 2001), it appears that the impact from interventions involving changes in social context may be most profound for those with the highest accumulation of risk. The mechanisms of influence may be consistent, but the size of the effect from an intervention may vary depending on the initial level of risk.

Given this, it makes sense that the core principles guiding the way that both less serious and more serious juvenile offenders are treated should flow from a developmental perspective. Farrington and Welsh (2007) call this risk-focused prevention, in which risk is examined from the appropriate developmental stage and appropriate domain of risk (Biglan et al., 2004). Viewing involvement in antisocial behaviors in light of what it means to be an adolescent, rather than in terms of what it might take to erase a deficit, puts a different light on how one might think about designing and administering the juvenile justice system.

For one thing, being an adolescent means living in a period of life when change, rather than behavioral consistency, is the norm. Adolescents, including juvenile offenders, undergo accelerated physical, emotional, psychological, and social context changes during the period of their potential involvement with the juvenile court. Despite involvement with the juvenile justice system, they are still growing up on multiple dimensions. In addition, based on our earlier review, being an adolescent also means that cognitive and emotional regulatory capacities are not yet synchronous enough to produce what would be considered logical judgments in times of emotional arousal. This means that adolescents may make reasonable judgments in some situations and not in others, or about some issues and not about others, and that their social learning can show considerable variability depending on the social context considered (Smetana and Villalobos, 2009). Developing the ability to regulate and integrate cognitive and emotional processes is one of the major tasks of this developmental period. These simple regularities have implications for how to most usefully frame and respond to criminal involvement.

Implications for Assessment

The fact that adolescents are moving targets has implications for how one characterizes and assesses adolescent offenders. Variability in adolescent behavior and perceptions means that mental health diag-

noses of adolescents are less reliable or valid and that the characteriza-
tions of adolescents as having certain immutable personality characteristics
(e.g., psychopathy) are less trustworthy. In addition, involvement in antisocial activity, like many other adolescent behaviors, changes over time and
has some relation to the developmental status of an adolescent. Considerable evidence exists that a high proportion of adolescent offenders reduce
or stop their antisocial behavior as they move into their mid-20s (Broidy et
al., 2003; Piquero, 2008b). This change appears to be attributable to some
combination of the positive effects of social transitions that occur during this
period (e.g., entry into the workforce, positive romantic relationships) (Laub
and Sampson, 2003), increases in psychosocial capacities (Monahan et al.,
2009), and decreases in substance use (Chassin, Fora, and King, 2004).
Qualitative work has also pointed up the importance of an increased sense
of personal agency in promoting these changes, with adolescents trying on
new, more prosocial identities as part of their adoption of an emerging adult
sense of self (Maruna, 2001; Giordano, Cernkovich, and Rudolph, 2002).

One implication of these observations is that depictions of an adolescent as having a fixed set of characteristics are highly likely to be inaccurate,
and assessments of adolescents' risk of future offending and suitability for
certain interventions have a limited shelf life (Mulvey and Iselin, 2008).
Categorization of adolescents according to their presenting offense alone,
without consideration of developmental factors, is particularly poor at
predicting later adjustment or outcomes (Loeber and Farrington, 1998),
except for the demonstrated low level of reoffending among juvenile sex
offenders (Zimring, 2004). Assessments of adolescents are most valid when
they focus on short-term outcomes and explicitly incorporate the types of
events that might precipitate or reduce the likelihood of a particular outcome. Thus, to be most informative, assessments of high-risk adolescents
should be done regularly and should consider the influential social factors
in the adolescent's life.

This approach stands in sharp contrast to some trends in juvenile justice legislation and programming. Over the last two decades, statutes limiting the jurisdiction of the juvenile court have relied on the commission of
one of a range of offenses to justify transfer or waiver of an adolescent to
the adult court. Other program foci at the less serious end of the juvenile
offender continuum have also taken an offense-oriented perspective for
identifying adolescents who should receive specialized services, such as
school truants and drug dealers. In these approaches, the overall risk profile
of the adolescent is secondary to the presenting offense. From the outset,
such approaches ignore the reality that the illegal behaviors of interest
occur in a developmental framework and that there is considerable relevant
variability among adolescents who commit the same offense or level of
offense (Schubert et al., 2010).

Implications for Designing Interventions

Recognizing the fluid nature of adolescence has implications for interventions promoted by the juvenile justice system. Some interventions are clearly and appropriately aimed at fixing an adolescent's deficits. For example, providing intensive schooling to increase the likelihood that an adolescent offender will graduate from high school certainly makes sense. Increasing human capital in terms of expanded skills or competencies is a key aspiration in any balanced set of interventions (as advocated by the balanced and restorative justice approach) (Office of Juvenile Justice and Delinquency Prevention, 1997a; Griffin, 2006). Just "fixing" an adolescent on one dimension of functioning, however, is unlikely to have a great impact on later adjustment. As seen in the review above, interventions with the most success at altering the level of subsequent offending provide opportunities for an adolescent to develop successfully in a supportive social world. Model programs like those cited above work systematically with multiple aspects of the adolescent's world, including the family, the school, and the community. While building the personal competencies of the adolescent (e.g., increasing problem-solving strategies), they also work on constructing a more supportive social environment for the adolescent.

This makes sense from a developmental perspective. The process of changing an adolescent's trajectory rests on the ability of the systems around the adolescent to support and direct the ongoing change process. In late adolescence, most individuals follow a pattern of individuating from parents, orienting toward peers, and integrating components of attitudes and behavior into an autonomous self-identity (Collins and Steinberg, 2006). These processes are occurring simultaneously in an overlapping fashion, with the success of one process dependent on the course of another. Navigating this developmental period successfully, in which the adolescent sees himself or herself as a prosocial, law-abiding person, requires supportive adults, healthy relationships with peers, and opportunities to make autonomous decisions (Scott and Steinberg, 2008).

The juvenile justice system could increase its impact by considering when it might be impeding or promoting these developmental processes. The most obvious example is the system's continued reliance on institutional placement. Being in an institutional environment for extended periods, away from community opportunities to experiment with developing conceptions of self, might not allow for the developmental experiences needed in adolescence. Spending time in an institutional setting provides few opportunities to freely develop skills and competencies like learning job-related expectations or discovering qualities in a life partner that are a good match. Regimented schedules and restrictions reduce opportunities to develop the skills critical to a successful adolescent transition to adulthood (Mulvey and Schubert, 2011). Although some adolescents may receive essential skills for later life relationships, a great many others may just not catch up when they return to the community. Following this logic, the longer they are out of the normal, developmental pattern, the more difficult this becomes.

An awareness of the developmental needs of adolescents also implies altered emphases in designing and assessing both institutional and community-based programming. If one adopts a developmental approach, the settings and regularities of programming environments take on increased importance. Instead of simply considering whether a program addresses a feature of internal change within the adolescent offender (e.g., promoting social skills that might reduce a reliance on aggression as a response), programs (both institutional and community-based) would become more focused on the mechanisms by which they are promoting positive development (e.g., encouraging adolescent involvement in program operations or the maintenance of a safe environment). Like many of the burgeoning efforts at promoting positive youth development, juvenile justice programs would become focused on how program environment and operations further the development of program participants to address the next set of challenges facing them. Assessment of programs would focus on aspects of program operations that contribute to the development of an environment that promotes positive outcomes (see the approach taken by the David P. Weikart Center for Youth Program Quality at http://www.cypq.org/ for an example of what such an orientation might entail).

SUMMARY

Adolescents who are involved in delinquency continue to develop during adolescence and early adulthood. This is true both physically, for example, with respect to brain development, and socially, for example, with respect to decision making and peer influence. In a real sense they are not yet complete.

It is thus only logical, but nonetheless imperative, that the services provided to adolescent offenders foster positive, prosocial development. The developmental differences between adults and adolescents should be an orienting consideration in how assessments and interventions are designed for the juvenile justice system and how this system should differ systematically from the adult criminal justice system. Adolescents require certain social conditions to emerge successfully from this period of development, whether they have committed a crime or not. Evidence indicates that building these factors into the interventions used with adolescents reduces their likelihood of reoffending.

This is best accomplished in the context of a juvenile justice system that is responsive to developmental concerns and not in the context of the adult criminal justice system with its often shared, but nonetheless differently ordered, set of priorities. For juveniles, policies and programs that are predominantly punitive neither foster prosocial development nor reduce recidivism (Howell, 2009; Lipsey, 2009). Although they may reaffirm societal values and respond to the emotional needs of the victimized, they are not consistent with a developmental perspective and are less likely to foster the primary objective of public safety. There is no convincing evidence that confinement of juvenile offenders beyond a minimum amount required to provide sufficiently intense services for them to benefit from this experience, either in adult prisons or juvenile correctional institutions, appreciably reduces the likelihood of subsequent offending. To the extent that preventing reoffending is the primary policy consideration, juvenile court dispositions should avoid lengthy confinement, adolescents should be tried in criminal court only in the most serious cases of personal violence, and criminal court sentences should avoid confinement of adolescents in adult prisons.

With exceedingly few exceptions, adolescent offenders (even serious offenders) who experience secure confinement will return to society while still relatively young but at a considerable disadvantage for success as an adult. Given this, it is in society's interest to reduce the likelihood of continued offending by providing developmentally appropriate interventions that are rooted in what is known about adolescent development (Biglan et al., 2004; Farrington and Welsh, 2007). Forestalling future crime and building developmental strengths for offenders makes more sense in the long run than handicapping offenders by removing them from society in harsh environments and forestalling positive development in the process. This evidence for the effectiveness of developmentally sensitive interventions is bolstered by analyses of the costs and benefits of these interventions. The most comprehensive and detailed analyses of the dollars spent and saved by putting these types of programs into place show that the public savings are considerable. The advantages of many programs are not small; broad-based community interventions and theoretically sound institutional approaches all show benefits several times the costs.

This is more than simple-minded ideology. Almost all of the model programs that demonstrate impressive reductions in reoffending are rooted in a developmental perspective. Successful programs attempt to reduce the risk factors that are associated with delinquency and violence by fostering prosocial development and by building promotive factors at the individual, family, school, and peer levels. Policies and programs for the range of adolescent offenders, including those that take place in secure confinement, should be based on these same core principles of successful intervention.

7

Accountability and Fairness

In the context of criminal punishment of adults, it is often said that just punishment must "fit the crime." Under the prevailing legal model of criminal sentencing, a legislature or sentencing commission establishes "presumptive" sentences that "fit the crime," while allowing sentencing judges some leeway for departure (in favor of greater leniency or greater severity) to "fit the offender." Legal scholars typically refer to the principle that punishment should fit the crime as "retribution" or "just deserts." The founding model of the juvenile court dispensed with offense-related considerations altogether in deciding what should be done with the delinquent youth; instead, interactions between the youth and the juvenile justice system, as well as the judge's choice of disposition, were supposed to be based solely on the goal of rehabilitating the offender. In theory, if not in practice, the seriousness of the offense was not even a relevant consideration, much less a determinative one, in choosing a juvenile court disposition.

In its pivotal decision in *In re Gault* (1967), the Supreme Court observed that rehabilitative ambitions for juvenile offenders were often unrealized and that delinquent youth were being "punished" in fact, if not in name. In so doing, the Court left the guiding precepts of the juvenile court in confusion. For example, is punishment a suitable aim of the modern juvenile court? Should a juvenile court disposition be designed to fit the offense as well as the offender? If so, how are preventive and punitive considerations to be accommodated or balanced? One way of understanding the instability of the law governing juvenile justice over the four decades since *Gault* is continuing puzzlement about the answers to these questions. As noted in Chapter 2, however, the committee thinks that a consensus on these basic

issues has finally been reached. We think that this emerging societal consensus can be summarized along the following lines:

Most fundamentally, reducing recidivism by youth before the juvenile
court should continue to be the primary goal of delinquency proceedings
(i.e., the dispositional intervention should be designed mainly to "fit the
offender"). At the same time, however, the juvenile justice system should
also ensure that adolescents are held accountable for their wrongdoing
and that, in doing so, they are treated fairly. A review of contemporary
juvenile justice statutes reveals that they typically declare dual objectives:
holding youth accountable and providing rehabilitative services to reduce
their risk of reoffending. Both of these goals are necessary to satisfy public
expectations that corrective action will be taken. In the committee's view,
both of these goals can and should be securely anchored in a developmental
approach to juvenile offending.

In the committee's understanding, saying that youth should be held
accountable is not the same as saying that they should be punished. The
concept of accountability is used in everyday speech to refer to a wide variety of mechanisms, both formal and informal, for declaring and enforcing
norms of personal and institutional responsibility and taking corrective
or remedial action. Formal mechanisms of accountability include being
ordered to compensate a victim for the harm that one has caused, being dismissed from a position in a company for embarrassing the company or
causing a loss to its shareholders, or even being turned out of office. Similarly, holding adolescents accountable for their offending vindicates the
just expectation of society that responsible offenders will be answerable
for wrongdoing, particularly for conduct that causes harm to identifiable
victims, and that corrective action will be taken. It does not follow, however, that the mechanisms of accountability are punitive or that they should
mimic criminal punishments. Condemnation, control, and lengthy confinement, the identifying attributes of criminal punishment, are not necessary
features of accountability for juveniles, and should be avoided except in the
rare instances when confinement is necessary to protect society.

Chapter 6 reviewed the evidence regarding the effects of interventions
available to the juvenile justice system in preventing recidivism. In this
chapter we address official actions taken by the juvenile justice system (and
by parallel disciplinary systems in schools) from the vantage point of ensuring offender accountability and healthy legal socialization. Although most
of the interventions addressed in Chapter 6 can serve both purposes, a key
objective of this chapter is to highlight the potentially useful role of official
actions other than juvenile court dispositions as instruments of accountability, particularly those associated with the process of adjudication itself.
It is helpful in this respect to have in mind the entire process of involvement
in the juvenile justice system, including all official interactions with law

enforcement authorities and judges. Both positive and negative interactions with legal authorities are likely to influence the way youth perceive the law and respond to juvenile justice interventions.

Making conduct illegal, disapproving its occurrence, apprehending suspected offenders, holding adjudicatory hearings, and administering sanctions communicate messages to the public, including adolescents, about the importance of adhering to a particular norm or to the law in general.[1] Cumulatively as well as in specific cases, these events and actions may affect the adolescents' beliefs about, and attitudes toward, personal responsibility for wrongdoing, obedience to law, obligations to victims, and fairness in the administration of justice

A key message of this chapter is that accountability practices in juvenile justice should be designed specifically for juvenile justice rather than being carried over from the criminal courts and should be designed to promote healthy social learning, moral development, and legal socialization during adolescence. If designed and implemented in a developmentally informed way, procedures for holding adolescents accountable for their offending can promote positive legal socialization, reinforce a prosocial identity, and facilitate compliance with the law. However, unduly harsh interventions and negative interactions between youth and justice system officials can undermine respect for the law and legal authority and reinforce a deviant identity and social disaffection.

ACCOUNTABILITY FROM A DEVELOPMENTÁL PERSPECTIVE

Accepting responsibility for oneself and one's behavior has consistently been regarded as a key measure of maturation in numerous studies involving participants from a variety of socioeconomic classes and ethnic groups, and it has been identified as a key outcome of socialization in Western societies (see Arnett, 2007). Socialization can be thought of as a succession of processes occurring at successive stages of development, in which individuals are taught the behaviors, values, and motivations needed for competent interaction with other individuals in a culture. It is an interactive process that involves dynamic relationships between socializing agents and developing youth. In the study of socialization and moral development, the focus has shifted from the behavior of authority figures and adolescents, respectively, to a greater concern with the interactions between

---

[1]This chapter emphasizes the declarative or expressive effects of prescribing and enforcing the law. As discussed in Chapters 5 and 6, the severity of the threatened sanction probably has little effect in motivating adolescents to refrain from offending. Although increasing the perceived probability of detection may deter adolescent offending, the committee regards deterrence as a secondary consideration in the design of juvenile justice adjudications and dispositions.

them (Maccoby, 2007). Indeed, as noted by Grolnick and colleagues (1997, p. 135), "whereas socializing agents can 'teach' their children the values and attitudes they hold dear, the important thing is having the children 'own' those attitudes and values."

This section briefly reviews both the practices of socializing agents and the unique characteristics of adolescents relevant to the development of their sense of accountability. An important point is that although a child's family of origin may be the first and most enduring socializing institution, peer groups, schools, religious institutions, and employers play important roles. Recent research also emphasizes the impact of legal actors on adolescent socialization. The literature summarized below suggests that, if implemented in a developmentally informed way, procedures for holding adolescents accountable for their offending by the juvenile justice system and by other disciplinary authorities can promote moral development and "legal socialization"—described by Fagan and Tyler (2005, p. 218) as a "a vector of developmental capital that promotes compliance with the law and cooperation with legal actors." The literature also indicates that procedures youth perceive as unfair and illegitimate may undermine legal socialization and compliance with the law (Fagan and Tyler, 2005).

Moral Development in Adolescence

Moral development during adolescence, as summarized by Kurtines and Gewirtz (1995), is characterized by developing identification with one's social groups, becoming responsive to the expectations of others, and defining one's place in the community as formal social roles are assumed. Rest and colleagues (1999, p. 15) describe adolescence as a time of a "dawning awareness" of the need to establish a system of cooperation, which involves accepting a balance between one's own rights or freedoms and one's responsibility to respect the rights of others as well as to contribute to society. Accepting responsibility for behavior is integral to moral development.

Identity formation (the development of an understanding of self as an individual and as a member of various groups) and the related process of moral identity formation (the slow and normally imperfect process of integrating morality and the self-concept) are key developmental tasks of adolescence (Damon, 1984, 1999). Longitudinal studies examining youth's participation in community volunteer work have demonstrated what Hastings and colleagues (2007, p. 640) refer to as "a kind of active internalization, of becoming prosocial by being prosocial." For example, Switzer and colleagues (1995) found that school-mandated involvement in community service over a year was associated with increases in self-perceptions of being altruistic and continued involvement in community activities. Likewise, Pratt and colleagues (2003) found that involvement in community helping activities at age 17 predicted stronger commitment to being kind and caring at age 19, over and above the stability of values. Thus, encouraging adolescents' enrollment in community service may be an effective way of promoting their prosocial development, as adolescents are especially primed to incorporate their prosocial activities as an element of their identities.

Importantly, identity formation also involves a pursuit of autonomy, which leaves adolescents sensitive to, and at times resistant to, social control efforts of authority figures that they regard as illegitimate (Fagan and Tyler, 2005). Thus, an understanding of the adolescent conception of legitimacy is crucial to informing effective mechanisms of accountability. Adolescent conceptions of morality are dominated by notions of fairness and by developing notions of reciprocity in which approval and respect are earned (Baumrind, 1996). According to Gilligan (1993), these factors, together with their tendencies to spot contradiction and seek absolute truths (Erikson, 1958, p. 121), make adolescents particularly attuned to "false claims to authority at the same time as they yearn for right answers or for someone who will tell them how they should live and what they should do." Indeed, research demonstrates that perceptions of fairness mediate the youth's acceptance or rejection of a message; for example, children who perceive their parents' disciplinary practices to be fair are more likely to internalize their family's values and beliefs and to behave accordingly (Grusec and Goodnow, 1994).

Agents of Socialization

As highlighted by Hastings and colleagues (2007), it is important to recognize that any socializing institution or mechanism of accountability that is linked to prosocial behavior requires an adolescent to actively process a message, assess its meaning and relevance, determine how it can be enacted, and then choose to do so. In this way, moral development is an interactive and integrative process in which adolescents internalize information not only from the attitudes of others, but, important for our purposes, from the specific ways in which others react and respond to them in holding them responsible for their behavior (Kurtines and Gewirtz, 1995).

Thus, accountability practices that are informed by an understanding of the adolescent mind are most likely to be effective in promoting prosocial development. This section addresses how socializing and disciplinary practices can be effective in promoting the development of accountability of adolescents, who, as described above, are striving to develop social identities, are interested in moral questions, and are sensitive to unfairness and impingements on their autonomy. Given these characteristics, procedures for holding adolescents accountable for their actions should be designed to promote positive moral development and legal socialization, while avoiding interactions that reinforce social disaffection and negative attitudes toward law and legal authority.

Parents

The dominant paradigm for studying the socialization of prosocial behavior in the real world has been the examination of parenting styles, which have been measured in terms of patterns of control, responsiveness, warmth, and punishment that parents use to manage their children's behavior (see Chapter 4). The parenting typology established by Baumrind and her colleagues in the 1960s (authoritarian, permissive, authoritative) provides a model of conceptualizing approaches to socialization and discipline that could be relevant to the juvenile justice system's challenge of promoting accountability.

Research reviewed by Maccoby (2007) demonstrates how parenting practices associated with permissive and authoritarian styles are ineffective at promoting accountability in children, as they either fail to instill any controls or instill only fear of punishment. Thus, the question underlying modern parenting research is not whether parents should exercise authority, but rather how parental control can best be exercised so as to support children's developing capacity for self-regulation. The identification of the authoritative parenting style has captured the combination of responsive, supporting parenting with firmness. Although there has been an unwavering emphasis on rule-setting, monitoring, and the importance of following up on infractions with discipline, there has also been an increasing emphasis on integrating warmth, humor, responsiveness, and politeness into these control functions. The authoritative style entails parents making age-appropriate demands on their children, modeling moral behavior, establishing clear and consistent expectations, and setting up firmly enforced rules of behavior, while also listening to their children, taking their viewpoints into account, providing explanations for parental demands, involving them in decision making, and creating opportunities for their moral reasoning (Laursen and Collins, 2009).

Gibbs (2003) highlights the role that "inductive discipline" encounters play in authoritative systems, asserting that although nurturance and role modeling foster receptivity in children, it is these discipline encounters that teach the impact of the child's selfish acts on others, which is crucial to the development of empathy and accountability (Bugental and Goodnow, 1998). Inductive reasoning in discipline encounters refers to parents informing their children of norms and principles, explaining why rules are necessary, highlighting the well-being of others, and illuminating the effects of children's actions. Discipline that emphasizes power does not cultivate empathy. Gilligan (1993) notes that the adolescent characteristics described above may be disorienting and frustrating to the adults who have to deal with them, which could lead them to adopt either permissive or authoritarian responses. Yet research indicates that adolescents are especially needy of authoritative parenting. Research indicates that adolescents who reported that their parents closely monitored their activities subsequently were more likely to engage in volunteer community work (Zaff et al., 2003), and those who described their parents as having clear rules and high expectations reported two years later that being kind and fairness to others were important qualities (Pratt et al., 2003). Other studies show that adolescents have positive responses when they believe they are being treated with dignity and respect and have their voices heard in the family decision-making process (see Fondarcaro, Dunkle, and Pathak, 1998). These parenting principles resonate in the justice context.

Schools

School and teacher characteristics can affect developmental processes (see Caldwell et al., 2009). Wentzel (2002) found that adolescents who perceived their teachers to have high expectations of them had higher levels of social responsibility. Research also indicates that the degree of emotional support from teachers perceived by adolescents predicts students' adherence to classroom rules and norms (Wentzel, 1998) and in part predicts whether students drop out of school (Rumberger, 1995). School-wide interventions in which teachers are taught to provide students with clear behavioral expectations, developmentally appropriate room for autonomy, and warmth and support have been shown to contribute to increased levels of students' sense of community and prosocial behavior (Watson et al., 1989).

As discussed in Chapters 3 and 4, a growing body of research has focused on school discipline, especially on the effectiveness of alternatives to zero-tolerance policies. These studies have a direct bearing on the challenge of implementing developmentally and culturally sensitive instruments of accountability in the juvenile justice system. For example, school principals who assume responsibility for managing their students' behavior and changing the attitudes, opinions, and behaviors of the teaching staff seem well positioned to offer wisdom and experiential learning opportunities to law enforcement and justice personnel that address the unique challenges of effectively interacting with oppositional adolescents (Rausch and Skiba, 2006). (For an illustrative example of how school discipline might be handled in a developmentally appropriate way, see Box 7-1.)

Scholars and practitioners have also extrapolated promising directions from evaluations of school-based problem behavior reduction programs

---

BOX 7-1
Developmentally Informed School Disciplinary Interventions

How would one describe a school that takes into account the developmental level of adolescents when dealing with discipline problems?

To begin with, a school that believes its disciplinary policies should reflect a developmental perspective builds its disciplinary strategy around certain premises. First, adolescents are susceptible to lapses in judgment, to taking risks, and to not thinking realistically about the consequences of their behavior. Second, adolescents are beginners at defining themselves vis-à-vis their community and at balancing their own rights or freedoms with their responsibilities. Third, adolescents are sensitive to perceived unfairness and react favorably to being treated with dignity and respect and having their voices heard.

The school does not rely on metal detectors, patting down by security personnel, or profiling to prevent disorder and crime from occurring on school grounds. Instead, its students are informed at the outset that some behaviors, such as possession of weapons or drugs or serious threat or assault, will not be tolerated. The school has a planned continuum of effective alternatives and works closely with parents, law enforcement, juvenile justice, and mental health professionals in order to develop an array of alternatives for those students whose behaviors threaten school safety or order.

The school has written disciplinary guidelines that have been drafted by a group of school leaders and students. Removal from school is the most severe sanction and is reserved for the most extreme circumstances. Consequences are geared to the seriousness and specific im-

---

implemented with black, Latino, urban, and low-income students and studies of successful teachers of black students, which might likewise hold lessons for juvenile justice system programs and actors. Commonalities among successful programs include an emphasis on student self-regulation and encouragement of "school connectedness" and "caring and trusting relationships" (Freiberg and Lapointe, 2006) between school officials and students. The principals interviewed by Rausch and Skiba (2006, p. 112) reported that a combination of high expectations and support for students can be effective "even for the toughest kids." Gregory and Weinstein (2008) found that an authoritative style of teaching, in which teachers showed both caring and high expectations, was effective in eliciting trust and cooperation among black students.

pact of the infractions. In setting discipline policies, the school weighs the importance of a particular consequence against the long-term negative consequences of more punitive intervention. It is understood that harsh discipline might create alienation, anxiety, rejection, and the breaking of healthy adult bonds for those subjected to it. Teachers handle infractions at the classroom level whenever possible and are trained to be aware of the potential for bias when issuing referrals for discipline.

When students get into trouble, the disciplinary response focuses on repairing the social injury or damage and having the student understand how the behavior has affected other people. Students are asked to take responsibility and to suggest ways to repair the harm. For example, instead of a scenario in which students might be arrested, handcuffed, and taken to jail for a food fight (Saulny, 2009), school personnel would move swiftly to bring the behavior under control and bring students together with cafeteria workers, custodians, and teachers to be given an opportunity to explain what had happened and to identify underlying issues. The group would discuss how the incident had affected them, learn about the costs that had been incurred, and identify appropriate ways to make amends. These amends might include cleaning the cafeteria for a specific time period, raising money to pay for damage, or working side by side with the cafeteria staff. Students might also be asked to develop a plan that included their own participation in monitoring student behavior at lunchtime.

SOURCE: This section draws on the American Psychological Association Zero Tolerance Task Force (2008); Ashley and Burke (2009); and Wald and Thurau (2010).

Legal Socialization

Adolescence, marked by the development of an understanding of self as an individual and as a member of various groups (Erikson, 1958), is a crucial time for legal socialization, which has been described as a developmental process that results in the internalization of legal rules and norms that regulate social and antisocial behaviors and create a set of obligations and social commitments that restrain motivations for law violation (Fagan and Piquero, 2007). Lind and Tyler (1988) argue that the development of values and beliefs about the legal system during childhood and adolescence forms the basis for a lifelong predisposition toward authority that is a more critical motivator of attitudes toward and compliance with authoritative directives than short-term self-interest.

As Fagan and Tyler (2005) observe, attention by researchers to developmental processes that promote compliance with the law has not been accompanied by equivalent interest in how the law itself can affect development. However, the hypothesis that people's views about the legitimacy of authorities arise out of social interactions and experiences has been tested under a variety of sampling and measurement conditions (see Tyler and Huo, 2002) in adult populations. Tyler's research (2006) has consistently shown that adults' treatment in the judicial process affects their attitudes about the law, and that they are more likely to regard legal authority as legitimate and feel obliged to obey the law if they have been shown respect and given an opportunity for meaningful participation in the proceedings (often characterized as "procedural justice"). Researchers have recently begun to explore how this process of legal socialization unfolds in adolescents, for whom formulating beliefs about themselves and society is a central developmental task. Although longitudinal studies of legal socialization are rare, a cross-sectional study by Fagan and Tyler (2005) suggested that perceived legitimacy of the law and legal authorities may decline as adolescents age, an interesting finding on its own. In addition, adolescents' procedural justice judgments about their personal interactions with legal actors predicted their attitudes toward the legitimacy of law, which, in turn, predicted self-reported delinquent behavior. Likewise, Woolard and colleagues (2008) found that adolescents who anticipated that they would be treated unfairly were less likely to comply with authorities than those who anticipated fair treatment. Moreover, Fagan and Piquero (2007) used interviews of adolescent felony offenders over time to demonstrate that these offenders' perceptions of procedural justice were a significant antecedent of their legal socialization, which influenced patterns of offending over time. The pattern demonstrated by these and other studies (Otto and Dalbert, 2005; Hines, 2007; Sprott and Greene, 2008) suggests that the well-documented connection between adults' perceptions about how fairly they have been treated by the justice system, regardless of the outcome of their case, and their subsequent compliance with the law also extends to adolescents.

Research in juvenile justice settings generally supports the procedural justice perspective. Levels of satisfaction with the fairness of the juvenile justice process among youth and their families in juvenile courts are often higher than those in criminal and civil courts, but the perceptions of participants in juvenile court may be diminished by overt bias and even excessive informality. In a recent survey of participants in North Dakota courts, the National Center for State Courts found that juvenile court participants had one of the highest satisfaction rates of any court type, with more than 80 percent of juvenile court participants reporting high levels of satisfaction on several dimensions of fairness and access. The ratings of juvenile court participants exceeded those of criminal and civil court participants (Nelsen, 2012, pp. 76-78). In juvenile court, however, perceptions of procedural justice can be fragile. A Minnesota study by Eckberg and colleagues (2004), used an experimental design to evaluate the procedures used to inform youth and parents about the sequence of events in juvenile court hearings. The study showed that juveniles and their families were generally satisfied with the fairness of the court process, but their satisfaction was lessened when the source of information was an administrative staff member rather than a judge or other judicial officer. Surveys of youth involved with the justice system show that "anticipatory injustice," or the expectation that the actions of justice authorities will be shaped by bias and discrimination, increases with the age of offenders and with the extent of their contact and experience in the justice system, especially among Latino youth and those of African American descent (Woolard, Harvell, and Graham, 2008). Studies of adolescents and their attitudes about the legitimacy of legal authorities indicate—not surprisingly—that older youth (ages 15-16) are more cynical of legal authority than their younger counterparts between the ages of 10 and 14 (Fagan and Tyler, 2005). The procedural justice benefits of the juvenile process, therefore, may be time limited.

Given the significant role that perceptions of procedural fairness play in legal socialization, it is important to understand how these perceptions manifest in adolescents. Fagan and Tyler's (2005) findings showed that adolescents' perceptions of procedural fairness are based on the degree to which they were given the opportunity to express their feelings or concerns, the neutrality and fact-based quality of the decision-making process, whether the youth was treated with respect and politeness, and whether the authorities appeared to be acting out of benevolent and caring motives. Fagan and Tyler (2005) discuss how ratings on these factors shape legitimacy, suggesting that one source of adolescent values is social experience with legal actors across a range of contexts, including police, school security personnel, and security staff in businesses and private, unregulated settings. Although these factors are in some ways similar to those that predict adults' perceptions of fairness, they take on special significance given adolescents' developmentally driven quest for autonomy as validated by a sense of being heard and sensitivity to fairness. Just as arbitrary enforcement of restrictive directives (authoritarian parenting) and avoidance of externally imposed rules (permissive parenting) are equally ineffective at instilling a sense of responsibility for actions in adolescents, neither the historic juvenile justice system, with its procedural shortcomings and crippled rehabilitative mission, nor the harsh criminal sanctions of the punitive era are likely to reinforce this important developmental lesson.

Importantly, research consistently shows (Tyler and Huo, 2002) that minority respondents have lower ratings of procedural justice than whites, and that these group differences reflect variant perceptions about fairness of the interactions as opposed to outcomes. Woolard and colleagues (2008) demonstrate that this pattern must be understood in a developmental context; their results indicate that older black adolescents anticipate less fair treatment in various justice contexts than younger black teens, and that anticipatory injustice about receiving help from a lawyer decreases with age among whites, but not for blacks.

One of the cardinal aims of juvenile justice policy is to promote respect for law and thereby reinforce inclinations toward a law-abiding way of life. Procedural justice theory and developmental research indicate that when adolescents feel that the system has treated them fairly, they are more likely to accept responsibility for their actions and embrace prosocial activities. A possible component of fairness may be timeliness and research exploring the implications of immediate consequences should be explored. Justice system practices that are perceived as unfair can have precisely the opposite effect, especially for adolescents, who tend to be especially sensitive to injustice by authority figures and to view their actions as illegitimate.

PROCEDURAL JUSTICE AND PERCEPTIONS OF FAIRNESS

Research on procedural justice and adolescents' perceptions of law and legal authority have significant implications for how key decisions should be made and how interactions between youth and legal actors should be structured in the juvenile justice system.

Adolescents become increasingly aware of obligations and consequences, and learning accountability, like other developmental tasks, needs to be understood as an ongoing process. When adolescents become involved in criminal activity, justice system personnel should view the ensuing proceedings as an opportunity for demonstrating the reciprocal obligations of the individual to respect the rights of others and to accept responsibility for wrongdoing and of the society to be fair and to respect the rights of those who may have offended. The importance of this developmental task suggests juveniles' interactions with justice system personnel, including police, judges, probation officers, and correctional agents, should in part be an exercise in moral education and positive legal socialization, designed to maximize the positive developmental impact of the intervention.

Police Contact and Arrest

Police interactions often provide youth with the earliest exposure to legal authorities. As observed in the research of Fagan and Tyler (2005), the negative observations and contacts that youth have with police may produce cynicism and undermine legal socialization. Researchers Ronald

Weitzer and Rod Brunson (2009) have identified several strategic responses youth employ to manage or reduce their interactions with police. Among them are systematic evasion, overt resistance with verbal or physical challenges, disregard for police commands, and resignation to perceived mistreatment. Minority youth, who tend to experience a significant share of police attention, hold more critical opinions of the police and are more likely to adopt protective responses, such as avoidance and resistance, than other groups (Woolard, Harvell, and Graham, 2008; Weitzer and Brunson, 2009). These negative reactions may be partly a result of the high rate of reports of verbal abuse, disrespect, excessive force, and unwarranted street stops experienced by minority young men compared with other groups (Weitzer and Tuch, 2002, 2006; Weitzer and Brunson, 2009). Minority youth are also socialized by peers, parents, and other community members, who urge them to avoid contact and conflict with the police (Weitzer and Brunson, 2009).

Strategies to improve police-youth relationships are necessary in light of this research. One potentially useful approach is training on adolescent development. For example, Strategies for Youth (SFY) has collaborated with the Psychiatry Department of Massachusetts General Hospital to provide assessments of individual police departments' youth–police interactions and context-specific training for police officers. These programs aim to translate research about adolescent development into practical skills for officers to use to improve and deescalate their interactions with youth (see http://www.strategiesforyouth.org). Although no evaluation of this training has yet been published, the services offered by SFY also include technical assistance and consultation, such as survey development and statistical analyses. Although the SFY website indicates that only three states require training of police officers in juvenile law and adolescent development, the development, implementation, and evaluation of such programs should be encouraged. (For an illustration of developmentally oriented policing, see Box 7-2.)

Another approach has been undertaken by the Philadelphia Police Department to build trust and reduce street-level conflict between police and youth, especially youth of color. Over the last decade, a multiagency working group of police leaders, public defenders, district attorneys, juvenile probation officers, and faith leaders have launched two significant initiatives: youth-focused training for new cadets in the Philadelphia Police Academy and Youth-Police Forums to facilitate dialogue between youth and local police officers.[2] The training curriculum for cadets focuses on

---

[2]Drawn from "Philadelphia Minority Youth-Law Enforcement Forums and Training Curriculum Case Study" (2012). Prepared by Alyssa Work and Yale Law School students in the Innovations in Policing Clinic. Paper on file with Professors Kristin Henning, Georgetown University School of Law, and James Forman, Yale Law School.

BOX 7-2
Developmentally Oriented Policing

How would a police officer's encounter with youth play out when shaped by a developmental perspective?

Depending on the reasons the youth comes to his or her attention, a police officer has available several referral strategies. For youth at risk of juvenile justice involvement or who are presenting problems to their parents, a police officer can refer the parents to a community-oriented and family-friendly program. The parents or guardian can access these referral programs by appointment or on a walk-in basis. In it their child receives an objective and thorough assessment and, on the basis of this assessment, the family members are referred to a number of available programs that address the needs of their child as well as the family.

The police officer brings a youth who is believed to have committed a crime to one central place where information on the youth is collected and verified. With the exception of youth who are perceived to be a danger to others, the youth is not handcuffed but instead is placed in pleasant surroundings with others for further processing and the arrival of a family member or other adult familiar with the youth and willing to take responsibility for him or her.

If the youth is a first-time nonviolent offender, the police officer issues a civil citation in lieu of turning the youth over to the juvenile justice

---

adolescent development, youth trauma, and effective strategies for communicating with youth. The youth–police forums seek to change the quality of low-level street contacts between youth and officers and reduce the likelihood that a street stop will escalate. The Philadelphia forums, held at schools, detention facilities, residential treatment centers, and community centers, provide youth with an opportunity to tell police how previous interactions with law enforcement affect their actions and allow officers to explain to teenagers how they are trained to respond to threats. These interactive exchanges lay the foundation for more productive police-community relationships by helping youth and police understand each other's motives and behaviors, altering negative perceptions, improving officers' responses to youth, and youth's reactions to police intervention.

Efforts to improve adolescents' perceptions of law, justice, and legal actors would be further enhanced by strategies that give youth a voice in reforming police practices and require police departments to model accountability for their own illegal or inappropriate behavior. Specifically, youth may benefit from a civilian complaint process that allows them to

system. The youth receives a structured assessment by a case manager who is not a law enforcement person. The case manager accesses the necessary welfare, health, and school records through an integrated management information system. The youth is asked about his or her daily activities and interests. An individual case plan that includes access to services and family, community, and school supports is developed. The family participates in the case plan's development and in monitoring the youth's progress, and the case manager follows up to ascertain the youth's level of participation. The case plan reflects restorative justice principles that call for accountability to the victim and positive youth development activities. If the youth completes the program successfully and commits no new offenses, the arrest is not recorded and no further action is required. There are consequences, including possible referral to the juvenile justice system, if the youth fails to comply with the plan or commits a new offense.

For youth who commit more serious crimes, the community has in place a system of graduated sanctions. The youth receives a validated risk/need assessment and, pending further disposition, is placed into the least restrictive placement setting (e.g., security level) that is consistent with community safety and his or her interests.

SOURCE: This section relies on information taken from Butts (2011) and Copeland (2011).

lodge complaints about police to a neutral body of citizens in an age-appropriate format (see Weitzer and Brunson, 2009). Other strategies to bolster perceptions of police legitimacy among apprehended youth include avoiding policing practices that rely on fear, control, and deterrence and encouraging police to explain their actions that have triggered complaints (Tyler, 2001).

Right to Counsel and Opportunity to be Heard

Accepting Lind and Tyler's (1988) core claim that children develop values and beliefs about the law and legal actors early in life and that these beliefs shape their behavior toward authority from adolescence through adulthood, it is likely that early youth–police interactions set the stage for how youth will perceive and interact with other actors in the juvenile justice system. After arrest, youth are often referred to the juvenile court for an intake assessment by the probation department and an arraignment and detention hearing before a judicial officer. In many jurisdictions, arraignment is the first opportunity for youth to have the assistance of counsel and to be heard regarding important pretrial decisions, such as alternatives to prosecution, pretrial detention, and conditions of release pending trial. As indicated by the research on procedural justice, youth and adults are more likely to accept the decisions of legal authorities and comply with the law when they experience the legal process as fair and respectful (see Woolard et al., 2008). Woolard and colleagues' (2008) findings that youth with more experience in the juvenile justice system are more likely to anticipate injustice compared with those with little or no experience suggest that improving perceptions of fairness is a major priority in juvenile justice reform.

Research involving adults indicates that litigants in legal proceedings evaluate fairness by opportunity for voice, validation, participation, choice, accuracy of outcomes, and access to information (Anderer and Glass, 2000; Fagan and Tyler, 2005; see also Tyler, 1990). Litigants have voice when they are given an opportunity to tell their story and express their own views and opinions before important decisions are made (Lind, Kanfer, and Earley, 1990). Validation goes further by ensuring not only that the litigant's story is heard, but also that the fact-finder has really listened to and considered his or her views. Meaningful participation in the legal process not only allows the litigant to feel like a valued member of society whose opinion is worthy of consideration, but also allows him or her to influence the judge's final decision and provides more confidence in the accuracy and legitimacy of the outcomes (see Lind, Kanfer, and Earley, 1990). In the juvenile justice system, the primary vehicle through which youth are afforded an opportunity to be heard and participate in the proceedings—from arrest through disposition—is the right to counsel. As a result, access to counsel and the quality of legal representation for accused youth merit special attention.

In the complex landscape of American juvenile courts, children need the assistance of a diligent and loyal advocate who will insist on substantive and procedural regularities and ensure that the child's voice is heard and validated at every stage of the juvenile justice process (see *In re Gault*). Yet as documented in multiple state assessments of the access to and quality of defense counsel for indigent youth, youth frequently appear without counsel or have inadequate representation in juvenile courts across the country (Mlyniec, 2008). Frequent waivers of the right to counsel, limited resources for defenders, high caseloads, and confusion about the appropriate role of youth's counsel and few opportunities for defender training are among the many challenges that impede effective advocacy for youth. When youth are represented by counsel, the lawyer is often appointed late in the juvenile justice process, leaving youth with little or no opportunity to be heard at the arraignment or detention hearing (Mlyniec, 2008). In some jurisdictions, counsel is not appointed until the day of trial, foreclosing any opportunity for the lawyer to meet with the client, investigate the facts, ascertain the client's views and meaningfully prepare to challenge the state's allegations (Mlyniec, 2008). In some jurisdictions, youth reported that they did not know their lawyer's name, had not been visited by their lawyer, and did not know how to get in touch with their lawyer (Mlyniec, 2008). Jurisdictions concerned about procedural justice, proper legal socialization, and developmentally appropriate strategies for holding youth accountable should alleviate barriers to timely appointment and effective representation by counsel.

Waiver of the Right to Counsel

Waiver of the right to counsel poses a significant barrier to a youth's opportunity to be heard and participate in delinquency proceedings. Although indigent youth in all 50 states have a statutory right to counsel in delinquency cases, the states vary widely in the accessibility of counsel. Mlyniec (2008) found that many youth who cannot afford to pay legal fees are denied court-appointed counsel by unreasonable eligibility criteria. For example, in Florida, youth must pay $40 just to apply for a determination of indigence and may be disqualified from appointed counsel if their parents have as little as $5 in the bank (National Juvenile Defender Center, 2006). In other states, youth are disqualified if their parents' income exceeds the federal poverty standard (Mlyniec, 2008, pp. 382-383). As evident in these examples, eligibility for appointed counsel is typically measured by the parents' financial status, even if the parent is unwilling to pay the fees.

Youth also face pressure from adults, such as parents, judges, or probation officers, to waive the right to counsel. Some parents encourage their children to waive counsel and plead guilty to avoid lengthy and expensive court proceedings, and others refuse to pay legal fees as punishment for the youth's alleged misconduct (Henning, 2006). Parents often fail to appreciate the risks associated with waiving counsel. As revealed in many state assessments, judges often do not thoroughly inquire into the validity of these waivers. In many jurisdictions, judges or probation officers encourage youth to waive counsel to expedite proceedings, save the jurisdiction money, or avoid the attorney's interference with the youth's treatment (Berkheiser, 2002, p. 581). Too often, these judges fail to discuss the consequences of waiving counsel or the value of having counsel to cross-examine government witnesses or present defense evidence (see, e.g., National Juvenile Defender Center, 2006). In some states, judges neglect to inform families that an attorney may be appointed at no cost to the youth and fail to advise the youth that a waiver must be voluntary (see, e.g., American Bar Association Juvenile Justice Center and Mid-Atlantic Juvenile Defender Center, 2002). In Louisiana, as many as 90 percent of youth waived their right to counsel (see, e.g., American Bar Association Juvenile Justice Center and Juvenile Justice Project of Louisiana, 2001, p. 60), and in many other states, including Florida, Georgia, and Kentucky, more than 50 percent of youth waived that right (see, e.g., American Bar Association Juvenile Justice Center and Southern Center for Human Rights, 2001, pp. 19-20; American Bar Association Juvenile Justice Center, 2002, p. 28; National Juvenile Defender Center, 2006, p. 28).

Youth often lack the cognitive and psychosocial capacity to knowingly, voluntarily, and intelligently waive counsel, given their limited knowledge of the law, impulsivity, and inadequate consideration of the long-term consequences. In order to alleviate the risks posed by adolescent waivers of counsel, state legislators should consider prohibiting waiver unless the child is allowed to consult with an attorney first (see, e.g., Md. Code. Ann. Cts. & Jud. Proc. § 3-8A-20, 2004; Tex. Fam. Code § 51.09; W. Va. Code § 49-5-9(a)(2)), establishing a rebuttable presumption against waiver of the right to counsel by juveniles (see, e.g., Md. Code. Ann. Cts. & Jud. Proc. § 3-8A-20, 2004), or precluding waiver altogether for youth under a certain age or in certain circumstances (Iowa Code Ann. § 232.11(2); Wis. Stat. § 938.23(1m)(a)). All states should require the juvenile court judge to notify youth of their rights and engage them in a comprehensive colloquy in age-appropriate language before accepting a youth's waiver (see, e.g., Fla. R. Juv. P. 8.165(b); Ky. Rev. Stat. Ann. § 610.060(2)(a)).

Investigation and Adjudication

The quality of representation a youth receives in the pretrial and adjudicatory phases may significantly impact his or her opportunity to be heard and perception of fairness. A lawyer who fails to investigate the factual allegations, declines to interview a client before the adjudicatory hearing, and neglects to file pretrial motions is unable to provide the youth with a meaningful voice in the proceedings. Lawyers in juvenile courts are often underresourced, overburdened by high caseloads, and untrained to adequately prepare for trial. Although the standard caseload recommended for delinquency cases is 200 cases per year (Spangenberg Group, 2001), defenders throughout the country may handle from 500 to 1,500 cases (see, e.g., American Bar Association Juvenile Justice Center et al., 2001; American Bar Association, 2002).

As a result of high caseloads and limited investigative support, defense attorneys are often unable to investigate cases or interview their clients in advance of the trial (Mlyniec, 2008). For example, in Maryland, most lawyers reported meeting their clients on the day of trial at the courthouse and not investigating the facts of the case or the underlying needs of the clients (American Bar Association Juvenile Justice Center and Mid-Atlantic Juvenile Defender Center, 2003). And 90 percent of youth interviewed for the

2003 assessment in Maryland reported not knowing their lawyer's name. In Indiana, more than half of the youth interviewed felt they did not have adequate time to consult with their lawyers (National Juvenile Defender Center and Central Juvenile Defender Center, 2006). In some counties in Washington, lawyers reported not using investigative support in any of their cases; statewide lawyers reported investigating only 50 percent of their cases (American Bar Association Juvenile Justice Center et al., 2003).

The paternalistic culture of the juvenile courtroom further interferes with zealous advocacy by juvenile lawyers during the pretrial and adjudicatory phases. For example, observers in Montana noted that zealous advocacy was met with hostility from judges, probation officers, and prosecutors, whereas other defenders who did not "rock the boat" were greeted positively (American Bar Association Juvenile Justice Center, 2003). In Kentucky, lawyers advocating for the "best interest of the child" engaged in little, if any, motions practice or trial preparation and did not seem to believe that delinquency cases warranted the use of investigators or experts (American Bar Association Juvenile Justice Center, 2002). Finally, in a nationwide survey conducted by the American Bar Association, only 30 percent of juvenile attorneys said they filed pretrial motions (Jones, 2004). To improve the quality of representation and enhance the youth's perception of justice, states must clarify the duties and obligations of juvenile defense counsel at every stage of the case. To this end, several states have adopted attorney practice standards that clearly delineate the lawyer's duties regarding investigation, client interviews, motions practice, and pretrial preparation (Burrell, 2012).

High Rates of Guilty Pleas

Meaningful participation in juvenile proceedings is often foreclosed to youth by the high rates of guilty pleas. Juvenile defenders face considerable systemic opposition to zealous advocacy of the child's stated interest and experience considerable pressure from judges and other legal actors to convince their clients to plead guilty (Mlyniec, 2008). As documented in a 2006 survey of juvenile courts, most juvenile cases are resolved by guilty pleas (Mlyniec, 2008). In Montana, for example, one judge reported that he only had 2-3 trials a year and defenders stated that cases rarely go to trial (American Bar Association Juvenile Justice Center, 2003). Although pleas will often be a favorable option for youth and may demonstrate their sense of accountability, they are often ill-informed about the decisions and implications of pleading guilty (see, e.g., Kaban and Quinlan, 2004). Lawyers fail to adequately explain options to the youth, and judges and lawyers speak to youth in complicated, legal language in client-counseling sessions and plea colloquies. Significant reforms are needed in the plea process to ensure that youth truly understand options available to them, have a meaningful choice about whether or not to plead guilty, and do not admit to having committed offenses they did not commit. At a minimum, client-counseling dialogues and plea colloquies should be conducted in age-appropriate language and youth should be afforded adequate time to understand information provided to them.

Appropriate Role of Counsel

The mere appointment of counsel does not ensure that youth will receive the quality representation to that which they are entitled, nor does it ensure that youth will have a meaningful opportunity to be heard in juvenile proceedings. Juvenile courts that are overly paternalistic have a crippling effect on the youth's right to participate. Too often, lawyers for juveniles see themselves as advocates for the youth's best interests instead of the youth's stated or expressed wishes or interests (e.g., American Bar Association Juvenile Justice Center, 2003). The lawyer may follow the views of parents or other adults, assuming that the youth lacks the capacity and good judgment to make important legal decisions in a delinquency case. In other cases, lawyers may subvert the youth's meaningful participation in decision making by withholding or manipulating information provided to the youth, controlling the content and sequence of meetings, limiting topics of conversation, or narrowing the alternatives from which the youth may choose (Henning, 2005). Attorneys may also undermine client autonomy and decision making by speaking in legalese, framing issues in a narrow and limiting fashion, or strategically arranging the list of options to exaggerate or emphasize negative or positive outcomes.

Lessons drawn from effective parenting styles (see Laursen and Collins, 2009) and fair family decision-making processes (see Fondacaro, Dunkle, and Pathak, 1998) are instructive for lawyers who must establish relationships with youth and parents in the juvenile justice system. Although parents are important allies for youth in a juvenile case, lawyers for juveniles must ensure that the parents' voice is not used to silence the youth. An attorney who defers entirely to the parent misses critical insight from the client, undermines the accuracy of juvenile court outcomes, and compromises the developmental value that would be gained from allowing the youth to meaningfully participate and be heard. The potential for conflicts of interest between youth and their parents further militates against allowing the parents' voice to substitute for that of the client (Henning, 2006).

Given Woolard and colleagues' (2008) findings that youth who anticipate they will not be treated fairly or receive help from their lawyers are less likely to comply with authorities, it is essential that lawyers become loyal and committed advocates who fairly represent the youth's voice in delinquency cases. Youth in the juvenile justice system generally have identifiable values and goals that are entitled to due weight and respect in court, especially as they relate to the issues of liberty and other important rights. Children as young as 10 or 12 will have the ability "to understand, deliberate upon, and reach conclusions about matters affecting [their] own well-being" (American Bar Association Model Rules of Professional Conduct R. 1.14 comment 1, 2012). Cognitive capacity varies widely among children and adolescents, and reasoned decision making is an acquired skill that varies according to context, experience, and instruction (see Steinberg et al., 2009). A youth who is well counseled in the trusting and safe environment of a lawyer's office may render thoughtful, well-reasoned insight even if he is likely to exercise poor judgment and make bad choices on the street or in peer-to-peer interactions (Henning, 2005; Steinberg et al., 2009a). The youth's decision-making capacity and voice may be enhanced by the lawyer's ability to create an appropriate environment for counseling, build rapport with the youth over time, engage the youth in one-on-one, age-appropriate dialogue, and repeat information as many times as the youth needs to hear it (Henning, 2005). By giving youth the opportunity to express views about important decisions in the juvenile justice system, lawyers may provide them with an opportunity to try on and enhance newly acquired decision-making skills and moral judgment (Buss, 2004). Respecting the youth's voice does not mean that he or she will be allowed to *decide* legal outcomes, only that they will be heard and meaningfully considered. Delinquency hearings are adversarial proceedings in which the judge makes the final decision about detention, innocence, and disposition. The youth's voice is but one of many in the court's calculus, but a concerted effort to elicit the youth's views and preferences promotes healthy legal socialization.

Disposition

The need for counsel and the opportunity to participate is no less important at the disposition hearing than at other stages of the case. As the Supreme Court noted in *Gault* (1967, p. 38) "in all cases children need advocates to speak for them and guard their interests, particularly when disposition decisions are made. . . . It is the disposition stage at which the opportunity arises to offer individualized treatment plans and in which the danger inheres that the court's coercive power will be applied without adequate knowledge of the circumstances." Reports across the country suggest that the quality of legal representation is especially uneven at the disposition stage. According to some reports, lawyers defer heavily to the views of juvenile probation officers and do little to bring the youth's voice and perspective to the court's attention (Mlyniec, 2008; see, e.g., American Bar Association Juvenile Justice Center and Mid-Atlantic Juvenile Defender Center, 2003).

The youth's opportunity to meaningfully participate in the disposition hearing is particularly relevant to his or her legal socialization and sense of accountability. Studies in the psychology of choice indicate that individuals who make choices for themselves engage more effectively in the rehabilitative process and with greater satisfaction (see Winick, 1998). Youth who design or actively participate in the development of their own treatment plans may have greater motivation to follow through and succeed (see Wexler, 2000). Paternalism, by contrast, is antitherapeutic because it breeds apathy, hinders motivation, and limits the potential for rehabilitation (see Winick, 1999). Thus, a youth who feels shut out or treated unfairly in a decision-making process that affects him or her may refuse to follow through with recommendations and court orders for counseling, probation meetings, curfew, and other treatment requirements made by a judge who has never heard or considered the youth's views (see Fagan and Tyler, 2005). Youth who anticipate that they will be treated unfairly in the legal system will also be less likely to disclose important information about themselves and their case (Woolard, Harvell, and Graham, 2008). Without critical insight from the youth, the diagnostic team assigned to develop the disposition plan is likely to rely on an inaccurate or incomplete picture of his or her needs.

It is particularly important to draw on the evidence summarized in Chapter 6 in designing and implementing developmentally oriented processes and dispositions in the juvenile justice system. For example, juvenile courts should involve families of youth at the disposition phase as constructively as possible to assist youth accept responsibility and to carry out whatever obligations are imposed by the court's dispositional order. Their opinions should be solicited regarding their needs, recommendations, and preferences for the youth's treatment. The youth's views should also be solicited during the proceedings (National Council of Juvenile and Family Court Judges, 2005, p. 135).

Postdisposition

Youth are held accountable long after the disposition hearing, yet they often lose the right to be heard after the disposition has been imposed. Lawyers frequently terminate representation after disposition and thus are not available to advise or advocate for youth in important postdisposition matters, such as probation revocation proceedings, appeals, early release from detention, or relief from poor conditions of confinement (Mlyniec, 2008). According to a state assessment in Indiana, for example, most juvenile attorneys believed their responsibility to clients ended after the disposition order was entered (Mlyniec, 2008). As a result, almost 57 percent of youth interviewed said they were not told of their right to appeal, and 77 percent said they did not discuss any possible issues on appeal. In Ohio, attorneys were not sure whether they had an obligation to provide postdisposition representation. And 41 percent of those interviewed claimed representation ended after the disposition hearing; 49 percent believed that representation continued until the disposition order was fulfilled. Given the rights at stake following disposition and the likely impact on the youth's perception of procedural justice, efforts should be made to ensure that youth are adequately represented from arrest through termination of juvenile court jurisdiction.

Measures of Perceived Fairness

Given the importance of the youth's perception of fairness, state offices of judicial administration should develop survey instruments and other qualitative methods for ascertaining the youth's attitudes toward and perceptions of the judicial process and experiences with the justice system. Once developed and evaluated, such survey measures can help juvenile courts assess an important aspect of system performance. Surveys of this kind are in their infancy and have some methodological issues to overcome (Henderson et al., 2010), but research to date is informing legal proceedings in the mental disabilities field (Swanson et al., 2006) and has potential for the juvenile justice field as well. Various national organizations, such as the National Center for State Courts and the National Conference of Juvenile and Family Court Judges, should help state courts develop and implement measures of perceived fairness.

In short, holding the youth accountable for his or her actions is a key aim of the juvenile justice system, one that should be examined closely, measured, and enhanced to make these interventions more developmentally appropriate and to enhance their effectiveness. As discussed earlier in the chapter, the same approach should be taken toward school discipline (see Box 7-1).

RECENT INNOVATIONS IN ACCOUNTABILITY

The committee attempted to identify innovations in juvenile court adjudication and other official disciplinary systems that have been grounded in a scientific understanding of legal socialization and moral development. Although initiatives by individual judges and attorneys were mentioned, the only two programmatic innovations that have been systematically implemented and evaluated are restorative justice programs and teen courts. We describe these activities below as promising illustrations of developmentally informed innovations, although it is premature to recommend either of them based on the current evidence. Developmentally informed training of law enforcement personnel, judges, and attorneys could also make an important contribution, but very little evidence now exists describing or evaluating such activities.

Restorative Justice Programs

A variety of juvenile justice programs have been developed under the rubric of "restorative justice" to encourage the development of account-ability on the part of juvenile offenders (Braithwaite, 1989; Bazemore and Umbreit, 1998; O'Brien, 2000) These programs, implemented in the United States and elsewhere, are aimed at involving the adolescent, the victims of crime, and the community in resolving the violation of community norms that has occurred. The use of restorative justice practices has been described as a "developmental aid" in promoting mature accountability. It does so by bringing the impact of one's behavior on other people into focus (as opposed to the abstract idea that the offense is "against the state"). Doing so is thought to promote deeper reflection on the injury to the victim and enhance motivation for change. These practices are comparable to those described as "scaffolding" from Vygotsky's theory on the zone of proximal development, which highlights the difference between what a learner can do without help and what a learner can do with help (Vygotsky, 1978). Sanctioning practices include victim–offender mediation and various com-munity decision-making or conferencing processes (Bazemore and Day, 2002). Community service is often integrated into this approach as a way for the adolescent to make amends for his or her criminal violation.

Proponents of restorative justice argue that this approach provides a strengths-based, experiential model for identity change, one that can pro-mote a realignment of self-image through reintegration into the community (Bazemore and Erbe, 2003). These proponents also highlight the potential for restorative justice practices to contribute to the recovery of victims who have been traumatized and to thereby reduce the risk of future offending by victims (Achilles and Zehr, 2001). The argument is that when offenders are held accountable in an integrative, prosocial way, *constructive accountabil-ity* serves both the offender's and the victim's needs. The general principles guiding the restorative justice movement (accountability, community safety, and competency development) have often been adopted as guidelines for orienting broader systems of juvenile justice. In many states, the principles of balanced and restorative justice have been adopted to guide program development, probation practice, and court dispositions (Office of Juvenile Justice and Delinquency Prevention, 1997a). Adopting these principles has often shifted the emphasis of the juvenile justice system toward more of a concern with community involvement and alternative interventions, focus-ing more on adolescent skill development than on more sanction-oriented approaches (Griffin, 2006).

Restorative justice programs are philosophically compatible with the general approach to juvenile justice reform envisioned in this report. Among the aims of holding adolescents accountable for their wrongdoing is inculcating fundamental norms of social morality, including the obligations to respect the rights and interests of the community, to take personal responsibility for one's conduct, and to rectify any harms that one may have caused to others.

Restorative justice programs appear to represent laudable efforts to operationalize these principles without relying on the concepts and practices of punishment. However, evaluating the impact of restorative justice interventions is difficult, given that it is not totally clear what constitutes a restorative justice program. A variety of interventions go under this name because they are guided by the general principles of this approach. However, whether a family conferencing meeting, for example, is following procedures that meet these guidelines is difficult to determine, because these standards are not rigorously defined. Moreover, restorative justice approaches may include a number of different specific elements (e.g., victim conferences, restitution, making amends), and which of these constitute the core elements of this approach are not specified. Thus, it is not surprising that randomized controlled studies (in which data are analyzed based on assignment rather than completion of programs to eliminate effects of self-selection) of the effectiveness of restorative justice interventions have generated mixed findings.

A summary of 36 direct comparisons (including six studies involving juvenile offenders) of restorative justice practices to conventional criminal justice practices indicates that restorative justice reduces repeat offending for some offenders, but not all (Sherman and Strang, 2007). The evidence reviewed in this summary suggests that restorative justice interventions are more likely to reduce future offending and improve outcomes for victims when they are focused on the kinds of offenses that have an individual victim who can be invited to meet with the offender and when they are focused on violent crime. Given that the examinations of restorative justice have involved small, randomized trials, there is a key evidence gap on its scaling up. It is unclear what would happen if restorative justice were delivered on a widespread basis, rather than in small pilot groups that affect a small fraction of cases in any local justice system.

Aside from its focus on changing behavior (to reduce recidivism), participation in restorative justice programs and conferences has ancillary effects on offender attitudes (see Umbreit et al., 2011, p. 276). In a review of four face-to-face restorative justice conferences in Australia and the United Kingdom, Strang and colleagues (2006) reported significant changes in victim and offender attitudes and emotions in the periods before and after the conference. Finally, in their review of restorative justice throughout the world, Sherman and Strang (2007) noted that restorative justice conferences provided victims and offenders with more satisfaction with justice than traditional criminal justice experiences and further that restorative justice conferences reduced the desire among crime victims for violent revenge. Additional research on the impact of these programs on legal socialization is warranted.

Teen Courts

Teen courts offer a dispositional alternative to the traditional juvenile justice system in which the juvenile offenders' teenage peers hear facts surrounding the incident, deliberate, and determine a disposition, which often includes community service or alcohol or drug treatment. They are based on the assumption that adolescents are more likely to be influenced by their peers as opposed to adult authority figures in the formal juvenile justice system (Butts and Buck, 2000). The well-documented finding that one of the strongest predictors of future acts of delinquency is the presence of delinquent peer associations (Snyder, Horsch, and Childs, 1997; Brendgen et al., 1999; Houtzager and Baerveldt, 1999; Newcomb et al., 1999) speaks to the role that peers play in socializing youth and provides the basis for the idea that peer pressure can be used to not only reinforce young people's delinquent behavior, but also to lead them out of delinquency. In this way, teen courts are designed to circumnavigate the pitfalls associated with adolescents' hypersensitivity to fairness and dominating perceptions of being mistreated by those in positions of authority (Matsueda, 1988) and to capitalize on the adolescents' desire for peer acceptance and approval.

Definitive studies about teen court outcomes have not been conducted (Butts et al., 2012), although there are numerous examples of positive results from teen court evaluations (Minor et al., 1999; Harrison, Maupin, and Mays, 2000; Garrison, 2001; LoGalbo and Callahan, 2001; Patrick and Marsh, 2005). Results are positive even when evaluations have included repeat offenders (Butts, Buck, and Coggeshall, 2002; Forgays and DeMilio, 2005; Forgays, 2008; see Harrison et al., 2000, for opposite findings), although the risk of recidivism has been found to increase with amount of time postcompletion (Rasmussen, 2004). However, the selection process of teen court participants has been shown to be biased (see Lanthier, 2006) in ways that could skew the results on the effectiveness of teen court participation. For example, Lanthier (2006) found that family status in the community was the strongest significant predictor of referral to teen court. Other factors would no doubt be fairer determinants of teen court placement, and they might also be more predictive of success. Smith and Blackburn (2011) argue that referrals of youth should instead be based on the likelihood that they will respond to positive peer influence, and they have begun to develop a tool to identify youth who are more likely to succeed in a teen court setting; more research is needed, however, to evaluate both the psychometric properties and the predictive validity of this screening tool. Of note, Smith and Blackburn (2011) found that younger teen court participants had more positive perceptions about peer influence and teen court than older participants, which could be due to developmental characteristics or a greater likelihood that older youth have more delinquent peer associations. Research is needed to evaluate whether older youth are more likely than younger youth to offend after teen court, and, if this is found to be true, the factors that mediate this relationship, so that those youth who are more likely to succeed in a teen court setting can be identified in advance by fair and accurate methods.

SUMMARY

Contemporary law reforms emphasize the importance of holding juveniles accountable for their criminal offenses. This is not a new theme—advocates for punitive reforms criticized the traditional juvenile court for its failure to hold youth accountable and aimed to correct this supposed deficiency. However, accountability does not require a moral model of retributive justice, as many advocates of "get-tough" policies seemed to assume. To be sure, accountability requires taking responsibility for one's own behavior and undertaking corrective action, but it does not entail the condemnatory messages and labels associated with "criminal" responsibility. Nor does holding youth accountable necessarily entail the use of confinement and other explicitly punitive sanctions.

Condemnation, control, and confinement—the identifying attributes of criminal punishment—are not necessary features of accountability for juveniles, do not deter or prevent reoffending, and should be avoided except in rare instances. Confinement ("serving time") should not be used, in itself, as an instrument of accountability in the juvenile justice system, although courts may sometimes find it necessary to restrain youth who pose a high risk of harming others or themselves or to use short-term detention for the purpose of deterring and responding to serious offending.

Interventions aiming to hold youth accountable must be firm and fair and informed by developmental knowledge, designed to improve the youth's future prospects rather than harming them. In short, juvenile justice must focus on the harm that the juvenile may have caused without harming the juvenile in response.

Developmental knowledge also suggests that the principle of accountability itself, if carefully implemented, can play a role in reducing juvenile offending—an important function not linked to accountability in earlier periods. This chapter has shown that being held accountable for one's wrongdoing and accepting responsibility for it are integral to the normal processes of social learning, moral development, and legal socialization during adolescence. If designed and implemented in a developmentally informed way, procedures for holding adolescents accountable for their offending by the juvenile justice system and other disciplinary authorities can promote positive moral development and promote respect for law. It must also be recognized, however, that processes of juvenile accountability, if perceived by youth as unfair, can reinforce social disaffection and negative attitudes toward law and legal authority. Thus, it is essential that police officers and other legal actors interact with youth in a way that is fair, inclusive, and respectful and that juvenile courts employ decision-making processes that provide youth with a meaningful opportunity to participate and be heard. Ensuring genuine access to developmentally informed counsel is an essential element of a reformed juvenile justice system. Designing and implementing effective mechanisms of accountability is one of the key challenges of juvenile justice reform in the 21st century. Several recent reforms based on developmental principles, such as restorative justice programs and teen courts, have yielded promising results, and further innovation is indicated.

Every aspect of the justice system's interactions with the adolescent— from a street encounter with a police officer through intake, petition, adjudication, disposition, and discharge from court supervision—should be viewed through a developmental lens. Throughout the process, juvenile justice professionals affect the youth's legal socialization and moral development through their demeanor, their framing of the legal situation, and their interactions with the youth and the family. The formal process of adjudicating wrongdoing and holding adolescents accountable for their wrongful choices can, if carried out properly, foster and reinforce the achievement of key developmental tasks, thereby nurturing healthy legal socialization and reduce the likelihood of future offending.

By emphasizing the importance of the processes of juvenile accountability, we do not mean to denigrate the formal events of the judicial process. To the contrary, the finding of guilt on the delinquency petition is a solemn and developmentally significant event. So too are the court's dispositional orders and any hearings that may subsequently be required to monitor and enforce compliance. If detention or custodial placement is ordered, the experience of a loss of freedom can have a penetrating impact on the identity and self-image of the youth. As noted earlier, however, these formal tools of accountability should be used as instruments of legal socialization and moral development, not as instruments of punishment.

8

Reducing Racial/Ethnic Disparities

A decade ago the National Research Council and Institute of Medicine report *Juvenile Crime, Juvenile Justice* pointed out that there were "major disparities in the extent of involvement of minority youth, particularly black youth, compared with white youth in the juvenile justice system" (2001, p. 228). A number of assessments over the ensuing decade continued to document this overrepresentation of minority youth, especially African Americans, in the juvenile justice system (Engen, Steen, and Bridges, 2002; Bishop, 2005; Lauritsen, 2005; Bishop and Leiber, 2012). Such overrepresentation immediately raises at least two types of concerns. First, this circumstance raises questions of bias, fairness, and legitimacy regarding the functioning of the justice system. Second, it raises questions about the larger life-course trajectories of many youth in minority communities who may become marked by criminal records early in life.

In part for these reasons, the question of disproportionate minority involvement has been an explicit federal policy priority. Congress first gave attention to racial disparities in 1988 when it amended the Juvenile Justice and Delinquency Prevention Act (JJDPA) of 1974 (P.L. 93-415, 42 U.S.C. 5601 *et seq.*) to require states that received formula funds from the Office of Juvenile Justice and Delinquency Prevention (OJJDP) to ascertain the proportion of minority youth detained in secure detention facilities, secure correctional facilities, and lockups compared with the general population and, if the number of minority youth was disproportionate, to develop and implement plans to reduce the disproportionate representation (Section 223(a)(23)). In 1992, the JJDPA was amended. Disproportionate minority confinement was made a core requirement, and 25 percent of a state's formula funds could be withheld if states did not comply. In 2002, Congress again modified the disproportionate minority confinement requirement and mandated states to implement juvenile delinquency prevention efforts and system improvement efforts designed to reduce, without establishing or requiring numerical standards or quotas, the disproportionate number of juvenile members of minority groups who come into contact with the juvenile justice system (P.L. 107-273, Sec. 12209). Thus, the disproportionate minority contact (DMC) core requirement was broadened from "confinement" to "contact," and states were required to implement strategies aimed at reducing disproportionality (Office of Juvenile Justice and Delinquency Prevention, 2009a). See Chapter 10 for a detailed description of OJJDP's DMC activities.

Public and scholarly discussions about race/ethnic inequities and the role they play in the genesis of antisocial and criminal behavior and in shaping societal responses have a very long history (Hawkins and Kempf-Leonard, 2005, p. 3). Given the long-standing discussions over race/ethnicity in the United States more generally (National Research Council, 2001a), it is not surprising that discussions oriented around race/ethnicity[1] and crime are among the most contentious of all (Sampson and Wilson, 1995; Kennedy, 2001; Peterson and Krivo, 2009).

Despite a research and policy focus on this matter for more than two decades, remarkably little progress has been made on reducing the disparities themselves or in reaching scholarly consensus on the root source of these disparities (National Research Council and Institute of Medicine, 2001). Volumes of data documenting disparities have been collected, but comparatively little progress has been made in addressing the problem (Kempf-Leonard, 2007; Piquero, 2008a; Bishop and Leiber, 2012). Thus, one assessment (Bell and Ridolfi, 2008, p. 15) observed with considerable irony:

> There's been a lot of motion but little movement in the last two decades. This inherited culture of the lowest common denominator in disparities

---

[1]Throughout this chapter and throughout the report, we have chosen to link race/ethnicity together because their definitions are often overlapping. The Office of Management and Budget recognizes a minimum of five racial categories: white, black (or African American), American Indian or Alaskan Native, Asian, and Native Hawaiian or other Pacific Islander. It also recognizes at least two ethnicities: Hispanic or Latino and non-Hispanic or Latino. People who identify themselves as Hispanic, Latino, or Spanish can be of any race. These racial/ethnic categories were also included in the 2010 decennial census. But an analysis of census data had this to say about the racial groupings: "The race categories included in the census questionnaire generally reflect a social definition of race recognized in this country and are not an attempt to define race biologically, anthropologically, or genetically. In addition, it is recognized that the categories of the race question include race and national origin or sociocultural groups" (Humes, Jones, and Ramirez, 2011, p. 2).

reduction has resulted in a class of decision makers who could have significant impact on racial and ethnic disparities, but are unmotivated to do so. Instead, they make-up a multi-million dollar cottage industry whose primary activity is to restate the problem of disparities, in essence, endlessly adoring the question of what to do about DMC, but never reaching an answer.

Several reasons can be identified as a means of understanding the lack of movement on this issue, including, but not limited to, lack of motivation, lack of cross-system collaboration, inadequate resources, and the extreme difficulties of disentangling the many complex, multilevel and interrelated factors that contribute to this problem (Kempf-Leonard, 2007; Bell and Ridolfi, 2008; Bell et al., 2009; Nellis and Richardson, 2010; Parsons-Pollard, 2011). Some observers have suggested that lack of progress may be related to the deeper continuing problem of racial injustice in American society. The current period has been characterized as a time of "laissez-faire racism," in which a "more covert, sophisticated, cultured-centered and subtle racist ideology, qualitatively less extreme and more socially permeable than Jim Crow racism," is influencing American culture and politics (Bobo, 2011, p. 15). Whatever the reason, a discomfort in discussing race and racial inequities noted by the National Academies a decade ago does not appear to have changed significantly (National Research Council and Institute of Medicine, 2001, p. viii).

In effect, racial disproportionality (and race generally) has become the elephant in the room: most people concede that racial disparities pose a huge problem but are reluctant to candidly discuss their underlying causes and possible remedies.

Several thorough reviews of the literature on racial/ethnic disparities in the juvenile justice system have been published (National Research Council and Institute of Medicine, 2001; Pope et al., 2002; Leiber, 2003; Bishop, 2005; Hawkins and Kempf-Leonard, 2005; Piquero, 2008a; Bishop and Leiber, 2012). Instead of presenting another detailed review, this chapter briefly summarizes the problem, reviews the two main frameworks that have been used to understand and explain the problem (differential offending and differential selection), and then addresses a variety of factors that may contribute to both offending and the juvenile system's response to it.

DEFINITIONS

The conceptual and definitional challenges associated with racial/ethnic differences in general (National Research Council, 2001a) are evident in the context of juvenile and criminal justice. The terms oft-associated with DMC are "disproportionate representation" (or disparity) and "discrimination" (or bias).[2] On one hand, *disproportionate (minority) representation*, or disproportionality, occurs when a minority group (historically the research has centered on black youth) comprises a far greater percentage of persons in the juvenile justice system than their numbers in the general population would predict. According to Bishop (2005, pp. 24-25), *disparity* is used to denote between-group differences in outcomes, irrespective of their origins. (Disparity might stem from differences in offending, from laws or policies that differentially impact minority youth, or from racism in the juvenile justice system.) If defined in this neutral way, the committee regards "disproportionate representation" and "disparity" as interchangeable terms. On the other hand, *discrimination* refers to "situations in which evidence suggests that extralegal or illegitimate factors are the cause of disparate justice system outcomes" (National Research Council, 2001, pp. 230-231; for other variants, see Walker et al., 2000, pp. 14-18).

Definitions take one only so far, however, and there are important distinctions to consider. For example, disparity, particularly large and persistent disparity, is often interpreted as indicative of unfair or illegitimate processes at work. It is critical analytically to stress that not all statistical disproportion is an immediate indicator of bias or discrimination. However, particularly in the domain of juvenile justice and when matters of race/ethnicity are concerned, persistent disparity should be taken as a strong signal that some underlying problematic circumstance and process are operating, whether or not direct race bias is the cause. Taking this concept one step further, when there is evidence that racial disparities are systematic and intentional, then they can be considered racial inequities (Chapin Hall Center for Children, 2009).[3]

MINORITY YOUTH INVOLVEMENT IN
THE JUVENILE JUSTICE SYSTEM

Researchers typically draw on three possible sources of data to gauge the extent of minority[4] youth involvement in crime and delinquency: official

---

[2]The term "disproportionate minority contact" is used to describe the disproportionate number of minority youth at various stages of processing in the juvenile justice system (Office of Juvenile Justice and Delinquency Prevention, 2009a, 2009b). Throughout the report, we use "racial disparities" to refer to racial/ ethnic disparities more generally and use DMC when it is common usage, for example, associated with OJJDP's core requirement or in a program initiative by the government or other organization, such as the MacArthur Foundation's Model for Change DMC Action Network.

[3]A very helpful graphic presentation of the relationship of disproportionality, disparities, and factors leading to disparity, can be found in Chapin Hall Center for Children (2009, p. 32).

[4]The term "minority" is not being used as a proxy for black or African American but is used when the term applies to minorities more broadly. The term "black or African American" is used when the statement applies specifically to that racial group.

statistics on arrests, criminal victimization surveys of the population, and self-report surveys and questionnaires administered to youth. Each potential source of data has limitations.

Official Records

We begin with a consideration of official statistics on juvenile arrests based on the Federal Bureau of Investigation's Uniform Crime Reports (UCR). (See Chapter 3 for a discussion of juvenile crime arrest data.) Table 8-1 reports official arrest results for people under age 18 by race for the year 2009, the most recent period for which these data were available to the committee. These results show disproportionate black arrests in most categories of offenses. The overrepresentation of black youth is greatest for violent crimes, particularly for homicide and manslaughter and for robbery. For homicide and manslaughter, black youth represent 58 percent of those arrested in 2009, although only 16 percent of youth under age 18 are in this age category. Similarly, blacks constitute 67 percent of those arrested for robbery.

Disproportionate arrests remain the pattern for black youth in most of the property crime offenses, although the extent of overrepresentation relative to their share of the total youth population is smaller. Thus, black youth constituted 37 percent of burglary arrests and 43 percent of motor vehicle thefts though only 16 percent of all youth. These percentages are half the extent of overrepresentation seen in some of the violent crime data.

Two further points are worthy of note. The one category in which black youth are underrepresented relative to their share of all youth is that of alcohol violations (6 percent of arrests). This is also the one type of offense for which white youth tend to be overrepresented. In addition, the degree of black overrepresentation is at its lowest in the category of drug abuse violations, in which blacks make up roughly 26 percent of youth arrests.

These data consistently show that there are important differences by race in rates of arrest—especially across offense type, with black youth arrested for violent index crimes at much higher rates than whites (Bishop, 2005; Bales and Piquero, 2012). These disparities tend to be smaller (but tend to persist) for property crime rates, with white rates being higher, on average, for other offenses, such as vandalism and offenses involving alcohol. The UCR does not produce data for offending rates across ethnic groups so, as a result, there is no official national arrest information relating to Hispanics—thus similar comparisons cannot be made between Hispanics and other racial/ethnic groups. Turning to the postarrest official data, blacks have higher rates than whites for ensuing juvenile and criminal justice decision stages, such as being referred to court, detained, formally

TABLE 8-1 Arrest of People Under 18 Years of Age by Offense Charged and Race, 2009

	White	Black	American Indian or Alaskan Native	Asian or Pacific Islander	Total
Population Under 18	57,563,627 (77.2)	12,045,688 (16.2)	1,081,363 (1.5)	3,857,537 (5.2)	74,548,218 (100)
Total Arrests	993,428 (65.9)	472,929 (31.3)	18,766 (1.2)	23,427 (1.6)	1,508,550 (100)
Murder and nonnegligent manslaughter	380 (40.4)	546 (58.0)	8 (0.9)	7 (0.7)	941
Forcible rape	1,501 (63.4)	818 (34.5)	19 (0.8)	30 (1.3)	2,368
Robbery	7,854 (31.1)	16,968 (67.3)	112 (0.4)	292 (1.2)	25,226
Aggravated assault	21,790 (55.4)	16,694 (42.4)	394 (1.0)	463 (1.2)	39,341
Burglary	36,073 (60.9)	22,082 (37.3)	511 (0.9)	571 (1.0)	59,237
Larceny/theft	164,701 (65.0)	80,670 (31.8)	3,148 (1.2)	4,948 (2.0)	253,467
Motor vehicle theft	8,454 (54.0)	6,765 (43.2)	234 (1.5)	213 (1.4)	15,664
Arson	3,222 (76.7)	865 (20.6)	56 (1.3)	60 (1.4)	4,203
Alcohol violations	98,113 (89.6)	6,946 (6.3)	3,105 (2.8)	1,343 (1.2)	109,507
Drug abuse violations	97,232 (72.4)	34,295 (25.6)	1,212 (0.9)	1,468 (1.1)	134,207
Weapons offenses	16,190 (60.7)	9,938 (37.3)	210 (0.8)	328 (1.2)	26,666

NOTE: Percentages in parentheses.
SOURCE: Federal Bureau of Investigation (2010).

charged, adjudicated delinquent, and placed out of the home (Bishop, 2005).

A second source of data is the Relative Rate Index (RRI), which was developed by OJJDP in order to measure disparity at each decision point in the system: arrest, court referral, diversion, detention, petitions/charge filing, transfer to adult court, delinquency findings, probation, and secure confinement.[5] Table 8-2 breaks down these processing stages by race. RRI data can be easily calculated on the basis of readily available data maintained by some states. Feyerherm (2011) recently examined RRI data from OJJDP's DMC website that included information from 1,043 jurisdictions (47 states and 996 substate jurisdictions, mainly counties). Based on these data, one is able to ascertain patterns among Hispanic youth and compare them to black and white youth. For example, RRI data suggest that Hispanic youth experience greater contact with the juvenile justice system than do white youth and that the extent of these differences (disparities) is not as great as those experienced in general by black youth (Feyerherm, 2011, p. 46).

These official records generate useful information, but they also suffer from some notable limitations (see Chapter 3). For example, official data and associated record-keeping systems are complex and not wholly integrated or infallible. For example, processing data may not be integrated with data from other child-serving systems with which the youth may have had contact or from which he or she may have been referred. Moreover, official records are contingent on the justice system responding to some action or call for service. Thus, official records do not include a large amount of criminal behavior that goes undetected and does not come to the attention of the formal justice system. Also as indicated above, the UCR data collection system treats race/ethnicity as two distinct characteristics and does not provide a means for identifying non-Hispanic and Hispanic members of different racial groups (Feyerherm, 2011, p. 46). This not only leads to difficulty in comparing arrest trends but also obfuscates the RRI because "arrest numbers cannot easily be traced into the juvenile justice system to follow the cumulative impacts of arrest, referral, detention, etc." (Feyerherm, 2011, p. 47).

An additional problem with the RRI calculations is that they do not come with any sort of statistical significance measure; thus, there is no way to measure whether an RRI of 1.0 is statistically significant—much

---

[5]Specifically, the RRI consists of three components: (1) a system map describing the major contact points or stages at which a juvenile may have additional contact or penetration into the justice system, (2) a method for computing rates of activity (by race/ethnicity) at each of the stages, and (3) a method to compare the rates of contact for different demographic groups at each of those stages (Feyerherm, Snyder, and Villarruel, 2009; Feyerherm, 2011, p. 37).

TABLE 8-2 The Processing of Juveniles by Race, 2008

	White	Black	American Indian or Alaskan Native	Asian or Pacific Islander	Total
Population Ages 10-17	25,251,300 (77.4)	5,437,700 (16.5)	455,700 (1.4)	1,549,000 (4.7)	32,963,700 (100)
Arrested	1,246,900 (66.7)	574,600 (30.8)	21,900 (1.2)	26,200 (1.3)	1,868,600
Arrest rate per 100,000 in population	4,886	10,567	4,806	1,637	
Relative risk black:white = 2.1:1					
Referred to Courts	1,043,600 (63.1)	563,500 (34.1)	23,500 (1.4)	22,700 (1.4)	1,653,300
Referral rate per 100,000 in population	4,089	10,363	5,157	1,465	
Relative risk black:white = 2.5:1					
Detained	194,100 (55.8)	143,300 (41.2)	5,300 (1.5)	5,100 (1.5)	347,800
Detention rate per 100,000 in population	761	2,635	1,163	329	
Relative risk black:white = 3.5:1					
Formally Charged	554,800 (60.0)	342,000 (37.0)	14,400 (1.6)	13,200 (1.4)	924,400
Petition rate per 100,000 in population	2,174	6,289	3,160	852	
Relative risk black:white = 2.9:1					
Adjudicated Delinquent	350,900 (62.2)	194,900 (34.6)	10,100 (1.8)	8,000 (1.4)	563,900
Adjudication rate per 100,000 in population	1,375	3,584	2,216	516	
Relative risk black:white = 2.6:1					
Placed Out of Home	91,000 (57.7)	61,500 (39.0)	3,200 (2.0)	2,000 (1.3)	157,700
Placement rate per 100,000 in population	357	1,131	702	129	
Relative risk black:white = 3.2:1					

NOTE: Percentages in parentheses.
SOURCE: Puzzanchera and Adams (2011a).

less whether an RRI of 1.38 is significantly different from an RRI of 2.53. As a result, these sorts of official statistics provide limited leverage on the larger question of disproportionate minority youth contact with the juvenile justice system.

Self-Report and Victimization Data

Other sources of racial/ethnic disparities emerge from data on offending patterns. Lauritsen's (2005) review of this line of work was based on victim reports from the National Crime Victimization Survey (NCVS) and a series of self-report surveys that gathered individual-level reports of offending. The analysis showed that "the most commonly occurring crimes exhibited few group differences, while more rare and serious crimes of violence showed generally higher levels of black and Latino involvement" (Lauritsen, 2005, p. 99). Thus, the salient message from Lauritsen's review is that data on youth violence are comparable across reporting sources because the same general patterns have emerged for the most serious but least common offenses (Lauritsen, 2005, p. 100). At the same time, an important difference emerged in relation to drug abuse violations. Lauritsen (2005, p. 96) reports that black youth are disproportionately involved in such offenses as measured via official records, whereas self-report data indicate that white youth report higher levels of drug abuse violations.

Similar to the Lauritsen study but using both UCR and self-report data sets, Piquero and Brame (2008) found little evidence of racial/ethnic differences in either self-reported offending (either in the frequency of offending or in the variety of offending) or officially based arrests leading to a court referral in the year preceding study enrollment.

Both victim and self-report data suffer from problems similar to those that plague official records. For example, the race/ethnicity of the offender may not be known in victim and self-report data. Furthermore, victim survey data are limited to the main race categories of black, white, and other. Self-report data suffer from both over- and underreporting, and these tendencies may vary across racial/ethnic groups. They are often collected from high school or general population samples, a practice that tends to limit reports of serious violence. Finally, there have been few comparisons of self-reports across racial/ethnic groups (Huizinga et al., 2007; Piquero and Brame, 2008), few data collection efforts focused on Hispanics (Maldonado-Molina et al., 2009), and even fewer studies examining the relationship of immigration status to offending (Lee, Martinez, and Rosenfeld, 2001; Nielsen, Lee, and Martinez, 2005; Bersani, 2012).

Research on the factors that might affect DMC at the police contact and court referral levels also has employed both official and self-report data with a common set of delinquency measures across data sources (on violence, property, weapons, and drug offenses). Huizinga and colleagues (2007) used data from the three delinquency studies in Pittsburgh, Pennsylvania; Rochester, New York; and Seattle, Washington, to examine DMC and the factors that might affect it at the police contact and court referral levels.

First, in all three cities, African American youth had the highest rate of contact/referral, and it was significantly greater than for white youth. Hispanics in Rochester had a significantly higher rate than whites; in Seattle, Asian American youth had a slightly higher rate of contact/referral compared with whites. These results were replicated in overall crime figures. Second, when the researchers examined race/ethnic differences in self-reported offending, they found that minority youth did exhibit higher self-reported offending than whites, but the differences were not so pronounced as they were with the official record data. In general, minority–white differences in the official record comparisons were roughly double what they were for the self-reported offending estimates. Thus, differences in self-reported offending were not able to completely eliminate the effects of race/ethnicity on official criminal records (Huizinga et al., 2007, p. 32). Third, Huizinga and colleagues examined the effect of race/ethnicity on contact/referral in the juvenile justice system after controlling for self-reported offending. Results from this analysis indicated that, across virtually all comparisons, although controlling for self-reported offending was itself significantly associated with official contact, it did not eliminate (nor very much reduce) any direct effect for race/ethnicity.

In sum, these results show that self-reported offending does not explain the differential rates of juvenile justice system contact by race/ethnicity.[6] When a risk factor composite (e.g., socioeconomic status, family structure, academic performance) was added to assess whether inclusion of this additional measure altered the significant race/ethnicity effect on official record representation, once again, with one exception (Pittsburgh), the results held: although both self-reported offending and the risk factor composite were significantly associated with disproportionate involvement as measured by official records, controlling for the risk factor composite did not affect the still-significant effect for race/ethnicity on official records (Huizinga et al. (2007).

Similarly, Bersani (2012) used self-report data from the National Longitudinal Survey of Youth 1997 (NLSY97) and official crime reports to

---

[6]Only a few other studies have examined self-reported delinquency and subsequent juvenile justice processing (Huizinga and Elliott, 1987, in the National Youth Survey; Fergusson, Horwood, and Swain-Campbell, 2003, in Australia; and Piquero and Brame, 2008, in the Research on Pathways to Desistance study). Although these studies contain longitudinal data, the methodological approaches thus far have not made explicit use of the longitudinal data in order to examine the racial disparity question in a developmental manner.

conduct trajectory analyses that examined immigrant offending histories from early adolescence to young adulthood. Her findings showed that first-generation immigrants had lower rates of criminal involvement compared to native-born persons. In fact, violence and drug crimes were virtually non-existent among first-generation immigrants while second-generation immigrants evinced offending patterns similar to native-born persons. These findings are consistent with those of other studies using other data sources that report a crime-suppression effect of immigrant concentration on crime rates even in areas marked by concentrated disadvantage (Lee et al., 2001; Nielsen et al., 2005; Sampson et al., 2005).

Reviews of DMC Research

A number of assessments over the years make it clear that minority youth are disproportionately represented in the system. Several recent careful reviews, in particular, have found that "race matters" beyond the characteristics of an offense. One recent major assessment that took stock of 72 quantitative studies of DMC had three major results (Cohen et al., 2011). First, it found that the vast majority of studies (82 percent) found some race effect that disadvantaged minority youth relative to white youth. Second, the evidence for race effects was greatest at earlier stages of the process, particularly at the stages of arrest, referral to court, and placement in secure detention. Third, although black youth are most likely to be disadvantaged, this is not uniformly the case and similar patterns tend to emerge for Hispanic youth as well.

Their review covered studies conducted in 2002-2010 on the official processing of minority youth at nine different decision points in the juvenile justice system (arrest, court referral, delinquency findings, detention, diversion, petition/charge filings, probation, secure confinement, and transfer to adult court). (Note: some decision points have been more intensively studied than others; i.e., arrest has been less thoroughly studied than the secure confinement decision and white-black disparities have been studied more often than others.) The analysis shows that the majority of reviewed studies indicated some race effects in the processing of minority youth, with the majority of those studies reporting mixed results (for some minority youth or at some processing points but not others). Black males were more likely to receive harsh treatment than females or whites, and minority youth, on average, were more likely to receive harsh treatment for certain but not all offenses. At the same time, the analysis also indicates a lower race effect in formal court processing, adjudication, and postadjudication.

In nearly all juvenile justice systems youth of color also remain in the system longer than white youth. From 2002 to 2004, although black youth accounted for approximately 17 percent of the youth population, they represented 28 percent of juvenile arrests, 37 percent of the detained population, 38 percent of those in secure placement, and 58 percent of youth committed to state adult prison (National Council on Crime and Delinquency, 2007, p. 3; The Sentencing Project, 2010, p. 1). Furthermore, 2008 case processing data for delinquency offenses from the Office of Juvenile Justice and Delinquency Prevention's National Disproportionate Minority Contact Databook (Puzzanchera and Adams, 2011a) indicate that black youth have much higher rates of arrests than their white coun- terparts, as well as higher rates of being detained, having petitions filed, and being placed, but lower rates of being diverted and referred to probation (see Table 8-2).[7] The pattern of differences for American Indian and Asian American youth compared with whites is not so straightforward. Both American Indian and Asian American youth have a higher rate of dispro- portionate contact at the case referral stage and the detention stage than whites. Asian youth have higher rates of processing than black youth in the referral, petition, and adjudication stages as well higher rates of transfer to adult court. Both groups are diverted at a lower rate than either white or black youth (see Table 8-2).

In sum, with few exceptions, data consistently show that youth of color have been overrepresented at every stage of the juvenile justice system, that race/ethnicity are associated with court outcomes, and that racial/ethnic differences increase and become more pronounced with further penetration into the system through the various decision points (Rodriguez, 2010).[8] When one includes the compound and cumulative character of racial/ethnic involvement throughout (and through progressive stages of) the juvenile justice system, it is no surprise that the issue has been subject to much discussion and, in turn, received persistent attention.

The remaining important question is *why* minorities are overrepre- sented in the juvenile and criminal justice systems. We begin with the two main perspectives (differential offending and differential selection by the justice system), which have often been viewed—incorrectly in the commit- tee's view—as competing, rather than complementary, explanations for the disparity (Piquero, 2008a; Bishop and Leiber, 2012). We then expand our

---

[7]In a different analysis of 2005 data from the National Juvenile Court Data Archive that include ethnicity data for about two-thirds of the nation's Latino population, Latino youth are 4 percent more likely than white youth to be petitioned; 16 percent more likely than white youth to be adjudicated delinquent; 28 percent more likely than white youth to be detained; 41 percent more likely than white youth to receive out-of-home placement; 43 percent more likely to be admitted to adult prison (Arya et al., 2009).

[8]The Rodriguez study appears to be at odds with the Cohen et al. (2011) review of 72 studies cited earlier. Although they are addressing similar issues, the Rodriguez study and others like it focus on a single site and study youth through various juvenile justice stages from beginning to end.

discussion to other explanations that either do not fit neatly into either of those two perspectives or may have relevance for both.

EXPLAINING RACIAL DISPARITIES

Accounts of DMC typically fall into one of two broad camps. Some scholars emphasize differential offending as the root source of disproportionate minority involvement in the juvenile justice system and of the system's differential response. This approach points, in effect, to real, underlying differences between white and minority youth in the actual extent of engaging in (or the severity of) law-breaking behaviors. Other researchers point to differential selection by the justice system (by the police in enforcement and by prosecutors, intake officers, judges, and other justice system officials thereafter) as the primary source of racial disparities. As discussed below, findings of differential selection have sometimes been interpreted as demonstrating systematic and often institutional bias, but differential enforcement and justice system processing are not necessarily or always attributable to bias or discrimination.

Differential Offending

As referenced by Lauritsen (2005), there are more similarities than differences among youth across races with respect to offending patterns in self-reported data, with the exception of participation in serious violence. As noted, minority youth (especially black youth)[9] tend to offend more with respect to serious person crimes, and they have also been found to persist in crime into early adulthood at a higher rate than whites (Elliott, 1994; Haynie, Weiss, and Piquero, 2008). This finding is important because research shows that serious violence is more likely to be reported to the police, more likely to result in the offender's apprehension, and more likely to trigger severe juvenile and criminal justice sanctions (Piquero, 2008a, p. 64). And although research shows that much of the minority overrepresentation in secure confinement and prisons can be attributed to differences among racial groups in arrests for crimes that are most likely to lead to confinement, this same research also shows that it is unlikely that behavioral differences account for all minority overrepresentation (Blumstein, 1982, 1993; Crutchfield, Bridges, and Pitchford, 1994; Sorensen, Hope, and Stemen, 2003).

---

[9]As previously noted, most disparity research is limited to comparisons between whites and blacks, largely because of the lack of data for Hispanics, Asian Americans, and American Indians in both self-reported and especially official records. The intersection of race and gender is even less frequently studied despite the rapid growth of black girls in the juvenile justice system (Sherman, 2012, p. 1617).

Although space precludes a detailed investigation and review of theoretical accounts of racial/ethnic differences in (serious) offending (Hawkins and Kempf-Leonard, 2005), these differences have been attributed to several risk factors that span the individual, familial, and neighborhood levels. (See Chapter 6 for an explanation of risk factors and risk markers.)[10] In general, these can be considered as "contexts for risk" (National Research Council and Institute of Medicine, 2001) so as to not be confused with another set of system-based factors that could also be implicated in disproportionality.

Minorities, especially blacks are more likely than whites to live in economically disadvantaged communities (Sampson and Wilson, 1995). Such communities have distressed education, child welfare, and public health systems (Sharkey and Sampson, 2010; Ryan, Chiu, and Williams, 2011). They also tend to have many social structural conditions that contribute to delinquency, crime, and violence, such as poverty, disorder, residential segregation, and neighborhood disadvantage (Wilson, 1987). These effects tend to compound and accumulate in mainly minority communities so that poor, inner-city residents find it to difficult to move out of this urban core and escape to more affluent neighborhoods that come with improved opportunities for education and employment.[11] The ramifications of these minority-centered contexts of risk include poor health care (and subsequent health)[12] and substance abuse problems and disparities (Piquero, Moffitt, and Lawton, 2005), low-performing schools, absence of recreation programs or other organized activities for youth (Bishop and Leiber, 2012), disadvantaged familial and community-level socialization and controls (Sampson, Morenoff, and Raudenbush, 2005), and greater exposure to violence and other negative experiences (Crouch et al., 2000). The totality of these risk factors is such that minority youth are born into and raised in severely compromised familial, community, and educational environments that set the stage for a range of adverse behaviors and outcomes, including problems in school, relationships, and engaging in prosocial behavior.

Investigating this phenomenon, Fite and colleagues (2009) noted that differences observed in offending across race/ethnicity (and in subsequent

---

[10]In this chapter, we are using "risk factors" instead of "risk markers" because of its usage by the writers we are citing.

[11]Massey and Denton (1993) argue that racial segregation is the principal organizational feature of American society that is responsible for the creation of the urban underclass.

[12]For example, based on available Canadian data, youth with fetal alcohol spectrum disorder, an umbrella term that covers the range of outcomes associated with all levels of prenatal alcohol exposure, are 19 times more likely to be incarcerated than are youth without the disorder in a given year (Popova et al., 2011). A similar study has not been done on minority youth in the United States, but, given the high rates of heavy alcohol consumption among African Americans and Native Americans (Galvan and Caetano, 2003), one can infer that minority youth would be at great risk for the disorder.

juvenile and criminal justice experience) could be traced to the fact that minority (especially black) youth display and experience more risk factors for offending and risk, such as poor health care and compromised education systems. They examined the effect of exposure to early risk factors on arrest rates and found that the risk factors themselves were predictive of a juvenile arrest. In fact, the risk factors accounted for 60 percent of the total effect between race and general arrest (Fite, Wynn, and Pardini, 2009, p. 921). Exposure to concentrated disadvantage can also have detrimental and long-lasting consequences even after a youth leaves a severely disadvantaged neighborhood (Sampson, Sharkey, and Raudenbush, 2008).

Differential Selection

The differential selection hypothesis asserts that a combination of differential enforcement (differing police presence, patrolling, and profiling in minority and nonminority neighborhoods) and differential processing by the juvenile justice system (differing dispositions and placements in the courts and correctional systems) leads to more minority youth being arrested, convicted, and subsequently confined than white youth (Piquero, 2008a, p. 65). This hypothesis may be especially pertinent to victimless crimes, such as drug use and sales and public order crimes, in which more discretion is available to formal social control agents, especially police, and virtually all interactions (especially among police and juveniles) are made out of the public eye (Piquero, 2008a, p. 65). Thus, the differential selection hypothesis would anticipate that minority youth emerge in official records at a disproportionate rate because of differential police, court, and correctional decisions.

To illustrate the differential selection hypothesis at the police level, consider a policy decision to differentially assign police to particular neighborhoods with higher reports of crime, especially serious and violent crimes. Because such neighborhoods often tend to be overrepresented in impoverished, minority locations, this places minority offenders at an increased risk of detection and potential arrest as a result of their encounters with the police. Increased police presence also creates greater opportunities for discretion to be exercised in street encounters and, as a result, for arrest decisions to vary across race/ethnicity.

As this example suggests, conventional enforcement practices or patterns of judicial administration can lead to racial/ethnic disparities even if they are not intended. Thus, it would be a mistake to regard differential selection by the juvenile justice system as equivalent to proof of bias. Bias or even intentional discrimination may well be operating, but disparities can also arise from otherwise legitimate justice system processes.

Differential Enforcement

Black youth who live in segregated communities tend to have more con-tacts with police than white youth (Brunson and Weitzer, 2009; Crutchfield, Bridges, and Pitchford, 2009). They are more likely to go to schools with police presence, more likely to be suspended or expelled from school (Skiba et al., 2002; Fabelo et al., 2011; Skiba et al., 2011), and more likely to have contact with officers as a result of disciplinary action. Children engaging in the same behavior in schools or in neighborhoods without a police pres-ence or who live where there are occasional patrols will have less contact (Crutchfield, Bridges, and Pitchford, 2009).

Many studies focus on institutional policy and practice around selective enforcement. Some focus on the role of drugs in minority communities (e.g., open-air drug markets, the passage of certain drug laws and punishment) as well as the controversial subject of racial profiling. With respect to the race–drugs relationship, Tonry (1995), for example, claimed that the passage of the crack cocaine sentencing laws was virtually known to differentially target minority—especially black youth—in urban communities because the sale and use patterns of crack cocaine (i.e., inner-city, open-air markets, violence-ridden streets) are largely race based. Thus, because the passage of the crack cocaine sentencing laws were made, in part, as a response to the violence that was permeating many inner cities in the mid- to late 1980s, and because the police had to selectively target certain communities and drug markets, an obvious by-product was that minority youth would be exceedingly more likely to fall under formal social control. Analyses of racial disparity in drug arrests in Seattle by Beckett and colleagues (2005, p. 419) centered on "the racialization of imagery surrounding drugs in gen-eral and crack cocaine in particular" as the driving force shaping police per-ceptions and practices, as well as disparities in drug possession in Seattle.

Turning to the potential effect of racial profiling on racial disparities, there is a large body of research that has examined a wide range of data on traffic stops, driving patterns, and public perceptions associated with racial/ethnic profiling by the police (Rice and White, 2010). Because space constraints preclude a detailed overview of this body of work, a few such studies are highlighted.

Fagan and colleagues have produced a comprehensive body of research on "order-maintenance policing" and its effect on racial profiling in New York City. In one recent report, Fagan and colleagues (2010) examined data on police street stops between 1998 and 2006 and focused on the rates of stops in New York City neighborhoods with the highest concentration of black residents. Their analyses showed that street stops were disproportion-ately concentrated in the city's poorest areas, that the most recent increases in stops were concentrated in predominantly minority neighborhoods, that minority residents were more likely to be disproportionately subjected to law enforcement contact based on the neighborhoods in which they lived rather than the crime problems in those areas, and that black citizens not only had an elevated risk of police contact compared with non-Hispanic whites and Hispanics, but also that the standards used to justify stops in their neighborhoods appeared to be lower than those in neighborhoods with larger white populations (Fagan et al., 2010, p. 311).

In short, there is a sizable literature indicating that minority youth are more likely than white youth to be stopped, arrested, and subsequently referred to court by police (Bishop and Leiber, 2012, p. 461). Although isolation of a single factor for this is beyond the reach of any study, it is fair to conclude that a range of factors—including differential deployment and police surveillance (Smith, 1986; Krivo and Peterson, 1996; Warren et al., 2006);[13] differential police suspicion (Alpert, MacDonald, and Dunham, 2005) and use of cognitive shortcuts and unconscious stereotypes in minority neighborhoods and on minority youth (Kennedy, 1997; Smith and Alpert, 2002); and juvenile demeanor ("Black and Hispanic youth tend to be [or are perceived to be] less cooperative, more gang-involved, and more threatening") (Bishop and Leiber, 2012, p. 461)—are implicated in differential policing handling of minority juvenile offenders (Piliavin and Briar, 1964).[14]

Race, police contact, and minority youth's behavior are also intertwined in complicated ways. When contacts with police occur early, the likelihood that a black youth will have future contacts with police is increased. For example, early contacts with police (by eighth grade) have been shown to increase the risk for arrest by high school by fivefold, even when accounting for all other environmental domains, including self-report criminal behavior (Crutchfield, Bridges, and Pitchford, 2009). These contacts with police also shape a youth's perception of and compliance with legal authorities (Fagan and Piquero, 2007). Lee and colleagues (2010) found that the stronger the sense of racial identification as a minority group, the higher the perceived discrimination by police. Race also affected perceptions of global police prejudice, procedural justice, and police legitimacy. (For a fuller discussion of youth's perceptions, see Chapter 7.) Youth who considered police contacts overly aggressive and confrontational tended to avoid police at all costs and were likely to perceive themselves as having been badly treated (Weitzer and Brunson, 2009). As a consequence, black youth have very

---

[13]For example, significant racial disparities in the implementation of marijuana law enforcement were observed in New York City during 2004-2008 (Geller and Fagan, 2010).

[14]At the same time, however, some additional evidence from traffic stops exploring citizens' demeanor and race shows that black and Hispanic motorists are not more likely than whites to be arrested during traffic stops when other legal and extra legal factors are considered (Engel, Klahm, and Tillyer, 2010).

troubled relationships with police compared with white youth (Brunson and Weitzer, 2009).

Differential Processing by the Justice System

A voluminous literature examines the decisions at each stage of the juvenile justice system in order to examine how minority and white youth are treated and the extent to which they receive similar or different outcomes (Bishop, 2005).[15] In the earlier cited review, Cohen and colleagues (2011) concluded that some race effects exist in the processing of some minority youth, in some locations, at some time periods, and for certain offenses; that minority youth are more likely to receive harsh treatment for certain but not all offenses; and that racial disparities can be documented for certain stages but not others. Here, a few studies are highlighted in order to show how this research has been conducted.

In a classic piece, Bridges and Steen (1998) examined the tone and value of word choices that were used to describe black and white juvenile offenders by probation officers. Officers attributed offenses by black juveniles more to negative attitudinal and personality traits. They attributed traits and offenses by whites more to the social environment. These authors also found that these differences contributed significantly both to the officers' differing assessments of the risk of reoffending and to their recommendations about sentencing, even after controlling for case and offender characteristics (Piquero, 2008a, p. 66).

In a related study in Washington, Bechtold and colleagues (2011, p. 5) examined juvenile probation at three sites with a mixture of black, Hispanic, and white youth by exploring whether judges set different conditions of probation and ordered different services for youth of different racial/ethnic groups and whether probation officers treated them differently according to their race/ethnicity. Results were mixed, but in general the authors reported no consistent pattern of discrimination. Specifically, all youth regardless of race/ethnicity received very similar conditions of probation, were cited for similar violations at similar rates, and received similar responses.

Graham and Lowery (2004) conducted two experiments in Los Angeles involving police officers and juvenile probation officers in order to examine unconscious racial stereotypes of decision makers in the juvenile justice system. Specifically, the sample was subliminally exposed to words related to the category black—such as ghetto, homeboy, and dreadlocks—or to

---

[15]It is important to point out that, although there is a body of research on the influence of race in police juvenile contacts, research on police arrest decisions is limited in comparison to what is known about the other stages of juvenile justice processing (Bishop and Leiber, 2012).

words neutral with respect to race. At the same time, the officers read two scenarios about a hypothetical adolescent who allegedly committed either a property (shoplifting) or violent (assault) crime. In addition to answering questions about conscious attitudes about race, the officers rated the offender on a number of individual characteristics and made judgments about culpability, expected recidivism, and deserved punishment. Findings showed that, compared with officers in the neutral condition, officers in the racial prime condition reported more negative trait ratings, greater culpability, and more expected recidivism and also endorsed harsher punishment. Significantly, the race primes had the same effect regardless of the officers' own race and consciously held attitudes about blacks. The findings held even among those who reported that they were tolerant and not biased toward nonwhites (Piquero, 2008a, pp. 66-67).

Using data from Black Hawk County, Iowa, Leiber (2009) examined the factors associated with pre- and postadjudication secure detention and subsequent decision making. His analysis showed that legal factors were strongly related in the expected direction to each type of secure detention and subsequent decisions but that race effects were also apparent for some juvenile justice decisions but not others. Moreover, his findings also revealed that race effects did not always result in more severe sanctions for minority youth.

In a sample of more than 23,000 Arizona youthful offenders, Rodriguez (2010) examined the cumulative effect of race/ethnicity via detention on various juvenile court outcomes. Her results showed that black, Hispanic, and American Indian youth were treated more severely in juvenile court outcomes than white juvenile offenders, both at the front-end court processes (diversion and detention) as well as the back-end processes and outcomes (out-of-home placement). The findings revealed that detention produces indirect racial/ethnic effects in subsequent stages of processing and that "youth who were detained pre-adjudication were more likely to have petitions filed, less likely to have petitions dismissed, and more likely to be removed from the home at disposition" (Rodriguez, 2010, pp. 391-392).

In examining differential involvement, it is also important to take account of the structural context of juvenile court administration in understanding racial/ethnic disparities in judicial processing. Some evidence suggests that urban courts tend to be more formal and bureaucratic and have greater access to detention facilities than rural courts and that these characteristics are associated with harsher sentences. Because they disproportionately reside in urban counties, black youth are at increased risk of being processed, detained, and punished than white youth in rural localities who have committed similar offenses. Thus, it is also possible that location, race, and punitiveness are intertwined (Feld, 1991; Sampson and Laub, 1993; Bray, Sample, and Kempf-Leonard, 2005; Rodriguez, 2010).

Other Explanations for Differential Involvement

As reflected in the discussion thus far, it remains difficult to appor-
tion documented disparities to either differential offending or differential
selection and to ascribe the role that bias plays. The research to date
has not attempted to do that, given that the impact of either perspective
is confounded by the effects of underlying social and cultural factors.
In addition, researchers have identified other factors that may contribute to differential juvenile justice outcomes that may not fit neatly into
either of those perspectives or may be distinct from both. These include
jurisdictional differences in the treatment of youth, such as case processing (Kempf-Leonard, 2007); organizational issues throughout the juvenile
justice system, including resources and agency roles (Bishop, Leiber, and
Johnson, 2010); "justice-by-geography," that is, local institutional culture
(Feld, 1991; Bray, Sample, and Kempf-Leonard, 2005); legislative decisions
(Tonry, 1995); and administrative policies, such as zero-tolerance policies in
schools that propel minorities into the system (Verdugo, 2002; Hirschfield,
2008). Several of these additional factors are discussed below.

Code of the Street

Anderson's (1999) code-of-the-street thesis, which contends that minority youth—especially black youth—form and espouse an attitude that is
organized around informal rules governing street behavior and response to
personal affronts. These attitudes form mainly in response to the economic
disadvantage, social isolation, and racial discrimination encountered by
black youth in the most disadvantaged urban communities. Adoption of
these codes, which center on the issue of respect (i.e., being treated right
or granted the deference one deserves), is deemed a virtual necessity for
respect and survival in the most disadvantaged, distressed, and impoverished minority—especially black—communities. But hanging out with
people who adopt the code of the street or being in places where such
people are known to congregate may increase the risk of greater involvement with the police (Crutchfield, Bridges, and Pitchford, 2009) as well
as actual crime. A study by Stewart and Simons (2010) using data on 800
black adolescents ages 10-15 in Georgia and Iowa showed that a youth's
expressed street code attitudes significantly predicted violence two years
later, so that youth who internalized and lived by the code were the most
likely to be involved in subsequent violence. It is important to note as well
that scholars have identified a similar respect-based code of the streets orientation among Hispanics (Bourgois, 2003).

Juvenile Justice System Feeders

A less investigated explanation for racial/ethnic differences in juvenile justice involvement concerns feeder systems and agencies that funnel youth into the juvenile justice system, including the school disciplinary system (Fabelo et al., 2011), the mental health system (Feld, 1998b; Teplin et al., 2002), and the child welfare system (Bowser and Jones, 2004; Herz et al., 2010). See Chapter 3 for a discussion of how these systems act as feeders for the juvenile justice system.

For example, a longitudinal study of almost a million adolescents in Texas schools found that 1 in 5 African American students had involvement with the juvenile justice system compared to 1 in 6 Hispanic students and 1 in 10 white students. The study controlled for 83 variables and found that African American students were more likely than students of other races to be disciplined and to receive a harsher punishment (Fabelo et al., 2011, p. 40). For example, African American youth were almost twice as likely as Hispanic students and three times as likely as white students to be placed on out-of-school suspension for the first violation (Fabelo et al., 2011, p. 42). This suggests that discretionary action by school officials is contributing to the higher rate of involvement with the juvenile justice system, with the Texas data showing that multiple discretionary disciplinary actions were more common among African American and Hispanic students than white students (Fabelo et al., 2011).

As with youth referred to the justice system by schools, race is an important predictor of whether youth cross over from the child welfare system to the juvenile justice system (Herz and Ryan, 2008a; Herz, Ryan, and Bilchik, 2010). This is not surprising, since African American youth are overrepresented in foster care at a rate of more than twice their proportion in the U.S. child population. African American youth in the child welfare system are up to two times more likely than white adolescents to experience at least one arrest (Ryan and Testa, 2005) and to be disproportionately represented in the arrest and detention population (Herz, Ryan, and Bilchik, 2010). As a result, previous child welfare contact is highly correlated with the overrepresentation of African American youth in the juvenile justice system (see also Chapter 3). Girls in the child welfare system are also more likely to be detained by the juvenile justice system than nonfoster care girls. Girls' histories of multiple foster home placements, child protection system policies that penalize girls for running away, and inadequate communication across the juvenile justice and child protection systems contribute to these disparities (Sherman, 2012).

Youth held in juvenile detention centers and other residential facilities exhibit high rates of mental disorder (see Chapter 3). Evidence suggests, however, that there are few differences between youth from different racial/

ethnic backgrounds on levels of symptoms at screening (Vincent et al., 2008) but African American youth may show greater levels of need than white youth on broader measures of mental health needs (Rawal et al., 2004). White youth are more likely to be ordered to services (Pumariega et al., 1998) or designated as severely mentally ill and referred for services than African American youth (Herz, 2001; Lopez-Williams et al., 2006; Maschi et al., 2008; Dalton et al., 2009), making them more eligible for smaller, more specialized treatment programs (Bishop, 2005). How much this differential in service involvement is attributable to juvenile justice system involvement is unclear (Garland et al., 2005).

Gender differences are more pronounced. Rates of symptoms at screening appear to be higher for girls than for boys (McCabe et al., 2002; Cauffman, 2004; Osterlind, Koller, and Morris, 2007; Vincent et al., 2008), and girls appear to have higher rates of prior maltreatment and family history of mental illness (McCabe et al., 2002). They are also more likely to be ordered to receive mental health services than boys (Yan and Dannerbeck, 2011).

As a general rule, studies documenting racial/ethnic differences suggest that blacks and other minorities experience a disproportionate amount of contact with these agencies than white youth. We turn again to these systems in our discussion of strategies for addressing racial/ethnic disparities.

Negative Stereotypes and Media Imagery of Minority Youth

Although negative stereotyping appears to have declined over the past two decades, negative images still remain quite commonplace (Bobo, 2011). Negative stereotypes and media imagery of minority youth may play a role in the differential treatment they receive from police and other actors in the juvenile justice system. For example, Bishop and Leiber (2012) suggest that although there is little evidence that police are overtly biased, they often do not have adequate information on which to base a decision to engage or arrest a youth and may be influenced by more subtle forms of bias arising from their perceptions of places and people.

Television crime reports contribute to negative stereotypes of minority youth. Iyengar's (2010) analysis of local news shows demonstrated a systematic overemphasis on violent crime and associated crime with the actions of racial minorities. Bjornstrom and colleagues (2010) showed that ethnic and racial portrayals in television news reports were influenced by the context of the story itself (the race of the victim and the race of the perpetrator as well as the social structural context). Their study also showed that victimization in minority communities was routinely minimized.

Social Structure and Culture

A macrosociological explanation of disparities looks to racial inequality and concentrations of "underclass" poverty that influence levels of offending, enforcement practices, and formal court processes. Building on earlier research that examined the structural variations in court administration (community-level variations, budget, personnel, availability of facilities, rates of referral) and their impact on court processes (Feld, 1991), research by Sampson and Laub (1993) examined such community attributes as underclass poverty, racial inequality, wealth, court referral rates, mobility, urbanism, youth density, and criminal justice resources on court processes.

Sampson and Wilson (1995) theorized that black-white disparities resulted from racially segregated neighborhoods in which members of minority groups were differentially exposed to key violence-inducing and violence-protecting social mechanisms. Wilson (2009) later expanded on this idea by acknowledging the prevalence of powerful structural factors impacting blacks, such as discriminatory laws, policies, hiring, housing, and education and the interplay of structural factors and the stereotypical attitudes and assumptions of various ethnic and racial groups, including social science researchers. To arrive at a fuller understanding of the causes of racial inequalities, he suggests that it is necessary to go beyond the independent contributions of social structure and culture and to focus on how they interact to shape different group outcomes that embody racial inequality, a view strongly endorsed by other researchers (Kempf-Leonard, 2007; Bishop and Leiber, 2012).

SUMMARY

The body of relevant evidence on racial/ethnic effects in the juvenile justice system demonstrates differential involvement of minorities in serious offending as well as differential selection and processing by the justice system. However, the race/ethnicity effects have been found to be both direct and indirect—operating both because of and through other factors. Moreover, the disparities are not uniform throughout the juvenile justice process (tending to be more common in the front-end processes, which afford much more discretion than back-end processes), and disparities seem to accumulate as youth are processed into the system (although studies of these trends are limited and may be hampered by various selection artifacts) (Engen, Steen, and Bridges, 2002; Leiber and Johnson, 2008). Other structural and contextual factors also may influence how minorities come to be disproportionately involved in the juvenile justice system, and these additional factors also need to be considered in designing possible strategies for reducing disproportionality.

More than a decade ago, the report *Juvenile Crime, Juvenile Justice* (National Research Council and Institute of Medicine, 2001, p. 229) concluded that the debate between the "behavior [differential offending] versus justice [differential selection]" positions has led to a "conceptual and methodological impasse." Following this, Piquero (2008b) concluded that future research should move beyond the "which matters more" debate and instead seek to understand how both hypotheses can explain the overrepresentation of minorities in the system and then to identify steps that can be taken to lower any disparate effect and treatment. Few steps have been taken in this regard. To be sure, there has been much attention devoted to racial/ethnic disparities over the past decades, yet the empirical research has primarily focused on assessing the effect of differential offending and differential enforcement (and to a lesser extent differential processing) in an isolated manner. There has been little effort to use statistical methods to quantitatively partition the various identifiable factors (differential participation in the crimes that lead to involvement with the juvenile justice system, socioeconomic/poverty effects, police patrol patterns in high-crime areas, family composition, etc.) that, in combination, produce racial/ethnic disparities.

The committee recognizes the challenges that must be overcome to quantify the various contributions to racial disproportionality, given the difficulty of assembling the necessary data, designing the study, and interpreting the findings. However, some progress seems possible by focusing separately on the sequential stages of the juvenile justice system. It is likely that some factors are more influential at spawning racial/ethnic differences at initial stages of the system (i.e., police decision to patrol and/or stop youth) compared with other stages of the system (i.e., prosecutor's decision to charge and/or judge's decision to institutionalize youth). Although this would entail a complex research effort, it should be undertaken for the purpose of helping to identify specific, actionable policy recommendations at each stage of the juvenile justice system. See Chapter 11 for a fuller presentation of research needs.

That said, the possibility of further research on the causes of racial/ethnic disparities should not delay policy actions aiming to reduce them. Many initiatives have been undertaken in recent years, and some promising strategies appear to have emerged. The next section highlights some of these efforts.

INTERVENTIONS AND PROMISING REFORM STRATEGIES

Several intervention efforts and policy reform initiatives and strategies have been developed to reduce DMC in the juvenile justice system. Little has been systematically documented about these strategies and their effectiveness—and even less has been published in the traditional academic literature. Evaluations of these strategies have typically been undertaken by agencies involved in the implementation of reform strategies rather than by independent researchers.

The committee agrees with the general conclusion that there is "little objective evidence that interventions designed to reduce DMC actually do so" (Poulin, Orchowsky, and Iwama, 2011, p. 118). However, two research studies are worth noting. An evaluation of community-based delinquency prevention programs designed in part to address racial/ethnic disparities found that programs were successful in reducing recidivism, that recidivism was lowest among the high-attendance group, but that program effects on school outcomes were negligible (Welsh, Jenkins, and Harris, 1999). A second study assessed how legal and extralegal factors changed in predicting outcomes at two decision-making stages (intake and judicial disposition) about 10 years before and 10 years after the DMC mandate. Their findings regarding the impact of the DMC initiative were equivocal. Specifically, they found direct effects for race at intake, but such effects were less pronounced than at judicial disposition largely because of the "wide latitude for discretion at the front-end of the system" (Leiber, Bishop, and Chamlin, 2011, p. 26).

Research on differential juvenile offending, differential processing, and the broader structural context that impacts both suggests possible strategies worthy of exploration.

Addressing DMC at the Front End

Focusing on Arrest and Detention

Given the evidence that race is strongly associated (both directly and indirectly) with decisions made at the front end of the system (Engen et al., 2002; Bishop and Leiber, 2012), strategies targeted at reducing the likelihood of arrest and detention, particularly from sources of referral to the juvenile justice system, offer a promising approach to reduce racial disparities.

Juvenile Detention Alternatives Initiative. Funded by the Annie E. Casey Foundation, the Juvenile Detention Alternatives Initiative was designed to reduce reliance on secure detention by promoting changes to policies, practices, and programs. (See Chapter 9 for a fuller description.) The initiative has been credited with assisting in the closure of detention units or entire facilities as well as leading to reductions in Latino youth detained in Santa Cruz due to the opening of an evening reporting center (Office of Juvenile Justice and Delinquency Prevention, 2009a; Annie E. Casey Foundation at http:www.aecf.org/initiatives/jdai).

The W. Haywood Burns Institute. The Burns Institute works with community stakeholders and local agencies in a data-driven, consensus-based approach to change policies, procedures, and practices that result in the detention of low-offending youth of color and poor youth. As part of its technical assistance function, Burns reports some successes in developing DMC-reduction policies to reduce the number of youth who were held in secure detention and to develop alternatives to detention that have been shown to be related to a significant decrease in detention among black youth (Bell and Ridolfi, 2008; Bell et al., 2009; Poulin, Orchowsky, and Iwama, 2011, p. 106).

Models for Change. The MacArthur Foundation Models for Change Initiative was launched in 2004 in Pennsylvania and expanded to several other states, including Illinois, Louisiana, and Washington, and in 2007 the foundation established a county-level Action Network to address specific DMC initiatives in eight states. (For a more detailed description of the Models for Change initiative, see Chapter 9.) Anecdotal evidence suggests that several jurisdictions have initiated efforts to collect and analyze data on race/ethnicity across key decision points and have taken steps to use data to inform policy and practice. A Model for Change site (Philadelphia) has developed a minority youth–law enforcement training curriculum that was a joint project of the district attorney and the police department; in Berks County, Pennsylvania, the DMC Action Network enhanced Spanish-language capability and cultural competence, developed workforce opportunities, and showed some signs of reducing minority detentions through improved assessment screening and diversion (Armour and Hammond, 2009, p. 6). Griffin (2008) reports that the DMC Action Network in Peoria, Illinois, found that many arrests of black youth were for aggravated battery and that once alternative conflict strategies were started, arrests for black youth dropped significantly.

Working with the Child Welfare and School Systems

As noted, the child welfare and school systems are contributors to the overrepresentation of minority youth in the juvenile justice system. Researchers supported by child welfare organizations, such as the Child Welfare League and Georgetown's Center for Juvenile Justice Reform, have been working for more than a decade to identify "crossover youth" and to develop an integrated, multisystem approach to program development and delivery of services (Wiig and Tuell, 2011). For those youth appropriately referred to the juvenile justice system, identifying appropriate services and placements for them at entry would aim to limit their deeper penetration into the system.

The differential treatment of minority students for disciplinary infractions is the object of close scrutiny by both the U.S. Department of Education and the Department of Justice. Publicly available data representing
85 percent of the nation's students are being used to determine disparate
discipline rates for suspensions and expulsions as well as arrests and referral to law enforcement.[16] A recent rollout of the expanded Department of
Education civil rights database and the Texas study showing the high degree
of discretion being exercised by school administrators in suspension and
expulsion decisions (Fabelo et al., 2011) have resulted in widespread media
coverage and a collaborative project between the Justice and Education
departments to address the "school to prison pipeline." Among the goals
of the initiative are to promote collaborative research and data endeavors,
including evaluations of alternative disciplinary policies and interventions
and to encourage positive discipline options and awareness of evidence-
based and promising policies and practices among each state's judicial and
education leadership (U.S. Department of Justice, 2011).

Heightening Awareness

An innovative legislative approach to reducing racial/ethnic disparities has been tried in Iowa and Connecticut. Iowa became the first state
to require "minority impact statements" for proposed legislation related to
crimes, sentencing, parole, and probation and for grants awarded by state
agencies, and Connecticut requires racial/ethnic impact statements for
bills and amendments that could, if passed, increase or decrease the pretrial or sentenced population of state correctional facilities (Armour and
Hammond, 2009, p. 6). Although these legislative efforts have yet to be
empirically evaluated for reducing DMC, they represent the kind of innovations that are needed in addressing a serious but admittedly complicated
problem. The minority impact statement challenges all participating agencies to inventory their policies and practices to heighten awareness of contributing factors and provide a tool for monitoring progress.

Characteristics of Promising Strategies

Soler and Garry (2009) have highlighted some traits that are characteristic of promising strategies to address disparities. First, these efforts need
to have community support, originate at the community level, and include
community stakeholders. Second, strategies need to rely on data from
several sources to paint a complete picture of the nature and extent of the
problem. Third, strategies need to be transparent about both successes and

---

[16]Available: http://ocrdata.edu.gov.

setbacks. Fourth, all interested parties need to be committed to long-term investment in lowering DMC that relies on evidence-based practices and follow-through with sustainable initiatives. It should also be added that a set of realistic expectations should be put in place so as to manage what stakeholders hope will happen and what is actually likely to happen in the short and long terms. Furthermore, DMC-related programs should have strong process evaluations in place prior to outcome evaluations being conducted on program effects because poorly implemented programs are likely to evince ineffective results and conclusions (Piquero, 1998).

Based on experiences in reducing disparities in the child welfare system and for crossover youth who enter the juvenile justice system, five general strategies have been identified (Chapin Hall Center for Children, 2009):

- Increase transparency—by building management information systems that collect race/ethnicity information.
- Reengineer structures and procedures—by reviewing processes and procedures routinely to determine whether they contribute to disparities.
- Change organizational culture—by influencing attitudes of agency staff and identifying the subtle ways attitudes can affect policy and practice.
- Mobilize political leadership—by building awareness and consensus among them.
- Partner with developing community and family resources to build political will.

The committee endorses these strategic suggestions and thinks they should be pursued.

CONCLUSIONS

Several National Academies reports have described with concern the differential handling of minorities by the justice system: *Juvenile Crime, Juvenile Justice* (National Research Council and Institute of Medicine, 2001); *Fairness and Effectiveness in Policing: The Evidence* (National Research Council, 2004a); and *Informing America's Policy on Illegal Drugs: What We Don't Know Keeps Hurting Us* (National Research Council, 2004b). Two reports have undertaken a broad review of the status of racial relations and racial trends (National Research Council, 1989, 2001a), and each contains thought-provoking chapters on racial trends in the administration of justice. Each aims for better understanding of the role that race and specifically racial disparities play in American culture and institutions.

Each reflects the complexity of the overrepresentation of minorities and the lack of easy solutions.

We know that racial/ethnic disparities are not reducible to either differential offending or differential selection. Many other factors affect disproportionality of minority youth in the juvenile justice system, including the troubling entrenched patterns of poverty, segregation, gaps in educational achievement, and residential instability. DMC exists in the broader context of a "racialized society" in which many public policies, institutional practices, and cultural representations operate to produce and maintain racial inequities.

The literature reflects continuing uncertainty about the relative contribution of differential offending, differential enforcement and processing, and structural inequalities to these disparities. However, the current body of research suggests that poverty, social disadvantage, neighborhood disorganization, constricted opportunities, and other structural inequalities—which are strongly correlated with race/ethnicity—contribute to both differential offending and differential selection, especially at the front end of juvenile justice decision making. Because bias (whether conscious or unconscious) also plays a role, albeit of unknown magnitude, juvenile justice officials should embrace activities designed to increase awareness of these unconscious biases and to counteract them, as well as to detect and respond effectively to overt instances of discrimination. Although the juvenile justice system itself cannot alter the underlying structural causes of racial/ethnic disparities in juvenile justice, many conventional practices in enforcement and administration magnify these underlying disparities, and these contributors *are* within the reach of justice system policy makers.

Based on the current knowledge base and the context in which DMC occurs, the committee identifies four reform strategies for moving the DMC agenda forward. We think, given the importance and persistence of the problem, that the existing data are sufficient to warrant serious consideration of these strategies.

First, reform efforts to reduce racial/ethnic disparities should pay special attention to the arrest and detention stages at the front end of the system. Reducing discretion by police and court officers through the use of written guidelines and risk assessment instruments; eliminating detention for youth who do not pose a danger; providing mental health, substance abuse, and other services up front so that youth can avoid penetrating deeper into the system; and providing alternatives to detention and alternatives to prosecution should all be part of an improved response to youth who are at the entry threshold of the juvenile justice system.

Second, a comprehensive reform strategy should encompass review of school disciplinary practices and elimination of those that are punitive and discretionary and are likely to result in a referral to the juvenile justice system. As indicated earlier, schools are the source of numerous minority youth who are caught up in the discretionary disciplinary practices of schools and are referred often to law enforcement for nonserious offenses. More research is needed to understand the pipeline process and the role that various actors play (school resource officers, school management) in these referrals. Similarly, policies and practices involving youth who have ties to the mental health and child welfare systems need to be carefully assessed to ensure that the reasons for their handling are legitimate and their subsequent processing by the juvenile justice system is appropriate and nondiscriminatory.

Third, any reform strategy should focus on eliminating formal and informal agency policies and practices that are shown to disproportionately disadvantage minority youth. To do so will require the identification of key decision points and decision-making criteria that appear in practice to fall disproportionately on minority youth and perhaps to reflect implicit bias. It will also require the availability of proper legal representation for all minority youth and, for Hispanic youth and their families, translators.

Fourth, reform efforts are needed to increase the accountability of national, state, and local governments for reducing racial/ethnic disparities. At the local level, political leaders need to take responsibility for identifying the extent of disproportionality in their communities. At the state level, cabinet-level leadership on juvenile justice administration should monitor efforts to address these disparities and to provide the necessary resources to enable the necessary data to be collected and reported. As mentioned earlier, state legislatures should consider statutes that would give heightened urgency and visibility to this problem, including establishing oversight bodies. Even though state policy makers do not control all the levers that must be engaged to address the problem, they do have the power to command attention. Part of the long-term solution is for state juvenile justice leaders to keep this issue at the forefront of the reform agenda. Finally, reform strategies at the national level, specifically those involving the OJJDP, the lead agency on this issue, are described in Chapter 10.

9

Achieving Reform

During the past two decades, major reform efforts in juvenile justice have focused on reducing the use of detention and secure confinement; improving conditions of confinement; closing large institutions and reinvesting in community-based programs; providing high-quality, evidence-based services for youth in the juvenile justice system; reducing racial/ethnic disparities; retaining most offending juveniles in the juvenile justice system rather than transferring them to the criminal justice system; improving delivery of defense services; and developing system-wide juvenile justice planning and collaboration (see Box 9-1).

These reform efforts have been frequently driven by the need to remediate harmful conditions of confinement, improve poor quality programs and services, and reduce costs—problems that are not mutually exclusive. More often than not, they exist simultaneously in a jurisdiction. Sometimes we found that innovations were initially focused on one particular aspect of the juvenile justice system, such as reduction in the use of detention, but in the process of addressing a particular problem, the initiative took on a larger focus and was scaled up geographically or was broadened to address other issues (e.g., reducing racial/ethnic disparities) and components of the system. Sometimes the reform was intended to address a fiscal crisis or some specific element of unfairness or program quality. And for some, the effort was targeted from the beginning at system-wide reform changes to the juvenile justice system.

The changes in public policy that have occurred are the result of a complicated interaction among government agencies, policy makers, and the particular characteristics of the policy itself. With this complicated

BOX 9-1
Typology of Reform Activities

Developing system-wide juvenile justice planning and collaboration— Illinois, Iowa, Kansas, Louisiana, North Carolina, Ohio, Pennsylvania, Virginia, and Washington.

Reducing detention—By the end of 2012, the Juvenile Detention Alternatives Initiative will be active in 40 states plus the District of Columbia and 150 jurisdictions.

Improving conditions of confinement—Over the past four decades, as a result of 57 lawsuits in 33 states plus the District of Columbia and Puerto Rico, states have initiated court-sanctioned remedies in response to alleged abuse or otherwise unconstitutional conditions in juvenile facilities (Mendel, 2011); 198 facilities in 27 states subscribe to the performance-based standards process (PbS Learning Institute, 2011).

Closing large institutions and reinvesting in community-based programs—These kinds of efforts may involve a shift to a network of small regional facilities (Massachusetts, Missouri, Utah) or a transfer of responsibility from the state to the counties (California, Illinois, Ohio).

Retaining juveniles in the juvenile justice system—Some states have raised the age of exclusive juvenile court jurisdiction (Connecticut, Illinois, Mississippi); 10 states have made changes to their transfer laws that keep more youth in the juvenile justice system (Arizona, Colorado, Connecticut, Delaware, Illinois, Indiana, Nevada, Utah, Virginia, Washington) (Campaign for Youth Justice, 2011).

Utilizing evidence-based programs that reduce recidivism—Several states have passed legislation or promoted state policies that require funded programs for youth be assessed for effectiveness (Florida, North Carolina, Pennsylvania, Washington) and/or that programs be evidence based (North Carolina, Oregon, Tennessee, Washington).

Improving access to and quality of mental health services—Reforms include statewide mental health screening for all youth (Minnesota) and for all youth on probation (Texas); special mental health courts (Washington); omnibus mental health legislation (Washington); and statewide multijurisdictional crisis intervention teams (Colorado). Colorado, Connecticut, Illinois, Louisiana, Ohio, Pennsylvania, Texas, and Washington are pursuing mental health reforms as members of the MacArthur Mental Health Action Network.

Providing quality defense services—Reforms to improve access to and quality of defense services are under way in California, Florida, Illinois, Louisiana, Massachusetts, New Jersey, Pennsylvania, and Washington—model sites in the MacArthur Indigent Defense Action Network. The National Juvenile Defender Center is working to promote a variety of reforms, such as standardizing indigence determination and statewide resource center (Pennsylvania), creation of a statewide system of defender offices (Massachusetts), and development of competency protocols and draft legislation (California).

Providing access to educational programs in detention and post release—Colorado requires local school districts to provide educational services during the school year to juveniles held in adult jails and to comply with the federal Individuals with Disabilities Education Act for all jailed juveniles with disabilities.

Reducing racial disparities—More than 40 jurisdictions have worked directly with the W. Haywood Burns Institute to undertake community-wide planning around reducing racial disparities. Specific initiatives have included reducing detention by developing alternatives to secure detention, reducing failure-to-appear rates, developing disciplinary policies that reduce referrals to law enforcement, and focusing on Latino youth initially detained by probation, available: http://www.burnsinstitute.org/article.php?id=56 [May 2013].

Modifying harsh sentencing laws for youth—Four states (Colorado, Georgia, Texas, Washington) have modified their sentencing laws. Colorado adjusted maximum sentences without parole that youth could receive; Georgia posed exceptions to mandatory minimum sentences for sex offenders; Texas abolished juvenile life without parole; and Washington eliminated mandatory minimum sentences for juveniles tried as adults (Arya and Ward, 2011).

Building multisystem approaches in child welfare and juvenile justice—Approximately 40 counties across the country are advancing the Crossover Youth Practice Model, developed by Casey Family Programs and the Center for Juvenile Justice Reform at the Georgetown University Public Policy Institute. The model is designed to reduce the flow of youth between the child welfare system and the juvenile justice system, the number of youth entering and reentering care, and the length of stay in out-of-home care (Center for Juvenile Justice Reform, available: http://cjrr.georgetow.edu/pm/practicemodel.htm [August 2012]).

interaction in mind, the committee was interested in identifying juvenile justice reforms that reflect a developmentally appropriate approach and in ascertaining how they had come about and what they had accomplished. We were interested in the lessons one might draw from these reforms— lessons that could be applied to future efforts to promote and sustain a developmental approach by the juvenile justice system.

We have focused on innovations that have been described in the literature or have made some effort to document their progress in moving the juvenile justice system from a punitive corrections model to a developmentally appropriate services model. See Box 9-1 for a broad typology of reform activities identified by the committee.

DRIVERS OF REFORM

A variety of organizations have provided the impetus for reform. We have organized the sequence of reform initiatives in a roughly chronological fashion. In identifying them and describing the changes they influenced, we are not suggesting that any driver by itself was the sole force for the particular change being described. Usually an innovation is affected by multiple forces, sometimes occurring concurrently and at other times sequentially. However, we think important lessons can be derived from this account.

The Office of Juvenile Justice and Delinquency Prevention

The federal government's interest in preventing and addressing juvenile crime and juvenile offenders is vested in the Office of Juvenile Justice and Delinquency Prevention (OJJDP). Its mandate is to provide the resources, leadership, and coordination to improve the quality of juvenile justice (Juvenile Justice and Delinquency Prevention Act of 1974, P.L. 93-415). OJJDP dollars have provided a strong incentive for communities to undertake several far-reaching juvenile justice reforms on a national scale. Primary among them are certain core requirements that states must fulfill if they are to receive funding. But as federal expenditures for domestic programs decline in the coming years, OJJDP's approach for promoting juvenile justice reforms is likely to be weakened and may disappear altogether. Organizations and stakeholders supporting the re-authorization of OJJDP strongly advocate for its continued role in promoting reform and an increase in grant support to the states to carry out OJJDP's mandated reform activities (Coalition for Juvenile Justice, 2008; National Juvenile Justice Delinquency Prevention Coalition, 2011a, 2011b). These issues are described in detail in Chapter 10.

OJJDP also offers a different financial incentive through its sponsorship of community-wide initiatives. During the 1990s, it sponsored several large multisite demonstration programs that provided resources to communities willing to tackle large problems, such as school safety, exposure of children to violence, gang prevention and intervention, and delinquency prevention. Along with programmatic support, the agency offered communities extensive training and technical assistance (TTA). In return for federal dollars, communities were required to develop a matrix of services and to match youth to those services through the use of risk/need assessments. Some current state reform efforts (Missouri, North Carolina, Pennsylvania) and local ones (Baton Rouge, Louisiana, and San Diego, California) also trace their beginnings to the partnerships established to implement this comprehensive strategy (Wilson and Howell, 1993; Howell, 1995a, 2003b).

OJJDP's capacity to impact the juvenile justice field through support of large-scale demonstrations has dramatically declined. With this decline, state and local governments, foundations, and other youth-serving and advocacy organizations have taken on the challenge of reform.

Transformational State Models

Some statewide innovations originate and are propelled by state policy makers rather than by outside change agents. In two widely touted examples of major statewide innovations, in Massachusetts and Missouri, the impetus for change came from elected officials and state administrators with juvenile justice oversight.

The Massachusetts Experiment

During the early 1970s, Jerome Miller, director of youth services in Massachusetts, conceived and led an effort to close the state's correctional training schools[1] and replace them with a network of decentralized community-based services and several small, secure units for violent juvenile offenders. His accomplishment has been described as "the most sweeping reform in youth corrections in the United States since the establishment of juvenile reformatories in the 19th century and juvenile courts in the 20th century" (Howell, 2003b, p. 200).

In a retrospective account of his experiences in Massachusetts, Miller freely admits that at first he had only hazy ideas about how to improve the harsh conditions (Miller, 1991). His effort to close the training schools grew out of the realization that his veteran staff, many of whom had received

---

[1]The term "training school" is one of several used to refer to facilities that house youthful offenders, usually those adjudicated for serious crimes. Originally these facilities were conceived of as places where youth would be educated or trained to be model citizens, hence the name "training" school.

their jobs through a patronage system, would vehemently oppose any steps to change the status quo. But as the notion of closing the schools began to take hold, he began to work in a more systematic way to bring a "therapeutic community" philosophy to one institution at a time, expanding training, structuring new kinds of programs, and setting up community-based alternatives. He gained the support of influential people and groups, including the League of Women Voters and the Massachusetts Council on Crime and Delinquency, gradually finding allies among the staff. Within a two-year period, he succeeded in closing all seven training schools, which housed approximately 1,000 youth, and replaced them with two 30-bed facilities, in-home services, group homes, and residential placements (Krisberg and Austin, 1998).

The Missouri Model

The Missouri model is a therapeutic treatment model for all youth in institutional placement. Its key elements include

- continuous case management, from postarrest processing to aftercare;
- small, decentralized residential facilities (no more than 50 youth with an average population of 20) within 50-75 miles of their homes;
- peer-led services for small groups of 10-12 youth who remain together for all activities, meals, and treatment throughout their stay; and
- a rehabilitative treatment approach in which no specific treatment model is used but each youth has his or her own treatment plan that stresses group processes.

The Missouri model has had a long history of acceptance and support by the Missouri legislature. Small-group staffing of residential facilities was piloted during the late 1950s and early 1960s. After the Department of Youth Services, a free-standing agency within the Department of Social Services, was established, the idea of regional treatment was expanded and two large training schools were closed during the 1970s and 1980s. A major milestone occurred in 1987, when the legislature created a bipartisan Youth Services Advisory Board composed of local and state lawmakers and experts with responsibility for planning the state's juvenile treatment and placement services. Credit for refining and sustaining the Missouri model also goes to its unusually stable leadership. Mark Steward led the Department of Youth Services from 1988 to 2005, and its current director, Tim

Decker, worked under Steward for nine years prior to returning to the agency to assume the directorship in 2007.

More than two dozen states have visited Missouri to learn about the model, and Louisiana, New Mexico, two counties in California, New York, and the District of Columbia, are actively engaged in adopting the model to their jurisdictions. Despite the public attention given to the Missouri model and many replication efforts, the committee found little scientific evidence supporting the model's effectiveness. Recidivism data, on which many claims are based, are purely descriptive and correlational in nature. An outside assessment of the Missouri model (Mendel, 2010), which compared Missouri's recidivism rates to those of other states, was also flawed methodologically. (See Appendix B for a detailed description of the methodological issues.) Similarly, there has been no systematic process evaluation to determine which aspects of the model contribute to its success.

Key elements of the Missouri model reflect a developmental perspective. Its strong and stable leadership, as well as legislative and stakeholder support, appear to be important strategic conditions for transformative changes. In the absence of better documented models, it has been embraced by the juvenile justice field.[2] But the case for its adoption would be strengthened if the model and its elements were systematically and rigorously evaluated.

Civil Rights Litigation

Traditionally, litigation has been a major tool for ameliorating unfair and harmful conditions of confinement. As the first step in what later may become a broader systemic effort, litigation or even the threat of litigation often serves as a powerful incentive for states and local jurisdictions to make significant changes in their juvenile justice systems. During the early 1970s and 1980s, litigation was primarily brought by juvenile law centers supported by private foundations, such as the Edna McConnell Clark Foundation. From 1979 to 1981, OJJDP also provided start-up funding to juvenile law centers. Two current legal centers funded during this period

---

[2]The committee acknowledges that there may be other statewide juvenile justice reform efforts that are more extensive or have had a greater impact than that of the Missouri model. We chose to highlight this reform because of the amount of documentation that exists, the favorable support it has received from the juvenile justice field and the efforts to widely replicate it. We note, however, that the model has not been objectively and independently supported with empirical research. Appendix B provides a review of the research to date and describes the requisites of a rigorous process and outcome evaluation.

are the Youth Law Center in San Francisco and the Juvenile Law Center in Philadelphia, Pennsylvania.[3]

The Youth Law Center

Established in 1978, the Youth Law Center has brought more than a dozen lawsuits aimed at removing youth from jails and improving conditions of confinement. The lawsuits are based on constitutional requirements relating to provision of health, mental health, and education services to youth in confinement. They were also aimed at excessive use of force, restraining devices, and other safety issues. Through the early 1990s, the Youth Law Center worked in close conjunction with OJJDP. After the center filed a suit, OJJDP would provide technical assistance and guidance as to how the defendant facilities and agencies could improve conditions and meet the demands of any settlement eventually negotiated. This partnership resulted in removing youth from jails and in several cases closing public training schools that had abusive practices (Soler, personal communication, South Dakota case).[4] Its work also has impacted private training schools (*Milonas v. Williams*, 1982), with the court ruling that even private facilities require state oversight and involvement.

Two recent cases involving the Youth Law Center demonstrate the broad impact a case can have on a state's juvenile justice system. *L.H. v. Schwarzenegger* (2007) was brought against the California Division of Juvenile Justice (DJJ) for its practice of routinely imposing, without proper or timely notice, lengthy parole periods when juveniles violated their initial paroles. The suit also alleged that juveniles were not allowed to have witnesses testify on their behalf, to present evidence, or to have an attorney. As a result of the settlement, DJJ was required to hold timely parole hearings, to desist from holding youth in "temporary detention" if they were continued on parole, to provide accommodations for mental and physical disabilities, to allow youth to present evidence and witnesses at their prob-

---

[3]There are numerous organizations throughout the country that litigate on behalf of youth who come in contact with the juvenile justice system. Some, like the National Youth Law Center in Oakland, California, receive support from their state bars; others are funded privately and work primarily within their own states. The Prison Law Office in San Francisco was responsible for bringing the *Margaret Farrell v. Mathew Cate* lawsuit, which resulted in a far-reaching consent decree requiring the state to implement six different remedial plans. The work of the Juvenile Law Center and the Youth Law Center is highlighted in this report because of their longevity and the scope of their activities.

[4]Telephone interview with Mark Soler, former executive director of the Youth Law Center and now current executive director, Center for Children's Law and Policy, June 13, 2011. Information on the Youth Law Center's legal activities is available from http://www.ylc.org [April 2013].

able cause and revocation hearings, and to provide a prompt administrative appeal process.[5]

The second case, *S.H. v. Reed* (2011) (formerly *S.H. v. Taft*), against the Ohio Department of Youth Services (ODYS) charged the department with abusive, inhuman, and illegal conditions, policies, and practices. According to the Youth Law Center's website, the settlement

> creates a long term investment in Ohio youth by infusing new resources into DYS operations, overseeing reform in the process for determining when youth should be released from DYS custody, and supporting evidence-based community programs for low-risk offenders. Changes included hiring up to 115 juvenile correctional officers. The agreement also supports improved mental health services, enhanced educational, medical and dental services and a capacity goal on the youth population.[6,7]

Juvenile Law Center

The Juvenile Law Center was established in 1975 to deal with issues affecting juveniles and dependent children.[8] Originally a walk-in clinic for any youth up to age 21 needing a lawyer, over the years it has broadened its scope to include not only on the juvenile justice system but also on the dependency and foster care systems, with a particular emphasis on youth aging out of foster care. Like the Youth Law Center, its litigation has addressed detention of youth (*Youth Study Center*, 1976; *A.M. v. Luzerne County Detention Center*, 2001); conditions of confinement (*D.B. v. Casey*, 1991); loss of liberty (*Coleman v. Stanziana*, 1981; *T.B. v. City of Philadelphia*, 1988); and access to such services as education (*D.C. v. School District of Philadelphia*, 2004) and health and mental health services (*Scott v. Snider*, 1991). Several cases have set important precedents regarding the use of isolation and lack of access to counsel and other postdispositional due process issues for incarcerated youth (*Troy D. and O'Neill S. v. Mickens et al.*, 2010). Most recently, its strong advocacy paid off in a class action suit brought on behalf of children and families of Luzerne County, Pennsylvania (*H.T. et al. v. Mark A. Ciavarella, Jr. et al.*, 2009) who were involved in the "kids-for-cash" corruption scheme. Judge Ciavarela was one of two judges who sentenced about 2,500 children during 2003-2008. Many were sent

---

[5] Available: http://www.ylc.org/viewDetails.php?id=69 [September 2011].

[6] Available: http://www.ylc.org/viewDetails.php?id=63 [June 2012].

[7] Ohio is an interesting example of a state that has been sued for poor conditions of confinement while at the same time it has been engaged in statewide efforts to lower the number of youth in state facilities and to provide quality community-based alternatives for them. See Box 9-4.

[8] Available: http://www.jlc.org [April 2013].

to a privately run juvenile facility in return for cash kickbacks. More than half of the youth lacked counsel, and 60 percent of them were removed from their homes. In December 2011, the plaintiffs were awarded partial settlement of more than $17 million subject to the court's approval.[9] The Juvenile Law Center regards its most importance contribution to be the attention it has brought to the need for systemic change.[10]

Prison Litigation Reform Act

Since the mid-1990s, privately funded juvenile law centers have found it more difficult to sue on behalf of their youthful clients (Mendel, 2011). In 1996, the Prison Litigation Reform Act of 1995 was passed. This law amends and supplements the U.S. Code in a number of ways that restrict and discourage litigation by prisoners. Detained and adjudicated delinquents held in both public and private juvenile facilities are considered prisoners under the act (42 U.S.C. § 1997e(h); 28 U.S.C. § 1915(h); 28 U.S.C. § 1915A(c)) (Boston, 2004). According to Mark Soler, the 1995 act makes it more difficult to sue and to negotiate agreements.[11] Parties must have exhausted all administrative remedies before bringing the suit and must agree to the least restrictive measures that can be used to resolve the problems. The act also sets very low limits on fees for attorneys and expert witnesses, thus discouraging attorneys from taking on cases.

CRIPA Litigation

Starting in the mid-1990s, the special litigation division in the civil rights division of the U.S. Department of Justice (DOJ) began stepping up its investigations of juvenile facilities. Its authority to litigate is derived from the Civil Rights of Institutionalized Persons Act of 1980 (CRIPA), Section 14141 of the Violent Crime Control Act of 1994, and Title III of the Civil Rights Act of 1964.[12] Advocates point to *U.S. v. Georgia* (1998) as a particularly significant investigation that reflected a more activist role for the Department of Justice. It addressed systemic practices as well as specific conditions of confinement. A total of 16 remedial measures were proposed to address the lack of health, dental, mental health, suicide prevention, and

---

[9] Available: http://www.jlc.org/current-initiatives/promoting-fairness-courts/luzerne-kids-cash-scandal [April 2013].

[10] Telephone interview on June 12, 2011, with Robert Schwartz, executive director of the Juvenile Law Center. Information on the Juvenile Law Center's activities is available from http://www.jlc.org [April 2013].

[11] Telephone interview with Mark Soler, former executive director of the Youth Law Center and now current executive director, Center for Children's Law and Policy, June 13, 2011.

[12] Available: http://www.justice.gov/crt/about/spl/cripa.php [September 2011].

education services; harsh disciplinary practices; poor access to recreation and visitation; and lack of training and supervision of staff.

According to a recent analysis of monitoring or enforcement actions pending as of September 1, 2010, juvenile facilities in 35 states have been investigated or sued by the Department of Justice since 1971. Eight distinct categories reflect the kinds of problems that the responsible states or facilities have agreed (or been ordered) to improve. In addition, these categories include problems documented in a federal CRIPA investigation whether or not a case settlement has been reached:

- abuse or excessive use of force;
- excessive use of restraint and/or isolation;
- failure to protect youth from harm;
- failure to provide therapeutic environment and rehabilitative treatment;
- failure to provide required services (education, mental health, health);
- inadequate staffing or staff training;
- environmental safety issues (fire safety, crowding); and
- failure to provide opportunity for communication (mail, attorney, telephone).

Of these categories, failure to provide required services and excessive use of restraint and use of force were the most common problems. Although some lawsuits deal with specific facilities, others target the statewide juvenile justice system (e.g., Georgia, Mississippi, New York, Ohio, and Puerto Rico).[13]

Impact of Litigation

Depending on the timing, litigation can spark system reform or lend additional support to changes that are already under way. A DOJ investigation of two training schools in Louisiana in 1996 sparked the beginning of an effort to address the high rates of confinement of juveniles in Louisiana and the violent conditions under which they were held (*U.S. v. Louisiana*, 1998). Through several settlement agreements, the state addressed numerous safety, education, and medical remedial measures.[14] Of great

---

[13]From information compiled by the Youth Law Center in May 2011 and made available to the committee in July 2011. Similar information is contained in Mendel (2011, p. 7)

[14]Settlement agreement (education) filed November 1, 1999; U.S. Jena Agreement filed April 1, 2000; settlement agreement for medical, dental, mental health, rehabilitation, and juvenile justice issues filed August 8, 2000; settlement agreement filed December 31, 2003; settlement agreement filed January 1, 2004. (Information provided to the committee by the Youth Law Center, May 2011.)

significance was the closing of the Tallulah Youth Correctional Center for Youth in 2004, a facility that had received national attention for being "an institution out of control" because of rampant violence and staff brutality (JI-LA-0001-0009 June 18, 1997). The DOJ consultants encouraged the state to seek major foundation support to improve its operations, and it subsequently became a MacArthur Foundation Model for Change site. Louisiana officials have also worked closely with the Annie E. Casey Foundation. (A fuller description of the foundations' initiatives is provided in the next section.) As a result of numerous changes in law and juvenile detention and corrections policies, the number of juveniles in secure care has been reduced to 350 from approximately 1,900 youth when the investigation first began in 1997.[15]

DOJ also initiated legal action against New York (*U.S. v. New York*, 2010), in the midst of efforts by the state's Office of Children, Youth, and Family Services (OCYFS) to carry out a reform agenda that included (among other things) closing numerous large residential facilities located in upstate New York and relocating juveniles to smaller community-based facilities. According to committee member Gladys Carrión, the commissioner of OCYFS:

> In New York State, the DOJ lawsuit served to buttress our transformation efforts that were already underway. In many ways, it gave legitimacy and confirmed what we were saying about the system's shortcomings and the approach to remedy the conditions. DOJ affirmatively lauded our efforts to reform the system and their intervention heightened the awareness and sense of urgency to implement change. It helped to widen the universe of interested parties and prompted Legal Aid to sue. To an extent, it muted the opposition that now had to address the DOJ findings and forced them to find other objections to the changes we were pursuing. . . . It required the investment of additional state resources in targeted areas for multiple years. Without DOJ, given the state's dire fiscal situation, it is doubtful the system would receive additional dollars and in fact would have faced substantial cuts. . . . Overall DOJ has given us political cover to make fundamental change that probably would have been much harder to undertake, freed up money to support the reforms and made it difficult for people to continue to support the status quo.[16]

DOJ's action did not aim to effect change across the entire system (e.g., pretrial) because the investigation involved only four facilities. It also focused narrowly on mental health and conditions of confinement and did not address inadequate educational programs or lack of compli-

---

[15]Telephone interview with Judy Preston, staff attorney, special litigation unit, civil rights division, U.S. Department of Justice, June 29, 2011.

[16]E-mail exchange with Gladys Carrión, commissioner, New York State Office of Children, Youth, and Family Services, September 6, 2011.

ance with federal law regarding special education and special needs youth. Often when a lawsuit focuses on one institution, DOJ's involvement ends once the institution is closed, and ongoing DOJ review and oversight are limited.[17] In the case of New York, however, DOJ continued to monitor youth after their facility was closed and they were moved to a different one. Furthermore, DOJ is requiring New York City to carry out the settlement and policies developed prior to it, after the city assumes responsibility for city youth in state custody.[18]

In conclusion, litigation provides an incentive to reform policies and practices of juvenile justice systems. As one might imagine, state juvenile justice agencies want to avoid unfavorable media attention and protracted litigation. According to Judy Preston, an experienced staff attorney in the special litigation unit at the DOJ, states are typically responsive to the threat of litigation, and it is seldom necessary for DOJ to go to trial.[19] However, reaching agreement or being ordered to do something is often the first step in a larger reform process. Cases can remain active for years afterward. Of the 57 federal CRIPA investigations over conditions of confinement in state-funded juvenile correctional facilities, 6 cases have remained active for as long as 11 years following the initial case disposition (e.g., a settlement, consent decree, order, or decision).[20]

DOJ is now in the process of expanding its investigative activities from a traditional focus on conditions of confinement and the postdispositional stage to the moment a youth enters the system. To do so, it is relying on Section 14141 of the Violent Crime Control and Law Enforcement Act of 1994, which gives the attorney general authority to file lawsuits to seek judicial remedies when administrators of juvenile justice systems engage in a pattern or practice of violating incarcerated juveniles' federal rights.[21]

Interestingly, the court's involvement can be a double-edged sword. While improving and moderating institutional conditions and reducing harsh discipline, it can also reinforce the reliance on an institutional model. Because there is the threat of ongoing litigation, legislators may use the

---

[17]E-mail exchange with Cheri Townsend, executive director, Texas Juvenile Justice Department, September 6, 2011.

[18]E-mail exchange with Gladys Carrión, commissioner, New York State Office of Children, Youth, and Family Services, April 23, 2012.

[19]Telephone interview with Judy Preston, staff attorney, special litigation unit, civil rights division, U.S. Department of Justice, June 29, 2011.

[20]Rhode Island has the distinction of having the longest open case. In 1971, the Department of Justice initiated an investigation of conditions in the Rhode Island Boys Training School, and, since 2000, a court-appointed master has monitored compliance with the court order (*Inmates of the Boys Training School v. Lindgren* [D.R.I. filed 1971]) (Mendel, 2011).

[21]Telephone interview with Judy Preston, staff attorney, special litigation unit, civil rights division, U.S. Department of Justice, June 29, 2011.

litigation as a reason to justify higher budgets and more staff and buildings (Miller, 1991).

Influential Foundation Initiatives

Beginning in the early 1990s, foundations became increasingly aware of and involved in activities aimed at addressing the harsh treatment of youth by the juvenile justice system. Their interest in juvenile justice was a natural extension of their interest in promoting the healthy development of children and their increasing concern about poor institutional conditions, unfairness, and ineffective practices. In particular, the Annie E. Casey Foundation (Annie E. Casey) and the John D. and Catherine T. MacArthur Foundation (MacArthur) have invested millions of dollars in research, demonstrations, and TTA to support jurisdictions willing to change the way they currently handle juvenile offenders. Employing different strategies and slightly different but overlapping objectives, these foundations have assumed the mantle of leadership during a time in which it appears that OJJDP's leadership role has waned.

Annie E. Casey Foundation and Detention Reform

Alarmed by the number of youth being detained, the deplorable conditions and the troubling effects of detention on youth (e.g., isolation, increased levels of violence, suicides, lack of services), the Annie E. Casey Foundation initiated in 1992 the Juvenile Detention Alternatives Initiative (JDAI)—perhaps the most widely replicated reform initiative since the passage of Juvenile Justice and Delinquency Prevention Act of 1974. From an initial demonstration program involving five sites, the initiative has been implemented in approximately 150 jurisdictions in 39 states plus the District of Columbia (Annie E. Casey Foundation, 2012). Four of them serve as model sites: Bernalillo, California; Cook County, Illinois; Multnomah County, Oregon; and Santa Cruz, California (Mendel, 2009; Annie E. Casey Foundation, 2012).

The chief goals of the initiative are to reduce detention and to use the detention process as a lever for broader system-wide reforms. It is characterized by collaboration between juvenile justice agencies and other community and governmental organizations; use of data to diagnose problems; objective admissions criteria and instruments to replace subjective decision making; new or enhanced nonsecure alternatives to detention; case processing reforms to expedite the flow of cases through the system; minimizing special detention cases; additional specific strategies aimed at reducing racial disparities; and improve the conditions of confinement (Mendel, 2009).

Assessing Effectiveness. JDAI places a great emphasis on the collection and analysis of data for the purpose of understanding the characteristics of youth going through the system and what is happening to them. In addition to quarterly submission of data (specified by race, ethnicity, and gender) on admissions, average length of stay, and average daily population, JDAI requires each site to collect information on current charge, prior adjudications, prior failures to appear in court, and aggravating and mitigating factors. Furthermore, sites report when a youth is detained despite being at low risk for failing to appear in court or for committing another offense prior to adjudication (Soler, 2010).

Annual Results Report. In fall 2011, JDAI released its first annual results report (Annie E. Casey Foundation, 2011).[22] Although JDAI sites had been submitting annual reports since 2004, many data-related problems needed to be overcome (Mendel, 2009). The JDAI Annual Report 2009 covered 102 local sites, with data from individual sites within a state being aggregated, for a total number of data from 34 grantees. Three core areas were measured:

- impact—quantifiable change in detention utilization, postdisposition commitments and placements, public safety (reoffending and failure to appear), and racial/ethnic disparities;
- influence—specific changes in policies, practices, and programs implemented by the sites; and
- leverage dollars invested in the reporting year to support detention reform activities, whether local, state, federal, or private.

JDAI sites reported a one-third decrease in the average daily population of detention facilities, a 30 percent decrease in detention admissions, and a 5 percent decrease in average length of stay across all JDAI jurisdictions in comparison to the baseline year. JDAI reported that annual commitments to state youth corrections by the JDAI sites decreased by one-third and out-of-home placements decreased by 16 percent across all sites in comparison to the baseline year. Finally, results with respect to the racial/ethnic disparities showed a 28 percent reduction in average daily population in detention among youth of color and a 12 percent average reduction in youth of color placed out of home at disposition. Interestingly, the findings reported that reductions for youth of color in average daily population in detention and in detention admissions were lower than reductions for the overall youth population for these indicators. Reductions in average length of stay in detention and in commitments to state corrections for youth of color were

---

[22]Despite its release date, the report is entitled *JDAI Annual Report 2009.*

higher than reductions reported for the overall population for these same indicators (Annie E. Casey Foundation, 2011).

Although the JDAI report represents a real advance in the foundation's effort to assess the impact of its path-breaking national reform effort, the evaluation has significant weaknesses. A great deal of attention is given to "reductions," but comparison periods are not clearly defined. Sites have different baseline years and have been allowed to determine whether the 12-month period is a calendar or a fiscal year (FY) as long as they remain consistent. The comparison of youth of color with all youth rather than with white youth reflects an inaccurate picture of the size of the effect. In a place like Chicago or the District of Columbia, youth of color may constitute half (or much more) of the total, so the comparison may miss the contrast between youth of color and white youth. Finally, the report does not deal with other changes in the jurisdictions that might account for changes in detention or commitment—for example, whether the overall use of commitment has dropped, regardless of whether the youth had pre-trial detention, and whether new laws have been enacted that increase the transfer of youth to adult court, making it more likely that a youth who is eventually incarcerated will not be handled through the juvenile system and therefore will not be reflected in the statistics that JDAI uses. The committee also notes that, in the absence of raw data, it was difficult to understand the calculations.[23]

Despite these shortcomings, what makes the report particularly note-worthy is the honesty with which it describes the data deficiencies. These include underreported or inaccurate data regarding failure-to-appear rates, preadjudication rearrest rates, out-of-home placements, and commitments and out-of home placement of youth of color. More than two-thirds of all local JDAI sites failed to report baseline and recent-period data for the failure-to-appear and rearrest indicators—the greatest single failing in the annual results reports. Defining admissions, out-of-home place-ments, and general indicators of public safety also proved to be problem-atic. Although the report explains some of the deficiencies, it concedes the importance of addressing these problems if the sites "are to credibly claim that their detention reforms do not undermine the integrity of the court pro-cess or jeopardize public safety" (Annie E. Casey Foundation, 2011, p. 5).

Future of JDAI. Since 2003, JDAI has been increasingly focused on state-level replication efforts. The Annie E. Casey Foundation has increasingly partnered with states enlisting cohorts of counties and then expanding as other counties come on board once they see progress being made. In 2009,

---

[23]E-mail from William Feyerherm, vice-provost for research and dean of graduate studies, Portland State University, September 8, 2011.

New Jersey became the first statewide model jurisdiction and has closed three detention facilities, saving an estimated $16.5 million a year (Mendel, 2009). Florida, Maine, New York, and Pennsylvania are the most recent state partners (Annie E. Casey Foundation, 2012).

While the Annie E. Casey Foundation remains firmly committed to expanding and sustaining JDAI, it concedes that its commitment is, in the long run, insufficient either to maintain fidelity or achieve scale. Although OJJDP has provided $1 million in discretionary funds over two years to support the strategic expansion of JDAI,[24] whether a long-term federal role will emerge remains uncertain. (See Chapter 10.)

John D. and Catherine T. MacArthur Foundation's Models for Change

In the period 1996-2011, the MacArthur Foundation has expended more than $140 million to improve the treatment of youth who come to the attention of the juvenile justice system. This investment in juvenile justice grew out of the foundation's interest in promoting adolescent development as a pillar of juvenile justice practice. It was informed by the MacArthur Foundation Research Network on Adolescent Development and Juvenile Justice (1996-2005), an interdisciplinary group of scholars, policy experts, and practitioners. The network's research efforts focused on understanding the capabilities and limitations of adolescents, their risk for public safety, and their potential for change.[25]

Among the important findings of the network's research was that a significant proportion of adolescents age 15 or younger are probably incompetent to stand trial, as judged by adult measures of competency; that there are significant age-related changes in a youth's ability to consider the consequences of his or her actions and susceptibility to peer pressure; that unconscious racial stereotyping causes African American adolescents to be seen as more "adult-like" and thus more blameworthy; and that the huge variability among serious offenders makes it difficult to predict future offending based on the presenting offense (MacArthur Foundation Research Network on Adolescent Development and Juvenile Justice, 2006).

MacArthur launched Models for Change in 2004 and selected Illinois, Louisiana, Pennsylvania, and Washington to develop "more rational, fair, effective and developmentally sound" juvenile justice systems that could then serve as models of successful system-wide reform elsewhere (John D.

---

[24]Presentation by Bart Lubow, director, juvenile justice strategy group, Annie E. Casey Foundation, to the committee, January 19, 2011.

[25]Presentation by Laurie Garduque, director of juvenile justice, program on human and community development, John D. and Catherine A. MacArthur Foundation, to the committee, October 11, 2010.

and Catherine T. MacArthur Foundation, 2010). Each state was provided with a total of $10 million for five years. Rather than propose a single model, MacArthur identified eight principles that constituted the framework of an ideal juvenile justice system (see Box 9-2). The strategy has been to fund different promising models in several states, to learn from those experiences, and then to come up with several models that could then be offered to other states for adoption (John D. and Catherine T. MacArthur Foundation, 2010).

BOX 9-2
Models for Change Principles

The Models for Change framework is grounded in eight principles that reflect widely shared and firmly held values related to juvenile justice:

1. *Fundamental fairness:* All system participants—including youthful offenders, their victims, and their families—deserve bias-free treatment.
2. *Recognition of juvenile-adult differences:* The system must take into account that juveniles are fundamentally and developmentally different from adults.
3. *Recognition of individual differences:* Juvenile justice decision makers must acknowledge and respond to individual differences in terms of young people's development, culture, gender, needs, and strengths.
4. *Recognition of potential:* Young offenders have strengths and are capable of positive growth. Giving up on them is costly for society. Investing in them makes sense.
5. *Safety:* Communities and individuals deserve to be and to feel safe.
6. *Personal responsibility:* Young people must be encouraged to accept responsibility for their actions and the consequences of those actions.
7. *Community responsibility:* Communities have an obligation to safeguard the welfare of children and young people, to support them when in need, and to help them to grow into adults.
8. *System responsibility:* The juvenile justice system is a vital part of society's collective exercise of its responsibility toward young people. It must do its job effectively.

SOURCE: John D. and Catherine T. MacArthur Foundation (2010).

MacArthur also provided support to jurisdictions in another 12 states through its Action Networks. Funded during 2007-2008, the networks focused on three separate issues: reducing disproportionate minority contact (DMC), improving access to mental health services for juvenile justice youth, and improving indigent defense services.[26] A National Resource Bank provides training, technical assistance, and consultation to the MacArthur sites.[27] To date, approximately 204 Models for Change grants have been made to 92 separate agencies and organizations. In all, MacArthur has spent almost $41 million of its Models for Change funding to support TTA for state and local governments (Griffin, 2011).

The MacArthur Foundation's reach and influence in the juvenile justice field extend beyond its Models for Change initiative. MacArthur also supports several activities related to the handling of "dually involved" or "crossover" youth who are involved in both the child welfare and juvenile justice systems, often with adverse effects. (See Chapter 3 for a discussion of crossover youth.) One of these related activities is the Child Welfare and Juvenile Justice Integration Initiative, an ongoing activity in the Model for Change states. Begun in 2000, this initiative focuses on cross-system coordination and integration of the child welfare and juvenile justice systems (Herz et al., 2012). A partnership between the Casey Family Program (a separate program from the Annie E. Casey Foundation) and Georgetown's Center for Juvenile Justice Reform is implementing and testing the Crossover Youth Practice Model, specific practices aimed at reducing the number of youth who cross over between the two systems, the number of youth entering and reentering care, and the length of stay in out-of-home care (Herz et al., 2012).

Assessing the Impact of Models for Change. To date, a formal cross-site evaluation of the impact of the Models for Change program has not been conducted.[28] The Models for Change initiative is a sprawling, complex set of activities involving more than 35 jurisdictions in 16 states (Griffin, 2011). Its four key states were funded at different times and are at different stages of development. Each state determined its own starting point in the

---

[26]Available: http://www.models for change.net/aboutAction-networks.html [April 2012].

[27]Available: http://www.models for change.net/about/National-Resource-Bank.html [April 2012].

[28]In 2009, MacArthur hired Bennett Midland LLC to design a database to be used for reporting on the totality of its investments, activities, and accomplishments of Models for Change. The first report, produced in December 2011, provides a broad description of the grants (size, goals, activities) and what it calls "progress events," such as publications, activities associated with community-based programs, training, data infrastructure/use/ sharing, establishment of collaborative infrastructure, screening and assessment, and fiscal commitment (Griffin, 2011).

juvenile justice system and targeted areas of improvement. Consequently, each site conducts different kinds of evaluation activities, usually reporting qualitative information as to what was achieved. There has been some attempt to collect information on five key outcomes from the four key states on a quarterly basis (John D. and Catherine T. MacArthur Foundation, 2010). These key outcomes include

1. impartial and unbiased decision making (reduced racial disparities);
2. retention of youth in the juvenile justice system (reduced transfer and waiver to adult criminal court);
3. prosocial development and engagement (increased participation in education and rehabilitation and treatment programs);
4. public safety (reduced recidivism); and
5. informal local handling of delinquency (reduced reliance on incarceration and increased use of community-based alternative sanctions).

To date, however, this information has not been made publicly available on a cross-site basis or in a comprehensive way.

Within the Action Networks, data are also being collected on impact (Soler, 2010). For example, 20 sites in the 4 core Models for Change states and the 4 DMC states (Kansas, Maryland, North Carolina, and Wisconsin) collect data on 35 indicators developed by the W. Haywood Burns Institute in San Francisco.[29] This information is used by the sites and the Center for Children's Law and Policy, the technical assistance provider, to monitor the sites' policies and practices (Soler, 2010).

In 2008, MacArthur also funded a study of system change strategies of its four key states to identify what strategies had been implemented, their outcomes and consequences, and the identifiable facilitators and barriers for the reform initiatives (Wiig et al., 2010). According to the lead researcher on the study, it was not possible to assess outcomes because of lack of data.[30] Recently, MacArthur released a report presenting composite information on grant characteristics, grantees, grant aims, and focus areas (Griffin, 2011). It is based on data taken from the foundation's grant files and grantees' annual and final reports as well as data entered retroactively online. Although helpful in categorizing the range and scope of activities supported under the mantle of Models for Change, the report concedes that

---

[29]Examples of indicators include admissions to detention, average length of stay, and average daily population on a quarterly basis. Data are broken down by race, ethnicity, and gender.

[30]Telephone conversation with Kimberly Isett, associate professor, school of public policy, Georgia Tech, November 14, 2011.

the summarized results "should be regarded as preliminary impressions, not facts" (Griffin, 2011, p. 11).

Future of Models for Change. MacArthur is now working with state and local jurisdictions to ensure that the foundation-funded reforms can be sustained and replicated (Wiig et al., 2010). More recently, it announced that it is creating a funding partnership with OJJDP in four areas: mental health screening and risk/need assessment, mental health training for juvenile justice staff, DMC reduction, and juvenile justice and child welfare system integration (U.S. Department of Justice, 2012). It also signaled that its focus will shift to promoting statewide legislative reforms and promoting state policy changes on a national scale.[31]

Community Advocacy

Changing the way youth are handled by the juvenile justice system depends heavily on public support and acceptance. Public support can influence juvenile justice policy (Cullen et al., 1998; Roberts, 2004), and sometimes previously adopted policies reflected in statutes become out of touch with developing public opinion (Mears et al., 2007). Community-based organizations also act as drivers of reform legislation. California, Connecticut, Louisiana, and New York are four states where community advocates have been pivotal in moving the reform agenda along.

Connecticut's Raise the Age Campaign

In the past six years, a combination of litigation activities, legislative action, and community organizing has been under way in Connecticut to improve services for youth in detention, reduce detention of status offenders who have violated court orders, increase community-based services, and develop regional family support centers. The issue most closely identified with community advocates, however, is the raising of the maximum age of juvenile jurisdiction from 15 to 18.[32]

During the 1990s, Connecticut was one of only three states that had lowered the maximum age of juvenile court jurisdiction to age 15. The Connecticut Juvenile Justice Alliance composed of various groups concerned with the treatment of youth in the juvenile justice system conducted

[31]Presentation by Laurie Garduque, director of juvenile justice, program on human and community development, John D. and Catherine T. MacArthur Foundation, to the committee, October 11, 2010.

[32]Abby Anderson, executive director, Connecticut Juvenile Justice Alliance, Children's Law Center webinar, July 11, 2011. Available http://www.childrenslawky.org/webcasts/2011/5/9/trends-and-challenges-in-juvenile-justice-reform-experiences.html [November 2011].

a "Raise the Age" campaign in which it undertook intensive efforts to inform the public, the media, and legislators of the need to raise the age of juvenile court jurisdiction.[33] In July 2007, legislation was passed that raised the age of juvenile court jurisdiction from age 15 to age 16 effective January 2010 and to age 17 effective January 2012. However, it was not until October 2009, after some hard-fought battles in the legislature over cost projections and the concerns of law enforcement, that the final timetable was established and the budget was approved. Community advocates are credited with keeping the issue on course through monthly statewide advocacy meetings, working closely with state legislators to lobby for the necessary funding, and providing continuous information on the positive effects of the changes as well as the failure of various concerns to materialize.[34] The activism has paid off. On July 1, 2012, the age of juvenile court jurisdiction was raised to age 18.[35]

California's Closure of State Facilities

In the 1960s and 1970s, California had an excellent reputation for its progressive handling of juvenile offenders, but by the late 1990s its reputation had become badly tarnished by evidence of harsh treatment in unsafe, overcrowded facilities (Skonovd, 2003). As in many other jurisdictions, the drop in juvenile crime rates and the concurrent escalation in costs ($252,000/year/bed) provided the impetus for change (McCracken and Teji, 2010).

Since the 1980s, community and advocacy groups had been feeding information to the media and the legislative staff on the abuses and identifying better options.[36] They testified before the legislature, educated juvenile justice professionals (including every presiding judge and every chief probation officer), and created a public record of abuses and failure to reform. Similar to Connecticut's experience, federal litigation and a resulting court decree (*Farrell v. Cate*, 2003; formerly *Farrell v. Harper*) played a critical role in challenging all aspects of conditions in California's facilities.[37] In

---

[33] Available: http://www.raisetheagect.org [April 2013].

[34] Abby Anderson, executive director of the Connecticut Juvenile Justice Alliance, Children's Law Center webinar, July 11, 2011 (Children's Law Center, Inc., 2011).

[35] Available: http://www.raisetheagect.org.html [November 2011].

[36] Sue Burrell, staff attorney, Youth Law Center, Children's Law Center webinar, July 11, 2011 (Children's Law Center, Inc., 2011).

[37] As a result of the Farrell litigation, the California Division of Juvenile Justice is required to implement remedial plans to correct problems associated with education, disabilities, medical care, sexual behavior treatment, safety and welfare, and mental health. Since April 2006, a special master has monitored implementation of these plans. Available: http://www.prisonlaw.com/cases.php#juvi [November 2011].

addition, ongoing evidence of the abuse compiled in joint expert reports and special master reports received huge media attention. The result was pressure on Governor Arnold Schwarzenegger to focus his attention on reorganizing and reforming the system.[38] Legislation was passed imposing sliding scale fees on localities for commitments to state facilities (SB 681, 1996) and providing program funds for counties (Juvenile Justice Crime Prevention Standards Act, AB 913, 2000), increasing the discretion of judges to reduce confinement time and to bring youth back to the community, restricting parole board powers, and increasing reporting requirements (SB 459, 2003). As the state struggled to make changes in line with the *Farrell* agreement, the legislature narrowed eligibility for commitment to state facilities (SB 81, 2007), and money was allocated to the counties to serve youth locally. SB 81 banned all future commitments of nonviolent youth to the state system, allowing state commitment only if the youth was found to have committed an offense on the statutory list of crimes for which juveniles could be tried as adults. The result has been a rapid decline in the training school population (see Box 9-3). Currently, the state is deciding whether to shut down the entire state system and to have all youth handled by the counties. It is unclear at this writing what the final outcome will be (Schiraldi, Schindler, and Goliday, 2011).[39,40]

Louisiana's Transformative Initiatives

The Juvenile Justice Project of Louisiana (JJPL), a public interest law firm and youth advocacy group, was formed in late 1997 on the heels of the U.S. DOJ's investigation of the inhumane and harsh treatment of juvenile offenders. Its stated goals include reducing the use of incarceration and investing in community-based alternatives while alleviating the unconstitutional conditions of confinement (Celeste et al., 2005). Although many claims arising out of the DOJ investigation were settled in 1999 and 2000, the notoriously dangerous Tallulah Youth Corrections Center remained open through the support of numerous powerful legislators, including a former head of the Department of Public Safety and Corrections. JJPL teamed with Family and Friends of Louisiana's Incarcerated Children (FFLIC), an organization formed in 2001 to serve as the collective voice of parents

[38]Sue Burrell, staff attorney, Youth Law Center, Children's Law Center webinar, July 11, 2011 (Children's Law Center, Inc., 2011).
[39]Ibid.
[40]In the January 2012 California state budget appropriation, the state declared it would not accept serious and violent youthful offenders from the counties. In May 2012, Governor Jerry Brown inserted language into the revised budget appropriation that reversed the earlier language and required that young offenders (up to age 23) would continue to be sentenced to the California Department of Youth Services (de Sá, 2012).

BOX 9-3
Closing State Juvenile Institutions

Declining numbers of juveniles being sentenced to secure state institutions, coupled with the need to respond to budget shortfalls, is resulting in the closing of state juvenile facilities and the shifting of youth to local community-based programs. This trend has been particularly dramatic in five states:

California: The California Youth Authority originally operated 11 facilities and 4 youth forestry camps. Currently, the Division of Juvenile Justice operates 4 institutions and 1 camp. In April 2011, 1,232 youth were under the Division of Juvenile Justice, which includes more than 200 youth housed in adult prisons. In 1996, the population peaked at 10,122. At the end of 2010, the population was 1,254, a nearly 88 percent decline.

Illinois: Commitment of youth to the Illinois Department of Juvenile Justice 1996-2010 declined from 902 to 400.

Ohio: Since 2002, the state has reduced its commitments to state facilities by more than 70 percent.

New York: During 2007-2012, the state closed 18 facilities and allocated $5 million from the cost savings to support local alternatives to detention.

Texas: In 2011, 3 of 10 youth prisons closed, and money was shifted to local rehabilitation programs. Texas has cut its 5,000 youth population by half within two years. The end-of-year secure population in fiscal year (FY) 2000 was 5,646; in December 2011 it was 1,267. A cautionary note when comparing states: some states, like Texas, have a determinate sentence option, which means that some youth who are committed to state youth facilities might be sent straight to prison in another state. There is also the issue of age of juvenile and adult jurisdiction. Still, since 2007, Texas has closed 2,232 secure beds.

SOURCES: Moore (2009); McCracken and Teji (2010); California Department of the Youth Authority (n.d., p. 4); California Department of Corrections and Rehabilitation, Division of Juvenile Justice; National Campaign to Reform Juvenile Justice Systems, Report on the 2011 States (fact sheet distributed at Models for Change meeting in December 2011); Felony Commitments and Revocations of Parole for FY2002-2011 spreadsheet provided in an e-mail from Ryan Gies, deputy director, Courts and Community Services, Ohio Department of Youth Services, August 24, 2012; e-mail from Cherie Townsend, former executive director, Texas Department of Juvenile Justice (December 14, 2011).

whose children were at that time (or formerly) incarcerated at Tallulah. FFLIC efforts were at first unsuccessful. It took another two years before a full-fledged legislative and public media campaign known as "Close Tallulah Now!" was begun in force. The campaign was undertaken by JJPL, FFLIC, and the Coalition for Effective Juvenile Justice Reform, with strong support from the Annie E. Casey Foundation, the Youth Law Center, the Justice Policy Institute, and the Grassroots Initiative. Two years of intense advocacy work resulted in the passage of the Juvenile Justice Reform Act of 2003 (known as Act 1225), calling for Tallulah's closing (Celeste et al., 2005). In 2004, the legislature passed a bill creating Youth and Children Services Planning Boards, composed of all stakeholders at the local level (Bervera, 2003). In 2006, Louisiana became a MacArthur Foundation Models for Change site, and five local sites (encompassing seven parishes) have been engaged since then in building an infrastructure of local alternatives to formal processing and secure confinement, promoting access to evidence-based services, and addressing the problem of DMC (Griffin, 2009). Today, FFLIC continues to monitor conditions of confinement and to advocate for numerous reforms, including an increased role for the family in several facilities in Louisiana.

New York's Transformative Initiatives

In September 2008, a Task Force on Transforming the Juvenile Justice System was convened by New York's governor, David Paterson. Chaired by Jeremy Travis, president of John Jay College, the task force was composed of 32 juvenile justice experts drawn from around the state. It is noteworthy that 20 of them represented private organizations—universities, TTA organizations, advocacy groups, and community service organizations. The focus of the task force was the treatment of adjudicated juveniles found guilty of committing a delinquent act (a crime committed by someone between ages 7 and 15) and subject to a dispositional order. The task force's recommendations called for reducing the use of institutional placement, reinvesting resources in community-based alternatives, eliminating racial disparities, improving services during custody and after release, and ensuring system accountability (Task Force on Transforming Juvenile Justice, 2009).

The New York task force came on the heels of a major effort already under way to reform juvenile justice services. With the support of Governor Paterson, Gladys Carrión, the commissioner of the state's Office of Children and Family Services, had begun the process of closing unneeded facilities and implementing a comprehensive system reform agenda. She was able to amass considerable support by working closely with community organizations to develop necessary programs, securing foundation money for programs, collaborating with the juvenile justice network (an organization of advocacy groups), producing data regarding the costs of operating facilities, and conducting a well-organized media campaign. The task force also played an important role in supporting and sustaining the momentum. According to Carrión:

> The Task Force was instrumental in moving the process along. Its report became the blueprint for reform and the effort was given credibility. The Governor viewed the Task Force as an antidote to anticipated backlash. Here was an independent prestigious body to counter the opposition. People were respectful of such a deliberative body that was also inclusive. Its report was embraced and was responsible for pushing forward the work. It was also reassuring to the advocates who tend to want quick results. It assured them that there would be no turning back.[41]

The task force disbanded after the release of its report, but its recommendations have continued to influence juvenile justice budget decisions, according to Carrión. By March 2012, New York had closed 18 facilities, eliminating 969 beds and 1,035 full-time positions (see Box 9-3). The secure population has been reduced by 23 percent, the limited secure population by 55 percent, and the nonsecure population by 56 percent. The numbers of youth in direct care have continued to decline. Expanded mental health services for youth in facilities, as well as those being maintained in communities, have been developed. New York City Mayor Bloomberg decided not to send New York City youth to upstate facilities (Bosman, 2010). Brooklyn to Brooklyn, a newly established program located in the community, offers a continuum of nonresidential and residential services based on the pillars of the Missouri model. Incentives have been offered to jurisdictions with the highest placement rates to divert youth from detention, and reinvestment funds have been targeted to community-based services in those jurisdictions that are home to the greatest number of youth placed in state custody.[42]

PROMOTING AND SUSTAINING REFORM

Previously reviewed evidence shows convincingly that reforming juvenile justice in accord with well-established principles of adolescent development can reduce offending and promote accountability while treating juvenile offenders fairly and serving their individual needs. There is no need to trade public safety for due process and individualized treatment.

Despite the momentum for developmentally grounded juvenile justice reform, it is disappointing, though perhaps not surprising, that the changes

---

[41]Telephone conversation with Gladys Carrión, commissioner, New York Office of Children, Youth, and Family Services, July 12, 2011.

[42]E-mail correspondence from Gladys Carrión, commissioner, New York Office of Children, Youth, and Family Services, March 16, 2012.

already put in place have not been evaluated in a sufficiently rigorous and systematic manner. This lack of evaluation impedes other reform-minded jurisdictions to undertake similar initiatives with the confidence that they can be implemented successfully and will achieve the desired effects. However, the committee is impressed with the reformers' ability to generate and consolidate stakeholder coalitions, build a consensus regarding the necessary changes, create the infrastructure needed to maintain momentum, and sustain the effort over the long run. This accumulated experience inspires optimism that juvenile justice reform can be achieved successfully on a national scale.

On the basis of this perspective, the reader is asked to assume that policy makers in a state are committed to transforming their juvenile justice system so that it is grounded in a developmental perspective. The following section aims to summarize what has been learned from efforts to implement policy change, what are the obstacles to successful innovation, and what can be done to address them.

Assembling and Using Data

The issue of data quality and inadequacy has been discussed throughout this report. In Chapter 3, we note the inadequacy of the juvenile arrest data, the incompleteness of court data and the lack of available juvenile justice data due to privacy restrictions. In Chapter 6, we attribute a failure to identify effective programs to the inadequate data for tracking youth outcomes. In Chapter 8, we note the lack of racial/ethnic data on youth at various processing stages.

An essential prerequisite to designing, implementing, and sustaining reform is the compilation of critical data and analytical tools. Many agencies lack data needed for their internal operations (individual, process, and outcome data) and across systems data (education, mental health, education, child welfare).[43] Without these data, it is difficult to see the true picture of who is detained, how the system operates, what the impact is on minority youth, whether the youth is receiving the designated services, and what the impact is of the treatment he or she does receive. Agencies need to distinguish between data required for routine monitoring of processes (i.e., outputs and outcomes, such as numbers served, services delivered, costs, and quality of services) and data that are required for empirically based research evaluations (i.e., treatment outcome data, comparison data for different youth samples). A common measure of performance for many

---

[43]Presentation by Laurie Garduque, director of juvenile justice, program on human and community development, John D. and Catherine T. MacArthur Foundation, to the committee, October 11, 2010.

juvenile justice systems is recidivism data. Yet 12 states still do not track recidivism outcomes of youth released from juvenile facilities statewide in any fashion; 6 states track only the share of youth who return to juvenile custody; and another 8 measure youth's success only for 12 months or less following release (Mendel, 2011). Data are also often not available on other measures of effectiveness that indicate whether progress has been made toward successful maturation, such as academic progress, enrollment in school, job placement and retention, and health and mental well-being (Mendel, 2011). Efforts are being made to improve data and to create integrated data systems, but the impact of these efforts has been very limited thus far (see Appendix B) (Mankey et al., 2006; Wiig and Tuell, 2008). Data tools are also needed to identify problems, develop responses, and then monitor and assess the impact of policies and programs.

Both Models for Change and the Juvenile Detention Alternatives Initiative acknowledge the importance of data and describe themselves as "data-run programs" that aim to use data to inform policy and practice at the organizational and system levels. Data are also a crucial element in demonstrating a program's effect on youth and their families, the juvenile justice and other child-serving systems, and the community. Data can be used to make the case for why reform activities are needed and then can be used to support the need to sustain them (Wiig et al., 2010). (For a useful discussion of evaluation methods and challenges for anticrime programs, see National Research Council, 2005.) In both cases, automated management information systems are urgently needed (Howell, 2003a). Data collection, aggregating data, and accessing data across systems have been identified as factors impeding an organization's ability to implement change (Isett, 2011).

In summary, resolving data issues and having good data systems appear to be paramount to launching reform activities. Yet this is a challenge that often goes beyond the capacity or capability of individual juvenile justice systems or even entire jurisdictions to address adequately. One need only look at state efforts to develop and implement Statewide Automated Child Welfare Information Systems (SACWIS), mandated by the federal government in 1993, to understand how expensive and difficult a challenge it is.[44] The committee repeatedly heard from national juvenile justice leaders that an appropriate role for the federal government is to help develop accurate and timely data systems and to provide TTA in their use. The committee strongly agrees.

---

[44]Since 1993, the federal government has expended $2.3 billion getting SACWIS up and running, and some states are still in the planning and development stage. See http://www.acf. hhs.gov/programs/cb/systems/sacwis/about.htm [April 2013].

Clarity of Mission

There are 51 different juvenile justice systems in the country. As observed in Chapter 3, policies and practices based on a correctional model in which youthful offenders are detained in facilities with varying degrees of security may exist side by side with policies rooted in a rehabilitative approach focused on serving the needs of young offenders. The committee doubts that reform based on a developmental model can be achieved and sustained without resolving this tension explicitly. Papering over the problem may allow a legislative victory to be achieved, but it will not establish the necessary foundation for enduring change. The fundamental case for reform is that public safety can be well-served—indeed, better served— by abandoning a confinement-oriented correctional approach in favor of community-based services for the majority of juveniles who can be safely supervised in the community.

Leadership and Organizational Culture

Strong leadership is required to articulate and build consensus concerning the goals of reform as well as its essential elements. Accommodations on specific issues will be needed, such as satisfying prosecutorial concerns about the jurisdictional borders between juvenile courts and criminal courts, but prosecutors are not institutionally or professionally opposed to the juvenile justice reforms described in this report if they are presented with the evidence and are convinced that interventions will be undertaken to ensure public safety and satisfy legitimate public expectations about accountability.

The organizational culture of juvenile justice agencies may impede innovation. Some state juvenile justice agencies fall under state-run criminal justice facilities (e.g., California), and in other states juvenile justice responsibilities are part of the broader child-serving agency (e.g., New York). It is likely that one reason for the sustainability of the Missouri system is the fact that the Division of Youth Services is under the Department of Social Services and separate from the adult correction system (see Appendix B). Even within juvenile justice agencies, it is sometimes difficult for managers and line staff to think about the long-term benefits and not be enticed by a piecemeal approach (Howell, 2003b). In places where reform is thriving, leaders with vision are working closely with multiple groups—including the legislature, other executive agencies, community stakeholders, and the media—to explain the desired changes and to keep them well informed. Sometimes the driving force is the director of the juvenile justice state agency; in other jurisdictions, the judicial official takes the lead in bringing about change. But there is always a need for someone who can take charge and has the necessary clout to call other youth-serving agencies to the table.

Changing institutional culture is difficult and can take a long time. A Models for Change assessment team noted that, even after four years, veteran staff remained ambivalent about the transition from an adult corrections model to a juvenile-centered and rehabilitation model and unclear about their roles (Illinois Models for Change Behavioral Health Assessment Team, 2010). Missouri officials credit the transparency of their programs and their activities as a critical ingredient in keeping the support of the legislature and the public (see Appendix B). They also attribute the longevity of the Missouri model to stable leadership, an unusual occurrence in the United States, where a juvenile corrections administrator serves an average of 2.8 years.[45]

One common feature of many successfully implemented reforms is a significant investment in TTA to address organizational culture and to smooth the way for implementation by teaching specific operational skills and techniques essential to implementing reforms. Missouri estimates that it spends approximately $500,000 annually in training its staff (see Appendix B). Training was viewed by JDAI as critical to retaining support among stakeholders and by Models for Change to ensure that new personnel have the knowledge and orientation to perform their new roles (Schwartz, 2001; Wiig et al., 2010). Technical assistance also continues to be an important component of reform activities. Both Models for Change and JDAI make heavy use of peers and consultants who offer technical assistance and allow for the sharing of experiences among the sites. Peer-to-peer technical assistance, as opposed to traditional technical assistance and training models, appears to be the more favored approach (Lubow, 2011).

Structural Barriers

Structural differences may exacerbate the difficulties of establishing and sustaining collaboration between the juvenile justice agency and the courts and among the courts, juvenile justice agency, and the family/welfare/schools/health agencies. We have already mentioned the difficulties associated with housing a juvenile justice agency within the adult corrections department. Key structural barriers can also arise from differences in mission, mandates, and goals among various youth-serving agencies (Osher, 2002). These differences have been particularly noted in the fields of education (Leone, Quinn, and Osher, 2002), mental health (Shufelt, Cocozza, and Skowyra, 2010), and child welfare (Siegel and Lord, 2004; Herz and

---

[45]E-mail from Darlene Conroy, Council of Juvenile Correctional Administrators, April 18, 2012.

Ryan, 2008a; Wiig and Tuell, 2008). Achieving buy-in from different agencies often requires structural changes and the recognition that collaboration not only will further each agency's mandate but also should contribute to a shared set of goals and vision (Shufelt, Cocozza, and Skowyra, 2010; Herz et al., 2012).

Some states have attempted to reform their systems by making structural changes. Texas passed legislation in 2011 combining two separate agencies, the Texas Youth Commission and the Texas Juvenile Probation Commission, into a unified state juvenile justice agency that has direct responsibility for youth committed to the state agency as well as responsibility to establish regulations and to pass through state funding to support youth who come to the attention of local juvenile justice agencies (Senate Bill 653, 82nd Regular Legislative Session [TX2007]).

Finally, structural issues also arise from the separation of legislative and executive powers. Even if reformers are able to establish new juvenile justice policies and missions, keeping all the agencies on board and collaborating are very difficult in light of these structural problems.

Accommodating Resistant Stakeholders

A more substantial impediment is to overcome the resistance of the staff of juvenile corrections agencies, who are concerned about the loss of job security that is inevitably associated with transitions from an institution-based model to a community-based services model, for which they have not been trained. (See the earlier description of Jerome Miller's experience in Massachusetts.) The opposition may arise from local governments, particularly in small communities that are dependent on facility jobs. Well-organized opposition tends to come from the unions that represent juvenile justice staff and from legislators who support the unions. The difficulty of closing state juvenile justice facilities is analogous to the well-documented problems associated with closing state prisons and mental health facilities.

Union response to closing state juvenile justice facilities in New York is an illustration of this fierce opposition. In 2006, the unions in New York were successful in getting the legislature to statutorily impose a 12-month advance notice provision of a significant service reduction before any facility could be closed. Although there is no longer a need for a facility, unless the governor is able to secure a waiver from the legislature, the state is required to keep the facility open and fully staffed for a year after its announced closing. Efforts to minimize the impact of facility closings failed to appease the union or dampen its opposition. Since 2007, fewer than 300 people have been terminated from state service due to the rightsizing of the juvenile justice system.[46]

According to New York officials, one key to reducing union influence and power was a media campaign that exposed the shortcomings of the system and highlighted the huge cost of incarcerating each youth and the poor system outcomes. A second factor was the influence of a strong advocacy community, which mobilized quickly and was strategic in engaging diverse constituencies and targeting the legislature. Finally, the commissioner's willingness to operate in a more transparent manner and share information about the youth in care, conditions, and costs generated support among a diverse group of stakeholders.

Costs of Restructuring

Even when the reform promises to save money in the long run, added costs are often associated with implementing change in the short run, particularly when the change calls for creating a new agency or establishing new programs. It is a challenge to manage and mobilize the necessary financial resources to pay for salaries, training, and the costs associated with new programs as well as for transitional costs associated with layoffs or retraining displaced personnel. During the past two decades, states have attempted to meet the economic challenges caused by rising costs by offering financial incentives to counties for prevention programs and community-based treatment for adjudicated youth. In return, the counties agree to reduce their juvenile commitments to state facilities and intervene with youth locally. This "reinvestment" strategy was tried in Pennsylvania and Wisconsin in the 1970s and 1980s, and in the past 15 years it has gained popularity as state governments have become increasingly strapped for funds. Today, California, Illinois, North Carolina, Ohio, Texas, and Deschutes County, Oregon, all have legislative programs calling for state reimbursement to counties for youth maintained in the local community (see Box 9-4 for a description of Ohio's reforms). Wayne County, Michigan, has moved further: in 2000 it abolished its county probation agency and replaced it with a private juvenile case management system. The private provider is now responsible for all juvenile services, including residential placement, with the state matching funds that the county spends on juvenile services (Butts and Evans, 2011).

---

[46]E-mail correspondence from Gladys Carrión, commissioner, New York Office of Children and Family Services, March 16, 2012.

Building and Sustaining Program Capacity

The desire to provide high-quality community programs is a driving force for many juvenile justice reform activities. This certainly is the case in states that are shifting the numbers of youth held in state institutions to community programs. It is also a key focus of states, including Florida, North Carolina, Tennessee, and Washington, that have passed legislation requiring evidence-based programs and practices (see Box 9-5).

Committing funding sources to evidence-based programs is one part of the challenge. But an equal challenge is identifying programs at the local level capable of providing the needed services. This was a huge problem for youth services director Jerome Miller in the 1970s in Massachusetts, who admits to having gambled on community-based programs that were not very experienced (Miller, 1991). One approach used in Missouri is the creation of community liaison councils in program sites. These councils have responsibility for managing the community-based treatment programs. In addition to providing treatment, they offer peer support and a general home base in the community (see Appendix B).

Replication and Scaling Up

Replicating and scaling up successful innovations requires documentation of the innovation itself and the contextual and organizational elements that contribute to its successful implementation. As Berman and Nelson point out, "A model that produces desirable outcomes in some locations by changing the organization is likely to require organizational change in another setting. . . . Knowing that a model produces desirable outcomes in one location is not the same as knowing what makes the model work" (Berman and Nelson, 1997, p. 329). Berman and Nelson (1997) believe that it is not even possible to replicate with any fidelity; instead, replication should be regarded as an effort to stimulate a process of adaptation whose results are most likely to produce effective outcomes. Increasingly, however, this view is being challenged (Fagan et al., 2008; Hawkins et al., 2008).

The Annie E. Casey Foundation has acknowledged that rigorous replication of its JDAI model has been a challenge and attributes the difficulty to the demands of the model itself and the lack of a single dedicated funding source. A 2008 survey of its 54 sites revealed that almost all had formed leadership collaborations, had site coordinators and annual work plans with measurable outcomes, and had developed a data capacity. But sites had much more difficulty implementing case processing reforms, reducing confinement of some kinds of detention cases, and identifying factors contributing to DMC. Furthermore, few sites had been able to monitor

---

BOX 9-4
Ohio's Reforms

Since 1995, the Ohio legislature and the state's juvenile justice leadership have undertaken far-reaching statewide reforms that include highly
incentivized reinvestment strategies, e.g., RECLAIM OHIO and Targeted
RECLAIM, which allow youthful offenders to be served in their local
communities; an expansion of community-based alternatives; an expansion of evidence-based programs in its state institutions; a focus on the
behavioral and health needs of its most serious juvenile offenders; efforts
to reduce collateral sanctions; and capacity-building components related
to the support of evidence-based programs and workforce capacity.
The results to date are impressive:

- Between 2002 and 2011, Ohio decreased its annual commitments
  to state facilities from 2,336 to 633 youth (felonies and revocations). Source: Felony Commitments and Revocations of Parole for
  FY2002-FY2011 spreadsheet provided in e-mail correspondence
  from Ryan Gies, deputy director, Courts and Community Services,
  Ohio Department of Youth Services, August 24, 2012.
- Between April 2009 and July 2012, Ohio more than halved the
  average daily population of its state facilities. Source: Ryan Gies,
  deputy director, Courts and Community Services, Ohio Department of Youth Services.

---

and improve conditions of confinement for youth in secure confinement
(Schwartz, 2001).

The Missouri model has also presented great challenges to jurisdictions
attempting to replicate it. Part of the challenge arises from the fact that
some jurisdictions find themselves unable to adopt the model in its entirety.
Another challenge is the inadequacy of documentation of the Missouri
model. New York's Office of Children and Family Services found it necessary to commission a detailed set of written policies and procedures for use
with its own developing program (New York State Office of Children and
Family Services, Vera Institute of Justice, and the Missouri Services Institute, 2011). In Louisiana, replication of the model has become a political
issue with the youth advocacy group, FFLIC, sharply criticizing the inadequacy of the state's efforts to replicate the model (Families and Friends of
Louisiana's Incarcerated Children, 2011).

- Since 2010, Targeted Reclaim (the six counties that have historically committed the most youth to ODYS as well as an additional 8 counties added in 2012) has funded evidence-based treatment programs in their counties and now participates in an extensive evaluation.
- Between 2006 and 2011, Ohio treated 1,758 charged or adjudicated youth with substantial mental health impairments as part of its Behavioral Health/Juvenile Justice Initiative (BHJJI). Operating in the largest urban counties, the program diverts youth from local and state detention centers who are primarily (76%) moderate or high-risk youth into community-based mental and behavioral health treatment. Nearly 62% of the youth terminated from the program were identified locally as successful treatment completers. One year after termination, 10% of successful completers and 19% of unsuccessful completers had a new felony charge. The average cost to the state of youth enrolled in BHJJI was $4,778 compared to $167,960, the estimated costs of housing the average youth at a state facility (Kretschmar, Flannery, and Butcher, 2012).
- The Collateral Sanctions Bill, S.B. 337, signed June 26, 2012, reduces those barriers that further impact juveniles, including breach of confidentiality involving juvenile records, educational hindrances for youth returning to their communities, and laws or administrative codes that impede a youth's ability to get a job (Ohio Department of Youth Services, 2012).

JDAI is now working to achieve state-scale replication of its model. New Jersey is serving as a learning laboratory for other JDAI states. The Annie E. Casey Foundation has indicated that it hopes JDAI can be replicated in jurisdictions serving at least three-fourths of the nation's youth by 2015. Expanding to additional states and localities, sustaining detention reform in existing sites, and doing both during difficult financial times remain difficult challenges (Mendel, 2009).

The committee thinks that scientifically valid evaluations could contribute to replication efforts by providing solid evidence of the impact of reform activities and identifying effective elements of any reform model. Research aimed at examining the quality of implementation efforts across many sites can also shed important light on the factors affecting the implementation process (Durlak and DuPre, 2008; Liberman, 2011).

BOX 9-5
Legislative Commitments to Evidence-Based,
Developmentally Appropriate Policies

Illinois—House Bill 83, signed by Governor Pat Quinn, directs judges to consider whether treatment in a youth's community would be a better option than sentencing to incarceration in a state juvenile prison. HB 83 was signed on August 15, 2011, and took effect on January 1, 2011. It is an amendment to the Illinois Juvenile Court Act. Advocates said it is intended to make certain that judges determine what sentence is best for the youth and the community.

Under Public Act 95-1031 (January, 2010), 17-year-olds charged with misdemeanors will now have access to the juvenile court's mental health, drug treatment, and community-based services.

In 2005, Illinois voted unanimously to repeal an "adult time for adult crime" law that required youth accused of drug crimes in or around public schools or housing projects to be transferred to the adult system.

Mississippi—Under S.B. 2969, 2010 Leg., Reg. Sess. (Miss. 2010), most 17-year-olds are removed from the adult criminal court. The new law, which went into effect on July 1, 2011, allows juveniles charged with arson, drug offenses, robbery, and child abuse to remain under the original jurisdiction of the juvenile justice system.

Sustaining Reforms

Sustaining juvenile justice reforms is regarded by at least one foundation as "the most challenging issue facing new and innovative juvenile justice programs today" (Wiig et al., 2010, p. 3). Some efforts have been made to document the factors influencing sustainability, but the research is limited and does not appear to be very rigorous (Wiig et al., 2010).

Sustainability certainly arose as an issue 40 years ago, following the closing of the facilities in Massachusetts by Jerome Miller. Miller experienced enormous pushback from the Massachusetts legislators, who were not able to find their constituents jobs. Miller's own peers, the National Conference of State Training School Superintendents, voted to censure him, and by November 1972 he was forced to vacate his position. During the next decade, commitments to institutions continued to fall, but by the beginning of the 1990s, the number of young people in secure care in Massachusetts had risen (Miller, 1991).

North Carolina—The Juvenile Justice Reform Act of 1998 called for adoption of Office of the Juvenile Justice and Delinquency Prevention's Comprehensive Strategy framework. It was preceded by North Carolina General Statute, Chapter 143B, Executive Organization Act of 1973, which called for programs and services to be planned and organized at the community level in partnership with the state. It also established the Juvenile Crime Prevention Council at the local level to undertake planning.

Ohio—HB 86 and HB 153, signed into law in 2011, provide for the investment of funds from closed facilities into local services; enhance research-based practices; extend juvenile court authority to permit judicial release throughout a youth's term of commitment; review mandatory sentencing to allow young people to be tried in juvenile court; and adopt uniform competency standards.

Tennessee—The Evidence-Based Law, signed by Governor Bredesen on July 1, 2007 (Public Chapter 585), provides for a five-year implementation timeline for all dollars spent on juvenile justice to go to evidence-based practices. The state is conducting a review of programs' ability to generate data elements to determine effectiveness of evidence-based practices.

The Annie E. Casey and MacArthur Foundations have recognized the importance of providing guidance to their sites regarding sustainability. Each has produced a publication that specifically addresses the issue (Schwartz, 2001; Wiig et al., 2010). Both reflect the view that strategies to sustain innovations should be part of every genuine reform effort from the very beginning. They also emphasize the importance of building an infrastructure to support long-term change. Among the elements of such an infrastructure that they both cite are: strong leadership and collaborative bodies; communication and marketing strategies; data systems that can be used, not only to highlight problems, but also to provide critical information about the impact of policies and programs as well as their cost-effectiveness; and administrative practices that include an emphasis on training and skill development. As described earlier, the reforms in Missouri have been sustained by four factors: stable leadership, organizational change, treatment strategies, and constituency buy-in. Critical to its political success has been a bipartisan Youth Services Advisory Board (see Appendix B). Created by the legislature, it is a collaborative advisory body with policy responsibility, oversight, and clout. As Decker (2010) has noted, constituency building is a key element to any successful program, particularly for long-term initiatives that span legislative cycles.

Stakeholder advocacy organizations can play a vital role to ensure that the pressure for sustaining the reformist vision and commitment is maintained through leadership changes. As shown in California, Connecticut, and Louisiana, commitment and single-mindedness have helped sustain the efforts in all the diverse ways that are necessary. Foundation priorities come and go. Good inspirational leaders come and go. But these advocacy groups remain.

SUMMARY

During the past 15 years, substantial progress has been made by numerous states and local jurisdictions in embracing and implementing a more developmentally appropriate way of handling youth in the juvenile justice system. Sometimes jurisdictions have been driven to make these changes by the threat of litigation or by cuts in funding that make current practices and policies untenable. Others have responded to incentives offered by the federal government and to financial, training, and technical support provided by foundations. Juvenile justice watchdog groups and stakeholder organizations (at the local, state, and national levels) have played an increasingly important role in building consensus around the need for reform and bringing reform activities to fruition. Collaboration among the foundations and reform-minded stakeholder organizations is urgently needed if the reforms achieved during the past decade are to be sustained.

A major impediment to reform has been the lack of critical data on youth characteristics, particularly racial/ethnic data, offense data, and process data. Data on program outcomes are also urgently needed both for individual programs and larger system-wide efforts involving major jurisdictions. Both the Annie E. Casey and MacArthur Foundations acknowledge the difficulties they have had in quantifying the impact of their programs, particularly in light of other forces at work at the same time (Mendel, 2009) and the broad and flexible range of system reform models (Griffin, 2011). The Missouri model is being replicated, but its policies and practices have not been thoroughly documented and outcomes have not been assessed with scientific rigor. Resources are clearly required to conduct such assessments, but first and foremost there needs to be a commitment to undertaking this work.

The committee is disappointed with the efforts to date to define goals and specify quantified outcomes. We could find no evidence of well-constructed, scientifically valid evaluations that present the underlying theories about expected program outcomes to guide the assessment. Despite the fact that the use of logic models has gained broad acceptance as a tool for constructing and conducting evaluations, and there have been examples of well-constructed multisite evaluations with jurisdictions as the unit of analysis, these methods have not been widely employed to assess the juvenile justice reforms described in this chapter.

The committee is puzzled about why systematic evaluation has not been undertaken and can only theorize that it has not been a priority given its expense and the practical difficulty of conducting them in sites that lack adequate research expertise and an infrastructure to conduct them successfully. The federal government can play an important role in facilitating efforts to improve data collection and analysis and supporting evaluations that will promote the adoption of developmentally appropriate policies and practices.

10

The Federal Role

We now turn our attention to the role that the federal government can play in promoting more developmentally appropriate juvenile justice policies and practices. We focus specifically on the Office of Juvenile Justice and Delinquency Prevention (OJJDP), the congressionally mandated lead agency for juvenile justice. Given the current state of the field, with its receptivity to change but need for assistance, two questions arise: Is OJJDP the appropriate federal agency to guide and assist state, local, and tribal jurisdictions toward the goal of a developmentally appropriate juvenile justice system? If so, how can its leadership role be strengthened? This chapter reviews the history of OJJDP, its relevant portfolio, its current status, and presents the committee's views about the agency's future role in promoting and facilitating juvenile justice reform.

THE HISTORY OF OJJDP

OJJDP is the only federal agency specifically directed to develop and disseminate knowledge to the juvenile justice field and to assist states in improving their systems. Established in 1974, the office has authority for federal programs under the Juvenile Justice and Delinquency Prevention Act (JJDPA), as amended. This legislation reflected basic understandings that delinquent behavior is preventable and that juveniles involved in the juvenile justice system should receive individualized treatment. It also acknowledged the deficiencies of juvenile courts and the services available to them, particularly the "critically needed alternatives to institutionalization" (P.L. 93-415, Sec. 102).

OJJDP and its predecessor agencies[1] came into operation during the due process reform period of juvenile justice change described in Chapter 2 and reflected a new federal commitment to help state and localities strengthen their juvenile justice systems to make them more fair and effective (Matsuda and Foley, 1981). Congress established OJJDP to provide immediate and comprehensive action by the federal government. OJJDP was given a broad mandate to provide technical assistance and training, conduct a centralized research and evaluation effort, develop national standards, and coordinate federal activities related to the treatment of juvenile offenders and those at risk of entering the juvenile justice system. It was also given authority to provide formula grants to participating states and territories to help them meet the goals of JJDPA and develop their juvenile justice programs.

Although formula funds could be applied to a wide variety of delinquency prevention and intervention programs, receipt of this funding was tied to compliance with core requirements. The original JJDPA included two core protection requirements. Subsequent revisions to the JJDPA expanded the list of core mandates to the four that exist today (see Box 10-1). In order to receive formula funds from OJJDP, states must submit a plan every three years, which guides the development, implementation, and funding of programs to address the core requirements of JJDPA and improves state juvenile justice systems. Demonstrating compliance with the requirements necessitated the creation of adequate systems for monitoring jails, detention facilities, and correctional facilities (Office of Juvenile Justice and Delinquency Prevention, 2010). States receiving formula funds are required to distribute most of the monies to local jurisdictions.

Total funding for OJJDP from 1974-2010 is shown in constant 2010 dollars in Figure 10-1. In the early years, funds for the State Formula Grant Program (also known as Title II, Part B) constituted about two-thirds of OJJDP's budget. These formula funds were awarded to states to encourage the separation of juveniles from adult inmates, the diversion of juveniles from the juvenile justice system to community-based alternatives to confinement, and the development of new and effective approaches to the treatment of juvenile offenders.

In the 1980s and 1990s, when state policies and programs were "getting tough" on juveniles (see Chapter 2), OJJDP continued to support

---

[1]In 1912, the Children's Bureau was created to investigate and report on juvenile courts. The Division of Juvenile Delinquency Services was created under the Children's Bureau 40 years later. With the passing of the 1961 Juvenile Delinquency and Youth Offenses Control Act, the Office of Juvenile Delinquency was established within the Department of Health, Education, and Welfare. The Juvenile Justice and Delinquency Prevention Act (JJDPA) of 1974 replaced previous legislation and established the Office of Juvenile Justice and Delinquency Prevention (OJJDP) within the Department of Justice to oversee efforts in the United States to prevent juvenile delinquency and improve the quality of juvenile justice (Matsuda and Foley, 1981).

BOX 10-1
JJDPA's Four Core Requirements

- **Deinstitutionalization of Status Offenders (DSO):** Juveniles who are charged with or who have committed an offense that would not be a crime if committed by an adult, and juveniles who are not charged with any offenses, are not to be placed in secure detention or secure correctional facilities.
- **Removal from Adult Jail and Lockup (Jail Removal):** Juveniles are not to be detained or confined in any institution in which they would have contact with adult inmates. In addition, correctional staff working with both adult and juvenile offenders must have been trained and certified to work with juveniles.
- **Sight and Sound Separation (Separation):** Juveniles are not to be detained or confined in any jail or lockup for adults, except for juveniles who are accused of nonstatus offenses. These juveniles may be detained for no longer than six hours as they are processed, waiting to be released, awaiting transfer to a juvenile facility, or awaiting their court appearance. In addition, juveniles in rural locations may be held for up to 48 hours in jails or lockups for adults as they await their initial court appearance. Juveniles held in adult jails or lockups in both rural and urban areas are not to have contact with adult inmates, and any staff working with both adults and juveniles must have been trained and certified to work with juveniles.
- **Disproportionate Minority Contact (DMC):** States are required to show that they are implementing juvenile delinquency prevention programs designed to reduce—without establishing or requiring numerical standards or quotas—the disproportionate number of minorities confined in their juvenile justice systems.

SOURCE: Nuñez-Neto (2008).

---

states' efforts to comply with the requirements of JJDPA and improve their juvenile justice programs. The office began to focus on issues that affect the system as a whole, such as drugs and serious juvenile offending, and to develop programs that would help coordinate system-wide responses. One of its training programs, the Serious Habitual Offender Comprehensive Action Program, called for the active participation and coordination of all agencies in the juvenile justice system—police, prosecution, courts, probation, corrections, aftercare, and human service agencies—to deal with serious juvenile offenders. OJJDP started looking outside the bounds of the juvenile justice system and, in efforts to prevent juvenile delinquency, supported research and development on school policies and family interventions (Office of Juvenile Justice and Delinquency Prevention, 1988). One of its projects examined existing school disciplinary policies and developed and tested new policies and procedures designed to reduce school crime and disorder. Another project identified promising programs that would strengthen families in ways shown to reduce delinquency (Alvarado and Kumpfer, 2000).

OJJDP was given additional authority to support programs relating to child victimization and exploitation through the Missing Children's Assistance Act (MCAA) and the Victims of Child Abuse Act (VOCA). These programs continue to receive support. Today, the National Center for Missing and Exploited Children as well as regional and local training for AMBER Alert activities are funded under MCAA. The Children's Advocacy Centers are funded under VOCA to provide assistance for the investigation, treatment, and prosecution of child abuse cases.

In the 1992 reauthorization of JJDPA, reducing DMC[2] was elevated to a fourth core requirement tied to formula and block funds. This reauthorization also established the Community Prevention Grants program, also referred to as the Incentive Grants for Local Delinquency Prevention, under Title V to encourage prevention efforts at the local level. This Title V program was designed to encourage local leaders to assess the risk factors in their neighborhoods and develop and implement data-driven delinquency prevention strategies. It provided additional funds to states, supplementing the formula funds but specifically directed at delinquency prevention at the local level. During the period of the 1980s and 1990s, the combination of Part B formula and Title V funds represented two-thirds of OJJDP's budget.

The 1992 reauthorization also focused OJJDP's attention on the legal representation of juveniles. It funded a study to examine problems facing public defenders and impeding legal representation (Puritz et al., 1995), which led to the development of training and technical assistance (TTA) for defenders in local jurisdictions. In addition, new language in the reauthorization directed states to use formula funds to identify gaps and biases in their systems in regard to gender-specific services. The increasing involvement of young women in the juvenile justice system was a significant concern at this time. OJJDP's mandate and available funding through the formula grants as well as the new Challenge Grant Program provided a vehicle for states to address the needs of adolescent girls (Larance, 2009).[3]

---

[2]In 1992, the DMC acronym referred to disproportionate minority confinement, but the scope was changed to disproportionate minority contact in the 2002 reauthorization after it was widely determined that disproportionally extended to all parts of the system.

[3]For a description of federal leadership on gender issues, see Sherman (2012, pp. 1586-1595).

Public concerns about juvenile crime were intensified during this period. As such, OJJDP was able to grow its portfolios on illegal drugs, gangs, and serious, violent offenders. At the same time, OJJDP undertook several activities to assess the available evidence to determine the most effective programs for preventing delinquency and strengthening juvenile justice systems. The result of its efforts was a position paper entitled *The Comprehensive Strategy on Serious, Violent, and Chronic Youth Crime* (Wilson and Howell, 1993), which refocused attention on early intervention and prevention. Once youth entered the juvenile justice system, the strategy called for jurisdictions to provide a continuum of graduated sanctions tailored for first-time nonserious offending through multiple offending and serious violent offending (Krisberg, Barry, and Sharrock, 2004). As interest and support for the strategy grew, OJJDP developed an implementation guide (Howell, 1995a) and embarked on intensive TTA initiatives to pilot and push forward the adoption of the *Comprehensive Strategy* by local and statewide jurisdictions.

The office also embarked on efforts to involve other child-serving systems that have critical roles in delinquency prevention. It became an active supporter of the Blueprints for Violence Prevention Project (Mihalic et al., 2004) and helped promote the adoption of research-based prevention programs. It provided funding for TTA to nationwide replications of Blueprint programs aimed at reducing adolescent violent crime, aggression, delinquency, and substance abuse.

Its Safe Futures Initiative, launched at demonstration sites in 1996, brought family and health services, education systems, and juvenile justice together in an effort to reduce juvenile delinquency and violence. It sought to establish public–private partnerships to leverage resources needed to provide a continuum of services appropriate for diverse needs of youth (Morley et al., 2000). Three years later, OJJDP undertook other federal collaborative efforts in the school violence and child victimization areas. The Safe Schools/Healthy Students Initiative, cofunded with the Departments of Education and Health and Human Services, provided federal funding to communities to create an infrastructure that would link and integrate existing and new services that promote student development, positive mental health, and prosocial behavior (Office of Juvenile Justice and Delinquency Prevention, 2001b). OJJDP also partnered with the Department of Health and Human Services to develop and support the Safe Start Initiative, designed to address child victimization (primarily birth to age 6). Again the initiative sought to create comprehensive systems, which incorporated community assessment and strategic planning across services (Kracke, 2001).

As pressure to "get tough" on youth mounted in the mid-1990s, OJJDP was authorized to provide additional resources to states to build their juvenile justice system infrastructure through the Juvenile Accountability Block

Grant (JABG) Program.[4] A core mandate of JABG is that states must show progress toward implementing a system of graduated sanctions in order to be eligible for funding. For five years, monies appropriated through JABG represented a significant boost to OJJDP's budget and, very important, was a source of funding states relied on to build and strengthen their juvenile justice system infrastructure. Congressional support of this program even in the face of opposition by the Clinton administration[5] reflected Congress's priorities and its desire that support to the states for their juvenile justice system infrastructures should receive precedence over prevention programming. The JABG program continues today, but its funding is about one-sixth of what it was when introduced. See Figure 10-1.

Around the same time as the introduction of the JABG program, Congress began to direct OJJDP to address other areas, such as underage drinking and tribal youth justice. Congress initiated the Enforcing Underage Drinking Laws (EUDL) Program in FY1998 and appropriated $25 million annually to EUDL through FY2010. The Tribal Youth Program (TYP) was established in FY1999 and awards funds to federally recognized tribal governments to improve their juvenile justice systems. The program addresses the chronic underfunding of juvenile justice systems and services in American Indian and Alaska Native communities and the limited training and assistance available to law enforcement and justice personnel in these areas. Both programs have been appropriated funds through carve-outs from Title V funding.[6] An example of carve-outs is illustrated in the 2009 appropriations language in Box 10-2.

During the late 1990s, OJJDP entered a new stage in its development. After 1998, its total operating budget nearly tripled. See Figure 10-1. However, funds for its hallmark State Formula Grant Program dropped to less than 20 percent of the agency's operating budget from 1998 to 2010. As the number of appropriated carve-outs continued to rise, OJJDP's portfolio was increasingly shaped by congressional priorities, and its ability to support the agency's original mission declined. See Figure 10-2. By 2008, the

---

[4]JABG was originally known as the Juvenile Accountability Incentive Block Grant (JAIBG) Program. JABG funds can be spent on local programs in distinct purpose areas: graduated sanctions, corrections/detention facilities, court staffing and pretrial services, prosecutors (staffing and/or funding equipment or training), training for law enforcement and court personnel, juvenile gun courts, juvenile drug courts, juvenile records systems, information sharing, accountability, risk/need assessment, school safety, restorative justice, juvenile courts and probation, corrections/detention personnel, and reentry (Office of Juvenile Justice and Delinquency Prevention, 2009c).

[5]OMB did not include JABG in its annual budget submissions.

[6]Carve-outs are programs that Congress requires an agency to support and for which it usually specifies the budget category from which the funds should come. For example, tribal youth justice and underage drinking programs are carve-outs, and the funds to support them come from the funds allocated to the delinquency prevention program area.

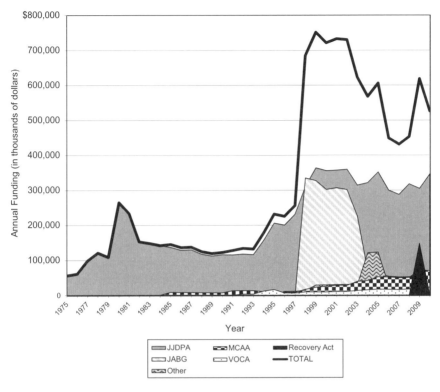

FIGURE 10-1 OJJDP annual funding 1975 to 2010 in constant 2010 dollars.
NOTES: Funding for Juvenile Accountability Block Grants, although it disappears in the graph after FY2004, has remained at about $50 million. JABG = Juvenile Accountability Block Grant, JJDPA = Juvenile Justice and Delinquency Prevention Act of 1974, MCAA = Missing Children's Assistance Act, OJJDP = Office of Juvenile Justice and Delinquency Prevention, VOCA = Victims of Child Abuse Act.
SOURCE: Created from financial information provided by OJJDP.

budget for its combined state formula and block grant programs[7] dropped to one-third of OJJDP's total budget.

JJDPA was last reauthorized in 2002 through the 21st Century Department of Justice Appropriations Authorization Act (P.L. 107-273), and, as of the writing of this report, has yet to be reauthorized. As a result, formal authorization for OJJDP's programs expired in FY2007 and FY2008.

---

[7]Combined state formula and block grant programs refers to the Title II Part B Formula Funds, Title V Incentive Grants, EUDL, and the Challenge Grants (old Title II, Part E) under JJDPA as well as block grants authorized under JABG.

BOX 10-2
Legislative Language from 2009 Appropriations (excerpt)

JUVENILE JUSTICE PROGRAMS
For grants, contracts, cooperative agreements, and other assistance authorized by the Juvenile Justice and Delinquency Prevention Act of 1974 ("the 1974 Act") . . . and other juvenile justice programs, $374,000,000, to remain available until expended as follows....
(3) $80,000,000 for youth mentoring grants;
(4) $62,000,000 for delinquency prevention, as authorized by section 505 of the 1974 Act, of which, pursuant to sections 261 and 262 thereof—
    (A) $25,000,000 shall be for the Tribal Youth Program;
    (B) $10,000,000 shall be for a gang resistance education and training program; and
    (C) $25,000,000 shall be for grants of $360,000 to each State and $4,840,000 shall be available for discretionary grants, for programs and activities to enforce State laws prohibiting the sale of alcoholic beverages to minors or the purchase or consumption of alcoholic beverages by minors, for prevention and reduction of consumption of alcoholic beverages by minors, and for technical assistance and training.

SOURCE: Omnibus Appropriations Act, 2009, H.R. 1105.

However, many of OJJDP's programs continue to receive support through appropriations. The remainder of this chapter highlights several of OJJDP's programs that have had a major impact on the juvenile justice field, and then turns to discuss its current status.

OJJDP'S PORTFOLIO

OJJDP's mandate is a broad one. Its responsibilities include collecting and documenting data on juveniles in the system, guiding and assisting efforts to prevent delinquency or improve state justice systems, ensuring states' compliance with the goals of the Juvenile Justice and Delinquency Prevention Act (JJDPA) of 1974, and sponsoring relevant research. We highlight some of its accomplishments in three areas: (1) data collection, (2) national standards, and (3) the core requirements of the JJDPA. We also provide an example of OJJDP's capacity to link research to practice.

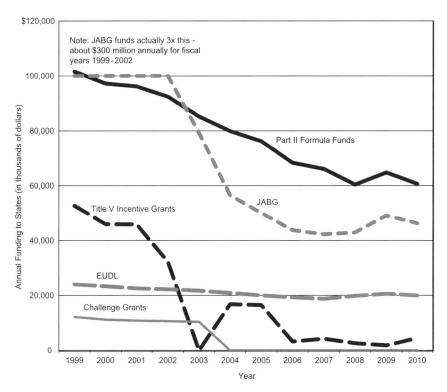

FIGURE 10-2 Trends in annual block/formula funding to states under JJDPA and JABG in constant 2010 dollars.
NOTE: In order to not distort the graph, JABG funding for fiscal years 1999-2002 is shown at one-third value. EUDL = Enforcing Underage Drinking Laws, JABG = Juvenile Accountability Block Grant, JJDPA = Juvenile Justice and Delinquency Prevention Act of 1974, OJJDP = Office of Juvenile Justice and Delinquency Prevention.
SOURCE: Created from financial information provided by OJJDP.

Data Collection

Since its inception, OJJDP has worked with other agencies both inside and outside the U.S. Department of Justice to develop a national statistics program that captures data on juvenile arrests, court cases, and placements. All these data are updated annually or biennially and made publicly available online through its Statistical Briefing Book (Office of Juvenile Justice and Delinquency Prevention, 2011b). With OJJDP's continued support, the statistics readily available to practitioners, policy makers, and researchers have steadily expanded to provide information on juveniles and cases at multiple points in the juvenile justice system.

Drawing on the FBI's Uniform Crime Reports, OJJDP produces the annual series *Juvenile Arrests* to document rates, patterns, and trends of arrests involving youth under age 18. The latest data reflect the continuing decline of both juvenile arrests overall and juvenile arrests for violent crime (Puzzanchera and Adams, 2011b).

OJJDP also funds the National Center for Juvenile Justice (NCJJ) to oversee the National Juvenile Court Data Archive. This archive currently contains more than 15 million automated case records from U.S. courts with juvenile jurisdiction; the majority of these records are delinquency and status offense records (National Center for Juvenile Justice, n.d.). The data archive produces the annual report *Juvenile Court Statistics* and maintains data sets for use by researchers as well as a web-based application tool for online access to analyze the databases from the report.

Finally, three OJJDP sponsored surveys provide data on youth in out of home placement. The biennial Census of Juveniles in Residential Placement (CJRP) is a one-day census of all youth in both private and public residential facilities. CJRP collects data on characteristics of juveniles (age, race, gender, and most serious offense), court of jurisdiction (juvenile or criminal), adjudicatory status (pre- or postadjudication), and the state or county with jurisdiction (Office of Juvenile Justice and Delinquency Prevention, 2001b). The biennial Juvenile Residential Facility Census (JRFC), first fielded in 2000, supplements the CJRP and captures facility-level information about the residential environments and the services juveniles receive while in facility placement. It requests data on facility ownership, security, capacity and crowding, as well as on injuries and deaths in custody (Hockenberry, Sickmund, and Sladky, 2011). Finally, the Survey of Youth in Residential Placement (SYRP) complements these two censuses by collecting information directly from youth through anonymous interviews. To date, the survey has been administered only once, but it has provided valuable data regarding youth characteristics and backgrounds, conditions of confinement, youth needs and services, and the nature and risk of victimization (Sedlak and Bruce, 2010; Sedlak and McPherson, 2010a, 2010b). It also provides information previously unavailable, such as the overall prevalence of all offenses for which youth are incarcerated as well as the characteristics (e.g., drug/alcohol use, accomplices) of these offenses and insight into the backgrounds, expectations, and beliefs of juveniles in custody (Sedlak, 2010).

National Performance Standards for Juvenile Facilities

OJJDP's role in developing national performance standards for juvenile facilities has been multifaceted, reflecting both its mission and its authority. It sponsored, at the request of Congress, the research study that examined the conditions of confinement and demonstrated the need for such standards (Parent et al., 1994). It provided the start-up funds for the development of standards, outcome measures, and tools. It sponsored pilot sites to test the program and provided incentives for participating facilities with funds for improvements identified by the program (Office of Juvenile Justice and Delinquency Prevention, 2001b).

The mandated study (Parent et al., 1994) found poor conditions at the turn of the 1990s—increased injuries to staff and youth due to overcrowding, high rates of suicidal behavior, few timely or professionally conducted health surveys, and high levels of staff turnover at detention and correctional facilities (Office of Juvenile Justice and Delinquency Prevention, 2001b). The study also found that existing national procedural standards, those that focus on developing policies and procedures and maintaining specific staff ratios, had no discernible effect on conditions (Parent, 1993).

OJJDP responded to these findings by initiating the Performance-based Standards (PbS) Program through a grant to the Council of Juvenile Correctional Administrators.[8] In 1998, the program was implemented in 20 facilities (Office of Juvenile Justice and Delinquency Prevention, 1999). As of April 2011, 198 facilities in 27 states subscribe to the PbS process (PbS Learning Institute, 2011). Although enrollment is increasing, current participation represents about 10 percent of total facilities in the United States.

The effects of the PbS Program have been promising. Facilities and jurisdictions that participate in PbS are in a position to make data-informed decisions and to monitor the progress of their changes. To date, the database contains more than 75,000 incident reports, more than 30,000 youth records, and more than 70,000 youth and staff surveys (PbS Learning Institute, 2011). The large volume of data allows the program to provide facilities with reliable averages and statistics for comparison. It also can be used for research. For example, Kupchik and Snyder (2009) used the PbS data to develop a model to predict victimization and fear among individual juvenile inmates.

Despite the fact that the PbS program has always been voluntary and its OJJDP support has dwindled, it continues to expand. In 2004, the PbS program transitioned from a free, federally supported program to an income-generating nonprofit, the PbS Learning Institute.

---

[8]National performance standards were developed and tested in critical areas—safety, security, order, health and mental health services, justice and legal rights, programming, and reintegration planning (PbS Learning Institute, 2011). In 2004, the Council of Juvenile Correctional Administrators was a recipient of the Innovations in American Government Award, bestowed by Harvard University's Ash Institute for Democratic Governance and Innovation and the Council for Excellence in Government, in recognition of the PbS program as an effective government program that inspires public confidence.

Core Requirements

The JJDPA, as amended, lays out four requirements that states must comply with to receive OJJDP's formula and block funds for improvements to their juvenile justice systems (see Box 10-1). Each of the core requirements reflects a developmentally appropriate practice.

States must submit a comprehensive three-year plan for meeting the JJDPA core requirements within the framework of their particular systems. Of the 56 eligible states and territories, only Wyoming has chosen not to participate in the formula grants program. Compliance with the deinstitutionalization of status offenders (DSO), jail removal, and separation is demonstrated through verified data from secure juvenile and adult facilities provided in the state's annual compliance monitoring report and a biannual monitoring audit. Determining compliance with the DMC requirement is less straightforward. It involves submission of a three-year DMC reduction plan, annual updates and the annual submission of data, known as Relative Rate Indices (RRIs) that measures disproportionality at different stages of juvenile justice system processing (see Chapter 8 for an explanation of RRIs). In addition, states must also submit updated DMC data in their three-year plan for at least three jurisdictions with the highest minority concentrations or, preferably, the localities with focused DMC reduction efforts. Failure to comply with each core requirement results in a 20 percent reduction in formula funds. Fifty percent of the remaining funds must then be used to support efforts to bring the state into compliance.

Deinstitutionalization of Status Offenders, Jail Removal, and Separation

OJJDP's greatest impact on the juvenile justice field has probably been its role in ensuring compliance with the core requirements (Howell, 1997). The JJDPA requirements spawned a permanent infrastructure for improvements (Howell, 1997). State advisory groups (SAGs) appointed by governors were created to develop and oversee state plans, and systems were established to monitor compliance. In 2010, 80 percent of the participating states and territories were in compliance with all four core requirements (Hornberger, 2010). Figure 10-3 shows the reduction in state violations of DSO, separation, and jail removal requirements between the baseline years[9] and 1993. Percentage reductions in violations for each mandate were 98 percent for DSO, 99 percent for separation, and 96 percent for jail removal.

Figure 10-4 shows the dramatic decrease in detention of status offenders since OJJDP was established. In 1975, 40 percent of status offense cases in juvenile court were detained; in 2008, only 5 percent of status offenders

---

[9]The baseline year is 1975 for DSO and separation and 1980 for jail removal.

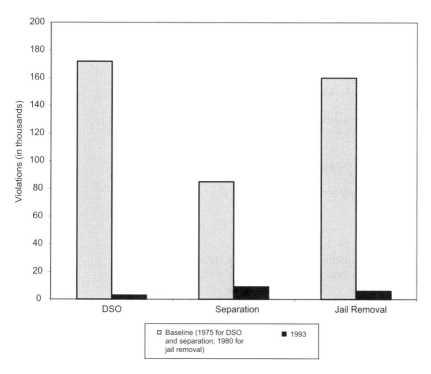

FIGURE 10-3 Violations of JJDPA mandates from baseline years to 1993.
NOTE: The baseline year is 1975 for DSO and separation and 1980 for jail removal. DSO = deinstitutionalization of status offenders, JJDPA = Juvenile Justice and Delinquency Prevention Act of 1974.
SOURCES: Office of Juvenile Justice and Delinquency Prevention (1995a); Howell (1997).

were detained. Throughout this period, about 20 percent of delinquency cases were detained. The decline in detention of status offenders represents the most significant change in the administration of juvenile justice brought about by the JJDPA.

These accomplishments are impressive, especially when one considers that the amount of federal funding states receive is a very small proportion of the overall state and local dollars going to support juvenile justice system services and consequently does not pose much of a financial incentive. Also, most states have maintained compliance with the core requirements even during periods when punishment and deterrence were emphasized.

This picture is mixed, however. During the past decade or so, many youth have not been afforded these protections because of exceptions in the JJDPA legislation, new state laws since JJDPA's passage, and policy inter-

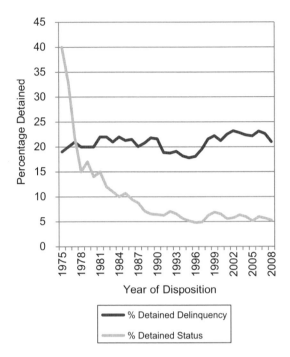

FIGURE 10-4 Trends in detention rates from court data for status cases and delinquency cases 1975-2008.
Data Sources: Authors' adaptation of NCJJ's National Juvenile Court Data Archive: Juvenile court case records for the years 1985-2008 [machine-readable data files] (National Center for Juvenile Justice, 2011) and National Juvenile Court Data Archive: Juvenile court case records for the years 1975-1984 [machine-readable data files] as presented in Office of Juvenile Justice and Delinquency Prevention (1995b).
SOURCE: Adams (2012).

pretations that have narrowed the categories of offenses that are considered status offenses and have changed the definition of an adult inmate thereby reducing the range of cases to which the protections apply.

Reclassification as Delinquent. In 1980, six years after its enactment, the JJDPA was modified because of pressure from judges to exclude youth who violated a valid court order (VCO) from the deinstitutionalization provision.[10] Today, although the federal legislation still excludes youth with

---

[10]For example, a youth who comes to the attention of the juvenile justice system because of truancy who then violates the judge's order to attend school regularly can be brought back before the judge and sentenced to detention even though truancy is considered a status offense.

VCO violations from the DSO protection, state practices vary. A total of 25 states and territories do not allow an exemption for a VCO violation, but 30 states do allow such an exception. OJJDP estimates that these jurisdictions use the exception about 12,000 times per year (Hornberger, 2010).

In the 2002 amendment of JJDPA, the provision was made to exclude juveniles held in accordance with the interstate compact on juveniles as enacted by the state.[11] It permits the temporary detention of status offenders, particularly runaways, in order to secure their return to the jurisdictions where they reside or where other appropriate custody exists while allowing states to remain in compliance with the DSO requirement and eligible for federal funding. Under interstate compact guidance, out-of-state youth placed in custody for a status offense can be detained if they are determined to be a threat to themselves or others (Montana Board of Crime Control, 2005; Interstate Commission for Juveniles, 2012).

Another factor that is affecting the detention of juveniles for status offenses is the passage of new laws that make what was formerly a status offense a criminal offense. For example, legislation passed in all 50 states and the District of Columbia classifying possession of alcohol by adults ages 18-20 as a criminal offense (minor in possession or MIP) eliminates MIP as a status offense because it is a criminal offense when committed by an adult.[12] In its direction to the states, OJJDP continues to maintain its policy that MIP offenders should not be securely detained (as either adults or juveniles) and is working with Congress to amend the language of the JJDPA.[13]

Furthermore, in the past two decades, the rise of domestic disputes charged as simple assaults, rather than incorrigibility or unruliness, has occurred particularly for girls (Stahl, Sickmund, and Snyder, 2004). Some researchers contend that the perceived increase in the delinquency of girls may actually reflect a relabeling of status offenses (Feld, 2009). With limited or nonexistent alternatives for girls who cannot or will not go back home, the juvenile court may be pressured to process girls as delinquents. As noted

---

[11]The interstate compact on juveniles is "a multi-state agreement that provides procedural means to regulate the movement across states lines of juveniles under court supervision" (Holloway, 2000).

[12]Memorandum to the states from OJJDP acting administrator, Jeff Slowikowski, regarding Status Offenders and Non-Offenders and the Juvenile Justice Delinquency Prevention Act (October 20, 2010); Memorandum to the states from OJJDP acting administrator, Jeff Slowikowski, regarding Status Offenders and the Juvenile Justice Delinquency Prevention Act, Follow-up on Data Reporting for Annual Core Requirements Determination (March 17, 2011).

[13]Guidance for Data Collection and Reporting for Minors in Possession of Alcohol Transcript, April 28, 2011. Available: http:www.ojjdp.gov/compliance/MIP_transcript.pdf [February 2012].

many times, the committee thinks confinement of noncriminal juveniles is not an acceptable solution and is likely to be more harmful.

Adult Inmate Label. In establishing the adult jail and lockup removal requirement, the JJDPA sought to promote the appropriate confinement of youth in juvenile facilities to provide for both public safety and the specific evaluation and treatment of youth needs. Exceptions in the act allow youth to be held in adult facilities for short periods of time; in these circumstances, the sight and sound separation requirement is in place to protect them from emotional and physical harm. However, currently these protections are afforded only to youth processed under the juvenile justice system and do not apply to youth under the jurisdiction of adult criminal courts.

The JDDPA currently defines an adult inmate as "an individual who has reached the age of full criminal responsibility under applicable State law; and has been arrested and is in custody for or awaiting trial on a criminal charge, or is convicted of a criminal charge offense." Under this definition, youth who are detained under criminal court jurisdiction are considered adult inmates, even in situations when they are younger than 18 at the time of offense and even when they are being held in juvenile facilities under progressive state laws. This classification has the perverse effect of requiring states to separate youth prosecuted as adults from other youth in juvenile facilities if they want to remain in compliance with the JJDPA.

Support for eliminating these exceptions to the JJDPA requirements continues to grow (Campaign for Youth Justice, 2007a, 2007b; Annie E. Casey Foundation, 2009; Coalition for Juvenile Justice, 2009; Soler, Shoenberg, and Schindler, 2009; National Juvenile Justice and Delinquency Prevention Coalition, 2010). Modifications to the JJDPA were previously considered in Senate bill S. 678 (111th Congress, 2009), that would (1) require all states participating in the formula grants program to phase out the VCO exception; (2) extend the jail removal and sight and sound core requirements to keep youth awaiting trial in criminal court out of adult lockups and to ensure sight and sound separation in some limited circumstances in which they are held in adult facilities; and (3) allow states to continue to serve youth tried in adult court in juvenile facilities without jeopardizing federal funding. Groups like the National Juvenile Justice and Delinquency Prevention Coalition (n.d.) are calling for even stronger measures that would better serve all youth under age 18, but they viewed Senate bill S. 678 as a good step toward more developmentally appropriate policies. However, the bill failed to pass and the JJDPA has yet to be reauthorized.

Disproportionate Minority Contact

Although historically few states have ever been out of compliance with this requirement, there is widespread agreement that it is still a significant, if not the most intractable characteristic, of the juvenile justice system (Pope and Feyerherm, 1990; Engen, Steen, and Bridges, 2002; Pope, Lovell, and Hsia, 2002; Bishop, 2005; Mendel, 2009). For a detailed review of the research on racial/ethnic disparities in the juvenile justice system, see Chapter 8.

OJJDP's Strategy. OJJDP carries out its federal mandate by requiring states to identify the extent to which DMC exists in their jurisdictions. Once its existence is verified, states must assess the reasons for DMC and develop and implement intervention strategies. States are then required to evaluate and monitor the effectiveness of chosen intervention strategies (Office of Juvenile Justice and Delinquency Prevention, 2009b). These five activities—identification, assessment, program implementation, evaluation, and monitoring—comprise OJJDP's DMC reduction model (Office of Juvenile Justice and Delinquency Prevention, 2010).

States are explicitly not held to any "numerical standard or quotas" (see Box 10-1)—that is, states are not required to actually reduce DMC. Instead, compliance is measured by a state's implementation of the DMC reduction model, which includes the annual submission of data known as RRIs.[14] OJJDP also reviews each state's annual report that describes its progress toward meeting the goals spelled out in its three-year DMC reduction plan.

Given that implementation of the model and progress toward carrying out the DMC reduction plan can be broadly construed, it is not surprising that noncompliance with DMC is a rare occurrence. Since 2007, only Mississippi and American Samoa have had their formula grant allocation reduced by 20 percent for failing to comply with the core requirement.[15] Each year OJJDP also identifies states that are at risk for noncompliance[16] and provides them a three-year window to act on their deficiencies. OJJDP does not make public the information on the at-risk states, but the numbers are not insignificant. In fiscal year (FY) 2011, 13 at-risk states were in the process of trying to achieve compliance. OJJDP staff acknowledged that, in

---

[14]The RRI compares the rate of juvenile justice contact experienced by different groups of youth. See Chapter 8 for a fuller explanation.

[15]Available: http://www.ojjdp.gov/compliance/compliancedata.html [February 2010].

[16]Some of the reasons states are determined to be at risk include failing to submit annual reports, submitting incomplete or nonverifiable RRIs for the different decision points, having fewer than three local jurisdictions in the state addressing DMC, or failing to follow through on interventions outlined in their three-year plans.

the past, the agency provided considerable leeway to states in determining their compliance, but in recent years it has been much stricter.[17]

To assist state and local jurisdictions, OJJDP now employs a full-time senior-level DMC coordinator and designated staff to review DMC plans and provide assistance and supports a network of consultants for TTA. In addition, it has created a DMC Best Practices Database and a DMC virtual resource center website. The agency has sponsored research on DMC measurement tools and state-of-the-art reviews of DMC research and evaluated DMC interventions. Recently, OJJDP made a sizeable investment from its limited research funds to support three grants to identify successful programs and strategies to assist states and local communities to achieve and maintain compliance with the DMC requirement.[18]

Impact of the DMC Core Requirement. By its own standards (Office of Juvenile Justice and Delinquency Prevention, 2009a), the DMC initiative has had only limited success and, in fact, OJJDP has conceded that "states and localities, except for a few jurisdictions, have not reduced DMC" (Coleman, 2011, p. 28).

This lack of progress is not surprising, given the nature and extent of disproportionality (see Chapter 8).[19] Nonetheless, OJJDP's efforts to ensure compliance with the DMC core requirement have had a positive impact on the states' willingness to address the problem. Almost half the states use formula funds to support full-time state-level DMC coordinators, and the remaining states (with one exception) have part-time or other state-level staff designated as DMC coordinators. About three dozen states have ongoing committees under their SAGs that give sustained attention to DMC (Office of Juvenile Justice and Delinquency Prevention, 2009b), and some states support DMC initiatives with their own dollars. Approximately 22 states submit RRI data to OJJDP for all contact points in their juvenile justice systems, and 39 states submit data for six or more (out of nine) contact points (Office of Juvenile Justice and Delinquency Prevention, 2009b).

---

[17]Remarks of Andrea Coleman, OJJDP DMC coordinator, at the NRC Committee on Assessing Juvenile Justice Reform meeting, October 11, 2010.

[18]The grants were 2009-JF-FX-0072 "Evaluating the Effectiveness of the Juvenile Detention Alternative Initiative to Decrease DMC and the Detention of Status Offenders," Chris Hartney, principal investigator, National Council on Crime & Delinquency: 2009-JF-FX-0103 "Expanding the Use of DMC Data: Analysis of Patterns to Identify Best Practices," Marcia I. Cohen, principal investigator, Development Services Group, Inc: 2009-JF-FX-0101 "An Impact Evaluation of Three Strategies Created to Reduce Disproportionate Minority Contact in the Detention Population," Nancy Rodriquez, principal investigator, Arizona State University.

[19]This should be juxtaposed with the fact that there are 3,033 organized county or county-equivalent governments in the United States according to 2007 Census of Governments. The OJJDP DMC initiative requires each state and three local jurisdictions to report on how they are addressing racial/ethnic disparities.

Several jurisdictions appear to have been effective in reducing DMC. In a recent analysis of three years of RRI data from more than 800 counties, Cohen and colleagues (2012) found that three states and seven local jurisdictions showed improved and/or stable and low RRI values at three of the five juvenile justice decision points (referral, diversion, detention, confinement, and transfer). When the number of decision points was reduced to two, 15 additional jurisdictions showed improvement and/or stable and low RRI values.

Obstacles to DMC Reduction. Several obstacles stand in the way of jurisdictions making greater progress toward reducing DMC. First, as described in Chapter 8, insufficiency of data needed to determine RRIs, especially data on ethnic groups, prevents jurisdictions from getting a clear picture of the extent of racial/ethnic disparities and their impact on specific minority groups.

A second obstacle is the failure of many jurisdictions to complete the critical analytical phase before initiating interventions (Coleman, 2011; Poulin, Orchowsky, and Iwama, 2011). The only states that OJJDP identifies as having conducted adequate assessments are Arkansas, Connecticut, Iowa, New Mexico, and Wisconsin. These assessments involve an investment of time, resources, and expertise that many jurisdictions have been unwilling or unable to make.

A third obstacle is the lack of rigorous evaluations and scientific evidence regarding the impact of interventions undertaken to reduce DMC (Poulin, Orchowsky, and Iwama, 2011). While some interventions at the detention stage show promise, studies to date are more likely to uncover the limitations of states' efforts than the effects of their interventions. These limitations include gaps in recordkeeping, misuse of RRI data, absence of assessments for the contributors to the RRI findings, and selection of generic prevention programs without considering their own jurisdiction's needs and the impact on racial/ethnic disparities (Coleman, 2010, 2011; Poulin, Orchowsky, and Iwama, 2011).[20]

---

[20]OJJDP's DMC Best Practices Database may be contributing to the confusion regarding the selection of interventions. The searchable database assists jurisdictions in "identifying both multicomponent jurisdictional DMC initiatives that have demonstrated a basic level of effectiveness in reducing DMC as well as single-component programmatic interventions that were not necessarily developed to reduce DMC but may prove useful as a tool in the arsenal against DMC." The committee had difficulty understanding the overall rationale for the database itself or the scientific basis for the interventions and questions whether the ease of conducting this kind of database search discourages jurisdictions from pursuing a more careful and thoughtful review.

OJJDP's Future Role in Addressing DMC. In the past four years, OJJDP has focused increased attention and resources on its DMC core requirement. But the scope of the problem and the complexities of addressing DMC call for a stronger federal policy and more intensive efforts. The committee agrees with juvenile justice advocacy groups that the DMC core requirement in OJJDP's authorizing legislation needs to be strengthened (Campaign for Youth Justice, 2007a; Coalition for Juvenile Justice, 2008, 2009; Annie E. Casey Foundation, 2009; Federal Advisory Committee on Juvenile Justice, 2009; Krisberg and Vuong, 2009; Soler, Shoenberg, and Schindler, 2009; National Juvenile Justice and Delinquency Prevention Coalition, 2010).

Recommendations by Nellis and Richardson (2010) for strengthening the federal DMC requirements, embraced in large measure by the Coalition for Juvenile Justice (2008) and the National Juvenile Justice and Delinquency Prevention Coalition (2011a, 2011b), require states to take concrete steps to reduce racial/ethnic disparities, including the improvement of data systems. Interestingly, Nellis and Richardson (2010) also suggested that the JJDPA be amended to require states to have a nongovernmental auditing body report on DMC initiatives and findings, a suggestion the committee thinks has considerable merit.

Strengthening the DMC core requirement will hold the states more accountable and will provide OJJDP with authority to monitor state progress more closely. Even in the absence of new legislation, OJJDP can increase the effectiveness of its DMC initiative by enforcing its own compliance guidelines and supporting evaluations of interventions.

OJJDP could be more transparent not only about the progress states are making but also the problems they are having. As mentioned earlier, information about states at risk for noncompliance of DMC is not made public. Nor are state plans or other compliance determination documents made available by OJJDP. In particular, the committee endorses greater transparency of all OJJDP and jurisdictional DMC activities because we think transparency will lead to greater accountability on the part of the states as well as OJJDP. However, we also recognize that decisions regarding transparency may need the support of the Office of General Counsel of the Office of Justice Programs (OJP). (For a discussion of OJJDP's relationship with OJP and its offices, see the section on reauthorization.)

The lack of empirical data on effective programs needs to be addressed by OJJDP, as does the tendency of jurisdictions to sponsor interventions that are not data driven or appropriate. OJJDP should actively assist jurisdictions to establish partnerships with universities or other research organizations to develop evaluations and carry them out. It should also clarify the limitations of its DMC Best Practices Database. Although support for research initiatives has become increasingly difficult, OJJDP should make evaluations of DMC interventions a priority and should continue its practice of an annual research solicitation on DMC.

Linking Research to Practice

Unlike many other agencies,[21] OJJDP is authorized to support a broad range of activities, including research and evaluation, TTA, and the dissemination of information, as well as to provide direct funding to state, local, and tribal jurisdictions. Over the years, it has developed a research-to-practice continuum in which it has been able to leverage research knowledge and statistics to inform program development and shape juvenile justice policies and practices. This continuum provides important feedback to guide future research.

From the beginning, OJJDP's research portfolio has focused on issues of interest to practitioners in the juvenile justice field. In the 1970s, OJJDP supported work to better understand youth gangs in America as well as violent and chronic juvenile offending. In the 1980s, OJJDP supported the initiation of two longitudinal studies that continue today, with additional funding from other federal and private sources: the Seattle social development project[22] and the Program of Research on the Causes and Correlates of Delinquency (see Box 10-3). In the 1990s, OJJDP turned its attention to juvenile justice systems and sponsored a study on the conditions of confinement as well as a study of the American Indian and Alaskan Native justice systems. It also collaborated with other federal agencies and private foundations to support a longitudinal component to the Northwestern Juvenile Project, which examined alcohol, drug, and mental health disorders. In 2000, OJJDP launched another longitudinal study, Pathways to Desistance, to investigate the factors that lead youth who have committed serious offenses to continue or desist from offending. The agency also developed research programs to respond to girls' involvement in delinquency and to bullying and its potential impact on truancy and delinquency. In each decade, OJJDP funded research to review the practice of transferring juveniles to the adult court system (Hamparian et al., 1982; Fagan, 1991; Snyder, Sickmund, and Poe-Yamagata, 2000; Lanza-Kaduce et al., 2002; Fagan, Kupchik, and Liberman, 2007; Griffin et al., 2011).

---

[21]For example, other agencies in the Office of Justice Programs—the Bureau of Justice Assistance, the Office for Victims of Crime, the Bureau of Justice Statistics—do not have this full complement of authorities.

[22]The Seattle social development project, primarily funded by the National Institute of Drug Abuse, is a longitudinal project that has tracked more than 800 youth from 1985 to present in order to examine aspects of youth development, such as substance use, delinquency, violence, school dropout, and changes in health status. For more information on the project, see http://www.ssdp-tip.org/SSDP/index.html [May 2012].

BOX 10-3
Longitudinal Studies

The Program of Research on the Causes and Correlates of Delinquency was begun in 1986 with three studies: the Denver Youth Survey, the Pittsburgh Youth Study, and the Rochester Youth Development Study. For each project, in addition to data collection from records, researchers conducted individual, face-to-face interviews with urban youth considered at high risk for involvement in delinquency and drug abuse (Browning et al., 1999). The repeated contact with youth during a substantial portion of their developmental years has generated knowledge about pathways to delinquency, chronic offending, substance use, and neighborhood influences, to name a few areas (Thornberry, Huizinga, and Loeber, 2004).

The Causes and Correlates research program reached great stature in part because it constitutes the largest shared measurement approach ever achieved in delinquency research. The three research teams worked together to ensure that certain core measures were identical across the sites. OJJDP encouraged the collaborative analyses across the sites, which in turn have advanced understanding of delinquency by replicating some findings across sites, distinguishing why certain other findings apply to one site or population rather than other sites or populations, and aggregating data across sites to study phenomena that otherwise could not be studied at one site because of its low base rate (e.g., illicit drug use other than marijuana) (Loeber, Huizinga, and Thornberry, 1996).

OJJDP initially funded the research program, but this longitudinal investigation is ongoing because of its continued support as well as funding from other sources.* This long-term support has extended data collection on the samples into adulthood, allowing examination of the transitions from adolescent to adult offending and desistance. From over two decades of research, a huge data set is available on young individuals as they grow up in inner cities from age 6 through their 20s (Loeber, Huizinga, and Thornberry, 1996).

The following findings from the Causes and Correlates program, in conjunction with statistical trends in juvenile crime and other research knowledge available at the time, guided the development of OJJDP's Comprehensive Strategy for Serious, Violent, and Chronic Juvenile Offenders:

- Three pathways to chronic delinquency can be distinguished: (1) the overt pathway from aggression to fighting then violence, (2) the covert pathway from minor covert behavior to property damage then serious delinquency, and (3) the authority conflict pathway from stubborn behavior to defiance then authority avoidance.
- Most chronic juvenile offenders start their criminal careers prior to age 12.
- Early-onset offenders tend to come from poorer, inner-city disadvantaged neighborhoods.
- Gang members are responsible for a very large and disproportionate share of delinquent acts, especially more serious and more violent acts.
- Membership in adolescent street gangs facilitates involvement in serious and violent delinquent behavior. That is, delinquent behavior is highest during periods of active gang membership compared with either before or after such periods.
- While relatively few in number, chronic violent delinquents self-report committing the majority of violent offenses.
- Any successful effort to reduce youth violence and juvenile delinquency must deal with chronic offenders.
- No current ability enables accurate prediction of who will be chronic offenders.
- Chronic violent offenders tend to be less attached to and less monitored by their parents; have less commitment to school and attachment to teachers; have more delinquent peers and are more apt to be gang members; and are more likely to reside in poor, high-crime areas.
- Coordination is often lacking among different agencies in their efforts to curtail the emerging delinquent career of early-onset offenders.

---

*Other sources of funding include the Centers for Disease Control and Prevention, the National Institute on Drug Abuse, the National Institute of Mental Health, and the National Science Foundation.

SOURCE: Wilson and Howell (1993), with findings from Huizinga, Loeber, and Thornberry (1992).

Throughout the years, OJJDP has supported the transfer of knowledge gained from research to practice through its many program demonstrations, evaluations, and technical assistance efforts. For example, early research examined strategies to remove status offenders from secure confinement and to prevent their entry. Based on the evaluation findings, TTA were formulated and provided to help states meet the DSO requirement. Similar efforts were made to link research on serious violent offenders to program development efforts.[23] In recent years, OJJDP has focused on developing online tools to assist practitioners with identifying relevant research as well as promising strategies and programs: the model programs guide and database; the national DMC databook; the strategic planning tool for youth gang programming; and the DSO Best Practices Database.

OJJDP funds an array of services to assist practitioners and to provide training to them, including a number of TTA centers. The National Training and Technical Assistance Center (NTTAC)[24] was established in 1995 to coordinate requests for assistance and to direct practitioners to appropriate resources and/or deliver customized assistance as applicable. It provides assistance relating to five of OJJDP's initiatives: the Title II formula grants program, the Title V community prevention grants program, the JABG program, the girls' delinquency and crime initiative, and the DMC initiative. Training has also been expanded to a wider juvenile justice audience. Other centers supported by OJJDP include the Center for Advancement of Mentoring, the National Center for Missing and Exploited Children, the National Center for Youth in Custody, the National Gang Center in collaboration with the Bureau of Justice Assistance, the Tribal Youth Training and Technical Assistance Center, and the Underage Drinking Enforcement Training Center.

Comprehensive Strategy

A signature program of OJJDP that evolved more than a decade ago, the Comprehensive Strategy for Serious, Violent and Chronic Juvenile Offenders, illustrates OJJDP's research-to-practice continuum. The comprehensive strategy started as a theory of reform (Wilson and Howell, 1993)

---

[23]These demonstration programs included the Violent Juvenile Offender R&D Program, with its focus on dispositional options for the treatment and reintegration of violent juvenile offenders; the Serious Habitual Juvenile Offender/Drug Involved Program, which examined justice system resources on serious crime by juvenile drug users; the Habitual, Serious, and Violent Juvenile Offender Program, which focused on swift, intensive prosecution and improved correctional programs; and the Intensive Aftercare Program for Serious, Violent Juvenile Offenders, which identified and tested a model for providing effective aftercare services for juvenilesz

[24]For more information on NTTAC, see https://www.nttac.org [February 2012].

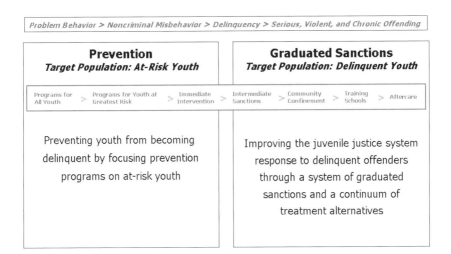

FIGURE 10-5 The comprehensive strategy for serious, violent, and chronic juvenile offenders.
SOURCES: Howell (1995a, 2011).

based on available research and evaluation. Findings from various lines of research, including OJJDP's Causes and Correlates research program (see Box 10-3), served as a basis for the strategy. The strategy framed a proactive response to juvenile delinquency as a continuum of programs aimed at both prevention and graduated sanctions (see Figure 10-5 and Box 10-4).

The development of the comprehensive strategy identified critical research gaps and served as a guide to three subsequent national research reviews supported by OJJDP and designed to fill these gaps (Howell, 2003c). The first review focused on research findings from prevention and intervention programs for juvenile offenders and youth at risk of offending and was incorporated in a guide for the comprehensive strategy (Howell, 1995a) and in the sourcebook (Howell et al., 1995). Both documents were intended to provide considerable detail about the strategy, its research underpinnings, and planning activities. The second review, conducted by the Study Group on Serious and Violent Juvenile Offenders (Loeber and Farrington, 1998), expanded on the earlier assessment, with particular attention to risk and protective factors for serious and violent juvenile offenders and promising and effective prevention and treatment programs for them. The third review, conducted by the Study Group on Child Delinquents, explored what was known about the causes and treatment of problem behaviors in children ages 12 and younger (Loeber and Farrington, 2000, 2001).

The comprehensive strategy spawned research on program interven-

---

BOX 10-4
Program Framework of the Comprehensive Strategy

In the Comprehensive Strategy Framework, program interventions and sanctions move from least to most restrictive.

- Community primary prevention programs oriented toward reducing risk and enhancing strengths for all youth.
- Focused secondary prevention programs for youth in the community at greatest risk but not involved with the juvenile justice system or perhaps diverted from the juvenile justice system.
- Intervention programs tailored to identified risk and need factors, if appropriate, for first-time minor delinquent offenders provided under minimal sanctions, such as diversion or administrative probation.
- Intervention programs tailored to identified risk and need factors for nonserious repeat offenders and moderately serious first-time offenders provided under intermediate sanctions, such as regular probation.
- Intensive intervention programs tailored to identified risk and need factors for first-time serious or violent offenders provided under stringent sanctions, such as intensive probation supervision or residential facilities.
- Multicomponent intensive intervention programs in secure correctional facilities for the most serious, violent, and chronic offenders.
- Postrelease supervision and transitional aftercare programs for offenders released from residential and correctional facilities.

SOURCE: Lipsey et al. (2010, p. 38).

---

tions supported by OJJDP. Meta-analyses of juvenile delinquency research were able to demonstrate the effectiveness of treatment programs (Lipsey, 1995); they also showed that there was a relatively small amount of variability by gender,[25] age, race, or ethnicity (Lipsey, 1992, 1995; Lipsey and Wilson, 1998). For a discussion of the findings from meta-analyses, see Chapter 6.

The comprehensive strategy was well received at both the national

---

[25]Note that intervention research has been heavily dominated by studies of male samples. Although the few studies with girls show similar variability as that among boys, there is not yet sufficient evidence to draw confident conclusions.

and the state levels by juvenile justice practitioners and researchers. OJJDP released the guide (Howell, 1995a) through a national summit and a series of workshops at annual association meetings. More than 70,000 copies of the guide were distributed (Krisberg, Barry, and Sharrock, 2004), and OJJDP undertook extensive TTA initiatives to help jurisdictions and communities engage stakeholders and develop plans that would lead to jurisdictions adopting a continuum of prevention and juvenile justice system programs and identifying additional funding sources for new programs. A critical role for technical assistance was to sustain enthusiasm for the difficult and time-consuming planning process (Krisberg et al., 2004). By 2001, 42 local comprehensive plans had been completed since the TTA initiatives began (Mondoro, Wight, and Thell, 2001).

Comprehensive Strategy as a Model for Reform

The comprehensive strategy demonstrates the importance of the planning model and the role that OJJDP plays in influencing the field. OJJDP's assistance to the states and localities focused on a four-phase planning process that included (1) mobilization of community groups (justice components as well as schools, social services, businesses, and parents); (2) inventory and assessment of risk factors and systematic responses to those factors; (3) development of a plan for creating new programs and enhancing existing services; and (4) implementation of the plan. It encouraged people to think about risk and protective factors and to tailor programs to specific youth. Participants in the comprehensive strategy planning reported improved communication and coordination among agencies and increased awareness of the prevention services and sanction options available for juveniles (Coolbaugh and Hansel, 2000). Local officials chose to reallocate resources to support effective programs, to avoid duplication of services, and to promote greater accountability (Mondoro et al., 2001). Plans were also used to secure funds from other state and federal sources (Krisberg et al., 2004).

The comprehensive planning strategy demonstrated that many communities had an interest in strengthening their services for youth and their families but often lacked information about delinquency and treatment patterns in their areas and needed the assistance in obtaining and interpreting accurate data (Krisberg et al., 2004). Data collection efforts proved to be challenging. Difficulties in identifying appropriate data and data sources as well as accessing these data were commonplace. Even when available, data were difficult to analyze because of the inconsistencies in definitions and recording mechanisms across agencies (Coolbaugh and Hansel, 2000). Communities expressed a need for continuing technical assistance to update their planning data, establish management information systems to track their progress, and to identify promising programs (Krisberg et al., 2004).

OJJDP supported the development of guides for TTA to communities in the comprehensive strategy process (Howell, 1995a; Crowe, 2000). For the comprehensive strategy initiatives, pilot sites received extensive multiday training to orient key leaders to the strategy, to provide the information and tools necessary to create a data-based profile of community strengths and needs, and to assist communities in developing an outcome-focused, data-driven five-year plan (Coolbaugh and Hansel, 2000). This model of extensive TTA was repeated in several OJJDP's initiatives, such as the Safe Futures, Safe Schools/Healthy Students, and Safe Start initiatives. For all these initiatives, OJJDP's support focused on a few pilot sites. Other states and jurisdictions took on the implementation of the comprehensive strategy on their own through efforts of state juvenile justice specialists and advisory groups, guided by OJJDP publications (Howell, 2003c). At this writing, the comprehensive strategy serves as a platform to help states translate research knowledge into policies and practices in the juvenile justice system improvement project conducted by Georgetown University's Center for Juvenile Justice Reform (Lipsey et al., 2010).[26]

OJJDP'S CURRENT STATUS

Over nearly four decades, OJJDP has compiled an impressive record of leadership and achievement. We now turn to OJJDP's current budget and political status.

Budget

The following sections examine how recent appropriations, which have included numerous carve-outs and earmarks, have diminished the capacity of OJJDP's authorized programs—particularly its state formula/block grant programs, mandate to coordinate federal efforts, nonearmarked research and data collection, and technical assistance—to carry out the core requirements of the JJDPA.

Funds for State Grant Programs

Earlier Figures 10-1 and 10-2 indicated that OJJDP funding authorized through JJDPA has been relatively stable over the last decade but that funding available to support juvenile justice improvements by state and local

---

[26]For more information on the Juvenile Justice System Improvement Project, see http://cjjr. georgetown.edu/jjsip/jjsip.html [February 2012].

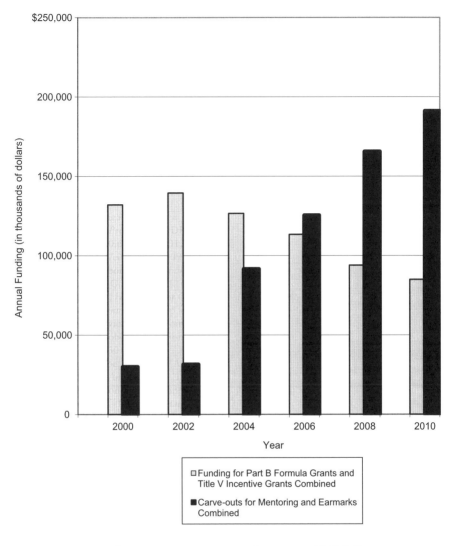

FIGURE 10-6 Trends in OJJDP appropriations in constant 2010 dollars, carve-outs for mentoring and earmarks, 2000 to 2010.
SOURCE: Created from financial information supplied by OJJDP.

governments has steadily declined by 83 percent from 1999 to 2010 in constant 2010 dollars. The reason for this decline is the dramatic decline in funding available through JABG since 2003 as well as the increase in appropriated carve-outs under Title II and Title V (e.g., Enforcing Underage Drinking, Tribal Youth Program, mentoring) and earmarked programs (see

Figure 10-6). Note that recent restrictions on earmarks have not restored OJJDP's base funding, as monies continue to be appropriated through carve-outs to special programs.

The 2002 reauthorization of JJDPA replaced the challenge grants program with the demonstration projects program under Part E, Title II.[27] Both programs authorized OJJDP to make grants to state, local, and tribal governments and private entities to carry out programs to develop, test, or demonstrate promising new initiatives that may prevent, control, or reduce juvenile delinquency. For FY2004 to FY2010, monies allocated under Part E went to awards directed by statutory earmarks. As such, funding was dedicated to specific programs in specific states and could not be directed otherwise by either OJJDP or the states. Significant portions of earmarked funds, particularly in the last two or three years, were directed toward mentoring programs for youth (Fitzpatrick, 2010). (The increase in appropriated funding specifically directed for mentoring programs is discussed later in the chapter.)

Funds for Federal Coordination

The original JJDPA established an independent organization in the executive branch known as the Coordinating Council on Juvenile Justice and Delinquency Prevention as a vehicle through which OJJDP was intended to exert its leadership to coordinate the federal government's juvenile delinquency programs. JJDPA, as amended, has changed the composition of the coordinating council[28] over the years but continues to address the need for coordination at the federal level.

The coordinating council holds quarterly meetings that are open to the public and serve as forums for member agencies to share information on their initiatives and to hear about relevant research efforts from guest presenters. These meetings serve to engage agencies and organizations that might not normally interact (Coordinating Council on Juvenile Justice and Delinquency Prevention, 2008).

Funding for federal coordination is appropriated under the JJDPA Part A. In the past, there was a cap of $200,000 to support coordinating council meetings, with additional funding to support other agency activities, usually at OJJDP's discretion, including some interagency projects. Appropriated funding for federal coordination under Part A dropped from $6.8 million in FY2002 to zero in FY2010. In 2005-2006, when OJJDP had

---

[27]See also OJJDP's report of awards for statutory earmarks at http://www.ojjdp.gov/Funding/fy10awards.html [May 2013] and http://www.ojjdp.gov/funding/fy09/earmarks.pdf [May 2012].

[28]The current composition of the coordinating council is available at http://www.juvenilecouncil.gov/members.html [March 2012].

more than $1 million in Part A funds, the agency was able to convene the 2006 coordinating council conference and to support various partnerships with coordinating council member agencies. As Part A funding decreased significantly between 2006 and 2008, it was used solely to support the coordinating council meetings and a few other specific interagency projects. With partial support from U.S. Department of Health and Human Services, OJJDP was able to develop the resource portal www.cciToolforFeds.org. In recent years, there has been no appropriation for the coordinating council, whose meetings have been funded by carryover, set-aside, and other discretionary funds to support continuation of meetings and basic cross-agency work. OJJDP doesn't have the resources to fund the necessary research, evaluation, and data collection on its own. It needs a strong mechanism to coordinate funding and activities among other federal agencies in pursuit of improving prospects for all youth.

Funds for Research, Evaluation, and Data Collection

The original JJDPA of 1974 established the National Institute for Juvenile Justice and Delinquency Prevention (NIJJDP) within OJJDP to conduct research and evaluation, development and review of standards, training, and collection and dissemination of information. A research institute of significant size and stature never materialized. Instead, from FY1975 to FY2003, OJJDP maintained a research and program development division to direct its research program, which was supported by appropriated funds to the NIJJDP, as well as set-aside funding (up to 10 percent) from its other programs.

The 2002 reauthorization of JJDPA amended Title II to eliminate NIJJDP and provide authority directly to the OJJDP administrator to oversee research, training, technical assistance, and information dissemination. Funding for this "new" research program (known as Title II, Part D) was appropriated in FY2004 and FY2005 but discontinued thereafter. Currently, OJJDP has to piece together funding from the set-asides across its programs and collaborations with other agencies in order to continue its mandated research program. As a result, research funding has been cut in half from $40 million in FY2002 to $23 million in FY2010 (in constant 2010 dollars).

OJJDP has been directed by Congress to use set-aside monies for research, evaluation, and statistics activities that benefit the authorized programs. Given the increasing carve-outs by Congress, OJJDP's research portfolio in the areas of youth mentoring and tribal youth have experienced a significant boost in the last three years. The set-aside money under the state formula program is primarily being used to support continuing efforts, like the statistics program discussed earlier, a research data archive, the model programs guide, and longitudinal studies begun in the 1980s. Very little funding is available to support new research that can inform states' efforts to improve their juvenile justice systems.

Funds for Training and Technical Assistance

Funding to support TTA is also drawn from appropriations to OJJDP's individual programs. Some set-asides for TTA are legislatively limited; others are not. For example, TTA programs under MCAA, VOCA, and Title V of JJDPA do not have a limit. The programs under Title II of JJDPA[29] and JABG had a 2 percent set-aside limit for TTA until FY2011, when that limit was increased to 5 percent. There is also an additional appropriation specifically for TTA directly to the states under the Title II Part B Formula Grant program, so that the TTA funds represent 4 percent (now 7 percent) of the total appropriation to the formula grant program.

Overall, OJJDP's funds for TTA have fluctuated modestly between $40 and $60 million annually in the past decade. However, because of the legislative restrictions and declining funds to the state grant programs, 75-80 percent of OJJDP's TTA dollars have supported training and technical assistance outside the scope of JJDPA since FY2004. Specifically, these funds support programs under MCAA and VOCA. Remaining funds support TTA to states related to the formula grants program (8 percent) and special initiatives under Title V (the carve-outs), such as EUDL and TYP (12 percent). Note, however, that from FY2008 to FY2010 there has been insufficient TTA funding available under the Title V community prevention grants program to support local assessment of prevention needs and development of appropriate programs. As funding for the state grant programs continues to decline, the set-aside limit for TTA is increasingly inadequate to support the needs of the field.

Juvenile justice practitioners have identified the need for more thorough guidance on complying with the core requirements, particularly the DMC requirement, citing the inadequacy of the guidance currently provided under the JJDPA and by OJJDP (Coalition for Juvenile Justice, 2009). Many states have turned to establishing partnerships with private foundations and organizations, such as the W. Haywood Burns Institute, that are engaged in DMC reduction efforts and can provide assistance. Given OJJDP's limited resources, it should continue efforts to partner with other organizations to provide TTA, such as its recent partnership with the MacArthur Foundation. The MacArthur Foundation is providing $1 million per initiative

---

[29]This would include the Part B State Formula Grant Program, the Part E Demonstration Projects Program (which generally does not use its TTA set-aside), and the Part G Mentoring Program.

in matching funds to OJJDP to support mental health screening and risk assessment, the integration of juvenile justice and child welfare services, mental health training in juvenile justice, and DMC. Among the activities the DMC initiative will support is intensive technical support and funding to two communities willing to engage in a "strategic, data-driven effort" to reduce DMC.[30]

OJJDP's Mentoring Portfolio

One can see how a weakened budget and lack of programmatic discretion might play itself out when one examines OJJDP's mentoring portfolio. Mentoring is an example of a program for which an extensive privately and publicly funded network has grown up to provide prosocial experiences to at-risk youth. OJJDP has supported this network through its grant programs for almost two decades. Mentoring has great congressional support and, in the last few years, OJJDP has been directed to increase its support of mentoring programs. At this writing, mentoring programs consume approximately 50 percent of funds appropriated to OJJDP under the JJDPA.

As discussed in Chapter 4, the committee recognizes that an authoritative, supportive adult plays a significant role in the healthy development of an adolescent. For many adolescents, this critical relationship happens naturally through engaged parents, relatives, teachers, and/or coaches. But for many at-risk youth, there is no one who fulfills this important role. Despite its recognition of the important role mentoring can play, the committee has serious reservations about the recent surge in funding for mentoring programs in OJJDP's portfolio. First, federal support for mentoring appears to have outpaced what is known about its effectiveness and second, OJJDP's core budget and portfolio are increasingly consumed by mentoring programs. The state of the research on mentoring as well as OJJDP's support for mentoring programs over the past two decades are discussed further in Appendix C.

The increase in funds directed at mentoring programs comes at a price (see Figure 10-6). Because funds to support OJJDP's hallmark state formula and block grants are declining, OJJDP is constrained from helping states and localities with other interventions that may better fit their local needs for preventing delinquency. Mentoring is but one intervention. Research has shown that it takes a succession of effective experiences (or interventions) for adolescents to develop into prosocial adults. No single program can serve all youth or incorporate every feature of positive developmental environments (National Research Council and Institute of Medicine, 2002).

[30]For more information, see http://www.cclp.org/apply.php#About [February 2012].

Therefore, excessive resources in one program, like mentoring, do a dis-service to the juvenile justice field more generally and to state, local, and tribal jurisdictions more specifically by overriding or ignoring their efforts to assess their own identified needs and efforts.

Reauthorization

Foundation executives, youth advocates, and juvenile justice practi-tioners, including a former OJJDP administrator, describe OJJDP as being in a state of decline in both capacity and stature (Bilchik, 2008, 2010).[31] A *Washington Post* editorial described OJJDP as being "hampered, to the point of being ineffectual, as a result of serial budget cuts; the absence of an administrator at the helm has only exacerbated its woes" (*The Washington Post*, 2011).

OJJDP's authorizing legislation (P.L. 107-273) expired in 2007 and 2008, although funding support has continued. Numerous efforts to reau-thorize the agency have been unsuccessful.[32] Since 2009, OJJDP has been without a presidentially appointed administrator—the only OJP bureau that does not have one.[33] Both circumstances have contributed to its weakened state. For that reason, the committee was very interested in the context in which reauthorization efforts have occurred, the views of the field regard-ing the reauthorizing legislation, and the implications for OJJDP's future.

OJJDP Management and Grant Administration Issues

At the same time that reauthorization of OJJDP has been under con-sideration, its grant monitoring and grant award processes have come under scrutiny (U.S. Government Accountability Office, 2009). OJJDP's reputation suffered serious damage in spring 2008 when it was discov-ered that the OJJDP administrator and OJP assistant attorney general

---

[31]Presentations by Laurie Garduque, director, Juvenile Justice Program on Human and Com-munity Development, John D. and Catherine T. MacArthur Foundation, to the committee, October 11, 2010, and Bart Lubow, director, Juvenile Justice Strategy Group, Annie E. Casey Foundation, to the committee, January 19, 2011. In addition, a written statement to the com-mittee, Nancy G. Hornberger, Coalition for Juvenile Justice, provided a field perspective on JJDPA compliance (August 4, 2010).

[32]Senator Patrick Leahy, chairman of the Senate Judiciary Committee, has sponsored reau-thorizing legislation for OJJDP. Known as the Juvenile Justice and Delinquency Prevention Reauthorization Act of 2009 (S. 687), it cleared the Senate subcommittee but was never voted on by the full committee. No new bill was introduced during the 113th Congress. Several House bills were also introduced during the same period. H.R. 1873 was closest to the Senate bill but never moved forward.

[33]In February 2012, Laurie Robinson, the assistant attorney general for the Office of Justice Programs resigned, and as of December 2012, a permanent appointee has not been nominated.

had overruled the recommendations of peer reviewers and program staff in awarding FY2007 grants. A number of well-publicized congressional hearings were held, and Congress requested a full investigation (June 27, 2008). The resulting report from the Department of Justice's Office of the Inspector General strongly criticized OJJDP for its poor review processes and nondocumentation of reasons for selecting grants that had not been highly rated.[34] The OJJDP administrator was also criminally investigated for his hiring practices, travel expenses, and personal ties to groups that receive funding from OJJDP (Johnson, 2008).

Relationship with the Office of Justice Programs. OJJDP's lack of an appointed leader affects its ability to negotiate and argue its position on numerous matters with its oversight agency, the Office of Justice Programs, and the assistant attorney general (AAG) who directs it. As described in the National Research Council report on the National Institute of Justice (National Research Council, 2010), the AAG wields a great deal of authority through oversight of the budget and control of the various offices that support the component agencies of OJP.[35] Since 2005, many functions and activities previously undertaken by the individual offices have been centralized. Examples of these functions include peer review and dissemination activities. In addition, numerous budgeting, staffing, and grant awarding documents must go through various OJP offices during review and must receive AAG approval. A strong OJJDP leader is necessary to maintain a balance between the interests and needs of an individual agency and those of its oversight agency.

Failure to Promulgate Regulations. Since the passage of the JJDPA reauthorizing OJJDP in 2002, OJJDP has failed to publish formal federal regulations to implement the law, despite the criticism of the juvenile field for failing to do so (Bilchik, 2008; Coalition for Juvenile Justice, 2009). Regulations prepared by OJJDP staff have been submitted several times to the Office of the General Counsel (OGC) but have failed to move forward.[36] In the absence of regulations, OJJDP relies on OGC for guidance, and the

---

[34]Department of Justice, Office of Inspector General, Audit Report 09-24, "Procedures Used by the Office of Juvenile Justice and Delinquency Prevention to Award Discretionary Grants in FY 2007" (April 2009).

[35]These include the Office for Administration, the Office for Audit, Assessment and Management, the Office of Civil Rights, the Office of Communications, the Office of the Chief Financial Officer, the Office of the Chief Information Officer, and the Office of the General Counsel.

[36]In 2003, regulations were prepared by Roberta Dorn, former director of the state relations and assistance division, OJJDP and recently by OJJDP's Kathi Grasso, attorney advisor. There may have been other versions of regulations that were submitted to OGC of which the committee's staff is unaware.

result has been described as "federal policy by executive memo" (Bilchik, 2008). This kind of policy making does not adhere to federal rule-making standards or to the JJDPA, which stipulates that the OJJDP administrator is required to consult with states when establishing rules, regulations, and procedures that affect the federal/state partnership and compliance with JJDPA requirements (JJDPA Sec. 299A).

In 2003, the juvenile justice field became particularly alarmed by an OGC ruling that youth convicted as adults in criminal court, including youth under the age of majority at the time of the offense, were classified as "adult inmates" under the JJDPA. This interpretation had perverse effects as applied to youth in states with so-called blended jurisdiction because youth under the age of majority who are tried in criminal court can be sent to a juvenile facility until they reach the maximum age of a state's juvenile court jurisdiction; the youth then finishes the sentence in an adult correctional facility. However, because the juveniles were adult inmates under the DOJ interpretation, states found themselves facing sanctions if they failed to remove these youth from juvenile facilities. This policy was reversed in 2008 after what has been described as "unrelenting education and advocacy efforts" by those who understood the devastating effect this "rule" would have on youthful offenders (Coalition for Juvenile Justice, 2009). States were particularly concerned that such a policy could be developed without seeking public comment or consultation from those in the juvenile justice field. Subsequently, the states have urged that JJDPA be amended to affirm that rule-making functions of the OJJDP administrator are subject to the Administrative Procedures Act of 1946 (Coalition for Juvenile Justice, 2008).

Challenges to OJJDP's Research and Statistics Functions. Even though OJJDP is mandated to undertake juvenile justice research and had a robust research program until 2002, questions have arisen as to whether it should retain its research function. In 1999, the assistant attorney general proposed a reorganization plan for OJJDP that placed responsibility for all criminal and juvenile justice research with the National Institute of Justice (NIJ). OJJDP successfully argued the case for retaining the research and the statistics function within OJJDP,[37] and although steps were taken to reorganize OJP, the proposed transfer of research to NIJ did not occur. Since 1999, there have been other challenges to OJJDP's research function. In 2002, NIJ staff was asked to develop a plan for phasing in OJJDP research to NIJ,[38] and in 2003 OJJDP was required to transfer funds to NIJ to conduct

---

[37]Terence Thornberry, recommendations to the Assistant Attorney General regarding Juvenile Justice Research, Statistics and Evaluation (January 14, 1999).

[38]Personal communication from Betty M. Chemers, former director of NIJ's evaluation division.

evaluability assessments and outcome evaluations of OJJDP juvenile justice program earmarks (National Research Council, 2010).

The most recent challenge occurred in FY2011 when the assistant attorney general sought and received approval for a policy requiring OJJDP, along with the Office for Victims of Crime and the Bureau of Justice Assistance—offices that do not have a legislatively authorized research and statistics function similar to OJJDP—to transfer 2 percent of their total program funds to the NIJ and the Bureau of Justice Statistics (BJS) to support their research and statistics activities.[39] An internal working group among the sister agencies is providing some input into the planning process for these dollars, but there is no requirement that their concerns or recommendations must be addressed by the directors of NIJ or BJS.

Support from the Field

The simplest explanation for why OJJDP has not been reauthorized is its lack of champions from the current administration or the Congress. In contrast, the juvenile justice field overwhelmingly supports OJJDP's reauthorization and its leadership role. More than 360 organizations support the Act 4 Juvenile Justice Campaign (Act4JJ), which has been leading the reauthorization effort for the past three years.[40] The Federal Advisory Committee for Juvenile Justice, the Coalition for Juvenile Justice, and the National Juvenile Justice Delinquency Prevention Coalition have issued statements urging Congress to reauthorize OJJDP and the president to appoint the OJJDP administrator (Coalition for Juvenile Justice, 2008; Federal Advisory Committee on Juvenile Justice, 2010; National Juvenile Justice and Delinquency Prevention Coalition, 2011a, 2011b).[41] In addi-

---

[39]Similarly to OJJDP, NIJ and BJS have also experienced budget reductions and increasingly less funding discretion. It is worth noting that OJP's Office for Victims of Crime, the Bureau of Justice Assistance and occasionally, OJJDP had transferred funds to NIJ and BJS for designated research activities. In an effort to provide more funding to them, the AAG determined that it was logical that states and local jurisdictions that benefit from the fruits of criminal justice research should support them. The congressional appropriators agreed.

[40]For a list of organizations participating in the Act4JJ campaign, see http://act4jj.org/participating_orgs.html [May 2012].

[41]The Coalition for Juvenile Justice was established by JJDPA, Sec. 223(f)(2)(A)-(E), and is a national organization of 1,500 members representing state advisory group members and juvenile justice practitioners. Its council is composed of 48 state advisory group chairs/chair-designees from states, territories, and the District of Columbia; the Federal Advisory Committee for Juvenile Justice (FACJJ) is a consultative body established by the JJDPA (Section 223—check for full citation) of appointed representatives of the state advisory groups that advise the president and Congress on matters related to juvenile justice and the progress and accomplishments of OJJDP. The National Juvenile Justice and Delinquency Prevention Coalition is a broad-based collaboration of youth- and family-serving, social justice, law enforcement, corrections, and faith-based organizations working to improve public safety by

tion, the committee heard from leaders in juvenile justice who voiced a strong commitment to the JJDPA and to the leadership role that OJJDP should play (Bilchik, 2010).

Although there are some variations in the specific recommendations of various youth advocacy groups supporting JJDPA, there is consensus that the reauthorizing legislation should substantially strengthen the core requirements; enhance OJJDP's capacity to advance best practices, promote prevention, and achieve and maintain compliance with the core protections; expand OJJDP's training, technical assistance, research and evaluation efforts; and enhance transparency and communication among OJJDP, the states, and Congress (see Box 10-5 for a list of specific recommendations by Act4JJ).

SUMMARY

OJJDP's authorizing legislation clearly envisions a strong partnership between the federal government and state juvenile justice agencies, as well as a strong leadership role for OJJDP. The Congress anticipated that OJJDP would "help states and communities prevent and control delinquency and strengthen their juvenile justice systems and coordinate and administer national policy in this area" (Office of Juvenile Justice and Delinquency Prevention, 2011a, p. 40394).

The Juvenile Justice and Delinquency Prevention Act of 1974 reflects several basic understandings that have set the nation on the path toward developmentally appropriate juvenile justice policies and practices. The guiding premises are that youth who offend should be treated differently and separately from adults who offend, that juvenile offending is preventable, and that youthful offenders should receive individualized treatment and services (P.L. 93-415, Sec. 102). The legislation's four core requirements reflect several normative principles that underlie developmentally appropriate policies and practices: youth who are not a risk to society or themselves should not be detained or removed from their existing support systems; youth are vulnerable and should not be in contact with adult criminals; and youth need to be treated fairly and equitably as a matter of justice.

The policies and principles reflected in JJDPA remain as valid today as they were almost 40 years ago. The core requirements of the JJDPA and OJJDP's efforts to ensure compliance have helped young people avoid detention when not warranted and unsafe conditions when detained. But progress has been impeded by new laws and policy interpretations that did not exist at the time JJDPA became law. In the case of the DMC require-

---

promoting fair and effective policies, practices, and programs for youth involved or at risk of becoming involved in the juvenile and criminal justice systems.

BOX 10-5
Act 4 Justice Recommendations for
Reauthorization Legislation

1. Extend the jail removal and sight and sound separation core protections to all youth under age 18 held pretrial, whether charged in juvenile or adult court.

2. Change the definition of "adult inmate" to allow certain states to continue to place youth convicted in adult court into juvenile facilities rather than adult prisons without jeopardizing federal funding.

3. Strengthen the disproportionate minority contact (DMC) core protection by requiring states to take concrete steps to reduce racial/ethnic disparities in the juvenile justice system.

4. Strengthen the deinstitutionalization of status offenders (DSO) core protection, which prohibits the locked detention of status offenders, by removing the valid court order and interstate compact exceptions.

5. Provide safe and humane conditions of confinement for youth in state and/or local custody by restricting the use of JJDPA funds for dangerous practices and encouraging states to promote adoption of best practices and standards.

6. Assist states in coming into compliance with the JJDPA and establish incentive grants to encourage states to adopt evidence-based or promising best practices that improve outcomes for youth and their communities.

7. Enhance the partnership between states and the federal Office of Juvenile Justice and Delinquency Prevention (OJJDP) by expanding training, technical assistance, research and evaluation, and the partnership between OJJDP and Congress by encouraging transparency, timeliness, public notice, and communication.

8. Expand juvenile crime prevention efforts by reauthorizing and increasing funding for JJDPA Title V and Mentoring.

SOURCE: National Juvenile Justice and Delinquency Prevention Coalition (n.d., p. 1).

---

ment, failure to set clearer expectations as to what is required and to monitor jurisdictions' progress in an objective and transparent way has limited its impact. The committee has noted the lack of publicly available reports on state plans, compliance status, and compliance determinations. It has also noted the desire on the part of juvenile justice policy makers for clear guidance on how to reduce racial/ethnic disparities. The committee concludes that greater transparency will lead to greater accountability on the part of OJJDP and state, local, and tribal jurisdictions for reducing DMC.

OJJDP currently is constrained from carrying out its legislative mandate to help jurisdictions work toward a fair and effective juvenile justice system. It has been weakened in the last decade by budgetary constraints as funds for its formula and block grant programs have declined and discretion to determine its programmatic priorities has narrowed. The biggest impact has been felt by jurisdictions that need the funds to address juvenile justice system needs. Because set-asides from formula and block grant funds are the biggest source of TTA dollars, the activities designed to provide guidance and assistance to improve juvenile justice infrastructures have also been greatly curtailed.

During its long history, OJJDP has responded to important needs of the juvenile justice field. OJJDP-funded research has enhanced understanding of juvenile crime and its prevention. OJJDP's training and technical assistance functions are greatly valued and needed by the juvenile justice field. Particularly during a time when state, local, and tribal governments are under pressure to adopt high-quality and cost-effective ways of dealing with juvenile crime, technical assistance and training are critical resources that communities need to identify and implement effectively evidence-based programs.

OJJDP will be able to draw on strategies that have been successful in the past to bring about change and improvements. But to do so will require that Congress remove the budgetary and political roadblocks that prevent OJJDP from making use of its legislative authority. As we have noted earlier, advocacy and juvenile justice practitioners continue to support OJJDP's mandate because they believe in the importance of a federal role in assisting state, local, and tribal jurisdictions to prevent crime and improve their handling of juvenile offenders. They believe that OJJDP should act as a bully pulpit to call attention to the needs of youth involved in the juvenile justice system and to get the Congress and jurisdictions to respond appropriately to those needs. Restoring OJJDP's authority and funding for its core mission will confirm the value of the purposes set forth in the legislation and will enable OJJDP to provide robust guidance for the developmentally appropriate treatment of juveniles in the justice system.

11

Moving Forward

Adolescent offenders are different from adult offenders, and their risk-taking behavior, including illegal activity, is often a predictable and transient feature of adolescence itself. Knowledge about the developmental features of adolescence has important implications for juvenile justice policy, providing the framework for a system that is fair to young offenders and effective in promoting legal socialization and reducing youth crime. An important opportunity for major policy reform exists because juvenile justice policy makers are increasingly aware of the developing body of research on adolescence and increasingly receptive to reforms grounded in a developmental perspective.

Many gaps in understanding remain. The experiential evidence is impressive in reform jurisdictions, but there is still little systematic empirical evidence that the major policy initiatives described in this report (see Chapter 9) have reduced delinquency and have done so at a reasonable cost. However, even in the absence of definitive evaluations of major reforms, the committee is convinced that the impressive body of research on adolescent development and the effects of juvenile justice interventions and programs is now sufficiently robust to provide a solid foundation for juvenile justice policy and for guiding policies and practices as knowledge continues to develop.

In this chapter, we describe several key components of an ongoing process for achieving and sustaining developmentally based juvenile justice reform: clarification of the goals of the juvenile justice system; robust interagency collaboration; strategic commitments by state, local, and tribal governments to an ongoing, transparent, multistakeholder process of designing, implementing and evaluating reform; a strengthened supporting role for the Office of Juvenile Justice and Delinquency Prevention (OJJDP); a comprehensive research program on adolescent development and juvenile justice; and an improved statistical system.

CLARITY OF PURPOSE

Juvenile justice is a complex, multiagency system with multiple goals that often are perceived to be in tension with one another. The formal goals and purposes of juvenile justice have varied from place to place and from era to era (Bernard and Kurlychek, 2010). The origins of modern juvenile justice can be traced back to the 19th century, but many salient features of the current system have emerged more recently. In the 1970s, juvenile proceedings became subject to the constitutional vision of fundamental fairness, a challenge that has not yet been fully met. In the 1980s and 1990s, many states modified the mission of their juvenile systems to incorporate a greater emphasis on punishment and incapacitation. Some states later reversed some of those policies, but the statutory mission of juvenile justice continues to evolve. Lawmakers today are more likely to require the juvenile system to hold young offenders accountable for their law violations and to include "proportionate" sanctions in the statutes setting forth the goals of juvenile courts—as the states of Arkansas, Georgia, Hawaii, Illinois, Iowa, Louisiana, Michigan, Missouri, and Rhode Island have done. Other states—Kentucky, Massachusetts, North Carolina, Ohio, South Carolina, Vermont, and West Virginia—still emphasize prevention and rehabilitation in their legal frameworks. In most states, the formal mission of the juvenile system is a mix of rehabilitation and public safety.

Despite these historical swings of emphasis, the basic legal structure of juvenile justice has survived since it was first conceived in 1899—a separate noncriminal court charged with responding to juvenile offending and emphasizing crime prevention rather than punishment. Tensions lie beneath the surface, and the interactions between law enforcement agencies and child welfare agencies will always reflect some differences in mission and perspective. However, the committee thinks that these complexities can be managed successfully within a developmental framework.

The overarching goal of the juvenile justice system is to support prosocial development of youth who become involved in the system and thereby ensure the safety of communities. The specific aims of juvenile courts and affiliated agencies are to hold youth accountable for wrongdoing, prevent further offending, and treat youth fairly. As we have explained in this report, these aims are compatible with one another and can all be achieved if they are implemented within a developmental framework. Guiding principles for implementing a developmentally informed approach to juvenile justice reform are set forth in Box 11-1.

INTERAGENCY COLLABORATION

A developmental approach to juvenile justice often requires a greater institutional reach than delivering court-ordered services or imposing sanctions for wrongdoing. The juvenile justice system has to devise interventions that help youth develop the strong sense of belonging that fosters positive attachments to prosocial adults, peers, and communities. To avoid criminal behavior, youth need access to positive and rewarding learning experiences. They need help navigating the school system and with gaining real work experience and developing sound job readiness skills. Like all adolescents, justice-involved youth also need to participate in vigorous physical activities and learn to have fun without breaking the law. They need access to a diverse array of activities, supports, and opportunities for normal development. These resources also need to be delivered in an environment that is itself developmentally appropriate and conducive to healthy development.

This complex mission makes it impossible for the agencies of the juvenile justice system to operate alone. Juvenile court judges typically cannot ensure that public schools work effectively with youth. Probation officers cannot guarantee that young people have access to stable housing. Prosecutors typically cannot provide youth and their families with access to the labor market and the personal resources to obtain and hold onto steady jobs. The very mission of the juvenile justice system requires it to be interorganizational, cross-sector, and multidisciplinary. In every one of these other systems and service sectors, however, justice-involved youth may be the least attractive, most troubling, and often most expensive clients encountered by an agency. Juvenile justice authorities must work with partners, but the partners may not be deeply motivated to work with them. Organizational partners may accept client referrals from juvenile justice authorities, but their first goal may be to jettison the most "noncompliant" youth they are asked to help. Thus, even a developmentally oriented juvenile justice system will confront challenges when it reaches across the boundaries of the child welfare, mental health, and education systems. An essential component of developmentally oriented juvenile justice reform is to establish genuine partnerships with the agencies that will be recruited to serve the needs of the youth who have become involved with the justice system or who are at risk of becoming involved (Cocozza and Skowyra, 2000; Bilchik, 2009; Shufelt, Cocozza, and Skowyra, 2010).

Collaboration among agencies at the federal level is also needed for systems change and for providing effective support and services (Lehman et al., 1998). Delinquency is one of several problem behaviors that share

BOX 11-1
Guiding Principles for Juvenile Justice Reform

The overarching goal of the juvenile justice system is to support prosocial development of youth who become involved in the system and thereby ensure the safety of communities. Juvenile courts and affiliated agencies specifically aim to hold youth accountable for wrongdoing, prevent further offending, and treat youth fairly. Actions taken to achieve these aims should be designed and carried out in a developmentally informed manner.

Accountability

- Use the justice system to communicate the message that society expects youth to take responsibility for their actions and the foreseeable consequences of their actions.
- Encourage youth to accept responsibility for admitted or proven wrongdoing, consistent with protecting their legal rights.
- Facilitate constructive involvement of family members in the proceedings to assist youth to accept responsibility and carry out the obligations set by the court.
- Use restitution and community service as instruments of accountability to victims and the community.
- Use confinement sparingly and only when needed to respond to and prevent serious reoffending.
- Avoid collateral consequences of adjudication, such as public release of juvenile records, that reduce opportunities for a successful transition to a prosocial adult life.

Preventing Reoffending

- Use structured risk/need assessment instruments to identify low-risk youth who can be handled less formally in community-based set-

many of the same risk markers. Thus, in addition to OJJDP, support by other federal agencies of research on adolescent development, on racial/ethnic disparities, and on evidence-based programs that are targeted at a variety of unhealthy and risky behaviors will also help inform juvenile justice policy and practice. Collaboration has been defined as "the process of individuals or organizations sharing resources and responsibilities jointly to plan, implement, and evaluate programs to achieve common goals"

tings, to match youth with specialized treatment, and to target more intensive and expensive interventions on high-risk youth.

- Use clearly specified interventions rooted in knowledge about adolescent development and tailored to the particular adolescent's needs and social environment.
- Engage the adolescent's family as much as possible and draw on neighborhood resources to foster positive activities, prosocial development, and law-abiding behavior.
- Eliminate interventions that rigorous evaluation research has shown to be ineffective or harmful.
- Keep accurate data on the type and intensity of interventions provided and the results achieved.

Fairness

- Ensure that youth are represented throughout the process by properly trained counsel unless the right is voluntarily and intelligently waived by the youth.
- Ensure that youth are adjudicated only if they are competent to understand the proceedings and assist counsel.
- Facilitate participation by youth in all proceedings.
- Intensify efforts to reduce racial/ethnic disparities, as well as other patterns of unequal treatment, in the administration of juvenile justice.
- Ensure that youth perceive that they have been treated fairly and with dignity.
- Establish and implement evidence-based measures for fairness based on both legal criteria and perceptions of youth, families, and other participants.

(Jackson and Maddy, 1992, p. 1). Coordination and cooperation are helpful, but collaboration is needed to move the juvenile justice field forward.

Given current fiscal constraints, collaboration among federal agencies should also be geared toward pooling resources and simplifying processes for the delivery of support and services. There are excellent examples of past collaboration on programs and policies occurring at the federal level. In the schools area, OJJDP, the Departments of Health and Human Services (the Substance Abuse and Mental Health Services Administration, the Administration for Children, Youth, and Families) and Education pooled funding and staff to support local community school violence reduction programs.[1] In the mental health arena, funding from OJJDP and the Center for Mental Health Services was combined to promote inclusion of youth with mental health needs involved in the juvenile justice system with other systems of care (Cocozza and Skowyra, 2000). In the disabilities area, the law reauthorizing the Individuals with Disabilities Education Act (IDEA) (34 CFR Part 300.244) allowed school districts to use their federal funding for programs that would improve results for children with disabilities and their families (Leone, Quinn, and Osher, 2002).

Sustained progress toward formulating and implementing developmentally appropriate juvenile justice policies and practices will depend on the willingness of state, local, and tribal juvenile justice policy makers and federal agencies to collaborate fully and share the responsibility for carrying out their important mission.

POLITICAL COMMITMENT TO REFORM BY STATE, LOCAL, AND TRIBAL GOVERNMENTS

Given the current fiscal realities regarding the role of OJJDP and the role of the federal government in general, the immediate momentum for change will need to come from the state, local, and tribal governments. Numerous state and local jurisdictions appear to be making progress toward more developmentally appropriate juvenile justice policies and practices. But many jurisdictions lack political support for reforms or the readiness to take the necessary first steps. Even among reform-minded jurisdictions, many have not yet undertaken system-wide improvements; they appear to be progressing on some fronts and backsliding on others. Moreover, some specific reforms, such as reducing racial/ethnic disparities and improving access to counsel, are being addressed at a very slow pace and by relatively few jurisdictions.

A key element to success in building and sustaining organizational and constituent support for reform has been the willingness of policy makers at all levels to be engaged in the process and to be transparent regarding the effectiveness and costs of their current programs and policies. Two strategies have been helpful: (1) the use of bipartisan, multistakeholder task forces or commissions to promote consensus and long-term follow-through and (2) collaboration with foundations, OJJDP, and other youth-serving organizations to leverage resources. In the past decade, several private

---

[1]For information on the Safe Schools/Healthy Student Initiative, see http://www.sshs.samhsa. gov [September 2012].

foundations have provided incentives, taken risks, seeded innovation, and added value to existing efforts in order to accelerate progress toward system reform. Foundation priorities may change, but the need for reform remains, and it is incumbent upon private organizations and the federal government to coordinate their activities so that dollars can go further and can be used more effectively to foster a developmentally appropriate juvenile justice approach.

Many reform activities have not been adequately documented or evaluated, particularly those aimed at reducing racial/ethnic disparities. State, local, and tribal juvenile justice policy makers should form partnerships with universities or other research organizations to measure performance and assess outcomes with scientific rigor. System-wide reform efforts as well as individual programs should have clearly stated goals and objectives that can be measured scientifically, either on an individual site basis or across many sites. A plan for collecting and analyzing the necessary data should also be developed and the assessment made public.

> **Recommendation 1: State and tribal governments should establish a bipartisan, multistakeholder task force or commission, under the auspices of the governor, the legislature, or the highest state court, charged with designing and overseeing a long-term process of juvenile justice reform. This body should**

a. Undertake a formal, authoritative, and transparent review of its juvenile justice system aiming to align laws, policies, and practices at every stage of the process with evolving knowledge regarding adolescent development and the effects of specific juvenile justice interventions and programs.

b. Develop a strategy for modifying current laws, policies, and practices, for implementing and evaluating necessary changes on an ongoing basis, and for reviewing any proposed juvenile justice legislation.

c. Intensify efforts to identify and then modify policies and practices that tend to disadvantage racial/ethnic minorities at various stages of the juvenile justice process and publish periodic reports on the nature and extent of disparities and the effects of specific interventions undertaken to reduce them.

STRONG SUPPORTING ROLE FOR OJJDP

The policies and principles reflected in the sequence of legislation establishing and authorizing OJJDP are now buttressed by a strong body of scientific knowledge regarding adolescent development as well as an impressive array of research on juvenile offending. Its core protections reflect developmentally appropriate policies and practice; however, many youth are not currently afforded the protections. Strengthening the legislation will send a strong message regarding the need for state, local, and tribal governments to assume greater responsibility for complying with the requirements and achieving a developmentally appropriate juvenile justice system. It will also enable OJJDP to redirect its resources in a way that best supports the efforts of state, local, and tribal jurisdictions.

Recommendation 2: The role of OJJDP in preventing delinquency and supporting juvenile justice improvement should be strengthened.

a. **OJJDP's capacity to carry out its core mission should be restored through reauthorization, appropriations, and funding flexibility. Assisting state, local, and tribal jurisdictions to align their juvenile justice systems with evolving knowledge about adolescent development and implementing evidence-based and developmentally informed policies, programs, and practices should be among the agency's top priorities. Any additional responsibilities and authority conferred on the agency should be amply funded so as not to erode the funds needed to carry out the core mission.**

b. **OJJDP's legislative mandate to provide core protections should be strengthened through reauthorizing legislation that defines status offenses to include offenses such as possession of alcohol or tobacco that apply only to youth under 21; precludes without exception the detention of youth who commit offenses that would not be punishable by confinement if committed by an adult; modifies the definition of an adult inmate to give states flexibility to keep youth in juvenile facilities until they reach the age of extended juvenile court jurisdiction; and expands the protections to all youth under age 18 in pretrial detention, whether charged in juvenile or in adult courts.**

c. **OJJDP should prioritize its research, training, and technical assistance resources to promote the adoption of developmentally appropriate policies and practices by jurisdictions throughout the country, particularly helping those that have not yet achieved a state of readiness to undertake reform.**

d. **OJJDP should support state and local efforts to reduce racial/ethnic disparities by using its technical and financial resources to expand the number of local jurisdictions currently participating in activities aimed at reducing disproportionate minority contact (DMC); support efforts to design and implement programs and policies aiming to reduce disparities; support scientifically valid methods** for understanding the causes of racial/ethnic disparities and for evaluating the impact of DMC interventions; and enhance the transparency of its oversight activities by identifying impediments being encountered and assisting localities to overcome them.

FEDERAL SUPPORT FOR RESEARCH

Traditionally, the Office of Juvenile Justice and Delinquency Prevention has been the primary funder of research on juvenile crime and juvenile justice, but its capacity is limited. Tremendous strides have been made in the past quarter-century to understand adolescent development and delinquency, and it is essential that OJJDP and other funding agencies continue to support research that has far-reaching implications beyond that of juvenile justice. Research on adolescent development has potential impact for a broad array of youth-related behaviors. The research agenda should include but not be limited to:

- Research that measures both neurobiological immaturity and psychological immaturity concurrently in the same individuals across a variety of legally relevant psychological capacities and across a broad age range.
- Research on the processes and utility of integrating structured risk/need assessments into court practice and service provision. This research should help to explain how these instruments are being used; their effectiveness with adolescents posing different risks; the congruence between identified needs and services actually delivered; the relation between assessment, system responses, and outcomes; and the impact of these assessment practices on minority youth.
- Research on the processes of family involvement in juvenile justice and methods for successfully involving parents and other family members in these processes.
- Research to investigate how far inclusion criteria for program involvement can be expanded to incorporate even more serious delinquents.
- Well-constructed and scientifically valid evaluations of system reform efforts, such as the Missouri model, the Juvenile Detention Alternatives Initiative (JDAI), and Models for Change.
- Empirical research on whether and how alternative adjudicative options and procedural strategies for holding juveniles accountable (e.g., timeliness) affect their sense of responsibility for wrongdoing and perceptions of fairness and whether and how they affect future offending.

- Principles of effective intervention, derived from analyses of evidence-based interventions.

As indicated above, a comprehensive research and data program designed to reduce racial/ethnic disparities is a critical research need. Whether undertaken as a stand-alone program or as part of a larger initiative on disparities in the administration of justice or in other youth-related fields that overlap with justice, the topics should include but not be limited to:

- Research that quantifies to the extent possible the influence of various identifiable factors (differential participation in the crimes that lead to involvement with the juvenile justice system, socioeconomic/poverty effects, police patrol patterns in high-crime areas, family composition, etc.) that, in combination, produce racial/ethnic disparities.
- Juvenile justice decision makers' attitudes and mechanisms by which individual perceptions influence decision making; legal decision making, including how court officials define and treat offenders.
- Possible racial/ethnic disparities connected with the use of any risk/need assessment strategy and how to make these instruments contribute to a larger vision of an effective and fair service involvement.
- The police decision to arrest; use of a variety of methodologies to address the wide range of discretionary policy practices of police in different neighborhood settings.
- Identification of juvenile justice system decision points and jurisdictional practices of urban and rural jurisdictions that contribute to racial/ethnic disparities; an understanding of cumulative effects of race across stages of process and over time through repeated encounters.
- Studies of school disciplinary, mental health, and child welfare system "crossover" youth, who move between the child welfare and juvenile justice systems, and how these youth fare at the charging stage.
- Scientifically valid evaluations of state and local initiatives to reduce racial/ethnic disparities.

The evidence-based movement in treatment and prevention did not gain traction until the programs were evaluated with experimental designs and rigorous benefit-cost analyses were undertaken. A similar effort is required to identify programs that work to reduce racial/ethnic disparities. Racial/ethnic disparities experienced by minority youth prevent the benefits of developmentally appropriate policies and practices from being achieved.

Even perceived discrimination on the part of minority youth can have a profound impact on the trajectories of their lives. After decades of little progress, an intensification of effort is called for.

> **Recommendation 3: Federal research agencies, including the National Science Foundation, the Centers for Disease Control and Prevention, and the National Institutes of Health, as well as OJJDP, should support research that continues to advance the science of adolescent development and expands our understanding of the ways in which developmental processes influence juvenile delinquency and juvenile justice responses.**

DATA IMPROVEMENT

Throughout the report, the committee has noted that poor, nonexistent, or inaccessible data impede efforts to improve the nation's response to juvenile crime and the treatment of youth in the juvenile justice system. State, local, and tribal governments are dependent on a variety of data sources from the federal government and from various agencies in their own jurisdictions, including law enforcement and juvenile justice agencies and courts, as well as education, social services, and health and mental health agencies. They often lack the clout to influence the providers of relevant juvenile justice and other systems' data. This challenge must be pursued at the federal level, and OJJDP is the logical agency to lead the effort and provide the training and technical assistance and support for a substantial, coordinated effort to improve the capacities of juvenile justice agencies and service providers to collect, manage, and analyze data on service provision and outcomes.

> **Recommendation 4: Under OJJDP's leadership, the Bureau of Justice Statistics and other governmental and private statistical organizations should develop a data improvement program on juvenile crime and juvenile justice system processing that provides greater insight into state, local, and tribal variations. OJJDP should also be involved in any effort undertaken by other U.S. Department of Justice agencies with the Federal Bureau of Investigation to improve the federal collection of juvenile arrest and incident data. At the state, local, and tribal levels, data should be collected on the gender, age, race/ethnicity of offenders as well as the offense charged or committed; arrest, detention, and disposition practices; and recidivism. OJJDP should provide training and technical assistance on data collection, automated data systems, and methods of preserving the confidentiality of juvenile records.**

References

Abrams, D.E. (2003). *A Very Special Place in Life: The History of Juvenile Justice in Missouri*. Jefferson City: Missouri Juvenile Justice Association.

Achilles, M., and Zehr, H. (2001). Restorative justice for crime victims: The promise, the challenge. In G. Bazemore and M. Schiff (Eds.), *Restorative Community Justice: Repairing Harm and Transforming Communities* (pp. 87-99). Cincinnati, OH: Anderson.

Adams, B. (2012). *Federal Requirements to Deinstitutionalize Status Offenders Have Been Effective*. Pittsburgh, PA: National Center for Juvenile Justice.

Advancement Project. (2010). *Test, Punish, and Push Out: How "Zero Tolerance" and High-stakes Testing Funnel Youth into the School-to-Prison Pipeline*. Washington, DC: Advancement Project. Available: http://www.advancementproject.org/sites/default/files/publications/rev_fin.pdf [June 2012].

Albert, D., and Steinberg, L. (2011). Judgment and decision making in adolescence. *Journal of Research on Adolescence, 21*(1), 211-224.

Alexander, J., and Parsons, B. (1973). Short-term behavioral intervention with delinquent families: Impact on family process and recidivism. *Journal of Abnormal Psychology, 81*(3), 219-225.

Alexander, J.F., Pugh, C., Parsons, B.V., and Sexton, T.L. (2000). Functional family therapy. In D.S. Elliott (Ed.) *Blueprints for Violence Prevention* (book 3, 2nd ed.). Boulder: Center for the Study and Prevention of Violence, Institute of Behavioral Science, University of Colorado.

Allen, F.A. (1964). *The Borderland of Criminal Justice: Essays in Law and Criminology*. Chicago, IL: University of Chicago Press.

Alpert, G.P., MacDonald, J.M., and Dunham, R.G. (2005). Police suspicion and discretionary decision making during citizen stops. *Criminology, 43*(2), 407-434.

Altschuler, D.M., and Armstrong, T. (1994). *Intensive Aftercare for High-risk Juveniles: A Community Care Model: Program Summary*. Washington, DC: Office of Juvenile Justice and Delinquency Prevention, Office of Justice Programs, U.S. Department of Justice.

Alvarado, R., and Kumpfer, K.L. (2000). Strengthening America's families. *Juvenile Justice Journal, VII*(3), 8-18.

American Academy of Child and Adolescent Psychiatry. (2012). *Solitary Confinement of Juvenile Offenders*. Available: http://www.aacap.org/cs/root/policy_statements/solitary_confinement_of_juvenile_offenders [August 2012].

American Bar Association Center for Professional Conduct. (2012). *ABA Model Rules of Professional Conduct*. Available: http://www.americanbar.org/groups/professional_responsibility/publications/model_rules_of_professional_conduct.html [February 2013].

American Bar Association Juvenile Justice Center. (2002). *Kentucky: Advancing Justice: An Assessment of Access to Counsel and Quality of Representation in Delinquency Proceedings*. Available: http://www.njdc.info/kentucky.php [September 2012].

American Bar Association Juvenile Justice Center. (2003). *Montana: An Assessment of Access to Counsel and Quality of Representation in Delinquency Proceedings*. Available: http://www.njdc.info/montana.php [September 2012].

American Bar Association Juvenile Justice Center et al. (2003). *Washington: An Assessment of Access to Counsel and Quality of Representation in Juvenile Offender Matters*. Available: http://www.njdc.info/washington.php [September 2012].

American Bar Association Juvenile Justice Center and Juvenile Justice Project of Louisiana. (2001). *The Children Left Behind: An Assessment of Access to Counsel and Quality of Representation in Delinquency Proceedings in Louisiana*. Available: http://www.njdc.info/louisiana.php [September 2012].

American Bar Association Juvenile Justice Center and Juvenile Law Center. (2003). *Pennsylvania: An Assessment of Access to Counsel and Quality of Representation in Delinquency Proceedings*. Available: http://www.njdc.info/pdf/pareport.pdf [August 2012].

American Bar Association Juvenile Justice Center and Mid-Atlantic Juvenile Defender Center. (2002). *Virginia: An Assessment of Access to Counsel and Quality of Representation in Delinquency Proceedings*. Available: http://www.njdc.info/virginia.php [September 2012].

American Bar Association Juvenile Justice Center and Mid-Atlantic Juvenile Defender Center. (2003). *Maryland: An Assessment of Access to Counsel and Quality of Representation in Delinquency Proceedings*. Available: http://www.njdc.info/maryland.php [September 2012].

American Bar Association Juvenile Justice Center and Southern Center for Human Rights. (2001). *Georgia: An Assessment of Access to Counsel and Quality of Representation in Delinquency Proceedings*. Available: http://www.njdc.info/georgia.php [September 2012].

American Psychiatric Association. (1994). *Diagnostic and Statistical Manual of Mental Disorders, Fourth Edition, Text Revision (DSM-IV-TR)*. Washington, DC: American Psychiatric Association.

American Psychological Association Zero Tolerance Task Force. (2008). Are zero tolerance policies effective in the schools? An evidentiary review and recommendations. *American Psychologist, 63*(9), 852-862.

Amso, D., and Casey, B.J. (2006). Beyond what develops when: Neuroimaging may inform how cognition changes with development. *Current Directions in Psychological Science, 15*(1), 24-29.

Andenaes, J. (1974). *Punishment and Deterrence*. Ann Arbor: The University of Michigan Press.

Anderer, S.J., and Glass, D.J. (2000). A therapeutic jurisprudence and preventive law approach to family law. In D.P. Stolle, D.B. Wexler, and B.J. Winick (Eds.), *Practicing Therapeutic Jurisprudence: Law as a Helping Profession* (pp. 207-236). Durham, NC: Carolina Academic Press.

Anderson, E. (1999). *Code of the Street: Decency, Violence, and the Moral Life of the Inner City* (1st ed.). New York: W.W. Norton.

Andrews, D.A., and Bonta, J. (1995). *Level of Service Inventory—Revised*. Toronto, Canada: Multi-Health Systems.

Andrews, D.A., and Bonta, J. (2010). *The Psychology of Criminal Conduct* (5th ed.). Cincinnati, OH: Anderson.

Andrews, D.A., Bonta, J., and Hoge, R.D. (1990). Classification for effective rehabilitation: Rediscovering psychology. *Criminal Justice and Behavior Criminal Justice and Behavior, 17*(1), 19-52.

Andrews, D.A., Bonta, J., and Wormith, J.S. (2006). The recent past and near future of risk and/or need assessment. *Crime and Delinquency, 52*(1), 7-27.

Annie E. Casey Foundation. (2009). *Reform the Nation's Juvenile Justice System*. Issue Brief. Available: http://www.aecf.org/~/media/PublicationFiles/Juvenile_Justice_issuebrief3.pdf [May 2012].

Annie E. Casey Foundation (2011). *JDAI Annual Report 2009*. Available: http://www.aecf.org/~/media/Pubs/Initiatives/Juvenile%20Detention%20Alternatives%20Initiative/JDAIResultsReport2009/JDAIResults2009.pdf [June 2012].

Annie E. Casey Foundation. (2012). *JDAI News Winter 2012*. Available: http://www.aecf.org/KnowledgeCenter/Publications.aspx?pubguid=%7B211E4FD2-2277-4A5D-A709-605FFC00E0D9%7D [April 2012].

Anwar, S., and Loughran, T.A. (2011). Testing a Bayesian learning theory of deterrence among serious juvenile offenders. *Criminology, 49*(3), 667-698.

Aos, S. (2002). *The Juvenile Justice System in Washington State: Recommendations to Improve Cost-effectiveness*. Olympia: Washington State Institute for Public Policy. Available: http://www.wsipp.wa.gov/rptfiles/WhatWorksJuv.pdf [March 2012].

Aos, S., and Drake, E. (2010). *WSIPP's Benefit-Cost Tool for States: Examining Policy Options in Sentencing and Corrections*. Olympia: Washington State Institute for Public Policy. Available: http://www.wsipp.wa.gov/pub.asp?docid=10-08-1201 [June 2012].

Aos, S., Phipps, P., Barnoski, R., and Lieb, R. (2001). *The Comparative Costs and Benefits of Programs to Reduce Crime*. Olympia: Washington State Institute for Public Policy.

Aos, S., Lieb, R., Mayfield, J., Miller, M., and Pennucci, A. (2004). *Benefits and Costs of Prevention and Early Intervention Programs for Youth*. Olympia: Washington State Institute for Public Policy.

Aos, S., Miller, M.G., and Drake, E. (2006). *Evidence-based Public Policy Options to Reduce Future Prison Construction, Criminal Justice Costs, and Crime Rates*. Document No. 06-10-1201. Olympia: Washington State Institute for Public Policy. Available: http://www.wsipp.wa.gov/rptfiles/06-10-1201.pdf [June 2012].

Armour, J., and Hammond, S. (2009). *Minority Youth in the Juvenile Justice System: Disproportionate Minority Contact*. Washington, DC: National Conference of State Legislators.

Armstrong, G.S., and MacKenzie, D.L. (2000). *Private versus Public Sector Operation: A Comparison of the Environmental Quality in Juvenile Correctional Facilities, Final Report*. Washington, DC: Office of Juvenile Justice and Delinquency Prevention, Office of Justice Programs, U.S. Department of Justice.

Arnett, J.J. (2000). Emerging adulthood. A theory of development from the late teens through the twenties. *American Psychologist, 55*(5), 469-480.

Arnett, J.J. (2007). Socialization in emerging adulthood: From the family to the wider world, from socialization to self-socialization. In J.E. Grusec and P.D. Hastings (Eds.), *Handbook of Socialization: Theory and Research* (pp. 208-231). New York: Guilford Press.

Arya, N., and Ward, J. (2011). *Recommendations for Juvenile Justice Reform: Opportunities for Action in the 112th Congress*. Washington, DC: National Juvenile Justice and Delinquency Prevention Coalition. Available: http://www.cclp.org/documents/Federal%20Advocacy/NJJDPC_Opportunies%20for%20the%20Obama%20administration.pdf [February 2012].

Arya, N., Villarruel, F., Villanueva, C., Augarten, I., Murguía, J., and Sánchez, J. (2009). *America's Invisible Children Latino Youth and the Failure of Justice*. Available: http://www.campaignforyouthjustice.org/documents/CFYJPB_InvisibleChildren.pdf [June 2012].

Asato, M.R., Terwilliger, R., Woo, J., and Luna, B. (2010). White matter development in adolescence: A DTI study. *Cerebral Cortex, 20*(9), 2122-2131.

Ashley, J., and Burke, K. (2009). *Implementing Restorative Justice: A Guide for Schools*. Available: http://www.icjia.state.il.us/public/pdf/BARJ/SCHOOL%20BARJ%20GUIDEBOOK. pdf [April 2012].

Aspy, C.B., Oman, R.F., Vesely, S.K., McLeroy, K., Rodine, S., and Marshall, L. (2004). Adolescent violence: The protective effects of youth assets. *Journal of Counseling and Development, 82*(3), 268-276.

Austin, J.B., Krisberg, B., and Joe, K. (1987). *The Impact of Juvenile Court Intervention*. San Francisco, CA: National Council on Crime and Delinquency.

Austin, J., Dedel, K., and Gregoriou, M. (2000). *Juveniles in Adult Prisons and Jails: A National Assessment*. Washington, DC: Bureau of Justice Assistance.

Baglivio, M.T., and Jackowski, K. (2012, April 3). Examining the validity of a juvenile offending risk assessment instrument across gender and race/ethnicity. *Youth Violence and Juvenile Justice, 11*(1), 26-43.

Baird, C. (2009). *A Question of Evidence: A Critique of Risk Assessment Models Used in the Justice System*. Madison, WI: National Council on Crime and Delinquency.

Baird, S.C., Storrs, G.M., and Connelly, H.N. (1984). *Classification of Juveniles in Corrections—A Model Systems Approach*. Washington, DC: Arthur D. Little.

Bales, W.D., and Piquero, A.R. (2012). Racial/ethnic differentials in sentencing to incarceration. *Justice Quarterly, 29*(5), 1-32.

Barnoski, R. (2002). *Washington State's Implementation of Functional Family Therapy for Juvenile Offenders: Preliminary Findings*. Olympia: Washington State Institute for Public Policy.

Barnoski, R.P. (2004). *Outcome Evaluation of Washington State's Research-based Programs for Juvenile Offenders*. Olympia: Washington State Institute for Public Policy.

Barton, C., Alexander, J.F., Waldron, H., Turner, C.W., and Warburton, J. (1985). Generalizing treatment effects of functional family therapy: Three replications. *American Journal of Family Therapy, 13*(3), 16-26.

Basile, K.C., Hertz, M.F., and Back, S.E. (2007). *Intimate Partner Violence and Sexual Violence Victimization Assessment Instruments for Use in Healthcare Settings: Version 1*. Atlanta, GA: Centers for Disease Control and Prevention, National Center for Injury Prevention and Control.

Bateman, I., Carson, R., Day, B., Hanemann, M., Hanley, N., Hett, T., Jones-Lee, M., Loomes, G., Mourato, S., Özdemiroglu, E., Pearce, D., Sugden, R., and Swanson, J. (2002). *Economic Valuation with Stated Preference Techniques: A Manual*. Northampton, MA: Edward Elgar.

Battin, S.R., Hill, K.G., Abbott, R.D., Catalano, R.F., and Hawkins, J.D. (1998). Contribution of gang membership to delinquency beyond delinquent friends. *Criminology, 36*(1), 93-115.

Baumeister, R.F., and Leary, M.R. (1995). The need to belong: Desire for interpersonal attachments as a fundamental human motivation. *Psychological Bulletin, 117*(3), 497-529.

Baumrind, D. (1985). Familial antecedents of adolescent drug use: A developmental perspective. *NIDA Research Monograph Series, 56*, 13-44.

Baumrind, D. (1991). The influence of parenting style on adolescent competence and substance use. *Journal of Early Adolescence, 11*(1), 56-95.

Baumrind, D. (1996). The discipline controversy revisited. *Family Relations, 45*(4), 405-414.

Bayer, P., Pintoff, R., and Pozen, D.E. (2003). *Building Criminal Capital Behind Bars: Social Learning in Juvenile Corrections*. New Haven, CT: Yale University, Economic Growth Center.

Bazemore, G., and Day, S.E. (2002). Restoring the balance: Juvenile and community justice. In W.R. Palacios, P.F. Cromwell, and R.G. Dunham (Eds.), *Crime and Justice in America: Present Realities and Future Prospects* (2nd ed., pp. 324-337). Upper Saddle River, NJ: Prentice Hall.

Bazemore, G., and Erbe, C. (2003). Operationalizing the community variable in offender reintegration: Theory and practice for developing intervention social capital. *Youth Violence and Juvenile Justice, 1*(3), 246-275.

Bazemore, G., and Schiff, M. (2005). *Juvenile Justice Reform and Restorative Justice: Building Theory and Policy from Practice*. Portland, OR: Willan.

Bazemore, G., and Umbreit, M. (1998). *Conferences, Circles, Boards, and Mediations: Restorative Justice and Citizen Involvement in the Response to Youth Crime*. Washington, DC: Office of Juvenile Justice and Delinquency Prevention.

Beaubien, J. (2007, October 30). *Missouri Sees Teen Offenders as Kids, Not Inmates*. Available: http://www.npr.org/templates/story/story.php?storyId=15784264 [June 2012].

Bechtold, J., Cauffman, E., and Monahan, K. (2011). *Knowledge Brief: Are Minority Youths Treated Differently in Juvenile Probation?* Chicago, IL: John D. and Catherine T. MacArthur Foundation.

Beck, A., Gilliard, D.K., Greenfeld, L.A., Harrell, C.W., Hester, T., Jankowski, L., Morton, D.C., Snell, T.L., and Stephan, J.J. (1993). *Survey of State Prison Inmates, 1991*. Washington, DC: Bureau of Justice Statistics, Department of Justice.

Becker, G.S. (1968). Crime and punishment: An economic approach. *Journal of Political Economy, 76*(2), 169-217.

Becker, G.S., and Decker, T. (2008). *Missouri DYS Integrated Treatment Process*. Jefferson City, MO: Department of Youth Services.

Beckett, K., Nyrop, K., Pfingst, L., and Bowen, M. (2005). Drug use, drug possession arrests, and the question of race: Lessons from Seattle. *Social Problems, 52*(3), 419-441.

Begley, S. (2000). Getting inside a teen brain. Hormones aren't the only reason adolescents act crazy. Their gray matter differs from children's and adults'. *Newsweek, 135*(9), 58-59.

Belknap, J. (2007). *The Invisible Woman: Gender, Crime, and Justice*. Belmont, CA: Thomson/Wadsworth.

Bell, J., and Ridolfi, L.J. (2008). *Adoration of the Question: Reflections on the Failure to Reduce Racial and Ethnic Disparities in the Juvenile Justice System*. San Francisco, CA: W. Haywood Burns Institute.

Bell, J., Ridolfi, L.J., Finley, M., and Lacey, C. (2009). *The Keeper and the Kept: Reflections on Local Obstacles to Disparities Reduction in Juvenile Justice Systems and a Path to Change*. San Francisco, CA: W. Haywood Burns Institute.

Belsky, J., Steinberg, L., and Draper, P. (1991). Childhood experience, interpersonal development, and reproductive strategy: An evolutionary theory of socialization. *Child Development, 62*(4), 647-670.

Benner, A.D., and Graham, S. (2011). Latino adolescents' experiences of discrimination across the first 2 years of high school: Correlates and influences on educational outcomes. *Child Development, 82*(2), 508-519.

Bennett, W.J., Dilulio, J.J., and Walters, J.P. (1996). *Body Count: Moral Poverty...and How to Win America's War against Crime and Drugs*. New York: Simon and Schuster.

Bergen, H.A., Martin, G., Richardson, A.S., Allison, S., and Roeger, L. (2004). Sexual abuse, antisocial behaviour, and substance use: Gender differences in young community adolescents. *Australian and New Zealand Journal of Psychiatry, 38*(1), 34-41.

Berk, R., Barnes, G., Ahlman, L., and Kurtz, E. (2010). When second best is good enough: A comparison between a true experiment and a regression discontinuity quasi-experiment. *Journal of Experimental Criminology, 6*(2), 191-208.

Berkel, C., Knight, G.P., Zeiders, K.H., Tein, J.-Y., Roosa, M.W., Gonzales, N.A., and Saenz, D. (2010). Discrimination and adjustment for Mexican American adolescents: A prospective examination of the benefits of culturally related values. *Journal of Research on Adolescence, 20*(4), 893-915.

Berkheiser, M. (2002). The fiction of juvenile right to counsel: Waiver in the juvenile courts. *Florida Law Review, 54*, 577-686.

Berman, P., and Nelson, B. (1997). Replication: Adapt or fail. In A.A. Altshuler and R.D. Behn (Eds.), *Innovation in American Government Challenges, Opportunities, and Dilemmas* (pp. 319-331). Washington, DC: Brookings Institution Press.

Bernard, T.J. (1992). *The Cycle of Juvenile Justice.* New York: Oxford University Press.

Bernard, T.J., and Kurlychek, M.C. (2010). *The Cycle of Juvenile Justice* (2nd ed.). New York: Oxford University Press.

Bersani, B.E. (2012). An examination of first and second generation immigrant offending trajectories. *Justice Quarterly,* 1-29

Bervera, X. (2003). *Reclaiming Children from the Prison System: The Juvenile Justice Reform Act (Act 1225), State of Louisiana.* Available: http://www.arc.org/pdf/281pdf.pdf [June 2012].

Berwick, D.M. (1989). Continuous improvement as an ideal in health-care. *New England Journal of Medicine, 320*(1), 53-56.

Beuttler, F.W., and Bell, C.C. (2010). *For the Welfare of Every Child—A Brief History of the Institute for Juvenile Research, 1909-2010.* Chicago: University of Illinois.

Bickman, L., and Hoagwood, K.E. (2010). Introduction to special issue. Making the real world ideal: Changing practices in children's mental health services. *Administration and Policy in Mental Health and Mental Health Services Research, 37*(1-2), 4-6.

Biglan, A., Brennan, P.A., Foster, S.L., and Holder, H.D. (2004). *Helping Adolescents at Risk: Prevention of Multiple Problem Behaviors.* New York: Guilford Press.

Bilchik, S. (2008, September 18). Statement before the U.S. House of Representative Committee on Judiciary's Subcommittee on Crime, Terrorism and Homeland Security. Available: http://judiciary.house.gov/hearing/pdf/Bilchik080918.pdf [February 2012].

Bilchik, S. (2009). Policy reforms to address racial and ethnic disparity and disproportionality in the child welfare and juvenile justice systems: Federal, state, and local action. In Chapin Hall Center for Children (Ed.), *Racial and Ethnic Disparity and Disproportionality in Child Welfare and Juvenile Justice: A Compendium.* Chicago, IL: University of Chicago, Center for Juvenile Justice Reform at the Georgetown Public Policy Institute and Chapin Hall Center for Children.

Bilchik, S. (2010). *Juvenile Justice Reform Efforts: The State of the Union.* Presentation to the Committee on Assessing Juvenile Justice Reform, August 5, National Research Council, Washington, DC.

Binder, A., Geis, G., and Bruce, D.D. (1997). *Juvenile Delinquency: Historical, Cultural, and Legal Perspectives* (2nd ed.). Cincinnati, OH: Anderson.

Bishop, D.M. (2005). The role of race and ethnicity in juvenile justice processing. In D.F. Hawkins and K. Kempf-Leonard (Eds.), *Our Children, Their Children: Confronting Racial and Ethnic Differences in American Juvenile Justice* (pp. 23-82). Chicago, IL: University of Chicago Press.

Bishop, D.M. (2006). Public opinion and juvenile justice policy: Myths and misconceptions. *Criminology and Public Policy, 5*(4), 653-664.

Bishop, D.M., and Frazier, C.F. (1992). Gender bias in juvenile justice processing: Implications of the JJDP Act. *Journal of Criminal Law and Criminology and Public Policy, 82*(4), 1162-1186.

Bishop, D.M., and Frazier, C. (2000). Consequences of transfer. In J. Fagan and F. Zimmerman (Eds.), *The Changing Borders of Juvenile Justice* (pp. 227-276). Chicago, IL: University of Chicago Press.

Bishop, D.M., and Leiber, M.J. (2012). The role of race and ethnicity in juvenile justice processing. In B.C. Feld and D.M. Bishop (Eds.), *The Oxford Handbook of Juvenile Crime and Juvenile Justice* (pp. 445-484). New York: Oxford University Press.

Bishop, D.M., Frazier, C.E., Lanza-Kaduce, L., and Winner, L. (1996). The transfer of juveniles to criminal court: Does it make a difference? *Crime and Delinquency, 42*(2), 171-191.

Bishop, D.M., Leiber, M., and Johnson, J. (2010). Contexts of decision making in the juvenile justice system: An organizational approach to understanding minority overrepresentation. *Youth Violence and Juvenile Justice, 8*(3), 213-233.

Bitan, T., Burman, D.D., Lu, D., Cone, N.E., Gitelman, D.R., Mesulam, M.M., and Booth, J.R. (2006). Weaker top-down modulation from the left inferior frontal gyrus in children. *NeuroImage, 33*(3), 991-998.

Bjork, J.M., Knutson, B., Fong, G.W., Caggiano, D.M., Bennett, S.M., and Hommer, D.W. (2004). Incentive-elicited brain activation in adolescents: Similarities and differences from young adults. *Journal of Neuroscience, 24*(8), 1793-1802.

Bjornstrom, E.E., Kaufman, R.L., Peterson, R.D., and Slater, M.D. (2010). Race and ethnic representations of lawbreakers and victims in crime news: A national study of television coverage. *Social Problems, 57*(2), 269-293.

Black, D.J., and Reiss, A.J., Jr. (1970). Police control of juveniles. *American Sociological Review, 35*(1), 63-77.

Bloom, B., Owen, B.A., and Covington, S. (2003). *Gender-responsive Strategies Research, Practice, and Guiding Principles for Women Offenders.* Washington, DC: National Institute of Corrections. Available: http://static.nicic.gov/Library/018017.pdf [June 2012].

Blumstein, A. (1982). On the racial disproportionality of United States' prison populations. *Journal of Criminal Law and Criminology, 73*(3), 1259-1281.

Blumstein, A. (1993). Racial disproportionality of U.S. prison populations revisited. *University of Colorado Law Review, 64,* 743-760.

Blumstein, A., and Nakamura, K. (2009). Redemption in the presence of widespread criminal background checks. *Criminology, 47,* 327-360.

Boardman, A., Greenberg, D., Vining, A., and Weimer, D. (2011). *Cost-Benefit Analysis: Concepts and Practice* (4th ed.). Upper Saddle River, NJ: Prentice Hall.

Bobo, L.D. (2011). Somewhere between Jim Crow and post-racialism: Reflections on the racial divide in America today. *Daedalus, 140*(2), 11-36.

Boisjoli, R., Vitaro, F., Lacourse, E., Barker, E.D., and Tremblay, R.E. (2007). Impact and clinical significance of a preventive intervention for disruptive boys: 15-year follow-up. *British Journal of Psychiatry, 191,* 415-419.

Bonnie, R.J., and Grisso, T. (2000). Adjudicative competence and youthful offenders. In T. Grisso and R.G. Schwartz (Eds.), *Youth on Trial: A Developmental Perspective on Juvenile Justice.* Chicago, IL: University of Chicago Press.

Bonnie, R.J., Coughlin, A.M., and Jeffries, J.C. (2010). *Criminal Law* (3rd ed.). New York: Foundation Press.

Bonta, J. (2002). Offender risk assessment: Guidelines for selection and use. *Criminal Justice and Behavior, 29*(4), 355-379.

Borum, R., and Verhaagen, D.A. (2006). *Assessing and Managing Violence Risk in Juveniles.* New York: Guilford Press.

Bosman, J. (2010, January 20). City signals intent to put fewer teenagers in jail. *The New York Times*. Available: http://www.nytimes.com/2010/01/21/nyregion/21juvenile.html?_r=1&pagewanted=print [June 2012].

Boston, J. (2004). *The Prison Litigation Reform Act*. New York: The Legal Aid Society. Available: http://www.wnylc.net/pb/docs/plra2circ04.pdf [September 2011].

Bottcher, J., and Ezell, M.E. (2005). Examining the effectiveness of boot camps: A randomized experiment with a long-term follow up. *Journal of Research in Crime and Delinquency, 42*(3), 309-332.

Botvin, G.J., Griffin, K.W., and Nichols, T.D. (2006). Preventing youth violence and delinquency through a universal school-based prevention approach. *Prevention Science, 7*(4), 403-408.

Bourgois, P. (2003). *In Search of Respect: Selling Crack in El Barrio* (2nd ed.). New York: Cambridge University Press.

Bowles, R. (2010). Valuing the benefits from criminal justice interventions. In J. Roman, T. Dunworth, and K. Marsh (Eds.), *Cost-benefit Analysis and Crime Control* (pp. 51-72). Washington, DC: Urban Institute Press.

Bowser, B.P., and Jones, T. (2004). *Understanding the Over-representation of African Americans in the Child Welfare System*. Hayward Hills, CA: Urban Institute Press.

Boyle, P. (2006, June 1). Are you my mentor? *Youth Today*. Available: http://www.youthtoday.org/view_article.cfm?article_id=627 [May 2012].

Brady, B., Dolan, P., O'Brien, M., and Canavan, J. (2005). *Big Brothers Big Sisters Ireland: Youth Mentoring Programme: Galway, Mayo & Roscommon. Evaluation Report*. Available: http://www.childandfamilyresearch.ie/sites/www.childandfamilyresearch.ie/files/big_brothers_big_sisters_ireland_youth_mentoring_programme_galway_mayo__roscommon.pdf [June 2012].

Brame, R., Mulvey, E.P., and Piquero, A.R. (2001). On the development of different kinds of criminal activity. *Sociological Methods & Research, 29*(3), 319-341.

Bratberg, G.H., Nilsen, T.I.L., Holmen, T.L., and Vatten, L.J. (2007). Perceived pubertal timing, pubertal status and the prevalence of alcohol drinking and cigarette smoking in early and late adolescence: A population-based study of 8,950 Norwegian boys and girls. *Acta Paediatrica, 96*(2), 292-295.

Bray, J. (2009, May 4). *Illinois Gov. Quinn Makes Pilot Redeploy Illinois Juvenile Justice Reform Permanent Program*. Available: http://www.modelsforchange.net/reform-progress/11 [June 2012].

Bray, T.M., Sample, L.L., and Kempf-Leonard, K. (2005). "Justice by geography": Racial disparity and juvenile courts. In D.F. Hawkins and K. Kempf-Leonard (Eds.), *Our Children, Their Children: Confronting Racial and Ethnic Differences in American Juvenile Justice* (pp. 270-299). Chicago, IL: University of Chicago Press.

Brendgen, M., Bowen, F., Rondeau, N., and Vitaro, F. (1999). Effects of friends' characteristics on children's social cognitions. *Social Development, 8*(1), 41-51.

Bridges, G., and Steen, S.S. (1998). Racial disparities in official assessments of juvenile offenders: Attributional stereotypes as mediating mechanisms. *American Sociological Review, 63*(4), 554-570.

Broidy, L.M., Nagin, D.S., Tremblay, R.E., Bates, J.E., Brame, B., Dodge, K.A., Fergusson, D., Horwood, J.L., Loeber, R., Laird, R., Lynam, D.R., Moffitt, T.E., Pettit, G.S., and Vitaro, F. (2003). Developmental trajectories of childhood disruptive behaviors and adolescent delinquency: A six-site, cross-national study. *Developmental Psychology, 39*(2), 222-245.

Broman, C.L., Mavaddat, R., and Hsu, S.-Y. (2000). The experience and consequences of perceived racial discrimination: A study of African Americans. *Journal of Black Psychology, 26*(2), 165-180.

Bronfenbrenner, U. (1979). *The Ecology of Human Development*. Cambridge, MA: Harvard University Press.

Bronfenbrenner, U., and Morris, P. (1998). The ecology of developmental processes. In W. Damon (Ed.), *Handbook of Child Psychology* (5th ed., pp. 993-1028). New York: John Wiley & Sons.

Brown, B.B. (2004). Adolescents' relationships with peers. In R.M. Lerner and L.D. Steinberg (Eds.), *Handbook of Adolescent Psychology* (pp. 363-394). Hoboken, NJ: John Wiley & Sons.

Brown, B.B., Bakken, J.P., Ameringer, S.W., and Mahon, S.D. (2008). A comprehensive conceptualization of the peer influence process in adolescence. In M.J. Prinstein and K.A. Dodge (Eds.), *Understanding Peer Influence in Children and Adolescents* (pp. 17-44). New York: Guilford Press.

Brown, T.T., Lugar, H.M., Coalson, R.S., Miezin, F.M., Petersen, S.E., and Schlaggar, B.L. (2005). Developmental changes in human cerebral functional organization for word generation. *Cerebral Cortex, 15*(3), 275-290.

Browning, K., Huizinga, D., Loeber, R., and Thornberry, T.P. (1999). *Causes and Correlates of Delinquency Program*. OJJDP Fact Sheet, No. 100. Available: https://www.ncjrs.gov/pdffiles1/fs99100.pdf [June 2012].

Brunson, R.K., and Weitzer, R. (2009). Police relations with black and white youths in different urban neighborhoods. *Urban Affairs Review, 44*(6), 858-885.

Bugental, D.B., and Goodnow, J.J. (1998). Socialization processes. In W. Damon and N. Eisenberg (Eds.), *Handbook of Child Psychology, Vol. 3: Social, Emotional, and Personality Development* (5th ed., pp. 389-462). New York: John Wiley & Sons.

Bunge, S.A., Dudukovic, N.M., Thomason, M.E., Vaidya, C.J., and Gabrieli, J.D. (2002). Immature frontal lobe contributions to cognitive control in children: Evidence from fMRI. *Neuron, 33*(2), 301-311.

Burgess, D., and Zerbe, R. (2011). Appropriate discounting for benefit-cost analysis. *Journal of Benefit-Cost Analysis, 2*(2). ISSN (Online), DOI: 10.2202/2152-2812.1065.

Burrell, S. (2012). Contracts for appointed counsel in juvenile delinquency cases: Defining expectations. *UC Davis Journal of Juvenile Law and Policy, 16*(1), 314-369.

Buss, E. (2004). Allocating developmental control among parent, child and the state, 2004. *University of Chicago Legal Forum, 27*, 36.

Butts, J. (2002). Juvenile justice and juvenile court. *Encyclopedia of Crime and Justice*. Available: http://www:encyclopedia.com/doc1G2-3403000164.html [September 2012].

Butts, J. (2010). *Juvenile Arrest Rates 1980-2009: National Arrest Estimates Calculated with Data from the FBI's Uniform Crime Reporting Program*. Powerpoint presentation. Available: http://jeffreybutts.wordpress.com/2010/10/25/ucrtrends [September 2012].

Butts, J.A. (2011). *Process Evaluation of the Chicago Juvenile Intervention and Support Center*. New York: John Jay College of Criminal Justice, Research and Evaluation Center. Available: http://jeffreybutts.files.wordpress.com/2011/04/jisc20112.pdf [October 2011].

Butts, J., and Buck, J. (2000, October). *Teen Courts: A Focus on Research*. OJJDP Juvenile Justice Bulletin. Washington, DC: Office of Juvenile Justice and Delinquency Prevention, Office of Justice Programs, U.S. Department of Justice.

Butts, J.A., and Evans, D.N. (2011). *Resolution, Reinvestment, and Realignment: Three Strategies for Changing Juvenile Justice*. New York: Research and Evaluation Center, John Jay College of Criminal Justice, City University of New York. Available: http://johnjayresearch.org/wp-content/uploads/2011/09/rec20111.pdf [April 2013].

Butts, J.A., and Roman, J. (2009). Juvenile crime interventions. In D. Weimer and A. Vining (Eds.), *Investing in the Disadvantaged: Assessing the Benefits and Costs of Social Policies* (pp. 103-126). Washington, DC: Georgetown University Press.

Butts, J.A., Buck, J., and Coggeshall, M.B. (2002). *The Impact of Teen Court on Young Offenders*. Washington, DC: Urban Institute Press. Available: http://www.urban.org/UploadedPDF/410457.pdf [June 2012].

Butts, J.A., Bazemore, G., and Meroe, A.S. (2010). *Positive Youth Justice: Framing Justice Interventions Using Concepts of Positive Youth Development*. Washington, DC: Coalition for Juvenile Justice.

Butts, J.A., Roman, J.K., and Lynn-Whaley, J. (2012). Varieties of juvenile court: Nonspecialized courts, teen courts, drug courts, and mental health courts. In B.C. Feld and D.M. Bishop (Eds.), *Oxford Handbook of Juvenile Crime and Juvenile Justice* (pp. 606-635). New York: Oxford University Press.

Caldwell, M.F., Vitacco, M., and Van Rybroek, G.J. (2006). Are violent delinquents worth treating? A cost-benefit analysis. *Journal of Research in Crime and Delinquency, 43*(2), 148-168.

Caldwell, M.F., Skeem, J., Salekin, R., and Rybroek, G.V. (2006). Treatment response of adolescent offenders with psychopathy features: A 2-year follow-up. *Criminal Justice and Behavior, 33*(5), 571-596.

Caldwell, L.D., Sewell, A.A., Parks, N., and Toldson, I.A. (2009). Guest editorial: Before the bell rings: Implementing coordinated school health models to influence the academic achievement of African American males. *Journal of Negro Education, 78*(3), 204-215.

California Department of Corrections and Rehabilitation. (2011). *Department of Corrections and Rehabilitation Division of Juvenile Justice Population Overview as of December 31, 2010*. Available: http://1.usa.gov/oiTt9x [June 2012].

California Department of the Youth Authority. (n.d.). *Table 1, Characteristics of the Youth Authority's Institution Population (CYA and CDC Cases) June 30 Each Year, 1993-2002*. Available: http://cdcr.ca.go/reports_research/docs/research/pops_93-02.pdf [June 2012].

Calkins, S.D., and Johnson, M.C. (1998). Toddler regulation of distress to frustrating events: Temperamental and maternal correlates. *Infant Behavior and Development, 21*, 379-395.

Campaign for Youth Justice. (2007a, March). *The Consequences Aren't Minor: The Impact of Trying Youth as Adults and Strategies for Reform*. Available: http://www.campaignforyouthjustice.org/documents/CFYJNR_ConsequencesMinor.pdf [May 2012].

Campaign for Youth Justice. (2007b, November). *Jailing Juveniles: The Dangers of Incarcerating Youth in Adult Jails in America*. Available: http://www.campaignforyouthjustice.org/documents/CFYJNR_ConsequencesMinor.pdf [May 2012].

Campaign for Youth Justice. (2011). *State Trends, Legislative Victories from 2005-2010, Removing Youth from the Adult Criminal Justice System*. Available: http://www.campaignforyouthjustice.org/documents/CFYJ_State_Trends_Report.pdf [April 2012].

Campbell, F.A., and Ramey, C.T. (1995). Cognitive and school outcomes for high-risk African-American students at middle adolescence: Positive effects of early intervention. *American Educational Research Journal, 32*(4), 743-772.

Carson, R. (2011). *Contingent Valuation: A Comprehensive Bibliography and History*. Northampton, MA: Edward Elgar.

Casey, B.J., and Jones, R.M. (2010). Neurobiology of the adolescent brain and behavior: Implications for substance use disorders. *Journal of the American Academy of Child and Adolescent Psychiatry, 49*(12), 1189-1201.

Casey, B.J., Cohen, J.D., Jezzard, P., Turner, R., Noll, D.C., Trainor, R.J., Giedd, J., Kaysen, D., Hertz-Pannier, L., and Rapoport, J.L. (1995). Activation of prefrontal cortex in children during a nonspatial working memory task with functional MRI. *NeuroImage, 2*(3), 221-229.

Casey, B.J., Trainor, R.J., Orendi, J.L., Schubert, A.B., Nystrom, L. E., Cohen, J.D, Noll, D.C., Giedd, J., Castellanos, X., Haxby, J., Forman, S.D., Dahl, R.E., and Rapoport, J.L. (1997). A pediatric functional MRI study of prefrontal activation during performance of a Go-No-Go task. *Journal of Cognitive Neuroscience, 9,* 835-847.

Casey, B.J., Tottenham, N., and Fossella, J. (2002). Clinical, imaging, lesion, and genetic approaches toward a model of cognitive control. *Developmental Psychobiology, 40*(3), 237-254.

Casey, B.J., Tottenham, N., Liston, C., and Durston, S. (2005). Imaging the developing brain: What have we learned about cognitive development? *TRENDS in Cognitive Sciences, 9*(3), 104-110.

Casey, B.J., Epstein, J.N., Buhle, J., Liston, C., Davidson, M.C., Tonev, S.T., Spicer, J., Niogi, S., Millner, A.J., Reiss, A., Garrett, A., Hinshaw, S.P., Greenhill, L.L., Shafritz, K.M., Vitolo, A., Kotler, L.A., Jarrett, M.A., and Glover, G. (2007). Frontostriatal connectivity and its role in cognitive control in parent-child dyads with ADHD. *American Journal of Psychiatry, 164*(11), 1729-1736.

Casey, B.J., Getz, S., and Galvan, A. (2008). The adolescent brain. *Developmental Review, 28*(1), 62-77.

Casey, B.J., Jones, R.M., Levita, L., Libby, V., Pattwell, S.S., Ruberry, E.J., Soliman, F., and Somerville, L.H. (2010). The storm and stress of adolescence: Insights from human imaging and mouse genetics. *Developmental Psychobiology, 52*(3), 225-235.

Catalano, R.F., and Hawkins, J.D. (1996). The social development model: A theory of antisocial behavior. In J. David Hawkins (Ed.), *Delinquency and Crime: Current Theories* (pp. 149-197). New York: Cambridge University Press.

Cauffman, E. (2004). A statewide screening of mental health symptoms among juvenile offenders in detention. *Journal of the American Academy of Child and Adolescent Psychiatry, 43*(4), 430-439.

Cauffman, E., and Grisso, T. (2005). Mental health issues among minority offenders in the juvenile justice system. In D.F. Hawkins and K. Kempf-Leonard (Eds.), *Our Children, Their Children: Confronting Racial and Ethnic Differences in American Juvenile Justice* (pp. 390-412). Chicago, IL: University of Chicago Press.

Cauffman, E., and Steinberg, L. (2000). (Im)maturity of judgment in adolescence: Why adolescents may be less culpable than adults. *Behavioral Sciences & the Law, 18*(6), 741-760.

Cauffman, E., Steinberg, L., and Piquero, A. (2005). Psychological, neuropsychological, and physiological correlates of serious antisocial behavior in adolescence: The role of self-control. *Criminology, 43*(1), 133-175.

Cauffman, E., Shulman, E.P., Steinberg, L., Claus, E., Banich, M.T., Graham, S., and Woolard, J. (2010). Age differences in affective decision making as indexed by performance on the Iowa gambling task. *Developmental Psychology, 46*(1), 193-207.

Caviness, V.S., Jr., Kennedy, D.N., Richelme, C., Rademacher, J., and Filipek, P.A. (1996). The human brain age 7-11 years: A volumetric analysis based on magnetic resonance images. *Cerebral Cortex, 6*(5), 726-736.

Celeste, G., Bauer, G., Bervera, X., and Utter, D. (2005). Just shut it down: Bringing down a prison while building a movement. In Building Blocks for Youth (Ed.), *No Turning Back: Promising Approaches to Reducing Racial and Ethnic Disparities in the Justice System* (pp. 69-77). Available: http://www.aecf.org/upload/PublicationFiles/ntb_fullreport.pdf [December 2011].

Chamberlain, P. (2003). *Treating Chronic Juvenile Offenders: Advances Made Through the Oregon Multidimensional Treatment Foster Care Model.* Washington, DC: American Psychological Association.

Chandra, A. (2010). *Children on the Home Front: The Experiences of Children from Military Families*. Testimony presented March 9 before the House Armed Services Committee, Subcommittee on Military Personnel.

Chang, J.J., Chen, J.J., and Brownson, R.C. (2003). The role of repeat victimization in adolescent delinquent behaviors and recidivism. *Journal of Adolescent Health, 32*(4), 272-280.

Chapin Hall Center for Children. (2009). *Racial and Ethnic Disparity and Disproportionality in Child Welfare and Juvenile Justice: A Compendium*. Chicago, IL: University of Chicago, Center for Juvenile Justice Reform at the Georgetown Public Policy Institute and Chapin Hall Center for Children.

Chase-Lansdale, P.L., Gordon, R.A., Brooks-Gunn, J., and Klebanov, P.K. (1997). Neighborhood and family influences on the intellectual and behavioral competence of preschool and early school-age children. In J. Brooks-Gunn, G.J. Duncan, and J.L. Aber (Eds.), *Neighborhood Poverty Context and Consequences for Children Volume I* (pp. 79-118). New York: Russell Sage Foundation.

Chassin, L.A., Fora, D.B., and King, K.M. (2004). Trajectories of alcohol and drug use and dependence from adolescence to adulthood: The effects of familial alcoholism and personality. *Journal of Abnormal Psychology, 113*(4), 483-498.

Chassin, L.A., Hussong, A.M., and Beltran, I. (2009). Adolescent substance use. In R.M. Lerner and L. Steinberg (Eds.), *Handbook of Adolescent Psychology* (3rd ed., pp. 723-764). Hoboken, NJ: John Wiley & Sons.

Chassin, L.A., Knight, G., Vargas-Chanes, D., Losoya, S., and Naranjo, D. (2009). Substance use treatment outcomes in a sample of serious juvenile offenders. *Journal of Substance Abuse Treatment, 36*(2), 183-194.

Chein, J., Albert, D., O'Brien, L., Uckert, K., and Steinberg, L. (2011). Peers increase adolescent risk taking by enhancing activity in the brain's reward circuitry. *Developmental Science, 14*, F1-F10.

Chesney-Lind, M. (1997). *The Female Offender: Girls, Women, and Crime*. Thousand Oaks, CA: Sage.

Children's Law Center, Inc. (2011, July 11). *Trends and Challenges in Juvenile Justice Reform: Experiences of Three States*. Available: http://www.childrenslawky.org/webcasts/2011/5/9/trends-and-challenges-in-juvenile-justice-reform-experiences.html [November 2011].

Chowanec, G.D. (1994). Continuous quality improvement: Conceptual foundations and application to mental health care. *Hospital and Community Psychiatry, 45*(8), 789-793.

Chung, H.L., and Steinberg, L. (2006). Relations between neighborhood factors, parenting behaviors, peer deviance, and delinquency among serious juvenile offenders. *Developmental Psychology, 42*(2), 319-331.

Chung, H.L., Little, M., and Steinberg, L. (2005). The transition to adulthood for adolescence in the juvenile justice system: A developmental perspective. In W. Osgood, M. Foster, C. Flanagan, and G. Ruth (Eds.), *On Your Own Without a Net: The Transition to Adulthood for Vulnerable Populations* (pp. 68-91). Chicago, IL: University of Chicago Press.

Chung, H.L., Schubert, C.A., and Mulvey, E.P. (2007). An empirical portrait of community reentry among serious juvenile offenders in two metropolitan cities. *Criminal Justice and Behavior, 34*(11), 1402-1426.

Cicourel, A.V. (1967). *The Social Organization of Juvenile Justice*. New York: John Wiley & Sons.

Coalition for Juvenile Justice. (2008). *Platform of Position on the Reauthorization of the Juvenile Justice and Delinquency Prevention Act (JJDPA)*. Available: http://www.juvjustice.org/reauthorization_platform.html [June 2012].

Coalition for Juvenile Justice. (2009). *A Pivotal Moment: Sustaining and Success and Enhancing the Future of the Juvenile Justice and Delinquency Prevention Act*. Available: http://www.juvjustice.org/announcement_140.html [February 2012].

Cocozza, J.J., and Skowyra, K.R. (2000). Youth with mental health disorders: Issues and emerging responses. *Juvenile Justice, 7*(1), 3-13.

Cohen, M.A. (2010). Valuing crime control benefits using stated preference approaches. In J. Roman, T. Dunworth, and K. Marsh (Eds.), *Cost-Benefit Analysis and Crime Control* (pp. 73-118). Washington, DC: Urban Institute Press.

Cohen, M.I., Feyerherm, W., Spinney, E., Stephenson, R., and Yerde, M. (2011). *Expanding Use of DMC Data Analysis of Patterns to Identify Best Practices*. Presentation at American Society of Criminology Annual Meeting, November 16-19, Washington, DC.

Cohen, M.I., Feyerhem, W., Spinney, E., Stephenson, R., and Yeide, M. (2012). *Expanding the Use of Disproportionate Minority Contact Data: Analysis of Patterns to Identify Best Practices (Semiannual Progress Report, July 1 through December 31, 2011)*. Washington, DC: Office of Juvenile Justice and Delinquency Prevention, Office of Justice Programs, U.S. Department of Justice.

Cohen, S. (1985). *Visions of Social Control*. Oxford, UK: Polity Press.

Cohen, S. (2002). *Folk Devils and Moral Panics* (3rd ed.). New York: Routledge.

Coleman, A. (2010). *Disproportionate Minority Contact: What Is Happening at the State and Local Levels*. Presentation to the Committee on Assessing Juvenile Justice Reform, October 11, National Research Council, Washington, DC.

Coleman, A.R (2011). Disproportionate minority contact (DMC): A historical and contemporary perspective. In N. Parsons-Pollard (Ed.), *Disproportionate Minority Contact, Current Issues and Practice* (pp. 19-33). Durham, NC: Carolina Academic Press.

Collins, W.A., and Steinberg, L. (2006). Adolescent development in interpersonal context. In N. Eisenberg, W. Damon, and R.M. Lerner (Eds.), *Handbook of Child Psychology: Vol. 3, Social, Emotional, and Personality Development* (6th ed., pp. 1003-1067). Hoboken, NJ: John Wiley & Sons.

Conduct Problems Prevention Research Group. (2010). Fast Track intervention effects on youth arrests and delinquency. *Journal of Experimental Criminology, 6*(2), 131-157.

Conger, D., and Ross, T. (2001). *Reducing the Foster Care Bias in Juvenile Detention Decisions: The Impact of Project Confirm*. New York: Vera Institute of Justice.

Connecticut Juvenile Jurisdiction Planning and Implementation Committee. (2007). *Final Report*. Available: http://www.ncdjjdp.org/resources/youthAccountabilityTaskForce/systemCosts/connecticut.pdf [June 2012].

Cook, P.J., MacCoun, R., Muschkin, C., and Vigdor, J. (2008). The negative impacts of starting middle school in sixth grade. *Journal of Policy Analysis and Management, 27*(1), 104-121.

Coolbaugh, K., and Hansel, C.J. (2000). The comprehensive strategy: Lessons learned from the pilot sites. *Juvenile Justice Bulletin*. Available: http://www.cantraining.org/BTC/docs/OJJDP/Comprehensive%20Strategy%20Lessons%20Learned.pdf [May 2012].

Coordinating Council on Juvenile Justice and Delinquency Prevention. (1996). *Combating Violence and Delinquency: The National Juvenile Justice Action Plan: Report*. Washington, DC: Office of Juvenile Justice and Delinquency Prevention, Office of Justice Programs, U.S. Department of Justice.

Coordinating Council on Juvenile Justice and Delinquency Prevention. (2008). *Report of Activities and Recommendations to Congress 2001-2008*. Available: http://www.juvenilecouncil.gov/reports.html [May 2012].

Copeland, M. (2011, October 13). *Miami-Dade Civil Citation Program*. PowerPoint Presentation at OJJDP's National Conference, Washington, DC.

Cose, E. (1993). *The Rage of the Privileged Class*. New York: HarperCollins.

Costanzo, P.R., and Shaw, M.E. (1966). Conformity as a function of age level. *Child Development, 37*(4), 967-975.

Counte, M.A., and Meurer, S. (2001). Issues in the assessment of continuous quality improvement implementation in health care organizations. *International Journal for Quality in Health Care, 13*(3), 197-207.

Cowell, A., Lattimore, P., and Krebs, C. (2010). A cost-benefit study of a breaking the cycle program for juveniles. *Journal of Research in Crime and Delinquency, 47*(2), 241-262.

Crockett, C.M., and Pope, T.R. (1993). Consequences of sex differences in dispersal for juvenile red howler monkeys. In M.E. Pereira and L.A. Fairbanks (Eds.), *Juvenile Primates: Life History, Development, and Behavior* (pp. 104-118). New York: Oxford University Press.

Crouch, J.L., Hanson, R.F., Saunders, B.E., Kilpatrick, D.G., and Resnick, H.S. (2000). Income, race/ethnicity, and exposure to violence in youth: Results from the national survey of adolescents. *Journal of Community Psychology, 28*(6), 625-641.

Crowe, A.H. (2000). *Jurisdictional Technical Assistance Package for Juvenile Corrections.* Washington, DC: Office of Juvenile Justice and Delinquency Prevention, Office of Justice Programs, U.S. Department of Justice.

Crutchfield, R.D., Bridges, G., and Pitchford, S. (1994). Analytical and aggregation biases in analyses of imprisonment: Reconciling discrepancies in studies of racial disparity. *Journal of Research in Crime and Delinquency, 31*(2), 166-182.

Crutchfield, R.D., Skinner, M.L., Haggerty, K.P., McGlynn, A., and Catalano, R.F. (2009). Racial disparities in early criminal justice involvement. *Race and Social Problems, 1*(4), 218-230.

Csikszentmihalyi, M., and Larson, R. (1987). Validity and reliability of the experience-sampling method. *Journal of Nervous and Mental Disease, 175*(9), 526-536.

Cullen, F.T. (2005). The twelve people who saved rehabilitation: How the science of criminology made a difference. *Criminology, 43*(1), 1-42.

Cullen, F.T., Golden, K.M., and Cullen, J.B. (1983). Is child saving dead: Attitudes toward juvenile rehabilitation in Illinois. *Journal of Criminal Justice, 11*(1), 1-13.

Cullen, F.T., Wright, J.P., Brown, S., Moon, M.M., Blankenship, M.B. and Applegate, B.K. (1998). Public support for early intervention programs: Implications for a progressive policy agenda. *Crime and Delinquency, 44*, 187-204.

Cullen, F.T., Jonson, C.L., and Nagin, D.S. (2011). Prisons do not reduce recidivism: The high cost of ignoring science. *The Prison Journal Supplement, 91*(3), 48S-65S.

Dalton, R.F., Evans, L.J., Cruise, K.R., Feinstein, R.A., and Kendrick. R.F. (2009). Race differences in mental health service access in a secure male juvenile justice facility. *Journal of Offender Rehabilitation, 48*, 194-209.

Daly, K. (1998). Gender, crime, and criminology. In M.H. Tonry (Ed.), *The Handbook of Crime and Punishment* (pp. 85-108). New York: Oxford University Press.

Daly, K., and Chesney-Lind, M. (1988). Feminism and criminology. *Justice Quarterly, 5*(4), 497-538.

Daly, M., and Wilson, M. (1987). The Darwinian psychology of discriminative parental solicitude. *Nebraska Symposium on Motivation, 35*, 91-144.

Damon, W. (1984). Self-understanding and moral development from childhood to adolescence. In W.M. Kurtines and J.L. Gewirtz (Eds.), *Morality, Moral Behavior, and Moral Development* (pp. 109-127). New York: John Wiley & Sons.

Damon, W. (1999). Reading between the lines: What do teenagers laws of life essays tell us about them? In P. Veljkovic (Ed.), *Laws of Life* (Winter, p. 2). Radnor, PA: John Templeton Foundation.

Davis, S.M., Scott, E.S., Wadlington, W., and Whitebread, C.H. (2008). *Children in the Legal System: Cases and Materials* (4th ed.). Westbury, NY: Foundation Press.

Dawes, R., Faust, D., and Meehl, P. (1989). Clinical versus actuarial judgment. *Science, 243*(4899), 1668-1674.

Dawson, R.O. (1990). The future of juvenile justice: Is it time to abolish the system? *Journal of Criminal Law and Criminology, 81*(1), 136-155.

de Ridder, D.T., Lensvelt-Mulders, G., Finkenauer, C., Stok, F.M., and Baumeister, R.F. (2012). Taking stock of self-control: A meta-analysis of how trait self-control relates to a wide range of behaviors. *Personality and Social Psychology Review, 16*(1), 76-99.

de Sá, K. (2012). Gov. Jerry Brown backtracks on plan to phase out the state's youth prison system. *Mercury News.* Available: http://www.mercurynews.com/california/ci_20631280/gov-jerry-brown-backtracks-plan-phase-out-states [May 2012].

Deardorff, J., Gonzales, N.A., Christopher, F.S., Roosa, M.W., and Millsap, R.E. (2005). Early puberty and adolescent pregnancy: The influence of alcohol use. *Pediatrics, 116*(6), 1451-1456.

Decker, T.C. (2010, August 2). *Tortoise or Hare? Slow Change Can Be Powerful, Here's How to Begin.* Available: http://www.governing.com/blogs/bfc/slow-change-powerful.html [June 2012].

Decker, T.C. (2011, May 13). *Engaging Families in Juvenile Justice: Workforce and Organizational Developmental Strategies.* Presentation to Georgetown Workforce Panel on Engaging Families at the Family Engagement Symposium, Washington, DC. Available: http://cjjr.georgetown.edu/pdfs/famengagement/FamEngSympoPowerPoint.pdf [June 2012].

Decker, T.C., and Steward, M. (2011, March 28). *Missouri DSS Division of Youth Services.* Presentation to the New York City Administration for Children's Services at the Residential Realignment Kick-Off Meeting, New York. Available: http://www.missouriapproach.org/storage/documents/OverviewMissouriDYSforNewYorkCity3-28-11.pdf [June 2012].

DeComo, R., and Wiebush, R.G. (2005). *Graduated Sanctions for Juvenile Offenders: A Program Model and Planning Guide.* Reno, NV: National Council of Juvenile and Family Court Judges, Juvenile Sanctions Center.

DeGarmo, D.S., and Martinez, Jr., C.R. (2006). A culturally informed model of academic well-being for Latino youth: The importance of discriminatory experiences and social support. *Family Relations, 55*, 267-278.

Dembo, R., Turner, G., Schmeidler, J., Sue, C.C., Borden, P., and Manning, D. (1996). Development and evaluation of a classification of high risk youths entering a juvenile assessment center. *Substance Use & Misuse, 31*(3), 303-322.

Deng, S., Kim, S.Y., Vaughan, P.W., and Li, J. (2010). Cultural orientation as a moderator of the relationship between Chinese American adolescents' discrimination experiences and delinquent behaviors. *Journal of Youth and Adolescence, 39*(9), 1027-1040.

Desai, R., Goulet, J., Robbins, J., Chapman, J., Midgole, S., and Hoge, M. (2006). Mental health care in juvenile detention facilities: A review. *Journal of the American Academy of Psychiatry and Law, 34*(2), 204-214.

Desai, R.A., Falzer, P.R., Chapman, J., and Borum, R. (2012). Mental illness, violence risk, and race in juvenile detention: Implications for disproportionate minority contact. *American Journal of Orthopsychiatry, 82*(1), 32-40.

DeWit, D.J., Lipman, E., Manzano-Munguia, M., Bisanz, J., Graham, K., Offord, D.R., O'Neill, E., Pepler, D., and Shaver, K. (2007). Feasibility of a randomized controlled trial for evaluating the effectiveness of the Big Brothers Big Sisters community match program at the national level. *Children and Youth Services Review, 29*(3), 383-404.

Dick, D.M., Latendresse, S.J., Lansford, J.E., Budde, J.P., Goate, A., Dodge, K.A., Pettit, G.S., and Bates, J.E. (2009). The role of GABRA2 in trajectories of externalizing behavior across development and evidence of moderation by parental monitoring. *Archives of General Psychiatry, 66*, 649-657.

Dilulio, J.J., Jr. (1995, November 27). The coming of the super-predators. *The Weekly Standard, 1*(11), 23.

Dishion, T.J., and Andrews, D.W. (1995). Preventing escalation in problem behaviors with high-risk young adolescents: Immediate and 1-year outcomes. *Journal of Consulting and Clinical Psychology, 63*(4), 538-548.

Dishion, T.J., Capaldi, D., Spracklen, K.M., and Li, F.Z. (1995). Peer ecology of male-adolescent drug-use. *Development and Psychopathology, 7*(4), 803-824.

Dishion, T.J., Spracklen, K.M., Andrews, D.W., and Patterson, G.R. (1996a). Deviancy training in male adolescent friendships. *Behavior Therapy, 27*(3), 373-390.

Dishion, T.J., Andrews, D.W., Kavanagh, K., and Soberman, L.H. (1996b). Preventive interventions for high-risk youth: The adolescent transitions program. In R.D. Peters and R.J. McMahon (Eds.), *Preventing Childhood Disorders, Substance Abuse, and Delinquency* (pp. 184-214). Thousand Oaks, CA: Sage.

Dishion, T.J., McCord, J., and Poulin, F. (1999). When interventions harm: Peer groups and problem behavior. *American Psychologist, 54*(9), 755-764.

Dishion, T.J., Dodge, K.A., and Lansford., J.E. (2006). Findings and recommendations: A blueprint to minimize deviant peer influence in youth interventions and programs. In K.A. Dodge, T.J. Dishion, and J.E. Lansford (Eds.), *Deviant Peer Influences in Programs for Youth: Problems and Solutions* (pp. 366-394). New York: Guilford Press.

Dodge, K.A. (2001). The science of youth violence prevention. Progressing from developmental epidemiology to efficacy to effectiveness to public policy. *American Journal of Preventive Medicine, 20*(1), 63-70.

Dodge, K.A., and Rutter, M. (2011). *Gene-environment Interactions in Developmental Psychopathology.* New York: Guilford Press.

Dodge, K.A., Lansford, J.E., and Dishion, T.J. (2006). The problem of deviant peer influences in intervention programs. In K.A. Dodge, T.J. Dishion, and J.E. Lansford (Eds.), *Deviant Peer Influences in Programs for Youth: Problems and Solutions* (pp. 3-13). New York: Guilford Press.

Doherty, B. (1998, May 31). When kids kill: Blame those who pull trigger. *Milwaukee Journal Sentinel.*

Donabedian, A. (1988). The quality of care. *Journal of the American Medical Association, 260*(12), 1743-1748.

Dosenbach, N.U., Nardos, B., Cohen, A.L., Fair, D.A., Power, J.D., Church, J.A., Nelson, S.M., Wig, G.S., Vogel, A.C., Lessov-Schlaggar, C.N., Barnes, K.A., Dubis, J.W., Feczko, E., Coalson, R.S., Pruett, J.R., Jr., Barch, D.M., Petersen, S.E., and Schlaggar, B.L. (2010). Prediction of individual brain maturity using fMRI. *Science, 329*(5997), 1358-1361.

Douglas, K.S., and Skeem, J.L. (2005). Violence risk assessment: Getting specific about being dynamic. *Psychology Public Policy and Law, 11*(3), 347-383.

Drake, E.K., Aos, S., and Miller, M.G. (2009). Evidence-based public policy options to reduce crime and criminal justice costs: Implications in Washington State. *Victims and Offenders, 4*(2), 170-196.

DuBois, D.L., Holloway, B.E., Valentine, J.C., and Cooper, H. (2002a). Effectiveness of mentoring programs for youth: A meta-analytic review. *American Journal of Community Psychology, 30*(2), 157-197.

DuBois, D.L., Burk-Braxton, C., Swenson, L.P., Tevendale, H.D., and Hardesty, J.L. (2002b). Race and gender influences on adjustment in early adolescence: Investigation of an integrative model. *Child Development, 73*(5), 1573-1592.

DuBois, D.L., Neville, H.A., Parra, G.R., and Pugh-Lilly, A.O. (2002c). Testing a new model of mentoring. *New Directions for Youth Development, 93*, 21-57.

DuBois, D.L., Portillo, N., Rhodes, J.E., Silverthorn, N., and Valentine, J.C. (2011). How effective are mentoring programs for youth? A systematic assessment of the evidence. *Psychological Science in the Public Interest, 12*(2), 57-91.

Duff, R.A. (1993). Choice, character, and criminal liability. *Law and Philosophy, 12*(4), 345-383.

Duggan, P. (1999, November 9). George W. Bush: The Texas record, youth feel the force of a vow kept; juvenile justice overhaul reflects tougher approach. *The Washington Post*, p. A01.

Durlak, J.A., and DuPre, E.P. (2008). Implementation matters: A review of research on the influence of implementation on program outcomes and the factors affecting implementation. *American Journal of Community Psychology, 41*(3-4), 327-350.

Durlauf, S.N., and Nagin, D.S. (2011). Imprisonment and crime: Can both be reduced? *Criminology & Public Policy, 10*(1), 13-54.

Durston, S., Davidson, M.C., Tottenham, N., Galvan, A., Spicer, J., Fossella, J.A., and Casey, B.J. (2006). A shift from diffuse to focal cortical activity with development. *Developmental Science, 9*(1), 1-8.

Eccles, J.S., and Roeser, R.W. (2009). Schools, academic motivation, and stage-environment fit. In R.M. Lerner and L.D. Steinberg (Eds.), *Handbook of Adolescent Psychology* (pp. 404-434). Hoboken, NJ: John Wiley & Sons.

Eccles, J.S., Midgley, C., Wigfield, A., Buchanan, C.M., Reuman, D., Flanagan, C., and Iver, D.M. (1993). Development during adolescence. The impact of stage-environment fit on young adolescents' experiences in schools and in families. *The American Psychologist, 48*(2), 90-101.

Eckberg, D.A., Podkopzacz, M.R., and Zehm, K. (2004). *Juvenile Court Fairness Study*. Minneapolis, MN: Fourth Judicial District Court of Minnesota. Available: http://www.mncourts.gov/Documents/4/Public/Research/Juvenile_Court_Fairness_Report_(2004).pdf [October 2012].

Eckenrode, J., Zielinski, D., Smith, E., Marcynyszyn, L.A., Henderson, C.R., Jr., Kitzman, H., Cole, R., Powers, J., and Olds, D.L. (2001). Child maltreatment and the early onset of problem behaviors: Can a program of nurse home visitation break the link? *Development and Psychopathology, 13*(4), 873-890.

Eddy, J.M., Whaley, R.B., and Chamberlain, P. (2004). The prevention of violent behavior by chronic and serious male juvenile offenders: A 2-year follow-up of a randomized clinical trial. *Journal of Emotional and Behavioral Disorders, 12*(1), 2-8.

Eder, D., Evans, C.C., and Parker, S. (1995). *School Talk: Gender and Adolescent Culture*. New Brunswick, NJ: Rutgers University Press.

Eisenberg, N., Fabes, R.A., Murphy, B.C. (1996). Parents' Reactions to Children's Negative Emotions: Relations to Children's Social Competence and Comforting Behavior. *Child Development, 67*(5), 2227-2247.

Elliott, D.S. (1994). Serious violent offenders: Onset, developmental course, and termination—the American Society of Criminology 1993 presidential address. *Criminology, 32*(1), 1-21.

Elliott, D.S., Huizinga, D., and Ageton, S.S. (1985). *Explaining Delinquency and Drug Use*. Thousand Oaks, CA: Sage.

Elliott, D.S., Huizinga, D., and Menard, S. (1989). *Multiple Problem Youth: Delinquency, Substance Use, and Mental Health Problems*. New York: Springer-Verlag.

Ellis, B.J., Del Giudice, M., Dishion, T.J., Figueredo, A.J., Gray, P., Griskevicius, V., Hawley, P.H., Jacobs, W.J., James, J., Volk, A.A., and Wilson, D.S. (2012). The evolutionary basis of risky adolescent behavior: Implications for science, policy, and practice. *Developmental Psychology, 48*(3), 598-623.

Ellis, D.A., Zucker, R.A., and Fitzgerald, H.E. (1997). The role of family influences in development and risk. *Alcohol Health & Research World, 21*(3), 218-226. Available: http://www.circle.wisc.edu/13-Eval/Tools/PDF-Documents/Family%20Influences%20and%20Risk.pdf [September 2012].

Emerson, R.M. (1974). Role determinants in juvenile court. In D. Glaser and S. Adams (Eds.), *Handbook of Criminology* (pp. 621-650). Chicago, IL: Rand McNally.

Emerson, R.M. (1991). Case processing and interorganizational knowledge: Detecting the real reasons for referrals. *Social Problems, 38*(2), 198-212.

Empey, L.T., and Rabow, J. (1961). The Provo experiment in delinquency rehabilitation. *American Sociological Review, 26*(5), 679-695.

Engel, R.S., Klahm, C.F., and Tillyer, R. (2010). Citizens' demeanor, race, and traffic stops. In S.K. Rice and M.D. White (Eds.), *Race, Ethnicity, and Policing: New and Essential Readings* (pp. 287-308). New York: New York University Press.

Engen, R.L., Steen, S., and Bridges, G.S. (2002). Racial disparities in the punishment of youth: A theoretical and empirical assessment of the literature. *Social Problems, 49*(2), 194-220.

Erikson, E.H. (1958). *Young Man Luther: A Study in Psychoanalysis and History* (1st ed.). New York: W.W. Norton.

Ernst, M., Nelson, E.E., Jazbec, S., McClure, E.B., Monk, C.S., Leibenluft, E., Blair, J., and Pine, D.S. (2005). Amygdala and nucleus accumbens in responses to receipt and omission of gains in adults and adolescents. *NeuroImage, 25*(4), 1279-1291.

Esbensen, F.A., Peterson, D., and Taylor, T.J. (2010). *Youth Violence: Sex and Race Differences in Offending, Victimization, and Gang Membership.* Philadelphia, PA: Temple University Press.

Ezell, M.E. (2007). The effect of criminal history variables on the process of desistance in adulthood among serious youthful offenders. *Journal of Contemporary Criminal Justice, 23*(1), 28-49.

Ezell, M.E., and Cohen, L.E. (2005). *Desisting from Crime: Continuity and Change in Long-Term Crime Patterns of Serious Chronic Offenders.* New York: Oxford University Press.

Fabelo, T., Thompson, M.D., Plotkin, M., Carmichael, D., Marchbanks, M.P., III, and Booth, E.A. (2011). *Breaking Schools' Rules: A Statewide Study of How School Discipline Relates to Students' Success and Juvenile Justice Involvement.* New York: Council of State Governments Justice Center.

Fagan, J. (1990). Treatment and reintegration of violent juvenile offenders: Experimental results. *Justice Quarterly, 7*(2), 233-263.

Fagan, J. (1991). *Comparative Impacts of Juvenile and Criminal Court Sanctions on Adolescent Offenders.* Report to the Office of Juvenile Justice and Delinquency Prevention. NCJ Number: 134377. Washington, DC: National Institute of Justice.

Fagan, J. (1999). Context and culpability in adolescent crime. *Virginia Journal of Social Policy and the Law, 6*(3), 507-583.

Fagan, J.A., and Piquero, A.R. (2007). Rational choice and developmental influences on recidivism among adolescent felony offenders. *Journal of Empirical Legal Studies, 4*(4), 715.

Fagan, J.A., and Tyler, T. (2005). Legal socialization of children and adolescents. *Social Justice Research, 18*(3), 217-241.

Fagan, J., Kupchik, A. and Liberman, A. (2007). *Be Careful What You Wish for: Legal Sanctions and Public Safety Among Adolescent Offenders in Juvenile and Criminal Court.* Columbia Law School, Pub. Law Research Paper No. 03-61. Available: http://ssrn.com/abstract=491202 [August 2012].

Fagan, A.A., Hanson, K., Hawkins, J.D., and Arthur, M.W. (2008). Bridging science to practice: Achieving prevention program implementation fidelity in the community youth development study. *American Journal of Community Psychology, 41*(3-4), 235-249.

Fagan, J.A., Geller, A., Davies, G., and West, V. (2010). Street stops and broken windows revisited: The demography and logic of proactive policing in a safe and changing city. In S.K. Rice and M.D. White (Eds.), *Race, Ethnicity, and Policing New and Essential Readings* (pp. 309-348). New York: New York University Press.

Fair, D.A., Dosenbach, N.U.F., Church, J.A., Cohen, A.L., Brahmbhatt, S., Miezin, F.M., Barch, D.M., Raichle, M.E., Petersen, S.E., and Schlaggar, B.L. (2007). Development of distinct control networks through segregation and integration. *Proceedings of the National Academy of Sciences of the United States of America, 104*(33), 13507-13512.

Families and Friends of Louisiana's Incarcerated Children. (2011). *A Failing System: Reminiscent of Tallulah.* Available: http://www.fflic.org/wp-content/uploads/2011/09/A-Failing-System-Report.pdf [June 2012].

Farrington, D.P. (1989). Early predictors of adolescent aggression and adult violence. *Violence and Victims, 4*(2), 79-100.

Farrington, D.P., and Welsh, B. (2007). *Saving Children from a Life of Crime: Early Risk Factors and Effective Interventions.* New York: Oxford University Press.

Feagin, J.R. (1991). The continuing significance of race: Antiblack discrimination in public places. *American Sociological Review, 56*(1), 101-116.

Federal Advisory Committee on Juvenile Justice. (2009, September). *Annual Report 2009.* Washington, DC. Available: http://www.facjj.org/annualreports.html [May 2012].

Federal Advisory Committee on Juvenile Justice. (2010). *Federal Advisory Committee on Juvenile Justice Annual Report 2010.* Available: http://www.facjj.org/annualreports/00-FACJJ%20Annual%20Report-FINAL%20508.pdf [June 2012].

Federal Bureau of Investigation. (2010). *Crime in the United States.* Washington, DC: U.S. Department of Justice. Available: http://www2.fbi.gov/ucr/cius2009/data/table_43.html [June 2012].

Federal Bureau of Investigation. (2011). *Crime in the United States, 2010.* Washington, DC: U.S. Department of Justice. Available: http://www.fbi.gov/about-us/cjis/ucr/crime-in-the-u.s/2010/crime-in-the-u.s.-2010/2010%20CIUS%20Summary.pdf [June 2012].

Federal Bureau of Investigation. (n.d.). *Crime Statistics.* Available: http://www.fbi.gov/stats-services/crimestats [June 2012].

Feeley, M.M., and Lazerson, M.H. (1983). Police-prosecutor relationships: An interorganizational perspective. In K.O. Boyum and L.M. Mather (Eds.), *Empirical Theories about Courts* (pp. 216-243). New York: Longman.

Feld, B.C. (1984). Criminalizing juvenile justice: Rules of procedure for the juvenile-court. *Minnesota Law Review, 69*(2), 141-276.

Feld, B.C. (1988). Juvenile court meets the principle of offense: Punishment, treatment, and the difference it makes. *Boston University Law Review, 68*(5), 821-915.

Feld, B.C. (1991). Justice by geography: Urban, suburban, and rural variations in juvenile justice administration. *Journal of Criminal Law and Criminology, 82*(1), 156-210.

Feld, B.C. (1998a). Juvenile and criminal justice systems responses to youth violence. *Crime and Justice, 24*, 189-250.

Feld, B.C. (1998b). The juvenile court. In M. Tonry (Ed.), *The Handbook of Crime & Punishment* (pp. 509-541). New York: Oxford University Press.

Feld, B.C. (1999). *Bad Kids: Race and the Transformation of the Juvenile Court.* New York: Oxford University Press.

Feld, B.C. (2009). Girls in the juvenile justice system. In M. Zahn (Ed.), *The Delinquent Girl* (pp. 225-264). Philadelphia, PA: Temple University Press.

Feld, B.C. (2012). Procedural rights in juvenile courts, competence, and consequences. In B.C. Feld and D.M. Bishop (Eds.), *The Oxford Handbook of Juvenile Crime and Juvenile Justice* (pp. 664-691). New York: Oxford University Press.

Feld, B.C., and Bishop, D.M. (2012). Transfer of juveniles to criminal court. In B.C. Feld and D.M. Bishop (Eds.), *The Oxford Handbook of Juvenile Crime and Juvenile Justice* (pp. 801-842). New York: Oxford University Press.

Feldman, R.A., Caplinger, T.E., and Wodarski, J.S. (1983). *The St. Louis Conundrum: The Effective Treatment of Antisocial Youths.* Englewood Cliffs, NJ: Prentice Hall.

Fergusson, D.M., Horwood, L.J., and Swain-Campbell, N. (2003). Ethnicity and criminal convictions: Results of a 21-year longitudinal study. *Australian and New Zealand Journal of Criminology, 36*(3), 354-367.

Feyerherm, W. (2011). Measuring DMC: The origins and use of the relative rate index. In N.Y. Parsons-Pollard (Ed.), *Disproportionate Minority Contact: Current Issues and Policies* (pp. 35-50). Durham, NC: Carolina Academic Press.

Feyerherm, W., Snyder, H.N., and Villarruel, F. (2009). *Chapter 1: Identification and Monitoring. Disproportionate Minority Contact Technical Assistance Manual* (4th ed.). Washington, DC: Office of Juvenile Justice and Delinquency Prevention.

Figner, B., Mackinlay, B.J., Wilkening, F., and Weber, E.U. (2009). Affective and deliberative processes in risky choice: Age differences in risk taking in the Columbia Card Task. *Journal of Experimental Psychology: Learning Memory and Cognition, 35*(3), 709-730.

Finckenauer, J.O., and Gavin, P.W. (1999). *Scared Straight!: The Panacea Phenomenon Revisited.* Prospect Heights, IL: Waveland Press.

Fisher, C.B., Wallace, S.A., and Fenton, R.E. (2000). Discrimination distress during adolescence. *Journal of Youth and Adolescence, 29*(6), 679-695.

Fite, P.J., Wynn, P., and Pardini, D.A. (2009). Explaining discrepancies in arrest rates between black and white male juveniles. *Journal of Consulting and Clinical Psychology, 77*(5), 916-927.

Fitzpatrick, E. (2010, January 4). OJJDP mentoring funds boosted by $20 million; $50 million also will assist children of prisoners. *Youth Today.* Available: http://www.youthtoday.org/view_blog.cfm?blog_id=272 [May 2012].

Flanagan, T.J., and Maguire, K. (1991). *Sourcebook of Criminal Justice Statistics, 1990.* Albany, NY: Hindelang Criminal Justice Research Center.

Fletcher, A.C., Steinberg, L., and Williams-Wheeler, M. (2004). Parental influences on adolescent problem behavior: Revisiting Stattin and Kerr. *Child Development, 75*(3), 781-796.

Foglia, W.D. (1997). Perceptual deterrence and the mediating effect of internalized norms among inner-city teenagers. *Journal of Research in Crime and Delinquency, 34*(4), 414-442.

Fondacaro, M.R., Dunkle, M., and Pathak, M.K. (1998). Procedural justice in resolving family disputes: A psychosocial analysis of individual and family functioning in late adolescence. *Journal of Youth and Adolescence, 27*(1), 101-119.

Forgays, D.K. (2008). Three years of teen court offender outcomes. *Adolescence, 43*(171), 473-484.

Forgays, D.K., and DeMilio, L. (2005). Is teen court effective for repeat offenders? A test of the restorative justice approach. *International Journal of Offender Therapy and Comparative Criminology, 49*(1), 107-118.

Forst, M., Fagen, J., and Vivona, T.S. (1989). Youth in prisons and training schools: Perceptions and consequences of the treatment-custody dichotomy. *Juvenile and Family Court Journal, 40*(1), 1-14.

Fox, J.A. (1996). *Trends in Juvenile Violence: A Report to the United States Attorney General on Current and Future Rates of Juvenile Offending.* Washington, DC: U.S. Bureau of Justice Statistics. Available: http://bjs.ojp.usdoj.gov/content/pub/pdf/tjvfox.pdf [June 2012].

Freiberg, H.J., and Lapointe, J.M. (2006). Research-based programs for preventing and solving discipline problems. In C.M. Evertson and C.S. Weinstein (Eds.), *Handbook of Classroom Management* (pp. 735-786). Mahwah, NJ: Lawrence Erlbaum Associates.

Friemel, C.M., Spanagel, R., and Schneider, M. (2010). Reward sensitivity for a palatable food reward peaks during pubertal developmental in rats. *Frontiers in Behavioral Neuroscience, 4*, 1-20.

Galvan, A., Hare, T.A., Parra, C.E., Penn, J., Voss, H., Glover, G., and Casey, B.J. (2006). Earlier development of the accumbens relative to orbitofrontal cortex might underlie risk-taking behavior in adolescents. *Journal of Neuroscience, 26*(25), 6885-6892.

Galvan, A., Hare, T.A., Voss, H., Glover, G., and Casey, B.J. (2007). Risk-taking and the adolescent brain: Who is at risk? *Developmental Science, 10*(2), F8-F14.

Galvan, F.H., and Caetano, R.C. (2003). *Alcohol Use and Related Problems Among Ethnic Minorities in the United States.* Washington, DC: National Institute of Drug Abuse, National Institute on Alcohol Use and Alcoholism.

Gamoran, A. (1992). The variable effects of high school tracking. *American Sociological Review, 57*(6), 812-828.

Gardner, M., and Steinberg, L. (2005). Peer influence on risk taking, risk preference, and risky decision making in adolescence and adulthood: An experimental study. *Developmental Psychology, 41*(4), 625-635.

Gardner, W. (1993). A life-span rational choice theory of risk taking. In N. Bell and R. Bell (Eds.), *Adolescent Risk Taking* (pp. 66-83). Newbury Park, CA: Sage.

Gardner, W., and Herman, J. (1990). Adolescents' AIDS risk taking: A rational choice perspective. *New Directions for Child and Adolescent Development, 50*, 17-34.

Garland, A.F., Lau, A.S., Yeh, M., McCabe, K.M., Hough, R.L., and Landsverk, J.A. (2005). Racial and ethnic differences in utilization of mental health services among high-risk youths. *American Journal of Psychiatry, 162*(7), 1336-1343.

Garrett, C.J. (1985). Effects of residential treatment of adjudicated delinquents. A meta-analysis. *Journal of Research in Crime and Delinquency, 22*, 287-308.

Garrison, A.H. (2001). An evaluation of a Delaware teen court. *Juvenile and Family Court Journal, 52*(3), 11-21.

Gatti, U., Tremblay, R.E., Vitaro, F., and McDuff, P. (2005). Youth gangs, delinquency and drug use: A test of the selection, facilitation, and enhancement hypotheses. *Journal of Child Psychology and Psychiatry, 46*(11), 1178-1190.

Gatti, U., Tremblay, R.E., and Vitaro, F. (2009). Iatrogenic effect of juvenile justice. *Journal of Child Psychology and Psychiatry, 50*(8), 991-998.

Geier, C.F., Terwilliger, R., Teslovich, T., Velanova, K., and Luna, B. (2010). Immaturities in reward processing and its influence on inhibitory control in adolescence. *Cerebral Cortex, 20*(7), 1613-1629.

Geller, A., and Fagan, J. (2010). Pot as pretext: Marijuana, race, and the new disorder in New York City street policing. *Journal of Empirical Legal Studies, 7*(4), 591-633.

Gendreau, P. (1996). The principles of effective interventions with offenders. In A. Harland (Ed.), *Choosing Correctional Options That Work: Defining the Demand and Evaluating the Supply.* Thousand Oaks, CA: Sage.

Gibbs, J.C. (2003). *Moral Development and Reality: Beyond the Theories of Kohlberg and Hoffman.* Thousand Oaks, CA: Sage.

Giedd, J.N. (2004). Structural magnetic resonance imaging of the adolescent brain. *Annals of the New York Academy of Sciences, 1021*, 77-85.

Giedd, J.N., Snell, W., Lange, N., Rajapakse, J.C., Casey, B.J., Kozuch, P.L., Vaituzis, A.C., Vauss, Y.C., Hamburger, S.D., Kaysen, D., and Rapoport, J.L. (1996a). Quantitative magnetic resonance imaging of human brain development: Ages 4-18. *Cerebral Cortex, 6*(4), 551-560.

Giedd, J.N., Vaituzis, A.C., Hamburger, S.D., Lange, N., Rajapakse, J.C., Kaysen, D., Vauss, Y.C., and Rapoport, J.L. (1996b). Quantitative MRI of the temporal lobe, amygdala, and hippocampus in normal human development: Ages 4-18 years. *Journal of Comparative Neurology, 366*(2), 223-230.

Gilligan, C. (1993). Adolescent development reconsidered. In A. Garrod (Ed.), *Approaches to Moral Development: New Research and Emerging Themes* (pp. 103-132). New York: Teachers College Press.

Giordano, P.C., Cernkovich, S.A., and Rudolph, J.L. (2002). Gender, crime, and desistance: Toward a theory of cognitive transformation. *American Journal of Sociology, 107*(4), 990-1064.

Glisson, C. (2007). Assessing and changing organizational culture and climate for effective services. *Research on Social Work Practice, 17*(6), 736-747.

Glueck, S. (1964). Some "unfinished business" in the management of juvenile delinquency. *Syracuse Law Review, 15*, 628-659.

Gogtay, N., Giedd, J.N., Lusk, L., Hayashi, K.M., Greenstein, D., Vaituzis, A.C., Nugent, T.F., Herman, D.H., Clasen, L.S., Toga, A.W., Rapoport, J.L., Thompson, P.M., and Ungerleider, L.G. (2004). Dynamic mapping of human cortical development during childhood through early adulthood. *Proceedings of the National Academy of Sciences of the United States of America, 101*(21), 8174-8179.

Goldstein, A.P., Glick, B., Reiner, S., Zimmerman, D., and Coultry, T. (1987). *Aggression Replacement Training: A Comprehensive Intervention for Aggressive Youth.* Champaign, IL: Research Press.

Gonzales, N., and Dodge, K. (2010). *Family and Peer Influences on Adolescent Behavior and Risk Taking.* Unpublished paper submitted to the National Research Council and Institute of Medicine's Board on Children, Youth, and Families. Available: http://www.BCYF.org/dodge_gonzales_paper.pdf [September 2012].

Goode, E., and Ben-Yehuda, N. (2009). *Moral Panics: The Social Construction of Deviance* (2nd ed.). Malden, MA: Wiley-Blackwell.

Gottfredson, D.C. (2010). Deviancy training: Understanding how preventive interventions harm. *Journal of Experimental Criminology, 6*(3), 229-243.

Gottfredson, M.R., and Hirschi, T. (1990). *A General Theory of Crime.* Stanford, CA: Stanford University Press.

Gottfredson, S.D., and Moriarty, L.J. (2006a). Clinical versus actuarial judgments in criminal justice decisions: Should one replace the other? *Federal Probation, 70*(2), 15-18.

Gottfredson, S.D., and Moriarty, L.J. (2006b). Statistical risk assessment: Old problems and new applications. *Crime and Delinquency, 52*(1), 178-200.

Graham, S., and Lowery, B.S. (2004). Priming unconscious racial stereotypes about adolescent offenders. *Law and Human Behavior, 28*(5), 483-504.

Grann, M., and Langstrom, N. (2007). Actuarial assessment of violence risk: To weigh or not to weigh? *Criminal Justice and Behavior, 34*(1), 22-36.

Greene, A. (1986). Future-time perspective in adolescence: The present of things future revisited. *Journal of Youth and Adolescence, 15*, 99-113.

Greenwood, P. (2006). *Changing Lives: Delinquency Prevention as Crime Control Policy.* Chicago, IL: University of Chicago Press.

Greenwood, P. (2008). Prevention and intervention programs for juvenile offenders. *The Future of Children, 18*(2), 185-210.

Greenwood, P.W., and Turner, S. (2011). Establishing effective community-based care in juvenile justice. In F.T. Sherman and F.H. Jacobs (Eds.), *Juvenile Justice: Advancing Research, Policy, and Practice* (pp. 477-504). Hoboken, NJ: John Wiley & Sons.

Gregory, A., and Weinstein, S.R. (2008). The discipline gap and African-Americans: Defiance or cooperation in the high school classroom. *Journal of School Psychology, 46*(4), 455-475.

Gregory, A., Skiba, R.J., and Noguera, P.A. (2010). The achievement gap and the discipline gap: Two sides of the same coin? *Educational Researcher, 39*(1), 59-68.

Griffin, P. (2006). *Ten Years of Balanced and Restorative Justice in Pennsylvania*. Pittsburgh, PA: National Center for Juvenile Justice. Available: http://www.ncjj.org/PDF/paprogress_june2006_10yrs_BARJ.pdf [June 2012].

Griffin, P. (2008). *Models for Change 2008 Update: Gathering Force*. Pittsburgh, PA: National Center for Juvenile Justice. Available: http://www.modelsforchange.net/publications/105 [June 2012].

Griffin, P. (2009). *Models for Change 2009 Update: Core State Progress*. Pittsburgh, PA: National Center for Juvenile Justice. Available: http://modelsforchange.net/publications/296 [May 2012].

Griffin, P. (2011). *Adding Up Models for Change: Initial Findings from the Models for Change Database*. Available: http://www.modelsforchange.net/publications/325 [June 2012].

Griffin, P., Addie, S., Adams, B., and Firestone, K. (2011). *Trying Juveniles as Adults: An Analysis of State Transfer Laws and Reporting*. Washington, DC: Office of Juvenile Justice and Delinquency Prevention, Office of Justice Programs, U.S. Department of Justice.

Grisso, T. (1980). Juveniles' capacities to waive Miranda rights: An empirical analysis. *California Law Review, 68*(6), 1134-1166.

Grisso, T. (1981). *Juveniles' Waiver of Rights: Legal and Psychological Competence*. New York: Plenum Press.

Grisso, T. (2006). *Double Jeopardy: Adolescent Offenders with Mental Disorders*. Executive Summary. Available: http://www.adjj.org/downloads/5314Double%20Jeopardy.pdf [April 2012].

Grisso, T. (2008). Adolescent offenders with mental disorders. *Future of Children, 18*(2), 143-164.

Grisso, T., Steinberg, L., Woolard, J., Cauffman, E., Scott, E., Graham, S., Lexcen, F., Reppucci, N.D., and Schwartz, R. (2003). Juveniles' competence to stand trial: A comparison of adolescents' and adults' capacities as trial defendants. *Law and Human Behavior, 27*(4), 333-363.

Grisso, T., Vincent, G., and Seagrave, D. (2005). *Mental Health Screening and Assessment in Juvenile Justice*. New York: Guilford Press.

Grolnick, W.S., Deci, E.L., and Ryan, R.M. (1997). Internalization within the family: The self-determination perspective. In J.E. Grusec and L. Kuczynski (Eds.), *Parenting and Children's Internalization of Values: A Handbook of Contemporary Theory* (pp. 135-161). New York: John Wiley & Sons.

Grossman, J.P., and Tierney, J.P. (1998). Does mentoring work? An impact study of Big Brothers/Big Sisters. *Evaluation Review, 22*(3), 403-426.

Grusec, J.E., and Goodnow, J.J. (1994). Impact of parental discipline methods on the child's internalization of values: A reconceptualization of current points of view. *Developmental Psychology, 30*, 4-19.

Hagan, J. (1975). The social and legal construction of criminal justice: A study of the pre-sentencing process. *Social Problems, 22*(5), 620-637.

Hagan, J., Shedd, C., and Payne, M. (2005). Race, ethnicity, and youth perceptions of criminal justice. *American Sociological Review, 70*(3), 381-407.

Hale, S. (1990). A global developmental trend in cognitive processing speed. *Child Development, 61*(3), 653-663.

Halemba, G.J., Siegel, G.C., Lord, R.D., and Zawacki, S. (2004). *Arizona Dual Jurisdiction Study: Final Report*. Pittsburgh, PA: National Center for Juvenile Justice.

Hallinan, M.T., and Williams, R.A. (1989). Interracial friendship choices in secondary schools. *American Sociological Review, 54*(1), 67-78.

Hamm, J.V., Brown, B., and Heck, D.J. (2005). Bridging the ethnic divide: Student and school characteristics in African American, Asian-descent, Latino, and white adolescents' cross-ethnic friend nominations. *Journal of Research on Adolescence, 15*(1), 21-46.

Hamparian, D.M., Estep, L.K., Muntean, S.M., Priestino, R.R., Swisher, R.G., Wallace, P.L., and White, J.L. (1982). *Major Issues in Juvenile Justice Information and Training Youth in Adult Courts—Between Two Worlds.* Report to the Office of Juvenile Justice and Delinquency Prevention. NCJ Number: 80823. Washington, DC: National Institute of Justice.

Handler, J. (1965). The juvenile court and the adversary system: Problems of function and form. *Wisconsin Law Review, 7,* 51.

Hardin, M.G., Mandell, D., Mueller, S.C., Dahl, R.E., Pine, D.S., and Ernst, M. (2009). Inhibitory control in anxious and healthy adolescents is modulated by incentive and incidental affective stimuli. *Journal of Child Psychology and Psychiatry and Allied Disciplines, 50*(12), 1550-1558.

Hare, T.A., O'Doherty, J., Camerer, C.F., Schultz, W., and Rangel, A. (2008). Dissociating the role of the orbitofrontal cortex and the striatum in the computation of goal values and prediction errors. *Journal of Neuroscience, 28*(22), 5623-5630.

Harp, T., and Walker, T. (2007, January 19). No justice for teens treated as adults. *Hartford Courant.*

Harrison, P., Maupin, J., and Mays, G. (2000). Teen court: An examination of processes and outcomes. *Crime and Delinquency, 47*(2), 243-264.

Hartman, R.G. (2000). Adolescent autonomy: Clarifying an ageless conundrum. *The Hastings Law Journal, 51*(6), 1265.

Hasenfeld, Y., and Cheung, P.P.L. (1985). The juvenile court as a people-processing organization: A political economy perspective. *American Journal of Sociology, 90*(4), 801-824.

Hastings, P.D., Utendale, W.T., and Sullivan, C. (2007). The socialization of prosocial development. In J.E. Grusec and P.D. Hastings (Eds.), *Handbook of Socialization Theory and Research* (pp. 638-664). New York: Guilford Press.

Hawkins, D.F., and Kempf-Leonard, K. (2005). Introduction. In D.F. Hawkins and K. Kempf-Leonard (Eds.), *Our Children, Their Children: Confronting Racial and Ethnic Differences in American Juvenile Justice* (pp. 1-19). Chicago, IL: University of Chicago Press.

Hawkins, J.D., Catalano, R.F., and Miller, J.Y. (1992). Risk and protective factors for alcohol and other drug problems in adolescence and early adulthood: Implications for substance-abuse prevention. *Psychological Bulletin, 112*(1), 64-105.

Hawkins, J.D., Herrenkohl, T., Farrington, D.P., Brewer, D., Catalano, R.F., and Harachi, T.W. (1998). A review of predictors of youth violence. In R. Loeber and D.P. Farrington (Eds.), *Serious and Violent Juvenile Offenders: Risk Factors and Successful Interventions* (pp. 106-146). Thousand Oaks, CA: Sage.

Hawkins, J.D., Catalano, R.F., Arthur, M.W., Egan, E., Brown, E.C., Abbott, R.D., and Murray, D.M. (2008). Testing communities that care: The rationale, design and behavioral baseline equivalence of the community youth development study. *Prevention Science, 9*(3), 178-190.

Haynie, D.L. (2003). Contexts of risk? Explaining the link between girls' pubertal development and their delinquency involvement. *Social Forces, 82,* 355-397.

Haynie, D.L., Weiss, H.E., and Piquero, A. (2008). Race, the economic maturity gap, and criminal offending in young adulthood. *Justice Quarterly, 25*(4), 595-622.

Heckman, J.J., Moon, S.H., Pinto, R., Savelyev, P.A., and Yavitz, A. (2010). The rate of return to the High/Scope Perry Preschool Program. *Journal of Public Economics, 94*(1-2), 114-128.

Heinemann, A.W., Fisher, W.P., and Gershon, R. (2006). Improving health care quality with outcomes management. *Journal of Prosthetic and Orthotics, 18*(Suppl. 1), S46-S50.

Henderson, H., Wells, W., Maguire, E.R. and Gray, J. (2010). Evaluating the measurement properties of procedural justice in a correctional setting. *Criminal Justice and Behavior, 37,* 384-399.

Henggeler, S.W., Melton, G.B., and Smith, L.A. (1992). Family preservation using multisystemic therapy: An effective alternative to incarcerating serious juvenile offenders. *Journal of Consulting and Clinical Psychology, 60*(6), 953-961.

Henggeler, S.W., Schoenwald, S.K., Borduin, C.M., Rowland, M.D., and Cunningham, P.B. (1998). *Multisystemic Treatment of Antisocial Behavior in Children and Adolescents.* New York: Guilford Press.

Hennigan, K., Kolnick, K., Poplawski, J., Andrews, A., Ball, N., Cheng, C., and Payne, J. (2007). *Juvenile Justice Data Project. Phase I, Survey of Interventions and Programs, A Continuum of Graduated Responses for Juvenile Justice in California.* Los Angeles, CA: University of Southern California, Center for Research on Crime.

Henning, K. (2005). Loyalty, paternalism and rights: Client counseling theory and the role of child's counsel in delinquency cases. *Notre Dame Law Review, 245*, 318-324.

Henning, K. (2006). It takes a lawyer to raise a child? Allocating responsibilities among parents, children, and lawyers in child delinquency cases. *Nevada Law Journal, 6*, 836-889.

Herrera, C., Grossman, J.B., Kauh, T.J., Feldman, A.F., and McMaken, J. (2007). *Making a Difference in Schools: The Big Brothers Big Sisters School-Based Mentoring Impact Study.* Philadelphia, PA: Public/Private Ventures.

Herz, D.C. (2001). Understanding the use of mental health placements by the juvenile justice system. *Journal of Emotional Behavioral Disorders, 9*(3), 172-181.

Herz, D.C., and Ryan, J.P. (2008a). Building multisystem approaches in child welfare and juvenile justice. In D. Barish, S. Hunter, A. Lee, B. Levin, and A. Light (Eds.), *Bridging Two Worlds: Youth Involved in the Child Welfare and Juvenile Justice Systems: A Policy Guide for Improving Outcomes* (pp. 27-113). Washington, DC: Center for Juvenile Justice Reform. Available: http://www.cjjr.georgetown.edu/pdfs/cypm/cypm.pdfw [June 2012].

Herz, D.C., and Ryan, J.P. (2008b). *Exploring the Characteristics and Outcomes of 241.1 Youth Crossing Over from Dependency to Delinquency in Los Angeles County. CFCC Research Update.* San Francisco: Judicial Council of California, Administrative Office of the Courts, Center for Families, Children and the Courts.

Herz, D.C., Ryan, J.P., and Bilchik, S. (2010). Challenges facing crossover youth: An examination of juvenile-justice decision making and recidivism. *Family Court Review, 48*(2), 305-321.

Herz, D.C., Lee, P., Lutz, L., Stewart, M., Tuell, J., and Wiig, J. (2012). *Addressing the Needs of Multisystem Youth: Strengthening the Connection between Child Welfare and Juvenile Justice.* Washington, DC: Center for Juvenile Justice Reform and the Robert F. Kennedy Children's Action Corps.

Hirschfield, P.J. (2008). Preparing for prison? The criminalization of school discipline in the USA. *Theoretical Criminology, 12*(1), 79-101.

Hoagwood, K.E. (2005). Family-based services in children's mental health: A research review and synthesis. *Journal of Child Psychology and Psychiatry, 46*(7), 690-713.

Hockenberry, S., Sickmund, M., and Sladky, A. (2011). *Juvenile Residential Facility Census, 2008: Selected Findings.* Washington, DC: Office of Juvenile Justice and Delinquency Prevention, Office of Justice Programs, U.S. Department of Justice.

Hoge, R.D., Andrews, D.A., and Leschied, A.W. (1996). An investigation of risk and protective factors in a sample of youthful offenders. *Journal of Child Psychology and Psychiatry, 37*(4), 419-424.

Holloway, C. (2000). *Interstate Compact on Juveniles.* OJJDP Fact Sheet. Washington, DC: Office of Justice Programs, Office of Juvenile Justice and Delinquency Prevention, U.S. Department of Justice. Available: https://www.ncjrs.gov/pdffiles1/ojjdp/fs200012.pdf [May 2012].

Hornberger, N.G. (2010, Summer). Improving outcomes for status offenders in the JJDPA reauthorization. *Juvenile & Family Justice TODAY*. Available: http://www.juvjustice.org/media/announcements/announcement_link_156.pdf [June 2012].

Houtzager, B., and Baerveldt, C. (1999). Just like normal. A social network study of the relation between petty crime and the intimacy of adolescent friendships. *Social Behavior and Personality, 27*, 177-192.

Howell, J.C. (1995a). *Guide for Implementing the Comprehensive Strategy for Serious, Violent and Chronic Juvenile Offenders*. Washington, DC: Office of Juvenile Justice and Delinquency Prevention, Office of Justice Programs, U.S. Department of Justice.

Howell, J.C. (1995b). *OJJDP Model Risk Assessment*. Washington DC: Office of Juvenile Justice and Delinquency Prevention, Office of Justice Programs, U.S. Department of Justice.

Howell, J.C. (1997). *Juvenile Justice and Youth Violence*. Thousand Oaks, CA: Sage.

Howell, J.C. (2003a). *OJJDP Model Risk Assessment*. Washington, DC: Office of Juvenile Justice and Delinquency Prevention, Office of Justice Programs, U.S. Department of Justice.

Howell, J.C. (2003b). *Preventing and Reducing Juvenile Delinquency: A Comprehensive Framework*. Thousand Oaks, CA: Sage.

Howell, J. C. (2003c). Diffusing research into practice using the Comprehensive Strategy for Serious, Violent, and Chronic Juvenile Offenders. *Youth Violence and Juvenile Justice: An Interdisciplinary Journal, 1*(3), 219-245.

Howell, J.C. (2009). *Preventing and Reducing Juvenile Delinquency: A Comprehensive Framework* (2nd ed.). Thousand Oaks, CA: Sage.

Howell, J.C. (2011). *Addressing Fiscal Constraints in Juvenile Justice System Reforms*. Presentation to the Committee on Assessing Juvenile Justice Reform, National Research Council, January, 19, 2011, Washington, DC.

Howell, J.C., Krisberg, B., Hawkins, J.D., and Wilson, J.J. (1995). *Sourcebook: Serious, Violent, and Chronic Juvenile Offenders*. Thousand Oaks, CA: Sage.

Hudley, C., and Graham, S. (1993). An attributional intervention to reduce peer-directed aggression among African-American boys. *Child Development, 64*(1), 124-138.

Huff, O. (2007, May 20). Imprisoning teens doesn't get the results that we want. *Asheville Citizen Times*.

Hughes, D., Rodriguez, J., Smith, E.P., Johnson, D.J., Stevenson, H.C., Spicer, P. (2006). Parents' ethnic-racial socialization practices: A review of research and directions for future study. *Developmental Psychology, 42*(5), 747-770.

Huizinga, D., and Elliott, D.S. (1987). Juvenile offenders: Prevalence, offender incidence, and arrest rates by age. *Crime and Delinquency, 33*(2), 206-223.

Huizinga, D., Loeber, R., and Thornberry, T.P. (1992). *New Findings on Delinquency and Substance Use in Urban Areas*. Congressional Briefing for the Committee on Education and Labor of the House of Representatives and the Judiciary Committee of the Senate, Washington, DC, May, 15 1992.

Huizinga, D., Loeber, R., and Thornberry, T.P. (1993). Longitudinal study of delinquency, drug use, sexual activity, and pregnancy among children and youth in 3 cities. *Public Health Reports, 108*, 90-96.

Huizinga, D., Loeber, R., and Thornberry, T.P. (1995). *Recent Findings from the Program of Research on Causes and Correlates of Delinquency*. Washington, DC: Office of Juvenile Justice and Delinquency Prevention, U.S. Department of Justice.

Huizinga, D., Schumann, K., Ehret, B., and Elliott, A. (2003). *The Effect of Juvenile Justice System Processing on Subsequent Delinquent and Criminal Behavior: A Cross-National Study. Final Report to the National Institute of Justice*. Boulder, CO: University of Colorado. Available: http:www.ncjrs.gov/pdffiles/nij/grants/205001.pdf [October 2012].

Huizinga, D., Thornberry, T., Knight, K., Lovegrove, P., and Farrington, D.P. (2007). *Disproportionate Minority Contact in the Juvenile Justice System: A Study of Differential Minority Arrest/Referral to Court in Three Cities.* Washington, DC: Office of Juvenile Justice and Delinquency Prevention, U.S. Department of Justice. Available: https://www.ncjrs.gov/pdffiles1/ojjdp/grants/219743.pdf [June 2012].

Humes, K.R., Jones, N.A., and Ramirez, R.R. (2011). *Overview of Race and Hispanic Origin. 2010 Census Briefs.* Washington, DC: U.S. Department of Commerce.

Huynh, V.W., and Fuligni, A.J. (2010). Discrimination hurts: The academic, psychological, and physical well-being of adolescents. *Journal of Research on Adolescence, 20,* 916-941.

Hwang, K., Velanova, K., and Luna, B. (2010). Strengthening of top-down frontal cognitive control networks underlying the development of inhibitory control: A functional magnetic resonance imaging effective connectivity study. *Journal of Neuroscience, 30*(46), 15535-15545.

Illinois Juvenile Justice Commission. (2005). Disproportionate minority contact in the Illinois juvenile justice system. *Annual Report to the Governor and General Assembly.* Springfield: Illinois Juvenile Justice Commission.

Illinois Models for Change Behavioral Health Assessment Team. (2010). *Report on the Behavioral Health Program for Youth Committed to the Illinois Department of Juvenile Justice.* Available: http://www.modelsforchange.net/publications/271 [April 2012].

Interstate Commission for Juveniles. (2012). *Bench Book for Judges and Court Personnel.* Available: http://www.juvenilecompact.org/LinkClick.aspx?fileticket=hP5YtZN5GWU%3D&tabid=647 [May 2012].

Irwin, C.E., and Millstein, S.G. (1986). Biopsychosocial correlates of risk-taking behaviors during adolescence. Can the physician intervene? *Journal of Adolescent Health Care, 7*(Suppl. 6), S82-S96.

Isett, K.R. (2011). *Analyzing Systems Change.* Available: http://www.modelsforchange.net/about/research/isett.html [June 2012].

Iyengar, S. (2010). Race in the news: Stereotypes, political campaigns, and market-based journalism. In H. Markus and P.M.L. Moya (Eds.), *Doing Race: 21 Essays for the 21st Century* (pp. 251-273). New York: W.W. Norton.

Jackson, D., and Maddy, W. (1992). *Introduction, Building Coalitions Fact Sheet.* Columbus: The Ohio Center for Action on Coalitions for Families and High Risk Youth. Available: http://edis.ifas.ufl.edu/pdffiles/FY/FY49300.pdf [May 2012].

Jacob, M. (2001). Getting tough: The impact of high school graduation exams. *Educational Evaluation and Policy Analysis, 23*(2), 99-121.

Jacobs, M.D. (1990). *Screwing the System and Making It Work: Juvenile Justice in the No-fault Society.* Chicago, IL: University of Chicago Press.

James-Burdumy, S., Dynarski, M., Moore, M., Deke, J., Mansfield, W., and Pistorino, C. (2005). *When Schools Stay Open Late: The National Evaluation of the 21st Century Community Learning Centers Program: Final Report.* Washington, DC: U.S. Department of Education, National Center for Education Evaluation and Regional Assistance. Available: http://www.mathematica-mpr.com/publications/pdfs/21stfinal.pdf [August 2012].

Jazbec, S., Hardin, M.G., Schroth, E., McClure, E., Pine, D.S., and Ernst, M. (2006). Age-related influence of contingencies on a saccade task. *Experimental Brain Research, 174*(4), 754-762.

John D. and Catherine T. MacArthur Foundation. (2008). *Models for Change: Research Initiative, Research Project Summaries.* Available: http://www.modelsforchange.net/about/research.html [December 2012].

John D. and Catherine T. MacArthur Foundation. (2010). *Models for Change: Systems Reform in Juvenile Justice Overview.* Available: http://www.modelsforchange.net/publications/291 [April 2012].

John D. and Catherine T. MacArthur Foundation. (2011). *Models for Change: Background and Principles.* Available: http://www.modelsforchange.net/about/Background-and-principles. html [June 2012].

Johnson, C. (2008, June 20). Justice Department grant overseer subject of criminal probe. *The Washington Post.* Available: http://www.//washingtonpost.com/wp-dyn/content/article/2008/06/19/AR2008061903132.html [June 2012].

Johnson, V., and Pandina, R. (1991). Effects of the family environment on adolescent substance use, delinquency, and coping styles. *American Journal of Drug and Alcohol Abuse, 17,* 71-88.

Johnston, L.D., O'Malley, P.M., Bachman, J.G., and Schulenberg, J.E. (2012). Table 6. Trends in annual prevalence of use of various drugs in grades 8, 10, and 12. In L.D. Johnston, P.M. O'Malley, J.G. Bachman, and J.E. Schulenberg (Eds.), *Monitoring the Future: National Results on Adolescent Drug Use. Overview of Key Findings, 2011* (pp. 56-60). Ann Arbor: University of Michigan, Institute for Social Research. Available: http://monitoringthefuture.org/pubs/monographs/mtf-overview2011.pdf [June 2012].

Jones, J. (1997). *Prejudice and Racism* (2nd ed.). New York: McGraw-Hill.

Jones, J.B. (2004). *Access to Counsel Juvenile Justice Bulletin.* Washington, DC: Office of Juvenile Justice and Delinquency Prevention, Office of Justice Programs, U.S. Department of Justice. Available: https://www.ncjrs.gov/pdffiles1/ojjdp/204063.pdf [August 2012].

Joyner, T. (2007, October 26). Genarlow Wilson rejoices over his release. *Atlanta Journal Constitution.*

Juvenile Justice Evaluation Center. (2002). *Cost-Benefit Analysis for Juvenile Justice Programs.* Washington, DC: Justice Research and Statistics Association.

Kaban, B., and Quinlan, J. (2004). Rethinking a "knowing, intelligent, and voluntary waiver" in Massachusetts juvenile courts. *Journal of the Center for Families, Children & the Courts, 5,* 35-55.

Kail, R. (1997). Processing time, imagery, and spatial memory. *Journal of Experimental Child Psychology, 64*(1), 67-78.

Kaltiala-Heino, R., Marttunen, M., Rantanen, P., and Rimpelä, M. (2003). Early puberty is associated with mental health problems in middle adolescence. *Social Science & Medicine, 57*(6), 1055-1064.

Karcher, M.J. (2005). The effects of developmental mentoring and high school mentors' attendance on their younger mentees' self esteem, social skills, and connectedness. *Psychology in the Schools, 42,* 65-77.

Karoly, L.A., Greenwood, P.W., Everingham, S.S., Hoube, J., Kilburn, M.R., Rydell, C.P., Sanders, M., and Chiesa, J. (1998). *Investing in Our Children: What We Know and Don't Know About the Costs and Benefits of Early Childhood Interventions.* Santa Monica, CA: RAND.

Katz, L.F., Kling, J.R., and Liebman, J.B. (2001). Moving to opportunity in Boston: Early results of a randomized mobility experiment. *The Quarterly Journal of Economics, 116*(2), 607-654.

Kazdin, A.E. (2008). Evidence-based treatment and practice: New opportunities to bridge clinical research and practice, enhance the knowledge base, and improve patient care. *American Psychologist, 63*(3), 146-159.

Kazemian, L., Farrington, D.P., and LeBlanc, M. (2009). Can we make long-term accurate predictions about patterns of de-escalation in offending behavior? *Journal of Youth and Adolescence, 38,* 384-400.

Keating, D.P. (2004). Cognitive and brain development. In R.M. Lerner and L. Steinberg (Eds.), *Handbook of Adolescent Psychology* (2nd ed., pp. 45-84). Hoboken, NJ: John Wiley & Sons.

Keating, L.M., Tomashina, M.A., Foster, S., and Allesandri, M. (2002). The effects of a mentoring program on at-risk youth. *Adolescence, 37*, 717-734.

Keenan, K., and Shaw, D.S. (2003). An early starter model of children's conduct problems. In B. Lahey, T. Moffitt, and A. Caspi (Eds.), *The Causes of Conduct Disorder and Serious Juvenile Delinquency* (pp. 153-181). New York: Guilford Press.

Kempf-Leonard, K. (2007). Minority youths and juvenile justice: Disproportionate minority contact after nearly 20 years of reform efforts. *Youth Violence and Juvenile Justice, 5*(1), 71-87.

Kempf-Leonard, K. (2012). The conundrum of girls and juvenile justice processing. In B.C. Feld and D.M. Bishop (Eds.), *The Oxford History of Juvenile Crime and Juvenile Justice* (pp. 485-525). New York: Oxford University Press.

Kempf-Leonard, K., and Sample, L. (2000). Disparity based on sex: Is gender-specific treatment warranted? *Justice Quarterly, 17*(1), 89-128.

Kempf-Leonard, K., Tracy, P.E., and Howell, J.C. (2001). Serious, violent, and chronic juvenile offenders: The relationship of delinquency career types to adult criminality. *Justice Quarterly, 18*(3), 449-478.

Kennedy, R. (1997). *Race, Crime, and the Law* (1st ed.). New York: Pantheon Books.

Kennedy, R. (2001). Racial trends in the administration of criminal justice. In N. Smelser, W.J. Wilson, and F. Mitchell (Eds.), *America Becoming: Racial Trends and Their Consequences* (vol. II, pp. 1-20). Washington, DC: National Academy Press.

Kennedy, S. (2000). Treatment responsivity: Reducing recidivism by enhancing treatment effectiveness. *Forum on Corrections Research*, 19-23.

Kerr, M., and Stattin, H. (2000). What parents know, how they know it and several forms of adolescent adjustment: Further support for a reinterpretation of monitoring. *Developmental Psychology, 36*(3), 366-380.

Kessler, R., Mickelson, K., and Williams, D. (1999). The prevalence, distribution, and mental health correlates of perceived discrimination in the United States. *Journal of Health and Social Behavior, 40*(3), 208-230.

Kim, C.Y., Losen, D.J., and Hewitt, D.T. (2010). *The School to Prison Pipeline: Structuring Legal Reform*. New York: New York University Press.

Klein, M.W. (2006). Peer effects in naturally occurring groups: The case of street gangs. In K.A. Dodge, T.J. Dishion, and J. Lansford (Eds.), *Deviant Peer Influences in Programs for Youth: Problems and Solutions* (pp. 234-252). New York: Guilford Press.

Klenowski, P.M., Bell, K.J., and Dodson, K.D. (2010). An empirical evaluation of juvenile awareness programs in the United States: Can juveniles be "scared straight"? *Journal of Offender Rehabilitation, 49*(4), 254-272.

Klietz, S., Borduin, C., and Schaeffer, C. (2010). Cost-benefit analysis of multisystemic therapy with serious and violent juvenile offenders. *Journal of Family Psychology, 24*(5), 657-666.

Kling, J.R., and Liebman, J.B. (2004, March). *Experimental Analysis of Neighborhood Effects on Youth*. Princeton Industrial Relations Section Working Paper 483. Available: http://dataspace.princeton.edu/jspui/bitstream/88435/dsp01m613mx58m/1/483.pdf [June 2012].

Kling, J.R., Ludwig, J., and Katz, L.F. (2005). Neighborhood effects on crime for female and male youth: Evidence from a randomized housing voucher experiment. *Quarterly Journal of Economics, 120*(1), 87-130.

Klingberg, T., Forssberg, H., and Westerberg, H. (2002). Increased brain activity in frontal and parietal cortex underlies the development of visuospatial working memory capacity during childhood. *Journal of Cognitive Neuroscience, 14*(1), 1-10.

Kochanska, G. (1995). Children's temperament, mothers' discipline, and security of attachment: Multiple pathways to emerging internalization. *Child Development, 66*, 597-615.

Kracke, K. (2001). *Children's Exposure to Violence: The Safe Start Initiative*. OJJDP Fact Sheet. Washington, DC: Office of Justice Programs, Office of Juvenile Justice and Delinquency Prevention, U.S. Department of Justice.

Kraemer, H., Kazdin, A., Offord, D., Kessler, R., Jensen, P., and Kupfer, D. (1997). Coming to terms with the terms of risk. *Archives of General Psychiatry, 54*, 337-343.

Kretschmar, J., Flannery, D.J., and Butcher, F. (2012). *An Evaluation of the Behavioral Health/ Juvenile Justice Initiative: 2006-2011*. Ohio Department of Youth Services and Ohio Department of Mental Health. Available http://mentalhealth.ohio.gov/assets/children-youth-families/system-of-care/bhjj-2011-evaluation-final-6-9-12.pdf [September 2012].

Krisberg, B., and Austin, J. (1998). What works with juvenile offenders: The Massachusetts experiment. In D. Macallair and V. Schiraldi (Eds.), *Reforming Juvenile Justice: Reasons and Strategies for the 21st Century* (pp. 173-196). New York: Kendall Hunt.

Krisberg, B., and Vuong, L. (2009, February). *Rebuilding the Infrastructure for At-risk Youth*. Special Report. Oakland, CA: National Council on Crime and Delinquency.

Krisberg, B., Barry, G., and Sharrock, E. (2004). *Reforming Juvenile Justice through Comprehensive Community Planning*. Oakland, CA: National Council on Crime and Delinquency.

Krivo, L., and Peterson, R.D. (1996). Extremely disadvantaged neighborhoods and urban crime. *Social Forces, 75*(2), 619-648.

Krueger, R.F., Caspi, A., Moffitt, T.E., White, J., and Stouthamer-Loeber, M. (1996). Delay of gratification, psychopathology, and personality: Is low self-control specific to externalizing problems? *Journal of Personality, 64*(1), 107-129.

Kuhn, D. (2009). Adolescent thinking. In R.M. Lerner and L.D. Steinberg (Eds.), *Handbook of Adolescent Psychology* (3rd ed., pp. 152-186). Hoboken, NJ: John Wiley & Sons.

Kupchik, A., and Snyder, R.B. (2009). Impact of juvenile inmates' perceptions and facility characteristics on victimization in juvenile correctional facilities. *The Prison Journal, 89*(3), 265-285.

Kurlychek, M.C., Brame, R., and Bushway, S. (2007). Enduring risk? Old criminal records and predictions of future criminal involvement. *Crime and Delinquency, 53*(1), 64-83.

Kurtines, W.M., and Gewirtz, J.L. (1995). *Moral Development: An Introduction*. Boston, MA: Allyn and Bacon.

Laird, R.D., Pettit, G.S., Bates, J.E., and Dodge, K.A. (2003a). Parent's monitoring-relevant knowledge and adolescents' delinquent behavior: Evidence of correlated developmental changes and reciprocal influences. *Child Development, 73*(3), 752-768.

Laird, R.D., Pettit, G.S., Dodge, K.A., and Bates, J.E. (2003b). Change in parents' monitoring knowledge: Links with parenting, relationship quality, adolescent beliefs, and antisocial behavior. *Social Development, 12*(3), 401-419.

Landenberger, N., and Lipsey, M. (2005). The positive effects of cognitive-behavioral programs for offenders: A meta-analysis of factors associated with effective treatment. *Journal of Experimental Criminology, 1*(4), 451-476.

Lansford, J.E. (2006). Peer effects in community programs. In K.A. Dodge, T.J. Dishion, and J. Lansford (Eds.), *Deviant Peer Influences in Programs for Youth: Problems and Solutions* (pp. 215-233). New York: Guilford Press.

Lansford, J.E., Dodge, K.A., Pettit, G.S., Bates, J.E., Crozier, J., and Kaplow, J. (2002). A 12-year prospective study of the long-term effects of early child physical maltreatment on psychological, behavioral, and academic problems in adolescence. *Archives of Pediatrics and Adolescent Medicine, 156*, 824-830.

Lanthier, F.M. (2006). *Teen Court: An Evaluation of the Selection Process in Producing "Good" Candidates*. Paper presented at the annual meeting of the American Society of Criminology (ASC). Available: http://www.allacademic.com/meta/p126036_index.html [June 2012].

Lanza-Kaduce, L., Frazier, C.E., Lane, J., and Bishop, D.M. (2002). *Juvenile Transfer to Criminal Court Study: Final Report*. Florida Department of Juvenile Justice. Available: http://www.prisonpolicy.org/scans/juveniletransfers.pdf [May 2012].

Larance, E.G. (2009). *Juvenile Justice: Technical Assistance and Better Defined Evaluation Plans Will Help Improve Girls Delinquency Programs (GAO-09-721R)*. Washington, DC: U.S. Government Accountability Office.

Latessa, E.J. (2004). Best practices of classification and assessment. *Journal of Community Corrections, 12*(2), 4-6, 27-30.

Latimer, J. (2001). Meta-analytic examination of youth delinquency, family treatment, and recidivism. *Canadian Journal of Criminology, 43*(2), 237-253.

Laub, J.H., and Boonstoppel, S.L. (2012). Understanding desistance from juvenile offending: Challenges and opportunities. In B.C. Feld and D.M. Bishop (Eds.), *The Oxford Handbook of Juvenile Crime and Juvenile Justice* (pp. 373-394). New York: Oxford University Press.

Laub, J.H., and Sampson, R.F. (2001). Understanding desistance from crime. In M.H. Tonry (Ed.), *Crime and Justice: A Review of Research* (vol. 28, pp. 1-69). Chicago, IL: University of Chicago Press.

Laub, J.H., and Sampson, R.J. (2003). *Shared Beginnings, Divergent Lives: Delinquent Boys to Age 70*. Cambridge, MA: Harvard University Press.

Lauritsen, J.L. (2005). Racial and ethnic differences in juvenile offending. In D.F. Hawkins and K. Kempf-Leonard (Eds.), *Our Children, Their Children: Confronting Racial and Ethnic Differences in American Juvenile Justice* (pp. 83-104). Chicago, IL: University of Chicago Press.

Laursen, B., and Collins, W.A. (2009). Parent-child relationships during adolescence. In R. Lerner and L. Steinberg (Eds.), *Handbook of Adolescent Psychology: Vol. 2. Contextual Influences on Adolescent Development* (3rd ed., pp. 3-42). New York: John Wiley & Sons.

Lee, J.M., Steinberg, L., and Piquero, A.R. (2010). Ethnic identity and attitudes toward police among African American juvenile offenders. *Journal of Criminal Justice, 38*(4), 781-789.

Lee, J.M., Steinberg, L., Piquero, A.R., and Knight, G.P. (2011). Identity-linked perceptions of the police among African American juvenile offenders: A developmental perspective. *Journal of Youth and Adolescence, 40*(1), 23-37.

Lee, M.T., Martinez, R., and Rosenfeld, R. (2001). Does immigration increase homicide? Negative evidence from three border cities. *Sociological Quarterly, 42*(4), 559-580.

Lee, V.E. (2000). Using hierarchial linear modeling to study social controls: The case of school effects. *Educational Psychologist, 35*(2), 125-141.

Lehman, C.M., Wolford, B., Stuck, Jr., E.M., and Kelly, R.E. (1998). Introduction. In D. Hammitt (Ed.), *Building Collaboration Between Education and Treatment for At-Risk and Delinquent Youth: An Interdisciplinary Approach with Action Plan* (pp. 1-6). Richmond: Eastern Kentucky University, College of Law Enforcement, National Juvenile Detention Association, Training Resource Center.

Leiber, M.J. (2003). *The Contexts of Juvenile Justice Decision Making: When Race Matters*. Albany: State University of New York Press.

Leiber, M.J. (2009, September 15). Race, pre- and postdetention, and juvenile justice decision making. *Crime and Delinquency, 10*(3), 333-353.

Leiber, M.J., and Johnson, J.D. (2008). Being young and black: What are their effects on juvenile justice decision making? *Crime and Delinquency, 54*(4), 560-581.

Leiber, M.J., Bishop, D., and Chamlin, M.B. (2011). Juvenile justice decision-making before and after the implementation of the disproportionate minority contact (DMC) mandate. *Justice Quarterly, 28*(3), 460-492.

Leone, P., Quinn, M.M., and Osher, D. (2002). *Collaboration in the Juvenile Justice System and Youth Serving Agencies: Improving Prevention, Providing More Efficient Services, and Reducing Recidivism for Youth with Disabilities.* Washington, DC: American Institutes for Research. Available: http://cecp.air.org/juvenilejustice/docs/Collaboration%20in%20the%20Juvenile%20Justice%20System.pdf [June 2012].

Levine, M., and Levine, A. (1992). *Helping Children: A Social History.* New York: Oxford University Press.

Liberman, A. (2011). *Implementation Research: Implications for Criminal & Juvenile Justice.* Presentation to the Committee on Assessing Juvenile Justice Reform, January 19, National Research Council, Washington, DC.

Lind, A.E., Kanfer, R., and Earley, P.C. (1990). Voice, control, and procedural justice: Instrumental and noninstrumental concerns in fairness judgments. *Journal of Personality & Social Psychology, 59,* 952-959.

Lind, E.A., and Tyler, T.R. (1988). *The Social Psychology of Procedural Justice.* New York: Plenum Press.

Lindsey, B.B., and Borough, R. (1931). *The Dangerous Life.* New York: H. Liveright.

Lindsey, B.B., and O'Higgins, H.J. (1970, reprint), *The Beast.* Seattle: University of Washington Press.

Lippman, J. (2010, May 3). Reforms proposed for juvenile justice. *New York Law Journal.* Available: http://www.newyorklawjournal.com/PubArticleNY.jsp?id=1202457430541&Reforms_Proposed_for_Juvenile_Justice [April 2013].

Lipsey, M.W. (1992). Juvenile delinquency treatment: A meta-analytic inquiry into the variability of effects. In H. Cooper, D.S. Cordray, H. Hartman, L.V. Hedges, R.J. Light, T.A. Louis, and F. Mosteller (Eds.), *Meta-Analysis for Explanation: A Casebook* (pp. 83-127). New York: Russell Sage Foundation.

Lipsey, M.W. (1995). What do we learn from 400 research studies on the effectiveness of treatment with juvenile delinquents? In J. McGuire (Ed.), *What Works: Reducing Re-Offending—Guidelines from Research and Practice* (pp. 63-78). Chichester, UK: John Wiley & Sons.

Lipsey, M.W. (1999). Can intervention rehabilitate serious delinquents? *The ANNALS of the American Academy of Political and Social Science, 564*(1), 142-166.

Lipsey, M.W. (2003). Those confounded moderators in meta-analysis: Good, bad, and ugly. *The ANNALS of the American Academy of Political and Social Science, 587*(1), 69-81.

Lipsey, M.W. (2006). The effects of community-based group treatment for delinquency: A meta-analytic search for cross-study generalizations. In K.A. Dodge, T.J. Dishion, and J.E. Lansford (Eds.), *Deviant Peer Influences in Programs for Youth: Problems and Solutions* (pp. 162-184). New York: Guilford Press.

Lipsey, M.W. (2009). The primary factors that characterize effective interventions with juvenile offenders: A meta-analytic overview. *Victims and Offenders, 4,* 124-147.

Lipsey, M.W., and Cullen, F.T. (2007). The effectiveness of correctional rehabilitation: A review of systematic reviews. *Annual Review of Law and Social Science, 3,* 297-320.

Lipsey, M.W., and Derzon, J.H. (1998). Predictors of violent or serious delinquency in adolescence and early adulthood: A synthesis of longitudinal research. In R. Loeber and D.P. Farrington (Eds.), *Serious and Violent Juvenile Offenders. Risk Factors and Successful Interventions* (pp. 86-105). Thousand Oaks, CA: Sage.

Lipsey, M., and Landenberger, N. (2006). Cognitive-behavioral interventions. In B.C. Welsh and D.P. Farrington (Eds.), *Preventing Crime: What Works for Children, Offenders, Victims, and Places* (pp. 57-71). Dordrecht, The Netherlands: Springer.

Lipsey, M.W., and Wilson, D.B. (1993). The efficacy of psychological, educational, and behavioral treatment. Confirmation from meta-analysis. *The American Psychologist, 48*(12), 1181-1209.

Lipsey, M., and Wilson, D. (1998). Effective intervention for serious juvenile offenders: A synthesis of research. In R. Loeber and D. Farrington (Eds.), *Serious and Violent Juvenile Offenders: Risk Factors and Successful Interventions* (pp. 313-345). Thousand Oaks, CA: Sage.

Lipsey, M.W., Wilson, D.B., and Cothern, L. (2000). *Effective Intervention for Serious Juvenile Offenders.* Washington, DC: Office of Juvenile Justice and Delinquency Prevention, Office of Justice Programs, U.S. Department of Justice.

Lipsey, M.W., Howell, J.C., Kelly, M.R., Chapman, G., and Carver, D. (2010). *Improving the Effectiveness of Juvenile Justice Programs: A New Perspective on Evidence-Based Practice.* Washington, DC: Georgetown University, Center for Juvenile Justice Reform.

Liston, C., Watts, R., Tottenham, N., Davidson, M.C., Niogi, S., Ulug, A.M., and Casey, B.J. (2006). Frontostriatal microstructure modulates efficient recruitment of cognitive control. *Cerebral Cortex, 16*(4), 553-560.

Lochman, J.E., and Wells, K.C. (2004). The coping power program for preadolescent aggressive boys and their parents: Outcome effects at the 1-year follow-up. *Journal of Consulting and Clinical Psychology, 72*(4), 571-578.

Loeber, R., and Farrington, D.P. (1998). *Serious and Violent Juvenile Offenders: Risk Factors and Successful Interventions.* Thousand Oaks, CA: Sage.

Loeber, R., and Farrington, D.P. (2000). Young children who commit crime: Epidemiology, developmental origins, risk factors, early interventions, and policy implications. *Development and Psychopathology, 12*(4), 737-762.

Loeber, R., and Farrington, D.P. (2001). *Child Delinquents: Development, Intervention, and Service Needs.* Thousand Oaks, CA: Sage.

Loeber, R., and Farrington, D.P. (2012). *From Juvenile Delinquency to Adult Crime: Criminal Careers, Justice Policy, and Prevention.* New York: Oxford University Press.

Loeber, R., Huizinga, D.H., and Thornberry, T. (1996). *Program of Research on the Causes and Correlates of Delinquency.* Annual Report 1995-1996 presented to the Office of Juvenile Justice and Delinquency Prevention. NCJ 170562.

Loeber, R., Farrington, D.P., and Waschbusch, D.A. (1998). Serious and violent juvenile offenders. In R. Loeber and D.P. Farrington (Eds.), *Serious & Violent Juvenile Offenders: Risk Factors and Successful Interventions* (pp. 13-29). Thousand Oaks, CA: Sage.

Loeber, R., Farrington, D.P., Stouthamer-Loeber, M., and White, H.R. (2008). *Violence and Serious Theft: Development and Prediction from Childhood to Adulthood.* New York: Routledge.

LoGalbo, A.P., and Callahan, C.M. (2001). An evaluation of teen court as a juvenile crime diversion program. *Juvenile and Family Court Journal, 52*, 1-12.

Logan, W.A. (1998). Proportionality and punishment: Imposing life without parole on juveniles. *Wake Forest Law Review, 33*, 681-725.

Lopez-Williams, A., Stoep, A.V., Kuro, E., and Stewart, D.G. (2006). Predictors of mental health service enrollment among juvenile offenders. *Youth Violence and Juvenile Justice, 4*(3), 266-280.

Lorion, R.P., Tolan, P.H., and Wahler, R.G. (1987). Prevention. In H.C. Quay (Ed.), *Handbook of Juvenile Delinquency* (pp. 383-416). New York: John Wiley & Sons.

Losen, D. (2011). *Discipline Policies, Successful Schools, and Racial Justice.* Boulder, CO: National Education Policy Center. Available: http://nepc.colorado.edu/publication/discipline-policies [June 2012].

Loughran, T., Mulvey, E., Schubert, C., Fagan, J., Losoya, S., and Piquero, A. (2009). Estimating a dose-response relationship between length of stay and future recidivism in serious juvenile offenders. *Criminology, 47*(3), 699-740.

Loughran, T.A., Mulvey, E.P., Schubert, C.A., Chassin, L.A., Losoya, S., Steinberg, L., Cota-Robles, S., Piquero, A.R., Fagan, J., and Cauffman, E. (2010). Differential effects of adult court transfer on juvenile offender recidivism. *Law and Human Behavior, 34*(6), 476-488.

Loughran, T., Piquero, A.R., Fagan, J., and Mulvey, E. (2011a). Deterring serious and chronic offenders: Research findings and policy thoughts from the pathways to desistance study. In N. Dowd (Ed.), *Justice for Kids: Keeping Kids Out of the Juvenile Justice System* (pp. 201-218). New York: New York University Press.

Loughran, T.A., Paternoster, R., Piquero, A.R., and Pogarsky, G. (2011b). On ambiguity in perceptions of risk: Implications for criminal decision-making and deterrence. *Criminology, 49*(4), 1029-1061.

Loughran, T.A., Pogarsky, G., Piquero, A.R., and Paternoster, R. (2012). Reassessing the certainty effect in deterrence theory using insight from prospect theory. *Justice Quarterly, 29*, 712-741.

Lowenkamp, C.T., and Latessa, E.J. (2005). Increasing the effectiveness of correctional programming through the risk principle: Identifying offenders for residential placement. *Criminology and Public Policy, 4*(2), 263-290.

Lowenkamp, C.T., Latessa, E.J., and Holsinger, A.M. (2006). The risk principle in action: What have we learned from 13,676 offenders and 97 correctional programs? *Crime and Delinquency, 52*(1), 77-93.

Lowenkamp, C.T., Latessa, E.J., and Smith, P. (2006). Does correctional program quality really matter? The impact of adhering to the principles of effective intervention. *Criminology & Public Policy, 5*(3), 575-594.

Lubow, B. (2010). *State of the Initiative.* Speech presented at the JDAI National Inter-site Conference, October 6, Kansas City, MO. Available: http://www.aecf.org/~/media/PDF Files/JDAI/2010StateOfTheInitiativeJan2011.pdf [May 2012].

Lucas, S.R. (1999). *Tracking Inequality: Stratification and Mobility in American High Schools.* New York: Teachers College Press.

Luckenbill, W., and Yeager, C. (2009). *Family Involvement in Pennsylvania's Juvenile Justice System.* Available: http://www.modelsforchange.net/publications/238 [May 2012].

Ludwig, J., and Duncan, G. (2006). Promising solutions in housing and the community. In K.A. Dodge, T.J. Dishion, and J.E. Lansford (Eds.), *Deviant Peer Influences in Programs for Youth: Problems and Solutions* (pp. 312-327). New York: Guilford Press.

Luna, B., Thulborn, K.R., Munoz, D.P., Merriam, E.P., Garver, K.E., Minshew, N.J., Keshavan, M.S., Genovese, C.R., Eddy, W.F., and Sweeney, J.A. (2001). Maturation of widely distributed brain function subserves cognitive development. *NeuroImage, 13*(5), 786-793.

Lynn, L.E., Jr. (1997). Innovation and the public interest: Insights from the private sector. In A.A. Altshuler and R.D. Behn (Eds.), *Innovation in American Government: Challenges, Opportunities, and Dilemmas* (pp. 83-103). Washington, DC: Brookings Institution Press.

MacArthur Foundation Research Network on Adolescent Development and Juvenile Justice. (2006). *Bringing Research to Policy and Practice in Juvenile Justice.* Available: http://www.adjj.org/downloads/552network_overview.pdf [June 2011].

Maccoby, E.E. (2007). Historical overview of socialization research and theory. In J.E. Grusec and P.D. Hastings (Eds.), *Handbook of Socialization Theory and Research* (pp. 13-41). New York: Guilford Press.

MacDonald, J.M., Haviland, A., and Morral, A.R. (2009). Assessing the relationship between violent and nonviolent criminal activity among serious adolescent offenders. *Journal of Research in Crime and Delinquency, 46*(4), 553-580.

Mack, J.W. (1909). The juvenile court. *Harvard Law Review, 23*(2), 104-122.

MacKenzie, D.L. (2001). Corrections and sentencing in the 21st century: Evidence-based corrections and sentencing. *Prison Journal, 81*(3), 299-312.

MacKenzie, D.L., Wilson, D., and Kider, S. (2001). Effects of correctional boot camps on offending. *The ANNALS of the American Academy of Political and Social Science, 578*, 126-143.

MacKinnon-Lewis, C., Kaufman, M.C., and Frabutt, J.M. (2002). Juvenile justice and mental health: Youth and families in the middle. *Aggression and Violent Behavior, 7*(4), 353-363.

Mahoney, J.L., and Stattin, H. (2000). Leisure activities and adolescent antisocial behavior: The role of structure and social context. *Journal of Adolescence, 23*(2), 113-127.

Mahoney, J.L., Stattin, H., and Magnusson, D. (2001). Youth recreation center participation and criminal offending: A 20-year longitudinal study of Swedish boys. *International Journal of Behavioral Development, 25*, 509-520.

Mahoney, J.L., Stattin, H., and Lord, H. (2004). Participation in unstructured youth recreation centers and the development of antisocial behavior: Selection processes and the moderating role of deviant peers. *International Journal of Behavioral Development, 28*, 553-560.

Mahoney, J.L., Larson, R., Eccles, J.S., and Lord, H. (2005). Organized activities as developmental contexts for children and adolescents. In J.L. Mahoney, R.W. Larson, and J.S. Eccles (Eds.), *Organized Activities as Contexts of Development: Extracurricular Activities, After-School and Community Programs* (pp. 3-22). Mahwah, NJ: Lawrence Erlbaum and Associates.

Maldonado-Molina, M.M., Piquero, A.R., Jennings, W.G., Bird, H., and Canino, G. (2009). Trajectories of delinquency among Puerto Rican children and adolescents at two sites. *Journal of Research in Crime and Delinquency, 46*(2), 144-181.

Mankey, J., Baca, P., Rondenell, S., Webb, M., and McHugh, D. (2006). *Guidelines for Juvenile Information Sharing.* National Criminal Justice, No. 215786. Washington, DC: Office of Juvenile Justice and Delinquency Prevention, Office of Justice Programs, U.S. Department of Justice.

Marsh, K. (2010). Economic evaluation of criminal justice interventions: A methodological review of the recent literature. In J. Roman, T. Dunworth, and K. Marsh (Eds.), *Cost-Benefit Analysis and Crime Control* (pp. 1-32). Washington, DC: Urban Institute Press.

Martin, J.A., Maccoby, E.E., and Jacklin, C.N. (1981). Mothers' responsiveness to interactive bidding inventory for African adolescents. *Perceptual and Motor Skills, 76*, 1001-1008.

Martin, M.J., McCarthy, B., Conger, R.D., Gibbons, F.X., Simons, R.L., Cutrona, C.E., and Brody, G.E. (2011). The enduring significance of racism: Discrimination and delinquency among black American youth. *Journal of Research on Adolescence, 21*, 662-676.

Martinson, R. (1974). What works?—Questions and answers about prison reform. *The Public Interest, 35*, 22-54.

Maruna, S. (2001). *Making Good: How Ex-convicts Reform and Rebuild Their Lives.* Washington, DC: American Psychological Association.

Maryland Department of Juvenile Services. (2008). *Department of Juvenile Services (DJS) Response to Juvenile Justice Monitoring Unit (JJMU), Second Quarter Report 2008, Sections I-V.* Baltimore: Maryland Department of Juvenile Services. Available: http://www.oag.state.md.us/JJMU/reports/CMR_08_Q2_DJS.pdf [June 2012].

Maschi, T., Hatcher, S.D., Schwalbe, C.S., and Rosato, N.S. (2008). Mapping the social service pathways of youth to and through the juvenile justice system: A comprehensive review. *Children and Youth Services Review, 30*(12), 1376-1385.

Massey, D.S., and Denton, N.A. (1993). *American Apartheid: Segregation and the Making of the Underclass* (9th ed.). Cambridge, MA: Harvard University Press.

Masten, A.S. (2001). Ordinary magic: Resilience processes in development. *The American Psychologist, 56*(3), 227-238.

Masten, A.S., and Coatsworth, J.D. (1998). The development of competence in favorable and unfavorable environments. Lessons from research on successful children. *The American Psychologist, 53*(2), 205-220.

Mather, L. (2003). Fundamentals: What do clients want? What do lawyers do? *Emory Law Journal, 52,* 1065-1086.

Matsuda, D., and Foley, J. (1981). *Profile of the Federal Effort in Juvenile Justice: A Report of the Youth Policy Institute of the Robert F. Kennedy Memorial.* Washington, DC: Youth Policy Institute.

Matsueda, R.L. (1988). The current state of differential association theory. *Crime and Delinquency, 34*(3), 277-306.

Matsueda, R.L., Kreager, D.A., and Huizinga, D. (2006). Deterring delinquents: A rational choice model of theft and violence. *American Sociological Review, 71*(1), 95-122.

Matza, D. 1964. *Delinquency and Drift.* New York: John Wiley & Sons.

Maxfield, M. (2001). *Guide to Frugal Evaluation for Criminal Justice, Final Report.* Washington, DC: National Institute of Justice.

May, J.C., Delgado, M.R., Dahl, R.E., Stenger, V.A., Ryan, N.D., Fiez, J.A., and Carter, C.S. (2004). Event-related functional magnetic resonance imaging of reward-related brain circuitry in children and adolescents. *Biological Psychiatry, 55*(4), 359-366.

Mays, V., Cochran, S., and Barnes, N. (2007). Race, race-based discrimination, and health outcomes among African Americans. *Annual Review of Psychology, 58,* 201-225.

McCabe, K.M., Lansing, A.E., Garland, A., and Hough, R. (2002). Gender differences in psychopathology, functional impairment, and familial risk factors among adjudicated delinquents. *Journal of American Academy of Child and Adolescent Psychiatry, 41*(7), 860-867.

McCracken, C., and Teji, S. (2010, October). *An Update. Closing California's Division of Juvenile Facilities: An Analysis of County Institutional Capacity.* Available: http://www.cjcj.org/files/An_Update_Closing_Californias_Division_of_Juvenile_Facilities.pdf [December 2011].

McElfresh, R., Yan, J., and Janku, A. (2009). *MO Juvenile Offender Recidivism Report: A 2009 Statewide Juvenile Court Report.* Jefferson City: Supreme Court of Missouri, Office of State Courts Administrator.

McGarvey, A. (2005, September 12). A culture of caring. *The American Prospect.* Available: http://prospect.org/article/culture-caring [December 2012].

McGowan, A., Hahn, R., Liberman, A., Crosby, A., Fullilove, M., Johnson, R., Moscicki, E., Price, L., Snyder, S., Tuma, F., Lowy, J., Briss, P., Cory, S., and Stone, G. (2007). Effects on violence of laws and policies facilitating the transfer of juveniles from the juvenile justice system to the adult justice system. *American Journal of Preventive Medicine, 32*(4), 7-28.

McShane, M.D., and Williams, F.P. (1989). The prison adjustment of juvenile offenders. *Crime and Delinquency, 35*(2), 254-269.

Mears, D.P. (2012). The front end of juvenile court: Intake and informal versus formal processing. In B.C. Feld and D.M. Bishop (Eds.), *The Oxford Handbook of Juvenile Crime and Juvenile Justice* (pp. 573-605). New York: Oxford University Press.

Mears, D.P., Hay, C., Gertz, M., and Mancini, C. (2007). Public opinion and the foundations of the juvenile court. *Criminology, 45*(1), 223-257.

Mendel, R.A. (2000). *Less Hype, More Help: Reducing Juvenile Crime, What Works—and What Doesn't.* Washington, DC: American Youth Policy Forum.

Mendel, R.A. (2009). *Two Decades of JDAI: From Demonstration Project to National Standard*. Baltimore, MD: Annie E. Casey Foundation. Available: http://www.aecf. org/~/media/Pubs/Initiatives/Juvenile%20Detention%20Alternatives%20Initiative/Two DecadesofJDAIFromDemonstrationProjecttoNat/JDAI_National_final_10_07_09.pdf [June 2012].

Mendel, R.A. (2010). *The Missouri Model: Reinventing the Practice of Rehabilitating Youthful Offenders*. Baltimore, MD: Annie E. Casey Foundation. Available: http://www.aecf.org/~/ media/Pubs/Initiatives/Juvenile%20Detention%20Alternatives%20Initiative/MOModel/ MO_Fullreport_webfinal.pdf [June 2012].

Mendel, R.A. (2011). *No Place for Kids, The Case for Reducing Juvenile Incarceration*. Baltimore, MD: Annie E. Casey Foundation. Available: http://www.aecf.org/OurWork/ JuvenileJustice/~/media/Pubs/Topics/Juvenile%20Justice/Detention%20Reform/NoPlace ForKids/JJ_NoPlaceForKids_Full.pdf [June 2012].

Meschke, L.L., and Silbereisen, R.K. (1997). The influence of puberty, family processes, and leisure activities on the timing of first sexual experience. *Journal of Adolescence, 20*(4), 403-418.

Mihalic, S.F., Irwin, K., Elliott, D., Fagan, A., and Hansen, D. (2001). *Blueprints for Violence Prevention*. Washington, DC: Office of Juvenile Justice and Delinquency Prevention, Office of Justice Programs, U.S. Department of Justice.

Mihalic, S.F., Irwin, K., Fagan, A., Ballard, D., and Elliot, D.S. (2004). *Successful Program Implementation: Lessons from Blueprints*. Washington, DC: Office of Justice Programs, Office and Juvenile Justice and Delinquency Prevention, U.S. Department of Justice. Available: https://www.ncjrs.gov/pdffiles1/ojjdp/204273.pdf [June 2012].

Milkman, H.B., and Wanberg, K.W. (2007). *Cognitive-Behavioral Treatment: A Review and Discussion for Corrections Professionals*. Washington, DC: U.S. Department of Justice, National Institute of Corrections.

Miller, J.G. (1991). *Last One Over the Wall: The Massachusetts Experiment in Closing Reform Schools*. Columbus: Ohio State University Press.

Miller, J., and Mullins, C. (2006). The status of feminist theories in criminology. In F.T. Cullen, J.P. Wright, and K.R. Blevins (Eds.), *Taking Stock: The Status of Criminological Theory* (pp. 217-250). New Brunswick, NJ: Transaction.

Miller, T., Cohen, M., and Wiersema, B. (1996). *Victim Costs and Consequences: A New Look*. Research Report NCJ-155282. Washington DC: National Institute of Justice. Available: https://www.ncjrs.gov/pdffiles/victcost.pdf [August 2012].

Minor, K., Wells, J., Soderstrom, I., Bingham, R., and Williamson, D. (1999). Sentence completion and recidivism among juveniles referred to teen courts. *Journal of Crime and Delinquency, 45*(4), 467-480.

Missouri Department of Social Services. (2011). *Annual Report: Fiscal Year 2010*. Jefferson City: Missouri Division of Youth Services.

Missouri Department of Youth Services. (2003). *Missouri Division of Youth Services: Programs and Services*. Jefferson City: Missouri Department of Social Services.

Mlyniec, W.J. (2008). *In re Gault* at 40: The right to counsel in juvenile court—A promise unfulfilled. *Criminal Law Bulletin, 44*, 371-412.

Moffeit, M., and Simpson, K. (2006). Research points to changing teen brain: The last area to develop, as late as in the 20s, affects impulse control and the grasp of consequences. *Denver Post*, p. A-11, February 19.

Moffitt, T.E. (1993). "Adolescence-limited" and "life-course-persistent" antisocial behavior: A developmental taxonomy. *Psychological Review, 100*(4), 674-701.

Moffitt, T.E., Arseneault, L., Belsky, D., Dickson, N., Hancox, R.J., Harrington, H., Houts, R., Poulton, R., Roberts, B.W., Ross, S., Sears, M.R., Thomson, W.M., and Caspi, A. (2011). A gradient of childhood self-control predicts health, wealth, and public safety. *Proceedings of the National Academy of Sciences of the United States of America, 108*(7), 2693-2698.

Monahan, K.C., Steinberg, L., Cauffman, E., and Mulvey, E.P. (2009). Trajectories of antisocial behavior and psychosocial maturity from adolescence to young adulthood. *Developmental Psychology, 45*(6), 1654-1668.

Mondoro, D.M., Wight, T., and Tuell, J.A. (2001). Expansion of OJJDP's comprehensive strategy. *OJJDP Fact Sheet*. Available: https://www.ncjrs.gov/pdffiles1/ojjdp/fs200118.pdf [May 2012].

Montana Board of Crime Control. (2005). *Montana Monitoring Standards for Juveniles in Custody for Law Enforcement Departments: A Guide to Compliance with the Juvenile Justice and Delinquency Prevention Act of 2002 and the Montana Youth Court Act*. Available: http://mbcc.mt.gov/JuvenileJustice/Compliance/law%20enforcement%20department%20monitoring%20standards.pdf [May 2012].

Moody, J. (2001). Race, school integration, and friendship segregation in America. *American Journal of Sociology, 107*(3), 679-716.

Moore, S. (2009). Missouri treats juveniles with lighter hand. *New York Times*, March 26. Available: http://www.nytimes.com/2009/03/27/us/27juvenile.html?pagewanted=all [June 2012].

Morash, M., Bynum, T.S., and Koons-Witt, B. (1998). *Women Offenders: Programming Needs and Promising Approaches*. Washington, DC: Office of Justice Programs, National Institute of Justice, U.S. Department of Justice.

Morley, E., Rossman, S.B., Kopczynski, M., Buck, J., and Gouvis, C. (2000). *Comprehensive Responses to Youth at Risk: Interim Findings from the Safe Futures Initiative*. Washington, DC: Office of Juvenile Justice and Delinquency Prevention, Office of Justice Programs, U.S. Department of Justice.

Multisite Violence Prevention Project. (2009). The ecological effects of universal and selective violence prevention programs for middle school students: A randomized-controlled trial. *Journal of Consulting and Clinical Psychology, 77*(3), 526-542.

Mulvey, E.P. (2005). Risk assessment in juvenile justice policy and practice. In K. Heilbrun, N.E. Goldstein, and R. Redding (Eds.), *Juvenile Delinquency: Prevention, Assessment, and Intervention* (pp. 209-232). New York: Oxford University Press.

Mulvey, E.P., and Iselin, A.R. (2008). Improving professional judgments of risk and amenability in juvenile justice. *Future of Children, 18*(2), 35-57.

Mulvey, E.P., and Lidz, C.W. (1998). The clinical prediction of violence as a conditional judgment. *Social Psychiatry and Psychiatric Epidemiology, 33*(Suppl. 1), S107-S113.

Mulvey, E.P., and Reppucci, N.D. (1988). The context of clinical judgment: The effect of resource availability on judgments of amenability to treatment in juvenile offenders. *American Journal of Community Psychology, 16*(4), 525-545.

Mulvey, E.P., and Schubert, C. (2011). Youth in prison and beyond. In B.C. Feld and D.M. Bishop (Eds.), *Oxford Handbook on Juvenile Crime and Juvenile Justice* (pp. 843-867). New York: Oxford University Press.

Mulvey, E.P., Steinberg, L., Fagan, J., Cauffman, E., Piquero, A.R., Chassin, L., Knight, G.P., Brame, R., Schubert, C.A., Hecker, T., and Losoya, S.H. (2004). Theory and research on desistance from antisocial activity among serious adolescent offenders. *Youth Violence and Juvenile Justice, 2*(3), 213-236.

Mulvey, E.P., Schubert, C.A., and Odgers, C.A. (2010). A method for measuring organizational functioning in juvenile justice facilities using resident rating. *Criminal Justice and Behavior, 37*(11), 1255-1277.

Mulvey, E.P., Steinberg, L., Piquero, A.R., Besana, M., Fagan, J., Schubert, C., and Cauffman, E. (2010). Trajectories of desistance and continuity in antisocial behavior following court adjudication among serious adolescent offenders. *Development and Psychopathology,* 22(2), 453-475.

Murray, C.A., and Cox, L.A. (1979). *Beyond Probation: Juvenile Corrections and the Chronic Delinquent.* Thousand Oaks, CA: Sage.

Nagin, D.S. (1998). Criminal deterrence research at the outset of the twenty-first century. In M. Tonry (Ed.), *Crime and Justice: A Review of Research* (vol. 23, pp. 1-42). Chicago, IL: University of Chicago Press.

Nagin, D.S., and Land, K.C. (1993). Age, criminal careers, and population heterogeneity: Specification and estimation of a nonparametric, mixed poisson model. *Criminology,* 31(3), 327-362.

Nagin, D.S., and Pogarsky, G. (2001). Integrating celerity, impulsivity, and extralegal sanction threats into a model of general deterrence: Theory and evidence. *Criminology,* 39(4), 865-892.

Nagin, D.S., and Pogarsky, G. (2003). An experimental investigation of deterrence: Cheating, self-serving bias, and impulsivity. *Criminology,* 41(1), 167-194.

Nagin, D.S., Piquero, A.R., Scott, E.S., and Steinberg, L. (2006). Public preferences for rehabilitation versus incarceration of juvenile offenders: Evidence from a contingent valuation survey. *Criminology & Public Policy,* 5(4), 627-652.

Nagin, D.S., Cullen, F.T., and Jonson, C.L. (2009). Imprisonment and reoffending. In M. Tonry (Ed.), *Crime and Justice: A Review of Research* (vol. 38, pp. 115-200). Chicago, IL: University of Chicago Press.

National Center for Juvenile Justice. (2011). *National Juvenile Court Data Archive: Juvenile Court Case Records 1985-2008* [machine-readable data files]. Pittsburgh, PA: National Center for Juvenile Justice.

National Conference of State Legislatures. (1996). *A Legislator's Guide to Comprehensive Juvenile Justice, Interventions for Youth at Risk.* Denver, CO: National Conference of State Legislatures. Available: https://www.ncjrs.gov/pdffiles1/Digitization/165150NCJRS. pdf [May 2012].

National Council of Juvenile and Family Court Judges. (2005). *Juvenile Delinquency Guidelines: Improving Practice in Juvenile Delinquency Cases.* Reno, NV: National Council of Juvenile and Family Court Judges. Available: http://www.ncjfcj.org/resource-library/publications/ juvenile-delinquency-guidelines-improving-court-practice-juvenile [June 2012].

National Council on Crime and Delinquency. (2007). *And Justice for Some: Differential Treatment of Youth of Color in the Justice System.* Oakland, CA: National Council on Crime and Delinquency.

National Institute on Drug Abuse. (2006). *Principles of Drug Abuse Treatment for Criminal Justice Populations: A Research-Based Guide.* Bethesda, MD: National Institutes of Health, U.S. Department of Health and Human Services.

National Juvenile Court Data Archive. (n.d). *History.* Available: http://www.ojjdp.gov/ ojstatbb/njcda/asp/history.asp [March 2012].

National Juvenile Defender Center. (2006). *Florida: An Assessment of Access to Counsel and Quality of Representation in Delinquency Proceedings.* Available: www.njdc.info/florida. php [September 2012].

National Juvenile Defender Center and Central Juvenile Defender Center. (2006). *Indiana: An Assessment of Access to Counsel and Quality of Representation in Delinquency Proceedings.* Available: http://www.njdc.info/indiana.php [August 2012].

National Juvenile Justice and Delinquency Prevention Coalition. (2010, August 9). *Letter to Attorney General Holder and Acting Adminstrator Slowikowski.*

National Juvenile Justice and Delinquency Prevention Coalition. (2011a). *Recommendations for Juvenile Justice Reform: Opportunities for the Obama Administration.* Available: http://www.cclp.org/documents/Federal%20Advocacy/NJJDPC_Opportunies%20 for%20the%20Obama%20administration.pdf [February 2012].

National Juvenile Justice and Delinquency Prevention Coalition. (2011b). *Recommendations for Juvenile Justice Reform: Opportunities for Action in the 112th Congress.* Washington, DC. Available: http://www.juvjustice.org/media/resources/public/resource_548.pdf [May 2012].

National Juvenile Justice and Delinquency Prevention Coalition. (n.d.). *Juvenile Justice and Delinquency Prevention Act (JJDPA) Recommendations and Background.* Juvenile Justice Fact Sheet. A Campaign of the Juvenile Justice and Delinquency Prevention Coalition. Available: http://www.act4jj.org/media/factsheets/factsheet_56.pdf [May 2012].

National Research Council. (1989). *A Common Destiny: Blacks and American Society.* G.D. Jaynes and R.M. Williams, Jr. (Eds.), Committee on the Status of Black Americans, Commission on Behavioral and Social Sciences and Education. Washington, DC: National Academy Press.

National Research Council. (2001a). *America Becoming: Racial Trends and Their Consequences* (Vol. 1). N. Smelser, W.J. Wilson, and F. Mitchell (Eds.). Washington, DC: National Academy Press.

National Research Council. (2001b). *Knowing What Students Know: The Science and Design of Educational Assessment.* Committee on the Foundations of Assessment. J. Pelligrino, N. Chudowsky, and R. Glaser (Eds). Board on Testing and Assessment, Center for Education. Division of Behavioral and Social Sciences and Education. Washington, DC: National Academy Press.

National Research Council. (2004a). *Fairness and Effectiveness in Policing: The Evidence.* Committee to Review Research on Police Policy and Practices. W. Skogan and K. Frydl (Eds.). Division of Behavioral and Social Sciences and Education. Washington, DC: The National Academies Press.

National Research Council. (2004b). *Informing America's Policy on Illegal Drugs: What We Don't Know Keeps Hurting Us.* Committee on Data and Research for Policy on Illegal Drugs. C.F. Manski, J.V. Pepper, and C.V. Petrie (Eds.). Division of Behavioral and Social Sciences and Education. Washington, DC: The National Academies Press.

National Research Council. (2005). *Improving Evaluation of Anti-crime Programs.* Committee on Improving Evaluation of Anti-Crime Programs. M. Lipsey (Ed.). Committee on Law and Justice, Division of Behavioral and Social Sciences and Education. Washington, DC: The National Academies Press.

National Research Council. (2010). *Strengthening the National Institute of Justice.* Committee on Assessing the Research Program of the National Institute of Justice. C.F. Wellford, B.M. Chemers, and J.A. Schuck (Eds.). Division of Behavioral and Social Sciences and Education. Washington, DC: The National Academies Press.

National Research Council and Institute of Medicine. (2001). *Juvenile Crime, Juvenile Justice.* Panel on Juvenile Crime: Prevention, Treatment and Control. J. McCord, C. Spatz Widom, and N.A. Crowell (Eds.). Committee on Law and Justice and Board on Children, Youth, and Families. Washington, DC: National Academy Press.

National Research Council and Institute of Medicine. (2002). *Community Programs to Promote Youth Development.* Committee on Community-Level Programs for Youth. J. Eccles and J. A. Gootman (Eds.). Board on Children, Youth, and Families, Division of Behavioral and Social Sciences and Education. Washington, DC: National Academy Press.

National Research Council and Institute of Medicine. (2009). *Preventing Mental, Emotional, and Behavioral Disorders Among Young People: Progress and Possibilities.* Committee on the Prevention of Mental Disorders and Substance Abuse Among Children, Youth, and Young Adults: Research Advances and Promising Interventions. M.E. O'Connell, T. Boat, and K.E. Warner (Eds.). Board on Children, Youth, and Families, Division of Behavioral and Social Sciences and Education. Washington, DC: The National Academies Press.

National Research Council and Institute of Medicine. (2011). *The Science of Adolescent Risk-Taking: Workshop Report.* Committee on the Science of Adolescence. Board on Children, Youth, and Families. Washington, DC: The National Academies Press.

National Research Council and National Academy of Education. (2011). *High School Dropout, Graduation, and Completion Rates: Better Data, Better Measures, Better Decisions.* Committee for Improved Measurement of High School Dropout and Completion Rates: Expert Guidance on Next Steps for Research and Policy Workshop. R.M. Hauser and J.A. Koenig (Eds.). Center for Education, Division of Behavioral and Social Sciences and Education. Washington, DC: The National Academies Press.

Neblett, E.W., Philip, C.L., Cogburn, C.D., and Sellers, R.M. (2006). African American adolescents' discrimination experiences and academic achievement: Racial socialization as a cultural compensatory and protective factor. *Journal of Black Psychology, 32,* 199-218.

Nellis, A., and Richardson, B. (2010). Getting beyond failure: Promising approaches for reducing DMC. *Youth Violence and Juvenile Justice, 8*(3), 266-276.

Nelsen, K. (2012). *Accessible and Fair? An Assessment of the Ramsey County Court System.* Williamsburg, VA: National Center for State Courts, Institute of Court Management. Available: http://www.ncsc.org/Educatipon-and-Careers/ICM-Fellows-Papers/ICM-Fellows-Papers-2012.aspx [October 2012].

New York Civil Liberties Union and Annenberg Institute for School Reform. (2009). *Safety with Dignity: Alternatives to the Over-Policing of Schools.* Available: http://www.nyclu.org/files/Safety_with_Dignity.pdf [October 2012].

New York State Office of Children and Family Services, Vera Institute of Justice, and the Missouri Services Institute. (2011). *Brooklyn for Brooklyn Initiative: Improving Outcomes for Youth in State Juvenile Justice Custody, Close to Home.* Draft Program Plan.

Newcomb, A.F., Bukowski, W.M., and Bagwell, C.L. (1999). Knowing the sounds: Friendship as a developmental context. In W.A. Collins and B. Laursen (Eds.), *Relationships as Developmental Contexts: 29th Minnesota Symposium on Child Psychology* (pp. 63-84). Hillsdale, NJ: Lawrence Erlbaum Associates.

Nielsen, A.L., Lee, M.T., and Martinez, Jr., R. (2005). Integrating race, place and motive in social disorganization theory: Lessons from a comparison of black and Latino homicide types in two immigrant destination cities. *Criminology, 43*(3), 837-872.

Nuñez-Neto, B. (2008). *Juvenile Justice: Legislative History and Current Legislative Issues.* CRS Report for Congress RL33947.

Nurmi, J. (1991). How do adolescents see their future? A review of the development of future orientation and planning. *Developmental Review, 11,* 1-59.

Oakes, J. (2005). *Keeping track: How Schools Structure Inequality* (2nd ed.). New Haven, CT: Yale University Press.

O'Brien, S. (2000). *Restorative Juvenile Justice Policy Development and Implementation Assessment: A National Survey of States.* Ft. Lauderdale: Florida Atlantic University, Balanced and Restorative Project.

Office of Justice Programs. (2006). *OJP Financial Report, 2006.* Washington, DC: Office of Justice Programs, U.S. Department of Justice.

Office of Juvenile Justice and Delinquency Prevention. (1988). *Achievements and Challenges: OJJDP's Annual Report Fiscal Year 1987.* Washington, DC: Office of Juvenile Justice and Delinquency Prevention, Office of Justice Programs, U.S. Department of Justice.

Office of Juvenile Justice and Delinquency Prevention. (1995a). *Guide for Implementing the Comprehensive Strategy for Serious, Violent, and Chronic Juvenile Offenders.* Washington, DC: Office of Juvenile Justice and Delinquency Prevention, Office of Justice Programs, U.S. Department of Justice.

Office of Juvenile Justice and Delinquency Prevention. (1995b). *Juvenile Offenders and Victims: A National Report.* Washington, DC: Office of Juvenile Justice and Delinquency Prevention, Office of Justice Programs, U.S. Department of Justice.

Office of Juvenile Justice and Delinquency Prevention. (1997a, August). *Balanced and Restorative Justice for Juveniles: A Framework for Juvenile Justice in the 21st Century.* Washington, DC: Office of Juvenile Justice and Delinquency Prevention, Office of Justice Programs, U.S. Department of Justice.

Office of Juvenile Justice and Delinquency Prevention. (1997b). *Juvenile Justice Reform Initiatives in the States: 1994-1996.* Washington, DC: Office of Juvenile Justice and Delinquency Prevention, Office of Justice Programs, U.S. Department of Justice.

Office of Juvenile Justice and Delinquency Prevention. (1999). *OJJDP's Annual Report 1998.* Washington, DC: Office of Juvenile Justice and Delinquency Prevention, Office of Justice Programs, U.S. Department of Justice.

Office of Juvenile Justice and Delinquency Prevention. (2000). *Evaluation of the Juvenile Mentoring Program (JUMP).* National Criminal Justice, No. 189127. Washington, DC: Office of Juvenile Justice and Delinquency Prevention, Office of Justice Programs, U.S. Department of Justice. Available: https://www.ncjrs.gov/pdffiles1/Digitization/189127NCJRS.pdf [May 2012].

Office of Juvenile Justice and Delinquency Prevention. (2001a). *OJJDP Research 2000.* Washington, DC: Office of Juvenile Justice and Delinquency Prevention, Office of Justice Programs, U.S. Department of Justice.

Office of Juvenile Justice and Delinquency Prevention. (2001b). *OJJDP's Annual Report 2000.* Washington, DC: Office of Juvenile Justice and Delinquency Prevention, Office of Justice Programs, U.S. Department of Justice.

Office of Juvenile Justice and Delinquency Prevention. (2004). *OJJDP Annual Report 2003-2004.* National Criminal Justice, No. 206630. Washington, DC: Office of Juvenile Justice and Delinquency Prevention, Office of Justice Programs, U.S. Department of Justice.

Office of Juvenile Justice and Delinquency Prevention. (2009a). *Disproportionate Minority Contact Technical Assistance Manual* (4th ed.). Washington, DC: Office of Juvenile Justice and Delinquency Prevention, Office of Justice Programs, U.S. Department of Justice. Available: https://www.ncjrs.gov/html/ojjdp/dmc_ta_manual/https://www.ncjrs.gov/html/ojjdp/dmc_ta_manual/index.html [May 2012].

Office of Juvenile Justice and Delinquency Prevention. (2009b). *Disproportionate Minority Contact.* Washington, DC: Office of Juvenile Justice and Delinquency Prevention, Office of Justice Programs, U.S. Department of Justice. Available: https://www.ncjrs.gov/pdffiles1/ojjdp/228306.pdf [June 2012].

Office of Juvenile Justice and Delinquency Prevention. (2009c, October). *Juvenile Accountability Block Grants Program.* Washington, DC: Office of Juvenile Justice and Delinquency Prevention, Office of Justice Programs, U.S. Department of Justice. Available: https://www.ncjrs.gov/pdffiles1/ojjdp/226357.pdf [June 2012].

Office of Juvenile Justice and Delinquency Prevention. (2010). *Guidance Manual for Monitoring Facilities Under the Juvenile Justice and Delinquency Prevention Act of 1974, as Amended* (3rd ed.). Washington, DC: Office of Juvenile Justice and Delinquency Prevention, Office of Justice Programs, U.S. Department of Justice. Available: http://www.ojjdp. gov/compliance/guidancemanual2010.pdf [March 2012].

Office of Juvenile Justice and Delinquency Prevention. (2011a). Final plan for fiscal year 2011. *Federal Register*, 76(131), 40394. Available: http://www.ojjdp.gov/about/Federal Register2011ProgramPlan.pdf [May 2012].

Office of Juvenile Justice and Delinquency Prevention. (2011b). *Statistical Briefing Book.* Available: http://www.ojjdp.gov/ojstatbb/default.asp [March 2012].

Office of Juvenile Justice and Delinquency Prevention. (2011c). *Upper Age of Original Juvenile Court Jurisdiction, 2009.* Available: http://www.ojjdp.gov/ojstatbb/structure_process/ qa04101.asp [March 2012].

Office of the Surgeon General. (2001). *Youth Violence: A Report of the Surgeon General.* Washington, DC: U.S. Public Health Service.

Ohio Department of Youth Services. (2012). *Ohio Department of Youth Services Annual Report, Fiscal Year 2012.* Available: http://www.dys.ohio.gov/DNN/LinkClick.aspx?file ticket=ITTby3%2fXF%2fw%3d&tabid+102&mid=544 [September 2012].

Olds, D., Henderson, C.R., Jr., Cole, R., Eckenrode, J., Kitzman, H., Luckey, D., Pettitt, L., Sidora, K., Morris, P., and Powers, J. (1998). Long-term effects of nurse home visitation on children's criminal and antisocial behavior: 15-year follow-up of a randomized controlled trial. *Journal of the American Medical Association, 280*(14), 1238-1244.

Olin, S.S., Hoagwood, K.E., Rodriguez, J., Ramos, B., Burton, G., Penn, M., Crowe, M., Radigan, M., and Jensen, P.S. (2010). The application of behavior change theory to family-based services: Improving parent empowerment in children's mental health. *Journal of Child and Family Studies, 19*(4), 462-470.

Oman, R.F., Vesely, S.K., Aspy, C.B., McLeroy, K., Rodine, S., and Marshall, L. (2004). The potential protective effect of youth assets on adolescent alcohol and drug use. *American Journal of Public Health, 94*(8), 1425-1430.

Onifade, E., Davidson, W., and Campbell, C. (2009). Risk assessment: The predictive validity of the youth level of service case management inventory with African Americans and girls. *Journal of Ethnicity in Criminal Justice, 7*(3), 205-221.

Orr, L., Feins, J.D., Jacob, R., Beecroft, E., Sanbonmatsu, L., Katz, L.F., Liebman, J.B., and Kling, J.R. (2003). *Moving to Opportunity: Interim Impacts Evaluation.* Washington, DC: U.S. Department of Housing and Urban Development, Office of Policy Development and Research.

Osborne, J. (2008). *Best Practices in Quantitative Methods.* Thousand Oaks, CA: Sage.

Osgood, D.W., and Chambers, J.M. (2000). Social disorganization outside the metropolis: An analysis of rural youth violence. *Criminology, 38*(1), 81-115.

Osgood, D.W., Wilson, J.K., Bachman, J.G., O'Malley, P.M., and Johnston, L.D. (1996). Routine activities and individual deviant behavior. *American Sociological Review, 61*, 635-655.

Osher, D. (2002). Creating comprehensive and collaborative systems. *Journal of Child and Family Studies, 11*(1), 91-99.

Osher, T., and Shufelt, J. (2006). *What Families Think of the Juvenile Justice System: Findings from a Multi-state Prevalence Study.* Available: http://www.rtc.pdx.edu/PDF/fpS0607 Corrected.pdf [June 2012].

Osterlind, S.J., Koller, J.R., and Morris, E.F. (2007). Incidence and practical issues of mental health for school-aged youth in juvenile justice detention. *Journal of Correctional Health Care, 13*(4), 268-277.

Otto, K., and Dalbert, C. (2005). Belief in a just world and its functions for young prisoners. *Journal of Research in Personality, 39*(6), 559-573.

Overton, W.F. (1990). *Reasoning, Necessity, and Logic: Developmental Perspectives.* Hillsdale, NJ: Lawrence Erlbaum Associates.

Owen, B. (1998). *"In the Mix": Struggle and Survival in a Women's Prison.* Albany: State University of New York Press.

Oxford, M., Harachi, T., Catalano, R.F., and Abbott, R.F. (2001). Preadolescent predictors of substance initiation: A test of both the direct and mediated effect of family social control factors on deviant peer associations and substance initiation. *American Journal of Drug and Alcohol Abuse, 27*(4), 599-616.

Pager, D., and Shepherd, H. (2008). The sociology of discrimination: Racial discrimination in employment, housing, credit and consumer markets. *Annual Review of Sociology, 34*, 181-209.

Parent, D.G. (1993). Conditions of confinement. *Juvenile Justice, 1*(1), 2-7.

Parent, D.G., Lieter, V., Kennedy, S., Livens, L.,Wentworh, D., and Wilcox, S. (1994). *Conditions of Confinement: Juvenile Detention and Corrections Facilities.* Research Report. Bethesda, MD: Abt Associates.

Parke, R.D., Burks, V., Carson, J., Neville, B., and Boyum, L. (1994). Family-peer relationships: A tripartite model. In R.D. Parke and S. Kellam (Eds.), *Exploring Family Relationships with Other Social Contexts* (pp. 115-140). Hillsdale, NJ: Lawrence Erlbaum Associates.

Parsons-Pollard, N.Y. (2011). *Disproportionate Minority Contact: Current Issues and Policies.* Durham, NC: Carolina Academic Press.

Paternoster, R. (2010). How much do we really know about criminal deterrence? *Journal of Criminal Law and Criminology, 100*(3), 765-824.

Patrick, S., and Marsh, R. (2005). Juvenile diversion: Results of a 3-year experimental study. *Criminal Justice Policy Review, 16*, 59-73.

Patterson, G.R. (1982). *Coercive Family Process.* Eugene, OR: Castalia.

Patterson, G.R., and Stouthamer-Loeber, M. (1984). The correlation of family management practices and delinquency. *Child Development, 55*(4), 1299-1307.

Patterson, G.R., Reid, J.B., and Dishion, T.J. (1992). *Antisocial Boys.* Eugene, OR: Castalia.

Paulsen, M.G. (1957). Fairness to the juvenile offender. *Minnesota Law Review, 41*(5), 547-576.

PbS Learning Institute. (2011). *Performance-based Standards.* Available: http://pbstandards.org/cjacaresources/93/PbS_InfoPacket2011.pdf [May 2012].

Peterson, R.D., and Krivo, L.J. (2009). Race, crime, and justice: Contexts and complexities. *The ANNALS of the American Academy of Political and Social Science, 623*.

Petrosino, A., and Soydan, H. (2005). The impact of program developers as evaluators on criminal recidivism: Results from meta-analyses of experimental and quasi-experimental research. *Journal of Experimental Criminology, 1*(4), 435-450.

Petrosino, A., Turpin-Petrosino, C., and Buehler, J. (2003). *"Scared Straight" and Other Juvenile Awareness Programs for Preventing Juvenile Delinquency.* Campbell Systematic Reviews 2004:2. The Campbell Collaboration. Available: http:www.campbellcollaboration.org/library.php [October 2012].

Petrosino, A., Turpin-Petrosino, C., and Guckenburg, S. (2010). *Formal System Processing of Juveniles: Effects on Delinquency.* Campbell Systematic Reviews 2010:1: The Campbell Collaboration. Available: http:www.evidencebasedassociates.com/reports/processing juvoffenders.pdf [October 2012].

Pettit, G.S., Bates, J.E., Dodge, K.A., and Meece, D.W. (1999). The impact of after-school peer contact on early adolescent externalizing problems is moderated by parental monitoring, perceived neighborhood safety, and prior adjustment. *Child Development, 70*, 768-778.

Piliavin, I., and Briar, S. (1964). Police encounters with juveniles. *American Journal of Sociology, 70*, 206-214.

Piquero, A.R. (1998). Applying an evaluability assessment tool to community-based programs in Pittsburgh. *Prison Journal, 78*(1), 74-89.

Piquero, A.R. (2008a). Disproportionate minority contact. *Future of Children, 18*(2), 59-79.

Piquero, A.R. (2008b). Taking stock of developmental trajectories of criminal activity over the life course. In A.M. Liberman (Ed.), *The Long View of Crime: A Synthesis of Longitudinal Research* (pp. 23-78). New York: Springer.

Piquero, A.R., and Brame, R. (2008). Assessing the race-crime and ethnicity-crime relationship in a sample of serious adolescent delinquents. *Crime and Delinquency, 54*(3), 390-422.

Piquero, A.R., Gomez-Smith, Z., and Langton, L. (2004). Discerning unfairness where others may not: Low self-control and unfair sanction perception. *Criminology, 42*, 699-734.

Piquero, A.R., Moffitt, T.E., and Lawton, B. (2005). Race and crime: The contribution of individual, familial, and neighborhood-level risk factors to life-course-persistent offending. In D.F. Hawkins and K. Kempf-Leonard (Eds.), *Our Children, Their Children: Confronting Racial and Ethnic Differences in American Juvenile Justice* (pp. 202-244). Chicago, IL: University of Chicago Press.

Piquero, A.R., Farrington, D.P., Welsh, B.C., Tremblay, R., and Jennings, W. (2009). Effects of early family/parent training programs on antisocial behavior and delinquency. *Journal of Experimental Criminology, 5*(2), 83-120.

Piquero, A.R., Cullen, F.T., Unnever, J.D., Piquero, N.L., and Gordon, J.A. (2010). Never too late: Public optimism about juvenile rehabilitation. *Punishment and Society-International Journal of Penology, 12*(2), 187-207.

Piquero, A.R., Paternoster, R., Pogarsky, G., and Loughran, T. (2011). Elaborating the individual difference component in deterrence theory. *Annual Review of Law and Social Science, 7*(1), 335-360.

Piquero, A.R., Hawkins, J.D., and Kazemian, L. (2012). Criminal career patterns. In R. Loeber and D.P. Farrington (Eds.), *From Juvenile Delinquency to Adult Crime: Criminal Careers, Justice Policy, and Prevention* (pp. 14-46). New York: Oxford University Press.

Pollock, J.M. (2002). *Women, Prison, and Crime.* Belmont, CA: Wadsworth.

Pope, C.E., and Feyerherm, W. (1990). Minority status and juvenile justice processing. *Criminal Justice Abstracts, 22*(2), 327-336 (part I); 22(3), 527-542 (part II).

Pope, C.E., Lovell, R., and Hsia, H.M. (2002). *Disproportionate Minority Confinement: A Review of the Research Literature from 1989 Through 2001.* Washington, DC: Office of Juvenile Justice and Delinquency Prevention, U.S. Department of Justice.

Popova, S., Lange, S., Bekmuradov, D., Mihic, A., and Rehm, J. (2011). Fetal alcohol spectrum disorder prevalence estimates in correctional systems: A systematic literature review. *Canadian Journal of Public Health, 102*(5), 336-340.

Porter, P.K., Thornberry, T.P., Huizinga, D., Loeber, R., and Stouthamer-Loeber, M. (1999). *Risk Factors for Serious Violent Offending.* Report prepared for the Office of Juvenile Justice and Delinquency Prevention, U.S. Department of Justice, November.

Posner, D. (2004). What's wrong with teaching to the test? *Phi Delta Kappan, 85*(10), 749-751.

Poulin, M., Orchowsky, S., and Iwama, J. (2011). Assessing DMC initiatives: A case study of two states. In N.Y. Parsons-Pollard (Ed.), *Disproportionate Minority Contact: Current Issues and Policies* (pp. 97-121). Durham, NC: Carolina Academic Press.

Pratt, M.W., Hunsenberger, B., Pancer, S.M., and Alisat, S. (2003). A longitudinal analysis of personal values socialization: Correlates of a moral self-ideal in late adolescence. *Social Development, 12*(4), 563-585.

Prelow, H.M., Danoff-Burg, S., Swenson, R.R., and Pulgiano, D. (2004). The impact of ecological risk and perceived discrimination on the psychological adjustment of African American and European American youth. *Journal of Community Psychology, 32*(4), 375-389.

Prentky, R., and Righthand, S. (2003). *Juvenile Sex Offender Assessment Protocol-II (J-Soap-II) Manual.* Washington, DC: Office of Juvenile Justice and Delinquency Prevention, Office of Justice Programs, U.S. Department of Justice. Available: http://purl.access.gpo.gov/GPO/LPS44913 [June 2012].

Prinstein, M.J., and Wang, S.S. (2005). False consensus and adolescent peer contagion: Examining discrepancies between perceptions and actual reported levels of friends' deviant and health risk behavior. *Journal of Abnormal Child Psychology, 33*(3), 293-306.

Pumariega A.J, Glover S., Holzer C.E., and Nguyen, H. (1998). Administrative update: utilization of services. II. Utilization of mental health services in a tri-ethnic sample of adolescents. *Community Mental Health Journal, 34*(2), 145-156.

Puritz, P., Burrell, S., Schwartz, R., Soler, M., and Warboys, L. (1995). *A Call for Justice: An Assessment of Access to Counsel and Quality of Representation in Delinquency Proceedings.* Report of the American Bar Association. Washington, DC: American Bar Association.

Puzzanchera, C., and Adams, B. (2011a). *National Disproportionate Minority Contact Databook.* Available: http://www.ojjdp.gov/ojstatbb/dmcdb/index.html [June 2012].

Puzzanchera, C. and Adams, B. (2011b, December). *Juvenile Arrests 2009.* Juvenile Offenders and Victims: National Report Series. Washington, DC: Office of Juvenile Justice and Delinquency Prevention, Office of Justice Programs, U.S. Department of Justice. Available: http://www.ojjdp.gov/pubs/236477.pdf [May 2012].

Puzzanchera, C., Stahl, A.L., Finnegan, T.A., Tierney, N., and Snyder, H.N. (2004). *Juvenile Court Statistics 2000.* Pittsburgh, PA: National Center for Juvenile Justice.

Puzzanchera, C., Adams, B., and Sickmund, M. (2011). *Juvenile Court Statistics 2008.* Pittsburgh, PA: National Center for Juvenile Justice.

Quadrel, M.J., Fischhoff, B., and Davis, W. (1993). Adolescent (in)vulnerability. *American Psychologist, 48*(2), 102-116.

Rabin, R.F., Jennings, J.M., Campbell, J.C., and Bair-Merritt, M.H. (2009). Intimate partner violence screening tools. *American Journal of Preventive Medicine, 36*(5), 439-445.

Rasmussen, A. (2004). Teen court, referral, sentencing and subsequent recidivism: Two proportional hazards models and a little speculation. *Crime and Delinquency, 50,* 615-635.

Rausch, M.K., and Skiba, R.J. (2006). Exclusion is not the only alternative: The children left behind project. In A.H. Reyes (Ed.), *Discipline, Achievement and Race.* Lanham, MD: Rowman and Littlefield Education.

Rawal, P., Romansky, J., Jenuwine, M., and Lyons, J.S. (2004). Racial differences in the mental health needs and service utilization of youth in the juvenile justice system. *Journal of Behavioral Health Services Research, 31*(3), 242-254.

Real, K., and Poole, M. (2005). Innovation implementation: Conceptualization and measurement in organizational research. *Research in Organizational Change and Development, 15,* 63-134.

Redding, R.E. (2008). Juvenile transfer laws: An effective deterrent to delinquency? *Juvenile Justice Bulletin.* Available: http://works.bepress.com/richard_redding/6 [August 2012].

Regnery, A. (1985). Getting away with murder: Why the juvenile justice system needs an overhaul. *Policy Review, 34,* 65-68.

Reiss, A., and Farrington, D. (1991). Advancing knowledge about co-offending: Results from a prospective longitudinal survey of London males. *Journal of Criminal Law and Criminology, 82,* 360-395.

Reiss, A.L., Abrams, M.T., Singer, H.S., Ross, J.L., and Denckla, M.B. (1996). Brain development, gender and IQ in children. A volumetric imaging study. *Brain, 119*(5), 1763-1774.

Rest, J.R., Narvaez, D., Bebeau. M.J., and Thoma, S.J. (1999). *Postconventional Moral Thinking: A Neo-Kohlbergian Approach.* Hillsdale: NJ: Lawrence Erlbaum Associates.

Reynolds, A.J., Temple, J.A., Ou, S.R., Arteaga, I.A., and White, B.A.B. (2011). School-based early childhood education and age 28 well-being: Effects by timing, dosage, and subgroups. *Science, 333*(6040), 360-364.

Rhodes, J., and DuBois, D. (2006). Understanding and facilitating the youth mentoring movement. *Social Policy Report, 20*(3), 3-19.

Rhodes, J.E. (2008). Improving youth mentoring interventions through research-based practice. *American Journal of Community Psychology, 41*(1-2), 35-42.

Rice, S.K., and White, M.D. (2010). *Race, Ethnicity, and Policing: New and Essential Readings.* New York: New York University Press.

Rivera, B., and Widom, C.S. (1990). Childhood victimization and violent offending. *Violence and Victims, 5*(1), 19-35.

Roberts, H., Liabo, K., Lucas, P., DuBois, D., and Sheldon, T.A. (2004). Mentoring to reduce antisocial behaviour in childhood. *British Medical Journal, 328*, 512-514.

Roberts, J.V. (2004). Public opinion and youth justice. In M.H. Tonry and A.N. Doob (Eds.), *Youth Crime and Youth Justice: Comparative and Cross-National Perspective* (Ch. 9). Chicago, IL: University of Chicago Press.

Robertson, A., Grimes, P., and Rogers, K. (2001). A short-run cost-benefit analysis of community-based interventions for juvenile offenders. *Crime and Delinquency, 47*(2), 265-284.

Rodriguez, N. (2010). The cumulative effect of race and ethnicity in juvenile court outcomes and why preadjudication detention matters. *Journal of Research in Crime and Delinquency, 47*(3), 391-413.

Roman, J., Dunworth, T., and Marsh, K. (2010). *Cost-Benefit Analysis and Crime Control.* Washington, DC: Urban Institute Press.

Romanelli, L.H., Hoagwood, K.E., Kaplan, S.J., Kemp, S.P., Hartman, R.L., Trupin, C., Soto, W., Pecora, P.J., LaBarrie, T.L., Jensen, P.S., and the Child Welfare-Mental Health Best Practices Group. (2009). Best practices for mental health in child welfare: Parent support and youth empowerment guidelines. *Child Welfare, 88*, 189-218.

Rosenbaum, P.R., and Rubin, D.B. (1983). The central role of the propensity score in observational studies for causal effects. *Biometrika, 70*(1), 41-55.

Rosenbloom, S.R., and Way, N. (2004). Experiences of discrimination among African American, Asian American, and Latino adolescents in an urban high school. *Youth and Society, 35*(4), 420-451.

Rosenfeld, R. (2008). Recidivism and its discontents. *Criminology and Public Policy, 7*(2), 311-318.

Ross, T., and Conger, D. (2009). Bridging child welfare and juvenile justice: Preventing the unnecessary detention of foster children. In T. Ross (Ed.), *Child Welfare: The Challenges of Collaboration* (pp. 173-192). Washington, DC: Urban Institute Press.

Rumberger, R. (1995). Dropping out of middle school: A multilevel analysis of students and schools. *American Educational Research Journal, 32*(3), 583-625.

Rutter, M., and Maughan, B. (2002). School effectiveness findings 1979-2002. *Journal of Social Psychology, 40*(16), 451-475.

Ryan, J.P., and Testa, M.F. (2005). Child maltreatment and juvenile delinquency: Investigating the role of placement and placement instability. *Children and Youth Services Review, 27*(3), 227-249.

Ryan, J., Chiu, Y.-L., and Williams, A. (2011). *Knowledge Brief: Is There a Link Between Child Welfare and Disproportionate Minority Contact in Juvenile Justice?* Models for Change System Reforms for Juvenile Justice. Chicago, IL: John D. and Catherine T. MacArthur Foundation.

Sampson, R.J., and Laub, J.H. (1993). Structural variations in juvenile court processing: Inequality, the underclass and social control. *Law and Society Review, 27*(2), 285-312.

Sampson, R.J., and Laub, J. (2005). A life-course view of the development of crime. *The ANNALS of the American Academy of Political and Social Science, 602*, 12-45.

Sampson, R.J., and Wilson, W.J. (1995). Toward a theory of race, crime, and urban inequality. In J. Hagan and R.D. Peterson (Eds.), *Crime and Inequality* (pp. 37-54). Stanford, CA: Stanford University Press.

Sampson, R.J., Morenoff, J.D., and Raudenbush, S. (2005). Social anatomy of racial and ethnic disparities in violence. *American Journal of Public Health, 95*(2), 224-232.

Sampson, R.J., Sharkey, P., and Raudenbush, S.W. (2008). Durable effects of concentrated disadvantage on verbal ability among African American children. *Proceedings of the National Academy of Sciences of the United States of America, 105*(3), 845-852.

Sanbonmatsu, L., Kling, J.R., Duncan, G.L., and Brooks-Gunn, J. (2007). New kids on the block: Results from the Moving to Opportunity experiment. *Education Next, 7*(Fall), 60-66.

Sanborn, J.B., Jr. (1998). Second-class justice, first-class punishment: The use of juvenile records in sentencing adults. *Judicature, 81*(5), 206-213.

Saulny, S. (2009). 25 Chicago students arrested for a middle school food fight. *New York Times*, November 10. Available: http://www.newyorktimes.com/2009/11/11/us/11foodfight.html [October 2011].

Saunders, D. (2011). *Virginia Juvenile Justice System Referrals: Have the 2002 ABA Recommendations Been Addressed?* Williamsburg, VA: National Center for State Courts. Available: http://www.ncsc.org/~/media/Files/PDF/Education%20and%20Careers/CEDP%20Papers/2011/Juvenile%20Justice%20System%20Referrals.ashx [May 2012].

Schaeffer, C.M., and Borduin, C.M. (2005). Long-term follow-up to a randomized clinical trial of multisystemic therapy with serious and violent juvenile offenders. *Journal of Consulting and Clinical Psychology, 73*(3), 445-453.

Schiraldi, V., Schindler, M., and Goliday, S. (2011). The end of the reform school? In F. Sherman and F. Jacobs (Eds.), *Juvenile Justice: Advancing Research, Policy and Practice* (Ch. 20, pp. 409-432). Hoboken, NJ: John Wiley & Sons.

Schneider, A. (1990). *Deterrence and Juvenile Crime: Results from a National Policy Experiment (Research in Criminology)*. New York: Springer-Verlag.

Schoenwald, S. (2008). Toward evidence-based transport of evidence-based treatments: MST as an example. *Journal of Child and Adolescent Substance Abuse, 17*(3), 69-91.

Schrader, J. (2007). Trying juveniles as adults: What age? *Asheville Citizen Times*, April 15.

Schubert, C., Mulvey, E., Loughran, T., Fagan, J., Chassin, L., Piquero, A., Losoya, S., Steinberg, L., and Cauffman, E. (2010). Predicting outcomes for youth transferred to adult court. *Law and Human Behavior, 34*(6), 460-467.

Schubert, C.A., Mulvey, E.P, Loughran, T., and Losoya, S. (2012). Perceptions of institutional experience and community outcomes for serious adolescent offenders. *Criminal Justice and Behavior, 39*(1), 71-93.

Schwalbe, C.S. (2004). Re-visioning risk assessment for human service decision making. *Children and Youth Services Review, 26*, 561-576.

Schwalbe, C.S. (2008). Strengthening the integration of actuarial risk assessment with clinical judgment in an evidence based framework. *Children and Youth Services Review, 30*(12), 1458-1464.

Schwalbe, C.S., and Maschi, T. (2009). Investigating probation strategies with juvenile offenders: The influence of officers' attitudes and youth characteristics. *Law and Human Behavior, 33*, 357-367.

Schwalbe, C.S., Fraser, M., Day, S., and Cooley, V. (2006). Classifying juvenile offenders according to risk of recidivism: Predictive validity, race/ethnicity, and gender. *Criminal Justice and Behavior, 33*(3), 305-324.

Schwalbe, C.S., Fraser, M., and Day, S. (2007). Predictive validity of the joint risk matrix with juvenile offenders: A focus on gender and race/ethnicity. *Criminal Justice and Behavior, 34*(3), 348-361.

Schwartz, R.G. (2001). *Promoting and Sustaining Detention Reforms. Pathways to Juvenile Detention Reform 11.* Baltimore, MD: Annie E. Casey Foundation.

Scott, E.S. (2000). The legal construction of adolescence. *Hofstra Law Review, 29*, 547-598.

Scott, E.S. (2009). *Taking a Therapeutic Approach to Juvenile Offenders: The "Missouri Model."* Cambridge, MA: Harvard University Press.

Scott, E.S., and Grisso, T. (2005). Developmental incompetence, due process, and juvenile justice policy. *North Carolina Law Review, 83*(4), 793-846.

Scott, E.S., and Steinberg, L.D. (2003). Blaming youth. *Texas Law Review, 81*(3), 799.

Scott, E.S., and Steinberg, L.D. (2008). Adolescent development and the regulation of youth crime. *The Future of Children/Center for the Future of Children, the David and Lucile Packard Foundation, 18*(2), 15-33.

Scott, E.S., and Steinberg, L.D. (2010, reprint). *Rethinking Juvenile Justice.* Cambridge, MA: Harvard University Press.

Scott, E.S., Reppucci, N.D., and Woolard, J.L. (1995). Evaluating adolescent decision making in legal contexts. *Law and Human Behavior, 19*(3), 221-244.

Scott, E.S., Reppucci, N.D., Antonishak, J., and DeGennaro, J.T. (2006). Public attitudes about the culpability and punishment of young offenders. *Behavioral Sciences & the Law, 24*(6), 815-832.

Sedlak, A.J. (2010). *Introduction to the Survey of Youth in Residential Placement.* Juvenile Justice Bulletin (NCJ 218390). Washington, DC: Office of Justice Programs, Office of Juvenile Justice and Delinquency Prevention, U.S. Department of Justice.

Sedlak, A., and Bruce, C. (2010). *Youth's Characteristics and Backgrounds: Findings from the Survey of Youth in Residential Placement.* Washington, DC: Office of Juvenile Justice and Delinquency Prevention, Office of Justice Programs, U.S. Department of Justice. Available: http://purl.fdlp.gov/GPO/gpo3250 [June 2012].

Sedlak, A.J., and McPherson, K. (2010a). *Survey of Youth in Residential Placement: Youth's Needs and Services.* Rockville, MD: Westat.

Sedlak, A., and McPherson, K.S. (2010b). *Conditions of Confinement: Findings from the Survey of Youth in Residential Placement.* Washington, DC: Office of Juvenile Justice and Delinquency Prevention, Office of Justice Programs, U.S. Department of Justice. Available: https://www.ncjrs.gov/pdffiles1/ojjdp/227729.pdf [May 2012].

Sellers, R.M., and Shelton, J.N. (2003). The role of racial identity in perceived racial discrimination. *Journal of Personality and Social Psychology, 84*(5), 1079-1092.

Sellers, R.M., Copeland-Linder, N., Martin, P.P., and Lewis, R.L. (2006). Racial identity matters: The relationship between racial discrimination and psychological functioning in African American adolescents. *Journal of Research on Adolescence, 16*(2), 187-216.

The Sentencing Project. (2010). *Disproportionate Minority Contact Fact Sheet.* Washington, DC: The Sentencing Project. Available: http://www.sentencingproject.org/doc/publications/jj_DMCfactsheet.pdf [February 2012].

Shadish, W.R., Cook, T.D., and Campbell, D.T. (2001). *Experimental and Quasi-experimental Designs for Generalized Causal Inference.* Boston, MA: Houghton Mifflin.

Shannon, L. (1980). Assessing the relationship of adult criminal careers to juvenile careers. In C. Abt (Ed.), *Problems in American Social Policy.* Cambridge, MA: Abt Books.

Shannon, L. (1985). *A More Precise Evaluation of the Effects of Sanctions.* Iowa City, IA: University of Iowa, Iowa Urban Community Research Center.

Sharkey, P., and Sampson, R.J. (2010). Destination effects: Residential mobility and trajectories of adolescent violence in a stratified metropolis. *Criminology, 48*(3), 639-681.

Shaw, D.S., Keenan, K., and Vondra, J.I. (1994). Developmental precursors of externalizing behavior: Ages 1 to 3. *Developmental Psychology, 30*(3), 355-364.

Shaw, D.S., Winslow, E.B., Owens, E.B., Vondra, J.I., Cohn, J.F., and Bell, R.Q. (1998). The development of early externalizing problems among children from low-income families: A transformational perspective. *Journal of Abnormal Child Psychology, 26*, 95-107.

Shepherd, R.E. (1996). *Juvenile Justice Standards Annotated: A Balanced Approach.* Chicago, IL: Criminal Justice Section, American Bar Association.

Sherman, F.T. (2012). Justice for girls: Are we making progress? *UCLA Law Review, 59*, 1584-1628.

Sherman, L.W. (1993). Defiance deterrence and irrelevance: A theory of the criminal sanction. *Journal of Research in Crime and Delinquency, 30*(4), 445-473.

Sherman, L.W., and Strang, H. (2007). *Restorative Justice: The Evidence.* London, UK: The Smith Institute.

Sherman, L.W., Gottfredson, D., MacKenzie, D., Eck, J., Reuter, P., and Bushway, S. (1997). *Preventing Crime: What Works, What Doesn't, What's Promising.* Washington, DC: Office of Justice Programs, National Institute of Justice, U.S. Department of Justice.

Short, J.F., and Nye, F.I. (1958). Extent of unrecorded juvenile delinquency, tentative conclusions. *Journal of Criminal Law, Criminology, and Police Science, 49*(4), 296-302.

Shufelt, J., and Cocozza, J. (2006). *Youth with Mental Health Disorders in the Juvenile Justice System: Results from a Multi-state Prevalence Study.* Delmar, NY: National Center for Mental Health and Juvenile Justice.

Shufelt, J.L., Cocozza, J.J., and Skowyra, K.R. (2010). *Successfully Collaborating with the Juvenile Justice System: Benefits, Challenges, and Key Strategies.* Washington, DC: Technical Assistance Partnership for Child and Family Mental Health. Available: http://www.tapartnership.org/docs/jjResource_collaboration.pdf [March 2012].

Sickmund, M., Sladky, A., and Kang, W. (2011). *Easy Access to Juvenile Court Statistics: 1985-2008.* Available: http://www.ojjdp.gov/ojstatbb/ezajcs/ [March 2012].

Siegel, G., and Lord, R. (2004). *When Systems Collide: Improving Court Practices and Programs in Dual Jurisdiction Cases.* Pittsburgh, PA: National Center for Juvenile Justice.

Simmons, R.G., and Blyth, D.A. (1987). *Moving into Adolescence: The Impact of Pubertal Change and School Context.* Hawthorne, NY: Aldine de Gruyter.

Simons, R.L., Murry, V., McLoyd, V., Lin, K.-H., Cutrona, C., and Conger, R.D. (2002). Discrimination, crime, ethnic identity, and parenting as correlates of depressive symptoms among African American children: A multilevel analysis. *Development and Psychopathology, 14*(2), 371-393.

Simons, R.L., Chen, Y.-F., Stewart, E., and Brody, G. (2003). Incidents of discrimination and risk for delinquency: A longitudinal test of strain theory with an African American sample. *Justice Quarterly, 20*(4), 827-854.

Simons, R.L., Simons, L.G., Burt, C.H., Drummund, H., Stewart, E., Brody, G.H., Gibbons, F.X., and Cutrona, C. (2006). Supportive parenting moderates the effect of discrimination upon anger, hostile view of relationships, and violence among African American boys. *Journal of Health and Social Behavior, 47*(4), 373-389.

Simons-Morton, B., Singer, J., and Lerner, N. (2005). The observed effects of teenage passengers on the risky driving behavior of teenage drivers. *Accident Analysis and Prevention, 37*(6), 973-982.

Singer, L.R. (1980). *Standards Relating to Dispositions. Juvenile Justice Standards Project of the Institute of Judicial Administration and the American Bar Association.* Available: http://www.americanbar.org/groups/criminal_justice/pages/JuvenileJusticeStandards.html [September 2012].

Singer, S.I. (1996). *Recriminalizing Delinquency: Violent Juvenile Crime and Juvenile Justice Reform.* New York: Cambridge University Press.

Sipe, C.L. (1996). *Mentoring: A Synthesis of Public/Private Venture's Research: 1988-1995.* Philadelphia, PA: Public/Private Ventures.

Sisk, C.L., and Zehr, J.L. (2005). Pubertal hormones organize the adolescent brain and behavior. *Frontiers in Neuroendocrinology, 26*(3-4), 163-174.

Skeem, J., Manchak, S., and Peterson, J. (2011). Correctional policy for offenders with mental illness: Creating a new paradigm for recidivism reduction. *Law and Human Behavior, 35*(2), 110-126.

Skiba, R.J., Michael, R.S., Nardo, A.C., and Peterson, R.L. (2002). The color of discipline: Sources of racial and gender disproportionality in school punishment. *Urban Review, 34*(4), 317-342.

Skiba, R.J., Horner, R.H., Chung, C.-G., Rausch, M.K., May, S.L., and Tobin, T. (2011). Race is not neutral: A national investigation of African American and Latino disproportionality in school discipline. *School Psychology Review, 40*(1), 85-107.

Skonovd, N. (2003). California youth authority. In M.D. McShane and F.P. Williams (Eds.), *Encyclopedia of Juvenile Justice* (pp. 40-42). Thousand Oaks, CA: Sage.

Small, S., Reynolds, A., O'Connor, C., and Cooney, S. (2005). *What Science Tells Us about Cost-Effective Programs for Juvenile Delinquency Prevention.* Madison: University of Wisconsin–Madison.

Smetana, J.G., and Villalobos, M. (2009). Social-cognitive development during adolescence. In R.L. Lerner and L. Steinberg (Eds.), *Handbook of Adolescent Psychology* (3rd ed., vol. 1, pp. 187-208). New York: John Wiley & Sons.

Smith, C., and Thornberry, T.P. (1995). The relationship between childhood maltreatment and adolescent involvement in delinquency. *Criminology, 33*(4), 451-481.

Smith, D.A. (1986). The neighborhood context of police behavior. *Crime and Justice, 8*, 313-341.

Smith, K.S., and Blackburn, A.G. (2011). Is teen court the best fit? Assessing the predictive validity of the Teen Court Peer Influence Scale. *Journal of Criminal Justice, 39*, 198-204.

Smith, M., and Alpert, G. (2002). Searching for direction: Courts, social science, and the adjudication of racial profiling claims. *Justice Quarterly, 19*(4), 673-703.

Smith, P., Gendreau, P., and Swartz, K. (2009). Validating the principles of effective intervention: A systematic review of the contributions of meta-analysis in the field of corrections. *Victims and Offenders, 4*, 148-169.

Smith, S.S. (2010). Race and trust. *Annual Review of Sociology, 36*, 453-475.

Snyder, H.N. (1998). Appendix: Serious, violent, and chronic juvenile offenders: An assessment of the extent of and trends in officially recognized serious criminal behavior in a delinquent population. In R. Loeber and D.P. Farrington (Eds.), *Serious and Violent Juvenile Offenders: Risk Factors and Successful Interventions* (pp. 428-444). Thousand Oaks, CA: Sage.

Snyder, H.N., and Mulako-Wangota, J. (2011). *Arrest Data Analysis Tool.* Washington, DC: Bureau of Justice Statistics. Available: http://www.bjs.gov/index.cfm?ty=datool&surl=/arrests/index.cfm [June 2012].

Snyder, H.N., and Sickmund, M. (1999). *Juvenile Offenders and Victims: 1999 National Report.* Washington, DC: Office of Juvenile Justice and Delinquency Prevention, Office of Justice Programs, U.S. Department of Justice.

Snyder, H.N., and Sickmund, M. (2006). *Juvenile Offenders and Victims: 2006 National Report.* Washington, DC: Office of Juvenile Justice and Delinquency Prevention, Office of Justice Programs, U.S. Department of Justice.

Snyder, H.N., Sickmund, M., and Poe-Yamagata, E. (2000). *Juvenile Transfers to Criminal Court in the 1990s: Lessons Learned from Four Studies.* Washington, DC: Office of Justice Programs, Office of Juvenile Justice and Delinquency Prevention, U.S. Department of Justice.

Snyder, J., Horsch, E., and Childs, J. (1997). Peer relationships of young children: Affiliative choices and the shaping of aggressive behavior. *Journal of Clinical Child Psychology,* 26(2), 145-156.

Soler, M. (2010). Missed opportunity: Waiver, race, data, and policy reform. *Louisiana Law Review, 71*(1), 17-34.

Soler, M., Shoenberg, D., and Schindler, M. (2009). Juvenile justice lessons for a new era. *Georgetown Journal on Poverty Law & Policy,* XVI, 538-541, Symposium Issue.

Soler, M.I., and Garry, L.M. (2009). *Reducing Disproportionate Minority Contact Preparation at the Local Level.* Washington, DC: Office of Juvenile Justice and Delinquency Prevention, Office of Justice Programs, U.S. Department of Justice. Available: http://purl.access.gpo.gov/GPO/LPS123421 [June 2012].

Somerville, L.H., Fani, N., and McClure-Tone, E.B. (2011a). Behavioral and neural representation of emotional facial expressions across the lifespan. *Developmental Neuropsychology, 36*(4), 408-428.

Somerville, L.H., Hare, T., and Casey, B.J. (2011b). Frontostriatal maturation predicts cognitive control failure to appetitive cues in adolescents. *Journal of Cognitive Neuroscience, 23,* 2123-2134.

Sorensen, J., Hope, R., and Stemen, R. (2003). Racial disproportionality in state prison admissions: Can regional variation be explained by differential arrest rates? *Journal of Criminal Justice, 31*(1), 73-84.

Sowell, E.R., Thompson, P.M., Holmes, C.J., Jernigan, T.L., and Toga, A.W. (1999). In vivo evidence for post-adolescent brain maturation in frontal and striatal regions. *Nature Neuroscience, 2*(10), 859-861.

Sowell, E.R., Peterson, B.S., Thompson, P.M., Welcome, S.E., Henkenius, A.L., and Toga, A.W. (2003). Mapping cortical change across the human life span. *Nature Neuroscience,* 6(3), 309-315.

Sowell, E.R., Thompson, P.M., and Toga, A.W. (2004). Mapping changes in the human cortex throughout the span of life. *The Neuroscientist, 10*(4), 372-392.

The Spangenberg Group. (2001). *Keeping Defender Workloads Manageable.* Prepared for the Office of Justice Programs, Bureau of Justice Assistance, U.S. Department of Justice. Available: https://www.ncjrs.gov/pdffiles1/bja/185632.pdf [August 2012].

Spear, L.P. (2010). *The Behavioral Neuroscience of Adolescence.* New York: W.W. Norton.

Spear, L.P., and Varlinskaya, E.I. (2010). Sensitivity to ethanol and other hedonic stimuli in an animal model of adolescence: Implications for prevention science? *Developmental Psychobiology, 52*(3), 236-243.

Sprott, J.B. (1998). Understanding public opposition to a separate youth justice system. *Crime and Delinquency, 44*(3), 399-411.

Sprott, J.B., and Greene, C. (2008). Trust and confidence in the courts: Does the quality of treatment young offenders receive affect their views of the courts? *Crime and Delinquency, 56*(2), 269-289.

St. Pierre, T.L., Mark, M.M., Kaltreider, D.L., and Campbell, B. (2001). Boys & girls clubs and school collaborations: A longitudinal study of a multicomponent substance abuse prevention program for high-risk elementary school children. *Journal of Community Psychology, 29*(2), 87-106.

Stahl, A., Sickmund, M., and Snyder, H.N. (2004). *Statistics on Violent Girls in the Juvenile Justice System: Facts, Myths, and Implications.* Paper presented at the annual meeting of the American Society of Criminology, Nashville, TN.

Stapleton, W.V. (1993). *Changing Patterns in the Administration of Modern Juvenile Justice.* Chico: California State University-Chico.

Stapleton, W.V., and Teitelbaum, L.E. (1972). *In Defense of Youth: A Study of the Role of Counsel in American Juvenile Courts.* New York: Russell Sage Foundation.

State of California Department of the Youth Authority. (n.d.). *A Comparison of the Youth Authority's Institution and Parole Populations: June 30 Each Year, 1993-2002.* Available: http://1.usa.gov/prwraw [June 2012].

Steffensmeier, D., Schwartz, J., Zhong, H.U.A., and Ackerman, J. (2005). An assessment of recent trends in girls' violence using diverse longitudinal sources: Is the gender gap closing? *Criminology, 43*(2), 355-406.

Steinberg, L. (2001). We know some things: Parent-adolescent relationships in retrospect and prospect. *Journal of Research on Adolescence, 11*(1), 1-19.

Steinberg, L. (2008). A social neuroscience perspective on adolescent risk-taking. *Developmental Review, 28*(1), 78-106.

Steinberg, L. (2009). Should the science of adolescent brain development inform public policy? *American Psychologist, 64*(8), 739-750.

Steinberg, L. (2010). A dual systems model of adolescent risk-taking. *Developmental Psychobiology, 52*(3), 216-224.

Steinberg, L., and Cauffman, E. (1996). Maturity of judgment in adolescence: Psychosocial factors in adolescent decision making. *Law and Human Behavior, 20*(3), 249-272.

Steinberg, L., and Monahan, K.C. (2007). Age differences in resistance to peer influence. *Developmental Psychology, 43*(6), 1531-1543.

Steinberg, L., and Scott, E.S. (2003). Less guilty by reason of adolescence: Developmental immaturity, diminished responsibility, and the juvenile death penalty. *American Psychologist, 58*(12), 1009-1018.

Steinberg, L., Chung, H.L., and Little, M. (2004). Reentry of young offenders from the justice system: A developmental perspective. *Youth Violence and Juvenile Justice, 2*(1), 21-38.

Steinberg, L., Albert, D., Cauffman, E., Banich, M., Graham, S., and Woolard, J.L. (2008). Age differences in sensation seeking and impulsivity as indexed by behavior and self-report. Evidence for the dual-systems model. *Developmental Psychology, 44*, 17764-17789.

Steinberg, L., Cauffman, E., Woolard, J., Graham, S., and Banich, M. (2009a). Are adolescents less mature than adults? Minors' access to abortion, the juvenile death penalty, and the alleged APA "flip-flop." *American Psychologist, 64*(7), 583-594.

Steinberg, L., Graham, S., O'Brien, L., Woolard, J., Cauffman, E., and Banich, M. (2009b). Age differences in future orientation and delay discounting. *Child Development, 80*, 28-44.

Stewart, A., Livingston, M., and Dennison, S. (2008). Transitions and turning points: Examining the links between child maltreatment and juvenile offending. *Child Abuse and Neglect, 32*(1), 51-66.

Stewart, E.A., and Simons, R.L. (2010). Race, code of the street, and violent delinquency: A multilevel investigation of neighborhood street culture and individual norms of violence. *Criminology, 48*(2), 569-605.

Stewart, E.A., Baumer, E.P., Brunson, R.K., and Simons, R. (2009). Neighborhood racial context and perceptions of police-based racial discrimination among black youth. *Criminology, 47*(3), 847-887.

Strang, H., Sherman, L., Angel, C.M., Woods, D.J., Bennett, S., Newbury-Birch, D., and Inkpen, N. (2006). Victim evaluations of face-to-face restorative justice conferences: A quasi-experimental analysis. *Journal of Social Issues, 62*, 281-306.

Substance Abuse and Mental Health Services Administration. (2011). *Results from the 2010 National Survey on Drug Use and Health. Summary of National Findings.* Rockville, MD: Substance Abuse and Mental Health Services Administration, U.S. Department of Health and Human Services.

Swanson, J., Burris, S., Moss, K., Ullman, M., and Ranney, L. (2006). Justice disparities: Does the ADA enforcement system treat people with psychiatric disabilities fairly? *Maryland Law Review, 66,* 94-139.

Swanston, H.Y., Plunkett, A.M., O'Toole, B.I., Shrimpton, S., Parkinson, P.N., and Oates, R.K. (2003). Nine years after child sexual abuse. *Child Abuse & Neglect, 27*(8), 967-984.

Switzer, G.E., Simmons, R.G., Dew, M.A., Regalski, J.M., and Wang, C.-H. (1995). The effect of a school-based helper program on adolescent self-image, attitudes, and behavior. *Journal of Early Adolescence, 15*(4), 429-455.

Szymanski, L.A. (2008). *Juvenile Delinquents Right to a Jury Trial.* Pittsburgh, PA: National Center for Juvenile Justice.

Tanenhaus, D.S. (2004). *Juvenile Justice in the Making.* New York: Oxford University Press.

Tanenhaus, D.S. (2012). The elusive juvenile court, its origins, practices, and reinventions. In B.C. Feld and D.M. Bishop (Eds.), *The Oxford Handbook of Juvenile Crime and Juvenile Justice* (pp. 420-441). New York: Oxford University Press.

Task Force on Community Preventive Services. (2007). Recommendation against policies facilitating the transfer of juveniles from juvenile to adult justice systems for the purpose of reducing violence. *American Journal of Preventive Medicine, 32*(4), 5-6.

Task Force on Transforming Juvenile Justice. (2009). *Charting A New Course: A Blueprint for Transforming Juvenile Justice in New York State.* Available: http://www.vera.org/download?file=2944/Charting-a-new-course-A-blueprint-for-transforming-juvenile-justice-in-New-York-State.pdf [September 2010].

Teplin, L.A., Abram, K.M., McClelland, G.M., Dulcan, M.K., and Mericle, A.A. (2002). Psychiatric disorders in youth in juvenile detention. *Archives of General Psychiatry, 59*(12), 1133-1143.

Texas Appleseed. (2010). *Texas' School-to-Prison Pipeline. Ticketing, Arrest and Use of Force in Schools: How the Myth of the "Blackboard Jungle" Reshaped School Disciplinary Processes.* Available: http://www.texasappleseed.net/images/stories/reports/Ticketing_Booklet_web.pdf [June 2012].

Theriot, M.T. (2009). School resource officers and the criminalization of student behavior. *Journal of Criminal Justice, 37*(3), 280-287.

Thomason, M.E., Henry, M.L., Hamilton, J.P., Joormann, J., Pine, D.S., Ernst, M., Goldman, D., Mogg, K., Bradley, B.P., Britton, J.C., Lindstrom, K.M., Monk, C.S., Sankin, L.S., Louro, H.M.C., and Gotlib, I.H. (2010). Neural and behavioral responses to threatening emotion faces in children as a function of the short allele of the serotonin transporter gene. *Biological Psychology, 85*(1), 38-44.

Thompson, R.A., and Nelson, C.A. (2001). Developmental science and the media. Early brain development. *American Psychologist, 56*(1), 5-15.

Thornberry, T.P. (2010, June). *A Strategy for Developing Evidence-based Gang Intervention Programs.* Paper presented at the Eurogang Conference, Neustadt an der Weinstrasse, Germany.

Thornberry, T.P., and Krohn, M.D. (2000). The self-report method for measuring delinquency and crime. In D. Duffee (Ed.), *Measurement and Analysis of Crime and Justice* (vol. 4). Washington, DC: Office of Justice Programs, National Institute of Justice, U.S. Department of Justice.

Thornberry, T.P., Krohn, M.D., Lizotte, A.J., Smith, C.A., and Tobin, K. (2003). *Gangs and Delinquency in Developmental Perspective.* Cambridge, UK: Cambridge University Press.

Thornberry, T.P., Huizinga, D., and Loeber, R. (2004). Causes and correlates studies: Findings and policy implications. *Juvenile Justice, 9*(1), 3-19.

Thornberry, T.P., Henry, K.L., Ireland, T.O., and Smith, C.A. (2010). The causal impact of childhood-limited maltreatment and adolescent maltreatment on early adult adjustment. *Journal of Adolescent Health, 46*(4), 359-365.

Thornberry, T.P., Giordano, P.C., Uggen, C., Matsuda, M., Masten, A.S., Bulten, E., and Donker, A.G. (2012). Explanations for offending. In R. Loeber and D.P. Farrington (Eds.), *From Juvenile Delinquency to Adult Crime: Criminal Careers, Justice Policy and Prevention* (pp. 47-85). New York: Oxford University Press.

Tierney, J.P., Grossman, J.B., and Resch, N.L. (1995). *Making a Difference: An Impact Study of Big Brothers/Big Sisters*. Philadelphia, PA: Public/Private Ventures.

Tiffan, S. (1982). *In Whose Best Interest? Child Welfare Reform in the Progressive Era.* Westport, CT: Greenwood Press.

Tonry, M.H. (1995). *Malign Neglect: Race, Crime, and Punishment in America.* New York: Oxford University Press.

Torbet, P.M. (1996). *Juvenile Probation: The Workhorse of the Juvenile Justice System.* Washington, DC: Office of Juvenile Justice and Delinquency Prevention. Available: https://www.ncjrs.gov/pdffiles/workhors.pdf [August 2012].

Torbet, P., Gable, R., Hurst IV, H., Montgomery, I., Szymanski, L., and Thomas, D. (1996). *State Responses to Serious and Violent Juvenile Crime.* Washington, DC: Office of Juvenile Justice and Delinquency Prevention, Office of Justice Programs, U.S. Department of Justice.

Tottenham, N., Hare, T.A., and Casey, B.J. (2011). Behavioral assessment of emotion discrimination, emotion regulation, and cognitive control in childhood, adolescence, and adulthood. *Frontiers in Psychology, 2*, 39.

Trulson, C.R., Marquart, J.W., Mullings, J.L., and Caeti, T.J. (2007). In between adolescence and adulthood: Recidivism outcomes for a cohort of state delinquents. *Youth Violence and Juvenile Justice, 3*, 355-377.

Trupin, E.W., Turner, A.P., Stewart, D., and Wood, P. (2004). Transition planning and recidivism among mentally ill juvenile offenders. *Behavioral Sciences & the Law, 22*(4), 599-610.

Tyler, T. (1990). *Why People Obey the Law.* New Haven, CT: Yale University Press.

Tyler, T. (2001). Trust and law and law abidingness: A model of social regulation. *Boston University Law Review, 81*(2), 361.

Tyler, T.R. (2006). Psychological perspectives on legitimacy and legitimation. *Annual Review of Psychology, 57*, 375-400.

Tyler, T.R., and Fagan, J. (2008). Legitimacy, compliance and cooperation: Procedural justice and citizen ties to the law. *Ohio State Journal of Criminal Law, 6*, 231-275.

Tyler, T.R., and Huo, Y.J. (2002). *Trust in the Law: Encouraging Public Cooperation with the Police and Courts.* New York: Russell Sage Foundation.

Uddin, L.Q., Menon, V., and Supekar, K. (2010). Typical and atypical development of functional human brain networks: Insights from resting-state fMRI. *Frontiers in Systems Neuroscience, 4.*

Umbreit, M.S., Vos, B., Coates, R.B., and Lightfoot, E. (2011). Restorative justice in the twenty-first century: A social movement full of opportunities and pitfalls. *Marquette Law Review, 89*, 251-304.

University of Massachusetts Donahue Institute. (2008). *Evaluation of the Department of Youth Services Education Initiative.* Hadley: University of Massachusetts.

U.S. Census Bureau. (2010a). *PINC-04. Educational Attainment—People 18 Years Old and Over, by Total Money Earnings in 2009, Work Experience in 2009, Age, Race, Hispanic Origin, and Sex* (Female). Available: http://www.census.gov/hhes/www/cpstables/032010/perinc/new04_019.htm [August 2011].

U.S. Census Bureau. (2010b). *PINC-04. Educational Attainment—People 18 Years Old and Over, by Total Money Earnings in 2009, Work Experience in 2009 Age, Race, Hispanic Origin, and Sex* (Male). Available: http://www.census.gov/hhes/www/cpstables/032010/perinc/new04_010.htm [August 2011].

U.S. Department of Education. (2012). *Revealing New Truths About Our Nation's Schools. The Office for Civil Rights, The Transformed Civil Rights Data Collection (CRDC).* Washington, DC: Office of Civil Rights, U.S. Department of Education. Available: http://www2.ed.gov/about/offices/list/ocr/docs/crdc-2012-data-summary.pdf [August 2012].

U.S. Department of Justice. (2011, July 21). *Attorney General Holder, Secretary Duncan Announce Effort to Respond to School-to-Prison Pipeline by Supporting Good Discipline Practices.* Available: http://www.justice.gov/opa/pr/2011/July/11-ag-951.html [September 2012].

U.S. Department of Justice. (2012, January 26). *Department of Justice, MacArthur Foundation Provide $2 Million to Support Juvenile Justice Reform.* Available: http://www.ojp.gov/newsroom/pressreleases/2012/ojppr012612.pdf [February 2013].

U.S. General Accounting Office. (1999). *Youth Mentoring Programs: Fiscal Year 1998.* GAO/HEHS-99-129R. Washington, DC: U.S. General Accounting Office.

U.S. Government Accountability Office. (2009, September 22). *A Time Frame for Enhancing Grant Monitoring Documentation and Verification of Data Quality Would Help Improve Accountability and Resource Allocation Decisions.* GAO-09-850R. Washington, DC: U.S. Government Accountability Office. Available: http://gao.gov/assets/100/96377.pdf [June 2012].

van den Bos, W., van Dijk, E., Westenberg, M., Rombouts, S.A.R.B., and Crone, E.A. (2011). Changing brains, changing perspectives: The neurocognitive development of reciprocity. *Psychological Science, 22*(1), 60-70.

van der Geest, V., Blokland, A., and Bijleveld, C. (2009). Delinquent development in a sample of high-risk youth. *Journal of Research in Crime and Delinquency, 46*(2), 111-143.

Van Leijenhorst, L., Zanolie, K., Van Meel, C.S., Westenberg, P.M., Rombouts, S.A.R.B., and Crone, E.A. (2010). What motivates the adolescent? Brain regions mediating reward sensitivity across adolescence. *Cerebral Cortex, 20*(1), 61-69.

Van Waters, M. (1925). *Youth in Conflict.* New York: Republic.

Vanneman, A., Hamilton, L., Baldwin-Anderson, J., and Rahman, T. (2009). *Achievement Gaps: How Black and White Students in Public Schools Perform in Mathematics and Reading on the National Assessment of Educational Progress.* (NCES 2009-455). Washington, DC: National Center for Education Statistics, Institute of Education Sciences, U.S. Department of Education. Available: http://nces.ed.gov/nationsreportcard/pdf/studies/2009455.pdf [September 2012].

Vega, W.A., Zimmerman, R.S., Khoury, E.L., Gil, A.G., and Warheit, G.J. (1995). Cultural-conflicts and problem behaviors of Latino adolescents in-home and school environments. *Journal of Community Psychology, 23*(2), 167-179.

Verdugo, R.R. (2002). Race-ethnicity, social class, and zero-tolerance policies: The cultural and structural wars. *Education and Urban Society, 35*(1), 50-75.

Vieraitis, L.M., Kovandzic, T.V., and Marvell, T.B. (2007). The criminogenic effects of imprisonment: Evidence from state panel data, 1974-2002. *Criminology and Public Policy, 6*(3), 589-622.

Vincent, G. (2011). *Risk/Needs Assessment for Recidivism: Implementation and Effectiveness Study.* Available: http://www.modelsforchange.net/about/research/vincent.html [June 2012].

Vincent, G., Grisso, T., Terry, A., and Banks, S. (2008). Sex and race differences in mental health symptoms in juvenile justice: The MAYSI-2 national meta-analysis. *Journal of the American Academy of Child and Adolescent Psychiatry, 47*(3), 282-290.

Vincent, G., Chapman, J., and Cook, N. (2011). Risk-needs assessment in juvenile justice: Predictive validity of the SAVRY, racial differences, and the contribution of needs factors. *Criminal Justice and Behavior, 38*(1), 42-62.

Vorrath, H.H., and Brendtro, L.K. (1985). *Positive Peer Culture* (3rd ed.). New York: Aldine.

Vygotsky, L. (1978). Interaction between learning and development. In L. Vygotsky and M. Cole (Eds.), *Mind and Society: The Development of Higher Psychological Processes* (pp. 79-91). Cambridge, MA: Harvard University Press.

Wagman, M.T. (2000). Innocence lost in the wake of green: The trend is clear: If you are old enough to do the crime, then you are old enough to do the time. *Catholic University Law Review, 49*(2), 643-677.

Wald, J., and Losen, D.J. (2003). Defining and redirecting a school-to-prison pipeline. *New Directions for Youth Development,* (99), 9-15.

Wald, J., and Thurau, L. (2010). Taking safety too far? *Education Week, 29*(22), 24-25.

Walker, S., Spohn, C., and DeLone, M. (2000). *The Color of Justice: Race, Ethnicity, and Crime in America* (2nd ed.). Belmont, CA: Wadsworth Thomson Learning.

Walkover, A. (1984). The infancy defense in the new juvenile court. *UCLA Law Review, 31*(3), 503-562.

Wallis, C. (2004). What makes teens tick? *Time Magazine*, p. 56, May 10.

Walters, G.D. (2011). Taking the next step: Combining incrementally valid indicators to improve recidivism prediction. *Assessment, 18*(2), 227-233.

Warren, P., Tomaskovic-Devey, D., Smith, W.R., Zingraff, M., and Mason, M. (2006). Driving while black: Bias processes and racial disparity in police stops. *Criminology, 44*(3), 709-738.

The Washington Post. (2011). Federal office of juvenile justice needs a leader—and fast. *The Washington Post*, July 22. Available: http://www.washingtonpost.com/opinions/federal-office-of-juvenile-justice-needs-a-leader-and-fast/2011/07/14/gIQAX0kHUI_story.html [February 2011].

Washington State Institute for Public Policy. (2011). *Return on Investment: Evidence-Based Options to Improve Statewide Outcomes.* Olympia: Washington State Institute for Public Policy. Available: http://www.wsipp.wa.gov/rptfiles/11-07-1201.pdf [June 2012].

Wasserman, G.A., McReynolds, L.S., Schwalbe, C.S., Keating, J.M., and Jones, S.A. (2010). Psychiatric disorder, comorbidity, and suicidal behavior in juvenile justice youth. *Criminal Justice and Behavior, 37*(12), 1361-1376.

Watkins, J.C. (1998). *The Juvenile Justice Century: A Sociolegal Commentary on American Juvenile Courts.* Durham, NC: Carolina Academic Press.

Watson, M., Solomon, D., Battistich, V., Schaps, E., and Solomon, J. (1989). The child development project: Combining traditional and developmental approaches to values education. In L.P. Nucci (Ed.), *Moral Development and Character Education: A Dialogue.* Berkeley, CA: McCutchan.

Waxman, H.A., and Collins, S. (2004). *Incarceration of Youth Who Are Waiting for Community Mental Health Services in the United States.* Washington, DC: U.S. House of Representatives, Committee on Government Reform.

Waylen, A., and Wolke, D. (2004). Sex 'n' drugs 'n' rock 'n' roll: The meaning and social consequences of pubertal timing. *European Journal of Endocrinology, 151*, 151-159.

Webster, R.A., Hunter, M., and Keats, J.A. (1994). Peer and parental influences on adolescents substance use: A path-analysis. *International Journal of the Addictions, 29*(5), 647-657.

Weick, K.E. (2001). *Making Sense of the Organization.* Malden, MA: Blackwell.

Weiss, B., Caron, A., Ball, S., Tapp, J., Johnson, M., and Weisz, J.R. (2005). Iatrogenic effects of group treatment for antisocial youth. *Journal of Consulting and Clinical Psychology, 73*(6), 1036-1044.

Weitzer, R., and Brunson, R.K. (2009). Strategic responses to the police among inner city youth. *The Sociological Quarterly, 50,* 235-256.

Weitzer, R., and Tuch, S. (2002). Perceptions of racial profiling: Race, class, and personal experience. *Criminology, 40,* 435-446.

Weitzer, R., and Tuch, S. (2006). *Race and Policing in America: Conflict and Reform.* New York: Cambridge University Press.

Welsh, B.C., Sullivan, C.J., and Olds, D. (2010). When early crime prevention goes to scale: A new look at the evidence. *Prevention Science, 11*(2), 115-125.

Welsh, W.N., Jenkins, P.H., and Harris, P.W. (1999). Reducing minority overrepresentation in juvenile justice: Results of community-based delinquency prevention in Harrisburg. *Journal of Research in Crime and Delinquency, 36*(1), 87-110.

Wentzel, K.R. (1998). Social support and adjustment in middle school: The role of parents, teachers, and peers. *Journal of Educational Psychology, 90*(2), 202-209.

Wentzel, K.R. (2002). Are effective teachers like good parents? Teaching styles and student adjustment in early adolescence. *Child Development, 73*(1), 287-301.

Wexler, D.B. (2000). Just some juvenile thinking about delinquent behavior: A therapeutic jurisprudence approach to relapse prevention planning and youth advisory juries. *University of Missouri at Kansas City Law Review, 69,* 96-105.

Whitbeck, L.B., Hoyt, D.R., McMorris, B.J., Chen, X.J., and Stubben, J.D. (2001). Perceived discrimination and early substance abuse among American Indian children. *Journal of Health and Social Behavior, 42*(4), 405-424.

White House Task Force for Disadvantaged Youth. (2003, October). *White House Task Force for Disadvantaged Youth Final Report.* Available: http://www.acf.hhs.gov/programs/fysb/content/docs/white_house_task_force.pdf [May 2012].

Widom, C.S., and Maxfield, M.G. (2001, February). An update on the "cycle of violence." *National Institute of Justice Research in Brief.* Available: https://www.ncjrs.gov/pdffiles1/nij/184894.pdf [June 2012].

Wiebush, R. (2002). *Graduated Sanctions for Juvenile Offenders: A Program Model and Planning Guide.* Reno, NV: Juvenile Sanctions Center, National Council of Juvenile and Family Court Judges.

Wiebush, R.G., Baird, C., Krisberg, B., and Onek, D. (1995). Risk assessment and classification for serious, violent, and chronic juvenile offenders. In J.C. Howell, B. Krisberg, J.D. Hawkins, and J.J. Wilson (Eds.), *Serious, Violent and Chronic Juvenile Offenders: A Sourcebook* (pp. 171-212). Thousand Oaks, CA: Sage.

Wiig, J.K., and Tuell, J.A. (2008, revised). *Guidebook for Juvenile Justice and Child Welfare System Coordination and Integration: Framework for Improved Outcomes.* Washington, DC: Child Welfare League of America.

Wiig, J.K., and Tuell, J.A. (2011). Celebrating 10 years of juvenile justice child welfare systems integration work. *The Connector, 1*(1). Available: http://www.rfkchildren.org/images/stories/the%20connector%20winter%202011.pdf [June 2012].

Wiig, J., Widom, C.S., and Tuell, J.A. (2003). *Understanding Child Maltreatment and Juvenile Delinquency: From Research to Effective Program, Practice, and Systemic Solutions.* Washington, DC: Child Welfare League of America.

Wiig, J.K., Cocozza, J.J., Morris, J.A., Shufelt, J.L., and Skowyra, K.R. (2010). *Sustaining Change: A Models for Change Guidebook*. Available: http://modelsforchange.net/publications/289 [June 2012].

Wilson, J.J., and Howell, J.C. (1993). *A Comprehensive Strategy for Serious, Violent and Juvenile Offenders*. Washington, DC: Office of Juvenile Justice and Delinquency Prevention, U.S. Department of Justice.

Wilson, J.Q. (1995). Crime and public policy. In J.Q. Wilson and J. Petersilia (Eds.), *Crime* (pp. 489-507). San Francisco, CA: Institute for Contemporary Studies Press.

Wilson, W.J. (1987). *The Truly Disadvantaged: The Inner City, the Underclass, and Public Policy*. Chicago, IL: University of Chicago Press.

Wilson, W.J. (2009). *More Than Just Race: Being Black and Poor in the Inner City*. New York: W.W. Norton.

Winick, B.J. (1998). Client denial and resistance in the advance directive context: Reflections on how attorneys can identify and deal with a psycholegal soft spot. *Psychology, Public Policy, and Law, 4*, 901-923.

Winick, B.J. (1999). Therapeutic jurisprudence and the civil commitment hearing. *Journal of Contemporary Legal Issues, 10*, 37-60.

Wolfgang, M.E. (1983). Delinquency in two birth cohorts. *American Behavioral Scientist, 27*(1), 75.

Wolfgang, M.E., Figlio, R.M., and Sellin, J.T. (1972). *Delinquency in a Birth Cohort*. Chicago, IL: University of Chicago Press.

Wolfgang, M.E., Thornberry, T.P., and Figlio, R.M. (1987). *From Boy to Man, from Delinquency to Crime*. Chicago, IL: University of Chicago Press.

Wong, C.A., Eccles, J.S., and Sameroff, A. (2003). The influence of ethnic discrimination and ethnic identification on African American adolescents' school and socioemotional adjustment. *Journal of Personality, 71*(6), 1197-1232.

Woolard, J.L., Harvell, S., and Graham, S. (2008). Anticipatory injustice among adolescents: Age and racial/ethnic differences in perceived unfairness of the justice system. *Behavioral Sciences & The Law, 26*(2), 207-226.

Yan, J., and Dannerbeck, A. (2011). Exploring the relationship between gender, mental health needs, and treatment orders in a metropolitan juvenile court. *Journal of Child and Family Studies, 20*(1), 9-22.

Yang, M., Liu, Y., and Coid, J. (2010). *Applying Neural Networks and Other Statistical Models to the Classification of Serious Offenders and the Prediction of Recidivism*. Ministry of Justice Research Series 6/10. Available: http://library.npia.police.uk/docs/moj/neural-networks-research.pdf [June 2012].

Yoshikawa, H. (1994). Prevention as cumulative protection: Effects of early family support and education on chronic delinquency and its risks. *Psychological Bulletin, 115*(1), 28-54.

Zaff, J.F., Moore, K.A., Papillo, A.R., and Williams, S. (2003). Implications of extracurricular activity participation during adolescence on positive outcomes. *Journal of Adolescent Research, 18*(6), 599-630.

Zahn, M.A., Hawkins, S.R., Chiancone, J., and Whitworth, A. (2008). *The Girls Study Group—Charting the Way to Delinquency Prevention for Girls*. Washington, DC: Office of Juvenile Justice and Delinquency Prevention, Office of Justice Programs, U.S. Department of Justice.

Zahn, M.A., Agnew, R., Fishbein, D., Miller, S., Winn, D., Dakoff, G., Kruttschnitt, C., Giordano, P., Gottfredson, D.C., Payne, A.A., Feld, B.C., and Lind, M.C. (2010). *Causes and Correlates of Girls' Delinquency*. Washington, DC: Office of Juvenile Justice and Delinquency Prevention, Office of Justice Programs, U.S. Department of Justice.

Zerbe, R. (2007). The legal foundation of cost-benefit analysis. *Charleston Law Review*, 2(1), 93-184.

Zerbe, R., and Dively, D. (1997). *Benefit Cost Analysis: In Theory and Practice.* New York: Addison-Wesley.

Zimring, F.E. (1978). *Confronting Youth Crime: Report of the Twentieth Century Fund Task Force on Sentencing Policy toward Young Offenders.* New York: Holmes and Meier.

Zimring, F.E. (1998). A youth violence epidemic: Myth or reality? In F.E. Zimring (Ed.), *American Youth Violence* (pp. 31-48). New York: Oxford University Press.

Zimring, F. (2004). *An American Travesty: Legal Responses to Adolescent Sex Offending.* Chicago, IL: University of Chicago Press.

Zimring, F.E., and Hawkins, G. (1973). *Deterrence: The Legal Threat in Crime Control.* Chicago, IL: University of Chicago Press.

Zuckerbrot, R.A., Maxon, L., Pagar, D., Davies, M., Fisher, P.W., and Shaffer, D. (2007). Adolescent depression screening in primary care: Feasibility and acceptability. *Pediatrics, 119*(1), 101-108.

Appendix A

Costs and Benefits of Juvenile Justice Interventions[1]

There is compelling evidence that a variety of intervention programs for juvenile offenders significantly reduce recidivism (Drake, Aos, and Miller, 2009; Lipsey, 2009). Lipsey (2009) reports that the mean effect represented a reduction in the one-year rearrest rate of about 6 percentage points for treated offenders compared with a control group of offenders. The most effective programs reduced rearrest rates by more than 40 percentage points.

If a juvenile offender intervention program is effective, a comprehensive evaluation can then ask: Is the program more valuable than other opportunities that could be pursued with the resources devoted to it? That is, does the value of its effects exceed the cost of producing them? Or, less comprehensively, is it more valuable than other programs that pursue the same objective? The techniques of benefit-cost analysis (BCA) and cost-effectiveness analysis (CEA) can offer partial but informative answers to these questions.

After summarizing the basic tenets of benefit-cost analysis, this section discusses how to apply it to juvenile offender programs. The discussion mainly addresses how to measure the benefits of programs that reduce crime, because doing so is the primary methodological challenge for BCAs of juvenile justice programs. The review of well-done BCAs that follows shows strong evidence that several juvenile justice programs are remarkably good investments: their benefits greatly exceed their costs. Indeed,

---

[1]We acknowledge the valuable assistance of Kyle Frankiewich, M.P.A., a student at the Daniel J. Evans School of Public Affairs, University of Washington, who developed background materials for this section.

some programs deliver $10 or more of benefits for each $1 of cost. These findings are actually conservative; although existing BCAs measure the interventions' costs very well, they omit some important and possibly large categories of benefits. We conclude the section by discussing the limitations of existing BCAs of juvenile justice programs and offering recommendations for improving the state of the art.

OVERVIEW OF BENEFIT-COST ANALYSIS

The fundamental idea of benefit-cost analysis is straightforward. Comprehensively identify and measure the benefits and costs of a program, including those that arise in the longer term, after the participants leave it, as well as those occurring while they participate. If the benefits exceed the costs, then the program improves economic efficiency, in the sense that the value of the output (i.e., the program's impacts) exceeds the cost of producing it. As a result, society is economically better off. If costs exceed benefits, then society would be economically better off not operating the program at all and devoting the scarce resources that would be used to run it to other programs with the same goal that do pass a benefit-cost test, or to other worthwhile purposes.

BCA may be viewed as a way to calculate society's "profit" from investing in an intervention. In a sense, it is the public-sector analog to private-sector decisions about where to invest resources. But it is more complex than private-sector decisions, because it should consider benefits and costs for all members of society, not just those for a single enterprise.

It is important to recognize that programs that lead to large reductions in recidivism or other measures of crime may fail a benefit-cost test. Failure could occur if the costs per offender of operating the program are so large that they exceed its benefits. That is, a program's effectiveness is necessary but not sufficient for its benefits to exceed its costs. By a similar logic, programs with small impacts may pass benefit-cost tests.[2]

Legislators and other public officials must allocate scarce public resources among many competing uses, such as criminal justice, education, health, environmental protection, transportation, and defense. There is competition for resources among programs in the criminal justice sector as well. Choices about how to allocate those resources inherently embody judgments about the relative benefits and costs. BCA seeks to make the basis of such choices explicit so that stakeholders can better weigh the difficult trade-offs.

---

[2]Indeed, a program with zero impact on crime relative to current practice could conceivably pass a benefit-cost test if its costs were less than those of the program it would replace. Drake and colleagues (2009) show that such a result is not just a theoretical possibility.

At the same time, BCA neither can nor should be the sole determinant of programmatic and funding decisions. Aside from the limitations of any specific study, this technique cannot take into account moral, ethical, or political factors that are crucial in determining juvenile justice policy and funding. For example, BCA offers little insight into the value of reducing racial/ethnic disparities in the juvenile justice system (beyond their effect on criminal behavior, if any).

Any BCA must consider several key issues. What counts as a benefit? What counts as a cost? How can one measure their monetary values? If a benefit or cost is not measurable in monetary terms, how can it enter the analysis? How can one extrapolate benefits or costs beyond the follow-up period, after a youth leaves a program, when impact data are gathered? The costs of juvenile justice programs occur mainly at the outset, although the benefits may be realized many years later. How should benefits and costs at different times be valued to reflect the fact that a dollar of benefit received in the far future is worth less than one received in the near future, and that both are worth less than a dollar of cost incurred in the present? How can one assess benefits and costs to juveniles who participate in the program, to victims and nonvictims, and to society? The people who bear the costs of a program may well differ from those who share in the benefits. How can one incorporate these distributional impacts into the analysis? An enormous literature has addressed these issues.[3]

As with other evaluation methods, any specific BCA has limitations. It can be questioned because its results rest on judgments about which impacts to quantify and various other assumptions needed to conduct an analysis. Time and resource constraints prevent investigation of all possible benefits and costs. Some effects may be inherently unquantifiable or impossible to assess in financial terms, yet they may be considered crucial to a program's success or political viability. Nonetheless, when carefully done with attention to the findings' sensitivity to different assumptions, BCA can improve the basis on which juvenile justice policy decisions rest.

Analysts, practitioners, and other stakeholders may be concerned that BCA will lead decision makers to focus narrowly on financial values and downplay or ignore important program impacts that cannot be translated into financial terms. For example, teen courts appear to foster prosocial attitudes and social engagement (Butts and Roman, 2009), but it is not known how to (and one may not care to) assign a financial value to such benefits. A careful analysis will discuss nonmonetary benefits and will emphasize that a complete assessment of programs, in which important social values, such as in juvenile justice, are at stake, must weigh such

---

[3]Excellent texts include Zerbe and Dively (1997) and Boardman and colleagues (2011). Juvenile Justice Evaluation Center (2002) provides a brief overview of the method.

benefits along with the monetary ones. Analyses that fail to do so present an incomplete picture.

Applying benefit-cost methodology to juvenile offender programs is complex,[4] but no more so than in other arenas of social policy in which it has made significant contributions to policy research and analysis. Examples are health and mental health, early childhood education, job training, and welfare-to-work programs. The primary methodological challenges lie in how to measure the benefits of programs that reduce crime.

MEASURING THE BENEFITS OF REDUCING JUVENILE CRIMINALITY

Crime imposes many costs on society, and a successful criminal justice program reduces those costs. Those cost reductions are the program's benefits. One can express the benefits of a program for juvenile offenders as:

Benefits per treated juvenile =

$$\sum_{j=1}^{J} \text{Average number of crimes of type j prevented per treated juvenile} \times \text{Economic value per juvenile crime of type j prevented.}[5]$$

The equation recognizes that juvenile offenders commit different types of crimes (e.g., car theft, shoplifting, vandalism, assault), where j represents the total number of different crimes.

The first term of this equation—the impact on crime—is derived from data gathered as part of a program evaluation. Evaluations may measure program outcomes with self-reports of criminal activity by juvenile offenders or as the number of arrests or convictions using criminal justice system records. The estimate is exogenous to the BCA and serves as its starting point.[6] If self-reports are available and deemed reliable, for each crime j one can readily compute this term as the difference between the average number of crimes committed by untreated and treated juvenile offenders.[7]

BCAs typically use administrative data on arrests or convictions. In

---

[4]Roman and colleagues (2010) provide extensive discussion of the methodological issues that arise when applying BCA to crime control.

[5]Nearly all juvenile programs focus on reducing recidivism among convicted juveniles. The approach is similar for programs that seek to prevent juveniles from initially offending.

[6]A BCA may later vary the estimated treatment impact as part of a sensitivity analysis, but generally it would start with the point estimate.

[7]This assumes the evaluation was sufficiently rigorous to yield an unbiased estimate of this difference. See Chapter 6 for a discussion of issues in the evaluation of juvenile justice programs.

this case, calculating the first term is more complicated because arrests and convictions are both inaccurate measures of the number of crimes actually committed. Arrest data are inaccurate, because not every arrest leads to conviction. Because many costs of the juvenile justice system start only after a conviction, equating convictions to arrests will overestimate the system costs associated with convictions. To adjust for this situation, when arrests are used to project benefits, analysts use scaling factors to estimate the first term (Aos et al., 2001).

Another complication is that a juvenile arrested for, or convicted of, one crime may well have committed multiple crimes before being caught. In that case, assuming that one fewer arrest means one fewer victim would understate the full reduction in crime attributable to a program that reduced arrests. Klietz and colleagues (2010) recognized this problem in a randomized clinical trial of multisystemic therapy that collected arrest data over a 13.7 year follow-up period. They translated arrests into crimes using both a conservative estimate of one victimization per arrest and an expansive one of multiple victimizations per arrest.

Because many juvenile recidivists commit crimes during a period extending into their 20s, the benefits of reduced crime from a successful program are realized over a multiyear period. This means that the first term (and hence the product of the two terms) needs to be calculated for each posttreatment year for which there are suitable crime data.[8] When program follow-up data are limited to a few years, a BCA may draw on other information to project reductions in crime over a longer time period.[9]

Drake and colleagues (2009) observe that programs that are closely controlled by researchers or program developers tend to have better results than those that operate in real-world administrative structures (Lipsey, 2003; Barnoski, 2004; Petrosino and Soydan, 2005). Loss of fidelity may arise if local practitioners modify "brand name" programs, or if the characteristics of the juveniles in a specific program differ from those treated by the program developers. It can also arise because the challenges of training the many staff members needed to broadly implement a program and then monitoring their adherence to program protocols can result in less stringent practice over time. This suggests that a BCA of a model, nonreal-world program would be likely to overestimate its benefits (and perhaps underestimate its costs) if it were widely implemented.

To take this situation into account, Drake and colleagues (2009) reduced the treatment impact by 50 percent for studies they judged not

---

[8]More formally, a fully specified equation would include a double summation over types of crime and years.

[9]It is good practice to assess the sensitivity of the final results to alternative assumptions used to project future crime.

to be real-world trials. Although the choice of 50 percent appears to be arbitrary, the general point has merit. Although evidence is largely lacking on the extent of slippage in impact owing to loss of fidelity, BCAs can test the sensitivity of the findings to different levels of slippage. For example, if a model program's benefits exceed its costs assuming no slippage, but are equal assuming slippage of 10 percent, one may question whether it would pass a benefit-cost test if widely implemented. But if the program continues to pass a benefit-cost test until the assumed slippage rises to 75 percent, one could be highly confident that its benefits would exceed its costs under real-world conditions.

Until there is more empirical evidence on the degree of slippage one can generally expect, analysts and decision makers need to choose a "break-even" percentage they are comfortable with. For example, risk-averse decision makers might adopt a model program only if it passes a benefit-cost test assuming 60 percent slippage, whereas decision makers willing to adopt promising programs before their effectiveness is firmly established might set the break-even point at 20 percent. Further research on this issue is clearly in order (Welsh, Sullivan, and Olds, 2010).

The second term—economic value per type of juvenile crime prevented—is, as suggested above, the savings in costs caused by a crime. Multiplying the two terms yields the expected economic value of the crimes of type j not committed by a treated juvenile compared with an untreated juvenile.

Who Receives the Benefits?

The savings in costs accrue to four groups: victims and their families, nonvictims, society, and offenders and their families. For victims and their families, the primary tangible costs of crime consist of costs not covered by private insurance, including property damage and loss, physical and mental health care costs, and earnings losses (including fringe benefits).[10] They also include the value of lost housework and school attendance and expenses to reduce the chances of future victimization (e.g., home alarms, time spent in neighborhood watch activity). Intangible costs include pain, suffering, greater fear, avoidance activities (e.g., fewer out-of-home nighttime activities), lower quality of life (e.g., caused by a permanently disabling injury), and loss of life.[11]

Specific costs to nonvictims include expenses to reduce the chances of future victimization, their share of insurance premiums used to reimburse

---

[10]The share of insurance premiums used to reimburse victims for part of their losses is another small tangible cost.

[11]See Miller, Cohen, and Wiersema (1996) and Cohen (2005) for comprehensive discussions of victim and society costs.

victims for tangible losses and health care costs, avoidance activities, fear, unhappiness, and grief when friends or relatives become victims, and the general lower quality of life caused by crime.

For society the tangible costs are mainly the resources used to operate the criminal justice system (police, prosecutors, courts, jails and prisons, jurors' time, parole officers, etc.). These costs also include the resources of nonprofit programs as well as public programs outside the criminal justice system used because of juvenile crime. For example, a victim without health insurance may seek health or mental health treatment from a public or nonprofit clinic. The costs of treatment beyond what the victim pays are borne by taxpayers or supporters of the nonprofit clinic. Fire services in response to arson and schools' costs of repairing vandalism are other examples. Fewer juvenile crimes and offenders means fewer resources need be devoted to these government and nonprofit activities.

Crime creates costs for juvenile offenders and their families. Juvenile offenders may obtain less schooling and be more prone to substance abuse, with negative consequences for their long-term employment, earnings, and health. An institutionalized offender loses personal freedom and risks being victimized. Offenders' parents who attend judicial proceedings and participate in treatment programs may bear time and out-of-pocket costs and suffer lost earnings. Their child's delinquency may increase stress and other psychological burdens on family members and damage the family's reputation. Friends or younger siblings of offenders may be encouraged to commit their own delinquent acts and join gangs. A successful intervention may reduce these costs.[12] If one of its effects is to increase offenders' long-term earnings, the higher direct and indirect taxes paid from those earnings are benefits to society.

A comprehensive BCA measures all four types of cost savings, thereby capturing a program's benefits for all members of society.[13] Decision makers in the criminal justice system will also be interested in the benefits to their agencies because their agencies bear the costs of operating juvenile justice programs. However, it is important to recognize that restricting attention to the criminal justice system's benefits excludes some of the benefits to

---

[12]Any gains to juveniles from their crimes, such as use of stolen money and property, should not be included in a BCA because illegal gains do not have "standing" (Zerbe, 2007).

[13]BCAs of other social programs typically divide benefits between program participants (juvenile offenders in this context) and taxpayers (everyone else). The sum of the two sets of benefits represents the full benefits to society. In applications to criminal justice, it is useful and important to separate victim benefits from those of other nonparticipants because the potential victims, not the participants, are the main beneficiaries of the intervention. Further dividing the taxpayer component between nonvictims and society recognizes the different types of cost savings received by each group. Many BCAs of criminal justice programs ignore participant (offender) benefits.

society in general (e.g., less school vandalism) and, because victim costs for some crimes are very large, often dramatically underestimates total benefits (Greenwood, 2008). Underestimated benefits, in turn, may lead decision makers to forgo interventions that would pass a benefit-cost test.

The benefits of preventing a crime in the year following treatment are worth more than the benefits of preventing the same crime in later years. This is because a dollar received sooner can either be used or invested immediately to earn additional income. Hence, a BCA must convert future benefits into their present value by discounting them using a standard formula. Although the appropriate discount rate for public programs is still debated (Burgess and Zerbe, 2011), values in the range of 3 to 8 percent are typical.[14]

Estimating the Economic Value Per Crime Prevented

Although methods for estimating the economic value per crime prevented have received extensive discussion and have steadily improved, they remain controversial and incomplete (Bowles, 2010; Cohen, 2010). The "bottom-up" approach, used in nearly all BCAs of juvenile justice programs, measures the various individual costs described above and sums them. Cohen (2010) observes that some elements are relatively straightforward to measure, such as police and court costs, obtained from administrative data, or medical expenses and lost earnings, obtained from victim surveys. Other elements pose difficult challenges or have yet to be successfully measured.[15] The careful, detailed, though admittedly incomplete bottom-up estimates of victim costs developed by Miller and colleagues (1996) are widely used.[16] For juvenile justice programs that pass a benefit-cost test, the bottom-up savings in victim costs per treated offender are at least double the savings in costs to society (Drake, Aos, and Miller, 2009).

"Top-down" approaches attempt to derive the total value per crime prevented from one source. Contingent valuation (CV) is the most widely used top-down approach. It relies on randomized surveys of the public in which respondents are asked to indicate their willingness-to-pay for a specified benefit—in this case, the reduction of juvenile crime. CV has gained favor in environmental BCAs and has been widely used to place dollar

---

[14]A thorough BCA would test the sensitivity of its conclusions to different discount rates.

[15]For example, a randomized controlled trial evaluation would not allow researchers to identify program impacts on criminal activity of treated offenders' friends who were outside the treatment and control groups (Butts and Roman, 2009).

[16]An analyst must inflate the estimates to represent the purchasing power for the period in which an intervention operated.

values on nonmarket goods, such as improved water quality, endangered species, and scenic beauty.[17]

The theory of CV is elegant in that willingness-to-pay captures all aspects of the cost of crime. If one accepts the theory and has confidence in the validity of the survey, there are no questions whether the resulting estimate omits some portion of social costs.[18] This stands in contrast to the wide variety of possible costs that the bottom-up method must attempt to calculate. With the bottom-up method, each specific cost is one component of the full array of costs, and estimating each one adds a degree of uncertainty to the overall estimate.

There are well-established protocols for conducting CV surveys that researchers can implement to estimate the value of reductions in specific types of crime. With only five CV studies of the costs of crime (and only one focused on juvenile crime), this method's potential for deriving sound estimates of the benefits of crime reduction has just begun to be explored (Cohen, 2010).[19] Cohen (2010) summarizes existing CV estimates of the costs of crime, discusses the many challenges to conducting valid CV surveys about crime reduction, and recommends a major program of research to refine and apply CV methods to this issue.

A second top-down method has estimated the benefits of crime reduction by estimating the relationship between property values and the level of crime. Other factors held constant, one would expect property values to be higher in low-crime neighborhoods. Data limitations prevent these kinds of studies from estimating the economic value of reducing a specific category of offense. Instead, they produce estimates of the value of lowering an aggregate measure of crime, such as a crime index (Cohen, 2010). Moreover, such estimates do not capture the value of reducing crimes to persons when they are outside their neighborhoods (Cohen, 2010). Because of these and other shortcomings, the property value approach has fallen out of favor for BCAs of criminal justice interventions.[20,21]

---

[17]See Bateman and colleagues (2002) and Carson (2011) for comprehensive introductions to CV.

[18]In practice, CV may better capture costs to victims and nonvictims than costs to offenders and of the criminal justice system, because respondents probably would have relatively little knowledge of the latter two types of costs.

[19]In principle, a BCA could compare the costs of an intervention to CV estimates of the benefits of the crime prevented by the intervention. No such study has yet appeared.

[20]Following the same logic and having the same limitations, some studies examine the relationship between local crime and local wages.

[21]A recent approach infers the value of less crime from life satisfaction surveys (Cohen, 2010). This method is much less developed than CV, and its promise remains to be seen.

Measuring the Costs of Juvenile Justice Programs

Compared with benefits, calculating average program cost per treated juvenile offender is more straightforward. The major cost typically is for the salaries (and fringe benefits) of staff members who deliver the program. Other readily identified and monetized costs include office expenses (e.g., supplies, rent, insurance, utilities), transportation, special staff training, depreciation, and any other expenses incurred to deliver program services. While BCAs have omitted hard-to-monetize minor costs, such as parents' time and out-of-pocket expenses to participate in a program, their cost estimates are more complete than their benefit estimates.

If all program costs occur in the first year, as is typical, they do not require discounting. Program costs that continue beyond the first year of service require discounting in the same manner as future benefits.

Findings from Benefit-Cost Analyses of Juvenile Justice Programs

Although there are more than 500 impact evaluations of juvenile offender programs (Drake, Aos, and Miller, 2009; Lipsey, 2009), BCAs of these programs are sparse. This section discusses only BCAs of programs explicitly designed to reduce juvenile crime and does not cover ones that have been shown to improve a range of outcomes for children and youth, including schooling, earnings, teen pregnancy, and sometimes crime (see Aos et al., 2004; Small et al., 2005; and National Research Council, 2009, for reviews of broader prevention programs).

The BCAs produced by the Washington State Institute for Public Policy (WSIPP) are widely regarded as the most thorough and comprehensive in the criminal justice literature. Drake and colleagues (2009) summarize WSIPP's methods and present its recent BCA results (Aos et al., 2001, 2004, 2006).

WSIPP's studies are notable for several reasons. They examine a wide variety of juvenile justice interventions that have been carefully evaluated. These include model programs endorsed by the Blueprints for Violence Prevention Project (http://www.colorado.edu/cspv/blueprints), such as multisystemic therapy, multidimensional treatment foster care, and functional family therapy. They also include other interventions that WSIPP judges to be effective, such as drug courts, as well as interventions shown to be ineffective, such as Scared Straight and juvenile intensive probation supervision. The studies use meta-analytic methods to combine findings from different evaluations of the same intervention to derive the effects on crime outcomes used in the BCAs (essentially, term one of the equation presented earlier). They use rigorous methods to project the reductions in crime that an intervention is likely to produce over a 13-year follow-up period.

They then use the projections to estimate the resulting cost savings for the criminal justice system and victims. The projected reductions in crime and the criminal justice system cost savings are meticulously derived from Washington State data. Victim costs are taken from Miller and colleagues (1996). Finally, WSIPP analysts are transparent in describing their assumptions and methods.

The top of Table A-1 presents the BCA findings for the juvenile justice programs analyzed by Drake and colleagues (2009). The message is clear: whether one chooses to intervene with juvenile offenders when they are institutionalized, in group or foster homes, or on probation, states and localities can adopt programs that produce remarkably large economic returns.[22] The same is true for programs that seek to divert juveniles before they are convicted of further crimes.

For institutionalized juveniles, the benefits of aggression replacement therapy, functional family therapy, and family integrated services respectively exceed their costs by roughly $65,500, $57,300, and $16,000, respectively. For the small group of juvenile sex offenders, sex offender treatment yields large benefits that exceed the high treatment cost by nearly $25,000 per participant. Boot camp programs do not reduce crime, but because they cost less than placing offenders in an institution, they also pass a benefit-cost test when the baseline is institutionalization.

For juvenile offenders in group or foster homes, multidimensional treatment foster care's benefits exceed its costs by $33,000.

For juveniles on probation, $1,467 spent to provide aggression replacement therapy returns nearly $36,000 in benefits. Functional family therapy and multisystemic therapy for such juveniles easily pass a benefit-cost test. A recent BCA of a multisystemic therapy program in Missouri also demonstrated large economic returns (Klietz et al., 2010).

Six program models intended to divert juveniles from further offending have benefits that substantially exceed costs. For adolescent diversion (for lower risk offenders), teen courts, restorative justice, and coordination of services, the benefit-cost ratio ranges from 10.6 to 25.6. Drug courts and victim offender mediation yield benefit-cost ratios of 4.2 and 6.9, respectively.

It is important to recognize that some programs are economically inferior to conventional practice (i.e., the benefits are smaller than the costs). This is the case for both alternative parole programs, wilderness challenge, intensive probation supervision, and Scared Straight.

Parole is the only custody status for which no alternative programs pass a benefit-cost test. There may be parole practices that are economically better than standard practice, but they have not yet been developed

---

[22]Greenwood (2008) reports similar results in his review of programs for juvenile offenders.

TABLE A-1 Benefits and Costs per Participant of Juvenile Offender Programs (net present value, 2010 dollars)

Custody Status of Juvenile Participants[a]	Program	Benefits to Victims and Criminal Justice System	Program Costs (compared with cost of alternative)	Benefits Minus Costs	Benefit-Cost Ratio	Probability That Benefits Exceed Costs
Institution	Aggression replacement therapy[c]	$66,954	$1,473	$65,481	45.5	.93
	Functional family therapy[c]	60,639	3,198	57,341	19.0	.99
	Family integrated transitions[c]	27,020	10,968	16,052	2.5	.86
	Sex offender treatment[b]	60,477	35,592	24,885	1.7	n/a
	Boot camp[b]	0	−8,661	8,661	n/a	n/a
	Wilderness challenge[b]	0	3,350	−3,350	n/a	n/a
Group or Foster Home	Multidimensional treatment foster care[c]	40,787	7,739	33,047	5.3	n/a
Parole	Regular surveillance oriented parole (versus no parole supervision)[b]	0	1,301	−1,301	n/a	n/a
	Intensive parole supervision[b]	0	7,015	−7,015	n/a	n/a
Probation	Aggression replacement therapy[c]	36,043	1,476	34,566	24.4	.93
	Functional family therapy[c]	37,739	3,190	34,549	11.9	.99
	Multisystemic therapy[c]	29,302	7,206	22,096	4.1	.91
	Intensive probation supervision[b]	0	1,735	−1,735	n/a	n/a

Diversion	Adolescent diversion project (for low-risk offenders)[b]	53,072	2,077	50,995	25.6	n/a
	Teen courts[b]	17,782	985	16,797	18.0	n/a
	Drug courts[c]	12,737	3,024	9,713	4.2	.80
	Restorative justice[b]	10,106	954	9,152	10.6	n/a
	Coordination of services[c]	5,270	386	4,884	13.6	.78
	Victim offender mediation[c]	3,922	566	3,357	6.9	.90
	Scared Straight[c]	−6,031	63	−6,095	n/a	n/a

Benefits (Costs not available)

Institution	Behavior modification[b]	42,706
	Cognitive-behavioral therapy[b]	7,744
	Counseling, psychotherapy[b]	50,304
	Education programs[b]	109,834
	Life skills education programs[b]	13,908
Diversion	Diversion with services (versus regular juvenile court)[b]	3,982
	Other family-based therapy programs[b]	40,281

NOTE: n/a = estimate not available. Monetary figures are converted into 2010 dollars.
[a]Adapted from Greenwood (2008).
[b]Adapted from Drake, Aos, and Miller (2009).
[c]Adapted from Washington State Institute for Public Policy (2011).

and successfully tested. Juvenile justice officials may consider supporting
the development and testing of new parole models that might prove successful and pass a benefit-cost test. Alternatively, they can use their scarce
resources to implement the already proven programs that intervene during
a different custody status.

The results in columns 3 and 4 of Table A-1 show the best point estimates of benefits and costs. However, bottom-line estimates of total benefits
and costs have a degree of uncertainty, because estimates of some of the
underlying parameters needed to conduct a BCA are themselves uncertain.[23] WSIPP's (2011) recent analyses take this uncertainty into account
using Monte Carlo methods, which provide an estimate of the probability
that benefits will exceed costs when parameters values are systematically
varied.[24]

The Monte Carlo results in the last column of Table A-1 imply that
one can be highly confident that aggression replacement therapy, family
integrated transitions, functional family therapy, multisystemic therapy,
and victim offender mediation are successful programs from a benefit-cost
perspective. The probabilities that these approaches pass a benefit-cost test
are all at least .86, and most exceed .90. The probabilities are somewhat
lower for drug courts and coordination of services (.80 and .78), but one
can still be quite confident that both are successful.

Because WSIPP uses Washington data to estimate changes in crime and
the costs of the criminal justice system, the findings technically are not generalizable to other states or the nation as a whole. However, Washington's
crime and the costs of its criminal justice system probably do not differ
substantially from other states, so the findings are likely to apply elsewhere.
Indeed, even if the savings in criminal justice costs and the benefits to victims (not shown separately in Table A-1) were both 25 percent smaller, all
programs that pass a benefit-cost test in the WSIPP analysis would still pass
by a wide margin. The WSIPP findings provide reliable guidance for other
states and localities.

Seven other types of programs examined by Drake and colleagues
(2009) also generate benefits to victims and the criminal justice system,
as shown in the lower panel of Table A-1. Four of the seven have benefits

---

[23]Suppose an evaluation reports that a program reduced crime by 12 percent, with a
standard error of 1.4. This means that, although the most likely impact is 12 percent, there is
a 95 percent chance that the true impact lies between 9.3 and 14.7 percent. Similarly, estimates
of program costs, estimates of victim costs, and the methods used by Drake and colleagues
(2009) to combine findings from several studies are not perfectly precise.

[24]The Monte Carlo method simultaneously varies the specific parameters used to compute
benefits and costs based on the degree of uncertainty of all parameters' estimates. Repeating
the computations under thousands of variations tests the sensitivity of the overall findings to
the inherent uncertainly of the underlying parameters.

exceeding $40,000 per participant, so they are likely to pass a benefit-cost test. But because WSIPP had not computed cost estimates at the time of publication, we cannot draw this conclusion with certainty.

Building on its methodological innovations, WSIPP is currently developing a tool that other jurisdictions can use to derive benefit-cost estimates of criminal justice programs (Aos and Drake, 2010). The tool will allow analysts to use crime and cost data for their jurisdictions and vary the assumptions needed to compute cost savings.

A NOTE ON COST-EFFECTIVENESS ANALYSIS

If the principal benefit expected from a juvenile justice program cannot be given monetary value, cost-effectiveness analysis can be an alternative to benefit-cost analysis (Boardman et al., 2011). Suppose, for example, that the primary goal is to reduce recidivism and that other possible program impacts are of little import to decision makers. In such a case, programs might be compared in terms of the decrease in the average probability of recidivism per dollar spent to assist a first-time juvenile offender. The most cost-effective program is the one that produces the largest decrease in the probability per dollar spent.

Focusing on one goal is a strength in that it obviates the need to express the value of the outcome in monetary terms. Yet when interventions have multiple goals and no single one has clear priority, cost-effectiveness data may offer little guidance (Marsh, 2010). Suppose intervention A decreases a juvenile offender's likelihood of nonviolent crime by 20 percent and of violent crime by 10 percent. Alternative intervention B is equally costly and has corresponding decreases of 30 percent and 8 percent. Although B performs slightly worse in reducing violent crime, it does much better in reducing nonviolent crime. Which intervention is better? When there are multiple types of benefits, none of which dominates, and when the most important of them can be cast in monetary terms, a BCA will usually provide more useful information than a cost-effectiveness analysis.

LIMITATIONS OF CURRENT BENEFIT-COST ANALYSES

The program cost estimates in Table A-1 are essentially complete, yet all benefit estimates are understated for several reasons. These shortcomings apply to all other BCAs of juvenile justice programs as well. First, they ignore possible benefits to nonvictims and to offenders and their families. The latter especially could be large if the programs help offenders to attain more schooling or if desistance lowers the likelihood that younger siblings engage in delinquent acts.[25] Second, they count the savings of less crime for the criminal justice system, but not for other public agencies or nonprofit organizations that may also have savings (e.g., less money needed to repair vandalism). Third, as noted earlier, methods for measuring some types of victim costs have not yet been developed.[26] Finally, because adolescent behavior, including delinquency, is heavily influenced by peers, programs that reduce a participant's delinquency may reduce that of his or her peers as well. Because program evaluations have not measured this "second round" impact on crime, BCAs cannot include its benefits.[27]

Recognizing these reasons why benefits are understated further strengthens our earlier conclusion: states and localities can choose from a portfolio of programs for juvenile offenders that, if implemented well, can reduce crime and produce extraordinarily large economic returns.

As noted above, bottom-line estimates of total benefits and costs have a degree of uncertainty. Most existing BCAs of juvenile justice programs do not take this uncertainty into account and hence may give a misleading impression of the confidence one can place on the reported point estimates of benefits and costs. The recent analyses of the WSIPP (2011) do take account of uncertainty and mark a significant step forward.

IMPROVING BENEFIT-COST METHODS FOR JUVENILE JUSTICE PROGRAMS

The leading BCAs of juvenile justice programs employ sophisticated estimation methods and complex data sets and provide valuable information to stakeholders in the juvenile justice system. Like other evaluation methods, however, the state of the art can be improved.[28]

Some categories of bottom-up costs have not been measured at all, and measurement methods for others have limitations (Cohen, 2010). The potential of the contingent valuation method for deriving improved esti-

---

[25]Suppose a program raises the probability of completing high school by .10. Since in 2009 male (female) high school graduates earned $11,600 ($8,900) more per year than those without a degree (U.S. Census Bureau, 2010a, 2010b), the average increase in earnings would be $1,160 or $890. Over a 40-year working life, the present value of $1,160 and $890, making the conservative assumption that it does not grow over time and using a discount rate of 5 percent, is $20,900 and $16,000.

[26]Some other studies are further limited because they estimate cost savings to the criminal justice system but not victim benefits (Robertson, Grimes, and Rogers, 2001; Cowell, Lattimore, and Krebs, 2010).

[27]Butts and Roman (2009) observe that some potentially valuable program models, such as community-based interventions, lack the rigorous evaluations required to assess benefits and costs. This is less a limitation of the technique of BCA per se than of the funding priorities of agencies and researchers.

[28]See Butts and Roman (2009) for other suggestions.

mates of the benefits of crime reduction has just begun to be explored. A program of research to improve bottom-up measures, refine and apply CV methods, and compare the results of these two approaches is in order.

As observed above, Monte Carlo analysis offers a way to address the uncertainty of estimates of benefits and costs. Monte Carlo analysis strengthens the credibility of a study's findings and needs to be a routine element of future BCAs. The WSIPP model under development (Aos and Drake, 2010), which will have the capacity to execute Monte Carlo simulations, will substantially improve BCAs of criminal justice programs.

Finally, because evaluations of juvenile justice interventions understandably focus on changes in criminal behavior, they generally do not collect data on changes in noncriminal behavior, such as education or employment attributable to an intervention. Because these changes typically have positive benefits, ignoring them underestimates an intervention's total benefits. A more complete BCA would quantify the economic value of changes in these outcomes as well as in ones directly related to crime. Future impact evaluations and BCAs of juvenile justice programs would be stronger if they routinely measured changes in important noncrime outcomes, quantified their economic value whenever possible, and included them in the benefit-cost calculations in addition to the benefits directly related to crime.

Appendix B

The Missouri Model:
A Critical State of Knowledge

Beth M. Huebner
Department of Criminology and Criminal Justice,
University of Missouri at St. Louis

Over the past two decades, the juvenile incarceration rate has increased steadily. On any given day, more than 368 of every 100,000 juveniles are serving time in correctional facilities, and nearly all of them will be released back into the communities from which they came (Snyder and Sickmund, 1999). A continuum of programming services is needed to aid the incarcerated juvenile population in preparing for release, leaving prison, and returning to the community so that the likelihood of successful community adjustment can be improved and the risk of recidivism reduced.

The Missouri model of juvenile corrections has been heralded as a leader in the area of juvenile reform; however, little empirical research on the program has been conducted. The primary goal of this appendix is to provide a critical assessment of the Missouri model. It begins with a brief historical description of juvenile corrections in Missouri. Next, the program model is described and linkages are made to the relevant best practices literature in the juvenile justice field. Included is a discussion of the feasibility of this model for implementation in other states and suggestions for sustainability. Finally, proposals for future research are outlined and the need for additional data and analysis is described.

HISTORY OF THE MISSOURI JUVENILE JUSTICE SYSTEM

The structure and tone of the juvenile justice system at any given point in time are governed by period-specific understandings of what causes delinquency and how best to correct delinquent behavior (Bernard, 1992). The philosophical ideas about what causes crime contain within them implicit policy implications for how to fix "the problem." Although there is period-specific variation in the understanding of causal influences, the juvenile justice system has followed identifiable cycles.

The state of Missouri has been strongly influenced by legal thinking on juvenile justice and delinquency. Like most states in the early part of the 20th century, juveniles were held in gender-segregated training facilities (Abrams, 2003). The state opened two facilities in 1889: Boonville held males, and Chillicothe females. The institutions were run as paramilitary organizations, and solitary confinement and other isolation techniques were used for discipline. Reports of violence were rampant. In 1948, two youth were killed in the Boonville facility. At the peak custody level, Boonville housed 675 youth.

During this time, the courts began to take a more active role in affecting the juvenile justice processes. In 1967, the U.S. Supreme Court extended the rights of juveniles through *In re Gault* and a series of high-profile cases. Similarly, in 1957, the Missouri legislature passed the Unified Juvenile Court Act. Under the act, the juvenile court was now given jurisdiction over all cases related to delinquency and status offenses, abuse and neglect, and adoption. Specifically, the act required the court to consider the least restrictive alternative in punishment and to stress the need for reduced out-of-home placement. One of the central proponents, Judge Robert G.J. Hoester of St. Louis City, argued that the new act was bold and made the court a "treatment center rather than a punishment center" (Abrams, 2003).

This legislation paved the way for constructing the W.E. Sears Youth Center in Poplar Bluff. This was the first dormitory-style juvenile correctional facility in the state and was designed around the positive peer culture model (Abrams, 2003). Two additional camps were opened in 1962 and 1964 to address the crowding and violence associated with the congregate facilities. This new model of small group staffing was to serve as an experiment until funds for a larger training school could be procured. Calls were made by the Missouri Law Enforcement Assistance Council, Attorney General John C. Danforth, and Governor Kit Bond to reform the juvenile system. However, in 1971, a bill to provide $3 million in funding to support the building of a new training school was defeated (Abrams, 2003). Although the original bill was defeated, Tim Decker, the current director of the Division of Youth Services (DYS), argues that the small pilot programs were instrumental in securing eventual legislator support. The pilot programs required little initial financial support but provided valuable evidence to frontline workers, legislators, and others that the new approach would work (Decker, 2010).

In 1974, under the Juvenile Justice and Delinquency Prevention Act, the federal government mandated that no juvenile could be detained in an institution for criminal offenders if she or he was not guilty of criminal behavior. This legislation expanded federal oversight of juvenile courts and correctional facilities.

During this time, there was a complete organizational change in the juvenile justice system in Missouri. The Missouri DYS was created as a new free-standing agency in the Department of Social Services through the Omnibus State Reorganization Act of 1974. The division was developed using a decentralized organizational design, and offices were separated into five geographic regions, enhancing administrative and service delivery at a local level. In 1975, DYS Director Max Brand called for a five-year reorganization plan that included building several additional dormitory-style facilities, based on the positive reports garnered from the original Poplar Bluff facility. During this time, several states were questioning the efficacy of the congregate punishment model for juvenile offenders. Most notable was the Massachusetts Experiment, in which Jerome Miller led the charge to close all training schools in the state, including the prototypical training school, the Lyman School for Boys (Miller, 1991). The changes in juvenile corrections also came on the heels of the larger deinstitutionalization movement of this era.

The biggest challenge to juvenile corrections in Missouri came in 1975, when the U.S. District Court for the Western District of Missouri filed a consent decree challenging the conditions at Boonville. The Missouri system continued to expand the dormitory-style system; Chillicothe was closed in 1981, and Boonville shut down in 1983. In 1983, as a partial result of the consent decree, the Missouri House of Representatives created a standing committee on children, youth, and families, one of the first of its kind. In 1987, a DYS blue ribbon panel was convened to explore the needs of youth. The panel recommended the development of a 15-member bipartisan Youth Services Advisory Board, consisting of local and state lawmakers and experts, to help plan for expanding the juvenile treatment and correctional services in the state. The board is legislatively mandated and initially included several high-ranking conservative stakeholders, such as Stephen Limbaugh, an influential judge. The diverse nature of the board helped bridge political gaps and negotiate scarce resources for DYS programming. The board was a catalyst for the system-wide implementation of the new juvenile corrections model and helped quadruple the budget from $15 million in 1985 to $60 million today (Abrams, 2003). The dynamic, enduring support of the board was a central element in the development and sustainability of the Missouri model.

The progressive juvenile justice era, however, was short-lived. Starting in the 1980s, there was a decisive change in the focus of the juvenile justice system. The change was fueled by the perception that the juveniles were more violent than ever, and the criminal justice system was too lenient on juvenile offenders (Dilulio, 1995; Wilson, 1995). Missouri was not immune to the "get-tough" movement. Missouri legislators filed numerous bills during the early 1990s seeking to stiffen juvenile sentences, broaden transfer to adult courts, and increase the number of youth sentenced to juvenile courts. The Missouri Juvenile Justice Association, working in conjunction with then-Governor Mel Carnahan, conducted a comprehensive analysis of the juvenile justice system. Instead of yielding to the pressure of legislators, the DYS and the governor worked together to educate the community and governmental stakeholders on the cost-effectiveness and success of the Missouri model. In addition, Governor Carnahan signed legislation in 1995 that created the juvenile and family court division within the Office of State Courts Administrator. This division was charged with collecting data on the juvenile courts and developing a standardized training and educational protocol for DYS staff (Abrams, 2003). It is through this evidence-based lens that Missouri continues today.

THE MISSOURI MODEL

The DYS is managed under the Missouri Department of Social Services. Established in 1974, the agency is currently under the direction of Director Tim Decker. Its mission is to "enable youth to fulfill their needs in a responsible manner within the context of and with respect for the needs of the family and the community" (see http://dss.mo.gov/dys). The state operates under a defined set of goals that stress the importance of positive youth development, through the provision of treatment services that maximize youth and community safety. This type of therapeutic treatment model, centered on coordinated services, restorative integration, and specialized counseling, is consistently found to be associated with reduction in recidivism (Lipsey, 2009).

The DYS has jurisdiction for youth mandated to its care by one of 45 Missouri juvenile courts (Missouri Department of Social Services, 2011). Juveniles supervised by circuit courts and youth under age 17 convicted in adult courts are not under the jurisdiction of DYS. The agency maintains a budget of $60.5 million and operates under a decentralized administrative structure with administrative centers in five regions of the state. DYS offers a broad range of services, including residential and community-based programming for youth and families.

Although the philosophy and beliefs of the Missouri DYS permeate the juvenile justice system, the Missouri model refers specifically to the services provided to youth in institutional confinement. In total, DYS operates 32 residential facilities (726 total beds), including secure and moderate care facilities and group homes (Missouri Division of Youth Services, 2003). Average per diem cost is $167.30 per child, for an annual cost of $61,064. Youth in secure and moderate care facilities typically serve 9-12 months in the facility, and the average length of stay in group homes is 4-6 months. All statistics are reported by Missouri and are contained in official technical reports (Missouri Department of Social Services, 2011).

Missouri DYS Population

Only a very small fraction (2.5 percent) of the 648,648 Missouri youth ages 10-17 have contact with juvenile or family courts each year. Approximately 15,000 youth annually are convicted in Missouri circuit, juvenile, or family courts. In total, 77 percent of referrals to juvenile courts in 2008 were informally disposed and required little, if any, further action by the court. Less than half of youth with a formal disposition were sent to out-of-home placement; 56 percent were placed under the supervision of the Children's Division, 22 percent (1,143) were committed to DYS, and the remaining resided with family or in a private agency. Data on youth referred to state courts are compiled by the Office of State Courts Administrator (McElfresh, Yan, and Janku, 2009). The Missouri Supreme Court oversees the circuit courts, which provide oversight for local family and juvenile courts.

A very small proportion of juvenile law offenders are remanded to DYS; the majority of youth served by DYS were committed to a youth institution. A total of 1,004 new commitments and 91 recommitments were made to DYS in 2010; DYS served another 155 youth in the community. During FY2010, DYS had custody of 2,111 youth (Missouri Department of Social Services, 2011).

The following statistics detail the population served by the DYS in Missouri. The DYS population is predominantly male (84.3 percent), with an average age of 15.2. Most youth were Caucasian (66.2 percent); 31.3 percent were African American, and 2.5 percent were of another race.[1] In total, 10.7 percent of all new commitments in 2010 were for serious, personal felonies (robbery, assault), and 42 percent of the population was serving time for lesser felonies, usually for property or drug-related offenses. In addition, 37 percent of the new commitments were for misdemeanors (probation violation and petty larceny), and 10.4 percent for juvenile status offenses (violation of court order).

Many youth come to DYS with histories of substance abuse, educational limitations, and other challenges. Youth report an average nine years of schooling at the time of commitment. More than half (57.8 percent) of youth have a history of substance abuse involvement, and 42.4 percent have had prior mental health services. Many (56 percent) youth lived with a single parent before commitment, and most youth lived in urban areas

---

[1]Information on ethnicity was not provided.

prior to incarceration. In total, 65 percent of youth resided in one of the state's five metropolitan statistical areas; 29.3 percent of the total population came from the St. Louis region.

Description of Program Model

The Missouri model of juvenile corrections includes four core elements: (1) continuous case management, (2) decentralized residential facilities, (3) small-group, peer-led services, and (4) a restorative rehabilitation-centered treatment environment. Each element of the program model is detailed below, and more information can be found in official DYS documents (Missouri Department of Social Services, 2011) or the DYS Missouri model website (see http://www.missouriapproach.org). There is also an Annie E. Casey Foundation report that provides details on the programmatic elements (Mendel, 2010).

Case Management

The Missouri model is based on a continuous care model of case management. Case managers are assigned at initial court contact and remain with the youth and family until discharge. In order to provide intense, individualized treatment, caseloads for youth specialists are capped at 15 to 18 families. The state maintains a system of indeterminate sentencing, so the duration of treatment in the facility and in the community is based on the evaluations of the case manager.

The case management process begins with a comprehensive risk assessment. The Missouri Office of State Courts Administrator has developed three classification tools.[2] The risk assessment and classification matrix examine the relative likelihood of future delinquency and provide suggestions for graduated sanctions. A needs assessment is conducted after sentencing and is designed to assist with case management and treatment planning. The use of validated needs assessment scales in conjunction with case management is consistent with the principles of the risk-need-responsivity (RNR) model (Andrews, Bonta, and Hoge, 1990; Lowenkamp and Latessa, 2005c; Lowenkamp, Latessa, and Smith, 2006a). The RNR model has become a benchmark for effective programs with adults and has gained support among juvenile programs.

The case management approach continues in secure confinement. The caseworker maintains contact with the youth and family during the term of confinement. The caseworker is part of a coordinated treatment team

---

[2]See the court website for more information and scales used (http://www.courts.mo.gov/page.jsp?id=1199 [April 2013]).

that can include representatives from the school, treatment services, and facility staff. The case manager facilitates communication with the youth and family, advocates for the needs of the youth, and works with the youth and family to develop a prerelease plan.

In addition to traditional case management and institutional supervision, the state provides intensive case monitoring for individuals released from institutional placement. Aftercare is an important component, as the early period after release from incarceration has been shown to be the most critical in determining recidivism outcomes for juveniles (Murray and Cox, 1979; Austin, Krisberg, and Joe, 1987; Fagan, 1990). Although DYS does not adhere to a specific aftercare program model per se, the services provided to youth in Missouri following secure confinement mirror that of the successful Intensive Aftercare Program (IAP) designed by Altschuler and Armstrong (1994). Like the IAP model, DYS provides a continuum of services to the juvenile from inception of confinement to community integration.

Intensive surveillance is also a key component of the aftercare model. The caseworker provides the primary point of contact throughout the adolescent's tenure in the system. The program also employs community mentors, typically a position filled by college students or local agency staff, to maintain consistent, frequent contact with youth. These individuals provide cost-effective case management assistance and facilitate small caseload sizes for case managers. Graduated sanctions and participant incentives are also a central part of the program model. Overall, 1,335 youth participated in the intensive case monitoring program in FY2010 (Missouri Department of Social Services, 2011).

DYS provides a number of community care services, including individual and family counseling, education services, and temporary housing. The DYS has set up community support networks in each of the communities where facilities are located. Staffed by volunteers from the community and local social services agencies, the goal of the networks is to link each youth with services in the community. Community residents are encouraged to volunteer and visit the facilities, and youth participate in local social service projects. In addition, 561 youth were provided employment training through a partnerships program with the Division of Workforce Development (Missouri Department of Social Services, 2011). Youth in this program participate in job training and receive minimum wage compensation for the duration of the program.

Decentralized Residential Facilities

As noted, the DYS operates 32 residential facilities, including 7 secure care facilities, 18 moderate care facilities, and 7 community residential group homes (Missouri Department of Social Services, 2011). All facilities are developed around a small-group, dormitory-style model; however, the architecture and design of the facilities vary widely. DYS has built some new residential facilities, but some institutions are reappointed schools, and two are part of college campuses. The residential facilities share several common characteristics. All of them are small, with no more than 50 youth and an average population of 20. In contrast, the original training schools were large, congregate institutions that housed more than 100 youth. Youth stay in a dedicated small group (10-12) throughout their stay, and the agency strives to maintain a 1:6 staff-to-youth ratio (Missouri Department of Social Services, 2011).

The juvenile institutions bear little resemblance to a traditional training school. The facilities were designed to reflect the rehabilitative ideal. Living areas have appointments similar to a college dorm, including bunk beds, dressers, and carpet. Most facilities also have a larger congregate area with recreational activities. Youth dress in street clothing and remain in small groups while in the facility. The institutions do not resemble high-security facilities and do not include perimeter razor wire or barred windows.

The small-group congregate system is important for two primary reasons. First, DYS has a defined goal of keeping youth within 50-75 miles of their homes. The traditional congregate facilities separated youth from family. Youth are now allowed home visits to maintain familial relationships and facilitate eventual reentry. DYS has identified the family as an integral part of the treatment process. Keeping youth near their family facilitates group participation, as the division views parents and families as the expert on their child (Becker and Decker, 2008).

Second, the cottage model allows for 24/7, eyes-on supervision in lieu of isolation and other physical controls typically used in training schools. Instead, the organization relies on active supervision by trained staff to maintain order and safety. The first stage of treatment in Missouri includes meeting the basic safety and security needs of youth. Safety and structure provide the backbone for effective treatment; therefore, the organizational design of the institution reinforces the rehabilitative ideal (Becker and Decker, 2008). Research suggests that smaller institutions are less crowded and are more likely to emphasize rehabilitation over control (Lipsey et al., 2010).

Peer-Centered Treatment Model

Residential facilities provide a wide range of treatment services (Becker and Decker, 2008). The department has developed an integrated treatment model theoretically based on Bronfenbrenner's (1979) ecological model of development. The treatment models rests on the assumption that successful services must address the cultural values of youth, intimate effects (school and peer), and extended family and work.

Peer-based treatment is a central element of the treatment model. DYS treatment is built on the assumption that change does not occur in isolation. Youth and staff work together throughout the treatment process. The staff facilitates a peer leadership and support culture that reinforces the importance of safety, support, and civility in the institution. Youth participate in a highly structured weekly schedule and all activities, meals, and treatment as a group. In addition, youth are asked to check in with each other during the day to express concerns or to praise positive behaviors.

DYS does not prescribe a specific treatment model. Instead, it has developed an integrated treatment plan that stresses group processes while providing treatment and services for individual and family needs. Treatment services vary by institution, group, and even adolescent. All youth must participate in youth-centered therapy and educational services. The division was heavily influenced by the Office of Juvenile Justice and Delinquency Prevention's Comprehensive Strategy for Serious, Violent, and Chronic Juvenile Offenders (Howell, 1995b; see Chapter 10). And it uses strategies suggested by the Full Frame Institute (see http://www.fullframeinitiative. org) to refine and shape youth interventions. Decker stresses that they are continually revising and changing programs based on the needs of youth.

Positive, Treatment-Centered Environment

As noted, DYS has identified a series of core beliefs that reinforce all treatment and staffing decisions. Training and staffing are central to maintaining a positive treatment environment. The residential facilities staff are considered counselors and youth specialists, not guards, as they are commonly called in juvenile training centers and adult facilities. Staff are present in the facility at all times, and managers work flexible schedules to address the needs of youth. Steps are taken to maintain consistency in staffing to help create a healthy group culture.

The division has increased the education requirements of staff to enhance and broaden the role and responsibilities of the traditional juvenile caseworker. Youth specialist positions now require 60 hours of college coursework, and the division actively recruits on college campuses to draw the best students (Mendel, 2010). Staff also undergo nearly 300 hours of training during the first two years of employment and must undergo additional in-service training each additional year. The training curriculum, overall, has been rewritten to reinforce rehabilitation instead of law enforcement or correctional techniques to manage behavior. Contractual services are integrated into the holistic treatment model, and leadership supervises implementation to ensure consistency and success (Becker and

Decker, 2008). Unlike some other states, Missouri DYS does not outsource the housing needs of youth; contractors are responsible only for specialized treatment needs.

DYS also runs an accredited school district, and each adolescent is placed in educational programming for six hours per day. DYS manages 42 educational programs in the institution and the community, employing approximately 150 teachers.[3] The staff is accredited using the same standards as all public schools in Missouri, and the state employs a pool of staff with experience working with children with diverse educational backgrounds. More than 40 percent of youth have special education needs. Educational staff are part of the unified treatment process as employees of DYS. And DYS has recently extended its educational model for youth in the community. Youth who feel more comfortable in the DYS education system are able to continue to graduation, even if they have been discharged from the system.

Although Decker contends that it is a challenge to provide services to such a diverse population, he feels that the integration of education into the total treatment package facilitates educational achievement. Decker and Steward (2011) report several positive outcomes of the DYS education model. In Missouri, 95 percent of youth in DYS care earned high school credits, and 30 percent go on to complete a General Educational Development (GED) certificate or earn a high school diploma; comparative national statistics indicate that 50 percent of youth in secure care earn credit and 11 percent graduate or earn a GED.

BEST PRACTICES FOR THE MISSOURI MODEL

Four Key Factors

The Missouri DYS has identified four key factors that they believe are critical for developing and sustaining a successful juvenile treatment model (Decker, 2011). First, strong organizational leadership is needed. Director Mark Steward was at the helm of the department for over 17 years, providing continuity of management. In addition, the youth system as a whole has received strong, continued support from state government. Change was not a quick process. The Missouri model has become an example for change because of decisions made in the 1970s and 1980s (Abrams, 2003).

The legislature continues to keep close tabs on the organization through the bipartisan Youth Services Advisory Board. In fact, the advisory board remains a central element in the political success of the model. Having the support of conservative leaders in the state helped gained legitimacy for

---

[3] See http://dss.mo.gov/dys/ed.htm [May 2013].

the program. The division to this day maintains an open door policy and preaches transparency in policy and practice. DYS leaders have actively sought out support from local, state, and national leaders. As Decker (2010) notes, constituency building is a key element to any successful program, particularly for long-term initiatives that span legislative cycles.

Second, an organizational culture change is needed. Several key factors facilitated change in Missouri. Mark Steward argues that it is critical that DYS be under the Department of Social Services and separate from the court and the adult correctional system. This organizational structure allows DYS to stay free from the philosophies underpinning most traditional adult carceral models. Decker agrees, arguing that "changing our end destination often involves starting from a fundamentally different place."

Training and staffing are also key components to organizational change. In fact, cultural change must precede programmatic change. Decker argues that many organizations adopt an evidence-based model without acknowledging the nature of the organizational culture. Effective change is not driven by a specific program. Success is accomplished by having the "right people who share a set of beliefs and philosophies" (Decker, 2010).

Both Decker and Steward note that there was substantial turnover in the beginning of the new model, and they agree that proper staffing and training are among the most important elements in the Missouri model. Enhancing educational requirements for staff and active recruitment from college campuses have revitalized staff in Missouri. Training and staff development do come with some costs. Former director Steward, who now helps translate the Missouri model into other jurisdictions, indicates that training staff is a very laborious process and can cost $500,000 per year. Although the investment in training is large, he contends that costs pale in comparison to those of traditional security measures.

Third, highly effective treatment strategies and approaches are essential to positive youth outcomes. Decker stresses the importance of continual change and improvement in programmatic models. Equally essential is having the courage to change or remove a program if it is not working.

Constituency building and buy-in is the final key element. One main example in Missouri is the use and funding of community liaison councils in program sites throughout the state. The councils help manage the day treatment centers in the community. Community centers are an integral part of the reentry process, providing treatment services, peer support, and a general home base in the community. Decker indicates that it is important to lay the groundwork with community agencies and the legislators to help insulate the organizational mission. He argues that it is not possible for one agency to address the myriad needs associated with juvenile delinquency. Instead, DYS has chosen to use funds as a catalyst to support best practices in the community. In turn, the community has an investment in juvenile success and supports the agency mission.

Outcome Analyses

The Missouri model is generally regarded as one of the best approaches to juvenile justice practice available today. It has found considerable support in media accounts, and the program has garnered popular acclaim (McGarvey, 2005; Beaubien, 2007; Moore, 2009). Lipsey and colleagues (2010) consider Missouri's comprehensive strategy as a model juvenile justice system; they highlight the state's commitment to providing a continuum of graduated sanctions under the guidance of a caseworker and the use of a structured decision-making model to make treatment and placement decisions informed by risk and needs assessment.

Despite this strong support, there is no credible scientific evidence demonstrating the effectiveness of this approach. Much is still to be learned about how the program model affects long-term youth trajectories and to whom this model is most applicable. As is true of any intervention program, the strongest way of demonstrating effectiveness is to conduct a randomized clinical trial or, short of that, to conduct a rigorous quasi-experimental study. These designs ensure, to the greatest extent possible, that one is comparing identical treatment and control participants and that outcomes, such as recidivism, are measured in identical ways. There is a robust scientific literature supporting this approach to evaluation (Shadish, Cook, and Campbell, 2001). Moreover, the field of juvenile justice is increasingly relying on rigorous standards of evidence-based studies before concluding that programs are effective (Mihalic et al., 2001; Aos, 2002). However, the little research that has been conducted on the Missouri model falls far short of these standards.

Part of the perceived success of the model comes from Missouri's reported relatively low recidivism rates. DYS provides a detailed annual report documenting patterns of recidivism (Missouri Department of Social Services, 2011). Data from the 2010 DYS annual report indicate that 89.8 percent of youth housed in detention facilities successfully completed the DYS program. The remaining failed for various reasons, including subsequent law violation while under supervision, new commitment to DYS, or absconding. The state also reports one-, two-, and three-year recidivism rates for youth who successfully complete DYS programming. According to data on a cohort of youth discharged from Missouri juvenile facilities in 1999, 33.9 percent of the sample recidivated within three years of completing the DYS program. In total, 29.3 percent were recommitted to DYS, were sentenced to adult 120-day shock incarceration, or were sentenced to probation, and 4.6 percent were committed to adult prison. The recidivism rates have been relatively static over the past five years (Scott, 2009). However, these data remain entirely descriptive, not evaluative—that is, they describe the situation in Missouri, but they do not evaluate whether or not the Missouri model is effective or is any better than other approaches to juvenile justice. In order to do that, an adequate comparison group would have to be followed in identical ways to place these recidivism rates in the proper evaluative context.

Only one outside assessment of the Missouri model has been conducted. The report, funded by the Annie E. Casey Foundation, included measures of institutional safety. Mechanical restraints and isolation were rarely used in Missouri, and very few assaults on youth or staff were reported. In fact, youth in Ohio juvenile facilities were 2.5 times more likely to have been placed under mechanical restraints. Finally, no youth suicides have occurred in Missouri because the training schools were closed; 110 youth suicides occurred nationally between 1995 and 1999. The Annie E. Casey report also documented differences in recidivism levels between Missouri and other states (Mendel, 2010). For example Arizona, Indiana, and Maryland reported that more than 20 percent of youth were sentenced to adult prison within three years of release from residential confinement in a juvenile facility, in comparison to 8.5 percent in Missouri. Similarly, Florida reported a one-year reconfinement rate of 28 percent; Missouri had a 17 percent recidivism rate during the same period. In New Jersey, 36 percent of youth were recommitted to juvenile custody for a new offense or sentenced to adult prison within two years of release; in Missouri the comparable figure was 14.5 percent.

Although these state differences are often pointed to as evidence of effectiveness by supporters of the Missouri model, their fundamental methodological weaknesses render them virtually meaningless. There is no evidence that the recidivism rates being compared in these different states reflect the behavior of similar youth. Youth can differ in prior offending histories, risk factors, demographic characteristics, and the juvenile justice process—to name just a few factors—that make it impossible to draw conclusions from gross comparisons such as these. In addition, the data were not evaluated on the basis of common reporting criteria (Scott, 2009), and the research did not rely on a common definition of recidivism. Scholars have cautioned against comparing recidivism rates across systems, particularly given the diversity of juvenile justice systems. The data were collected from eight states using aggregate data presented in official reports downloaded from the Internet. No independent data verification was conducted. The size, nature, and age range of the juvenile samples varied across states. For example, the Missouri data represent youth under age 17, whereas Ohio tracks youth until age 20, probably inflating the statistics presented for this state.[4] In addition, Missouri does not include the approximately 11 percent of youth who fail to complete programs in their outcome analysis, and the measure of recidivism does not include rearrests.

Since the Annie E. Casey report has been published, Maryland has responded to the apparent disparity between Maryland and Missouri, pointing out differences in measurement schemes that include the age of youth, the length of follow-up, and measures of recidivism (Maryland Department of Juvenile Services, 2008). Finally, static (e.g., age, gender, education status) and dynamic (e.g., gang membership, mental health status) predictors of juvenile recidivism were not evaluated.

It is essential to collect data on factors that may simultaneously influence selection into deviance and increase the likelihood for juvenile detention and eventual recidivism. Independent data verification is needed before broad claims can be made based on the statistical data presented by Missouri—or any other state. Because of these and other serious methodological limitations, it is impossible to use the Annie E. Casey report to draw any conclusions about the effectiveness of the Missouri model. That is indeed unfortunate, given its popularity and the possibility that it may well be an effective program. But in order to inform policy, it is incumbent upon the model developers to convincingly and compellingly demonstrate the effectiveness of a program. That is not the case at the present time with respect to the Missouri model.

As is the case with the outcome evaluation, there has been no systematic process evaluation to determine whether the best practices for the Missouri model described above are actually essential for the development of the model. Although strong leadership, organizational culture change, and so forth are certainly plausible ingredients for success, the case for the dissemination of the Missouri model would be greatly strengthened if those aspects were systematically and rigorously evaluated as well.

NEEDS FOR FUTURE RESEARCH

The need for substantive information and examples of successful programs is a paramount concern for policy makers. Evidence-based practices are increasingly important, not only for line level personnel such as program managers or individual treatment specialists, but also for federal, state, and local policy makers seeking to promote investment in proven treatment strategies. At the national level, the federal government has made substantial investments in disseminating information about effective programs. A few examples of these efforts have included funding the development of

---

[4]See http://www.dys.ohio.gov/DNN/LinkClick.aspx?fileticket=percent2fjIektmoWxApercent3d &tabid=117&mid=879 [April 2013].

influential research documents, such as that prepared by Sherman and colleagues (1997), and, at the programmatic level, long-term commitment to such efforts as Blueprints for Violence Prevention, housed in the Center for the Study and Prevention of Violence at the University of Colorado (http://www.colorado.edu/cspv/blueprints/index.html). The notion of model programs has gained momentum as local, state, and national policy makers have placed their ideological and fiscal commitments behind establishing frameworks for effective programs.

Much remains to be learned about best practices in juvenile detention and subsequent reentry. The following sections detail suggestions for the enhancement of knowledge of juvenile confinement and youth outcomes. Several policy suggestions are presented, including further documentation of the Missouri model that encompasses both process and outcome evaluations. In addition, the development of group-specific treatment modalities and enhanced studies of desistance and reentry programming for youth is encouraged.

Process Evaluation

There has been a growing interest among criminal justice professionals to identify "what works" in criminal justice programming. Researchers and practitioners alike have called for the compilation of data regarding why certain programs work, how successful programs are implemented, and what can be done to replicate successful programs in other cities (Sherman et al., 1997). Replication of programs, particularly with rigorous controls, is needed before practitioners can be confident in investing in a new model. As noted, implementation of a Missouri-style model requires a significant initial investment among staff and administrators, often resulting in dramatic change in organizational philosophy. The development of a rigorous process evaluation can help identify the factors that impede or enhance implementation of a program model. This type of analysis is particularly important among line staff, as they are the foundation of successful implementation. Process evaluations also allow researchers to separate execution breakdowns from program failure. Programs implemented contrary to plans may compromise outcomes.

Process evaluation can include a number of phases and modalities. An ideal process evaluation would first include observation and documentation of the correctional treatment modalities and services. Separate from the research methodology used, it is important to assess program fidelity, identify implementation success, and provide general programmatic benchmarks for future interventions and sustainability. Because the treatment provided to the youth varies by institution and even by dormitory and adolescent, a program assessment component is needed to evaluate the particular aspect of treatment programming that is the most successful. The correctional program checklist (CPC) has been tested with juvenile populations and can help generate an estimate of program effectiveness based on established correctional and treatment protocols (Lowenkamp and Latessa, 2005c; Lowenkamp, Latessa, and Smith, 2006a). The effectiveness of programming can also be assessed using the standardized program evaluation protocol for assessing juvenile justice programs introduced by Lipsey et al. (2010). The score is based on five domains, including the nature of the primary treatment service, supplemental service, treatment amount (duration and contact hours), treatment quality, and youth risk level.

Similarly, a thorough evaluation should include an examination of the DYS education system. Although the educational results denoted by DYS are encouraging, many states have grappled with the challenges of providing comprehensive educational services to a high-risk and high-needs population. For example, the Massachusetts DYS underwent a complete reorganization because of high staff turnover, inconsistent educational quality, and lack of services for youth with special education needs (University of Massachusetts Donahue Institute, 2008). Given the size of the Missouri DYS population and the centrality of education for long-term success, it is critical to understand how educational needs are addressed in Missouri.

The use of structured interviews of principals at regular intervals can also help provide insight into program operation. These interviews should focus on the perceptions of those interviewed about project performance compared with expectations, implementation and operational issues, areas of needed improvement, perceptions of accomplishments, and suggestions for modifications. Replication rests on a detailed understanding of the program model and an ability to implement similar programming in diverse agencies.

Next, it is important to document the nature of the juvenile population sentenced to correctional supervision. As noted, very few youth who enter the Missouri juvenile and family court center enter a DYS facility. Some youth are handled informally, and others participate in diversionary programs. One global concern with juvenile justice models is that new programming models will bring more youth into the system than before program implementation, hence widening the net of correctional intervention. Documenting the flow of youth into the juvenile correctional system will help better illuminate the nature of the population served by Missouri institutions. The Missouri Office of State Courts Administrator, under the supervision of the Supreme Court of Missouri, maintains a Judicial Information System (JIS) database that tracks all juvenile law referral cases managed in state courts. These data should be used to compare youth diverted from confinement with youth in secure care. In turn, these data can be used for the outcome analysis to help select appropriate comparison groups in comparable states.

Several states are currently in the process of considering adopting a Missouri-style model. Most of this work has been guided by the Missouri Youth Services Institute (see http://www.mysiconsulting.org) under the leadership of Mark Steward, former director of the Missouri Division of Youth Services. Steward led the DYS for over 17 years and was one of the key staff responsible for designing and implementing the Missouri model. The agency is currently working with Louisiana; New Mexico; Santa Clara County, California; and the District of Columbia to replicate the model. Steward has not published case studies of the challenges agencies typically face in the implementation phase; doing so in a rigorous manner would be an excellent first step in a comprehensive program evaluation.

Outcome Analyses

There continues to be a pressing need for methodologically rigorous program evaluations in the area of juvenile justice. Because the Missouri model requires a complete system change, a true experimental evaluation would be very difficult to implement. Other alternatives, however, are available. One strategy would be to identify key components of the Missouri model and randomly assess their effectiveness. For example, one could assess the effectiveness of the DYS case management approach or its educational component using experimental methods. Although this approach would not provide a total evaluation of the Missouri model, it would inform the understanding of important aspects of it. A second strategy, given the complexity of the model, is to use rigorous quasi-experimental designs and to rely on relatively new statistical modeling techniques, such as regression-discontinuity analysis (Berk et al., 2010) or propensity score modeling, to evaluate and compare the outcomes of the Missouri model with that of other states (Osborne, 2008).

For example, propensity score matching can be used to account for differences between groups and to parcel out some of the unobserved heterogeneity in the statistical models, thereby reducing the likelihood of sample selection bias (Rosenbaum and Rubin, 1983). The propensity score can be seen as a balancing score, as it allows one to isolate the effects of correctional treatment models on recidivism by comparing the outcomes of the Missouri sample with a comparable sample of juveniles from other states who have a similar risk of delinquency. Given the costs of the model and limited funding availability, it is important to understand the efficacy of this program for diverse groups. It is important to consider if this program works and for whom. Additional analyses on recidivism patterns by gender, educational status, and criminal history profile are warranted.

FUTURE DIRECTIONS

The heterogeneity in youth offender populations has been well documented. However, as Lipsey and Wilson (1998) aptly observed, there is "little systematic attention . . . given to reviewing the evidence for effectiveness with distinct type of offenders." Future research should also explore what works for whom and under what circumstances when designing and replicating future programming. There are several populations and needs groups to be explored. Missouri has identified two particular subgroups in need of review: girls and youth who return to rural areas. Researchers have documented gendered pathways to crime and imprisonment (Daly and Chesney-Lind, 1988; Chesney-Lind, 1997; Daly, 1998; Owen, 1998; Bloom, Owen, and Covington, 2003; Miller and Mullins, 2006; Belknap, 2007). As noted in the DYS 2010 annual report, females account for only 15.7 percent of commitments, yet the agency notes that the population is a challenge given increasing populations and limited resources. Interestingly, females are more likely to be placed in custody than males. Females were most often committed to DYS for misdemeanors (43.6 percent) and juvenile offenses (21.5 percent). In contrast, males were most often serving time for felonies (55.9 percent). This finding is consistent with earlier work by Kempf-Leonard and Sample (2000), who found that prehearing detention and out-of-home placement were used for less serious crimes when compared with similar juvenile males.

Director Decker notes that the division has taken several steps to attend to the unique needs of girls, particularly in the area of reentry programming. DYS has recently implemented the Girls' Circle (see http://www.girlscircle. com) as part of their community aftercare program. Research suggests that most institutional programs implemented for adult female offenders fail to address their unique needs, and even less is known about appropriate programming for girls in and out of the institution (Morash, Bynum, and Koons-Witt, 1998; Pollock, 2002). This area is particularly important for reform, as girls often enter criminality through different pathways than boys and take unique trajectories following imprisonment.

Missouri has also faced challenges in providing care to youth in rural areas, particularly given the agency's goal of providing youth services close to home. The state has been able to maintain services for rural populations through the diversionary program and has provided transportation to families of youth who are housed in faraway institutions, but it will need to continue to develop innovative ways in which to serve this population. In terms of practice and policy, much of the current research centers on metropolitan contexts of reentry. Although large numbers of youth return to more populated areas, a significant number come home to rural communities. Some researchers have raised questions about the applicability of theoretical models of criminal justice practice to both urban and rural settings (Osgood and Chambers, 2000).

In conclusion, this appendix has described the nature of the Missouri model, a model that is consistent with best practices in juvenile justice. What remains to be learned, however, is whether the program is actually effective in reducing recidivism when subjected to a scientifically credible evaluation. We also need to learn which elements of the program are most successful and the best manner in which similar program models can be replicated in other communities. In a time of scarce resources, implementation and outcome measures must be collected to ensure that effective programming is continued and ineffective programming is eliminated (Maxfield, 2001). That is particularly important for programs with the popular acclaim of the Missouri model. Similarly, it remains important to see if this model works well for all juveniles. As Rosenfeld (2008) suggests, future research should attempt to isolate offenders who are most amenable to treatment, given that many first-time offenders desist without additional correctional interventions, and still others do so regardless of intervention and treatment. Similarly, it is essential to enhance data collection efforts at both the national and the state levels. Doing so will also pave the way for better understanding of the particular needs of special populations in the system.

Appendix C

Mentoring

RESEARCH ON MENTORING

Given the huge federal investment in mentoring, it is useful to lay out what is known about mentoring and its impact on behavior. Research provides support for the prosocial benefits young people receive from having at least one close, enduring relationship with a caring adult during adolescence (Butts, Bazemore, and Meroe, 2010). Such benefits include fewer risky behaviors, like substance abuse and delinquency (Aspy et al., 2004; Oman et al., 2004). Many believe that at-risk youth, like those who grow up in poverty and/or are in contact with child welfare, foster care, or the juvenile justice systems, lack such a relationship (Rhodes and DuBois, 2006). As such, mentoring is a widely used approach to match at-risk youth with a prosocial adult in an enduring and supportive relationship.

Most youth mentoring programs serve the broad purpose of developing competencies and future potential of mentees through ongoing, structured relationships with trusted individuals. Today, mentoring programs can take several forms: traditional mentoring (one adult to one young person); group mentoring (one adult with a small group of young people); team mentoring (several adults working with small groups of young people, in which the typical adult-to-youth ratio is not greater than 1:4); peer mentoring (trained, caring youth mentoring other youth); and even e-mentoring (mentoring via e-mail and the Internet). They can also take place in a number of settings, such as the workplace, a school, a faith-based organization or other community setting, a juvenile corrections facility, or a virtual community.

Evaluations of formal one-to-one mentoring programs have provided evidence of improvements in self-efficacy and social competence and academic success, as well as measurable reductions in problem behavior (Tierney, Grossman, and Resch, 1995; Grossman and Tierney, 1998; DuBois et al., 2002b, 2002c; Keating et al., 2002; Karcher, 2005; DeWit et al., 2007; Herrera et al., 2007). A highly cited study of the Big Brother, Big Sister Program demonstrates that positive outcomes were sustained for both boys and girls and across races (Tierney et al., 1995; Sipe, 1996). Meta-analytic results comparing studies across a range of program types and youth populations also support the general effectiveness of mentoring programs; however, effect sizes are relatively modest, particularly when compared with effects sizes found in meta-analyses of other prevention programs (DuBois, et al., 2002a; Rhodes, 2008). Positive social, academic, and behavioral outcomes are more likely to occur when programs have best practices in place. Such practices include procedures to screen then train volunteers, supervise the matches, provide ongoing support to the mentors, and ensure a relationship of at least 12 months with frequent meetings (Sipe, 1996; Brady et al., 2005; Rhodes, 2008).

Although mentoring programs have been shown on average to promote positive outcomes in adolescents' development, there is also evidence that (1) some programs are less effective, most notably those that do not have the structures to support the best practices; (2) some youth are less likely to benefit from mentoring; and (3) the measured benefit among different outcomes (e.g., academic, behavioral, social) varies within and across different types of programs. In other words, the current state of research can show only that mentoring works for some youth, in some settings, and for some outcomes (Roberts et al., 2004; Rhodes, 2008). Most of what is known about effective mentoring comes from evaluations of one-to-one mentoring programs. Other types of programs are just starting to be rigorously studied.

There is very little known about the limits of mentoring programs. The modest improvements in youth outcomes have not been tested to see if they hold up over time. Mentoring does seem to provide immediate academic success, such as improved test scores and school behaviors, but there is little known about its impact on other relevant outcomes, such as overall educational attainment, substance use, or juvenile offending (DuBois et al., 2011). The field has limited understanding of the characteristics of youth that are best served by mentoring and how many adults can be reasonably expected to serve as mentors (Sipe, 1996).

FEDERAL SUPPORT OF MENTORING

In 1992, the Juvenile Justice and Delinquency Prevention Act (JJDPA) was amended to establish the Juvenile Mentoring Program (JUMP). The program competitively awarded three-year grants to community-based nonprofit organizations or local education agencies to provide one-to-one mentoring for youth at risk of delinquency, gang involvement, or educational failure. At the same time, Congress instructed the Office of Juvenile Justice and Delinquency Prevention (OJJDP) to conduct an ongoing evaluation of JUMP (Office of Juvenile Justice and Delinquency Prevention, 2000).

The 1992 reauthorization defined mentoring specifically as a one-to-one relationship between a unpaid volunteer age 21 or over (mentor) and a juvenile (mentee) that occurs over an extended period of time. The program had clear expectations of one mentor for one mentee, and in the first few years JUMP grantees complied with this requirement (Office of Juvenile Justice and Delinquency Prevention, 2000). In addition to individual grants to organizations, JUMP supported mentoring across the nation in other ways. OJJDP was not the only federal agency to support mentoring programs. In 1999, the U.S. General Accounting Office identified 45 programs in 10 agencies that included mentoring services for at-risk or delinquent youth as part (if not all) of the program. OJJDP administered four of the nine programs identified within the U.S. Department of Justice. One was JUMP; the other three[1] had the authority to support mentoring programs although mentoring was not their primary focus (U.S. General Accounting Office, 1999).

FY2002 was the last year for which a JUMP solicitation was issued. In the 2002 reauthorization, Congress consolidated JUMP with other program areas under the Title II, Part C, Juvenile Delinquency Prevention Block Grant Program. This new block grant program never received funding. However, OJJDP continued to support previous JUMP applicants and grantees (Office of Juvenile Justice and Delinquency Prevention, 2004) and subsequently turned to supporting different types of juvenile mentoring initiatives. From 1995 to 2005, more than $50 million was awarded to 261 programs through JUMP (Boyle, 2006).

In response to recommendations from the White House Task Force for Disadvantaged Youth (2003), the Federal Mentoring Council was established in 2006 to strengthen support for mentoring, coordinate federal efforts, and minimize duplication. The council is chaired by the Corporation for National and Community Service and includes representatives of the U.S. Departments of Agriculture, Defense, Education, Health and Human Services, Housing and Urban Development, Justice, and Labor.

To continue to support juvenile mentoring, congressional appropriators began carving out such funds from appropriations under JJDPA. Carve-outs for juvenile mentoring started at about $10 million in FY2006; one-third of this was available for discretionary awards, and the rest was congres-

---

[1]The other three programs were Title II Formula Grants, Title V Incentive Grants for Delinquency Prevention Program, and Gang-Free Schools and Communities: Community-Based Gang Interventions.

sionally directed toward specific organizations (Office of Justice Programs, 2006). In its 2008 annual report, OJJDP reports spending more than $60 million on mentoring in FY2008. OJJDP was appropriated $80 million and $100 million respectively for juvenile mentoring programs in FY2009 and FY2010. All totaled, more than $300 million has been expended by OJJDP on mentoring.

At the time of this writing, OJJDP has six separate discretionary programs[2] that support youth mentoring activities. In addition to these discretionary grants, OJJDP has also been tasked with administering congressional earmarks, many of which were directed to mentoring partnerships (Fitzpatrick, 2010). In FY2011, OJJDP also received a $20 million transfer from the U.S. Department of Defense to support mentoring for youth with a military parent. It is beyond the charge and resources of this study to examine the quality of mentoring programs supported by OJJDP and other agencies.

Recent solicitations from OJJDP indicate that the scope of mentoring support has broadened. Eligibility for awards now extends to organizations that include adults or trained peers as mentors, that provide one-to-one or group mentoring services, and that target not only youth at risk of delinquency and offending but also those more broadly at risk of unhealthy development (Office of Juvenile Justice and Delinquency Prevention, 2010). OJJDP is currently mandated to support mentoring for tribal youth, sexually exploited children, youth with disabilities, and youth in military families. Although these are notably youth groups in need of services, there is no research that supports the notion that they are more in need of mentoring than other groups or that these groups will stand to benefit more than other groups (Chandra, 2010).

One advantage of having received increased funding support for mentoring is that OJJDP has been able to use set-aside funds for research on mentoring. However, this is a case of the cart before the horse, with needed research being undertaken after an expansion of federally supported mentoring programs has occurred. Targeted solicitations went out in FY2009, FY2010, and FY2011 requesting research proposals to identify the components of mentoring programs with the greatest impact toward reducing juvenile delinquency and offending. Some proposals were open to field-initiated ideas regarding the selection of components, and others were targeted to specific programmatic characteristics, such as paid versus volunteer mentors or specific group mentoring programs.

---

[2]The FY2011 discretionary grant programs on mentoring included OJJDP's Mentoring for Child Victims of Commercial Sexual Exploitation Initiative; the Mentoring for Youth with Disabilities Initiative; the Multi-State Mentoring Initiative; the National Mentoring Program; the Second Chance Act Juvenile Mentoring Initiative; and the Tribal Youth National Mentoring Program.

Appendix D

Biographical Sketches of Committee Members and Staff

Robert L. Johnson (*Chair*) is the Sharon and Joseph L. Muscarelle endowed dean, professor of pediatrics, professor of psychiatry, and director of the Division of Adolescent and Young Adult Medicine at the New Jersey Medical School of the University of Medicine and Dentistry of New Jersey (UMDNJ). His research focuses on adolescent physical and mental health, adolescent HIV, adolescent violence, adolescent fatherhood, and risk prevention/reduction programs with specific emphasis on substance and alcohol abuse, sexuality and sexual dysfunction, male sexual abuse, suicide, and AIDS. He currently serves on the U.S. Department of Health and Human Services' Council on Graduate Medical Education and chairs the Governor's Advisory Council on HIV/AIDS and Related Blood Borne Pathogens and the Newark Ryan White Planning Council. He is a fellow of the American Academy of Pediatrics. He has published widely and conducts an active schedule of teaching, research, and clinical practice at the New Jersey Medical School. He has an M.D. from the New Jersey Medical School of UMDNJ.

Richard J. Bonnie (*Vice Chair*) is the Harrison Foundation professor of medicine and law, professor of psychiatry and neurobehavioral sciences, professor of public policy, and director, Institute of Law, Psychiatry and Public Policy at the University of Virginia. He was elected to the Institute of Medicine (IOM) in 1991. He teaches and writes about criminal law, bioethics, and public policies relating to mental health, substance abuse, aging, and public health. He was associate director of the National Commission on Marijuana and Drug Abuse (1971-1973), secretary of the first National Advisory Council on Drug Abuse (1975-1985), and chief advisor for the American Bar Association's Criminal Justice Mental Health Standards Project (1981-1988). He currently chairs a Commission on Mental Health Law Reform at the request of the chief justice of Virginia. He has also served on the MacArthur Foundation's Research Network on Mental Health and the Law and a successor Network on Mandated Community Treatment and is currently participating in the foundation's Project on Law and Neuroscience. He received the Yarmolinsky Medal in 2002 for his contributions to the IOM and the National Academies. In 2007, Bonnie received the University of Virginia's highest honor, the Thomas Jefferson Award. He has a B.A. from Johns Hopkins University and an LL.B. from the University of Virginia School of Law.

Carl C. Bell is clinical professor of psychiatry and public health and director of the Institute for Juvenile Research at the University of Illinois at Chicago (UIC) where the field of child psychiatry originated. He is president and chief executive officer of the Community Mental Health Council and Foundation, Inc., in Chicago. He is a former member of the National Institute of Mental Health's National Mental Health Advisory Council and currently codirector of the UIC Interdisciplinary Violence Prevention Research Center. He received the E.Y. Williams Distinguished Senior Clinical Scholar Award of the National Medical Association's section on psychiatry in 1992; the American Psychiatric Association President's Commendation regarding violence in 1997; the Solomon Carter Fuller Award in 2011; the Agnes Purcell McGavin Award for Prevention in Child and Adolescent Psychiatry in 2012; and the Special Presidential Commendation for outstanding advocacy for mental illness prevention and for person-centered mental health wellness and recovery in 2012. He is also a current and founding executive committee member of the National Action Alliance for Suicide Prevention. Over 40 years, he has published numerous articles, chapters, and books on mental health. A 1967 graduate of UIC, he has an M.D. from Meharry Medical College. He completed a psychiatric residency in 1974 at the Illinois State Psychiatric Institute/Institute for Juvenile Research in Chicago.

Lawrence D. Bobo is the W.E.B. Du Bois professor of the social sciences at Harvard University. He holds appointments in the Department of Sociology and the Department of African and African American Studies. His research focuses on the intersection of social inequality, politics, and race and has appeared in the *American Sociological Review*, the *American Journal of Sociology*, *Social Forces*, the *American Political Science Review*, the *Journal of Personality and Social Psychology*, *Social Psychology Quarterly*, and *Public Opinion Quarterly*. He is the founding editor of the *Du Bois Review: Social Science Research on Race* published by Cambridge University Press. His most recent book, *Prejudice in Politics: Group Position, Pub-*

lic Opinion, and the Wisconsin Treaty Rights Dispute, was a finalist for the 2007 C. Wright Mills Award. Bobo is an elected member of the National Academy of Sciences as well as a fellow of the American Academy of Arts and Sciences, the American Philosophical Society, and the American Association for the Advancement of Science. He has M.A. and Ph.D. degrees in sociology from the University of Michigan.

Jeffrey A. Butts is executive director of the Criminal Justice Research and Evaluation Center at John Jay College of Criminal Justice, City University of New York. Previously, he was a research fellow with Chapin Hall at the University of Chicago, director of the Program on Youth Justice at the Urban Institute, and senior research associate at the National Center for Juvenile Justice (NCJJ) in Pittsburgh. NCJJ is the national repository for state juvenile court records and is the main producer and analyzer of juvenile justice system statistics. His work focuses on research and evaluation projects designed to discover and improve policies and programs for at-risk and disconnected youth, especially those involved with the justice system. He has more than 25 years of experience in research, program evaluation, policy analysis, and direct services. He has authored two books, dozens of reports for the U.S. Department of Justice and other agencies, and articles in such journals as the *American Journal of Criminal Law, Crime and Delinquency, Criminal Justice Policy Review, Judicature, Law & Policy, Juvenile and Family Court Journal,* and *Youth & Society.* He began his career in 1980 as a drug and alcohol counselor with the juvenile court in Eugene, Oregon. He has a Ph.D. in sociology and social work from the University of Michigan.

Gladys Carrión is commissioner of the New York State Office of Children and Family Services (OCFS), which has oversight of child welfare, including child preventive and protective services, foster care, and adoption; manages the state's juvenile justice system; and regulates and licenses child care. During Carrión's tenure, OCFS has earned national recognition for her initiative to transform the juvenile justice system she inherited from a "custody and control" model with a reputation for using excessive force on children; no oversight and few resources; and an 89 percent recidivism rate, to an evidence-based, trauma-informed, community-centered therapeutic model with significantly better outcomes for children and for maintaining community safety. Carrión's reform of New York's juvenile justice system also has included the closing of 13 empty or underutilized, but fully staffed, residential centers in local counties. Other positions she has held include staff attorney at the Bronx Legal Services Corporation, commissioner of the New York City Community Development Agency, chair of the New York City School Chancellor's Task Force on Latino Educational Opportunity, executive director of Family Dynamics, and program officer in community development at the Ford Foundation. She has a J.D. from the New York University School of Law.

B.J. Casey is director of the Sackler Institute for Developmental Psychobiology and the Sackler professor of developmental psychobiology at Weill Cornell Medical College. She has been examining the normal development of brain circuitry involved in attention and behavioral regulation and how disruptions in these brain systems give rise to a number of developmental disorders. Recently she has begun to examine the effects of gene-environment interactions in the development of affect and behavioral regulation and related brain systems, using both human and mouse genetics. She has a Ph.D. in experimental psychology from the University of South Carolina.

Betty M. Chemers (*Study Director*) is a senior project officer at the National Research Council. Previously, she held numerous positions at the U.S. Department of Justice, including director of the evaluation division of the National Institute of Justice (NIJ) and deputy administrator for discretionary programs at the Office of Juvenile Justice and Delinquency Prevention, where she oversaw its research, demonstration, and training and technical assistance activities. Her nonfederal service includes directing the planning and policy analysis division of the Maryland Department of Public Safety and Correctional Services and consulting on strategic planning, finance, and management issues with nonprofit organizations. She has an M.A. in history from Boston University and a B.A. in education/sociology from the University of Maryland.

Kenneth A. Dodge is the William McDougall professor of public policy and professor of psychology, social and health sciences, at Duke University. As the first director of the Center for Child and Family Policy at Duke, he leads an effort to bridge basic scientific research in children's development with public policy affecting children and families. His particular area of scholarship has addressed the development and prevention of chronic violence in children and adolescents. He is the recipient of a research scientist award from the National Institute of Mental Health as well as several awards from the American Psychological Association, including the Distinguished Scientific Award for Early Career Contribution to Psychopathology. He has conducted both laboratory and longitudinal studies of how chronic aggressive behavior develops across the life span. His work has identified early family experience factors (such as child physical abuse), peer relations factors, and social-cognitive patterns that serve as catalysts for aggressive behavioral development. With colleagues, he developed the Fast Track Program, a comprehensive effort to prevent the development of chronic violence in high-risk children. He has a Ph.D. in psychology from Duke University.

Sandra A. Graham is a professor and the Presidential Chair in Education and Diversity within the Department of Education at the University of California, Los Angeles (UCLA). Her major research interests include the study of academic motivation, peer aggression, and juvenile delinquency, particularly in African American children and adolescents. She has published widely in developmental, social, and educational psychology journals. She currently is principal investigator on grants from the National Science Foundation and the National Institute of Child Health and Human Development. She is the recipient of an Independent Scientist Award, funded by the National Institute of Mental Health, and she is a former recipient of the Early Contribution Award from Division 15 (Educational Psychology) of the American Psychological Association (APA). She was a fellow at the Center for Advanced Study in the Behavioral Sciences, Stanford, California. Among her professional activities, she is an associate editor of *American Psychologist* and a member of the advisory committee of the Minority Fellowship Program of APA. She previously served as a member of the MacArthur Foundation Network on Adolescent Development and Juvenile Justice and the Governing Council of the Society for Research on Adolescence. She has a Ph.D. in education from UCLA.

Ernestine Gray is chief judge of the Orleans Parish Juvenile Court in New Orleans. She was elected in 1984 and has since been reelected to three full eight-year terms on that court. Previously, she was employed by the Baton Rouge Legal Aid Society, the attorney general of the state of Louisiana, and the U.S. Equal Employment Opportunity Commission as a trial attorney. Throughout her career, Gray has held leadership positions with children's advocacy, judicial, and bar organizations. She is past president of the National Council of Juvenile and Family Court Judges and the National CASA (Court Appointed Special Advocates) board of trustees. At National CASA, she serves on the Inclusion and Outreach, Education and Public Awareness, and Standards committees. She has a J.D. from Louisiana State University.

Edward P. Mulvey is professor of psychiatry and director of the Law and Psychiatry Program at the Western Psychiatric Institute and Clinic at the University of Pittsburgh's School of Medicine. His research has focused on issues related to how clinicians make judgments regarding the type of risk posed by adult mental patients and the development and treatment of serious juvenile offenders. He is a fellow of the American Psychological Association and the American Psychological Society, a recipient of a faculty scholar's award from the William T. Grant Foundation, a member of two MacArthur Foundation Research Networks (one on mental health and the law and another on adolescent development and juvenile justice), and a member of the Steering Committee of the National Consortium on Violence Research. He currently serves on the Science Advisory Board of the Office of Justice Programs of the U.S. Department of Justice. He has a Ph.D. in community/clinical psychology from the University of Virginia. He also did postdoctoral training in quantitative methods in criminal justice at Carnegie Mellon University.

Robert D. Plotnick is professor of public affairs and associate dean at the Daniel J. Evans School of Public Affairs at the University of Washington. He serves as an adjunct professor in the University of Washington's Department of Economics and is a research affiliate with the West Coast Poverty Center and the Center for Studies in Demography and Ecology at the university as well as the Institute for Research on Poverty at the University of Wisconsin. He has written extensively on poverty, income inequality, nonmarital childbearing, income support policy, and related social policy issues in the United States. Previously, he served on the faculty at Bates College (1975-1977) and at Dartmouth College (1977-1984). He has been a visiting scholar at the Russell Sage Foundation, Cornell University, the University of New South Wales, and the London School of Economics; he served as director of the Center for Studies in Demography and Ecology from 1997 to 2002. He has a Ph.D. in economics from the University of California, Berkeley.

Julie A. Schuck is a senior program associate with the National Research Council and has worked in the Division of Behavioral and Social Sciences and Education for more than 10 years. She has provided analytical and editorial support for a number of projects and workshops, including those on improving undergraduate instruction in science, technology, engineering, and mathematics; understanding the technical and privacy dimensions of information for terrorism prevention; employing the science of human-systems integration in home health care and mine safety; and strengthening the research program of the National Institute of Justice. Previously, she was a research support specialist at Cornell University. She has an M.S. in education from Cornell University and a B.S. in engineering physics from the University of California, San Diego.

Elizabeth S. Scott is the Harold R. Medina professor of law at Columbia University Law School. In 2007-2009, she served as the law school's vice-dean. She teaches family law, property, criminal law, and children and the law. She has written extensively on marriage, divorce, cohabitation, child custody, adolescent decision making, and juvenile delinquency. Her research is interdisciplinary, applying behavioral economics, social science research, and developmental theory to family/juvenile law and policy issues. Previously, she served as legal director of the Forensic Psychiatry Clinic, Institute of Law, Psychiatry and Public Policy at the University of Virginia. She is the founder and was co-director of the University of Virginia's interdisciplinary Center for Children, Families and the Law. In 1995-2006, she was involved in empirical research on adolescents in the justice system as a member of the MacArthur Foundation Research Network on Adolescent Development and Juvenile Justice. In 2008, she published *Rethinking Juvenile Justice* with developmental psychologist Laurence Steinberg. She is also the coauthor of two casebooks on family law and children in the legal system. She has a J.D. from the University of Virginia School of Law.

Terence P. Thornberry is a distinguished university professor in the Department of Criminology and Criminal Justice at the University of Maryland. He was formerly director of the Problem Behavior Program at the Institute of Behavioral Science and professor of sociology at the University of Colorado (2004-2009) and prior to that held numerous positions at Albany, State University of New York (1984-2003). In 1995 he was elected a fellow of the American Society of Criminology and in 2008 he was the recipient of that society's Edwin H. Sutherland Award. His research interests focus on understanding the development of delinquency and crime over the life course, the consequences of maltreatment, and intergenerational continuity in antisocial behavior. He is the principal investigator of the Rochester Youth Development Study, a three-generation panel study begun in 1986 to examine the causes and consequences of delinquency and other forms of antisocial behaviors. He has a Ph.D. in sociology from the University of Pennsylvania.

Cherie Townsend recently retired from public service after nearly 40 years as a juvenile justice practitioner and leader. Prior to her retirement, she served as the executive director of the newly created Texas Department of Juvenile Justice, which replaced the Texas Youth Commission and the Texas Juvenile Probation Commission. In 2008-2011, she served as executive director or executive commissioner of the Texas Youth Commission. In this position she oversaw the state-operated juvenile corrections system. Her responsibilities included leading more than 4,000 employees in a reform effort and daily operations of this system. Previously, she served as director of juvenile justice services in Clark County, Nevada (Las Vegas), and as director of juvenile court services in Maricopa County, Arizona (Phoenix). In 2010, she was recognized for her leadership in juvenile justice by the Texas Corrections Association and by the Council of Juvenile Correctional

Administrators. In 2003, she received the Juvenile Court Administrator Award from the National Juvenile Court Services Association and in 2001 the Sam Houston State University Award as the Outstanding Probation Executive. She has an M.P.A. from Southern Methodist University and an M.B.A. from the University of Texas.